Best Practice Procurement

Best Practice Procurement

Public and Private Sector Perspectives

EDITED BY ANDREW ERRIDGE, RUTH FEE AND JOHN MCILROY

Gower

Published by
Gower Publishing Limited
Gower House
Croft Road
Aldershot
Hampshire GU11 3HR
England

Gower Publishing Company
131 Main Street
Burlington VT 05401-5600 USA

British Library Cataloguing in Publication Data
Erridge, Andrew
    Best practice procurement : public and private sector
    perspectives
    1. Purchasing   2. Business logistics
    I. Title   II. Fee, Ruth   III. McIlroy, John, 1973-
    658.7'2

ISBN 0 566 08366 3

Library of Congress Cataloging-in-Publication Data
Best practice procurement : public and private sector perspectives / [edited by] Andrew Erridge, Ruth Fee, and John McIlroy.
        p. cm.
    ISBN 0-566-08366-3 (hardback)
    1. Business logistics.   2. Delivery of goods--Management.   I. Erridge, Andrew.   II. Fee, Ruth.   III. McIlroy, John, 1973-

HD38.5 .B47 2000
658.7'2--dc21

00-059609

Typeset in Utopia and Frutiger by Manton Typesetters, Louth, Lincolnshire and printed in Great Britain by T.J. International Ltd, Padstow, Cornwall.

Contents

List of figures

List of tables

Notes on contributors

Frances Bowen is a lecturer in the Strategy, Systems and Management Division of Sheffield University Management School. When this chapter was written, she was a research officer at the School of Management, University of Bath, working on an EPSRC-funded project on Environmentally Sound Supply Chain Management (ESSCMo). She is currently writing up her PhD thesis on the implementation of environmental initiatives at the operating unit level of large, multiunit firms in the UK. Frances' other research interests include corporate social responsibility, organizational slack and R&D strategy.

Professor Dr Walter H. Brenner is Professor of Information Management at the University of Essen, Germany. Walter has published in the areas of management information systems, business process redesign, computerized information and electronic commerce. He holds a PhD from the University of St Gallen, Switzerland. He has published over 70 articles in journals such as *The European Journal of Purchasing and Supply Management, Telematics and Informatics, Wirtschaftsinformatik* and *Information Management.* Walter has written over 10 books, most of them published in German, but two of them published with John Wiley and Springer in the US. He has consulted widely in industry and the administration in the areas of strategic information planning and project management.

Tom Chadwick has over 20 years' experience in production and materials management in the defence sector with Ferranti and GEC Marconi. He became director of procurement at the University of Edinburgh in 1993, and in 1998 took up his current position in the new post of director of procurement development for the Joint Procurement Policy and Strategy Group (JPPSG) for UK higher education. A Fellow of the Chartered Institute of Purchasing and Supply, he is a member of the CIPS Appointments Board, and a trustee director of EduServ, a not-for-profit company working with education for education. He also holds a part-time lectureship in purchasing at Heriot-Watt University.

Dr Daniel Corsten is senior lecturer at the University of St Gallen and research manager for logistics and supply chain management at the Institute for Technology Management. The Research Centre pursues the development of theories, concepts and methods in the field of logistics in collaboration with renowned European companies and international publications. Current research focuses on supply chain management, electronic commerce and efficient consumer response (ECR). Daniel holds a University diploma from the University of Cologne and a PhD from the University of St Gallen. He has worked as an international sales and marketing manager at Bayer AG, Leverkusen and as a project manager at Agfa AG, New Jersey. Daniel is a Member of the Board of the Swiss Association for Logistics, the ECR Europe Academic Advisory Panel and the ECR Switzerland Board.

Pat Costello returned to education after raising a family and obtained a first class honours degree in business information systems. She then worked in industry implementing network solutions for SMEs to support business cases and has been a lecturer at the University of Wolverhampton for the past three years. She completed a pilot project in the use of the Internet and e-mail at 21 companies within the West Midlands, UK, in 1998 which has since been extended to a further 100 companies. Further IT-related courses include short courses for SMEs to improve their use of ICT with an emphasis on R&D and exports. She has written several papers on the subject of technology transfer involving SMEs, particularly on supply chain management and pedagogical aspects based around case study material of real business scenarios. She has also spoken at several conferences on this subject, including keynote speeches at Coventry University as part of the 'Cascade' ADAPT Project.

Paul Cousins is a senior lecturer in Operations Management in the School of Management, University of Bath, from where he obtained an MBA and a Doctorate. Previously Paul worked as a chief buyer with Westland Helicopters, and as a chief contracts negotiator for Sikorsky Aircraft in Connecticut, USA. He has also worked as senior consultant in the European Supply Chain practice of A.T. Kearney, Management Consultants, for whom he still consults on a part-time basis, and currently works with a range of other blue-chip firms. Paul worked with Professor Lamming on the RAP project developing methodologies for assessing and developing supplier–buyer relationships; on the ESSCMo (Environmentally Sound Supply Chain Management) project; and is currently designing and developing relationship assessment models for SCRIA, an Aerospace initiative. He continues to research and publish in the areas of collaboration, supply strategy, performance measurement and outsourcing, and has authored a wide range of academic papers, as well as two books.

Andrew Cox is Professor of Business Strategy and Procurement and director of the Centre for Business Strategy and Procurement at Birmingham University's Business School. He is also director of the MBA in strategy and procurement management. He is currently working with a number of multinational firms worldwide and has written on a wide range of topics related to procurement and business strategy. He has authored numerous books including *Business Success,* and has published articles in many journals including the *European Journal of Purchasing and Supply Management, Journal of Common Market Studies, Public Procurement Law Review,* and *Journal of Public Policy.* He was Organizing Chair of the 1995 IPSERA Conference at the University of Birmingham, and is a former IPSERA committee member.

Dr Simon Croom, FCIPS, is a lecturer at Warwick Business School in the UK. He is research officer for IPSERA and has advised over a dozen international corporations in the areas of supply chain management, electronic business and global strategy. He is the lead researcher of the International Global Account Management Study.

Valerie Cupples is Belfast City Council procurement officer with 12 years' experience. She holds a BA(Hons) in Public Policy with purchasing specialisms from the University of Ulster, and is a member of the Chartered Institute of Purchasing and Supply. Valerie is currently acting as an internal consultant and leading the implementation of ISO 14001 in Belfast City Council Procurement Unit.

Andrew Erridge is a Professor in the School of Public Policy, Economics and Law at the University of Ulster, Northern Ireland, where he runs courses in strategic procurement management. His main research interest is public procurement. His publications include *Managing Purchasing: Sourcing and Contracting* and articles in refereed journals including the *European Journal of Purchasing and Supply Management,* of which he is a member of the Editorial Committee. He is a Committee member and former chair of IPSERA. He advised the National Audit Office on their report on modernizing procurement, and is a member of the steering group for the review of government procurement in Northern Ireland.

Ann Esain is a senior research fellow with the Lean Enterprise Research Centre, part of Cardiff Business School. The Welsh Development Agency sponsors her post. The objective of her work is to establish breakthrough research, which can be translated into practical applications for Welsh organizations. She has worked in a wide range of sectors including the automotive, packaging and the public sector and has researched a number of key processes including new product introduction and order fulfilment. Ann was the joint winner (along with Professor Peter Hines and Nick Rich) of the European Best Practice Benchmarking Award for best academic paper in 1998.

Adam Faruk was a research officer on the ESSCMo project in CR*i*SPS at the University of Bath, UK, and now holds a position at Ashridge Management College.

Harold Fearon PhD, CPM, is NAPM Professor Emeritus and Founding Director of the Center for Advanced Purchasing Studies in Tempe, Arizona. Author of *The Purchasing Handbook*, a best-seller for over 30 years, he was the founder and first editor of the *International Journal of Purchasing and Materials Management* (now the *Journal of Supply Chain Management*), and has published numerous journal articles and CAPS reports.

Ruth Fee is a lecturer in Government and course director for the LLM and MSc in European Law and Policy in the School of Public Policy, Economics and Law at the University of Ulster, Northern Ireland. Ruth was formerly a research officer in public procurement working with Professor Andrew Erridge. Her qualifications include an LLB and MPhil. Her teaching and research interests are in public procurement law and policy and European law and policy, and she has published in journals including *Public Policy and Administration*, *Policy and Politics* and *Public Money and Management*. Ruth is on the board of the Public Procurement Law Review responsible for best value issues.

Dr Laura B. Forker, CPM, is an Associate Professor of Management at the University of Massachusetts Dartmouth. She received her PhD in Business Administration from Arizona State University. Dr Forker teaches courses in Manufacturing and Service Operations Management, Operations and Organizational Processes, and in Logistics and Supply Management. She has conducted research and published numerous articles in the areas of supplier quality management, supply chain management, and in international trade, especially countertrade. Her publications have appeared in many journals including the *Journal of Operations Manage-*

ment, *International Journal of Production Research*, *International Journal of Operations and Production Management* and *International Journal of Purchasing and Materials Management*.

John Fraser has worked in the marketing profession for more than 10 years, almost all of which have been spent in the IT industry working for a software author and more recently a software reseller in Manchester. John is a widely published author and contributor to industry publications such as the *VAR*, *Logistics Focus* and *MCB Journals* as well as a contributor to IPSERA conferences. In his current role as marketing manager of General Systems, John has responsibility for the market development of a number of solutions from established software authors such as Systems Union and Epicor.

Dr Nuran Fraser has established a respected position for herself in the International Business Unit of the Manchester Metropolitan University. As a lecturer in the department, Dr Fraser has had responsibility for the teaching of distribution and logistics in particular and has developed a keen interest on the impact of new technologies on the industry. She has contributed to a number of academic journals and is a member of IPSERA.

Steve Garner is a lecturer in the School of Computing and Information Technology at the University of Wolverhampton, having previously lectured at Coleg Powys. His qualifications include BSc(Hons) Computer Science and MSc in Advanced Software Technology. Steve is currently working on the Autolean project, providing Internet and e-mail training to 120 SMEs in the West Midlands.

Florence Gregg, a mathematics graduate and chartered secretary, has been involved in purchasing for some 20 years. She joined the purchasing office of Queen's University Belfast in 1990 and became its head of purchasing in 1998. In 1993, Florence was one of the first MSc graduates in purchasing and supply management at the University of Ulster. Over the last 5 years she has worked with colleagues in the UK higher education sector developing performance measurement tools, maintaining her interest in both practical and academic research.

David Griffiths is Head of the Procurement and Accommodation Services Group at the Driver and Vehicle Licensing Agency, and has spent some 18 years in the purchasing and contracts field within the Department of the Environment, Transport and the Regions and the former Property Services Agency. David is responsible for policy and planning, including the contractual aspects of better quality services; procurement excellence model; public expenditure report on civil government procurement; and the professional development of staff. In addition, he is responsible for policy on and procurement of estates services. David is a graduate member of the Chartered Institute of Purchasing and Supply and a member of IPSERA.

Dr Christine Harland is Senior Research Fellow at the Centre for Research in Strategic Purchasing and Supply (CRiSPS) in the School of Management, University of Bath, UK. She directs a partnership programme of action research in supply strategy with the NHS Purchasing and Supply Agency in addition to conducting private sector-based research. Previously Christine lectured on the Warwick Business School MBA and worked in supply chain management with GEC Telecommunications and the Dowty Group. As a business consultant Christine has worked with many companies including BT, Ericsson, Hewlett Packard, Volvo and Telia. She has been an advisor to HM Treasury on strategic procurement and contributed to the 1999 Cabinet Office review of civil government procurement. She is co-author of the world's leading text on operations management and has published articles in many journals including the *European Journal of Purchasing and Supply Management* and the *British Journal of Management*.

Professor Peter Hines is co-director of the Lean Enterprise Research Centre at Cardiff Business School where he holds a chair in Supply Chain Management. Peter followed a successful career in distribution and manufacturing industry before joining Cardiff Business School in 1992. He has written or co-written five books including *Value Stream Management* published by FT Prentice Hall in 2000. He has also both written and spoken widely on an international stage. He is editor-in-chief of the *International Journal of Logistics: Research & Applications* and the current chairman of the Logistics Research Network.

Dr Garry Homer initially trained as a metallurgist before joining the computer profession as a systems analyst in 1970. After a lengthy period working in both small and large companies, Dr Homer joined the lecturing staff of Wolverhampton University, UK. Here, his role as Head of Technology Transfer within the School of Computing has seen him lead many large, industry-based R&D projects. Garry has presented numerous papers at both national and international conferences on diverse topics ranging from computer learning to e-business and the Internet. Recently, his research has focused on the dual domains of statistical process control in the cold rolling industry, and e-business and ICT within the automotive supply chain.

Jon Hughes is senior partner of the Windsor Foundation for Business Development, specializing in change management and strategic relationships across the supply chain. Worldwide consulting over a period of 15 years provided insights for his book, *Transform Your Supply Chain*, co-authored with Mark Ralf and Bill Michels and available from International Thomson Publishing. He is active in the operationalization of leading edge business practices and holds visiting professorships at the Institut du Management de l'Achat Industriel at the University of Bordeaux, France, and the Supply Chain Competence Centre at the Vlerick Leuven Gent Management School, Belgium. He is also on the faculty of the American Management Association's base within Management Centre Europe in Brussels.

Dr Fraser Johnson is assistant professor at the Richard Ivey School of Business, the University of Western Ontario, Canada, where he earned a

MBA and a PhD, specializing in operations management. Prior to this, Fraser has held a number of senior management positions in both finance and operations in the automotive parts industry, was president of Elan Corporation for six years, and was an assistant professor at the University of British Columbia. Fraser has published articles in a wide variety of magazines and journals, and has authored a number of teaching cases. He is currently working with Professor Michiel Leenders on a study supported by the Center for Advanced Purchasing Studies, Arizona, USA, examining the roles and responsibilities of purchasing in *Fortune 500* service and manufacturing firms. Fraser was awarded the National Association of Purchasing Management Senior Research Fellowship in June 1999, and has worked actively with the Purchasing Management Association of Canada in developing material for the PMAC Accreditation Program.

Martyn Jones is Principal Lecturer in Construction Management at the School of Construction Economics, Management and Engineering at the University of the West of England, Bristol. Previously he was Director of Studies for the School of Construction Management. His research interests focus on the management of change in construction, supply chain management, and alternative procurement strategies including prime contracting. Recent research projects have included *Unlocking specialist potential: a more participative role for specialist contractors*, and *Best practice in partnering in the housing sector*. He is a consultant to a range of construction organizations comprising clients, management and cost consultants, and main contractors.

Dr Danuta Kisperska-Moron is Assistant Professor in the Department of Business Logistics, Academy of Economics, in Katowice, Poland. She obtained her PhD in 1987. Her major research interests are business logistics, materials management, inventory management and customer service. She had a fellowship, from 1998 to 1999, at the Centre for Logistics and Transportation at Cranfield University in the UK, with a project on benchmarking for supply chains. She was a Fulbright Senior Scholar at the Department of Business Logistics at the Pennsylvania State University from 1994 to 1995, and visiting researcher at the Department of Business Administration at Lund University, Sweden, in 1985. She is a co-ordinator of two international educational TEMPUS projects in the field of business logistics sponsored by the European Commission. She is a member of the national executive committee and vice president of the regional branch of the Polish Logistics Association and a member of the International Society for Inventory Research and the Global Manufacturing Research Group.

Dr Robert D. Klassen is an Assistant Professor at the Richard Ivey School of Business, University of Western Ontario, Canada. He earned his PhD in operations management from the University of North Carolina at Chapel Hill, USA, and has worked in the steel, oil and consumer products industries in the areas of environmental management and product development. His research interests include international operations, operations strategy, and linkages between operations and the natural environment. He has had papers published in *Management Science, Academy of Management Journal, Journal of Operations Management* and *Decision Sciences*, among other journals.

Louise Knight worked for nine years in a variety of human resource development roles in management and purchasing, prior to joining the Centre for Research in Strategic Purchasing and Supply (CRiSPS) at the School of Management, the University of Bath, in 1996. She specializes in organizational and network learning, and network management competence, in the context of supply networks. She is a member of a CRiSPS research programme conducted in partnership with the NHS Purchasing and Supply Agency on supply strategy in health sector supply networks. One of the programme's themes is outsourcing policy and strategy at the sector level.

Dr Richard Lamming is CIPS Professor of Purchasing and Supply Management at the School of Management, the University of Bath, where he is Director of the Centre for Research in Strategic Purchasing and Supply (CR*i*SPS). Author of the book *Beyond Partnership: Strategies for Innovation and Lean Supply*, Richard played a leading role in the International Motor Vehicle Programme, and has subsequently led numerous research projects including RAP and ESSCMo. Richard has published articles in many leading journals, including the *British Journal of Management, European Journal of Purchasing and Supply Management, International Journal of Purchasing and Materials Management* and *Business Policy*. He is founder editor of the *European Journal of Purchasing and Supply Management*, and a former chair of IPSERA.

Michiel R. Leenders is the Purchasing Management Association of Canada Professor of Purchasing Management and Chairman of Operations Management at the Richard Ivey School of Business at the University of Western Ontario, Canada. He received a degree in mining engineering from the University of Alberta, a MBA from the University of Western Ontario, and his doctorate from Harvard Business School. He is a former director of the School's PhD program. His supply texts have been translated into eight different languages and include: *Value-Driven Purchasing, Managing the Key Steps in the Acquisition Process* (with Anna Flynn) published by Irwin Professional Publishing; *Reverse Marketing: The New Buyer–Supplier Relationship* (with David Blenkhorn), published by The Free Press; *Improving Purchasing Effectiveness Through Supplier Development*, published by the Harvard Division of Research; and *Purchasing and Supply Management* (with Harold Fearon) now in its 11th edition and published by Richard D. Irwin.

Dr Johan J.C. Lilliecreutz is responsible for the business area of purchasing and supplier analysis at the Centre for Market Analysis in Linkoping, Sweden. He is involved in ongoing research projects in the supply chain management area within the automotive, telecom and aerospace industries, as well as e-procurement and e-business projects, with a special interest in Internet-based purchasing solutions. He is currently project leader for the Lean Aircraft Research Program (LARP), which collaborates with the Lean Aerospace Initiative (LAI) and previously the International Motor Vehicle Program (IMVP) at the Massachusetts Institute of Technology (MIT). He has a PhD from Linkoping Institute of Technology in industrial marketing focusing on buyer and supplier relationships.

Dr Chris Lonsdale is a lecturer in supply chain management and programme director of the MBA in strategy and procurement management in the Centre for Business Strategy and Procurement at Birmingham University's Business School. His specialist area of interest is the boundary of the firm decision. In 1998 his book *Outsourcing: A Business Guide to Risk Management Tools and Techniques* was published. During the 1990s he has taught both on MBA programmes and in a number of global corporations.

John McIlroy was research assistant in public procurement in the School of Public Policy, Economics and Law at the University of Ulster until June 2000, where he carried out PhD research on supply chains in the public sector, as well as contributing to research and publications on electronic procurement, SMEs and public procurement, and competitive tendering. He now works for Best Value Community Ltd in Antrim, Northern Ireland, a company providing Internet services to local government.

Howard McCulloch is Deputy Director (in Professional Development) at JPPSG (the Joint Procurement Policy & Strategy Group) and has a keen interest in the development and use of National Vocational Qualifications as a means of developing the business skills of university staff. Originally from a buying background, Howard entered education when he accepted a position as lecturer in purchasing at the Central College of Commerce, Glasgow in Scotland. He was responsible for the development and delivery of a wide range of structured procurement courses and seminars across every sector of business and for the past four years he has been heavily involved in coaching and assessing candidates who choose to develop competence through vocational qualifications in management and procurement.

Frank McDonald is Head of the International Business Unit at Manchester Metropolitan University. He has research interests in the area of the impact of economic integration on business strategies and operations and assessing the importance of the development of industrial districts in the process of internationalization. He has also worked on the implications of the development of e-commerce for supply chains.

J. Gordon Murray is procurement manager for Belfast City Council and has 25 years of local government purchasing experience. He developed, and is lead officer for implementation of, the council's purchasing strategy. Gordon holds an MSc in purchasing and supply management, is a Member of the Chartered Institute of Marketing and CIPS, and is currently pursuing a part-time DPhil at the University of Ulster, primarily on local government purchasing strategy and sustainable procurement. Previous work has been published in *Public Policy and Administration, European Journal of Purchasing and Supply Management*, and *Supply Chain Management: An International Journal.*

Eleftheria Noula was a research associate at the Centre for Business Strategy and Procurement at Birmingham University's Business School, working on an EPSRC-sponsored project examining the effectiveness of management tools and techniques within major UK and global companies. She now works for a Greek shipping company.

Johanna Rantala (née Stenberg) took her MSc (Economics) degree at Turku School of Economics in Finland in January 1998. She worked in Lappeenranta University of Technology in the Department of Business Administration until June 1999 as an assistant and researcher in purchasing. She has carried out research for a doctoral thesis on service purchasing and purchasing value chains since September 1998.

Currently she is working at Andersen Consulting's office in Helsinki as a change management consultant.

John Ritchie is director of London Universities Purchasing Consortium. As director of a large purchasing consortium in the UK higher education sector, John is responsible for developing the consortium's commercial effectiveness. His career spans a range of disciplines including logistics and project management as well as procurement, with experience gained in both the public and private sectors in the UK. John is a member of the Chartered Institute of Purchasing and Supply and has presented papers to conferences including the IPSERA and Institute of Purchasing and Supply (South Africa) international conferences as well as UK seminars and workshops. His themes have principally been associated with developing the effectiveness of purchasing and providing added value services.

Frank Rozemeijer graduated from the University of Amsterdam with an MSc in Economics in 1994, and had a book on managing outsourcing relationships published on behalf of a large maintenance services provider in the Netherlands. In 1995 he was involved in an international research project on the future of purchasing, which brought him into contact with a number of large companies in both the USA and Europe. Together with Professor Dr Arjan van Weele, he summarized the results of this study in *Revolution in Purchasing*, published in 1996. In 1996 he started both as a lecturer and PhD researcher at the Institute for Purchasing & Supply Development (IPSD) at Eindhoven University of Technology, in the Netherlands. Currently, he is also working part-time for Compendium, an international consultancy firm, in the areas of purchasing and resource management.

Dr Mohammed Saad is Principal Lecturer and Head of the School of Operations Management at the Bristol Business School at the University of the West of England. He is also Director of Innovation in the Business Systems Research Unit. His research, consultancy and teaching interests focus on the management of Novato, supply chain management and technology transfer to developing countries. Recent research projects have included *Unlocking specialist potential: a more participative role for specialist contractors, Innovation in management in developing countries* and *A report on the first thematic seminar on telecommunications technologies in the construction industry*.

Donna Samuel is a research associate at Cardiff University within the Lean Enterprise Research Centre. Donna gained several years' industrial experience before joining the university. Since joining she has been involved in a number of research programmes. Early programmes included the co-ordination of a network of SMEs on behalf of the DTI and execution of the UK element of a pan-European study into subcontracting on behalf of the EU. In more recent years the Centre has concentrated on applied research, focusing on improvement methods.

Peter Stannack is director of Sourcing Performance Ltd, a procurement consultancy based in Ashington, UK. He has researched and published widely, mainly in the areas of customer supplier relationships and supply chain management, and is a regular contributor to IPSERA and NAPM conferences.

Diana Thompson initially entered the teaching profession after graduating with a mathematics degree from Imperial College London, before joining the lecturing staff of the School of Computing at the University of Wolverhampton. At Wolverhampton, Diana has been instrumental in leading several novel initiatives, including the University's successful 'Women into Computing' programme and the marketing activities of the School. In addition to publishing widely, Diana has co-managed the University's e-Business Automotive Supply Chain programme.

Professor Hannu Vanharanta began his professional career in 1973 as technical assistant at the Turku office of the Finnish Ministry of Trade and Industry. Between 1975 and 1992 he worked for Finnish international engineering compa-

nies, including Jaakko Pöyry, Rintekno and Ekono as a process engineer, section manager and leading consultant. His doctoral thesis was approved in 1995. From 1995 to 1996 he was Professor in Business Economics in the University of Joensuu, and from 1996–1998 he was Purchasing and Supply Management Professor in the Lappeenranta University of Technology. Since 1998 he has been Professor in Industrial Management and Engineering at Pori School of Technology and Economics, at Tampere University of Technology. He is a member of IPSERA and Research Fellow in the Institute for Advanced Management System Research.

Veli-Matti Virolainen is Professor of Purchasing and Supply Management at the Lappeenranta University of Technology in Finland. He earned his MSc, Licentiate degree, and PhD at the Lappeenranta University of Technology. He has been visiting researcher at the University of Nottingham, UK. His research interests are in the areas of purchasing and supply management; in particular, strategic partnership

Dr Glyn Watson is a lecturer in the Centre for Business Strategy and Procurement at Birmingham University's Business School. He is also Director of the Centre's Certificate Programme in Advanced Procurement Management. His areas of research expertise include supply chain management, supply chains and the impact of regulation, and marketing for procurement. Glyn also works with a number of global companies undertaking in-house competence development programmes for their procurement personnel.

Arjan van Weele holds the NEVI Chair in Purchasing and Supply Chain Management, both at Nyenrode, The Netherlands School of Business (since 1998) and at Eindhoven University of Technology (since 1989). He has published widely on his scientific and consulting work. His book *Purchasing in Strategic Perspective* is the leading textbook within his country. His best-known books in English are *Purchasing and Supply Chain Management* (Thomson, 2000), *Purchasing Management Handbook* (with Prof Dr David Farmer, 1993) and *Revolution in Pur-*

chasing (with Frank Rozemeijer, 1996). Since 1994 he has been a member of the editorial board of the *International Journal of Purchasing and Materials Management* (USA); since 1995 of the editorial board of the *European Journal of Purchasing and Supply Management.*

Dipl.-Wirtsch.-Inf. Georg Wilking has been working on the subject of Internet-based business applications since 1992 and is currently finishing his PhD thesis on this subject. Georg holds a diploma in business administration and computer science from the University of Mannheim. He has been working at IBM's European Networking Centre (ENC) in Heidelberg, as well as for various publishing companies, where he has introduced Internet-based publication. Georg Wilking is currently responsible for the Competence Centre's IT and Purchasing course at Essen University, Germany, and has published several papers and articles on Internet-based procurement.

Lars Ydreskog graduated with an MSc in mechanical engineering 1986 from Linköpings University Sweden, and continued with a PhD in manufacturing engineering. He began his indus-

trial career at Saab Aircraft AB where he was a project manager for a Lean Enterprise project covering the entire operation. He went on to work as logistics director followed by a position as plant manager for commercial aircraft. In 1999 Lars started as a project manager and researcher for LARP (Lean Aircraft Research Program), a collaborative research program between Saab, Volvo, Ericsson and LAI at MIT. Today he works as a consultant in supply chain management.

Michael Zagler is research associate at the Institute for Technology Management (ITEM) and PhD student at the University of St Gallen, Switzerland. He holds a degree in business administration from the University of St Gallen. At ITEM Michael worked on the development and management of the Buy2gether consortium network. His other projects include target planning for material costs and an international benchmarking project on strategic purchasing with the TECTEM Benchmarking Centre. Research for his PhD thesis focuses on strategic purchasing, the management of purchasing synergies and Internet technology. Michael has co-authored a book (in German) on commodity management and purchasing consortia.

Introduction

This book is based on a selection of the papers presented at the 8th International Annual IPSERA Conference, held on 28–31 March 1999 in Belfast and Dublin. The quality of papers submitted for the Conference was higher than ever before, judging by the ratings given by our panel of referees. Of the 78 papers presented at the Conference, 24 have been selected for this book on the basis of referees' assessment of the initial paper proposal, sessional chairs' comments at the Conference, rankings awarded by an expert panel of academics and practitioners, and the editors' judgement as to the papers' suitability for the readers of this book.

In sequence and in terms of subject matter, the chapters are organized into five sections dealing with: supply chain management; outsourcing and partnership; organization and management; electronic procurement; and performance evaluation. This collection of chapters makes a contribution to most of the important issues confronting both practitioners and academics in purchasing and supply:

- how to structure supply chains and manage supplier relationships so as to achieve competitive supply;
- how to determine whether to 'make/do or buy'; what kind of relationships to develop and maintain with suppliers in different markets for the wide range of goods and services you buy;
- how to organize internally to get the best out of your purchasing function; when and how to collaborate with other buying organizations;
- how purchasing can make effective use of the opportunities provided by electronic means of doing business, especially the Internet;
- how purchasing performance may be evaluated both in terms of its internal activities and also in terms of the overall effectiveness of the supply chain.

The content of the chapters is discussed in more detail in the introduction to each section.

BEST PRACTICE PROCUREMENT

The title of the book reflects the editors' belief that the components of 'best practice' cannot be identified and set out as a blueprint to be applied regardless of the context within which your company or organization operates. Organizational contexts and individuals' experiences result in differences both in 'objective reality' (the facts upon which different observers in different contexts may agree) and in the 'conceptual lenses' through which reality is perceived. The latter may also result in distortion of the former, in that certain data is examined, and others ignored, resulting in different perspectives even on issues which appear to rely on hard facts. Thus, rather than claim to be able to offer a blueprint of best practice tools and techniques, the book offers a wide variety of perspectives on the constantly developing ideas and evidence about what may be successful ways of thinking about, analysing and managing effectively the complexities of the procurement function now and for the future. Drawing together in one collection papers reflecting a range of perspectives enables readers to decide which issues of those discussed are relevant to their practical or academic context, to balance their perceptions against those of others, and to come to a considered judgement about what steps to take in order to advance knowledge and practice.

PERSPECTIVES

The range of perspectives represented in the book includes the following:

- academic and practitioner, in some cases combined as joint authors;

- different countries with a variety of business and research cultures;
- public and private sector; and
- manufacturing and service sectors.

This range of perspectives provides a breadth of coverage of topics included in the papers presented at the Conference. First, of the twenty-four chapters, fourteen are authored solely by academics, five by practitioners, and five by combinations of academics and practitioners. This balance of interests and experience ensures that chapters deal both with conceptual or theoretical issues, and also address practical steps to deal with situations facing managers within the purchasing function.

Second, the book is aimed at reflecting the truly international nature of both IPSERA and the Conference itself. In total, some 20 countries were represented amongst the authors of papers presented at the Conference: of these, English was the first language of 57 per cent, with Italian, Swedish, German, Dutch and Finnish the most frequently represented amongst authors for whom English was not the first language. The 50 authors contributing to this text come from 12 different countries. The increasing internationalization of IPSERA is reflected in these figures, but more significant is the greater breadth of experience of different cultural, organizational and knowledge traditions increasingly recognized as contributing to debates about purchasing and supply. This strengthens and challenges the existing body of knowledge, stimulating wider cross-national collaboration to produce more soundly based theories and practical methods for analysing common problems arising from the globalization of markets.

The third element of breadth relates to sectoral perspectives, whether public or private, manufacturing or service. Fourteen chapters focus on the private sector, six on the public sector, and four cover organizations from both sectors, while eight chapters relate solely to manufacturing, eleven to services, and five cover both manufacturing and service sectors. Whilst this demonstrates cross-sectoral coverage in respect of both ownership and process, what is of greater interest is the extent to which lessons learned, or tools and techniques developed, from research in one sector can be applied in other sectors. Specific examples of the application of techniques developed in the private sector to public sector organizations are provided by Murray and Cupples in relation to 'green vendor appraisal' (Chapter 4), and Esain et al. (Chapter 20) in relation to evaluating effective order fulfilment within the Driver and Vehicle Licensing Agency (DVLA). Other chapters are explicitly cross-sectoral in their conceptual approach or empirical research, as a result of which the models developed and findings presented are more likely to be applicable regardless of ownership or process. Even those chapters which are specifically related to the public or private, manufacturing or service sectors should be examined for their potential synergies with other organizations or sectors. Many of the most successful innovations in product development, technology and service processes have emerged as a result of applying developments in one sector to others, often as a result of innovation by suppliers serving customers from different sectors. In addition, there is a long history of the public sector adapting private sector best practice to suit its own political, financial and socio-economic context, which is increasingly true in respect of purchasing. Thus supply chain management concepts and techniques initially derived from manufacturing are beginning to be examined for their relevance to the public sector. Rich rewards may therefore result from the chapters included in this book for both academics and practitioners, by thinking beyond the context and constraints of any one sector.

This range of perspectives benefits not only academics, who can build upon and further develop the ideas and empirical findings of the authors represented here, but also practitioners in terms of more broadly based methods, techniques and tools. Rather than a single best way which may be based upon one company's successful performance in a particular market at a particular time, these chapters draw upon the literature to provide an insight into the existing evidence, to which they then contribute with their own original research, thus demonstrating the complexity of most of the issues facing practitioners. Rather than following a set of prescribed steps whose derivation is unknown, these chapters provide a clear indication of the basis for their ideas, the organizations and settings from which their information is drawn, a clear explanation of their results and their deficiencies and, in most cases, present models, tools or techniques which may be applied in different ways to a wide range of different buyer–supplier contexts and relationships, thus providing a means of managing complexity.

ACKNOWLEDGEMENTS

On behalf of the Organizing Committee, the editors would like to take this opportunity to thank all those who contributed to the success of the Conference, organizationally, academically and socially. First the sponsors, Belfast City Council, Northern Ireland Tourist Board, Niceday and the Chartered Institute of Purchasing and Supply. Second, our colleagues on the Organizing Committee: Gordon Murray (Belfast City Council), Margaret Farrell (Dublin Institute of Technology), Steffan Bungart (National Institute of Transport and Logistics, Ireland) and Gerry Davis (Irish Institute of Purchasing and Materials Management). Third, all those who helped with the smooth running of the Conference: Beth and Jim Sinclair (University of Western Ontario), Jill Gayton (CIPS), Martin Sayliss and his staff (SCPDU, University of Ulster), and students and technical staff of the University of Ulster and Dublin Institute of Technology.

Finally, thanks are due to the authors of papers submitted to and presented at the Conference, as well as to the referees and colleagues who agreed to chair paper sessions, whose comments and recommendations made the very difficult task of selecting the papers for inclusion in this book considerably easier than it would otherwise have been. Many of the other papers presented at the Conference are worthy of publication, and no doubt are in the process of publication elsewhere. As with previous IPSERA conferences, a special edition of the *European Journal of Purchasing and Supply Management* (**6**(1), March 2000) is being published, containing papers from the Conference not included here. In total, 32 of the 78 Conference papers will be published under the auspices of IPSERA, thus contributing to its aim of 'developing and disseminating research in purchasing and supply'. Once again, many thanks to all those who have made this possible.

Andrew Erridge, Professor of Public Policy and Management (Chair, Organizing Committee)
Ruth Fee, Lecturer in Government (Conference Manager)
John McIlroy, Research Assistant, Public Sector Supply Chain Management (Member, Organizing Committee)

School of Public Policy, Economics and Law, University of Ulster

PART ONE

SUPPLY CHAIN MANAGEMENT

Introduction to supply chain management

John McIlroy

This section of the book provides a balanced assessment of supply chain management demonstrating both limitations and opportunities. The early chapters show how limitations can exist due to the nature of the specific industry, issues of cost and the distribution of power along the chain. The last two chapters in this section describe a brighter picture of supply chain management as providing opportunities for purchasing to play a key role in organizational strategy through the selection and management of suppliers and key supply chains.

In Chapter 1 Forker and Stannack take the view that supply chain management is a costly process which prevents most organizations from correctly implementing it. This would explain the industry-specific nature of supply research that tends to focus on large automobile and electronics companies. Costs discussed here by the authors include the need for new systems and 'reach', the idea that the size of supply chains prevent their correct management. For example, a firm could be affected by a fifth or sixth tier supplier they did not know existed.

The solution suggested by the authors is based on the premise that the more effective the information the more effective the management strategy. Therefore if organizations can better manage information they should be able to reduce the costs mentioned earlier. They argue that information that will predict, rather than describe, network behaviour will reduce costs by enabling preventative or avoiding action to be taken. Forker and Stannack provide a model to reduce supply chain costs through better information management.

In Chapter 2 Watson et al. suggest other limiting factors on supply chain management including the nature of the market and the issue of power, or lack of it. They argue that most supply chain research is based on an 'operational efficiency' theory which assumes that competition is a universal or near universal phenomenon centred on creating cost advantages and delighting the customer. Such a strategy ignores the 'centrality of power' where success depends on a firm's ability to appropriate value and not pass it on.

A case study of direct mail publishing is used to show the limitations of the efficiency type strategy. Whilst such efficiency is necessary for profitability within the direct mail publishing industry, it is not capable of delivering sustainable commercial success. Watson et al. provide a number of reasons to support their argument with reference to the structure of the direct mail supply chain; the lack of knowledge/resources valued by downstream customers; monopoly suppliers in certain markets; and the problem that in areas where there is scope for cost savings – for example, postage – there is no way of obtaining them.

The issue of power and the nature of the industry are also key topics for Saad and Jones in Chapter 3. Here they look at the construction industry and the role of the main contractor who is in a pivotal position to link the supply chain both up- and down-stream. They provide a rationale for developing supply chain management within construction. They suggest it will better manage and co-ordinate construction; develop greater synergy through collaboration; reshape relationships; and provide a more holistic approach. The authors show improvements resulting from more attention being paid to the supply chain through case studies of two main contractors. These improvements include enhanced quality, reduction in defects, increased tendering success and a more favourable perception of contractors by their clients. The case studies also identify problems which the previous chapters have discussed, including contractors fearing a loss of power and influence, the costs of implementation and the problem of more powerful clients not wanting to fully implement the strategy. At present the use of supply chain management is still a relatively new concept within construction, with only a few construction clients involved. Therefore it represents an interesting research area to follow to discover whether, as the authors believe, the existing inhibitors can be overcome.

The final two chapters suggest strategic opportunities for purchasing, which has a major contribution to make in improving the environmental performance of organizations. Both chapters agree that environmental information is not easily comprehensible to non-specialists and therefore there is a need to develop more user-friendly tools. Murray and Couples (Chapter 4) believe this can be done by further developing the familiar and incrementally adapting existing supplier appraisal tools. A questionnaire survey of local authority purchasers in the UK showed the limited extent to which green supplier appraisal is carried out currently. The authors develop a green supplier appraisal model which recognizes the costs involved with supply chain management and suggests a portfolio approach based on environmental risk and financial cost.

In Chapter 5 Lamming et al. outline their research on developing a model for environmentally sound purchasing based on an assessment of environmental risks and costs. This examines the complete supply chain covering the entire life cycle of a product including customer use and disposal. Once again there is no single approach recommended, as the nature of the product or industry is likely to affect the strategy decided on. Instead, the model presented by the authors will allow firms to develop their own working versions adapted to suit their own circumstances. The model was developed as a result of ongoing research with 30 leading companies, both publicly and privately owned, including London Underground.

These chapters demonstrate that there is no one supply strategy suitable for all circumstances. When deciding upon a supply strategy, an organization needs to look at costs involved; their power relative to others in the chain; risk; and the nature of the industry in which they operate. Relating this back to the discussion in Chapter 2, once these issues have been considered an organization may develop an operationally efficient strategy such as supply chain management, or they may choose a different strategy based on the centrality of power.

The chapters in Part I therefore reflect the perspectives discussed in the Introduction. A wide range of sectors is covered, including specific research on supply chain management in construction, direct mail publishing and local government, whilst Chapter 5 is based upon a wide range of public and private, manufacturing and service companies. The evidence and arguments presented, especially in Chapters 1 and 2, demonstrate that there is difficulty in transferring supply chain concepts developed in manufacturing, specifically for consumer products, to the public and service sectors. These chapters also challenge the value of applying supply chain management at all, without careful analysis of the cost and power implications. However, models and techniques are also developed to assist in making judgements about when and how to apply supply chain management, case studies that demonstrate best practice in developing customer focus in construction are presented (Chapter 3), and specific tools are discussed, particularly in respect of environmental purchasing (Chapters 4 and 5).

CHAPTER ONE

Co-evolutionary purchasing: several steps beyond supply chain management?

Laura Forker and Peter Stannack

CONCEPTUALIZING THE MANAGEMENT OF SUPPLY

It seems stupid to ask, 'Where did supply chain management (SCM) come from?' After all, there are so many possible answers. One can suggest that SCM is a response to competition, or to improved manufacturing techniques such as those described by Monden (1993). It is perhaps even a business response to more 'civilized' social values such as partnership and collaboration. The problem is that none of these explanations is complete. Within the literature no one seems to have asked this question. This lack does, we believe, have very real consequences for both practitioners and academics. Practitioners demand tools with which they can take action. Academics are often forced to produce tools based on a somewhat simplistic view of the world, such as the suggestion that a supply chain can be conceived in the form of an organization chart.

Nonetheless, a minimum requirement for human action is a conceptual model of the action you wish to take and the environment in which it will be taken. Such a model acts as a blueprint that can be used to plan, implement and take corrective action for designing a supply management programme. The better this blueprint describes and explains the phenomenon, the more likely it is to manage the phenomenon. Others have called this description and explanation 'theory' but we would suggest that theory is only a part of the overall blueprint.

The concept of a blueprint (in itself a blueprint) is common to many disciplines. In man-

agement, it is often referred to as a 'paradigm' drawing on Kuhn's (1970) work on the epistemology of science. Although Kuhn himself used the word in a number of ways, a paradigm in this sense is a shared view of an event or series of events. Similar concepts are employed in sociology where the word 'Weltanschauung' meaning world-view is employed to describe a similar shared view. In the burgeoning field of history, the word 'mentality' is employed to describe the same type of concept. Of course, all of these terms are linked to what we might call 'ideology', which Louis Althusser (1971) defined as 'the imaginary relationship of individuals to their real conditions of existence'.

Many supply 'chain' blueprints are borrowed from practice in the automotive or electronics sectors. These models are often culture-, or even industry-, specific and have developed in response to technological drivers such as improved production systems or functional drivers such as increasing speed of competition. The theoretical background of supply chain management does not really provide us with sufficient information to help develop an alternative model. Most of this theory rests upon transaction cost economics, which deals with the design and placement of organizational boundaries.

We shall discuss below the fact that supply management activity tends to take place in stages – spend aggregation, supply base rationalization, increases in proportional spend, and so on. In order to design an effective management blueprint, we need to consider the way in which we conceptualize supply management and 're-engineer' the concept.

RE-ENGINEERING SUPPLY MANAGEMENT

Within the field of economics a growing body of research can be identified, which suggests that demand does not arise purely from human needs and desires but is, in fact, co-created by the interaction of the buyer and the seller. This interactionist approach (see also Popper 1987) can also be seen in other disciplines. These include the study of service quality in management where there seems to be a growing recognition that customer satisfaction is created *jointly* by the interaction of the customer and the company. Poor products and services may well lead to 'lower' levels of customer satisfaction, but equally so may poor customer skills in using and evaluating the product or service. Low levels of customer satisfaction can also be caused by third party interactions beyond the control of the service provider or product supplier. Understanding both the levels of relative satisfaction and the reasons for these results is, therefore, equally important.

If we were to ignore legacy systems in SCM and redesign the discipline from scratch, we can see that there are a number of useful points that we can incorporate in our blueprint. The first, and most important, is that purchasing needs information in order to manage the supply base properly. Traditional purchasing has always been poor at acquiring information. SCM is improving its information acquisition activities, but quality is often still poor.

In this sense the task of SCM, and the task of marketing, are very similar. Both disciplines base their operations in networks. This is both their strength and their weakness. In order to improve the strength of their networks both disciplines need to manage the behaviour of large numbers of entities (people, groups or organizations). For a global marketing programme organized by a company such as Coca-Cola, the potential customer network can run into millions. Even in industrial marketing, the poten-

tial customer base can be in the hundreds of thousands. For a global sourcing programme, the supply base can reach tens of thousands. Even a 'local' programme can have ten thousand suppliers.

Networks have generally been much better at moving resources than information. Where resources can be processed and value added, information is all too often distorted and malformed. More recently, there has been a growing recognition that networks also involve the movement of information. Efforts have taken place in both SCM and marketing to improve information quality. These include 'relationship marketing' and 'partnership sourcing'. It should be recognized that these strategies represent a need for better information. The transition from classic to customer relationship marketing (CRM) involves a shift in emphasis from demographic (what type of entities they are working with) to psychographic (why entities behave in particular ways) information. The transition from 'adversarial' to 'partnership' relationships often involves longer contracts, and improved 'supplier assessment'. This shift also requires enhanced explanatory capability and therefore information with enhanced predictive power. Similar shifts can be seen in a number of professions including accounting where 'control accounting' acquired much of its power from the ability to predict trends in organizations (Brown 1927).

Acquiring, sorting and processing information is, however, expensive. The quality of information that a manager receives also has an impact upon the cost of management strategies. Poor information can lead to very expensive management mistakes such as Coca-Cola's introduction of 'new Coke'. Of course, catastrophic mistakes such as this one are not the norm, but even low-level management costs that are perceived as 'normal' can significantly erode profits.

Any effective SCM information based blueprint should recognize a number of principles:

● Information within the network should be both credible and relevant. Information can be controlled at the point where it enters the network (broadcast), or at the point that it leaves the network (pointcast) or throughout the network by managing the 'language' used.

- Existing network information-sharing disincentives need to be replaced with incentives.
- Actual and potential costs should be (relatively) fairly distributed across the network.
- There are two clear roles in improving network effectiveness – the role of the network manager and the role of the network information manager. This latter role should be occupied from outside the network.
- Information management needs a framework that can be used to assess information effectiveness. Criteria for such a framework should include accuracy, stability over time and across instances, and operational and predictive validity.

The better the information available to managers in whatever discipline, the more effective their management strategies are likely to be. Shifting from a commodity- and resource-based view of networks to an information-based view is, however, difficult. Before we consider the way in which a new blueprint might be operationalized, it may be useful to consider the consequences of continuing with the existing approach.

GROWTH IN SUPPLY CHAIN MANAGEMENT

Supply chain management (SCM) is seen as a 'hot' new area of professional expertise. The development and marketing of SCM solutions has grown dramatically in the last five years. Within this area, we can identify two product types. The first of these is supply chain software. AMR Research has forecast that the market for supply chain planning and execution software in the USA is expected to grow to $13.6 billion by the year 2002. The second is in the field of supply chain consultancy (which may or may not be related to information systems consulting). Although accurate market figures are difficult to obtain, most of the 'Big Five' accounting and consultancy companies have invested heavily in marketing supply chain management solutions.

Many of these solutions are focused on companies' internal constituencies involving the aggregation of expenditure. Such aggregations can produce immediate impacts on the cost of bought in goods and services (BIGS). External operations such as the rationalization of company supply bases can reduce purchasing costs, but their long term effects are more difficult to predict.

It is possible to suggest that these strategies are limited, and attempts to extend the effectiveness of such strategies may result in increases in purchasing consortium activity as managers attempt to extend the boundaries of their aggregation strategies. There is some evidence from the USA that there has recently been an increase in this type of activity (Kendrick 1998).

MATURITY

There are, however, some worrying signals for the market in supply chain management. The sheer scale of managing the supply base (and a company's position within that supply base) is beyond the resources of most, if not all, companies. Even companies that are seen as 'leading edge adopters' in highly competitive industrial sectors such as electronics or automotive manufacture and assembly are facing problems as their supply bases soak up more and more time, effort and money. The penetration of SCM solutions has therefore been limited to larger organizations in particular industrial sectors. Many factors contribute to the increasing cost of managing supply.

These costs often mean that the management of the supply base often falls into a number of stages. The first involves bringing acquisition activities within the company under control (see Table 1.1). This may involve the introduction of an Enterprise Resource Planning (ERP) system or some type of controlled purchasing procedure. The cost of introducing such systems is, however, high.

In order to ensure compliance, supply base reduction may also involve attempts to 'lock' suppliers in to contracts in the same way that 'Chaebol' such as Samsung manage their supply bases (Chao et al. 1996). Traditionally such organizations have ensured that their spend with a supplier is a high proportion of the supplier's total turnover. This stage also may involve seeking consortia purchasing. This increased spend gives the Original Equipment Manufacturer (OEM) high levels of leverage that can be used to dramatically reduce costs.

Supply base rationalization naturally follows from purchasing consolidation as the purchasing company seeks to deploy its purchasing power. Selection for these projects, and indeed selection for overall supply management strategy, is often carried out on the basis of two-dimensional matrix analysis or segmentation with 'cost' or expenditure being one axis of the matrix and 'criticality' being the other.

Purchasing power rarely, of itself, will bring the improvements in performance required, and some companies have embarked on exploratory projects to develop suppliers from the first 'tier' (see Table 1.2). These projects often involve the

Table 1.1 Purchasing consolidation

Activity	Actual Cost	Potential Cost	Risk
Introduction of ERP and SCP systems	System cost	Consultancy cost	Y2K costs
Increase in consortia purchasing	Administration, legal costs	Forced harmonization	Legal risks
Supply base reduction	Cost of managing rather than administering supply base including assessment process mapping, and re-engineering costs.	Potential cost creep in longer term contracts as an element in 'partnership' management strategies	Supplier complacency

Table 1.2 Supply management

Activity	Actual Cost	Potential Cost	Risk
Ongoing process management and lean methods	Management costs	Wider socio-economic costs of 'slash and burn' sourcing policies	Potential political or legal intervention
Increase supplier dependency	Management costs	Loss of innovation. Costs of introducing management systems to meet new market conditions	Risks of supplier failure
Introduce external measures	Cost of developing measures. Cost of misplaced management strategies	Inadvertent trade-offs between cost, quality, delivery, and so on. Hidden costs of failure in one or more of these domains	Inadequate measures may lead to major supply base failure
Introduce communication programmes	Cost of supplier conferences, workshops and so on	Miscommunication costs leading to cost analysis redirection	Mismanagement of supplier expectations
Manage inheritance of adversarial relationship legacy	Management costs for meetings to create 'partnerships', setting up separate 'company' for project, cost of consultants, monitoring costs	Legal costs, failure costs	Higher management costs as a result of role confusion

introduction of some sort of measurement systems such as Unipart's Ten(d) to Zero programme. This may also involve a range of process mapping and re-engineering projects that rely heavily on the use of traditional purchasing power to actively isolate supplier processes and manage these processes to target.

SCENARIOS FOR DECLINE

It is possible to place supply chain management in a wider context, and to suggest that the commercial drivers that have caused such growth may also lead to decline. Although, understandably, critical reviews of the effectiveness of supply chain management are difficult to find, there seems to be a feeling amongst some practitioners that these efforts have stumbled or stalled. Increasingly one can hear the question 'Where is supply chain management going next? '. It is possible to suggest that the type of SCM strategies identified above may have stalled. The costs of supply management, and its relative ineffectiveness, may mean that the use of the discipline may rapidly decline. It is on one hand too expensive to become a 'mass market' product; but on the other hand, after preliminary 'quick wins', sustainable efficiency improvements may be difficult to achieve. This may lead to SCM being abandoned.

One common way of managing the resource problem is through selective action. Many organizations claim to segment their supply network on the basis of 'cost' (that is, spend) and criticality (that is, risk). Although such methods can bring 'quick wins' they can also be less than effective in the long run. There are a number of potential costs. The first of these is 'reach'. Selectively managing sections of the supply base can lead to problems. If, for instance, we were to say that managers within organizations only managed 'key employees' and left the rest to do as they pleased, the results can be predicted. Practically, because of the limited range of these projects, the OEM can end up being affected by suppliers in the fifth or sixth 'tier' that they never knew existed. As well as failure cost, management costs are also a problem. Presumptions that costs will be minimized because suppliers

will 'pass on' the quality or cost message are somewhat difficult to support. The message seems to become both weaker and more distorted as it passes down the 'chain'.

Supply management is also hampered by the way in which traditional accounting systems are set up. In the same way that just in time (JIT) inventory management faced problems with traditional accounting systems, supply management faces problems in measuring cost effectiveness. As well as broader definitions of cost, there are also costs over time and potential costs, both of which impact on SCM effectiveness. Risk may be defined as a potential cost arising from unforeseen circumstances. Supply chain management strategies can lead to a number of such risks. These may range from the costs of introducing new management systems in the supply chain through to the wider economic costs of so-called 'slash and burn' sourcing policies. Such policies may well give an organization a competitive advantage, but they can have a major impact on home markets, as supply networks are worn out and supply companies make staff redundant. They may also include the inability of SCM to anticipate and manage risk within the network.

The overall economic effect of supply chain management is largely unrecognized. There is some anecdotal evidence to suggest that supply management strategies in the retail sector have had a negative effect on local economic growth as suppliers have been 'slimmed down' using lean management strategies, and then abandoned by their main customers. This evidence has been gathered in talks with local economic development staff and suppliers in the north east of England.

MANAGING INFORMATION WITHIN THE NETWORK

There seems to be a simple way to avoid the type of scenario identified above. Whilst marketing is also seen as a discipline which needs to 'reinvent' itself (Brown 1997, 1998; Shorris 1995), marketing seems to make both more extensive and 'better' use of information than purchasing. One framework of criteria which we might use to assess the 'quality' of information is that used by Stannack and Osborn (1997).

CRITERIA

Cost: How much does it cost to obtain the information?

Accuracy: How accurately does the information reflect the phenomenon it describes?

Stability 1: How well does the measure used transfer across instances?

Stability 2: How stable does the information remain over time?

Operational validity: How 'usable' is the information in dealing with existing situations?

Predictive validity: How 'usable' is the information in dealing with future situations?

Perceived relevance: How relevant is the information perceived as being by those involved in the information-gathering process?

Supplementation: How well does the information supplement what you already know?

In creating an information-based blueprint for supply management, we can identify a number of possible activities (Stannack 1999). Information is a commodity like any other. Raw data goes through a number of processing stages, adding 'value' at each stage (see Table 1.3). It may be useful to consider these stages, shown in the table below:

Many purchasing staff, however, fail to recognize this process. Instead they act like degenerate gamblers. They 'stop' their information-gathering and processing at activity three or four, or limit this information-

gathering to personalities within the supplier rather than the supplier as a whole (Stannack and Osborn 1997). They replace information with power – control – strategies such as contracting. Unfortunately, they do not have the information to ensure that those strategies will work effectively anywhere other than the first 'tier'.

In terms of turning this set of criteria and theoretical processing activities into practical network design and co-management we can identify two strands. The first, information management, deals with the type of information needed for supply management, and how it might be managed. The second, operations management, looks at how the information can be used to develop an operational strategy.

INFORMATION MANAGEMENT

Information management should reduce or redistribute the cost of data acquisition and handling. Data gathering and handling costs money. Any such activity needs to take these costs into account and also to carry out the following:

● Ensure that the right type of information is collected. Data about performance can be assessed in two ways. The first is external validity or assessment against context – a framework or baseline. The second is internal validity to establish how different elements of the information can be reconciled. In the case of performance, this may be how certain proc-

Table 1.3　Stages of information processing

Material		Description and Processing Activity
A.	*Raw data*	1. For example, numbers, sensory impressions. Add context to create:
B.	*Information*	2. Add comparators to create:
C.	*Measures*	3. Add other information dimensions to create:
D.	*Descriptive information*	4. This describes what happens. Add enquiry to this to create:
E.	*Explanatory information*	5. This explains how things happen. Add rules to create:
F.	*Causal information*	6. This reliably explains why things happen. We then add tools and relationships to create:
G.	*Operational information*	7. This can be used to change what happens. To this we add generalization to create:
H.	*Predictive information*	8. This can be used to consistently predict what is going to happen.

esses lead to particular outcomes, such as in what circumstances team-working leads to improved product reliability, or how activity-based costing contributes to improved cost transparency and improved cost management.

- Make sure information is relevant. Data needs to be set against a useful and measurable performance baseline. Although customers' needs and wants are highly unstable, it is possible to develop an external framework of these needs and wants against which performance can be measured.
- Make sure information is managed to give best value. Information needs to be processed to make it more useful and 'valuable'. Information that will predict network behaviour is clearly more useful than information that merely describes it.
- Increase management leverage. The type of information gathered about the network as a whole should increase management leverage.
- Decrease risk. Information should contribute to decreased risk in the network by enabling preventative or avoiding action to be taken.
- Contribute to the growth of community within the network. Such a growth will, as in marketing, reduce transaction costs.
- Ensure that information within the network can be channelled. This may be at the point where it enters the network (broadcast), or at the point that it leaves the network (pointcast) or throughout the network by managing the 'language' used.

OPERATIONS MANAGEMENT

Once the relevant information has been collected and processed, this can support operations.

- Replace existing network information sharing disincentives with incentives. This means starting to talk about the network as a whole, and creating and controlling an information pool about the network.
- Ensure information distributed across the network is both credible and relevant. Information relevance can be improved by cus-

tomizing information to the individual needs of network members.

- Ensure that information supports targeted action in the form of supplier development, supplier assessment and supply management.
- Ensure that the network takes ownership of this management action.
- Ensure that actual and potential costs should be (relatively) fairly distributed across the network.
- Create two clear roles in improving network effectiveness – the role of the network manager and the role of the network information manager. This latter role should be occupied from outside the network.

CONCLUSION

In closing this paper, we can suggest that the better the information that is available to managers in whatever discipline, the more effective their management strategies are likely to be. The transition from traditional accounting to control accounting has placed accounting professionals in a strong organizational position. Once purchasing managers develop and obtain better quality information, they can create the tools to manage supply networks.

REFERENCES

Althusser, L. (1971), *Lenin and Philosophy, and Other Essays*, London: NP.

Brown, D. (1927), 'Decentralized operations and responsibilities with co-ordinated control', *Management and Administration*, May.

Brown, S. (1997), *Postmodernist Marketing*, London: Routledge.

Brown, S. (1998), Marketing Apocalypse, London: Routledge.

Chao C. (1996), 'Supplier nurturing. Samsung's strategy for supplier development', Paper presented at the *81st NAPM International Purchasing Conference*.

Kendrick, T. (1998), 'Consortium purchasing' Workshop delivered at the *83rd NAPM International Purchasing Conference*.

Kuhn, T.S. (1970), *The Structure of Scientific Revolutions*, Chicago: University of Chicago Press.

Monden, Y. (1993), *The Toyota Production System – An Integrated Approach to Just in Time*, Atlanta: Institute of Industrial Engineers.

Popper, K. (1987), *In Defence of Interactionism*, London: Routledge.

Shorris, E. (1995), *A Nation of Salesmen. The Tyranny of the Market and the Subversion of Culture*, New York: W.W. Norton.

Stannack, P. and Osborn, M. (1997), 'Forensic Purchasing. The Purchasing Manager as Detective', *Proceedings of the 5th IPSERA Conference*, Ischia, Italy.

Stannack, P. (1999), 'Info-merchants and info-mercenaries. The role of procurement in E-commerce', Paper presented to the *84th NAPM International Purchasing Conference*, San Diego.

CHAPTER TWO

Power, cost and value appropriation in the publishing supply and value chain

Glyn Watson, Andrew Cox and Eleftheria Noula

The subject of strategy, while being one of great importance, is simultaneously a source of great confusion. Its importance arises out of a changing and increasingly hostile commercial environment that has put the profitability and even survival of many firms at risk. In the face of such competition firms are having to take a long hard look at what they do and the way they do it to assess its commercial relevance. The confusion arises out of the intellectual response to these challenges. Strategy has invited contributions from a myriad of functional specialists as well as business generalists. It has also invited contributions from a diverse range of academic disciplines: business, economics, political economy and sociology. Such has been the resultant confusion that the concept itself is in danger of being debased, reduced to a tag that is attached to any half-hearted attempt to find a structured response to a commercial problem. There is a desperate need, therefore, for clarity on the issue. One way that a number of academics have attempted to provide this clarity is by undertaking the structured categorization of these diverse strands of thought. In doing so, some have found it useful to divide the literature into two main camps of related thinkers: one that focuses on the importance of operational efficiency as a determinant of business success, and a second that focuses on the centrality of power.

Of these two broad approaches it is the first that has the longer lineage. It has its roots in mainstream economics and its central contention is that the state of economic nature is an essentially competitive one. Ergo, it is argued, the profitability of firms and even their survival is contingent upon their capacity to be operationally efficient and to use the resultant cost advantages to delight the customer. Debates within this school of thought centre on how these cost advantages can best be achieved. Amongst procurement and supply chain academics this has taken the form of wrangles over the relative merits of adversarial versus collaborative exchange. Despite the obvious influence of this school, particularly amongst procurement specialists, it sits somewhat outside the mainstream of strategic writing. For this mainstream the 'efficiency school' turns business logic on its head. Business success, it would argue does not rest on the capacity of firms to pass value to the customer. Indeed, this might be taken to be an indicator of business failure. Rather, business success depends on a firm's capacity to close markets and the best measure of success is a firm's ability to appropriate value, not pass it on. Strategic management, in short, is about power.

This chapter attempts to demonstrate the relative merits of these two schools of business strategy by showing the limitations of an efficiency-type strategy in a supply chain context. It will argue that while strategies built around the principle of operational efficiency may be necessary to a firm's profitability they are not capable of delivering it sustainable commercial success. This is for two reasons; first, because the competitive pressures that necessitate the approach in the first place, force the firm onto an innovation treadmill, in which the benefits of the sometimes costly, speculative investment accrue to the customer rather than the firm. Second, the firm's capacity to get the cost savings that it needs from its supply base is severely constrained by its suppliers' own ability to close markets. Where this ability exists, suppliers are likely to use their power to push up their margins. Expecting them to drop their prices to improve the cost profile of their customers is rather akin to expecting a turkey to vote for Christmas.

This chapter looks at the direct mail (DM) publishing supply chain. Publishing in the UK is a multi-billion pound business that enjoys significant cultural as well as economic significance. Historically, the chain has consisted of a series of discrete, well-established stages that run from concept origination and editorial generation, through component production, aggregation and marketing, to distribution and retail. DM publishing is novel in that it seeks to bypass retail outlets by delivering published output directly to the end-customer.

This chapter is divided into three sections. The first section elaborates on the academic debates that were briefly described above. The second section turns to the DM-supply chain, mapping the discrete stages necessary to bring a product to market as well as describing the participants operating at each stage. The third section addresses the question of value: which firms are able to get which deals and why. The chapter concludes by drawing these discussions together and suggesting an agenda for further research.

POWER VERSUS EFFICIENCY: SUCCESSFUL BUSINESS STRATEGY

The idea that business strategy centres on firms' capacity to pass value to the customer has existed since the eighteenth century. Indeed, it can be more or less precisely dated to the publication of Adam Smith's *Wealth of Nations* in 1776. According to Smith, every industry consists of identical firms producing goods and services that are only differentiable from one another in terms of their price (Blaug 1996). The reason for this stems from the basic economic condition. In Smith's model all information is freely avail-

able and relatively costless to obtain. This forces firms onto an innovation treadmill. In order to obtain a commercial advantage over competitors they must innovate. However, any advantage that they obtain through such innovation can only ever be temporary. Because of the abundance of cheaply available knowledge, new product developments are quickly communicated to the innovator's competitors who then copy (or even improve upon) the innovation, thus eroding the first mover's early advantage. Profits, consequently, always tend towards zero.

Although this basic model has been subject to considerable refinement since Smith's time, this refinement has been more in relation to means rather than ends. For Smith, economic nature is essentially antagonistic. Firms exist in quite distinct, albeit related universes. Vertically, they might come together to exchange but co-operation between them is impossible. No firm will voluntarily lock itself into a set of permanent upstream relationships if this means that the firm will be tied to a set of suppliers which mere months down the line might be industry laggards rather than industry leaders. Furthermore, what is true for a firm and its suppliers is also true for the firm's customers. They too, possess the same footloose attitude towards the firm.

A number of writers have questioned the extent to which a process of adversarial exchange is an effective mechanism for maximizing a firm's operational efficiency, however. From within the discipline of procurement, the major refinement to Smith's insights has come from the lean enterprise school (Lamming, 1993; Womack and Jones 1996). While the lean enterprise school retains Smith's strong customer focus and, with it, his emphasis on efficiency, the specifics of how the school regards the customer differs markedly from its predecessor. Whereas the orthodox perspective had defined customers as those actors with whom the firm has a direct and immediate downstream association, the lean enterprise model takes an extended view of the customer. It asserts that the performance of the firm depends not just on its ability to delight its own customers but its customers' capacity to delight them, and so on. Suppliers are similarly regarded. The performance of its suppliers' suppliers is just as important to the firm as the performance of its own suppliers. Using this logic, the lean enterprise school developed the concept of the supply chain. This they define as an interlocking set of exchange relationships that marks the physical transformation of a good or service from raw material to finished good.

Where the lean enterprise school really differs from its predecessor, however, is in relation to its attitude to exchange relationships. Adversarial exchange produces false economies, it is argued. Contrary to what Smith assumes, information is neither freely available nor costless to obtain. Supplier performance, therefore, is difficult to monitor and the process of exchange is characterized by bad faith and opportunism. This introduces considerable waste into the production process. As a corrective, advocates of the lean philosophy argue for partnership and co-operative buyer–supplier relationships. In such an environment, the different exchange partners can work together to eradicate waste from the supply chain. The 'value dividend' that results can then be passed to the customer, thus guaranteeing the survival of the partners into the next phase of competition.

Despite the obvious influence of lean enterprise thinking within the area of supply chain management and commercial practice, it has yet to have the same impact on mainstream strategic thinking. For the mainstream, all of the efficient operations-style approaches are flawed in a number of crucial respects. First, a question mark hangs over the long-term utility of their prescriptions. Lean thinking does not take the firm off the innovation treadmill; it just offers it a different way of innovating. Its techniques may push back the firm's productivity frontier but, as other firms follow suit, the initial advantages that flow from it are soon lost. Consequently, the technique ceases to be a source of strategic differentiation (Porter 1996).

More importantly, however, the efficiency school's prescriptions might have more force if its core assumption were true; that is, that intense competition is a universal or near universal phenomenon. Even a casual glance at the make-up of many industries indicates that there are considerable differences in the relative competitiveness of different firms. Furthermore, these differences persist, sometimes for considerable periods of time. Some firms, in effect, find ways to close markets. Those that do, use their resultant market power to earn high and sustainable returns. Furthermore, where this power runs in favour of a supplier, it is hard to see how the supplier can be persuaded to see the virtues of lean thinking.

The mechanisms to effect market closure and to give a firm or its suppliers power are quite varied. Some of the more critical ones, however, are natural monopoly, government licence and protection, predatory behaviour, oligopoly and resource-based innovation. Natural monopoly and government licence tend to go hand in hand. Natural monopolies occur when the economies of scale in an industry are so high as to only be capable of supporting a single producer efficiently. Frequently, where this occurs, governments will formalize the firm's *de facto* dominance by protecting it in law. Although this licence is granted on a *quid pro quo* basis, governments will expect to exert some influence over the way in which the firm operates in return for its regulatory protection. Firms may also achieve market power through predation, by destroying the competition. Microsoft is the latest and one of the most conspicuous examples of a predatory monopolist. More common than the monopolist, however, is the oligopolist. As industries start to mature they concentrate. As the number of competitors fall the remaining producers find it easier to co-ordinate (whether formally or informally) their pricing strategies. They will then increase prices. Occasionally, such price-fixing arrangements break down. However, such occurrences tend to be infrequent and short-lived. The commercial advantages of horizontal co-operation drive the participating firms back to their previously quiet and very profitable existences. The final and most common form of market closure comes through resource-based innovation. In order to produce anything firms must make use of factor inputs, or resources. Firms innovate when they use new factor inputs or combine existing factor inputs in new ways. Firms enjoy a sustainable commercial advantage when these novel uses of resources can be made unique. Here, government licence also plays a part in that it can be used to protect the firm's Intellectual Property Rights (IPR) (Cox 1997; Watson and Sanderson 1997; Watson, Cox and Sanderson 1999).

From the power perspective it is not that strategies directed at improving operational efficiency contribute nothing to the success of the firm. Indeed, in some instances (for example, where firms face intense competition), they may be a prerequisite to a firm's survival. At the very least they will contribute to the firm's bottom line. They are generally not sufficient, however, to deliver high and sustainable returns – not least because of their fixation with passing value to the customer rather than retaining it and appropriating it for the firm. The principal positions in this strategic debate are summarized in Figure 2.1.

MAPPING THE DIRECT MAIL (DM) PUBLISHING SUPPLY CHAIN: STAGES AND ACTORS

Publishing is a major sector in the UK. It involves all those activities and industries necessary to produce, transform and distribute a piece of creative writing, art or information into a product that can be made available to the general public, commercial organizations, educational establishments, and so on. Finished products include books, magazines, daily and periodical press, maps and musical scores. More recently, output has come to include non-printed matter, CD-ROMs and on-line information services. In the past products were marketed separately. Increasingly however, they are starting to be bundled together (for example, books with CD-ROMs) or integrated with other products (for example, magazines with videos). In 1997 industry experts estimated that the industry had a conservative annual value of £12 billion.

Direct mail publishing constitutes both a specialized channel of distribution for publishing

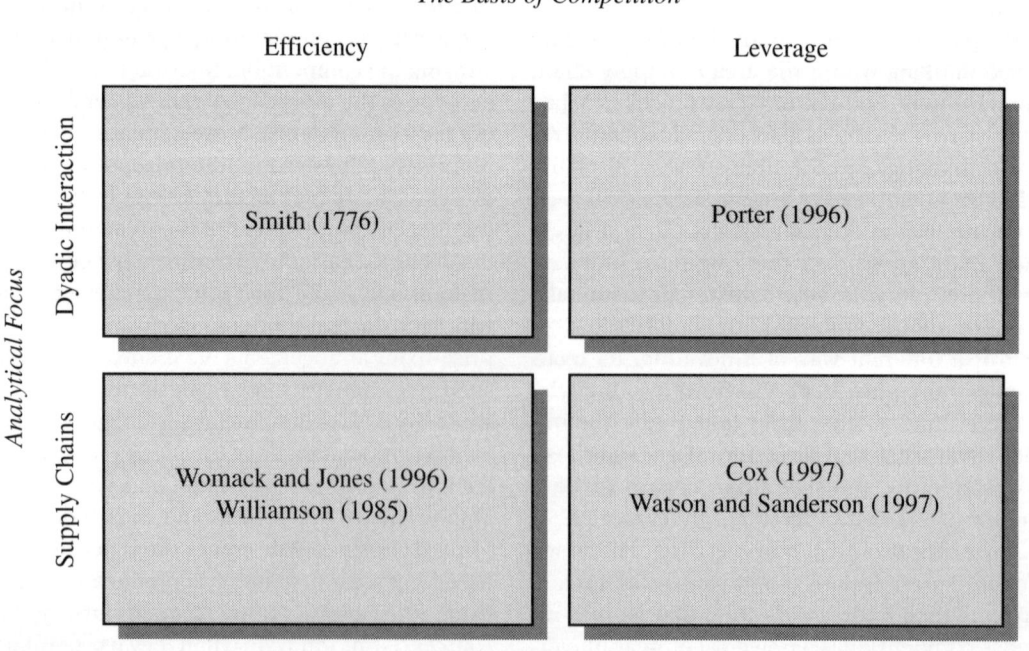

The Basis of Competition

Efficiency   Leverage

Analytical Focus — Dyadic Interaction	Smith (1776)	Porter (1996)
Analytical Focus — Supply Chains	Womack and Jones (1996) Williamson (1985)	Cox (1997) Watson and Sanderson (1997)

Figure 2.1   Supply chains and strategy

and a distinct utility proposition. As a distribution and advertising channel it offers a different way for publishers to get their products to the marketplace. Historically, publishers distributed their products through a standardized route: to the end-customer through a retail outlet. These outlets included independent newsagents and bookshops and the large multiples (WH Smiths, John Menzies, Waterstones, and so on). Such a route, however, creates two problems for the publisher. First, and particularly since the scrapping of the Net Book Agreement (NBA) which regulated the relationship between publisher–retailer–consumer, it exposed the publisher to a number of new commercial pressures. Secondly, it made it difficult for publishers to differentiate their products from those of their competitors. Unless a particular volume had been singled out for special promotion it tended to get lost amongst the hundreds of volumes that sat closely juxtaposed to each other. Consequently, a number of publishers have begun to explore the possibility of finding new channels for distributing their products. Some publishers have begun to sell direct to their customers, either via the Internet or by using direct mail techniques. To some, however, the concept of direct mail is synonymous with 'junk mail'. In fact, it represents a highly sophisticated promotional and distribution channel that has brought into existence a completely new set of industries (list, database, mailing and fulfilment houses), as well as greatly expanding the business of a number of existing firms (especially post and distribution companies). Currently, direct mail is worth over a £1 billion a year in its own right and accounts for over 10 per cent of all advertising expenditure.

The DM publishing industry, however, also provides the opportunity for publishers to offer the consumer a new utility proposition. Although some DM-publishers still offer standardized books, some experiment with new formats. For example, they can market their published output on a part-work basis whereby the customer receives the product as a series of regular instalments. Furthermore, the media can be varied and combined. Binder offers can be mixed with videos, books with CD-ROMs etc. The value of this to the publisher is that non-standardized products make it difficult for customers to make proper product comparisons. In the past, this has allowed publishers to charge a price premium.

The supply chain for direct mail publishing brings together two distinct sets of actors and consists of five distinct stages of production and distribution (see Figure 2.2). The two sets of actors are clearly those firms that have historically been associated with the generation of the written word plus the newer set of organizations that make possible the alternative channel of distribution. The five distinct transformation and distributive stages are concept origination, software production, component production and integration, production co-ordination and branding and distribution.

The chain begins with concept origination or the basic idea around which the published material will be produced. This may come from one of two sources: either the publisher itself or one of a number of independent packagers. Where the publisher generates the original utility-value proposition, the ownership of the idea is unequivocal. It belongs to the publisher. Publishers enjoy the option, however, of obtaining

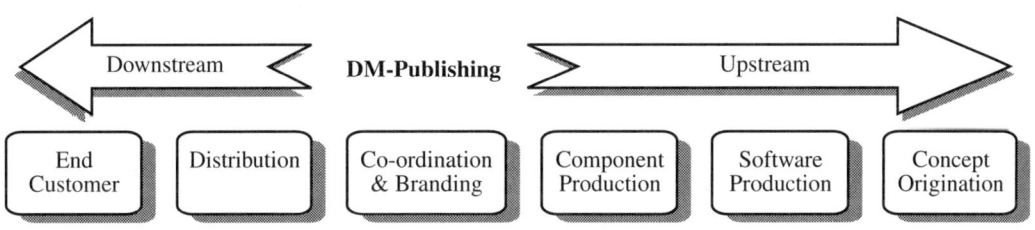

Figure 2.2 Mapping the direct mail publishing supply chain: stages and actors

their ideas from an external contractor. Here, Intellectual Property Rights are harder to define. The publisher will generally own the idea as it links to a particular format. The packager, however, may be free to sell a slightly modified idea in a modified format to one of the publisher's competitors. Notionally, when it comes to using an external contractor for this part of the production, there are hundreds of independent packagers from which the publisher might source. In reality, however, the specialized nature of the products (and sometimes also their content), means that the potential supply base can be relatively limited.

Once a concept has been agreed on, the editorial (or software) itself has to be produced or obtained. What the structure of the supply market looks like here obviously depends on the nature of the content but also on whether it has to be produced or can be obtained. If it is produced then the publisher can either undertake the production itself or pass it to a packager who will then work under the direction of the publisher. If a packager was responsible for generating the original idea it will usually also put together the editorial. If the editorial is being obtained, however, this means that it has been pre-produced and is offered to the publisher under licence. A variety of sources offer such material, including media production and phonographic companies. Where publishers contract from such companies they are usually contracting with very large companies in their own right. In the phonographic industry, for example, just five companies dominate the global supply of recorded material: CBS, EMI, Polygram, WEA and BMG supply 85 per cent of all recorded output. If the publisher's requirement for pre-published material is very specific, frequently it will mean obtaining it from a monopoly provider.

Component production involves the transfer of the editorial into its consumable form: putting words and pictures onto paper, music onto CDs etc. This requires the acquisition of commodity and quasi-commodity components. Examples of commodity components are items like paper and print. Both are mature industries with little scope for product innovation and only limited scope for market closure by other means. In the case of a quasi-commodity component like a CD its quasi-status arises out of the patterns of ownership within the industry. There are about 60 CD pressing plants worldwide and in the normal course of events CDs would be a commodity also. However, most of the phonographic companies own their own pressing plants. Where a publisher is seeking to obtain access to the phonographic company's software, that same company will also insist on undertaking the pressing itself. Where this occurs they will insist on charging a considerable mark-up for the privilege.

The publisher itself is at the fourth stage of the chain. There are no hard and fast rules as to what will constitute its core range of activities. At a minimum, however, the publisher might be expected to undertake the co-ordination of the enterprise, as well as market the product. There are four main DM publishing companies in the UK, Readers Digest, Time Life, IMP and the Book Club Association (BCA). Their product portfolios vary widely, with the Book Club Association offering books only while Readers Digest and IMP both offer a diverse range of multimedia products.

The final stage in the chain, prior to the end user, is the distribution mechanism. A diverse range of companies offer DM services. The industry's peak association, the Direct Mail Association (DMA), has a membership of around 700. For the publisher the most important firms are the list and database companies (of which there are around three or four capable of meeting the publisher's needs), and the mailing and fulfilment houses (of which there are around 50). The list brokers are critical to the publisher. DM has a typical response rate of around five per cent. This means that 95 per cent of marketing effort is wasted. List brokers not only provide the publisher with the names and addresses of prospective customers but they will 'clean' the list to take out names of people who are unlikely to respond. This can have a substantial impact on the level of wasted effort and therefore the publisher's costs. The other major group of actors involved in distribution are the mail and postage companies. There are about six companies capable of offering publishers the required geographical reach when sending parcels. There is only one company capable of handling its general post. This is the Royal Mail, which owes its position to the monopoly licence granted to it by the government for all post with a distribution cost of under £1.

EFFICIENCY AND PROFIT IN THE DM PUBLISHING SUPPLY CHAIN

DM publishing is a treadmill business in which operational efficiency, while being the only available strategic option, is a non-viable one. The utility of an operational efficiency-style approach arises out of the fact that publishers cannot close their markets thus making product innovation and cost control business necessities. The non-viability of the approach arises out of the expense of this innovation coupled with a supply chain structure in which certain key suppliers can close their markets to the detriment of publishers' attempts to control their unit costs.

There are few barriers to entry in the DM publishing industry. DM publishers enjoy no regulatory protection. They possess no proprietorial knowledge or resources valued by customers but which cannot readily be acquired by competitors. Furthermore, competition is fierce, not just between DM publishers but also between DM publishers and the publishing mainstream. In the past they were afforded some protection by virtue of the fact that the marketing channel itself made publishers' products distinct and attractive to customers. This allowed them to charge a price premium. This novelty has long since worn off, however, and publishers have had to try to find new ways to differentiate themselves. Consequently, levels of product innovation and experimentation in this industry are high and risky. Innovation can take one of two quite distinct forms. First, publishers now experiment with product formats. In the early days of the industry, publishers offered a high quality but no-frills product. For example, they would offer a simple range of books or partwork binders. Today it is common to experiment extensively with different media (many of which

are expensive), and this can incur substantial R&D costs. Second, publishers have had to significantly expand the deals that they make to their customers. For example, in the area of new business, where in the past a publisher would have typically offered customers one or two volumes at a greatly reduced rate in order to hook them, these days it is more likely to be three or four free book/CD packages. Often these free offers come without any commitment on the part of the prospective customer to buy additional material.

These high costs of innovation are significantly amplified by a further factor. This relates to the basic inefficiency of the marketing medium. Despite all their efforts, direct marketers have failed to make the medium attractive to their customers. What was once seen as a novelty is now seen as an intrusion. Given that the average response rate for direct mail is five per cent, 95 per cent of the initial marketing effort is wasted (this includes all of the free videos, books, and so on). The cost of this has to be written off. Profit margins in the industry are at zero and falling.

Not surprisingly, much of the strategic focus in this industry currently centres on cost. Here too, however, there are difficulties. These difficulties take two forms. First, in some important areas of spend, the scope for cost control has largely been exhausted. For example, paper and print represent two major areas of spend. Both are commodity businesses, although for different reasons. For example, commoditization in print has occurred because product differentiation in the industry is technologically driven but does not come from the printers themselves. Rather, it comes from the manufacturers of the presses that they use. Since these manufacturers make their innovations freely available to any printer who has the money to pay for them, these innovations quickly diffuse throughout the industry. Like publishing, this is an industry with low margins. Printers have been forced down the path of strategies of operational efficiency. However, with processes already standardized in a mature industry, there are few additional cost savings to come.

The other difficulty that publishers face is that in those areas where there is scope for cost savings, there is no way to obtain them. This has always been the case for postage, which represents DM publishers' greatest cost. Publishers spend in this area every time they undertake a product test, every time they go to a full product launch, every time they process orders and every time they bill customers. The supply of postal services is dominated by just one company, however, the Royal Mail. Given that most of the publishers' postal requirements fall into this category, this makes them dependent on a monopolist for their key area of spend.

The problem of monopoly supply is also starting to creep into other areas, however. As publishers have begun to develop new formats, this has brought them into contact with the media conglomerates that control phonographic output. These conglomerates have been able to close their markets through a combination of ownership or control of unique resources (the output of recording artists) and through a process of market concentration. If DM publishers wish to offer pre-recorded material to their customers they must do so on the terms set by the Media Company. Unrolling programmes of lean supply in this part of the supply chain is simply not an option.

CONCLUSIONS

There are two strategic options facing firms wishing to compete in their market place: one based on competition and operational efficiency, and a second based on market closure and power. Of these two approaches, strategy as efficiency is clearly the second-best option since it forces firms onto a treadmill in which value cannot be retained by the organization but must be passed to the customer. At times operational efficiency may become a strategic necessity – particularly in extreme cases where the firm cannot close its market and must control costs just to survive. Even where it is a necessity, however, there may be limits to a firm's capacity to apply it in a supply chain context. If an absence of power downstream is mirrored by a similar absence of power upstream, then the desire to control cost may represent little more than a wish list. The case of the Direct

Mail publishing supply chain represents a graphic example of this point. The levels of horizontal substitution that characterize competition in this market have reached such a pitch that no new innovation appears to be able to satisfy the customer. Rather, each new product development simply raises the pre-qualification levels for firms wishing to stay in the market place. The response of participants has been to embark on aggressive cost management exercises. Such policies have stalled, however, because many of the most important cost inputs cannot be controlled. Cost levels are determined by suppliers, who have no incentive to modify them because such modification impacts directly on their own bottom lines. They are able to reject publishers' entreaties to co-operate because it is they, rather than their suppliers, who possess the market power.

ENDNOTE

This chapter forms part of a broader research initiative currently being undertaken by the authors and their colleagues at the University of Birmingham, UK, on the subject of supply chains and supply chain types. The initiative seeks to draw out the links that exist between the analytical properties exhibited by particular exchange networks and the strategic performance of those actors operating within them. The data used in this study was obtained from an extensive series of structured interviews with participants in the publishing supply chain.

REFERENCES

Blaug, M. (1996), *Economic Theory in Retrospect*, 5th edn, Cambridge: Cambridge University Press.

Cox, A. (1997), *Business Success*, Boston: Earlsgate Press.

Lamming, R. (1993), *Beyond Partnership*, London: Prentice Hall.

Porter, M. (1996), 'What is Strategy?', *Harvard Business Review*, November-December.

Smith, A. (1776), *The Wealth of Nations*, Harmondsworth: Penguin (1985 edition).

Watson, G. and Sanderson, J. (1997), 'Collective

Goods Versus Private Interest: Lean Enterprise and The Free Rider Problem', in Cox, A. and Hines, P., *Advanced Supply Management*, Boston: Earlsgate Press.

Watson, G., Cox, A. and Sanderson, J. (1999), 'Thinking Strategically about Supply Chain Management' in D. Waters (Ed.) *Global Lo-gistics and Distribution Planning*, 3rd Edition, London: Kogan Page, pp. 125–37.

Williamson, O. (1985), *The Economic Institutions of Capitalism*, New York: The Free Press.

Womack, J. and Jones, D. (1996), *Lean Thinking*, New York: Simon and Schuster.

CHAPTER THREE

The role of main contractors in developing customer focus up and down construction's supply chain

Mohammed Saad and Martyn Jones

The chapter argues the case for a pivotal role for main contractors in aligning and integrating upstream and downstream construction processes in order to increase customer focus.

The first two sections of this chapter highlight the specific nature of construction and the need for change and innovation to increase customer focus. The following three sections argue the case for a new pivotal role for main contractors in managing construction's supply chains. Two case studies illustrating the shifting role of main contractors in increasing customer focus are provided in section 6, and the concluding comments provide a critique of the progress of the two main contractors in adopting this new pivotal role.

THE NATURE OF CONSTRUCTION

Construction embraces the efforts of a large number of participants including contracting firms, specialist contractors, consulting architects and engineers, quantity surveyors, suppliers of building materials, manufacturers of equipment and clients. Construction also involves a wide range of activities including planning, regulation, design, manufacture, construction, maintenance and eventual decommissioning of buildings and other structures (Saad and Jones 1998).

The organizations involved in the construction process often have very different aims, objectives, processes and cultures. These differences provide the basis of the benefits to be derived from collaborating and improving relationships, but also explain the reluctance of many construction organizations to meet the challenges and complexities of working more closely with other organizations.

Another defining characteristic of construction is that it is a project-based industry. This means that it is geared to flexibility, responsiveness and agility rather than ultimate product performance, which may well be more readily achieved in the longer-term, more stable processes associated with other industries. For each project a series of decisions has to be taken which take into account the context in which the tasks are to be executed; temporary organizational structures have to be created, strategies developed and plans achieved. Many decisions are often of a technical nature, but many are more related to the logistics of procurement, the problems of communication, the application of scarce or expensive resources, legal constraints, and the motivation of diverse groups of individuals and organizations.

Competition is inherent in construction's culture with price as the primary determinant of success. Supplier competition is good but it has evolved into one based almost entirely on price as contracts are systematically awarded to the lowest bidder. Time plays a role, as does quality, but price most frequently dominates customer–supplier relationships. The following findings from our research (Jones and Saad 1998) confirmed that these weaknesses in construction act against the adoption of a customer-focused approach and thus impede improvements in its overall performance:

- undue emphasis on price rather than value;
- poor communication and ambiguous project information;
- adversarial approaches leading to disputes, conflict and a lack of trust between project partners;
- insufficient focus on external and internal customer relationships;
- lack of clarity of agreed requirements with internal customers and suppliers;
- unfair unloading of risk; and
- fierce competition and reduced margins.

However, it needs to be recognized that these weaknesses can be attributed in part to the complexity of the construction process and the diversity, discreteness and uniqueness of its projects which sets it, in some respects, apart from the processes associated with other industries. Construction project outcomes are often considered difficult to predict because of the significant number of stages and actors, from both the public and private sectors, involved in the process.

The interdependency, complexity, fragmentation and uncertainty which characterize the construction process explains construction's strong reliance on more and more procurement systems and contracts, rather than developing stable relationships based on mutual understanding, appropriate sharing of risk and the development of trust. During the 1990s parts of the industry began to shift the emphasis from a contractual to a partnership approach. This has been led by a number of key partici-

pants in the construction process, including main contractors who are well placed to play a part in unifying and aligning both upstream and downstream processes. This chapter argues that main contractors are uniquely positioned to ensure the greater participation and integration of specialist contractors and their suppliers in the downstream processes, as illustrated in Figure 3.1.

THE NEED FOR CHANGE

From developing practice, already advanced in other sectors, the message for construction organizations is to work together in a more integrated way to develop greater customer focus, add value, reduce waste and achieve mutual advantage (Hellard 1995; Benett and Jayes 1995, 1998). The Latham Review (1994), the Technology Foresight Programme for Construction (1995) and the Egan Report (1998) are among many influential calls for innovation based on aligning processes and improving relationships in order to raise the performance and competitiveness of construction projects, and to help construction become a world-class industry. The research project recently completed by the authors has also confirmed the need for greater collaboration between the individuals and organizations involved. This research, which focused on the role of specialist contractors in construction, associated the poor performance of the construction industry with its adversarial relationships, the insufficient understanding of

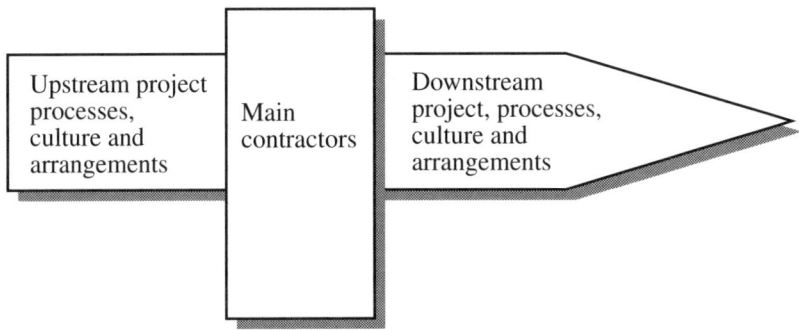

Figure 3.1   Positioning of main contractors in the supply chain

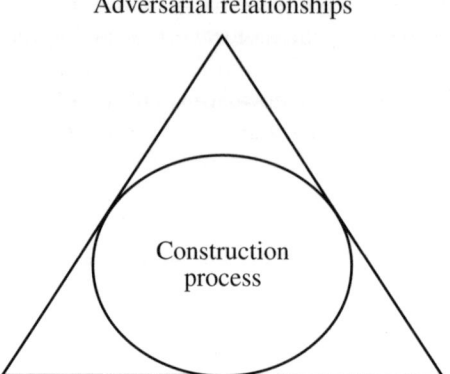

Adversarial relationships

Construction process

Poorly understood processes   Lack of customer focus

Figure 3.2 Problems with the construction contracting process

processes and the lack of customer focus, as illustrated in Figure 3.2.

As a consequence of increasing competition and a growing awareness of the need to innovate, more and more construction companies have, in recent years, sought to change their external as well as their internal relationships by developing closer and more harmonious links with specialist contractors and suppliers, in order to increase customer focus both up and down the construction process. These changes are taking place due to a growing climate of opinion that project participants working co-operatively must be more beneficial to both internal and external customers than adversarial relationships and the lack of understanding of processes that have characterized construction in the past.

However, working with others is not easy. It can be more complex and difficult when inter-organizational relationships have to be developed. Different aims, culture and perceived power imbalances often lead to conflicts (Huxman 1996). In the context of construction, where the dominant culture is adversarial and based on power rather than co-operation and mutual development (Jones and Saad 1998), then the necessary openness and the long term shared strategic perspective will be lacking, and will inhibit the effectiveness of such a change (Bessant 1991).

THE CASE FOR GREATER CUSTOMER FOCUS IN CONSTRUCTION

A customer-centred approach is increasingly seen as being at the core of improving performance and overall business effectiveness (Cooper et al. 1997). Peters (1993) also strongly argues that the customer must be brought into the centre of the business. Albrecht (1993) suggests that customer-focused businesses are built on key characteristics including a deep understanding of the customers' needs and aligning their organization with evolving customer needs and expectations. It therefore includes elements that reflect customers' perceptions of quality and value for money as well as expectations (Rosenberg 1996). From our research in construction, there is evidence of an increasing awareness of the need to understand customers and to know their needs through the following:

● adopting an internal and external customer-centred approach;
● identifying and meeting the external customer's objectives;
● negotiating a complete and clear external customer brief;
● providing incentives for team working;
● adopting partnering agreements rather than formal contracts;
● developing shared project objectives;
● providing payment for design input;
● involving specialist contractors early in the process;

- providing intra-company feedback;
- improving exchange of information; and
- making the process known and visible.

There is strong evidence that competitiveness is increasingly associated with the adoption of a more customer-focused approach. Our research in other sectors of the economy (automotive, aerospace and retailing) also indicates an even stronger emphasis on the customer and the necessity to develop strong customer–supplier relationships through:

- recognizing that there is a purchaser–supplier relationship which needs adequate time and resources to properly develop;
- clarifying customer–supplier relationships and developing clear statements of requirements;
- negotiating and agreeing goals and the mechanisms for measuring performance in relation to individual transactions, performance of the supplier or customer, and the overall value added through the relationship;
- substantially reducing the number of suppliers;
- changing the internal relationships, culture, behaviour and infrastructure within each organization in order to facilitate appropriate inter-organizational relationships;
- capitalizing on the cascade effect through which each inter-organizational link influences the whole supply chain or network;
- using contracts and agreements designed to reflect the benefits of the purchaser–provider partnership and which are not simply based on a narrow range of elements such as price;
- developing high levels of trust and honesty;
- ensuring openness, transparency and more sharing of information;
- working towards a more equal distribution of power within relationships; and
- developing compatible values and strategies.

However, it is important to recognize that developing such purchaser–supplier relationships needs considerable time and resources and is difficult in the present context and culture of construction. Developing mutual trust is clearly a critical factor for effective partnering, but time and resources need to be invested in order to create and sustain it. Huxham (1996) argues that there are two sorts of time required. The first is actual time invested in achieving mutual understanding, gaining goodwill, negotiating and co-ordinating. The second is the lapsed time necessary to cope with accountability issues and other organizational priorities and arrangements. Time and resources should also be allocated for learning to work with others. If this commitment of time and resources is not recognized and budgeted for, the partnering is unlikely to succeed and can lead to frustration and conflict.

THE ROLE OF THE MAIN CONTRACTOR IN ACHIEVING GREATER CUSTOMER FOCUS

To achieve customer focus it is necessary to have a clear and global view of the whole process or value chain, the actors involved and their relationships, and to recognize the importance of internal as well as external customers (Jones and Saad 1999). As illustrated in Figure 3.1, main contractors are well placed to provide a global view of the whole value chain because of their position between upstream and downstream processes. They can help link the customer to the supplier and negotiate, define and agree the customer's requirements. Using this approach means the output of the relationship can be determined and measured. As both the customer and supplier have negotiated and defined the requirements they also know whether the output meets the initial requirements. Another benefit of this approach is that main contractors can facilitate and encourage frequent and direct communication upstream and downstream in the process. This can provide a basis for the development of trust, continuous improvement in reducing waste and adding greater value to the external customer.

Customer satisfaction is increasingly being seen as dependent upon the move towards a better understanding of deeper values which are developed and nurtured by ongoing relationships and experiences between customers and suppliers in the whole process (Coulson-Thomas 1997). Main contractors can play a key role in determining what is important to both internal and external customers by engaging them in an ongoing process of discovering what real, sustained satisfaction means to them and how their requirements change over time. This would lead to both parts of the process working more closely together across the customer–supplier boundary to identify and resolve areas of mutual interest or concern. Clearly it is difficult and expensive to develop such deep relationships with the large numbers of customers and suppliers which currently exist in construction. This is why many organizations, including main contractors, have begun to reduce their numbers of customers and suppliers.

A significant difficulty in construction is that customers often have unclear and rapidly changing requirements. All construction's customers are to some extent unique, and seek and expect a degree of tailoring to their particular requirements. The high variability of customer requirements can make it difficult to identify and satisfy their needs, or measure accurately and precisely the degree of satisfaction achieved. This variability in customer requirements is compounded by a further difficulty related to the wide range of customers from regular to irregular users of construction services.

SUPPLY CHAIN MANAGEMENT (SCM) AS A MEANS TO DEVELOP CUSTOMER FOCUS IN CONSTRUCTION

SCM is a concept that extends the view of operations from a single business unit to a whole supply chain or network (Jones and Saad 1998). It is increasingly seen as a set of practices aimed at managing and co-ordinating the whole construction supply chain from raw materials suppliers to end customers (Vollman et al. 1997). The objective is to develop greater synergy through collaboration along the whole construction supply chain rather than focusing improvement on an individual business unit (New and Ramsay 1997). The holistic approach associated with SCM is essentially motivated by the benefits to be derived from a more effective man-

agement of the interfaces between all the organizations involved (von Hippel 1986; New and Ramsay 1997).

Research in a number of sectors of the economy has provided evidence of the significant benefits to be gained from the synergies developed from the successful implementation of SCM (Lamming 1993; Sako et al. 1994; Hines 1994; Lipparini and Sobrero 1994; Womack and Jones 1996; Towill 1996). These include:

- cost reduction;
- more innovation in products, processes and organization;
- more compatible and integrated processes;
- greater sharing and dissemination of information;
- better communication;
- increased shared learning based on joint problem-solving;
- greater predictability;
- greater flexibility and more responsiveness to changes in the external environment;
- more customer focus;
- greater transparency in transactions leading to greater trust and commitment;
- intra-supply chain collaboration and inter-supply chain competition;
- shorter cycle times including design to market;
- quality improvement through a better understanding of requirements and capability;
- better understanding of resource requirements and more effective utilization;
- better and longer-term planning which helps reduce cycle times and ensures more even flow from the supply chain;
- clear understanding of the role individuals and firms play within the supply chain; and
- greater contractual, competence and goodwill trust.

Successful implementation of SCM in construction is seen as strongly dependent upon the ability to create, manage and reshape relationships between individuals and organizations along the supply chain. In the case of frequent customers of construction services, closer long-term relationships lead to greater transparency in transactions which, in turn, increases trust and commitment which is seen as being central to the success of relationships between customers and suppliers. Applying SCM in the case of the infrequent customer is more problematic.

Effective SCM in other sectors suggests the need for a company to co-ordinate the whole supply chain and champion changes for improvement (Lamming 1993). In the context of construction, and in the case of regular and irregular external customers, main contractors are well positioned to co-ordinate both the upstream processes to the client and the end user, and downstream processes involving specialist contractors and their suppliers. However, it is clear that main contractors respond to severe competition by placing greater customer focus on the upstream side of the chain whilst largely underutilizing the potential in the downstream side of the process, as shown in Figure 3.3.

As a result of growing awareness of the changes introduced in other organizations and sectors of the economy, and fierce upstream competition, more and more main contractors are playing proactive roles in increasing customer focus through SCM. They are also beginning to use their downstream influence to develop greater customer focus throughout the whole supply chain.

CASE STUDIES OF TWO MAIN CONTRACTORS UTILIZING SCM

The two case studies discussed here have been selected to reflect differences in terms of size, the type of clients and the time of adoption of SCM. A small main contractor, A, has been implementing SCM through most of its organization since 1997. After a long period of preparation and planning, the larger main contractor B, has only recently begun to implement its SCM strategy. It aims to implement SCM throughout the whole organization by 2001.

MAIN CONTRACTOR A

Like many general contractors in the early 1990s, main contractor A was facing severe competition resulting in uncertainty of workload and low profitability. Having analysed a number of studies in construction, approaches being adopted in other sectors of the economy, and undertaken an analysis of the profitability of their customer base, they began to focus their efforts on three sectors of the construction market, including retailing, rather than chase after non-profitable work across the whole construction market.

In 1996 main contractor A began partnering with a major supermarket chain which had already begun the process of reducing and

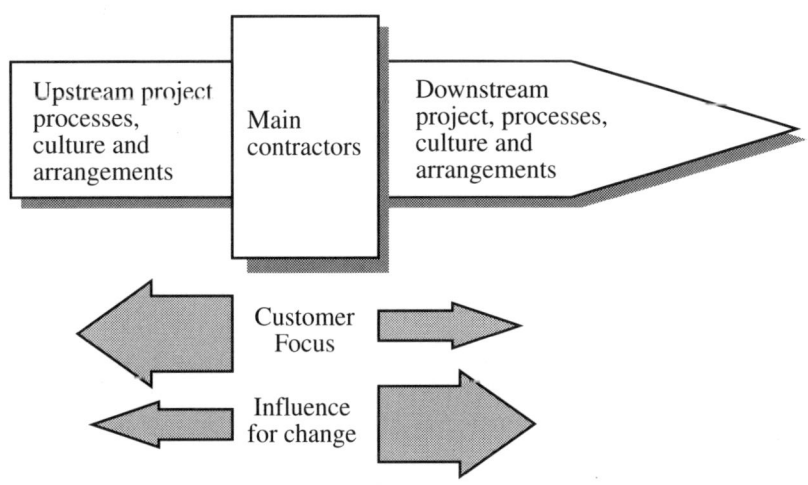

Figure 3.3 Extent of customer focus upstream and downstream

consolidating their main contractor base from 39 in 1995 to four in 1998. This was driven by the supermarket chain's increasing focus on their core business and their target to reduce overheads by 10 per cent per annum. This meant they could no longer afford the costs associated with their own, large, in-company property development and construction department. However, they were looking for performance improvements across a broad range of performance criteria including quality, flexibility, reduced customer impact, faster times from inception to completion – and all at reduced cost.

The supermarket's four main contractor partners (now termed 'partnering contractors') are beginning to exhibit some of the characteristics associated with a supplier alliance. Continuous improvement is encouraged through the supermarket's supply chain champion who meets with the partnering contractors on a monthly basis to exchange information, share problems and suggest improvements. The contractor partners are encouraged to focus their construction expertise on the changing needs and tastes of the supermarket's customers.

SCM has been championed in main contractor A by the managing director and through the appointment of a supply chain manager who reports directly to him. The SCM strategy is also being disseminated within contractor A's project teams through a major training programme and workshops. A senior manager with company A's retail division says: 'Working closely with the supermarket chain has increased our confidence in our future workload. This is providing us with the scope to plan the growth of our company and implement essential culture and process changes aimed at adding greater value for our client and constantly enhancing our relationship.'

Tangible and intangible benefits have come about from the programme, which has been running for two and a half years. One major tangible benefit of the strategy is improved specialist contractor performance. Enhanced evaluation and reporting of specialist contractor performance has improved their selection process. Consequently, core specialists now achieve an overall 'good–excellent' rating for 80 per cent of projects whilst non-core contractors achieve this rating for only 20 per cent of projects.

Further tangible benefits include a reduction in defects from an average of 80 per project in 1996/97 to 30 in 1998/99. Also the conversion of tender opportunities to orders has improved from 1 in 7 before the introduction of the SCM strategy through 1 in 4.5 in the first year of its implementation to 1 in 1.5 in the current year. There has also been more innovation through increased opportunities for value engineering. The less tangible benefits include significantly improved commitment at all levels of authority from specialist contractors, joint ownership of core objectives, improved risk management, improved productivity and quality.

The costs of the SCM strategy can be divided into direct and indirect. Direct costs of £24,000 per year include a senior manager for two days per week, a database manager for one day per week, supplier days, contractor visits and entertainment. Indirect costs of £6,000 include communication, project workshops and benchmarking procedures.

There are a number of barriers to implementing the SCM strategy. These include the insistence of clients and their consultants that competitive tendering to at least four specialist contractors is the only way to ensure best value for money bids. Also the focus is still on tender costs as opposed to final cost. The forms of contract and the allocation of risk are also not conducive to developing the relationships and processes needed for SCM. The volatility of workload and inability to accurately predict future and ongoing workload presents difficulties, as does the reluctance or inability of specialist contractors to invest resources in measuring and improving their performance in the context of the supply chain strategy. It can be suggested that this client-led approach to SCM has resulted in an unbalanced integration of upstream and downstream processes and relationships. Although main contractor A wants to play a proactive role in extending its SCM approach downstream this is being resisted by the supermarket chain and its advisors.

MAIN CONTRACTOR B

In 1995, main contractor B decided to introduce radical changes to its culture in order to improve profitability, provide non-linear growth in operating margins, and add more value for the external customer and end user. The initial focus was therefore on the need to change its own organizational culture. Given the size of the organization, its strong emphasis on 'command and control' and its anticipated resistance to change, it was decided to use an external consultant to help to transform their management approaches. This new culture is based on improving relationships and developing trust through the removal of barriers, more effective communication, addressing the causes of conflict and stimulating ongoing learning.

It was also realized that this new culture needed to transcend the boundaries of the organization and engage with other key players in the construction process. This is why in 1997 the organization commissioned a survey to investigate the nature of their relationships with their specialist contractors. As a consequence of the results of this survey, main contractor B is now actively investigating the implementation of SCM as a means of increasing customer focus both up and down the construction process, in order to differentiate itself from its main competitors.

Adoption of SCM is being built on previous work undertaken by the company aimed at improving relationships with specialist contractors and their suppliers. This is why main contractor B is currently involved in strengthening its relationships with preferred specialist contractors and suppliers in order to improve mutual understanding of needs, problems and business processes. Main contractor B is committed to establishing the following code of practice in all areas of its business:

- to select supply chains based on value;
- to invest in developing and sustaining long-term relationships with supply chains based on mutual trust and mutual benefits;
- to share intelligence throughout the supply chain;
- to design processes to identify and manage risk, backed up with quick and fair problem resolution; and
- to develop and coach all those involved in the building process to 'give and take' and respect each other.

Main contractor B has started to reduce their customer base to increase upstream customer focus. It has also encouraged customers to shift from price competition and lump sum contracts to two-stage, negotiated contracts. Selection of specialist contractors and suppliers is essentially based on three criteria – right first time, completion on time and right price – which are defined as the way to create greater value to the customer. Main Contractor B is planning to help its preferred specialist contractors and suppliers in terms of learning and enabling them to get involved earlier within the process in order to achieve right first time. Regular workshops are being held in order to build trust, better understand each other and consider how to build and develop a profitable working relationship.

A greater emphasis is being placed both on up-front thinking and planning and the post-construction stage. Analysis of main contractor B's in-house documents and proposed strategy reveal that quality at all stages and levels of business processes is to be enhanced through better planning and relationships within the supply chain. Procedures and tools aimed at preventing defects at each stage of the construction process are clearly defined. This suggests that main contractor B is in the process of making the transition from price competition to quality competition. A detailed SCM action plan has been produced to suggest better, fairer and earlier selection of specialist contractors and suppliers. This action plan places significant emphasis on team-building, communication, training, providing feedback and information on time, keeping winning teams, paying on time, and sharing risk and profit.

The introduction of SCM is being championed through a series of road shows by the chairman and the managing director. A company director is driving the initiative within the organization and the supply chain. He reports directly to the managing director and is assisted in this task by a newly appointed manager. Given their regional structure, facilitators are to be appointed in each region. The next stage is to select a pilot project in each region to help disseminate this strategy throughout the whole organization and supply chains. Team-building coaches have also been appointed with the task of assisting the selected projects and helping to develop a new culture to support and sustain the new strategy. Main contractor B is attempting to use these improved downstream relationships to play a leading and pivotal role in aligning and integrating both parts of the construction process.

The adoption of this strategy is based on an improvement action programme, in-house training, use of external services and learning from a wide range of customers who have been leading initiatives such as partnering, two-stage tendering, value engineering, sustainability and zero defects. However, in spite of the greater upstream selectivity, clients are still characterized by a wide range of requirements.

Since a substantial proportion of main contractor B's future workload will be awarded on the basis of lowest price, there is an awareness of the need for the company and its supply chains to be both lean and agile in order to be best prepared to deal with the wide range of construction markets. In this context, being lean is essentially about close collaboration, reducing waste and adding value through aligning and integrating processes, whilst agility is necessary to respond effectively to price-competitive projects and the needs of the irregular client.

Although it is too early to see the benefits of the SCM strategy, according to a senior manager of contractor B, this approach is already helping to reduce defects and improve quality through greater preventive awareness and actions at the project level. It is also helping to improve business results. Upstream, the adoption of this strategy is being favourably perceived by a number of leading clients, and downstream by specialist contractors and suppliers. Hence it is already being perceived as improving both their upstream and downstream marketing.

There have been significant direct costs in formulating the strategy. It is anticipated that the direct and indirect costs of implementing the strategy throughout the whole organization, its projects and supply chains will be substantial. Disseminating the new culture throughout the whole organization is proving to be a long and difficult task. Barriers which need to be overcome include a lack of champions throughout the whole organization, the continuing blame culture and the resistance of individuals to change, all of which are detrimental to forming better relationships with other organizations throughout the supply chains. In addition, more emphasis is being placed on developing technical skills rather than softer skills for supporting the strategy. Furthermore, the organization is not yet capturing and sharing learning from its different projects, functions and regions.

BARRIERS TO THE EFFECTIVE IMPLEMENTATION OF SCM IN CONSTRUCTION

It is clear that the present complexity, fragmentation, interdependency and uncertainty which characterizes the construction process will influence the way in which SCM is used to increase customer satisfaction. Given the variation in customer base, SCM as a means to deliver greater customer focus will need to be applied in a number of ways to reflect the wide range of factors which feature in construction, including the needs of regular and irregular external customers. Main contractors need, for instance, to prepare themselves and their supply chains to become both lean and agile.

Although SCM is being encouraged upstream in the process, it has yet to be fully extended to the specialist contractors and their suppliers downstream in the process, even though they often represent 80 per cent of project costs. From our fieldwork, there is also some evidence that efforts to cascade the new SCM approach downstream to specialist contractors is inhibited by external customers concerned about losing their competitive edge; their advisors fearing a loss of power and influence; main contractors who are not yet sufficiently prepared and committed; and specialist contractors who lack the resources and learning required to embrace this approach. As a consequence there is, as yet, limited evidence of the activities normally associated with supply chain development in some other sectors of the economy.

In partnering arrangements in construction, creative tension between co-operation and competition is maintained within the alliance of partnering contractors and there is considerable inter-supplier rivalry to find a favoured position in a project's overall network of consultants and suppliers. A partnering contractor who is judged to be underperforming can be 'punished' by missing its turn for a project as it is passed to the next contractor in line. Pressure for improvement is also maintained by the number of possible new entrants anxious to join the developing supplier alliances.

Possibilities for the spread of cross-network benefits are limited because of the very small number of construction clients adopting supply chain management. Also, there are still limited efforts to make partnering contractors and downstream suppliers more aware of shifts in end-users' changing needs and tastes. Furthermore, the whole of construction's supply chain is coming under increasing pressure due to changes in the client's external environment and government policies.

CONCLUSION

As argued in this chapter and illustrated in the two case studies, if appropriately implemented, SCM can offer a way forward for improving relationships, integrating processes and increasing customer focus. The benefits to all participants can include improvements in quality and delivery, more repeat work, reductions in overheads associated with obtaining work, increasing profitability, and the acquisition of new specialist knowledge and skills in significant sectors of the construction market.

A successful implementation of SCM in construction can only be achieved if greater emphasis is placed upon co-ordinating and integrating upstream and downstream processes in the supply chains. Main contractors are well positioned to ensure an effective alignment and integration of both upstream and downstream construction processes. However, they need to:

- establish a clear strategy at top level and ensure senior management commitment and support;
- set clear targets towards which all participants can aim;
- review their own internal organization, arrangements and culture to support extensive co-ordination and information management, participation and a sharing of knowledge;
- develop an ongoing programme of innovation and learning within their own organization and the supply chains to create an alternative organization which understands why changes are happening and is capable of managing the behavioural processes involved;
- reduce customer and supplier bases both up and down the supply chain and work towards establishing longer-term and more stable relationships to reduce complexity and increase customer focus, and match the degree of upstream interest and customer focus in the downstream processes through early involvement in the change process to ensure relevance, ownership and commitment;
- ensure that change strategies are sensitive to context and culture and that the strength of existing cultural forces is not underestimated; and
- maintain an overview of the dynamic, complex and long-term process of change, and recognize that change takes time.

ENDNOTE

This chapter is based on a completed research project funded by the Department of the Environment and the Reading Construction Forum. It is also drawn from consultancy work undertaken by the authors for construction organizations.

REFERENCES

Albrecht, K. (1993), *The Only Thing That Matters*, London: Harper Business.

Bennet, J. and Jayes, S. (1995), *Trusting the Team: The Best Practice Guide to Partnering in Construction*, Reading: Centre for Strategic

Studies in Construction at the University of Reading with the Partnering Task Force of the Reading Construction Forum.

Bennett, J. and Jayes, S. (1998), *The Seven Pillars of Partnering: A Guide to Second Generation Partnering*, Reading: Centre for Strategic Studies in Construction at the University of Reading with the Partnering Task Force of the Reading Construction Forum.

Bessant, J. (1991), *Managing Advanced Technology – The Challenge of the Fifth Wave*, Oxford: Blackwell.

Cooper, M.C., Lambert, D. and Pagh, J.D. (1997), 'Supply chain management: more than a new name for logistics', *The International Journal of Logistics Management*, **8**(1), pp. 1–4.

Coulson-Thomas, C. (1997), *Achieving Excellence Through Business Transformation*, London: Kogan Page.

Egan, Sir J. (1998), *Rethinking Construction*, London: Department of the Environment, Transport and the Regions.

Hellard, R.B. (1995), *Project Partnering – Principle and Practice*, London: Thomas Telford.

Hines, P. (1994), *Creating World Class Suppliers*, London: Financial Times/Pitman.

Huxham, C. (Ed.) (1996), *Creating Collaborative Advantage*, London: Sage.

Jones, M. and Saad, M. (1999), *Unlocking Specialist Potential: A More Participative Role for Specialist Contractors in Construction*, London: Thomas Telford Publishing.

Lamming, R. (1993), *Beyond Partnership: Strategies For Innovation And Lean Supply*, New York: Prentice Hall.

Latham, Sir M. (1994), *Constructing the Team: Final Report of the Government/Industry Review of Procurement and Contractual Arrangements in the UK Construction Industry*, London: HMSO.

Lipparini, A. and Sobrero, M. (1994), 'The glue and the pieces: entrepreneurship and innovation in small firms' networks', *Journal of Business Venturing*, 9, pp. 125–140.

New, S. and Ramsay J. (1997), *A Critical Appraisal of Aspects of the Lean Approach, European Journal of Purchasing and Supply Management*, **3**(2), pp. 93–102.

Peters, T. (1993), *Liberation Management*, Pan Books.

Rosenberg, J. (1996), Five myths about customer satisfaction, *Quality Progress*, December, pp. 57–60.

Saad, M. and Jones, M. (1998), 'Improving the performance of specialist contractors in construction through a more effective management of their supply chains', *Proceedings of the 7th International IPSERA Conference, Supply Strategies: Concepts and Practice at the Leading Edge*, London.

Sako, M., Lamming, R. and Helper, R.S. (1994), 'Good news – bad news', *European Journal of Purchasing and Supply Management*, **1**(4), pp. 237–248.

Technology Foresight Panel on Construction (1995), *Progress Through Partnership*, London: HMSO.

Towill, D.R. (1996), 'Time compression and supply chain management – a guided tour', *Supply Chain Management*, **1**(1), pp. 15–27.

Vollman, T., Cordon, C., and Raabe, H. (1997), *Supply Chain Management. Mastering Management*, London: Financial Times/Pitman, pp. 316–322.

von Hippel, E. (1986), 'Co-operation between rivals: informal know-how trading', *Research Policy*, **16**(5), pp. 291–302.

Womack, J.P. and Jones, D.T. (1996), *Lean Thinking: Banish Waste And Create Wealth In Your Corporation*, New York: Simon and Schuster.

CHAPTER FOUR

Environmental purchasing: tools of engagement

J. Gordon Murray and Valerie E. Cupples

In recent years it has been increasingly recognized that purchasing must contribute to environmental sustainability (Baily et al. 1994; Saunders 1994; van Weele 1994; Erridge 1995; Welford and Gouldson 1993; Dobler and Burt 1996; Lamming et al. 1996) and exert 'demand side pressure' to bring about supply chain environmental improvements (Green et al. 1996; Min and Galle 1997). Lamming and Hampson (1996) go further, advocating that 'the environment' provides a strategic opportunity for purchasing.

Unfortunately, this recognition of purchasing's contribution has not been reciprocated with the development of required, practitioner-friendly 'tools' (Noci 1997; and as discussed by Lamming et al. in Chapter 5). Such tools are necessary, for example, to assist purchasing managers to identify where attention should be focused, to develop strategies for action and then guide others on appropriate supplier appraisal methodologies. The absence of suitable tools is likely not only to restrict progress, but also to lead to costly mistakes as a result of inappropriate approaches being adopted (Cox 1997). This chapter offers two models as remedies to those specific problems.

BREEZES OF CHANGE IN PURCHASING

Clearly major changes are confronting purchasing managers and, as with all change, resistance can be expected (Graham 1978; Johnson and Scholes 1993). However, it is the view of the authors that change can be hastened as a result of emphasizing the familiar and incrementally adopting existing 'purchasing tools' to the new situation.

The strategic purchasing manager's core competence lies in supplier selection, management and development; Lamming describes this as 'external resource management' (1993). With that in mind, we set out first to establish where attention should be focused prior to discussing how purchasing managers currently evaluate potential suppliers' credentials (what purchasing managers refer to as 'supplier appraisal') and then adapt those processes to reflect environmental management.

SUPPLIER APPRAISAL: WHEN SHOULD IT BE APPLIED?

Supplier appraisal is a risk measurement tool used to establish whether or not it is wise to purchase from a particular firm (Baily et al. 1994). Its application is fundamental if risks relating to quality, environment, on time delivery, and so on are to be minimized. Therefore the effective use of supplier appraisal should reduce procurement costs and assist in achieving better value for money (Burt 1989). Having said that, the extent to which time, effort and cost is incurred in carrying out an appraisal should be contingent upon the potential risks.

Kraljic (1983), in his seminal paper, advocated a portfolio approach, with the variables of 'supply market complexity/supplier strength' and 'company attractiveness/strength'. This enabled the categorization of purchases into the four segments of bottleneck, strategic, non-critical and leverage items. Using the matrix, cost-effective identification can be made regarding which types of purchases are most appropriate for supplier appraisal.

A PORTFOLIO APPROACH TO IDENTIFYING GREEN PURCHASING STRATEGY

It is our belief that building on the principles of Kraljic's model is sensible, since it enables purchasing managers to approach the steep learning curve of green purchasing incrementally, from a position of familiarity. On that basis we have developed two models which can assist purchasing managers, first in identifying where and how attention should be focused, and second in teaching them how to approach the green supplier appraisal process.

MODEL 1: WHERE SHOULD ATTENTION BE FOCUSED

The first model sets out to fill a gap by helping purchasing managers consider some of the risks associated with 'green purchasing' and then acting as a decision-making tool for the development of 'green purchasing strategies'. Furthermore, it is our belief that the approach has wider business applications for other functions pursuing green business strategies. 'Green purchasing risk' varies according to the environmental impact of the purchase and also according to the perception of those outside the organization.

A purchase can be classified as having a high or low 'environmental risk', for example, in terms of the following:

● the sustainability of the raw materials used;
● energy consumed in the conversion process;
● environmental impact 'in use';
● its ability to be reused or recycled; and
● its biodegradability at the end of its useful life.

Equally, a purchase can be classified as having a high or low 'profile risk', for example, in terms of the following:

● public perception of whether or not the purchase is 'environmentally friendly';
● potential for adverse publicity associated with the purchase; and
● its potential to detract from the organization's 'good environmental practice'.

Essentially 'environmental risk' is relative and is concerned with actual knowledge and the 'precautionary principle' (Hanley et al. 1997). The precautionary principle is based on the reality that there exists a level of uncertainty about the environmental impact of some actions. Cognizant of that uncertainty and until confirmation can be obtained, society should make decisions based on preventative action being taken now as opposed to later. 'Profile risk' is concerned with the perceptions of those outside the organization, what they think the organization 'should be doing' (albeit perhaps from an uninformed point of view) and the potential for adverse publicity to detract from the other good environmental work in which the organization is engaged. To gain an insight into what we refer to as 'profile risk', one need only consider the adverse 'profile' impact that the Brent Spar disposal had on Shell who, with the benefit of hindsight, were actually behaving in an environmentally responsible manner!

As a result of identifying risk against each of the variables ('environmental risk' and 'profile risk') it is possible to identify where attention should be focused and what may be considered appropriate 'green purchasing strategies'. The first stage of applying the model rates purchases by a 'tick' against both the environmental and profile risk (see Table 4.1). The purchase of paper has been taken as an example to illustrate this. Paper has a comparatively low environmental risk in that a debate is still going on as to whether recycled paper is 'good for the environment' *per se*. However, to those outside the organization, what the firm is perceived to be doing about 'paper' and whether or not recycled paper is used, has the potential to un-

Table 4.1 Table for the categorization of green purchasing risk

Purchase	Environmental Risk		Profile Risk	
	Low	High	Low	High
Paper	✓			✓
Purchase B		✓	✓	
Purchase C		✓		✓
Purchase D	✓		✓	

High	*Priority 2* Reduce consumption Green supplier appraisal Green specifications Green options sought Cost/benefits evaluated Whole life costs Preference to green supplier	*Priority 1* Reduce consumption Green supplier appraisal Green specifications Green options sought Cost/benefits evaluated Whole life costs Preference to green supplier Gain commitment to future action

Low	*Priority 4*
	Reduce consumption
	Exercise caution re. Green
	  'marketing'
	Nominal preference to
	  green suppliers
		Priority 3
		Reduce consumption
		Green specifications only
		  on basis of cost/benefits
		Increase awareness and
		  encourage via
		  questionnaire and referral
		  to policy
		Nominal preference to
		  green suppliers
		Minimum green supplier
		  appraisal (third party)

Environmental risk (vertical axis) — Profile risk: Low / High (horizontal axis)

Figure 4.1 Green purchasing risk matrix strategies

dermine the firm's other environmental actions.

Having categorized the potential risks, it is possible to place the 'purchases' within a 'green purchasing risk matrix' (Figure 4.1).

THE GREEN PURCHASING RISK MATRIX: A GREEN PURCHASING STRATEGY TOOL

The green purchasing risk matrix helps us to develop appropriate purchasing strategies. Most attention should be focused on the high environmental/high profile risk with a view to minimizing impact and 'being seen' to demonstrate good corporate stewardship. With this category of purchase the organization will carry out detailed green supplier appraisal and purchase from 'greener suppliers', that is, those who are proactively addressing environmental management.

For all those purchases which are 'above the line' (high environmental risk) attention will be focused on ensuring good environmental supplier performance and seeking to generate 'green specifications'. It is our belief that the optimum specification can only be developed in collaboration with suppliers. Such collaboration provides a mechanism not only for suppliers to bring forward innovative, cost reducing solutions (Erridge and Murray 1998) but also provides a tool for reinforcing the environmental message. However, such collaboration must be well managed by the purchasing manager and can only be expected to be meaningful within a relationship of mutual respect and existing dialogue.

For those purchases identified as high profile/low environmental risk, clearly cost/benefit analysis will be a consideration and 'green specifications' will be sought on the basis of the cost/benefit risk analysis. The organization will want

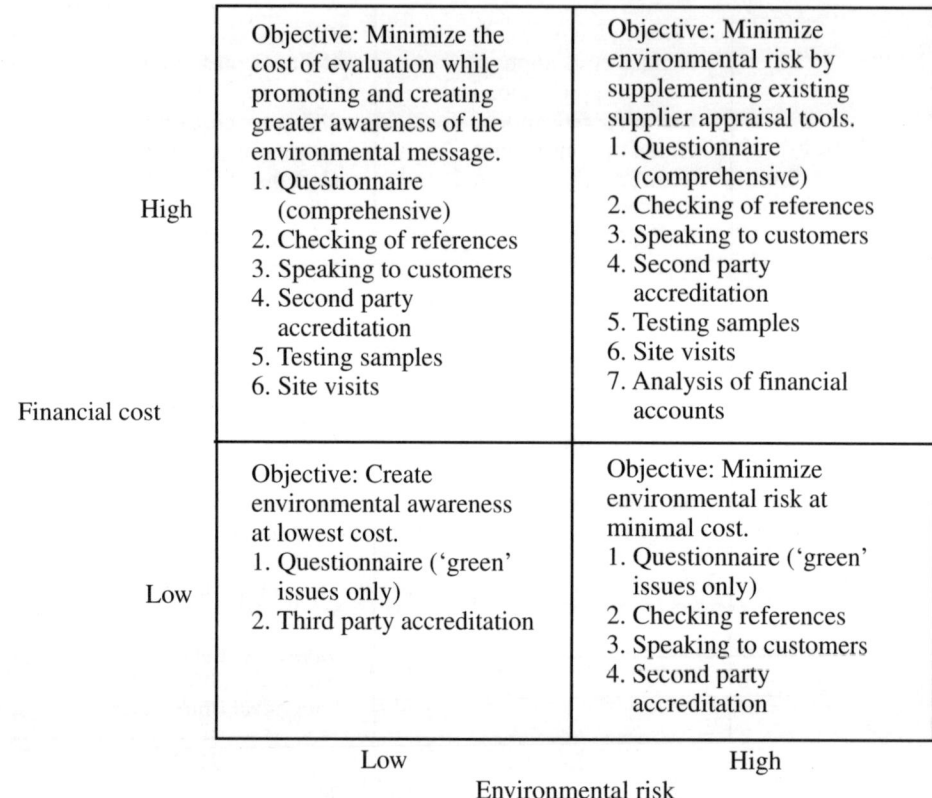

	Objective: Minimize the cost of evaluation while promoting and creating greater awareness of the environmental message. 1. Questionnaire (comprehensive) 2. Checking of references 3. Speaking to customers 4. Second party accreditation 5. Testing samples 6. Site visits	Objective: Minimize environmental risk by supplementing existing supplier appraisal tools. 1. Questionnaire (comprehensive) 2. Checking of references 3. Speaking to customers 4. Second party accreditation 5. Testing samples 6. Site visits 7. Analysis of financial accounts
High		
Low	Objective: Create environmental awareness at lowest cost. 1. Questionnaire ('green' issues only) 2. Third party accreditation	Objective: Minimize environmental risk at minimal cost. 1. Questionnaire ('green' issues only) 2. Checking references 3. Speaking to customers 4. Second party accreditation

Financial cost (vertical axis, High / Low)

Low   High
Environmental risk

Figure 4.2   Green supplier appraisal approaches

to have in place justification for stakeholders as to why it is not going down the 'pressure group line'. Little detailed green supplier appraisal will be required. However, that which is applied will be considered as a green supplier development tool aimed at increasing environmental awareness and encouraging environmental management from the supplier.

For those purchases which are considered low risk, with a view to 'greening the supply chain', suppliers will be encouraged to improve their own performance. These purchases will not be of great environmental concern, but could be vulnerable to opportunistic green marketing strategies. These purchases are likely to be of the 'back office' type, not seen by those outside the organization.

This model was tested on five separate focus groups, each of which had a different level of understanding of green purchasing. Each of the groups easily grasped the principles and

achieved consensus on the positioning of a test group of purchases. It is therefore our opinion that this first model satisfied the criteria of being practitioner-friendly. Since no equivalent core decision-making tool has been identified we also believe the model fills a gap. An overview of the particular strategies advocated and the associated priorities is presented in Figure 4.2.

EMPIRICAL INVESTIGATION INTO CURRENT APPROACHES TO SUPPLIER APPRAISAL AND GREEN SUPPLIER APPRAISAL

For traditional supplier appraisal, which does not consider environmental credentials, Erridge (1995) advocates that any or all of the following methods may be used:

- checking of references;
- speaking with previous and current customers;
- third-party certification;
- testing of samples;
- analysis of trading accounts;
- questionnaires;
- visits to supplier;
- audit of supplier;
- analysis of product costings;
- analysis of management structures, staffing and administrative procedures;
- analysis of production and quality processes; and
- analysis of overall financial viability and business performance.

A postal, self-administered questionnaire survey was carried out to establish empirically how purchasing managers currently approach supplier appraisal. Continuing to apply our principles of incrementally changing existing approaches, those methods used for supplier appraisal should therefore form the basis of green supplier appraisal. The questionnaire was sent to a stratified random sample of 118 'purchasers' from local authorities within the UK. While it is acknowledged that this is a unique market, it provided the benefits of being the subject of wider research currently being carried out by the authors and one which is under increasing pressure to apply environmental criteria in its decision making (Department of the Environment, Transport and the Regions (DETR) 1998). A response rate of 56 per cent was achieved, with 54 per cent of the total sample being usable (64 responses), which we consider to be representative. The survey findings identified that 79.7 per cent of purchasers (51 respondents) currently evaluate suppliers. Of these, the methods used included all those suggested by Erridge (1995). The most commonly used of those methods are as follows:

1. Checking of references: 76.5 per cent (39 respondents)
2. Speaking with previous and current customers: 76.5 per cent (39 respondents)
3. Testing samples: 72.5 per cent (37 respondents)

4. Visit to supplier: 72.5 per cent (37 respondents)
5. Analysis of product costings: 52.9 per cent (27 respondents).

Only 25.8 per cent, just 16 of the respondents, are currently evaluating suppliers' environmental performance (one of the respondents did not provide information on how they carried out supplier appraisal, therefore only 15 responses relating to green supplier appraisal were usable). Once again the methods used to evaluate suppliers' green credentials included all of those suggested by Erridge (1995). The most commonly used of those methods are:

1. Questionnaires: 73.3 per cent (11 respondents)
2. Third party certification: 66.7 per cent (10 respondents)
3. Visits to supplier: 60 per cent (nine respondents)

Table 4.2 provides a comparison of the various mechanisms used for supplier appraisal with those used in green supplier appraisal.

It is evident from Table 4.2 that methods used in traditional supplier appraisal have been transferred and are now used in green supplier appraisal. However, it is interesting to note the significant differences between them. Checking of references and speaking to customers appears to be largely underdeveloped in the latter, with only 33.3 per cent (five respondents) checking references and 40 per cent (six respondents) speaking with previous and current customers. This is compared to traditional supplier appraisal with 76.5 per cent (39 respondents) using both methods. Checking references is a method that is widely used for traditional supplier appraisal and would be a cost-effective way of sourcing information from the green supplier appraisal perspective.

Over 66 per cent of green supplier appraisals make use of third party certification (10 respondents) compared to 31.4 per cent of traditional supplier appraisals (16 respondents). This high percentage for green supplier appraisal may indicate that there is an illusion among purchasing practitioners that this is an effective method of evaluating a supplier. However,

Table 4.2   A comparison of supplier and green supplier appraisal methodologies currently used

Methods Suggested by Erridge	Supplier Appraisal		Green Supplier Appraisal	
	No.	%	No.	%
Checking references	39	76.5	5	33.3
Speaking with previous and past customers	39	76.5	6	40.0
Third-party certification	16	31.4	10	66.7
Testing samples	37	72.5	7	46.7
Analysis of trading accounts	25	49.0	2	13.3
Questionnaires	22	43.1	11	73.3
Visit to supplier	37	72.5	9	60.0
Audit of supplier	14	27.5	6	40.0
Analysis of product costings	27	52.9	4	26.7
Analysis of management structures, staffing and administrative procedures	17	33.3	5	33.3
Analysis of production and quality processes	17	33.3	7	46.7
Analysis of overall financial viability and business performance	21	41.2	2	13.3
Life cycle analysis	6	11.8	3	20.0

Netherwood (1996) and Starkey (1996) do not believe this to be an accurate assessment since it does not necessarily reflect superior environmental performance. It has already been noted that purchasing's focus is in sourcing quality suppliers. However, third party certification can mean the evaluation of either the quality system or the product. Therefore, if the supplier's accreditation is for the product, the evaluation of the supplier still remains outside the appraisal. It may also be the case that the requirement for third party accreditation provides a 'safety blanket' effect for the purchaser in that a need is identified but the purchasing manager lacks the required skills to carry out the evaluation. Perhaps it is also that EMAS/ISO 14001, the international environmental standards, are comparatively new, and at the present time are suffering from the fall in popularity of quality standards such as BS 5750/ISO 9001.

Over 72 per cent of traditional supplier appraisals (37 of respondents) test samples, compared to 46.7 per cent of green supplier appraisals (seven respondents). Supplier appraisals may be testing samples to establish value for money. The lower number of green supplier appraisals may indicate the belief that third party certification provides assurance regarding the product. Only 13.3 per cent of green supplier appraisals (two respondents) carry out an analysis of trading accounts compared to 49 per cent of supplier appraisals (25 respondents). Our research did not ask 'What was being looked for', but we can speculate that the reason was to identify any court judgements against the supplier, particularly in relation to the environment.

Questionnaires are the most widely used tool in green supplier appraisal with 73.3 per cent (11 respondents) using this method compared to 43.1 per cent of those who carry out traditional supplier appraisals (22 respondents). With questionnaires, the emphasis is on the supplier, therefore their use is relevant in any appraisal, particularly green supplier appraisal, in that specific questions based around environmental systems and procedures can be addressed. A visit to the supplier is being utilized in both types of appraisals at a significant level and therefore both have identified the benefits that can be accrued through this method.

78.9 per cent of questionnaires (12 respondents) used for green appraisals are issued as contracts are let, with the majority of evaluations made by a combination of purchasing and environmental staff. In 35.7 per cent (five respondents) of authorities green supplier appraisal is applied to high environmental risk purchases, with another 50 per cent (eight respondents) of authorities applying it to all purchases.

MODEL 2: THE APPROPRIATE APPROACH TO GREEN SUPPLIER APPRAISAL

The role of purchasing is to focus on the selection of quality suppliers and therefore a successful green supplier appraisal system should evaluate the supplier rather than the product. The survey evidence suggests that green supplier appraisal could evaluate suppliers' environmental performance by using traditional tools already being applied in supplier appraisal.

In deciding to which contracts green supplier appraisal should be applied, consideration must be given to the cost of carrying out this process. This cost would include the opportunity costs of purchasing and supplier staff, the production, data collection and analysis costs of questionnaires, the process costs associated with 2nd Party Accreditation, the travel costs associated with site visits, and so on. It is our belief therefore that green supplier appraisal should primarily be applied to those purchases identified in model 1 as 'above the line', relating to high environmental risk. However if a comprehensive supplier appraisal is already being carried out on high value purchases, it would make sense that a green supplier appraisal should be integrated, but what methodology should be applied?

We recommend that the model shown in Figure 4.2 be used to establish the appropriate approach to green supplier appraisal.

Within each of the quadrants we have identified the constituent parts of the methodology. The parts are listed in order of application, progressing from the lower cost approaches. This means that, if an unsatisfactory result is achieved and a decision is made not to consider the supplier further, the process has stopped at the optimum position from a cost perspective.

All of the methods advocated for 'high financial cost/high environmental risk' purchases, with the exception of the analysis of trading accounts, were also suggested for 'high financial cost/low environmental impact' purchases. However, as already identified, this area represents the greatest environmental risk. The methods indicated for use are those already being applied in supplier appraisal and therefore characterize a cost-effective technique for green supplier appraisal. Analysis of trading accounts should be used by the purchaser to discover whether there are any court orders against the supplier, specifically on issues relating to the environment.

WHO SHOULD EVALUATE SUPPLIERS?

The portfolio approach recognizes a mixture of commercial and environmental priorities and can be used to identify the appropriate method to be used for evaluating suppliers. The identification of those purchases which represent high financial expenditure would be the responsibility of purchasing. However, the task of identifying high environmental impact purchases would lie with the specifier. The specifier will effectively embrace the environmental culture of the organization through this proactive role in the process and must, in our opinion, play such an active role if long-term environmental purchasing performance is to be improved. Conversely, if purchasing take on this role they risk trespassing on others' territory and finding themselves criticized should the performance fall short of expectations.

In the short term, for high environmental risk, the evaluation should be carried out by a combination of both purchasing and environmental practitioners, thereby gaining an endorsement of the process, while for those purchases which have low environmental risk, the evaluation should primarily be carried out by purchasing in liaison with environmental practitioners. The justification for this is that, in our view, traditional purchasing training does not at present provide the necessary skills on which to base a robust decision to 'delist' a supplier on environmental grounds. Until such times as purchasing professionals gain that competency and confidence they risk compromising their own professional status.

In the long term, purchasing practitioners must develop sufficient skills to carry out environmental appraisal by themselves; we therefore believe a need exists for specific training in environmental purchasing. A possible route to developing these skills may be to become EMAS/ISO 14001 assessor accreditation qualified, a route we are aware that a number of proactive environmental purchasers have chosen to pursue.

CONCLUSION

We believe the models presented will fill a gap, one which must be closed if practitioners are to provide a level of professional expertise consistent with the growth in business trends towards the sustainable environmental management. Both models are incremental developments on approaches currently used by purchasing managers: therefore the only increase in knowledge required relates to the environment. The green purchasing risk matrix provides a method of categorizing and prioritizing purchases, an approach which could also be used for other forms of environmental management. Having positioned purchases, a portfolio of appropriate environmental purchasing strategies were presented.

The second model is founded on empirical evidence relating to how purchasers currently carry out supplier appraisal. The evidence indicates that purchasing managers use a variety of approaches when evaluating suppliers' ability to delivery a quality service, yet when seeking to evaluate suppliers from an environmental perspective, the choice of techniques differs from that traditionally used. We question why that is so and advocate much more transference of the traditional techniques. In response a model is presented which provides cost-effective strategies for green supplier appraisal.

At present, it is our belief that purchasing managers do not, in general, possess the necessary level of environmental expertise to carry out robust green supplier appraisal by themselves. A short-term solution lies in a collaborative approach with environmental experts; however, that knowledge, we believe, will soon become a requirement of purchasing managers for tomorrow's environmentally sustainable organization.

REFERENCES

Baily, P., Farmer, D., Jessop, D., Jones, M. (1994), *Purchasing Principles and Management*, 7th edn, London: Pitman Publishing.

Burt, D.N. (1989), 'Managing product quality through strategic purchasing', *Sloan Management Review*, Spring, pp. 39–48.

Cox, A. (1997), 'Business Success and Critical Supply Chain Assets: A Theoretical Framework for Analysing Business Strategy and Operational Best Practice', in Cox, A. and Hines, P. (Eds), *Advanced Supply Management: The Best Practice Debate*, Boston, UK: Earlsgate Press, pp. 301–345.

Department of Environment, Transport and the Regions (DETR) (1998) *Modernising Local Government: In Touch with the People.* London: HMSO.

Dobler, D.W. and Burt, D.N. (1996), *Purchasing and Supply Management*, New York: McGraw-Hill.

Erridge, A. (1995), *Managing Purchasing*, Oxford: Butterworth Heinemann.

Erridge, A., and Murray, J.G. (1998) 'The application of lean supply in local government: the Belfast experiments', *European Journal of Purchasing and Supply Management*, 4(4), pp. 207–221.

Graham, H.T. (1978), *Human Resources Management*, Plymouth: MacDonald and Evans.

Green, K., Morton, B. and New, S. (1996), 'Purchasing and environmental management: interactions, policies and opportunities', *Business Strategy and the Environment*, 5(3).

Hanley, N., Shogreu, J.F. and White, B. (1997), *Environmental Economics*, London: Macmillan Press.

Johnson, G. and Scholes, K. (1993), *Exploring Corporate Strategy*, London: Prentice Hall.

Kraljic, P. (1983), 'Purchasing must become supply management', *Harvard Business Review*, September-October, pp. 109–117.

Lamming, R.C. (1993), *Beyond Partnership: Strategies for Innovation and Lean Supply.* Hemel Hempstead: Prentice Hall.

Lamming, R., Warhurst, A. and Hampson J. (1996), *The Environment & Purchasing: Problem or Opportunity?* Easton on the Hill: Chartered Institute of Purchasing & Supply Management.

Lamming, R. and Hampson, J. (1996), 'The environment as a supply chain management issue', *British Journal of Management*, 7 (Special Issue), S45–S62, March.

Min, H. and Galle, P. (1997), 'Green purchasing strategies: trends and implications', *International Journal of Purchasing and Materials Management*, August, pp. 10–17.

Netherwood, A. (1996), 'Environmental Management Systems', in Welford, R. (Ed), *Corporate Environmental Management*, London: Earthscan.

Noci. G. (1997), 'Designing 'green' supplier rating systems for the assessment of a supplier's environmental performance', *European Journal of Purchasing & Supply Management*, 3(2), pp. 103–114.

Saunders, M. (1994), *Strategic Purchasing and Supply Chain Management*, London: Pitman Publishing.

Starkey, R. (1996), 'The Standardisation of Environmental Management Systems', in Welford, R. (Ed.), *Corporate Environmental Management*, London: Earthscan.

van Weele, A.J. (1994), *Purchasing Management*, London: Chapman & Hall.

Welford, R.J. and Gouldson, A.P. (1993), *Environmental Management and Business Strategy*, London: Pitman Publishing.

CHAPTER FIVE

A comprehensive conceptual model for managing environmental impacts, costs and risks in supply chains

Richard Lamming, Paul Cousins, Frances Bowen and Adam Faruk

A NOTE ON TERMINOLOGY

Inevitably, the subject of environmental soundness involves specialist, sometimes scientific, terms. In supply management, too, it is often necessary to truncate phrases into mnemonics in order to avoid fatigue in reading. In developing this research we have dealt with such terms but have avoided the more scientific ones in this chapter. We do use a few acronyms, simply to shorten the text and make it more palatable. This starts with the subject itself: environmentally sound supply chain management, which we have shortened to ESSCMo, for convenience (we explain 'environmental soundness' in the text) and, latterly, the sobriquet 'green supply' has been used; 'environmental related supplier initiatives' – an expression clear in itself but something of a mouthful – are called 'ERSI' for the purposes of this paper, while the tool we have developed to conduct 'streamlined, integrated life cycle analysis' we call SILCA. All have the advantage of being pronounceable as words but they are actually only 'working titles' for us – we do not seek to install them in management lexicon.

The objective of the Environmentally Sound Supply Chain Management research project (ESSCMo) is to develop a methodology to enable purchasing and supply managers to assess environmental business risks and costs, and biophysical impacts which result from sourcing decisions and the day-to-day management of the supply chain. The nature of the work has been both theoretical and practical, with the latter aimed at providing approaches that avoid the complexity which often renders the existing tools and methods impractical for purchasing managers.

An increasing number of organizations are implementing environment-related supplier initiatives, that is, a strategic, operational, or managerial practice which incorporates environmental considerations into purchasing decisions or supply management practices. These initiatives range from incorporating environmental conditions into contracts, to joint development of cleaner technologies with specific suppliers. Such initiatives are often undertaken in a well-intentioned, but *ad hoc*, fashion so do not necessarily lead to systematic, environmentally sound supply chain management. One of the aims of the ESSCMo project is to develop a methodology for supply managers to analyse and implement environment-related supplier initiatives (ERSIs) to improve the environmental soundness of their supply chains.

RESEARCH APPROACH

This research was conducted by a team of four researchers. The work on ecological aspects entailed an extensive survey of available information concerning the contributions which organizations make to identified categories of biophysical impact. These included ecosystem loss and degradation, the loss of exhaustible/ renewable resources, human health, global climate change, ozone depletion, water quality, acid rain, smog and the disposal of waste. This information was collated and interpreted with the objective of providing easily comprehensible information for the non-specialist; that is, purchasing and supply chain managers were envisaged as the eventual users of the tool, rather than environmental specialists or scientists.

A series of semi-structured interviews was undertaken during May-October 1998 in 30 business units within major UK companies, in order to assess the occurrence of types of economic environmental risk and how they might be overcome by implementing environment-related supplier initiatives. Interviews were conducted with senior representatives, including managing directors, directors or heads of safety, health and environment, and directors or heads of purchasing. The interviews were conducted in a broad cross-section of industries in order to capture managerial interpretations of 'green supply' and potential management strategies and tactics across a wide variety of business activity. The firms' positions in the supply chain varied, from extraction through pre-production, manufacture, distribution and retail. Various support activities, such as civil engineering and transport, were also included. The sample of business units included industries considered both 'clean' and 'dirty' and all the business units in the sample were parts of large corporations (which have an annual turnover greater than £300 million).

The main topics of discussion were environmental pressures and risks, environmental management strategies and tactics, supply chain pressures and environment-related supplier initiatives. Each interviewee was also sent a brief company profile questionnaire to aid in comparison across cases. The interview series was followed up by a questionnaire to several operating units in each business unit to supplement the strategic level data. The aim of this stage was to gather data from the operational front line – to begin to develop benchmarks for green supply management practices.

The role of the main industrial sponsor, London Underground, and the 25 member companies of the ESSCMo club has been crucial throughout this research in the development of the conceptual model for the methodology. Development of the tools, including piloting the prototypes, is currently underway.

THE LITERATURE

Much of the background literature which has informed the ESSCMo project was discussed in papers presented at IPSERA conferences (Bowen et al. 1997, 1998). We build on three specific themes generated in the earlier papers: the complexity of biophysical impacts, the necessity of analysing environmental impacts across the entire extended supply chain, and the role of risk in environmentally sound supply chain management.

From the outset, it was recognized that the management of biophysical impacts at any level is a complicated matter. A survey of the pertinent literature including environmental science, industrial ecology, environmental management and sustainable development, pointed to the possibility of contributing to knowledge in a number of key areas. Firstly, it was clear that ideas surrounding 'greenness', environmental responsibility and sustainable development were ambiguous. This lack of rigour and related clarity was seen as a real problem. As a consequence, the concept of environmental soundness has been described (see below). This definition has certain important practical implications when analysing the biophysical load associated with supply chains.

Further, no pragmatic, systematic means for mapping and analysing environmental impacts along supply chains existed. A product-based tool to do just that has been constructed. It should be stressed that this tool is applicable only to *extended* supply chains, that is, those involving the entire life cycle of products. Preliminary research demonstrated that stopping the analysis at delivery to the customer, without taking into account subsequent use and disposal, is not justifiable when assessing the environmental load associated with providing a product or service.

We have discussed elsewhere the role of environmental risk in supply management activity (Bowen et al. 1998), and concluded that it is analogous to environmental risk management in other business areas (Matten 1995). Supply managers face exposure both to ecological risks which may arise out of hazards in the natural environment, and to economic risks which may result from uncertainty in the business surroundings. Thus our project work maintained the separation in environmental supply risk between the exposure to causing biophysical damage and the exposure to being held to account for perceived damage (by consumers, regulatory agencies, insurers and so on). Assessment of biophysical impacts across extended supply chains was addressed in the development of a specific management tool (see SILCA, below). The project also aimed at further understanding environmental economic risk in sourcing decisions and how these interact with ecological risks.

ENVIRONMENTAL SOUNDNESS

Elsewhere, we have defined the term 'environmental soundness' as those aspects of sustainability that might be expected of a line manager in business (Lamming et al. 1999) (see Figure 5.1). Our contention is that, while managers may be expected to take some responsibility for the economic and environmental aspects of sustainable development, it is the role of government to oversee and direct social justice and co-ordinate progress in all three over very long-term time horizons.

The problem here for purchasing and supply managers is that many of the genuine aspects of sustainability are actually matters of public policy, not corporate responsibility. A small company cannot influence public policy, and a large corporation should not: in a democracy, public policy and social justice should be the responsibilities of elected representatives and their closely linked public officers (civil servants). Commercial organizations must comply with policy and its related legislation, of course, and be 'good corporate citizens', but they are answerable to shareholders and many of the aspects of sustainability, for good or ill, are in conflict with shareholders' interests (for example, provision for long-term considerations may reduce short-term financial returns).

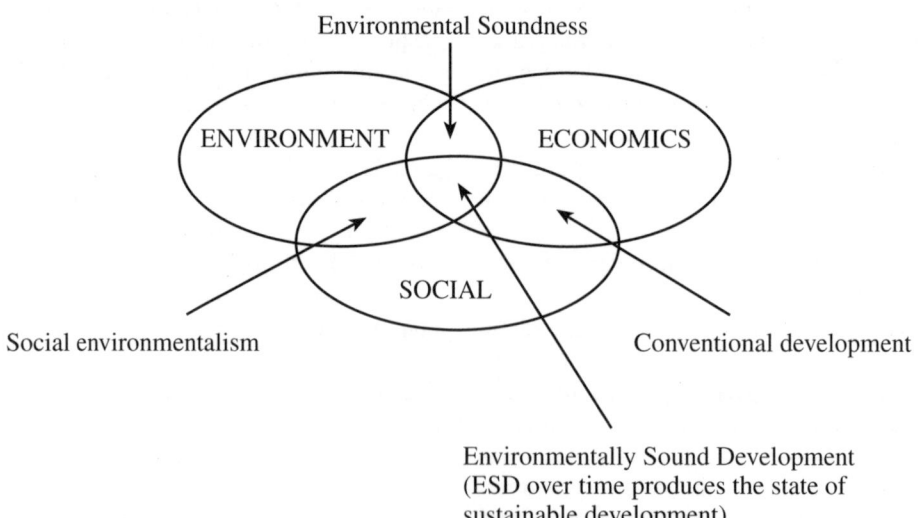

Figure 5.1 Defining environmental soundness in relation to sustainability
Source: Lamming, R.C., Faruk, A.C. and Cousins, P.D. (1999), 'Environmental soundness: a pragmatic alternative to expectations of sustainable development in business strategy', *Business Strategy and the Environment*, **8**(3). ©1999 John Wiley and Sons Limited. Reproduced with permission.

Thus, for example, large firms wishing to exploit local natural mineral resources in developing countries will build schools, roads and hospitals for the host government as a means of getting to the minerals. The problem here is that the large firm will often impinge on national sovereignty and legitimate government responsibilities, and may not achieve the highest standards in the delivery of something far removed from its core competence. There are a host of other drawbacks for society and companies which may result from requiring corporate strategists to take responsibility for social development; these include the possibility (particularly in developing countries) of creating dramatic social inequalities and, from a corporate perspective, inviting criticism in an area fraught with sensitivities (for example, accusations of cultural imperialism). For a full discussion of the proper limits of companies in progress towards social justice in a sustainable development framework, see Lamming et al. (1999). The environmental and economic areas of concern may be seen as the responsibility of the firm: on the one hand complying with – or exceeding – regulatory requirements on biophysical impacts and, on the other, behaving in an appropriate manner to ensure value is returned to its shareholders.

Within this context, then, supply managers who are asked to consider sustainability issues in sourcing decisions might reasonably argue that some of them lie beyond their domain. Environmental soundness, however, (defined as the combination of economic and environmental considerations) clearly does lie within such a domain and may thus be expected of a purchasing manager. The nature of these expectations is discussed below.

In seeking to achieve environmental soundness, a manager is concerned with the degree to which the actions of the firms in the supply chain (up and down stream, and within the firm itself) result in environmental or biophysical impacts (pollution, loss of biodiversity, and so on). When the concept is applied to the practice of supply chain management, the focus must include environmental soundness itself and the degree of environmental risk and related cost

that is taken on by the firm in making sourcing decisions, given specific choices. The ESSCMo methodology provides a way of comparing available supply chains, with a view to understanding and managing these factors. It is important to stress, however, that achieving environmentally sound supply chain management may not be synonymous with having a supply chain that is itself environmentally sound: the sourcing decision – a strategic choice between two supply chains – may simply leave the supply manager with the lesser of two evils.

Within the ESSCMo methodology lie the templates for several techniques and tools, designed to support supply managers in sourcing decisions. We refer to these as environment-related supplier initiatives (ERSI); they reflect both current practices, as observed from fieldwork, and those newly developed within this research to address perceived needs and gaps in the array of techniques that are available.

MANAGING BIOPHYSICAL IMPACTS ALONG EXTENDED SUPPLY CHAINS: STREAMLINED INTEGRATED LIFE CYCLE ASSESSMENT (SILCA)

Within the ESSCMo methodology lies an ERSI designed for gauging biophysical impacts. It goes under the working title of the Streamlined Integrated Life Cycle Assessment (SILCA). SILCA may be considered a variant of streamlined life cycle assessment which itself evolved from life cycle assessment (Faruk and Lamming 1998), both of which are cornerstone concepts of environmental management. The SILCA maintains a product life cycle perspective but with several important innovations such as the novel and systematic use of sustainability indicators and independent certification schemes to address some of the conceptual and practical deficiencies of existing techniques.[1] This has the objective of producing a structured means for analysing the biophysical impacts associated with the generality of products purchased by supply chain managers. There is not space to discuss SILCA at length in this chapter: the final version of the tool will be released at the end of the project. Some further details are provided in Faruk et al. (2000).

ASSESSING ENVIRONMENTAL ECONOMIC RISK IN SOURCING DECISIONS

In developing the conceptual model for the ESSCMo methodology, it is necessary to incorporate ERSIs related to assessing cost and managing risks. This leads to a dilemma in modelling predictions for the consequences, probabilities and outcomes of environmental risk exposure in the market place; the broad nature of the subject and its propensity for 'knock-on' effects means that such predictions would quickly become very complicated and unreliable. One way of approaching this would be to construct some sophisticated statistical models – but that would be to depart from the essential practical nature of the ESSCMo deliverables. Instead, techniques for the assessment of environmental risk were developed using concepts from service management – an area replete with models for this type of management problem.

From the literature we concluded that assessment of economic environmental risk would involve investigating the expectations of stakeholders (shareholders, customers, employees, suppliers, the community). The level of risk exposure might be thought of as the difference between stakeholders' expectations and their perception of associated causal actions (Matten 1995). This finds resonance in the concepts of service management systems (Normann 1984) and service quality (Parasuraman et al. 1985). Combining this with Kotler's (1997) definition of a service as 'any act or performance that one party can offer to another that is essentially intangible and does not result in the ownership of anything', leads us to view the 'delivery' of improved environmental performance by a supplier to a customer as a service (that is, something provided to the customer in addition to the delivery of, say, a physical product). This conclusion leads to the connection between service quality models and the development and measurement of environmental soundness.

The ERSIs within the ESSCMo methodology that deal with economic risk within environmentally sound supply chain management are therefore designed on the principles of service quality. This is in keeping with the nature of quality as a sustainable facet of a service, as opposed to satisfaction, which is considered to be a temporary outcome of a successful transaction.

TOWARDS A CONCEPTUAL MODEL FOR THE ESSCMO METHODOLOGY

Two sets of observations arose out of the data collection exercises. The first set are substantive research findings about the way in which firms are (or are not) modifying their supply activities in response to the environmental agenda. The second set are more pragmatic suggestions to help to build a new, practical, set of tools to aid in making supply chain management more environmentally sound.

Our substantive research findings suggest that firms are currently undertaking a wide variety of activities to make their supply chain management more environmentally sound (see Table 5.1). Such environment-related supplier initiatives range from introducing environmental conditions into contracts, through packaging waste reduction at the customer–supplier interface and supplier environmental audits, to advanced measures such as joint development of cleaner technology or the formation of supply chain clubs. The range of activities included in ERSI activity is much broader than has been portrayed in previous, more specialized studies (for example, Noci 1997; Carter et al. 1998).

Three main motivations for undertaking different types of ERSI were identified: cost reduction, economic risk management, and an attempt to manage biophysical impacts. Undertaking a supplier environmental questionnaire survey, for example, might highlight potential exposures to economic risk but might not, of itself, alter the supply chain's biophysical impact. Other ERSIs can serve more than one motive – many examples were encountered where reducing packaging led to both a reduction in the use of material resources and a net cost reduction.

Despite the wide range of initiatives currently undertaken in different firms, it was evident that managers do not undertake a systematic process of examining different options and choos-

Table 5.1   Examples of environment-related supplier initiatives (ERSI)

Supplier environmental questionnaires
Supplier environmental audits and assessments
Environmental criteria on approved supplier list
Require suppliers to undertake independent environmental certification
Jointly develop cleaner technology with supplier(s)
Engage suppliers in design for environment product innovation
Reduce packaging waste at the customer/supplier interface
Reuse/recycling of materials requiring co-operation with supplier
Reuse initiatives (including buy-backs, leasing)
Conduct life cycle analyses with co-operation from suppliers
Seek to influence legislation in co-operation with suppliers
Create supply club to collaborate on environmental issues
Co-ordinate minimization of environmental impact over the extended supply chain
Build environmental criteria into supplier contract conditions

ing the combination of ERSIs which best matches their circumstances. No one single supply management response is appropriate in all contexts and practitioners appear to lack a 'toolkit' which might enable them to discriminate between ERSIs and find the mixture which might maximize business benefits resulting from a sourcing decision.

This is particularly problematic when it is recognized that the success of any ERSI – generic or bespoke – depends on its appropriateness (perceived as well as actual; the acceptability of the technique must be established). For example, good work on managing biophysical impacts across the supply chain in a particular product area can all too easily be undone by a reputational problem in another area (which may have been more appropriately dealt with by a supplier environmental questionnaire).

One important conclusion from the survey, therefore, was that purchasing and supply managers appear to lack the knowledge and decision support mechanisms necessary for them to make informed decisions. It was also recognized that some specific tools are missing from the existing range of approaches. Crucially, this includes a practical way to assess biophysical impacts across extended supply chains – a concern identified in our earlier work, which inspired the development of SILCA.

Insights from the literature, ESSCMo Club meetings, desk work, interviews and question-naires were combined in the development of the conceptual model for the ESSCMo methodology (see Figure 5.2). The principles developed during the research permeate both the overall shape and specific elements of the ESSCMo methodology. The definition of environmental soundness developed in the research sets the limits of supply managers' responsibility. Given the responsibility of purchasing managers to incorporate both environmental and economic aspects in their sourcing decisions, the ESSCMo methodology aims to systematize and support the decision-making process.

The early stages of the methodology cover the economic and ecological risks inherent in the firm's activities and its supply chain. Assessing the economic risk requires the investigation of stakeholders' expectations and the supply chain's current performance. Based on a comprehensive analysis of the current situation (Stage 1), the main foci of ESSCMo activity are identified in Stage 2 (whether they are cost reduction, risk management or biophysical impact assessment) and priorities for consideration (Stage 3). The most appropriate ERSIs for the situation and focus of activity are suggested (Stage 4). A specifically developed tool – SILCA – may be employed at this stage if a biophysical impact focus is selected.

The main advantage of following the ESSCMo methodology over current approaches is that all ERSIs are considered valid approaches in

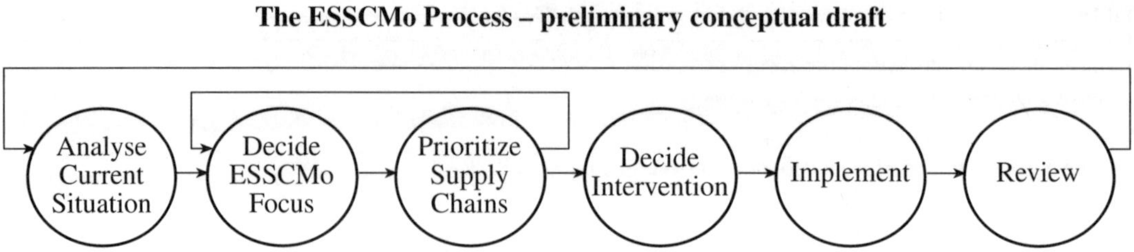

The ESSCMo Process – preliminary conceptual draft

Analyse Current Situation	Decide ESSCMo Focus	Prioritize Supply Chains	Decide Intervention	Implement	Review
Level: • strategic • managerial • operational	**Level:** • strategic • managerial • operational	**Level:** • strategic • managerial • operational	**Level:** • managerial • operational	**Level:** • managerial • operational	**Level:** • strategic • managerial • operational
Input: • corporate context • business context • purchasing's position • supply market context • environmental threats and opps.	**Input:** • motives for ESSCMo • existing capabilities	**Input:** • decision criteria • supply situation • environmental situation	**Input:** • ESSCMo focus • prioritized supply chains	**Input:** • 'Just do it!'	**Input:** • What did we do? • Was it worth it? • Was it the right thing to do?

Output:
• understand own motives for ESSCMo
• understand own capabilities
	Output:
	• balanced focus
	  – cost reduction
	  – risk management
	  – environmental impact
		Output:
		• decide on supply chains for:
		  – products
		  – product groups
			Output:
			• ERSI plan of action:
			  – cost
			  – risk
			  – environmental impact
				Output:
				• results of ESSCMo project
					Output:
					• ongoing ESSCMo activity

Figure 5.2 Conceptual model for the ESSCMo methodology

environmentally sound supply chain management. The exact combination of ERSIs implemented will be tailored to the characteristics of the firm, its supply management activity, its biophysical impacts, and its stakeholders' expectations. Implementing appropriate ERSIs is more likely to yield environmentally sound supply chain management in firms than the *ad hoc* introduction of initiatives commonly seen in current practice.

DEVELOPING THE METHODOLOGY FOR APPLICATION IN PRACTICE

The research is designed to develop a generic methodology for achieving environmentally sound supply chain management. From the methodology, firms will be able to develop their own working versions of ESSCMo. As principal sponsor, London Underground is being assisted in this process by the research team, providing in return an opportunity to pilot the design. The ESSCMo club members will also be able to develop early versions, before the final results are made public. Customization is always an important part of developing managerial tools from concepts but in the case of environmental management this is especially so. The nature of the environmental risks that are faced may depend heavily upon the type of business. Moreover, the terminology that is acceptable (and thus practical) may also vary widely with company and industry culture.

The final phase of the project will result in customized tools being employed by a range of firms in pursuit of environmentally sound supply chain management, adding to the integrity of their commercial, technical and logistical expertise and reputation.

CONCLUSION

In pursuing its objective, this research has revealed that current practices in supply management which are aimed at improving environmental credentials of purchased products appear to lack a cohesive framework. We have defined environmental risk as the combination of economic risk and risk of biophysical impacts, and environmental soundness as a subset of sustainability that stakeholders might reasonably expect of commercial organizations. Using these definitions, this project has enabled the construction of a practical methodology for managing supply chains, which may be developed into tools for managers to use in pursuing environmentally sound supply chain management. The methodology contains a process of decision-making, supported by a set of environment-related supplier initiatives. The conceptual model, presented here, illustrates this methodology and the potential for the development of tools.

ENDNOTE

1. Sustainability indicators are used since they apply to the constituent parts of the concept; their use in SILCA does not therefore detract from the focus on environmental soundness rather than sustainability itself. There are many independent certification schemes: an example would be the approval of the Forestry Stewardship Council (FSC) which indicates that any wood in a product has come from a responsibly managed forest.

REFERENCES

Bowen, F.E., Cousins, P.D. and Lamming, R.C. (1998), 'The role of risk in environment-related supplier initiatives', *Proceedings of the 7th Annual International IPSERA Conference*, London, April 1998.

Bowen, F.E., Faruk, A.C. and Stuart, F.I. (1997), 'A firm's environmental strategy and supply chain impacts', *Proceedings of the 6th Annual International IPSERA Conference*, Naples, March 1997.

Carter, C.R., Ellram, L.M. and Ready, K.J.' (1998), 'Environmental purchasing: benchmarking our German counterparts', *International Journal of Purchasing and Materials Management*, Fall, pp. 28–38.

Faruk, A.C. and Lamming, R.C. (1998), 'Streamlined integrated life cycle assessment: development of a pragmatic environmental management tool for supply chain managers', *Proceedings of the International Society for Ecological Economics Conference*, Santiago, Chile, November 1998.

Faruk, A.C., Lamming, R.C., Cousins, P.D. and Bowen, F.E. (forthcoming), 'Analyzing, mapping and managing environmental impacts along supply chains', *Journal of Industrial Ecology*.

Kotler, P. (1997), *Marketing Management: Analysis, Planning, Implementation and Control*, New Jersey: Prentice Hall.

Lamming, R.C., Faruk, A.C. and Cousins, P.D. (1999), 'Environmental soundness: a pragmatic alternative to expectations of sustainable development in business strategy', *Business Strategy and the Environment*, 8(3).

Matten, D. (1995), 'Strategy follows structure: environmental risk management in commercial enterprises', *Business Strategy and the Environment*, 4, pp. 107–116.

Noci, G. (1997), 'Developing "green" vendor rating systems for the assessment of suppliers' environmental performance', *European Journal of Purchasing and Supply Management*, 2(2), pp. 103–114.

Normann, R. (1984), *Service Management*, Chichester, UK: John Wiley & Sons.

Parasuraman, A., Zeithaml, V.A. and Berry, L.L. (1985) 'A conceptual model of service quality and its implications for future research', *Journal of Marketing*, 49, pp. 41–50.

PART TWO

OUTSOURCING AND PARTNERSHIP

Introduction to outsourcing and partnership

Andrew Erridge

The chapters in Part II focus on what has become the most common purchasing strategy in both the public and private sectors – outsourcing – and the most commonly advocated relationship style for strategic purchases – partnership. The two are linked in that many of the services outsourced are of either high value or carry high risk, which in theory may be managed most effectively by having very close, co-operative relationships with suppliers. The main themes are:

- the process of outsourcing and implementing partnerships;
- classification of services and suppliers;
- instruments to assess the effectiveness of outsourcing and partnership; and
- power in buyer–supplier relationships.

In Chapter 6, Louise Knight and Christine Harland argue that outsourcing has been the subject of a substantial amount of research, predominantly on outsourcing of particular support services, notably information technology (IT) provision, and focusing on the outsourcer and the outsource transaction (Benson and Ieronimo 1996). The chapter reports on the first stage of a new research project which adopts a higher level perspective on outsourcing, focusing on sector and national systems level issues. The project is aimed at improving decision-making in public sector organizations, and at building a bridge between policy and its implementation. Stage one, on which the chapter reports, consists of a critical review of prior research on outsourcing in both the public and private sectors in the UK and the USA, by academics from many fields including business and management, economics and public manage-

ment. The authors argue that outsourcing organizations are at risk of losing core competences and functions which cannot be brought in-house, and from increasing supplier power as a result of concentration in the supply market. Thus there may be a lack of alignment between initial objectives and eventual outcomes, especially in the public sector when the cumulative effects of many organizations' outsourcing decisions are examined. A conceptual framework is formulated and initial propositions for best practice that form the basis for the second stage are developed.

In Chapter 7, Johanna Rantala and Veli-Matti Virolainen develop a classification of services to assist in the choice of the most effective purchasing strategy for particular services. They argue that in many European countries the service sector dominates economic activity, accounting for more than half of total employment, and this share is increasing as more European economies enter the post-industrial era. Economic growth has fuelled the expansion of the service sector, as increasing prosperity means that companies, institutions and individuals have become more willing to trade money for time and to buy services rather than spend time doing things themselves. The aim of this chapter is to examine how services can be classified and grouped to make the most of differentiated purchase strategies. The authors suggest that services should be classified according to their type and the strategy of purchasing. A framework is developed which proposes suitable purchasing strategies for different service characteristics and different groups of classified services in order to gain long-term benefits, achieve a value-added approach and improve the organization's competitive position. For more complex, professional services, the authors advocate the use of partnership or lean supply, and argue that network sourcing provides an effective framework for the delivery of services.

The purpose of Chapter 8, by Johann Lilliecreutz and Lars Ydreskog, is to develop and test a supplier classification model for continuous improvement, in order to assist the buyer in the design and management of the extended organization. The model is developed from the authors' work with Saab Gripen, the Swedish aircraft manufacturer. The chapter shows that there is a need for more dynamic theories in the area of purchasing strategy, organization and relationship issues. If there is a serious focus on lean supply and supply chain management, there should also be a focus on how to treat the supplier base. Findings from many studies in the area of partnerships indicate a need for purchasing strategies with an ability to focus on specific buyer–supplier relationships. The model developed by the authors enables the measurement of the actual and the desired state of specific buyer–supplier relationships, pointing to areas where corrective action is required.

In Chapter 9, Andrew Cox, Chris Lonsdale and Glyn Watson strike a cautionary note, arguing that a renewed focus on boundary of the organization decisions is the obvious consequence of the changes and shocks that have characterized the development of the international economy over the last 20 years. In the private sector these may be defined in terms of the twin pressures of trade liberalization and deregulation. In the public sector it has been recession coupled with constraints on the public purse that have stimulated the initiatives to contract out. The authors argue that much of this outsourcing has been predicated upon a fairly crass logic that insists that organizations (both public and private) should focus on a set of core activities, outsourcing the rest. These approaches have failed both to adequately define core activities and to recognize that the outsourcing of certain non-core activities can place a firm at a real commercial disadvantage. This chapter attempts to go beyond the core competence model to look at a contingency model based around the idea of strategic and operational dynamism. The authors argue that

as markets are characterized by opportunism, there is a genuine risk of dependence on the supplier resulting from a loss of buyer competence and a build-up of dedicated assets, and they advocate a dynamic approach to outsourcing decisions to reduce the risk and achieve competitive advantage.

In Chapter 10, Arjan van Weele and Frank Rozemeijer show that despite many academics advocating the idea of partnership in buyer–seller relationships, empirical studies have demonstrated that partnership relationships are not widespread and in many cases are difficult to achieve. The empirical study described in this chapter, based on interviews with senior managers in manufacturing companies in the Netherlands, reveals that attempts to strive for partnership relationships, both from the buyer and the supplier perspective, often fail due to a lack of understanding of the power position of the parties involved. Moreover, failure is due to a lack of understanding of the conditions that should be met in order to make such relationships successful. The authors suggest that the role of power in buyer–seller relationships is more important than has been reflected in recent academic studies and requires more careful analysis, and they present a framework for analysing prospective partnership relationships.

Thus the chapters in this section acknowledge the risks inherent in outsourcing, and the difficulties encountered in establishing the kind of close working relationships necessary for effective service delivery. These problems are common to both public and private sectors, although the risks are perhaps greater in the public sector, as suggested by Knight and Harland, as a result of the cumulative effect of many organizations' outsourcing decisions. Nevertheless, three of the chapters present helpful frameworks to assist the outsourcing decision based upon more precise classification of services, suppliers and supply markets, whilst the other two offer models for assessing either prospective or actual partnership relationships. Thus, there is much in these chapters to guide the decisions of practising managers, as well as to stimulate further development of ideas and practical tools in these critical areas.

CHAPTER SIX

Outsourcing: a national and sector level perspective on policy and practice

Louise Knight and Christine Harland

'Outsourcing' became common business parlance during the 1990s; the term has been used to refer to a range of different arrangements with suppliers for activities that were originally conducted in-house. Outsourcing has been the subject of a substantial amount of research, predominantly concentrating on particular support services, notably information technology (IT) provision, and on the outsourcer and the outsource transaction (Benson and Ieronimo 1996). This chapter reports on a research project which extends the consideration of outsourcing to include the likely impact of outsourcing on whole sectors and at a national level. Focusing on policy and practice in the public sector, it identifies potential benefits and disadvantages not normally recognized in management literature. The research project draws on prior research by academics from many fields including business and management, economics and public management, but retains a management focus. It is aimed at improving decision-making in public sector organizations, and at building a bridge between policy and implementation. It is not about defining policy *per se*, but rather in developing our understanding of whether the steps that are taken to implement policy actually deliver as intended, or whether they have unexpected, and unrecognized, consequences that run counter to the original objectives. The first stage of the project, which is the subject of this chapter, involved a review of prior research and the development of a conceptual framework to shape the forthcoming empirical phase.

This chapter is presented in four parts. Following this introductory part, the project research questions and the research method used in this first research stage are described. The third part of the chapter critically reviews the findings of prior research. The final part covers the findings and conclusions from stage one, setting out the resultant conceptual framework and propositions for practice which form the basis for the second stage of the project.

RESEARCH PROJECT: QUESTIONS AND METHODOLOGY

The research questions on which this study is centred are:

1. From a management perspective, what are the implications of outsourcing at sector and national levels, and how do these fit with the objectives of outsourcing?
2. Based on this analysis of the implications, what lessons, guidance or models can be derived to aid future policy making and practice in the public sector?

A literature review is the core of the first stage of the research project. A search of the literature was undertaken to identify any papers which, directly or indirectly, considered the consequences of outsourcing at any unit of analysis higher than the level of the individual firm or public sector organization. To conduct this review a broad definition of outsourcing was adopted, to encompass any change in arrangements where some previously in-house activity was then contracted for externally. The literature has been critically evaluated to assess authors' method, empirical evidence, findings and any conclusions drawn that might influence future policy and practice. The literature review (Knight and Harland 1998) was complemented by a recent qualitative study which also expressly addressed the higher-level implications of outsourcing (Harland et al. 1998). To close the first stage of the project, a conceptual framework and a number of propositions have been developed as the basis for the second, empirical stage. The final project findings will be used to formulate a series of recommendations for those who develop and implement public sector policy. In the next section, prior research on outsourcing is critically evaluated.

FINDINGS OF REVIEW OF PRIOR RESEARCH

Remarkably little research has been undertaken that explicitly covers outsourcing at sector and national levels, and whose findings can be applied to developing outsourcing policy and practice at a collective level. In general, the strategic management literature (on private sector) and the purchasing and supply literature (on public and private sectors) focuses on the potential risks and benefits to the organization (for example, Sharpe 1997; Hendry 1995; Earl 1996) and/or the process of outsourcing (for example, McFarlan and Nolan 1995). Public sector research more often addresses sector and national level issues, but the findings tend to focus on challenging either government policy which leads to outsourcing, or the method of calculating the costs and benefits of outsourcing (Uttley 1993; Kerr and Radford 1994; Quiggin 1996; Patterson and Pinch 1995). Only one paper (Bettis et al. 1992) was identified which specifically addressed the aggregated consequences of individual organizations' outsourcing decisions, suggesting that individually logical and rational decisions can be counter-productive when considered collectively and cumulatively. In the main, the issues that were identified in the qualitative study (Harland et al. 1998) were similar to those from the literature, though terminology

differed and the distinct foci of the exercises were evident (with a strong practitioner bias in the qualitative study, and an academic bias in the literature). Many examples of evaluations of outsourcing, both favourable (such as Sharpe 1997) and unfavourable (such as Stein 1997), are founded more or less explicitly on ideology and management fashion (Hendry 1995). It appears that those in favour deploy primarily economic arguments, whilst those against focus on the social consequences of outsourcing. This split makes it more difficult to systematically compare the benefits and costs.

It is not the intention of this chapter to provide a full summary of the literature review (Knight and Harland 1998), but rather to present the key findings that relate directly to the research questions and thus form the basis for the design of the second part of the project. This review is organized around three inter-linked themes: economic and commercial issues; employment; and socio-political issues.

ECONOMIC AND COMMERCIAL CONSEQUENCES OF OUTSOURCING

Most of the reviews of the impact of compulsory competitive tendering (CCT) considered only the consequences for the public sector, as the outsourcer. However, Milne (1993) studied the effect of CCT on the contract cleaning industry serving the National Health Service (NHS). He found that it led to many firms trying to enter the market but also that many of those which were initially successful at winning contracts made large losses; and most contract cleaners withdrew from the market (because of losses, or because contracts were usually awarded to those firms which had a track record). From data for 1993 on seven commonly contracted-out local government services, Patterson and Pinch (1995) found that in each sector the five largest companies provided over 45 per cent of the service (by value), and in five of the seven sectors there were fewer than 50 private companies holding contracts (excluding management buy-outs). They argue that the dominance of a few firms in certain sectors can be explained by how capital-intensive the service is. For services such as refuse collection, only firms which are part of a major parent group can carry the losses that arise from the need for investment in the early years of the contract.

The extent of outsourcing in certain sectors, such as facilities management, catering, Information Technology/Information Systems (IT/IS) and cleaning has led to the substantial growth of various supply markets. Sharpe (1997) goes so far as to refer to the 'outsourcing industry', suggesting it is a sector in its own right, and argues that proposed regulation of the industry in the USA is unnecessary and inappropriate as it would have a detrimental effect on organizations' ability to respond to economic change: 'a key advantage of outsourcing is that it allows adjustment to change to occur with remarkably little in the way of labour market and other costs' (p. 548).

In contrast to Sharpe's (1997) optimistic view, Bettis et al. (1992) (who conceive of outsourcing as the international sourcing of components/ systems/whole production to [Asian] firms) argue that 'the improper use of outsourcing is playing an important role in the continuing competitive decline of many Western firms', and that firms make a series of outsourcing decisions which cumulatively 'represent the surrender of the business's capability to compete'.

OUTSOURCING AND EMPLOYMENT

The loss of jobs from the UK public sector in the 1980s and 1990s as a result of privatization and compulsory competitive tendering is well catalogued (Kerr and Radford 1994; Beaumont 1991). In the private sector, jobs have shifted from manufacturing to service sectors as a result of outsourcing (Postner 1990). Government statistics do not however permit researchers to assess the net effect of outsourcing on employment levels (Postner 1990; Kerr and Radford 1994), and no studies have been identified that attempted to do so by other means. Comparative studies of public and private sector tend to focus instead on relative terms and conditions of employment for staff transferred from the public to the private sector.

Kerr and Radford's (1994) review did not find a wide and consistent disparity between basic wages of personnel in the public sector when compared to basic wages of personnel employed by contractors. However they found that wide disparities have been identified when considering the full employment package. Private contractors have been able to reduce employment costs through changes to bonus schemes and other 'hidden' pay structures, leading to lower gross pay, sick pay, maternity pay and holiday entitlement; more part-time posts with many employees' hours falling below the level of National Insurance contributions and employment protection legislation thresholds; and changing shift patterns.

Furthermore, loss of jobs in the public sector has had a disproportionately high effect on ethnic minorities, women and lower skilled workers (Kerr and Radford 1994), thus amplifying socio-economic inequalities. Mayhew et al. (1997) found that outsourcing is associated with poorer levels of occupational health and safety. These findings lend support to Quiggin (1996) who questioned whether the savings accruing to public sector outsourcers actually lead to any net social welfare gain once the cost to the state of the lower conditions of employment and the costs of unemployment have been taken into account (see also Uttley 1993).

SOCIO-POLITICAL IMPLICATIONS OF OUTSOURCING

The impact of contractorization (contracting-out to the private sector and the establishment of quasi-contracts within the public sector) on health care, on politics and on public administration has been studied. Cousins (1987, p. 169, cited in Gustaffson 1995) found that staff experienced:

> ...the loss of values of compassion and caring in the service, for others it was reduced public accountability in a service already unresponsive to democratic control, and for others it was the loss of trust and motivation of lower-level members of the organization. The implementation of specific government policies, such as for instance the contracting out of ancillary services, also had the effect of lowering the

trust and commitment of staff, and re-moving the caring contribution that ancillary workers have traditionally made to patient care.

Gustafsson (1995) argues that in health care services 'care rationality' is replaced by 'wage rationality'. On local government, Patterson and Pinch (1995) conclude that 'CCT establishes a separation of a concern for the service to be provided from a concern for the people who will provide that service'.

Many (such as Sharpe 1997) argue that one benefit of outsourcing is the greater flexibility it offers in responding to economic downturns and to new opportunities. But it is increasingly widely recognized that firms are also at risk of losing flexibility if they outsource unwisely, or over-outsource. Because outsourcing can reduce an organization's ability to learn (Hendry 1995), it is possible that it loses the necessary skill to manage contracts, and it can make itself more susceptible to competition. Lei and Hitt (1995) label this corporate atrophy the 'hollowing out' of manufacturing organizations.

A similar problem arises with the public sec-tor though this is not so widely recognized. If the public sector gets it wrong, the impact is national and political/societal. Boston (1996, p. 109) notes that contracting-out is advocated by many people; some of them 'extolling the vir-tues of "hollow government" or "virtual govern-ment"'. These alternative phrases draw out the opposing views: 'hollow' has negative connota-tions, whilst 'virtual' can be interpreted as more positive. Overall, Boston advocates serious re-flection on the limits of contracting out, and the drafting of guidelines on the types of serv-ice that should not be contracted out, and those which should not be wholly contracted out.

However, defining these boundaries is not easy, and they can be expected to shift over time. Hood (1997) shows that what constitutes over-outsourcing depends on the nature of the con-tracting state (for example, whether the ability to govern, or the citizen as consumer, or the citizen as equal participant, predominate in the culture and values of the nation state). So a 'con-sumerist' contract state might undertake ex-

treme outsourcing, and this would not be inap-propriate. However, in doing so, much of the power of the state could be dispersed. Govern-ment's ability to influence would be reduced, and a new government elected under a differ-ent mandate (that is, a different contract state ethos) would have greater difficulty in imple-menting change. Public sector outsourcing on a large scale can affect local and national demo-cratic control (Hood 1997; Patterson and Pinch 1995; Boston 1996).

Even if there were no desire for change in policy, outsourcing can reduce flexibility in policy implementation. Whilst detailed specifi-cation of outcome/performance requirements might help to improve standards of quality, long term contracts reduce the purchaser's flexibility to adapt requirements and redeploy resources to meet any changes in policy (Boston 1996).

CONCLUSIONS FROM REVIEW OF PRIOR RESEARCH

From the literature on this subject, there is clear evidence that the debate surrounding outsourcing has, in recent years, moved on from its earlier, more partisan (Hendry 1995) nature to become more complex and subtle. More au-thors are presenting integrated discussions of the potential advantages and disadvantages of outsourcing, for both the private and the public sectors. It is notable that the risks and advan-tages are very similar for both sectors (compare, for example, Boston 1996 and Hendry 1995), and that most potential advantages are mirrored by a potential pitfall. Quality may improve, but it may also be jeopardized; local authority ex-penditure may be reduced, but this may be off-set by increased welfare spending by central government; this year's desirable flexibility may set off next year's atrophy. Furthermore, the outsourcing dogma that tends to portray outsourcing as an end in itself rather than as the means to achieve other objectives has been recognized and is increasingly disputed (see, for example, Hendry 1995; Alexander and Young 1996; Cant and Jeynes 1998).

Only very limited research was found which directly addressed the central issues in this project. The growth and changing structure of the sectors that are taking on the outsourced activities and the implications for outsourcers of increasing dependency on provider firms are not adequately addressed through research. The literature review points clearly to the lack of alignment between initial objectives and eventual outcomes of outsourcing decision, for the public sector and various industrial sectors, resulting from the failure to monitor and act upon the cumulative impact of outsourcing decisions. There is a paucity of normative research on assessing the impact of outsourcing, weighing direct costs against other, chiefly socio-economic, factors, which might enable public policy makers and corporate strategists to identify the limits of outsourcing (Boston 1996) and to achieve better alignment between objectives and outcomes.

RESEARCHING AND MANAGING OUTSOURCING

This next section reviews the current literature on the subject and discusses future action to be taken to minimize the problems and maximize the benefits of outsourcing.

THE CASE FOR HIGHER-LEVEL ANALYSIS AND ACTION

In terms of practice, the limited empirical evidence on the social and economic consequences (such as changes to employment levels and conditions, and the competitiveness of industrial sectors) clearly indicates that it is necessary to develop a more holistic view of outsourcing. Such a perspective would provide a better integrated view of the different types of benefit and risk (social, economic, political). Some would argue that private sector managers, and indeed public sector administrators, cannot and should not seek to take into account specifically socio-economic and socio-political issues, but even here a higher level perspective is still relevant. For example, the IT/IS, contract catering and contract cleaning supply markets are highly concentrated. Whilst current competition levels may be low but acceptable, a very low number of mergers and acquisitions could tip the balance towards unacceptable levels of dependence of the purchasers on the providers. However, because of the high capital costs in all these sectors, and the rate of technological change and the lack of outsourcer expertise in IT/IS, the outsourcers' scope to insource in the future is often very limited. Each organization would benefit from considering the possible long-term outcomes of their own *and* other organizations' outsourcing decisions.

The argument for further, high-level research is compelling, but the obstacles are substantial. Firstly, where data are gathered on costs and employment in the public sector, they can be of poor quality and may be confidential. There is no complementary body of data on costs and employment for the relevant parts of the private sector. It is therefore very difficult to assess the net impact of outsourcing on employment levels and conditions, and to determine whether localized efficiency gains in the public sector are outweighed by reductions in social welfare. Secondly, many of the issues raised above are only *potential* disadvantages; a higher-level analysis requires assessment of risk, a complex task, especially as the importance of risks is likely to change over time. Finally, as most of the sector and national level consequences described above are only apparent in the long term, this higher-level research would need to be longitudinal and, ideally, prospective.

Nevertheless, it may be possible for different parts of the public sector (such as local government or defence), and the private sector (acting through, for example, trade associations), to develop a more strategic approach to outsourcing, which is longer-term, shown to be in line with policy, adopts a holistic perspective of the potential benefits and risks, and is dynamic, adjusting as necessary to internal and external developments. The challenge lies in identifying ways to move towards achieving this strategic approach that are pragmatic and incremental, not bureaucratic and dogmatic.

CONCEPTUAL FRAMEWORK AND INITIAL PROPOSITIONS-FOR-PRACTICE

Based on the findings from the literature review, a conceptual framework has been developed to provide a structure for the second, empirical phase of this research project (see Figure 6.1).

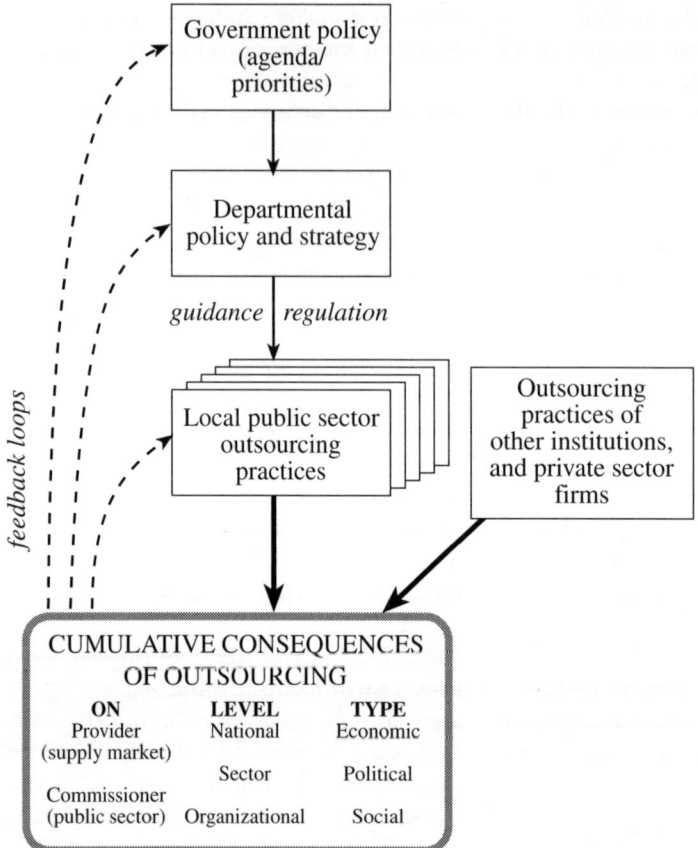

Figure 6.1 Conceptual framework based on the public sector and illustrating the key aspects of outsourcing, at different system levels

The framework focuses on the public sector, and indicates that high level government policy (agenda/priorities), departmental policy and strategy, and outsourcing at a local level are linked. Whilst the alignment between these three elements may be imperfect, there are guidance and regulation mechanisms designed to influence and control local practice. This framework focuses on the public sector because here there exists an infrastructure which regulates local practice and through which it would be possible to consider the actual and potential cumulative consequences of outsourcing. In the private sector, a more proactive and collective approach might be adopted by firms within a sector through, say, a trade association, but their coverage of the sector and their ability to influence organizational decisions would be limited.

The cumulative consequences of outsourcing are generated by outsourcing across many sectors. Whether they are considered to be favourable or negative depends on the nature of the consequence, and also from whose perspective it is considered. Outsourcing decisions that are logical and rational at the level of the individual organization (operating unit) can have detrimental and unforeseen consequences for the sector, or nationally. For example, a local public sector organization might take a proactive and strategic approach to outsourcing and successfully achieve its planned objectives, whilst nevertheless contributing to an unplanned and unobserved (at least in the early stages) impact on the service as a whole, at regional or national level.

The feedback loops are a key aspect of the framework. In the public sector, although decisions are taken at the organizational level, the guidance and regulations on outsourcing should not be static, but regularly updated and adapted if necessary, in the light of cumulative consequences. The feedback loops are required for a more strategic approach to outsourcing in the public sector; the investigation of prior research has demonstrated that these are lacking in current practice. Whilst the findings suggest that it is appropriate to adopt a more proactive and higher-level approach to managing outsourcing, it would be important to prioritize the areas in which this is done. For example, in the public sector, a collective, high-level view of outsourcing in, say, defence could prove more worthwhile than in more administrative public services, where recovery costs if poor decisions are made might be expected to be lower. In the next stage of this project, the propositions-for-practice outlined above will be developed and tested through interviews, focus groups and case studies, to seek to establish guidance and tools on outsourcing for use in the public sector to enable analysis and action at the higher systems levels.

CONCLUSION

This review has explored prior research that addresses the sector and national level implications of outsourcing across the private and public sectors. The limited way in which the topic has been addressed has been demonstrated, and a number of important gaps have been identified. It has been shown that further research on outsourcing at a higher-level of analysis would be worthwhile, even though difficult to undertake. Based on the prior research, a conceptual framework and initial propositions for practice around which the second stage of the project will be structured have been developed.

Whether or not it could be shown that the competitive tendering policies of the UK Conservative government of the 1980s and 1990s led to greater efficiency in the public sector, their policies undoubtedly helped to achieve other objectives such as reducing public sector employment levels, boosting certain parts of the private sector, and reducing the power of the unions (Kerr and Radford 1994). If one interprets the Labour government's policy as seeking good value and efficiency, but without pursuing competitive tendering as an end in itself (in Hood's (1997) terms, moving away from a 'consumerist' contract state), then questions of how to assess all forms of benefits and risks, evaluate outcomes at a higher level than the transaction, and monitor developments in order to respond proactively to new and changing risks must be addressed.

REFERENCES

Alexander, M. and Young, D. (1996), 'Outsourcing: where's the value?', *Long Range Planning*, **29**(5), pp. 728–730.

Beaumont, P. (1991), 'Privatization, contracting-out and public sector industrial relations: the Thatcher years in Britain', *Journal of Collective Negotiation*, **20**(2), pp. 89–100.

Benson J. and Ieronimo, N. (1996), 'Outsourcing decisions: evidence from Australia-based enterprises', *International Labour Review*, Jan-Feb, **135**(1), pp. 59–74.

Bettis, R., Bradley, S. and Hamel, G. (1992), 'Outsourcing and industrial decline', *Academy of Management Executive*, **6**(1), pp.7–22.

Boston, J. (1996), 'The use of contracting in the public sector – recent New Zealand experience', *Australian Journal of Public Administration*, **55**(3), pp. 105–110.

Cant, M. and Jeynes, L. (1998), 'What does outsourcing bring you that innovation cannot?', *Total Quality Management*, **9**(2&3), pp. 193–201.

Cousins, C. (1987), *Controlling Social Welfare*, Sussex: Wheatsheaf Books.

Earl, M. (1996), 'The risks of outsourcing IT', *Sloan Management Review*, Spring, pp. 26–32.

Gustafsson, R. (1995), 'Open the black box: paradoxes and lacunas in Swedish health care reforms', *International Journal of Health Services*, **25**(2), pp. 243–258.

Harland C.M., Lamming R.C. and Knight L. (1998), *A Strategic Study on Outsourcing: Organisation, Sector and National Level*

Implications and Issues, Working Paper, CRiSPS, School of Management, University of Bath, UK.

Hendry, J. (1995), 'Culture, community and networks: the hidden cost of outsourcing, *European Journal of Management*, **13**(2), pp. 193–200.

Hood, C. (1997), 'Which contract state? Four perspectives on over-outsourcing for public services', *Australian Journal of Public Administration*, **56**(3), pp. 120–131.

Kerr, A. and Radford, M. (1994), 'TUPE or not TUPE: competitive tendering and the transfer laws', *Public Money and Management*, Oct-Dec, pp. 37–45.

Knight, L.A. and Harland, C.M. (1998), *The Impact of Outsourcing: A Literature Review of Outsourcing's Sector and National Level Implications*, Working Paper, CRiSPS, School of Management, University of Bath, UK.

Lei, D. and Hitt, M. (1995), 'Strategic restructuring and outsourcing: the effect of mergers and acquisitions and LBOs on building firm skills and capabilities', *Journal of Management*, **21**(5), pp. 835–859.

Mayhew, C., Quinlan, M and Ferris, R. (1997), 'The effects of subcontracting/outsourcing on occupational health and safety: survey evidence from four Australian industries', *Safety Science*, **25**(1-3), pp. 163–178.

McFarlan, F. and Nolan, R. (1995), 'How to manage an IT outsourcing alliance', *Sloan Management Review*, Winter, pp. 9–23.

Milne R.G. (1993), 'Contractors' experience of compulsory competitive tendering: a case study of contract cleaners in the NHS', *Public Administration*, Vol 71, Autumn, pp 301–321.

Patterson, A and Pinch, P. (1995), '"Hollowing out" the local state: compulsory competitive tendering and the restructuring of British public sector services', *Environment and Planning*, A27, pp. 1437–1461.

Postner, H. (1990), 'The contracting-out problem in service sector analysis: choice of statistical unit', *Review of Income and Wealth*, Series 36 (2), June, pp. 177–186.

Quiggin, J. (1996), 'Competitive tendering and contracting in the Australian public sector', *Australian Journal of Public Administration*, **55**(3), pp. 49–57.

Sharpe, M. (1997), 'Outsourcing, organizational competitiveness, and work', *Journal of Labor Research*, **XVIII**(4), pp. 535–549.

Stein, H. (1997), 'Death imagery and the experience of organizational downsizing', *Administration and Society*, **29**(2), pp. 222–247.

Uttley, M. (1993), 'Contracting-out and market-testing in the UK defence sector: theory, evidence and issues', *Public Money and Management*, Jan-Mar, pp. 55–60.

CHAPTER SEVEN

A framework for classification of services to gain strategic purchasing insights

Johanna Rantala (née Stenberg) and Veli-Matti Virolainen

Purchasing of services has developed over a relatively long period of time in consumer markets and in high-volume services such as banking and insurance services, transportation and information services. There is, however, much undeveloped potential in the field of service contracting between organizations. Only recently have the supporting activities of purchasing and market networks been developed and the supply of purchase services augmented so that the services market can be better exploited and the network economy developed (Koskinen et al. 1995). Also the proportion of services in industrial enterprises has been augmented. Management, design, and other professional occupations are services by nature and they are more frequently procured from markets outside the company. As the level of attention paid to purchasing and supply increases, the work tends to become more strategic in emphasis, concentrating more upon such activities as negotiating longer-term relationships, supplier development, and total cost reduction, rather than ordering and replenishing routines (Baily et al. 1994).

Services today have a growing significance for organizational success, and service purchasers have a key role in making the supply chain work. Service marketing and selling challenges have been broadly discussed in marketing literature, but purchasers seldom have a clear and stable purchase strategy for buying services, although the value-added approach can be adopted and the end customers made satisfied only by obtaining and developing a strategic view to purchasing. This chapter builds on past research by examining the characteristics and classification of services in the marketing and purchasing literature. Service classifications are very dispersed and they are mainly discussed only in marketing literature. The aim of this critical review is to examine past research in order to develop a sensible framework for classifying services from the purchasing perspective. The framework suggested is the result of studying, applying and modifying the classifications discussed in literature to better meet the challenges in procurement and strategies for purchasing services.

SERVICE CHARACTERISTICS

Kotler and Bloom (1984) describe a 'service' as any activity or benefit that one party can offer to another that is essentially intangible and does not result in ownership. Its production may or may not be tied to a physical product. The overall objective of purchasing should be the same in any commercial organization: to generate competitive advantage through effective acquisition of the goods and services required by the organization. However, one key difference between the manufacturing and service sectors is that in service organizations the process is knowledge-based and most of the purchasing function's activity is inevitably involved in supporting and servicing people, the key to organizations' success (Smith 1996). Table 7.1 points out the basic differences between the purchase of goods and services.

Table 7.1   Differences between goods and services

Services	Physical Goods
Intangible	Tangible
Heterogeneous	Homogeneous
Production, distribution and consumption are simultaneous processes	Production and distribution are separate from consumption
An act or a process	An item
Core value produced in the interaction between buyer and seller	Core value produced in facility
Customers participate in production process	Customers do not usually participate in production process
Cannot be stored	Storable
Ownership is not passed	Ownership is passed

Reproduced with kind permission from Grönroos, C. (1990), *Service Management and Marketing*, Lexington, Mass: Lexington Books, p. 280.

When production and consumption, instead of being sequential processes, are parallel processes, the foundation for purchasing changes, compared to what we are used to in traditional buying models. In the service context the customer consumes the process itself, where the service is simultaneously emerging in an interaction between the customer, possible fellow customers and employees, physical resources, technologies and systems that are managed by the service provider (buyer–seller interactions or service encounters). The consumption of services can be characterized as process consumption; the customer consumes the process, not only its outcome (Grönroos 1998).

Purchasing of services differs from purchasing of goods mainly because of the four common factors that characterize all services. Services are said to be *intangible* because they are performances rather than objects, and they cannot be touched or seen in the same manner as goods. *Inseparability* of production and consumption refers to the fact that goods are first produced, then bought and consumed, whereas services have to be bought first and then produced and consumed at the same time. *Heterogeneity* refers to the potential for variability in the performance of services and problems of lack of consistency that cannot be eliminated in services as they frequently are with goods. *Perishability* means that services cannot be saved; unused capacity in services cannot be

claimed, and services themselves cannot be inventoried (Zeithaml et al. 1985).

The above characteristics of services distinguish the nature and scope of purchasing goods and services. These characteristics call for huge flexibility from the supplier, and the buyer must also be able to foresee the service need and inform the supplier about it. Without good cooperation and communication things are left undone and the production of the firm might be stopped while waiting for the required service (Koskinen et al. 1995). Whilst it is useful to look at the supply of services separately from the supply of goods, few contracts are purely for the supply of goods and, equally, few are for services alone (Baily et al. 1994).

SERVICE CLASSIFICATION

Defining the term 'service' in the purchasing context is not as simple as it might at first seem. The range of possible services is extremely broad, but organizations need only a part of the total. Furthermore, there are distinctive patterns of service needs for different types of organizations. A comprehensive definition of services in the purchasing context should not only include the broad array of services, but should also recognize the purchasing patterns of different organizational types (Maples et al. 1994).

Services can be classified according to their basic demand characteristics, service content and benefits; delivery procedures; service investments; to whom a service is directed; or according to the service relationship. Lovelock (1983) suggests that the following questions should be asked to determine into which category a service fits:

1. What is the nature of the service act?
2. What type of relationship does the service organization have with its customers?
3. How much room is there for customization and judgement on the part of the service provider?
4. What is the nature of demand and supply for the service?
5. How is the service delivered?

The thrust of Lovelock's argument is that services should be considered not for the factors that set them apart, but for the factors that draw them together. His concern is less to provide an organizational schema than to provide a series of guidelines for marketing managers. Identifying the factors that different kind of services have in common helps marketing managers to better understand their products, their organizations, and the relationship their organizations have with their customers (Bateson 1995). Likewise, identifying the factors that different services share helps purchasing managers to understand the purchase process and the service bought, their organization and their relationship with the suppliers.

The insights of different researchers on service classifications are presented in Table 7.2. By combining and emphasizing these service characteristics in different ways, services are found to vary between mass services and tailor-made professional services. As the table shows, the uniting factors on service characteristics to classify services systematically are the following (definitions from Silvestro et al. 1992):

1. *People vs. equipment* Equipment-focused services are those where the provision of certain equipment is the core element in the service delivery. People-focused services are those where the provision of contact staff is the core element in service delivery.
2. *Customer presence in the service operation*

(contact time) Customer presence means the degree of customers' participation, time spent and effort in the service process.
3. *Degree of customization* A high degree of customization exists where the service process can be adapted to suit the needs of individual customers. A low degree of customization exists where there is a non-varying standardized process.
4. *Degree of discretion* A high degree of discretion is found where front office personnel can exercise judgement in altering the service package or process without referring to superiors. A low degree of discretion is found where changes to service provision can be made only with authorization from superiors.
5. *Product vs. process orientation* A product-oriented service exists where the emphasis is on what the customer buys. A process-oriented service exists where the emphasis is on how the service is delivered to the customer.

Developing classification schemes is not enough. The most important aspect is to find the best division of services to best serve the needs and conditions of purchasing. Lovelock (1983) argues that classification schemes can only be of value if they offer strategic insights into the services themselves. It is important for such schemes to highlight the characteristics that certain types of service have in common, and to analyse the implications of these common factors for marketing managers. Like marketing managers, purchasing managers also need to understand the implications of service characteristics in order to buy those services successfully.

The service process model presented by Silvestro et al. (1992) has the same five service characteristics as the ones pointed out in Table 7.2, plus the characteristic of *the source of value added in front office versus back office oriented service*. A back office-oriented service is where the proportion of customer contact staff to total staff is small. A front office-oriented service is where the proportion of front office staff to total staff is large.

Table 7.2 Summary of previously proposed schemes for classifying services (the shaded areas show the most frequently cited characteristics of services)

Service Characteristics	Kotler 1980	Lovelock 1980, 1983	Lehtinen 1986	Grönroos 1990	Silvestro et al. 1992	Maples & Graw 1994	Koskinen et al. 1995	Burt & Pinkerton 1996	Tinnilä 1997	Grönroos 1998
People vs. equipment	x	x			x		x		x	
Customer presence	x	x	x		x	x	x	x	x	
Personal vs. business needs	x			x						
Public vs. private	x									
Profit vs. non-profit	x									
Degree of customization		x	x		x	x	x	x	x	
Degree of discretion		x			x	x	x		x	
Back vs. front office					x	x				
Product vs. process		x			x	x				x
Single vs. bundle		x								
Extent of imbalances		x								

In this model, services are divided into three categories. *Mass services* are equipment-focused, contact time is short, levels of customization and discretion low and the product-oriented service is produced in the back office. In *service shops* both people and equipment orientation is used, contact time, customization and discretion are medium and little process orientation is seen in a service provided by both back and front office staff. *Professional services* are people- and front office-focused processes, which require long contact time and a high degree of customization and discretion.

The model is analogous to the production process model and it is proposed that the three types of service process, professional service, service shop and mass service, give rise to different management concerns, and that the service strategy, control and performance measurement will differ significantly between the three (Silvestro et al. 1992). The next section examines the differences in purchase strategies between these three types of service processes.

THE SERVICE PURCHASE PROCESS

Efficient procurement of services is a new challenge for traditional purchasing. Often a certain amount of service is also required when purchasing goods, and service level is one criterion for evaluating and choosing the supplier. Organizations use many traditional, essential services like banking, insurance and catering, which are almost always bought in from outside the organization. Today it is more usual to buy whole service functions and also to outsource services traditionally carried out inside the company to external service providers (Koskinen et al. 1995).

The model of service processes by Silvestro et al. presented in Chapter 6 is analogous to Kraljic's (1983) purchase product portfolio technique, which can also be applied to services. In Kraljic's portfolio, adjusted to services, the purchasing service assortment is analysed on the basis of the importance of the purchase to the company and the supply risk. The combination of these two dimensions yields four service groups, each offering different interests to the company:

● strategic services, purchasing through partnership strategies (*professional services*);

- bottleneck services, whose supply continuity must be secured (*service shops*);
- leverage services obtained from various suppliers by competitive bidding (*service shops*); and
- routine services, which are best obtained by systems contracting, because they have few technical or commercial problems from the purchasing point of view (*mass services*).

Tinnilä's (1997) service process analysis matrix evaluates the efficiency of matching the type of service being offered with alternative types of delivery channels. Tinnilä suggests the categorization of service mix from simple to complex (shown in Figure 7.1 as the type of service) analogous to mass services, service shops and professional services presented by Silvestro et al. The delivery channel classification is based on the length of the channel, that is, the number of different units and interorganizational linkages constituting the channel. Four channel types, shown in Figure 7.1, can be defined.

Four efficient service processes are defined along the diagonal of the SPA matrix:

1. *Fast routine processes* are a combination of mass transaction service and market network channel. These processes include purchasing standard components from a catalogue, or purchasing transport services electronically, and the advantages are low cost and availability.

2. *Flexible integrated processes* represent standard service contracts provided by service personnel. The service is standardized by defining several options and the modules of process are pre-determined by the definition of service, such as the conditions of a loan in banking services.

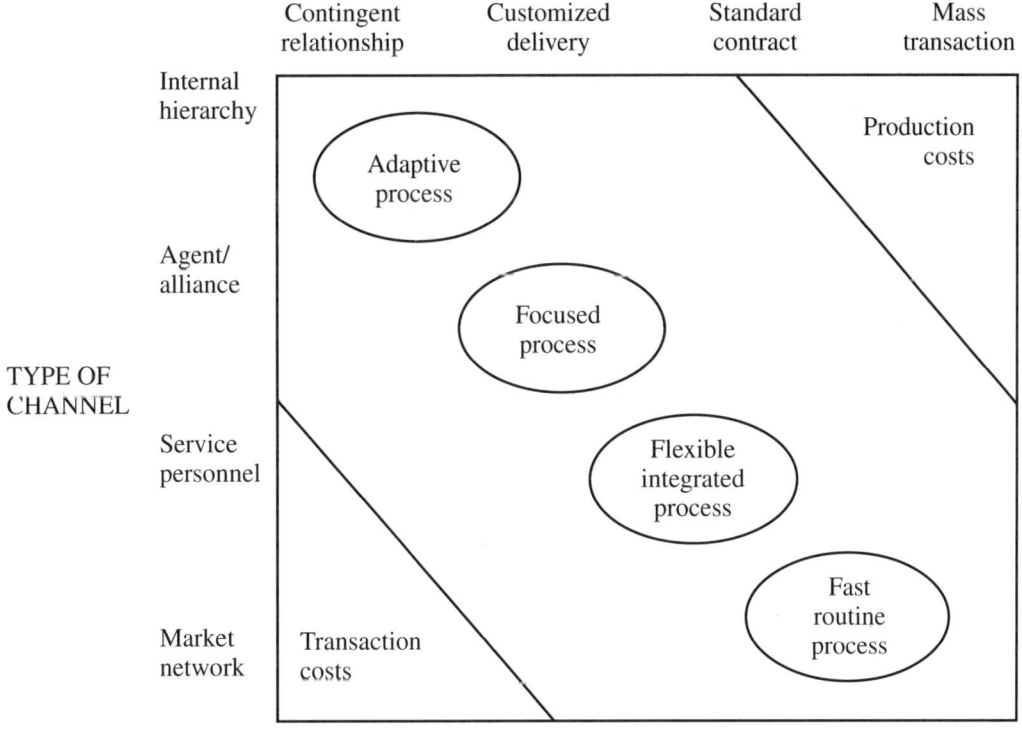

Figure 7.1 Service process analysis matrix with generic processes
Source: Tinnilä, M. (Ed.) (1997), Division of Service and Business Processes, Helsinki: Helsinki School of Economics and Business Administration.

3. *Focused processes* combine customized delivery and agent or alliance channel. They provide a degree of expertise and customization according to individual customer needs, such as printing and publication services, travelling services, or some training and education services.

4. *Adaptive processes* require confidential communication and flexible access to a customer's resource base. Contingent relationships deal with complex problems with a need to adapt to changing customer requirements and often call for modification of service processes, for example, professional services like legal services, consulting, most training and education services.

Efficient processes in the matrix are located along the diagonal. This preference for diagonal positions arises from the consideration of economic efficiency following the arguments of transaction cost economics (Williamson 1985). According to this view, economic transactions should be arranged so as to minimize the sum of production costs and transaction costs.

Production costs focus on internal operations of the service firm and the costs associated with them. Transaction costs are caused by the establishment and maintenance of external customer relationships and related co-ordination activities. These include negotiation costs, search costs, and costs of incentive contracts as well as the risks involved. These costs depend predominantly on the uncertainties and monitoring problems present in the marketplace (Tinnilä 1997).

Although price/cost should always be a factor in selecting a service supplier, it may not be the most important factor. A logical mix of technical/management and price/cost/business evaluation criteria may be more appropriate. The more technical the work, the more weight the technical criteria should be given (Maples et al. 1994).

The service ability of a firm is based on the distribution channels it uses to serve different customers. Firms have to develop their service processes and secure the efficiency of those processes by observing and evaluating charac-

teristics of the processes from the service purchaser's point of view (Koskinen et al. 1995). Successful service purchasing means managing to find criteria for good service and constantly evaluating the performance of the service supplier against those criteria (Koskinen et al. 1995). Thus, to make the buyer–supplier relationship work, the supplier's distribution channel type must match with the buyer's purchase strategies. Several different types of channel may be used to deliver the same type of service, and one service may be provided through several channels (Tinnilä 1997). Several different service purchase strategies may also be used to procure one type of service. The question is, which purchase strategy is the most efficient in terms of cost, availability, purchase risk, service quality and ultimate customer satisfaction?

Traditionally, purchase strategies and relationships between buyers and suppliers have been divided into adversarial and partnership relationships. The nature of services is turning more and more towards professional services, and a closer relationship between the service buyer and seller is needed. The unique nature of services and the inseparability of the service process challenges existing supplier and customer relationships and forces them to adapt new purchasing strategies in order to maintain and improve their performance.

Koskinen et al. (1995) have defined three different purchase strategies for the procurement of the four effective service processes shown in Figure 7.1. In the framework shown in Figure 7.2 we propose four different purchase strategies, one for each generic service process. Fast routine processes have to provide good availability at low cost. Purchasing is conducted through *competitive bidding* by different suppliers, but in order to minimize transaction and production costs several automation, rationalization and routine purchases are needed. Flexible integrated processes are to some degree standardized by defining several options and the modules of the process are pre-determined by *annual contracting*. Focused processes provide a degree of expertise and customization according to individual customer needs. These are best procured by *traditional partnership sourcing*,

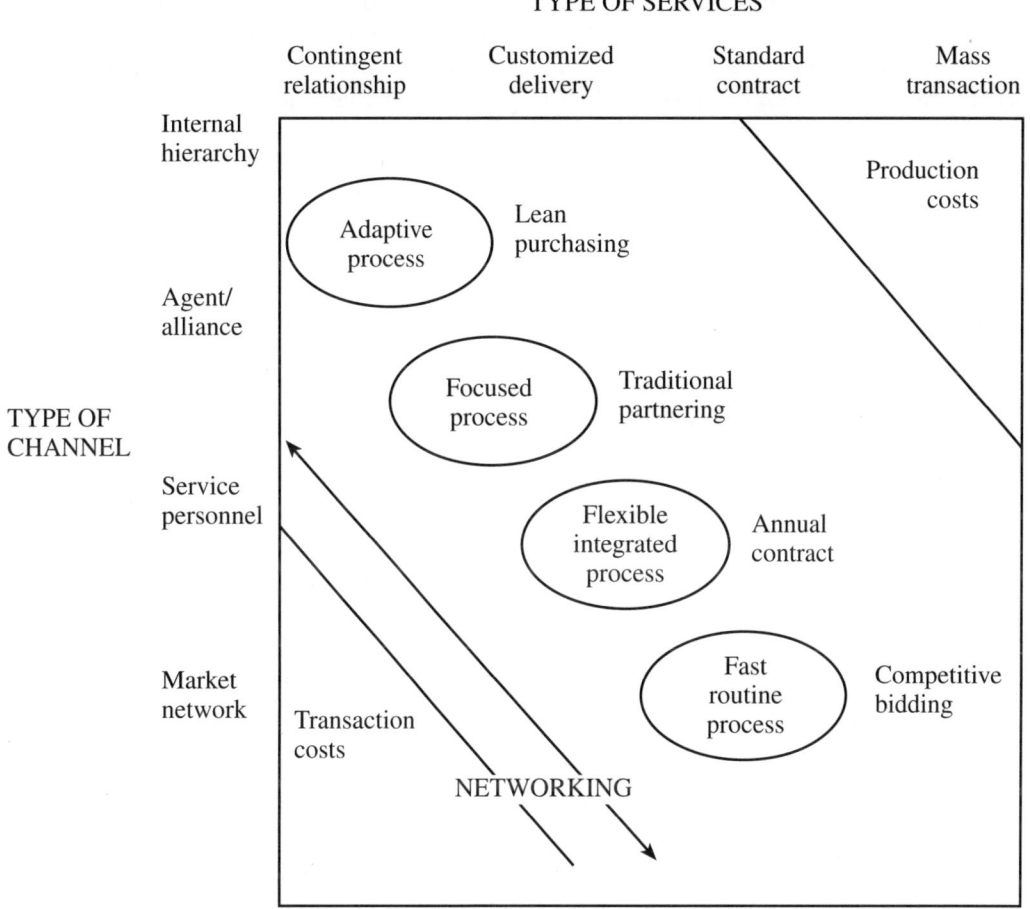

Figure 7.2 A framework for strategic purchase of services

which works only when both parties feel that they are not being exploited. They must feel secure that the relationship is on a sound footing and that it will continue for the foreseeable future. Both parties must be able to discuss problems frankly and constructively; a disagreement does not signify the end of a relationship, rather the beginning of its improvement. The power in this long-term co-operation is still somewhat on the purchaser's side. Adaptive processes require commitment between the customer and the supplier to have an equal, longer term relationship based on trust and clear, mutually agreed objectives and uniform strategies. Professional services are often critical in nature for the buyer's business performance and lean purchasing (presented by Lamming (1993), which calls for the supplier and buyer to share common goals of world-class capability and competitiveness) is the best and most effective way to procure complex, tailor-made professional services.

Although correlations between service processes and purchase strategies are difficult to measure and test, it can still be said that the adaptive service process, in particular, needs a close relationship with the supplier and lean purchasing gives the best premise on which to base consistent strategy and the development of shared strategic objectives between the buyer and the supplier.

THE NETWORK APPROACH

Regardless of the service process type, we propose that network sourcing provides an efficient sourcing solution. A network can be classified as a specific type of relation linking a defined set of persons, objects or events (Harland 1996). According to Hakanson and Johanson (1993) the components of networks are actors, resources, and activities or transactions. The network approach has its root in the Japanese economy. The primary tools employed by the Japanese to implement closer supplier co-ordination and individual supplier development are the cross-exchange of staff between buyers and suppliers. Generally speaking, by networking, firms aim to reduce financial and technological risks and improve their competitive advantage through greater specialization.

Japanese corporations rarely operate independently without connections to wider corporate groups. The modern business groups called *keiretsu* are the heart of the Japanese enterprise system, since they direct a vast majority of business activities in almost all sectors of industry. They share some common characteristics, no matter what type of organizational structures they represent. Each has a core financial institution as a member, the member corporations share resources and co-operate in mutual benefits and, finally, they rely on cross-shareholding to strengthen the sense of belonging together and preventing hostile takeovers.

The Japanese corporate network represents a relatively well ordered structure of relationships among highly differentiated firms. From one perspective *keiretsu* is seen as an attempt to spread industrial risk and reduce performance variability among group members. This creates strong incentives for managers to stabilize their external business relationships and to create implicit insurance arrangements with other companies, should their own companies face financial difficulties. In reality, Japan's diversified group structure probably represents an attempt by member firms to gain benefits both of sharing downside risks and creating strategic complementarities for upside gains (Gerlach 1992).

The new purchasing approaches such as network sourcing and lean purchasing are based on the Japanese network economy. The deliverables of network sourcing developed by Hines (1995) can be summarized as quality, cost, new product development and delivery. The key elements in network sourcing include supplier co-ordination and individual supplier development, and the primary tools to implement these elements are the cross-exchange of staff between buyer and supplier, one-to-one supplier development and, most importantly, the Japanese *kyoryoku kai* or supplier association. The supplier association is used as the vehicle to help align the supplier with the policy set by the customer's senior management team. In addition, it provides suppliers with an awareness of what they need to do to satisfy the customer, as well as an education on the individual techniques that they should use. This helps to lead to the successful implementation and continued improvement of all members of semi-formal, many-tiered supplier networks (Hines 1996).

Lean purchasing is similar to Japanese network sourcing, but with more equal relationships between the manufacturer and first-tier suppliers, with the supply base acting as a coherent entity to innovate, add value and reduce waste throughout the supply chain. The purchaser's attention is drawn away from logistics and technical details towards external resource management. A company can concentrate on its core competencies and procure the rest from its partnership network without the traditional competitive bidding of suppliers (Lamming 1993).

CONCLUSION

Services are a heterogeneous procurement group, which has implications for the purchasing process. Purchases that companies focus on include travel, transportation, insurance, information and advertising services. The purchasing of more simple services like cleaning and office services resembles the purchasing of goods, because you can easily assess the quality of the service and compare different service suppliers, and the service process is visible. The main problem with buying services is that the value and quality of a service can only be evaluated after the service is consumed. That is why it is important to work closely with a certain service producer for a long period of time. It is a question of trust, interaction, quality and learning.

The Japanese *keiretsu* is one of the most extensive applications of networking. By linking different enterprises it is possible to gain synergy benefits and reduce costs by co-operation and effective communication. The network sourcing model has many advantages over vertically integrated systems or the market driven systems more typical in the West (Hines 1995). Yet the benefits gained from efficient networking of service purchases have so far gained very little interest and attention in the Western world. This is probably why networking as a part of strategic purchasing has not been mentioned in the models of service processes presented in this paper. In our model we proposed lean purchasing, an example of network strategy, as a purchasing strategy for adaptive processes, but the network principles of the Japanese *keiretsus* should also be applied to purchases of focused processes, flexible integrated processes and even the partly automated, fast routine processes. Therefore the framework is now expanded, as shown in Figure 7.2 above, to include networking as a common strategy through all the proposed service purchase strategies.

In Japan the network economy is far more developed than in the West, and we should learn from the benefits and results gained in the East. Because of the complexity and the process nature of services, the effective use of networks as strategic purchasing options result in even greater benefits when purchases concern services only or services as a part of an integrated whole. The evidence from Japanese sourcing practices shows that only by combining an efficient and suitable purchase strategy with organized networking can true competitive advantage be gained and progress made towards the development of the 'virtual corporation'.

REFERENCES

Baily, P., Farmer, D., Jessop, D. and Jones, D. (1994), *Purchasing Principles and Management*, London: Pitman Publishing.

Bateson, J.E.G. (Ed.) (1995), *Managing Services Marketing*, Orlando: The Dryden Press.

Burt, D.N. and Pinkerton, R.L. (Eds) (1996), *A Purchasing Manager's Guide to Strategic Proactive Procurement*, New York: AMACOM.

Gerlach, M. (1992), 'The Japanese corporate network: a blackmodel analysis', *Administrative Science Quarterly*, 37 (March), pp. 105–139.

Grönroos, C. (Ed.) (1990), Nyt kilpaillaan palveluilla, Jyväskylä: Weilin & Göös.

Grönroos, C. (1998), *Service Marketing Theory: Back to Basics*, Working paper of Swedish School of Economics and Business Administration 369, Helsinki.

Hakanson, H. and Johanson, J. (1993), 'The Network as a Governance Structure. Interfirm Co-operation beyond Markets and Hierarchies', in Grapher, G. (Ed.), *The Embedded Firm*, London: Routledge, pp. 35–51.

Harland, C. (1996), 'Supply chain management: relationships, chains and networks', *British Journal of Management*, March, pp. 63–80.

Hines, P. (1995), 'Network sourcing: the concept explained', in Lamming, R. and Cox, A. (Eds), *Strategic Procurement Management in the 1990s, Concepts and Cases*, Boston, UK: Earlsgate Press.

Hines, P. (1996), 'Network sourcing in Japan', *The International Journal of Logistics Management*, 7(1), pp. 13–28.

Koskinen, A., Lankinen, M., Sakki, J., Kivistö, T. and Vepsäläinen, A.P.J. (Eds) (1995), Ostotoiminta yrityksen kehittämisessä, Porvoo: Weilin & Göös Oy.

Kotler, P. (Ed.) (1980), *Principles of Marketing*, New Jersey: Prentice Hall.

Kotler, P. and Bloom, P.N. (Eds) (1984), *Marketing Professional Services*, Englewood Cliffs, New York: Prentice Hall.

Kraljic, P. (1983), 'Purchasing must become supply management', *Harvard Business Review*, September/October, pp. 109–117.

Lamming, R. (1993), *Beyond Partnership. Strategies for Innovation and Lean Supply*, Hemel Hempstead: Prentice Hall.

Lehtinen, J.R. (1986), *Quality Oriented Services Marketing*, Tampere: University of Tampere, Series A2: studies and reports 44.

Lovelock, C.H. (1980), 'Towards a Classification of Services', in Lamb, C.W. and Dunne, P.M. (Eds), *Theoretical Developments in Marketing*, Chicago: AMACOM, pp. 72–76.

Lovelock, C.H. (1983), 'Classifying services to gain strategic marketing insights', *Journal of Marketing*, 47 (Summer), pp. 9–20.

Maples, D.M. and Graw, LeRoy H. (Eds) (1994), *Service Purchasing: What Every Buyer Should Know*, New York: Van Nostrand Reinhold.

Silvestro R., Fitzgerald L., Johnston R. and Voss, C. (1992), 'Towards a classification of service processes', *International Journal of Service Industry Management*, **3**(2), pp. 62–75.

Smith, P. (1996), 'Procurement Re-engineering in a Service Business: The Dun and Bradstreet Experience', in Cox, A. (Ed.), *Innovations in Procurement Management*, Boston, UK: Earlsgate Press, pp. 127–151.

Tinnilä, M. (Ed.) (1997), *Division of Service and Business Processes*, Helsinki: Helsinki School of Economics and Business Administration.

Williamson, O.E. (Ed.) (1985), *The Economic Institutions of Capitalism*, New York: Free Press.

Zeithaml, V.A., Parasuraman, A. and Berry, L.L. (1985), 'Problems and strategies in services marketing', *Journal of Marketing*, **49**(2), pp. 33–46.

CHAPTER EIGHT

Supplier classification as an enabler for a differentiated purchasing strategy

Johan Lilliecreutz and Lars Ydreskog

BACKGROUND TO THIS CHAPTER

In recent years, a considerable restructuring of the aerospace industry has taken place owing to the reduction of military budgets, market recession and increased competition confronting makers of regional commercial aircraft. The aerospace industry is characterized by a high degree of technical complexity, long product life cycles, high development costs, low volume series and continuous system upgrading. At present, many aircraft producers make only 20 to 40 per cent of the components and systems in an aircraft themselves; suppliers are responsible for the rest.

This situation has forced the entire aerospace industry to improve their supply and value chain. The proportion of outsourcing of both design and production has been increased in order to reduce risk exposure and costs in new aerospace programmes. Gadde and Håkansson (1993) argue that increased outsourcing is a consequence of increased specialization. Technology develops rapidly and it has become more difficult for a single company to possess all the necessary competences. Therefore there is a strong incentive for aircraft producers to improve relationships with their suppliers.

Such improvement has been achieved in the automotive industry, which today seems to be ahead of the aerospace industry in introducing integrated product development processes and order-to-delivery processes with its suppliers. In the extensive International Motor Vehicle Programme (IMVP) of research in the late 1980s a large number of researchers made a comparative study of the automotive industry worldwide. The project has so far resulted in numerous articles and in the best-seller 'The Machine that Changed the World' (Womack et al. 1990). The authors summarize the conclusions and explain why Japanese car corporations are superior to those in the West. In the Japanese lean production system fewer suppliers are used than in the Western mass production system. The suppliers have a responsibility for larger modules and join in the product development work at an earlier stage (Lamming 1993). The Japanese way of working with suppliers requires a high level of integration between the supplier and the car manufacturer.

When analysing the supplier base in the aerospace industry, we see a broad spectrum of system and technology levels – from the traditional sub-contractor of components to a sophisticated and closely integrated systems supplier. Every relationship has different characteristics and therefore a different need for integration. Treating every relationship in the same way is not an efficient purchasing strategy.

THE PURPOSE OF THIS CHAPTER

The supplier base has become more and more important as a resource base for the organization. The rapid change towards mega suppliers increases the need for greater knowledge of how to treat different supplier relations in order that the production system may become even leaner. The purpose of this chapter is to develop and implement, from the buyer's perspective, a supplier classification model for continuous improvement of the design and management of the extended organization. The hypothesis is that in order to develop a differentiated purchasing strategy, there is a need for more sophisticated supplier classification models.

IS THE LEAN CONCEPT MISLEADING?

Lean production has in numerous studies been presented as 'the way of the future' to handle increased competition. The key characteristic of the lean supply relationship is a clearer integration between buyers and suppliers, not necessarily implying cross-ownership. Lean suppliers are involved early in product development and are expected, therefore, to participate actively in the buyer's development of new models. The suppliers are geographically close to the buyer's assembly plants and at the same time ready to act in the global market. This means that the suppliers and the relationship between buyers and suppliers should be put under pressure for limited periods in order to develop. The increased focus on lean production also indicates a need for breaking each relationship into its component parts, a strategy that affects both buyer and supplier. The lean supply strategy indicates that the entire supplier base should be treated similarly in order to obtain full efficiency, but how can a supplier be lean if not treated in a specific or even individual way? In a sense, differentiation could be a way to achieve efficiency.

CLASSIFICATION CATEGORIES

Classification of the supplier base can mean that a specific strategy can be developed for each class. In the literature, many ways to categorize or classify the supplier base have been proposed. One way to accomplish a differentiated purchasing strategy is a more thorough classification of the supplier base. Brandes et al. (1995, 1999) show in two surveys (of 273 and 261 Swedish companies) that one single criterion has dominated the classification of the supplier base, for instance quality, product-related factors, volume or value of the purchased product. In the literature combinations of criteria are also suggested (van Weele 1997; Kraljic 1983; Brege et al. 1995;

Gadde and Håkansson 1993). In a broad sense, three groups of classification variables can be identified (Hedsund and Petersson 1998).

The first group of variables is related to the purchased product. Gadde and Håkansson (1993) distinguish between five types of goods: raw materials, components, maintenance/repair/operating supplies, investment goods and services. The authors state that each type requires a certain purchasing process. A frequently cited way to classify the supplier base is purchase portfolio analysis, proposed by Kraljic (1983). Kraljic distinguishes between two variables: the strategic importance of the purchase; and the complexity of the supply market (or risk profile). These two variables result in four different groups of suppliers/items: leverage items, non-critical items, bottleneck items and strategic items. Each of these groups has its own characteristics and the suppliers of each should be treated accordingly. For example, suppliers who are regarded as strategic should be treated as partners.

The second group has a more position-based approach and concerns variables connected to the supplier's position in the vertical market system. Strategies that are based solely on Kraljic's matrix lack the dynamics of the power that the suppliers can obtain. Brege et al. (1995) discuss the importance of taking the supplier's situation into account. According to the supplier's position in the network two dimensions are identified, actor network (primary supplier and tier level) and production system network (final assembly and raw material). On the basis of the supplier's position in these networks a supplier's role can be identified and placed against the supplier's customer base in order to develop different supplier strategies. In all, Brege at al. describe nine supplier strategies.

The third group is more relationship-orientated and concerns factors connected to co-operation with the supplier. Traditionally, Western manufacturers have tried to create a competitive atmosphere among their suppliers, in combination with high delivery, security and quality standards. Therefore the large manufacturers have chosen to have multiple suppliers for the same component, and thus have the option of comparing suppliers before choosing the right one. Buyer–supplier partnerships are a trend in many industries, especially the automotive industry, and convincing arguments have been presented that early supplier involvement and supplier partnerships constitute a large part of the explanation of the fact that Japanese companies outperform Western manufacturers in product development (Womack et al. 1990). Support for the importance of suppliers and groups of suppliers can also be found in the literature (Turnbull et al. 1993; Nishiguchi 1994). Ellram (1995) defines a strategic partnership between a buying and a supplying firm as 'a mutual, ongoing, relationship involving a commitment over an extended time period, and a sharing of information and the risks and rewards of the relationship'. This definition indicates the need for integration on all levels of the company if the expected outcome is to be achieved. Buyer–supplier partnership is also a long-term relationship between buyer and supplier based on trust, open communication and close interaction (Hammarkvist et al. 1982). Several authors try to make the partnership concept and its building blocks operational. In most cases the discussion is based on case histories regarding success or failure. Sako et al. (1995) suggest that a partnership exists when the supplier provides the automobile manufacturer with detailed information about manufacturing; the supplier believes that there is high prob ability that it will continue to provide products for the customer for more than three years; and the supplier does not expect to be replaced because another supplier offers a lower price on one occasion. In some other partnership models the supplier is involved earlier on in projects, which leads to a reduced number of modifications in later stages of the projects and thereby lower costs.

A SUPPLIER CLASSIFICATION MODEL

Economic profile and complexity and risk profile, as Kraljic proposes, are not enough to capture the dynamics needed in today's buyer–supplier relationships. In this chapter we propose that the lean concept also represents a differentiated purchasing strategy and therefore also a supplier classification. On the basis of the knowledge and experience gained from partnership relations and the increased focus on systems and system integration, we propose a second step involving three areas of focus: performance assessment, relationship characteristics and network position. Each of these areas is divided into variables based on measurable subvariables. The model must handle many different aspects. One major driving force is to establish inputs to a differentiated purchasing strategy. Another is to create a model that also is an operational tool for persons who work in the existing or developing relationship. Therefore the model must capture changes over time. The desired situation could be seen as a snapshot of the relationship from the perspective of the buying company. The situation should be changed by different purchasing initiatives into the desired situation.

METHOD AND EMPIRICAL STUDY

The study on which this chapter is based was conducted between April and September 1998 as a combination of an in-depth case study and survey, both focusing on the aerospace industry. The survey was sent to 87 suppliers to a systems integrator, Saab AB Gripen. The survey served primarily as a supplier attitude survey, but questions related to classification of the suppliers were included. The in-depth case study was a dyad study, including both a buyer and a supplier. It was performed at Saab AB Gripen, a business unit within Saab AB, which develops, produces and sells a fourth-generation fighter aircraft, Gripen. Gripen has been delivered to the Swedish air force and the next challenge is to export it to other countries.

EMPIRICAL FINDINGS

HISTORY AND BACKGROUND OF SAAB GRIPEN

Saab Gripen's major role in the development and production of the JAS 39 Gripen is to act as a systems integrator. Saab Gripen has focused on its core competencies, applying a holistic view of development and production of the aircraft. Most of the development and production of systems, equipment and components have been delegated to suppliers, representing about 60 per cent of product value. This situation, together with the characteristics of the aircraft industry, imposes very specific demands on the purchasing organization and supplier relations. The long product life cycle (between 25 and 45 years) necessitates good and reliable relations with suppliers. Systems, components and spare parts are subject to continuous upgrading and are in production for a long period, which emphasizes the need for long-term contracts with suppliers. The complexity of the product as well as demanding certification routines makes it difficult to change major system suppliers. Put together, these characteristics impose specific demands on the buyer–supplier relationship. Both parties benefit from a close and open co-operation.

The purchasing organization at Saab Gripen has faced many changes during the last few years, and there are more to come. Saab Gripen has always been very technically orientated owing to the complexity of its product. Most of the time, when the purchaser became involved in a specific project, a detailed product specification had already been thoroughly developed and a preferred supplier had been chosen. The role of the purchaser was then to make the best possible deal with respect to price agreements. A new purchasing director started working at the Saab Gripen purchasing department in 1996. He brought with him new ideas about how to create a more efficient and modern purchasing organization adapted to a new situation of global export markets and horizontal partnerships. New customers place new demands on the systems and components of the JAS 39 Gripen. Some customers may also require that certain systems and components be developed and produced in certain countries and by certain suppliers as well, as part of an offset deal. The new purchasing director sought to convey an overall purchasing strategy and vision, not only to the purchasing department itself but also to the whole Saab Gripen organization, under which Saab Gripen was to adopt an holistic view and

continuously measure new performance criteria along the value chain.

TOWARDS DIFFERENTIATED SUPPLIER STRATEGIES AT SAAB GRIPEN

The first step in implementing a new vision and strategy was to analyse Saab Gripen's performance in the supply chain. To accomplish this, a supplier attitude survey was carried out. A questionnaire was sent to 83 of Saab Gripen's suppliers, covering different fields. The suppliers were given the opportunity to identify Saab Gripen's major strengths and weaknesses. The questions were grouped into ten areas, for example, human relations and personnel, trust and confidence, efficiency of product development and specification and commitment. According to the survey, large system suppliers were in general more critical and negative than other suppliers were. The component suppliers on the other hand have in general given a greater proportion of positive answers than the average of the total group of respondents. One of the explanations of the higher degree of dissatisfaction felt by the large system suppliers might be found in a problem that Saab Gripen itself has identified: a lack of clearly spelled out differentiated strategies and working procedures for different groups of suppliers. The complexity of the relationship as well as of the product provided is larger with a large system supplier than with a component supplier; different types of suppliers therefore require different approaches and handling of relationships. To a certain extent, differentiated ways of working with different groups of suppliers were of course applied at Saab Gripen, for example management review meetings with suppliers of high volume purchases. But there were no well-defined strategies for differentiation or other classification criteria than the volume price of the product. To achieve greater efficiency in the supply chain both from the Saab Gripen perspective and from the supplier perspective, differentiated supplier strategies and working procedures needed to be applied.

CLASSIFICATION MODEL

The need for differentiated supplier strategies implies that some sort of classification is necessary. Since Saab Gripen's supplier relationships are generally complex and long term, we argue that it is necessary not only to classify the purchased product but also to evaluate the co-operation with the specific supplier. It is also important that the classification is dynamic in relation to changed conditions in the overall strategies. Therefore it should be a living document and act as a day-to-day tool for the organization. It should also serve as a tool for the improvement of both the supplier base and the purchasing organization. Put together, these demands stress the need for a different approach to a classification model than for a classification model for the selection of suppliers.

The model presented in this chapter is based on the Saab Gripen situation, and the variables used are relevant to that. Not all secondary variables are presented in this chapter and additional weighting of certain variables is probably needed. The classification model is a two-step approach (see Figure 8.1).

The first step is to distinguish groups of products and their characteristics. The evaluation of the product is divided into two main variables: *Economic profile* and *Complexity and risk profile* of the purchased product. Each of these is divided into a number of sub-variables (not shown in Figure 8.1), which should all be evaluated and given a value from 1 to 5 depending on how closely they correspond to the product to be classified. The main variable *Economic profile* has four sub-variables: product cost per shipment, total cost, value added on end-product and impact on total cost (again these are not shown in the figure). The main variable *Complexity and risk profile* is divided into five sub-groups with different sub-variables: supply market, uniqueness of product, technical complexity of product, influence from outside parties, and other risks related to the product.

The values of the main variables, *Economic profile* and *Complexity and risk profile* of the purchased product, are calculated as the mean values of the sub-variables. When the values are placed in the matrix (see Figure 8.1) the purchased product will be classified into one of the four groups of products: non-critical, leverage, bottleneck or strategic. For each of the four

groups it is possible to define the main characteristics of the *desired co-operation* with the supplier of the product (see Figure 8.1).

After the classification of the product and the related, desired co-operation are established, the next step is to analyse actual co-operation. This is evaluated according to three dimensions in relation to a specific supplier: *Performance assessment, Relationship characteristics* and *Network position*. Each of the three dimensions is divided into a set of main variables, and each of the main variables is divided into a set of sub-variables (not shown in Figure 8.1) given a value from 1 to 5 where 5 is the most positive value. By marking dots and drawing lines between the dots, areas are formed in the diagram (see figure) which indicate co-operation with the supplier.

The variables in the first dimension are production and delivery, product development, experience, quality, time focus, price and cost, organization and personnel. All suppliers should get a high score in this dimension even though some dimensions are more important with certain products according to the product classification.

The main variables in the second dimension, *Relationship characteristics*, are financial and economic issues, supplier's customer base, communication and information sharing, technological possibilities, confidence and win–win focus, historical aspects and strategic direction (of the supplier) and organization. The variables in this dimension are focused on long-term relationships. For strategic products this dimension is of the utmost importance. All main variables should have a high score and only minor differences between desired co-operation and actual co-operation are acceptable.

The main variables to consider in the third dimension, *Network position*, are size in the market, reputation, influence on and by other relationships. These variables are especially important for companies in the military aircraft industry, since a high level of regulation and political intervention characterizes this type of industry. This dimension is of the utmost importance not only for strategic products but also for some bottleneck products.

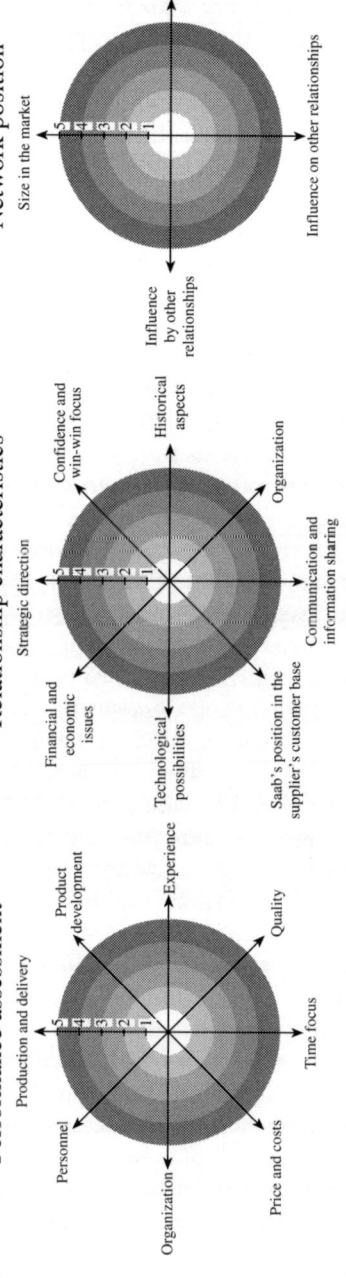

1 Product characteristics → Desired co-operation

	Leverage products	Strategic products
High		
Economic profile		
Low	Non-critical products	Bottleneck products

Low   High
Complexity and risk profile

2 Co-operation characteristics → Actual co-operation

Performance assessment

Relationship characteristics

Network position

Figure 8.1 Classification model
Source: Hedsund, A. and Petersson, K. (1998) *Towards Differentiated Supplier Strategies*, Linköpings Universitet.

Evaluation of the three dimensions will identify the actual co-operation with the supplier and is comparable with a desired state. If there are low scores or big differences between the actual state and the desired state, further analysis of the problems and remedial actions is necessary.

IMPLICATIONS AND PRACTICAL USAGE OF THE MODEL

The purpose of the classification model was to create a dynamic model as a day-to-day tool for the organization. It should also serve as a tool for improvement of both the supplier base and the purchasing organization. Therefore it was tested by Saab Gripen and also by two suppliers. It is also important to make it easily accessible and easy to use. To achieve this, the model should be computerized and coupled to other measurements of suppliers, especially performance measurement. For measurement of co-operation variables, the model serves as a structured and visual tool that was previously lacking.

The suppliers who tested the model found that it could be a very important tool in discussions between buyer and supplier. One supplier emphasized the importance of communicating the results of the classification to the suppliers and using it as a common tool for improvement.

RESULTS AND DISCUSSION

The increased focus on lean production also indicates a need for breaking each relationship into its component parts, a strategy that influences both customers and suppliers. Thus differentiation is one way to achieve efficiency. By categorizing and grouping the supplier base, a specific strategy can be developed for each category or group. Saab Gripen is currently taking various actions to achieve differentiated supplier strategies.

In the aerospace industry there is a broad spectrum of system and technology levels, from the traditional sub-contractor of components to a sophisticated and closely integrated systems supplier. We believe that every relationship has different characteristics and therefore a different need for integration. Treating every

relationship in the same way is not an efficient purchasing strategy. This indicates the need for a differentiated purchasing strategy. The model presented should not be seen as complete, but preliminary results show that it could serve as an important tool to achieve the aim. The most important thing is not to assign exact figures to the product–supplier relationships that are identified, but to start working with suppliers in a more structured and differentiated way. The results shown so far are as follows:

1. The supplier classification models in the literature are too general. The results indicate that by viewing the classification process as different continuous steps, company- and relationship-specific criteria could be added. Criteria focusing on 'soft' issues such as partnership-related topics are easily added and can be continuously updated. The suggested supplier classification model also distinguishes between 'actual state' and 'desired state'.

2. The supplier classification model could be made operational in different ways. One way is by making the model a day-to-day tool for the purchaser involved. The model also serves as a history of the relationship. Linked to the database infrastructure of the companies involved, the model becomes even more reliable.

3. The classification model now serves as an important tool for improvements in both the supplier base and the purchasing organization. Previously ignored areas of the relationship with the supplier are now highlighted. The classification also serves as a base for the restructuring of the purchasing organization. Strategic suppliers are in future handled by purchasers with higher managerial and relationship-orientated skills while other supplier groups are handled by purchasers with other skills (negotiation, business, price-oriented and so on).

4. Based on the classification, the buyer's purchasing strategy is dramatically influenced. The overall strategy is now differentiated, with different strategies for different supplier groups. In each of the supplier groups the

individual supplier is treated with its own strategy – often made operational in focus areas for improvements. The study also indicates ways to measure the efficiency of the individual purchaser.

5. By testing the model in a specific relationship between Saab Gripen and one of their major systems suppliers we found that it also provides a tool for the supplier's own strategic and operational development. If the dialogue between buyer and supplier includes elements of self-assessment or self-evaluation, different perspectives can be identified. One problem, though, is that many of the 'soft issues' are hard to assess as a number between 1 and 5. One example is 'feeling of trust'. How do you create a mutually accepted and objective measure of that?

CONCLUSION: THEORETICAL AND MANAGERIAL IMPLICATIONS

The lean concept is accompanied by differentiated strategies. Some theoretical and managerial implications can be deduced. Our study shows that there is a need for more dynamic theories in the area of purchasing strategy, organization and relationship issues. If there is a serious focus on lean supply and supply chain management, there also should be a focus on how to treat the supplier base. Kraljic's model is an efficient base model, but it does not capture the dynamic and increased demands on the supplier relationships. Findings from many studies in the area of partnerships indicate a need for purchasing strategies capable of focusing on specific buyer–supplier relationships. We believe that combinations of different theoretical models better capture today's organizational dynamics. Some managerial implications can be highlighted.

First, different supplier relationships need different purchasing strategies and should be managed accordingly. It is a waste of both time and competence to set up a purchasing team based on purchasers with a focus on price cutting when the supplier is supposed to be treated as a strategic supplier. Management of each relationship is a key issue.

Second, the supplier should be responsible for the benchmarking that has to take place continuously. Measurements made public via the model could easily be used as benchmarking for best practice.

Third, the area of supplier relationships is suitable for the implementation of IT. Some communications could take place via an extranet. By establishing relationship-specific Web solutions, a high momentum of development could be created.

Finally, buyer and supplier relationships are very much about face to face meetings. The social dimension should not be forgotten. It is through a combination of normative models and open discussion that creative and differentiated solutions are reached. These solutions lead to a practical realization of the lean concept and greater competitive advantage in the long run.

ENDNOTE

This chapter derives from research carried out by a research group in LARP (the Lean Aircraft Research Programme) at Linköping University, Sweden, where Anna Hedsund and Karolina Petersson (Hedsund and Petersson 1998) contributed considerably to the discussion as a part of their Masters' theses.

REFERENCES

Brandes, H., Jonsson, S. and Lilliecreutz, J. (1995), *Purchasing Barometer 1995*, Linköpings Universitet (in Swedish).

Brandes, H., Jonsson, S. and Lilliecreutz, J. (1999), *Purchasing Barometer 1998*, Linköpings Universitet, MTC AB (in Swedish).

Brege, S., Brandes, O., Lilliecreutz, J. and Brandes, H. (1995), *Supplier Strategies in Buyer-Dominated Hierarchies*, Dept. of Management and Economics, Linköpings Universitet.

Ellram, L. (1995), 'Partnering pitfalls and success factors', *International Journal of Purchasing and Materials Management*, **31**(2), pp. 36–44.

Gadde, L-E. and Håkansson, H. (1993), *Professional Purchasing*, London: Routledge.

Hammarkvist, K-O., Håkansson, H. and Mattson, L-G. (1982), *Marknadsföring för konkurrenskraft*, Liber (in Swedish).

Hedsund, A. and Petersson, K. (1998), *Towards Differentiated Supplier Strategies*, Linköpings Universitet.

Kraljic, P. (1983), 'Purchasing must become supply management', *Harvard Business Review*, Sept-Oct.

Lamming, R. (1993), *Beyond Partnership*, Hemel Hempstead: Prentice Hall.

Nishiguchi, T. (1994), *Strategic Industrial Sourcing*, Oxford: Oxford University Press.

Sako, M., Helper, S. and Lamming, R. (1995), *Supplier Relations in the UK Car Industry*, Report prepared for the Vehicles Division, Department of Trade and Industry.

Turnbull, P. Delbridge, R., Oliver, N. and Wilkinson, B. (1993), 'Winners and losers – the "tiering" of component suppliers in the UK automotive industry', *Journal of General Management*, **19**(1), pp. 48–63.

van Weele, A.J. (1997), *Purchasing Management – Analysis, Planning and Practice*, International Thomson Publishing.

Womack, J., Jones, D. and Roos, D. (1990), *The Machine that Changed the World – the Story of Lean Production*, New York: Harper Collins.

CHAPTER NINE

Beyond the 'core versus non-core' logic: the need for a contingency model for effective outsourcing in the public and private sectors

Andrew Cox, Chris Lonsdale and Glyn Watson

OUTSOURCING AND THE DYNAMIC BUSINESS ENVIRONMENT

Stimulated by the continuing trend towards trade liberalization and by technological advances – which have pushed down transport and communication costs – the scale of international economic activity has reached unprecedented levels in recent years. For the firm operating in this new environment, this drive towards globalization presents both an opportunity and a threat. The opportunities can be seen in terms of the firm's downstream ability to extend its operations overseas and its upstream capacity to source cheaper factor inputs. The threat stems from increased competition as national firms find that hitherto protected domestic markets are invaded by foreign rivals. These rivals are increasingly capturing market share and driving down prices.

This phenomenon has had two direct consequences. First, it has focused the attention of firms on their cost bases. Second – albeit sometimes belatedly – it has raised the profile of strategy in their thinking. Both of these consequences bear directly upon the issue of outsourcing and have guided practice in the area. In this chapter, current outsourcing practice is evaluated. It is argued that the majority of firms are outsourcing on the basis of a fairly crude logic and that the results achieved have been correspondingly moderate. Following this evaluation, an alternative model for outsourcing is presented, which deals more effectively with what are regarded as the main risks of the practice.

ALTERNATIVE APPROACHES TO OUTSOURCING

Outsourcing has been a prominent concept in the business world in the 1990s. Many consultants, academics and government advisory bodies have presented the practice as a cure-all to companies struggling with declining current profitability and uncertain future prospects. It has been facilitated by the decline in the strength of the trade unions, who would in the UK of the 1970s, for example, have blocked many outsourcing plans. Managers have reacted to this increasing profile in a number of different ways.

SHORT-TERM COST CUTTING

A first approach has been based on short-term cost cutting. Faced with a short-term need to cut costs many managers looked around their internal operations to ask themselves whether the goods and services they currently sourced internally might be obtained more cheaply from external suppliers. Typically, within such organizations the process of outsourcing has proceeded on a reactive, iterative basis. It has begun with the external sourcing of low profile support activities such as cleaning, security, catering and printing and, providing this has proven to be successful, has been extended into areas that relate directly to production – such as debt management, logistics and workshop maintenance. Then, if this too has proven to be a success, the outsourcing of some areas of production have been contemplated.

OUTSOURCING AND THE BUSINESS STRATEGY LITERATURE

A second approach, by contrast, has turned to strategic thinking to provide a model to guide outsourcing practice. The literature on business strategy is, of course, diverse. Not only does it encompass many different functional areas in business – marketing, finance, production and supply – but it is also genuinely interdisciplinary in nature. Some of this literature touches only tangentially on the question of outsourcing, whilst some of it does not touch on it at all. However, an increasingly important strand is linked directly to boundary of the firm decisions.

Crudely, this strand holds that a short-term focus on cost cutting, as evidenced in the first approach, should not be the basis on which a firm creates a sustainable competitive advantage or makes effective boundary of the firm decisions. Rather, sustainable competitive advantage is contingent upon three factors. First, a firm's ability to produce a product that is honed to user need (so that it has customers). Second, its ability to offer something that is unique (so that these products and services can be priced without too much regard to competition). Third, its ability to offer something that is difficult to replicate (so that profits will not immediately be competed away).

A model, founded on these three principles, is provided by the resource-based school. Peteraf (1993) argued that there were four cornerstones to competitive advantage: resource heterogeneity (uniqueness), ex-post limits to competition (or defences against replication), ex ante limits to competition and resource immobility.

Resource Heterogeneity

For this school, the central condition that underpins competitive advantage is resource heterogeneity – the aforementioned uniqueness. Business strategists in this school, in contrast to traditional economic thinkers, have always op-

erated under the assumption that firms within industries are heterogeneous in terms of their resources and capabilities. This heterogeneity presents itself in two main respects. First, a firm can possess superior productive processes that are *limited in supply*. These allow the firm to produce a good or service at lower cost than its competitors. So even in a competitive market where there is a market price, firms with superior productive resources will earn rents, as their lower costs allow supernormal profits – which due to the finite nature of the resources, their competitors cannot touch.

Second, rents can also be earned through market closure, which is most commonly achieved through product differentiation. Here the uniqueness comes not in the productive arena, but in the market offering itself. Firms which can offer customers a unique and superior functionality – *that is valued* – will be able to change a premium price and thus earn rents.

However, resource heterogeneity only deals with the issue of providing distinctiveness at any given time. Other conditions are necessary in order to turn that distinctiveness into a sustainable rent-earning position. As the next three sub-sections outline, resource positions must be protected from competition, achieved without high cost and retained within the firm.

Ex-Post Limits to Competition

The second condition necessary for a firm to achieve sustainable competitive advantage, therefore, is the existence of ex-post limits to competition. The firm's resource position needs to be protected over time against two main phenomena: imitation and substitution. Both of these factors will reduce the rent-earning potential of the firm – substitutes will allow customers to 'sidestep' the powerful market position of the firm by providing entirely different means of satisfying their functional requirement, and imitators will reduce the firm's rents by creating competition.

How imitation can be resisted has been an issue of considerable interest to business strategists and a range of concepts has been developed. Rumelt, for example, has coined the phrase 'isolating mechanisms' to describe factors that hold imitators at bay. His mechanisms include firm or product reputation, information asymmetry, causal ambiguity, buyer switching costs, economies of scale, producer learning and channel crowding (Rumelt 1987).

Ex-Ante Limits to Competition

The third condition required for sustainable competitive advantage focuses upon the need for managers to be entrepreneurial. Resource-based thinkers argue that firms must take risks with uncertainty if they are to earn rents. This view is based upon the belief that it is only possible to earn rents from scarce resources if they are acquired before their value is widely understood by other actors in the market. Once the value of a resource does become widely recognized, intense competition for it – and the potential revenues that could flow from it – will take place. The consequence of this will be that any future revenues will be offset by the high cost of acquisition. A critical skill firms need, then, is that of foresight.

Imperfect Mobility

The final condition is resource mobility. Firms, once they have obtained valuable resources (which could be certain people, or the skills and knowledge they possess), need to retain these resources within their boundaries. This will be easier if the resources are to a lesser or greater extent 'firm-specific', that is, if they have a diminished value outside that particular firm (Williamson 1985), or are 'co-specialized', such that they are only valuable if they are used in combination with other resources within the firm (Teece 1987).

BUSINESS STRATEGY AND OUTSOURCING

Business strategists, therefore, have outlined what they believe to be the causes of sustainable competitive advantage. As far as outsourcing is concerned, it logically follows that the firm should draw its boundary around those skills and capabilities that comply with these principles. While other things *may* be safely outsourced with little or no cost (and potentially even significant gain), if the firm loses control over its strategic core, as defined, it risks seeing the value that it had hitherto appropriated being passed to its suppliers.

THE DEBATE OVER THE LONGEVITY OF THE RENT-EARNING POTENTIAL OF FIRM RESOURCES

Whilst many strategy writers, including those from the resource-based school, agree that it is a firm's ability to offer the market something that is both *valued* and *unique* that will determine its ability to create an effective strategy, there is sharp disagreement over the permanence of the advantage that will result. Along with this disagreement is a parallel dispute over the relative fluidity of the firm's boundary. Resource-based thinkers, like Peteraf, argue that strategic positions can be sustained through the creation of high barriers to market entry, which typically involves an aggressive property rights approach. For such writers the firm's boundary, once set, is likely to remain relatively immobile.

By contrast, a second view, emphasizing the prevalence of global competition, is more sceptical about a firm's capacity to stave off competition over the medium to long-term. Thinkers holding this view argue that, rather than attempting, like King Canute, to hold back the tide, firms should recognize that it is coming in and shift their position accordingly. In order to do this, internally, the firm must become adept at identifying or even anticipating entrepreneurial opportunities as they are presented. Externally, the firm must be prepared to shift its boundary each time it becomes necessary to refocus its strategic direction. Failure to demonstrate such flexibility, in the face of an ever-changing commercial environment, will run the risk of a Darwinian-like extinction.

This view led to the development of the 'dynamic capabilities theory of the firm':

> Well known companies appear to have followed a resource-based strategy of accumulating valuable technology assets, often guarded by an aggressive intellectual property stance. However, this strategy is often not enough to support a significant competitive advantage. Winners in the global marketplace have been firms that can demonstrate timely responsiveness

and rapid and flexible product innovation (Teece and Pisano 1998 p. 193).

Teece and Pisano argued that the key to achieving this responsiveness and innovation was the effectiveness of the firm's 'processes'. In this respect, the firm needed three capabilities: integration, learning and transformation. In terms of integration they argued that firms need to develop 'special organizational routines' for gathering and processing information, for co-ordinating internal functions, for co-ordinating external suppliers and for matching customer experiences with design choices. In the case of the need for effective gathering and processing of information, the authors commented: 'Learning is a process by which repetition and experimentation enable tasks to be performed better and more quickly [over time], and means that new production opportunities are identified [more effectively]' (Teece and Pisano 1998 p. 200).

SUB-OPTIMAL APPROACHES TO OUTSOURCING

From the above, it is possible to distinguish between three distinct approaches to the issue of outsourcing: *ad hoc*, descriptive-strategic and dynamic-strategic. *Ad hoc* outsourcing, as the name implies, refers to the largely reactive/iterative practice whereby a firm's outsourcing programme evolves according to a series of piecemeal initiatives rather than as a function of a more or less coherent plan. It is driven by calculations of short-term financial gain, outsourcing designed to reduce organizational headcount, and outsourcing aimed at removing organizational headaches. Descriptive-strategic outsourcing, by contrast, represents an attempt by organizations to undertake a more coherent approach to the make-buy decision. This is the category that equates most closely to the static view of strategy outlined above.

From our research we have found that most outsourcing practice falls into either the *ad hoc* or descriptive-strategic categories (Cox and Lonsdale 1998). At the same time, most outsourcing has also been of somewhat questionable value to the organizations that have undertaken it. In 1996, the PA Consulting Group published its report on outsourcing. Among other things, this report considered firms' experience of the practice. It asked them to set any gains they felt they had obtained from the practice against the drawbacks. The results of this admittedly unscientific trawl were interesting, if not altogether surprising. Of those surveyed, only 29 per cent of respondents reported that they had enjoyed a trouble-free experience, whilst fewer still, a mere five per cent, reported that the experience had been both relatively trouble-free and had delivered significant performance gains for their organizations (PA Consulting Group 1996).

Perhaps somewhat predictably (certainly from the perspective of the descriptive-strategic approach), a number of the problems with the practice have arisen as outsourcing has moved into key areas of spend. This may well have been due to the fact that the resources or activities that were, at the time of outsourcing, judged to be 'non-core' had, due to changes in the business environment, become of greater significance. The classic example of this is, of course, the view that IBM took in the early 1980s about the relative importance of the operating system and microprocessor to the personal computer. When such misjudgements are made, firms can find themselves being leveraged by the new suppliers of those resources, or being denied supply of the resources altogether.

However, this cannot explain all or, indeed, even most of the difficulties experienced. This is not least as most of the outsourcing undertaken up until this time has consisted of non-core items – defined in terms of the relative centrality of a particular activity to the primary good or service that the firm delivers to its customers. Indeed, some of the greatest problems have arisen in the so-called less sensitive areas of business. The outsourcing of IT is a case in point and whole volumes have been dedicated to the difficulties that organizations have experienced in trying to manage these contracts.

The wide range of difficulties organizations have experienced with outsourcing, over such a wide range of goods and services, might raise the suspicion that there is a great deal of 'dumb luck' involved in outsourcing. However, a more detailed analysis suggests that firms have not been the victim of random mismanagement but that there are a set of deeper, underlying, principles that dictate whether or not the organization's initiatives are likely to be successful.

The weakness of both the *ad hoc* and descriptive-strategic approach is that they are overly static in their conception. This is in two respects. First, as we have discussed, neither approach is based around the need for the firm to possess dynamic capabilities to deal with an ever-changing business environment. Indeed, in the case of *ad hoc* approaches there is no internal logic at all. Yet beyond this there is also a second static element, which relates to the way in which these approaches deal with upstream risk – that is, the risk arising out of the firm's supply base. The inadequacy of the two approaches in this respect puts at risk the very benefit that inspired the decisions to outsource in the first place – cost reduction.

POST-CONTRACTUAL DEPENDENCY: THE FATAL FLAW IN THE 'CORE VERSUS NON-CORE' LOGIC

The most serious omission of these two approaches in dealing with upstream risk concerns the possibility of post-contractual dependency. Here, the important concepts are *uncertainty*, *asset specificity* and *myopic contracting*. Many outsourcing arrangements are entered into under conditions where there is considerable speculation as to whether the conditions that pertained when the agreement was first made will still hold true months, or even years, further down the line. Conventional economic thinking has often assumed in the past that managers are perfect calculating machines who make all of their decisions on the basis of perfect information.

Increasingly, however, writers in the area reject such a simple-minded view. Instead, they assert that a manager's rationality tends to be *bounded* – that is, although managers attempt to behave rationally, limits on their ability to receive, store and process information mean

that these attempts can only ever be imperfect. Not surprisingly, therefore, outsourcing contracts drawn up under such circumstances are necessarily incomplete – with the blanks left where the potential for uncertainty is greatest. While this leaves scope for flexibility in the relationship and holds out the possibility for revision – as and when the future becomes better understood – these advantages are counterbalanced by a number of risks. Principally, there is the risk that when it becomes necessary to renegotiate the terms of exchange, the contracting parties will fail to reach agreement.

This failure might arise for entirely honest reasons. However, this will not always be the case. Many firms are opportunistic – that is, they will pursue their self-interest with guile. A firm that wins an outsourcing contract may use the uncertainty and the gaps in the agreement to renegotiate the terms in its favour. This risk would not be serious if, upon detecting opportunistic behaviour in the actions of the supplier, the firm could switch vendors.

However, this is not always possible. Many transactions require a firm to make substantial, dedicated investments to support them. These investments are usually referred to as *asset specific*. They can involve specialized personnel, equipment or locations. If the firm contracts unwisely, and does not share the costs of such investments with the vendor, it can become locked into a relationship with that vendor, and find itself exploited as a consequence. Figure 9.1 provides a similar example of how a post-contractual dependency scenario might develop.

Indeed, it is crucial when discussing outsourcing that one has a view on what Williamson calls the 'behavioural context'. Many of the outsourcing programmes that the authors have discovered in their research would have been credible had it not been for the fact that, in Anglo-Saxon economies at least, many firms are opportunistic in their dealings with third parties. If firms were not opportunistic then this would alter fundamentally the way in which they interacted with each other. For example, it could be argued that contracts would not be necessary, as problems would be dealt with whenever

- At the point of the firm outsourcing there is a wide range of supply options. There is intense competition and the firm acquires a good deal.
- During the course of the contract, the supplier acquires information about the service or product provision and the firm's IT and production systems are adapted to be compatible with the supplier's. This adaptation is undertaken in order that the interaction be operated at maximum efficiency.
- When the contract expires, because of the large investment the firm has made in the relationship, and because of the supplier's superior knowledge vis-à-vis other suppliers, the effective level of competition at the re-contracting stage is severely reduced. This is because the costs associated with switching suppliers are very high and, in any case, the other suppliers are in a poor position to challenge the incumbent.
- This puts the existing supplier in an advantageous bargaining position. As a result, the terms the firm is able to obtain are far inferior to those written into the original contract and the firm is faced with rising costs, falling quality and declining innovation.
- On some occasions, attempts to renegotiate begin during the course of the first contract. Indeed, it may be that the supplier's strategy is based on lock-in pricing. Suppliers are helped in these circumstances by the fact that many outsourcing deals are undertaken by employees of the firm who have little or no procurement competence.

Figure 9.1 Transaction specific asymmetry: a development of Williamson's fundamental transformation
Source: Adapted from Lonsdale, C. and Cox, A. (1998), *Outsourcing: A Business Guide to Risk Management Tools and Techniques*, Boston, UK: Earlsgate Press, p. 50.

they arose in a 'gentlemanly' fashion. It is the authors' view on opportunism that makes them sceptical about the ability of the UK government's Private Finance Initiative (effectively an outsourcing policy) to deliver value for money to the public sector in the UK.

DYNAMIC APPROACH TO OUTSOURCING

For this reason, to *ad hoc* and descriptive-strategic approaches to outsourcing it is also necessary to add our third category – dynamic-strategic. This category takes into account both cost and strategic issues, but does not define the two variables in the static fashion that characterizes its rivals. In terms of cost, it is not concerned with the savings that can be made today, but rather with the costs that accrue over the lifetime of the association with a supplier. What this means is that the approach takes into account the risk of post-contractual dependency.

In terms of the strategic core, the approach is not concerned just with protecting the core but, rather, is concerned with understanding the competitive dynamics of the marketplace and shifting the boundary of the firm accordingly. This element of the approach, therefore, is in accordance with the dynamic capabilities theory of the firm, outlined earlier. If pursued as a strategy, dynamic-strategic outsourcing should be capable of delivering the most reliable results from outsourcing.

An example of dynamic-strategic outsourcing was encountered recently by the authors in their research. This example concerns Hewlett-Packard (HP) at its mobile phone testing equipment operation. In the early 1980s, managers at HP recognized that the company could no longer compete as a highly vertically integrated company, such was the pace of technological innovation. As a result, a make-buy policy was developed that was applied to the whole of the operation.

Despite the increasing pressures, HP's management did not direct their make-buy policy towards short-term cost savings (such savings were considered a virtuous by-product, when made). Rather, outsourcing was seen as one element in a process of reconfiguring the operation in line with the new competitive and technological en-

Table 9.1 Outsourcing risk and outsourcing strategy

	ACTIVITY		
STRATEGY	Residual	Complementary	Core
Ad hoc	Risk of outsourcing non-core activities of high asset specificity	Risk of outsourcing non-core activities of high asset specificity	Risk of outsourcing core activities
Descriptive-strategic	Risk of outsourcing non-core activities of high asset specificity	Risk of outsourcing non-core activities of high asset specificity	Risk of outsourcing future core
Dynamic-strategic	Lower/ limited risk	Lower/ limited risk	Lower/ limited risk

Source: Adapted from Londsdale, C. and Cox, A. (1998), *Outsourcing: A Business Guide to Risk Management Tools and Techniques*, Boston, UK: Earlsgate Press, p. 50.

vironment. Crudely speaking, the make-buy policy was based on the following questions:

- Does the activity make a significant contribution to the technological functionality which HP's products will need to possess in the medium term?
- Does the activity make a significant contribution to the quality (real and perceived) of HP's products?
- Does the activity make a significant contribution to cost reduction, whilst retaining the quality HP requires and demands?
- Are there acceptable market options?

Where the answer to the first three questions was 'no' and the answer to the fourth question was 'yes', then the activity was outsourced. The outsourcing was undertaken, however, with an awareness of the need to keep HP's switching costs low. Suppliers produce to HP's own designs, sometimes on its own equipment. The policy has proved a success, dramatically reducing cycle times without compromising quality or endangering control over cost. Finally, the position of the boundary of the firm is regularly re-evaluated, in response the constant change in their markets.

CONCLUSION: A HIERARCHY OF APPROACHES TO OUTSOURCING

What this chapter has developed is a hierarchy of approaches to outsourcing. It is our view that there are certain key principles which should be addressed when undertaking this practice. In many of the approaches we have encountered in our research these have been absent. At the bottom of the hierarchy are approaches that conform to the *ad hoc* categorization. These approaches to outsourcing clearly create the greatest scope for commercial vulnerability. In the outsourcing of complementary (and even residual) activities this overly static focus makes them vulnerable to cost miscalculation. Good deals can turn sour as the need for dedicated investments lock the firm into a long-term association with the supplier, making it vulnerable to leverage by the comparatively 'footloose' vendor. Even more seriously, however, *ad hoc* outsourcing offers no internal logic that allows the firm to distinguish between those key competencies and skills that should never be outsourced from those activities that may profitably pass to external suppliers. Without this the firm risks outsourcing those things upon which its long term survival depends.

Descriptive-strategic methodologies, by contrast, do insulate the firm from the risk of outsourcing those activities that are currently instrumental to its profitability. However, the emphasis here is on the present. With more than one eye on existing practice, and an excessively reverential attitude towards sunk investments, the firm risks attaching itself to a set of core activities long after they have ceased to be profitable. Furthermore, like *ad hoc* methodologies, the approach contains no internal mechanism for distinguishing static from dynamic costs when complementary and residual activities are outsourced.

In our view, at the top of the hierarchy are dynamic-strategic approaches. On the one hand, this approach focuses on the need for organizations to be flexible in the face of rapid technological development. On the other, it deals with both pre- and post-contractual dependency issues. Unfortunately, at the time of writing, very few firms have developed such an approach (despite the fact that relevant literature is freely available) which goes some way towards explaining the varied results firms experience.

REFERENCES

Cox, A. and Lonsdale, C. (1998), *Strategic Outsourcing Methodologies in UK Companies*, CBSP Working Paper, Birmingham: The University of Birmingham.

PA Consulting Group (1996), *Strategic Sourcing: International Survey 1996*, London: PA Consulting Group.

Peteraf, M. (1993), 'The cornerstones of competitive advantage: a resource-based view', *Strategic Management Journal*, 14, pp. 179–191.

Rumelt, R. (1987), 'Theory, Strategy and Entrepreneurship', in Teece, D. (Ed.), *The Competitive Challenge: Strategies for Industrial Innovation and Renewal*, New York: Harper and Row , pp. 137–158.

Teece, D. (Ed.) (1987), *The Competitive Challenge: Strategies for Industrial Innovation and Renewal*, New York: Harper and Row.

Teece, D. and Pisano, G. (1998), 'The Dynamic Capabilities of Firms: An Introduction', in Dosi, G., Teece, D. and Chytry, J. (Eds), *Technology, Organization and Competitiveness: Perspectives in Industrial and Corporate Change*, Oxford: Oxford University Press, pp. 193–200.

Williamson, O. (1985), *The Economic Institutions of Capitalism*, New York: Free Press.

CHAPTER TEN

The role of power in partnership relationships: an empirical investigation of the current body of knowledge

Arjan van Weele and Frank Rozemeijer

In 1998 a research project was started at Eindhoven University of Technology on behalf of the Dutch Chamber of Commerce and a number of major manufacturing companies in the Netherlands. A major objective was to study why opportunities for collaboration on joint product development and innovation had not materialized, notwithstanding the good intentions of the companies involved and the large body of knowledge on this subject. The study was conducted by the Institute for Purchasing and Supply Development (IPSD). We started with a survey of current literature on partnership relationships and concurrent engineering. The results of this part of the study have been published in a position paper. Next we conducted in-depth interviews with the technology leaders both in manufacturing and the first tier supplier industry. This chapter summarizes the findings of this study.

DEFINING THE FIELD: EXPLORATION OF THE EXISTING BODY OF KNOWLEDGE

The rapidly changing international competitive arena can explain major developments going on in relationships between manufacturers (subcontractors) and their suppliers (van Weele and Rozemeijer 1996). Globalization of world trade, the rapid development of information technology and trends towards concentration in many industries force large manufacturers to adapt

their market and competitive strategies and to adopt more flexible and productive manufacturing organizations. In doing so top managers critically review their business activities in terms of core and non-core activities. In many cases they may decide to outsource their non-core activities to specialized suppliers (see Figure 10.1). As a result manufacturers have gradually become more and more dependent on their suppliers, not only in terms of operational performance but certainly also in the area of product- and process-innovation. This has led manufacturers in many cases to reconsider the role and position that suppliers play in their value chains.

This reorientation of the role and position of suppliers in supply networks can be observed in many industries today. Examples are the retail sector where due to the large concentration that has taken place on the buyer side, suppliers are confronted with ever-higher demands in terms of financial contributions and logistics performance. Other examples can be found in the automotive and consumer electronics industry where suppliers are made responsible for supplying components during the life of the final product type against prearranged prices. In general, manufacturers have adopted more differentiated relationship patterns in business-to-business markets. From the literature we have found two different approaches on how such business-to-business patterns may be studied and structured: the supply chain approach (see

Developments in environment	Consequences for industrial manufacturers	Impact on supplier relations
• globalization of world trade • information technology/ possibilities of communication • trends towards concentration in many industries • trends towards consumer revolution	• focus on core activities • increased sub-contracting • internal and external benchmarking • reduced time-to-market • faster development • global sourcing	• higher demands in terms of quality, logistics and (integral) product costs • availability of innovation potential • specialization: focus on technological and customer specialities
⇩	⇩	⇩
Constant competitive pressure	*Continuous productivity improvement*	*Reorientation of role and position in supply chain*

Figure 10.1   How competitive and environmental changes impact the role and position of suppliers

among others Ellram and Cooper 1990, 1993; van Goor 1998); and approaches where supplier relationships are studied from a network perspective (see among others Hakansson 1982 and Wijnstra 1998).

From the perspective of the subcontractor, supplier relationships may be structured in different ways. Over the years many subcontractors have learned to use some kind of portfolio approach in order to develop differentiated and dynamic supplier strategies. This type of analysis enables subcontractors to differentiate between whether to pursue a partnership relationship with one specific supplier or to go for a more competitive type of relationship with another supplier (see also Laseter 1998).

Similar approaches have been applied for some years from the marketing perspective. In business to business marketing the concept of market segmentation has gained wide recognition (Anderson and Narus 1998). Market segmentation in business markets can be applied at different levels of abstraction. In general business marketeers may differentiate between macro-segmentation ('which markets do we focus on?') and micro-segmentation ('what customers do we focus on?'). Market segmentation

defines the position of a certain client in the portfolio of relationships, which a supplier may hold. One of the possible relationships to pursue from the point of view of a supplier is a partnership relationship.

Following Hendrick and Ellram (1993), we define partnership here as follows:

> ...the building and proactive maintenance of a relationship with a limited number of suppliers from a performance-oriented business perspective. This relationship is based on mutual trust and on the intention of subcontractor and supplier to work together for an extended period of time based upon a fair sharing of both risks and rewards. This makes it possible to work jointly on continuous optimization of processes and products throughout the entire chain of production (Rozemeijer 1996).

From this definition we can derive the following important characteristics of a partnership relationship:

● long term orientation;

- open exchange of information;
- equality in relationship; balance of power between parties involved;
- pattern of mutual contact on various levels of the organizations involved;
- possible only with a limited number of customers or suppliers; and
- risks and rewards resulting from the relationship are shared between parties.

Partnership demands that both parties invest in the relationship while the final results cannot be quantified exactly. Figure 10.2 shows how supply managers and business marketeers use these concepts to develop, manage and monitor their business relationships.

Customer- and supplier-portfolios are dynamic in nature. It is hypothesized that a central, but often underlying, element in business to business relationship management is how to develop a strong, relative power position vis-à-vis the other party. This is illustrated in Figure 10.3.

We state that partnerships can only grow when there is a certain balance of power between both parties. This was illustrated clearly by one of our executives who, when asked about the value of working towards trust in business-to-business relationships, stated that 'trust is against the nature of any businessman'. Based upon our personal observations of a large number of business-to-business relationships we hypothesize that in our Western culture business parties will generally try to dominate each other. As Hendrick and Ellram (1993) have demonstrated, a true balance of power is only present in a very limited number of cases. In most cases there is an imbalance in the power relationships: either the buyer or the supplier organization is in the driver's seat. Partnership relationships are possible, though in a very limited number of cases and among very specific circumstances. They may develop in the area marked by the low left–upper right diagonal in the portfolio.

Apart from the fact that the conditions for partnership relationships are present in very few cases, the development of such a relationship requires much effort and time. Based upon our literature survey we have conceived the steps set out in Figure 10.4 (Rozemeijer 1996).

This scheme illustrates that developing partnership relationships with suppliers (and with customers) takes time. Over time, (confidential) information is exchanged on various levels between the organizations involved. Learning to do so effectively puts specific demands on meth-

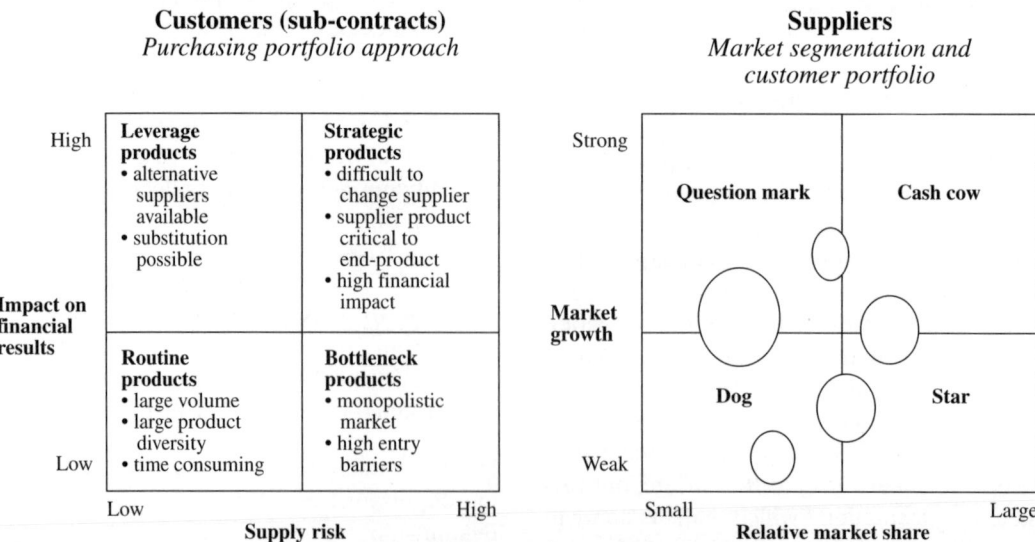

Figure 10.2   Portfolio techniques used in supply management and business marketing

Power strategies: customers
- purchasing co-ordination: combining volumes
- multiple sourcing
- competitive bidding
- cost down programmes
- 'open-cost' approach
- consortium buying

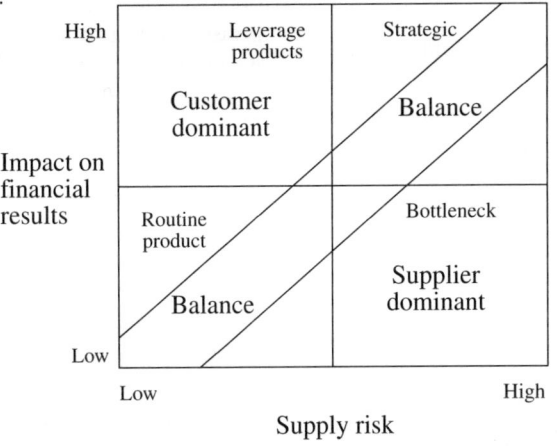

Power strategies: suppliers
- technological innovation
- value added services
- take over tasks of customer
- offer technical support

Figure 10.3 Power positions in the purchasing portfolio and how to influence them
Source: van der Hart, H.W.C. and van Weele, A.J. (Eds) (1997), Dynamiek in Commerciele Relaties, F & G Publishers, The Netherlands.

Steps	Dominant theme
Step 1	Acknowledge suppliers as a real source of added value
Step 2	Rationalize supplier base
Step 3	Partnering: streamlining operational relationship with best-in-class supplier
	• continuous improvement in the area of quality, logistics and costs
	• mobilization of supplier knowledge in innovation and development projects
Step 4	Active involvement of suppliers in technological development projects
Step 5	Integration: tuning future product and investment plans

Figure 10.4 Steps towards partnership relationships

ods of working (project management), business systems (EDI, CAD/CAM) (Electronic Data Interchange, Computer Aided Design/Computer Aided Manufacturing) ways to resolve conflicts (ethics) and management style (discipline, coaching). Developing effective partnership relationships therefore requires a sound 'fit' with respect to the various management aspects of the organizations involved.

Next, we observed that the five steps are not worked through in all cases: it seems that the more tailor-made and high tech the component, the higher the need for integrating the supplier into development, manufacturing and operational processes. In the case of simple commodities, the need for supplier integration in these processes seems much lower.

Our conclusion is that where specific market circumstances may support the development of a partnership relationship, the prospective partners need to investigate the degree to which both meet the conditions for a successful partnership in terms of business policy, organization, systems and culture. Another conclusion is that partnership and integration with suppliers is commodity- and situation-specific.

EXPLORING THE FIELD: FIELD RESEARCH

As we set out to prepare our field study, our main objectives were to develop a relational model and/or developmental typology to characterize and classify relationships between enterprises. Next we wanted to develop guidelines to help support technological co-operation between manufacturers and suppliers. Finally, we wanted to offer concrete suggestions on how to improve relationships between subcontractors and suppliers.

Due to the qualitative character of this study a limited number of manufacturers (9) and main-suppliers (8) was selected. Also, representatives from researchers and intermediary organizations (5) were interviewed. The manufacturers operated in the following sectors: medical systems, fibre optics, high tech equipment, lighting, automotive and office equipment. All main suppliers delivered 'high tech' components to these manufacturers. In depth, semi-structured interviews were held with executives from research and development (R&D), development and purchasing (manufacturers); and chief executive officers (CEOs) and executives from R&D and development (main suppliers). In most cases two or more managers were interviewed per company in order to prevent functional bias towards the research outcome. The initial research results have been fed back to the participants in round table discussions and were subsequently refined. For practical reasons the empirical investigations were limited to manufacturing and supplier companies in the southern part of the Netherlands. All companies agreed to participate. Discussions were open and straightforward.

Interviews focused on the following subjects: (a) market developments that can be identified; (b) the impact of these developments on the organization, its systems and culture; and (c) the changes resulting from these developments in commercial business relationships. These issues will be discussed now in more detail.

MARKET DEVELOPMENTS

The respondents observed a number of important developments in their customer markets.

Globalization of competition leads to sourcing on a global scale by manufacturers in many industries resulting in an ever-expanding international supply base. Technological developments lead to changes in the balance of power between manufacturers and suppliers. In this respect the following trends were reported: (a) new information and communication technology enabling effective communications and information exchange with suppliers over large distances (CAD/CAM, EDI, PDI, Internet); (b) digital technologies leading to new product innovations in medical equipment, automotive and scanning systems and an increasing need to integrate suppliers in product development processes; (c) the increasing influence of embedded software on product design ('intelligent products') affecting the traditional cost and supplier base of components purchased; and (d) miniaturization as a result of the application of new electronics leading to new sources of supply and development partners.

All manufacturers interviewed agreed that mass customization in many industries will be necessary in order to offer tailor-made products (requiring customer-specific product development) and 'value added services' (technical and product services and logistics services) as a result of a more demanding customer base. Consequently product offerings by suppliers as required by manufacturers are becoming more service intensive.

IMPACT ON MANUFACTURING ORGANIZATIONS

How do these changes influence manufacturing processes and organizations? In this respect manufacturers reported the following issues. All agreed that these trends forced them to differentiate between core and non-core activities. This is not only true for production and development activities but also for support activities within companies. Many companies were in the process of contracting out non-core activities. This trend towards focus and specialization could also be observed in their relationships with suppliers. Most companies reported that they focused on the supply of modules and/or subsystems from a smaller number of (main) suppliers. In selecting their suppliers all applied an approach based upon global sourcing: given the multi-business unit character of the manufacturers (which had manufacturing sites in different parts of the world) in general relationships with suppliers who have 'global presence' (see Box 1 below) were favoured. In their dealings with suppliers manufacturers increasingly adopt a supply chain and network orientation when it comes to product development and streamlining logistics processes. Finally, most respondents reported a strong emphasis within their companies on both internal and external cooperation (cross-business and cross-functional teams in both customer and supplier relationships).

BOX 1   DEVELOPING A 'GLOBAL PRESENCE' IN SUPPLIER NETWORKS

Inalfa, as a main supplier of sunroofs to car manufacturers, decided that they needed to expand their capacity in order to be able to meet the growing volume of orders requested by their customers. Economies of scale is a key success factor in this type of business in order to be able to cover overhead charges and to be able to invest continuously in new equipment. Instead of adding capacity to its main plant in Venray, the Netherlands, Inalfa decided to set up new manufacturing facilities abroad, located near its main customers. In some cases smaller firms were acquired for this purpose. In this way Inalfa was also able to meet the growing need for a 'global presence' as communicated by large automotive manufacturers.

In many cases it was argued that competitive pressure drives the need for integration in areas of operations management and technological development with severe and lasting consequences for internal methods of working, procedures and structures. Many companies reported that they were currently undergoing an important transitional phase.

CHANGES IN COMMERCIAL BUSINESS RELATIONSHIPS

How did the companies involved experience the commercial aspects of the buyer–supplier rela-

tionship? This subject was studied from both perspectives.

Based upon the interviews with *manufacturer representatives* we made the following observations. The purchasing portfolio approach is a much-used instrument for arriving at systematic, differentiated supplier strategies. In their dealings with supplier relationships, manufacturers move from one to one relationships to managing and steering (international) supply networks. Hence, the need occurs for main suppliers who are able to assume responsibility for and have the capability of managing the underlying supplier network (see Box 2 below). From the point of view of technological development there seems to be a strong preference by manufacturers to involve existing and experienced suppliers in their development projects; the selection of future development partners is increasingly becoming a joint decision made by development and purchasing departments. However, notwithstanding these trends, most supplier relationships at present still seem to be based on 'historically' developed and personal relationships. It is generally expected that this type of relationship will become less frequent in future.

BOX 2   MAIN SUPPLIERS UPGRADE THEIR PURCHASING FUNCTION

Main suppliers such as Te Strake, Frencken and KMWE have recognized and anticipated the current changes in the sourcing strategies of their large customers. These suppliers have recently reorganized their purchasing departments in order to be able to translate the ever-increasing customer demands to their suppliers. Suppliers (mostly specialized jobbers) are now working with these main suppliers in a similar way as the latter work with their large manufacturers. Hiring experienced strategic buyers was necessary in order to make this happen.

Based upon the interviews with *supplier respondents* we found that most suppliers admit they do not have sufficient marketing plans or customer portfolios to guide their future commercial strategies and policies. This is a handicap in their discussions with large manufacturers' buyers who increasingly want to discuss future perspectives based on sound business plans with their suppliers. Furthermore all respondents agreed that a thorough and critical screening is necessary before entering into a technology partnership with a customer. However, they admit that such screening is seldom applied, thus leading to disappointment and frustration once the relationship has been established. In their presentations and commercial approaches to attract new customers, advantages for the customer are not given sufficient attention. Most of the suppliers interviewed still appear to take a product- or capacity-oriented approach in this respect.

SOURCING PHILOSOPHIES

The way in which different manufacturers work with suppliers varies considerably. Purchasing approaches or sourcing philosophies may be classified into three categories:

1. *Control orientation*: the manufacturer attempts to build up a power position in the relationship with his suppliers through his subcontracting policy and also uses this power to his advantage, without an eye for the interests of the supplier organization.
2. *Support orientation*: the purchasing policy is primarily focused on supporting, developing and coaching suppliers; however, supplier relationships are based on strict commercial agreements indicating well defined improvement goals.
3. *Supply orientation*: the subcontractor's primary focus in his steering of suppliers is on quality and logistics without, however, active monitoring of and follow up on actual performance.

Although our sample was too small to generalize, the majority of the manufacturers involved seemed to exert a control-oriented attitude towards their suppliers. None of the companies seemed to apply a support orientation in their dealings with suppliers. This is one important reason, as we see it, why partnership as a concept has not (yet) matured within the Netherlands.

REQUIREMENTS FOR FOSTERING ENTREPRENEURIAL CO-OPERATION

Many companies involved in partnership relationships seem to lack a common understanding of the term partnership. This term is often used without taking into account the requirements that should be met by both parties in terms of the relative power position and organizational characteristics.

Respondents indicated that many bottlenecks could be observed at present in the relationship between subcontractors and suppliers. Both manufacturers and suppliers reported on a lack of timely and comprehensive forecasts of future purchasing needs. As a consequence organizations are confronted with unnecessary stock and logistics costs. Significantly, both parties noted a lack of co-operation on both sides. This resulted in all kinds of communication problems between the hierarchical levels of the parties. Furthermore, manufacturers criticized their suppliers for their lack of expertise on project management. Basic principles of project management were often neglected, leading to misunderstandings on responsibilities. This was aggravated by a further unclear definition of tasks, responsibilities and authority among the companies involved for development work. Finally, suppliers reported abuses of power by the manufacturer, which resulted in frustration and a loss of trust in the other party.

Next, we discussed the most basic preconditions for successful co-operation with our respondents. Having a clear market vision and strategic vision reflected in formal business policy documents was considered to be a prerequisite for both parties. Next, both parties should have an organization capable of fulfilling mutual expectations. In this respect manufacturers preferably should have a support-oriented purchasing and supplier policy which is supported and communicated jointly by development and purchasing departments. Suppliers, on the other hand, should make clear choices about the customers they want to work for (see Box 3), should be able to work in cross-functional account teams, and should have the ability to provide adequate

'Entrepreneurial partnership' from customer perspective

Step 1   Analyse current product/market strategy

- Vision on non-core activities present?
- Sub-contracting policy supported by development & purchasing?
- Purchasing involved in product development?
- Vision present regarding for which technologies, which suppliers to involve in development?

Step 2   Determine position of suppliers in purchasing portfolio

- Are suppliers in strategic segment?
- What is the balance of power?
- To what degree does supplier in question measure up technologically to best-in-class?

Step 3   Determine future role of partner/supplier

- Why are we doing business with these suppliers now?
- Why should we do business with them in the future?
- Why should they (want to) do business with us in the future?

Step 4   Establish areas for co-operation

- Formulate concrete, verifiable tasks.
- What improvements do we expect from the suppliers involved in terms of:
  - Contributions to development projects
  - Operational process improvements (quality, logistics, costs, efficiency).
- How will we reward suppliers for their efforts?
- What can we do to enable the suppliers to realize the formulated tasks?

Step 5   Establish internal conditions

- Are we ready to direct the process of co-operation with the suppliers involved in terms of:
  - Management attention?
  - Information systems?
  - Communication?
  - Quality of staff?

Step 6   Implementation

- If all previous steps are 'go', concrete goals and action plans must be formulated jointly to work on enterprising co-operation!

'Entrepreneurial partnership' from supplier perspective

Step 1   Analyse current product/market strategy

- Strategic policy plan and marketing plan present?
- Core technologies determined?
- What specific expertise do you have?
- Vision regarding non-core activities determined?

Step 2   Determine your position in customer's purchasing portfolio

- In which segment is your strategic activity located?
- In which segment are you as supplier located?
- Do both provide the position you desire?
- What is the balance of power?
- How effective do you think the co-operation is between development and purchasing in the customer organization?

Step 3   Determine future role of partner/sub-contractor

- Why are we doing business with this customer now?
- Why should we do business with them in the future?
- How do we rate their strategic importance as a future customer?
- Why should they (want to) do business with us in the future?

Step 4   Establish areas for co-operation

- Formulate concrete, verifiable tasks.
- In which areas do we feel we can offer concrete results to the customer involved? What concrete possibilities do you see:
  - Contributions to development projects
  - Operational process improvements (quality, logistics, costs, efficiency).
- What do we expect from our customer so that we can realize the formulated tasks?

Step 5   Establish internal conditions

- Are we ready to direct the process of co-operation with the customer involved in terms of:
  - Management attention?
  - Information systems?
  - Development capacity?
  - Communication?
  - Project management?
  - Quality of staff?

Step 6   Implementation

- If all previous steps are 'go', concrete goals and action plans must he formulated jointly to work on enterprising co-operation!

Figure 10.5   Step-by-step plan towards entrepreneurial partnership

project management. Finally, all respondents agreed that is was necessary to have adequate (electronic) systems and structures in place, aimed at communication and the exchange of information among all levels of the organization.

BOX 3   FOCUS ON CORE CUSTOMERS

Nebato is a successful supplier, located in the Netherlands, with several business units specializing in mechanical engineering and manufacturing of high-tech components. Some years ago Nebato Module Group was founded, to serve as a partner for manufacturers who wanted to subcontract systems and modules. NMG is selective in accepting new customers. In all assignments, its engineering personnel should be actively involved in the customer's engineering and development processes. The general manager says: 'As soon as a customer is going to treat us in a traditional purchasing way – prescribing specifications and only willing to discuss price – we will immediately refer him to one of our other business units. What we want to do is add value to the design process. That is what we are good at, and that is what we want to be paid for.'

Co-operation between organizations essentially involves social exchanges among people. Many respondents pointed out the importance of the 'chemistry' factor. There has to be a certain chemistry between the managers and employees involved all through the organization. If the chemistry in a specific team does not work, or is missing, management should not hesitate to change the composition of the team.

FOSTERING CONCURRENT ENGINEERING IN THE SUPPLY CHAIN

In conclusion we present a step-by-step plan (see Figure 10.5) on which effective technological collaboration might be based. The following steps may be used to decide whether or not to engage in a partnership relationship:

- Analyse your relative power position vis-à-vis the other party. Be careful if the other party has much more power in the relationship than you. He is probably going to use it at some stage of the relationship.
- Indicate which requirements need to be met in terms of organization, people, communication, systems and organizational culture, to facilitate the process of collaboration between organizations. Is there sufficient 'cultural fit' between both parties; do information systems have sufficient compatibility and sophistication; do both organizations view the relationship in the same way? When organizations are not sufficiently compatible, it is better not to enter into a partnership.
- Where there is a balanced power relationship and organizations are sufficiently compatible both parties may discuss future business opportunities, using the steps as indicated in our scheme.

Both supplier and manufacturer can influence the outcome of this process. However, we believe that by following the steps above, manufacturers and suppliers will gain a more realistic view of their organization and others, which could prevent partnerships from going wrong.

REFERENCES

Anderson, J.C. and Narus, J.A. (1998), *Business market management, Understanding, creating and delivering value*, New Jersey: Prentice Hall.

Cooper, M.C. and Ellram, L.M. (1993), 'Characteristics of Supply Chain Management and the implications for purchasing and logistics strategy', *International Journal of Logistics Management*, 4(2), pp. 13–24.

Ellram, L.M. and Cooper, M.C. (1990), 'Supply Chain Partnerships and the Shipper-Third Party Relationship', *International Journal of Logistics Management*, 1(2), pp. 1–10.

Hendrick, T. and Ellram, L.M. (1993), *Strategic Supplier Partnering: An International Study*, Tempe, AZ: Center for Advanced Purchasing Studies.

Goor, A.R. van (1998), *Partnership door Ketenlogistiek*, Handboek Logistiek, Alphen a/d Rijn: Samsom Bedrijfsinformatie (in Dutch).

Hakansson, H. (Ed.) (1982), *International Marketing and Purchasing of Industrial Goods*, New York: John Wiley and Sons.

Hart, H.W.C. van der and Weele, A.J. (Eds) (1997), Dynamiek in Commerciele Relaties, The Netherlands: F. & G. Publishers (in Dutch).

Laseter, T.L. (1998), *Balanced Sourcing: Cooperation and Competition in Supplier Relationships*, San Francisco: Jossey Bass Publishers.

Rozemeijer, F.A. (1996), *Zicht op partnerships: methoden en technieken voor het opbouwen van een partnership*, Eindhoven University of Technology, working paper (in Dutch).

Weele, A.J. van and Rozemeijer F.A. (1996), *Revolution in Purchasing*, Eindhoven: Eindhoven University of Technology/Philips Electronics.

Wijnstra, J.Y.F (1998), *The Role of Purchasing in Product Development*, Eindhoven University of Technology, PhD dissertation.

PART THREE

ORGANIZATION AND MANAGEMENT

Introduction to organization and management

Ruth Fee

Part III examines the organization and management of procurement in both the public and the private sectors. The success of any organization depends on its organizational structure and the effective management of both operations and staff. The theory of organization and management is diverse and extensive, encompassing many practical issues in purchasing and supply management. Part III focuses on the following issues: driving and managing change, staff development, the use of purchasing teams and the use of consortia in procurement.

Chapter 11 by Jon Hughes analyses the 'options, issues, roadblocks and realities of driving change in purchasing and supply'. Hughes acknowledges the academic debate in the area of the management of change but wishes to move, in his words, 'beyond ... ideology into considered action'. Indeed, he comments that academic theory on managing change in purchasing has a relatively low influence on practitioners, even amongst those who are leading change agents within major UK companies. From a survey of 60 global corporations and 119 UK based practitioners, Hughes examines the practical issues of design and implementation of sustainable change and the 'people issues' associated with building commitment. The research findings give an example of the gap between practitioners and academics in the field of purchasing and supply. In discussing the factors rated important for organizational success, strengthening teamwork across the business rated highest, with outsourcing and privatization ranking 14th in the list despite the high profile of these issues in the professional press and academia. One theme running throughout Part III is the experience and training of staff. Hughes examines the poor experience of respondents and questions the sustainability of change programmes when there is a high movement of staff between organizations: 'clearly the transformation of purchasing in an organization is a long haul task'. Finding suitably skilled staff is a problem but the chapter ends on the positive note that securing the support of high level sponsors and the coaching of staff in process thinking and handling conflict may help deal with resistance to change.

Staff development and training is a core factor outlined in Hughes' chapter as a driver for change in organizations, and this theme is further examined in Howard McCullough's chapter. McCullough examines the role of the Joint Procurement Policy and Strategy Group (JPPSG) in higher education (HE) to illustrate the importance of a professional, motivated workforce. He notes that one of the main reasons for the reluctance of institutions to collaborate in purchasing is the perceived low status of procurement within many institutions and, as a consequence, the existence of low self-esteem in purchasing and supply departments. Adams' equity theory is used to illustrate how procurement staff perceive their job as a 'dead end' without the prospect for advancement. The theory is applied to purchasing case studies in the higher education sector to show what can be achieved through professional training of staff. McCullough discusses the exodus of professional procurement staff in the public sector that threatens to undermine the government's best practice plans, where career development is clearly an important factor. This is an issue that also affects the private sector, as noted by Hughes. The chapter develops a training strategy for procurement staff in HE institutions and identifies two types of staff that will result from this strategy – first, a composite business manager and second, buyers in various departments. The price to pay for this 'utopia' is a commitment to meaningful, focused training. What sort of training should be provided? According to McCullough it is not training 'relying on a syllabus based course of instruction'. Training is based on an examination of the Purchasing and Supply Lead Body (PSLB) Standards of Competence and the use of National Vocational Qualifications (NVQs) to allow the individual to analyse how well he or she is performing in relation to the performance standard. McCullough uses three case studies to illustrate his contention that 'training staff trains the organization'; in each case study substantial savings were made for the organization by staff undergoing professional training programmes. In conclusion, the chapter makes reference to a report by the National Audit Office (1999) which suggests that a principal driver for change is a systematic and comprehensive method of training that will meet the challenge of effective procurement in universities.

As noted above, Hughes found that the highest rated factor for the importance of organizational success was the strengthening of teamwork across the business. Chapter 13 examines the influence of the industry sector, firm size and organizational structure on the use of purchasing teams. Based on a sample of 269 large North American supply organizations, this chapter examines the use of seven different approaches to team-based purchasing: purchasing councils, supplier councils, commodity teams, cross-functional teams, teams involving suppliers, teams involving customers and teams involving both suppliers and customers. Factor analysis was used to classify seven team-based purchasing techniques into two groups: internal and external. The authors examine whether certain combinations of teams tend to be more common and whether certain types of teams are used more frequently in the service, process and discrete goods industries. Why use purchas-

ing teams? The motivation to use purchasing teams is well established – they combine the skills and resources of several stakeholders, they are temporary and they are frequently created to focus resources on the completion of a temporary project. However, there is little research into the extent to which purchasing teams are used and no research that investigates how firms approach team use by combining various forms of purchasing teams as a method of influencing team or firm performance. Literature cited suggests that team-based purchasing is expanding – a reflection of flatter and leaner organizations and the benefits of cross-functional input into decisions. However, the reported level of use of team-based purchasing techniques was lower than anticipated, indicating that many firms are still hesitant to use purchasing teams extensively. The respondents cited cross-functional purchasing teams, commodity teams and purchasing councils as the most frequently used team-based purchasing techniques. The authors recognize the need for further research in the area: whilst the indications are that size and sector influences purchasing team use, how and why this occurs has not been addressed.

In Chapter 14 John Ritchie and Tom Chadwick examine the use of purchasing consortia using the experiences of the Joint Procurement Policy and Strategy Group (JPPSG) as an example. Progress and problems in moving from a price-based approach to a strategy of achieving overall best commercial value monitored by effective performance measures are described. The paper sets out the current and future roles for the HE purchasing consortia including step changes such as the 'one-stop shop' system for supplies that even third party suppliers are encouraged to join: the benefits of this agreement include price/cost reductions on services and products, and the ability to analyse supplier and product ranges. The next logical step, according to the authors, is the provision of value added services to include professional procurement and recruitment advice. In addition there is a number of supporting activities or objectives that need to be achieved, such as customer focus, business planning, marketing strategy and benchmarking. The authors acknowledge that there are barriers to optimum effectiveness: individual institutions may not wish to participate in the process and insecure purchasing staff may fear a loss of status. The importance of performance measurement, both qualitative and quantitative, is emphasized, along with the need for all consortia and constituent member institutions to use performance measurement in a consistent way. The authors recognize that these measures will evolve over time.

Together these chapters provide a wealth of insights into best practice in building an effective purchasing organization, drawing upon a range of UK and North American empirical evidence from both surveys and case studies. The issues examined are common to most organizations regardless of industry sector and ownership, although it might be argued that they are more relevant to medium or large, rather than small, organizations. The conundrum remains, however, that the more resources provided to develop staff towards professional qualifications, particularly in the public sector, the greater the risk of poaching from other organizations providing either higher levels of pay, better conditions or a more stimulating role for their professional buyers. Thus the context within which newly professionalized buyers operate must also change to allow the full deployment of their talents, especially in developing relationships with suppliers, customers and senior management, if such staff are to be retained.

REFERENCE

National Audit Office (1999), *Procurement in the English Higher Education Sector*, London: The Stationery Office.

CHAPTER ELEVEN

From ideology to action: options, issues, roadblocks and realities of driving change in purchasing and supply

Jon Hughes

CHANGE MANAGEMENT IN PURCHASING

During recent years there has been considerable academic debate about purchasing and supply, together with concerted attempts to 're-define the profession'. For many practitioners, however, there is a desire to move beyond such ideology into considered action. Rather than focusing on single prescriptions or the merits and demerits of one perspective of the supply chain over another there is a preference for a flexible approach and one that more effectively recognizes the internal cultural constraints that invariably have to be faced. Accordingly, over the last 18 months, the Windsor Foundation for Business Development has been conducting practical research into the various change options that are available, together with an identification of generic themes and the potential differentiators of effective versus ineffective change (Hughes 1998a; 1998b; 1999).

No attempt has been made within the research to adopt an unrealistically normative or prescriptive approach. Rather, the focus of study has been on the delineation and assessment of tentative linkage between broad business context and the macro factors within which a firm operates; the emerging drivers of competitive position; stakeholder requirements for differing types of financial contribution; the range of relational options available to various players within the supply chain; and, most importantly, the internal organizational competences and

capabilities that may, or may not, be in place to trigger, enable and sustain effective change in purchasing and supply. This approach broadly segments change, therefore, into (1) approaches that are essentially led by functionally positioned line managers in purchasing, where these goals are more traditionally focused on narrower definitions of operational improvement related to cost management and value delivery from suppliers, and (2) approaches that are implemented on a broader cross-business basis and which are driven by business managers pursuing mission critical goals. Again, it is not implied that either approach is exclusive or independent of the other, just that the leadership roles and the organizational positioning within business may vary.

It is argued that the meaning of change within purchasing and supply should be defined and evaluated in a variety of ways across the above continuum. Further, the specific tasks being pursued by the various 'change drivers' and their associated outputs and business valued deliverables will vary greatly, depending on the locus of activity and overall positioning within this change spectrum.

METHODOLOGY

A three part methodology has been pursued throughout the two year research study. First, an in-depth study was made of 60 global corporations to develop a high level model of supply chain transformation (see Figure 11.1 and

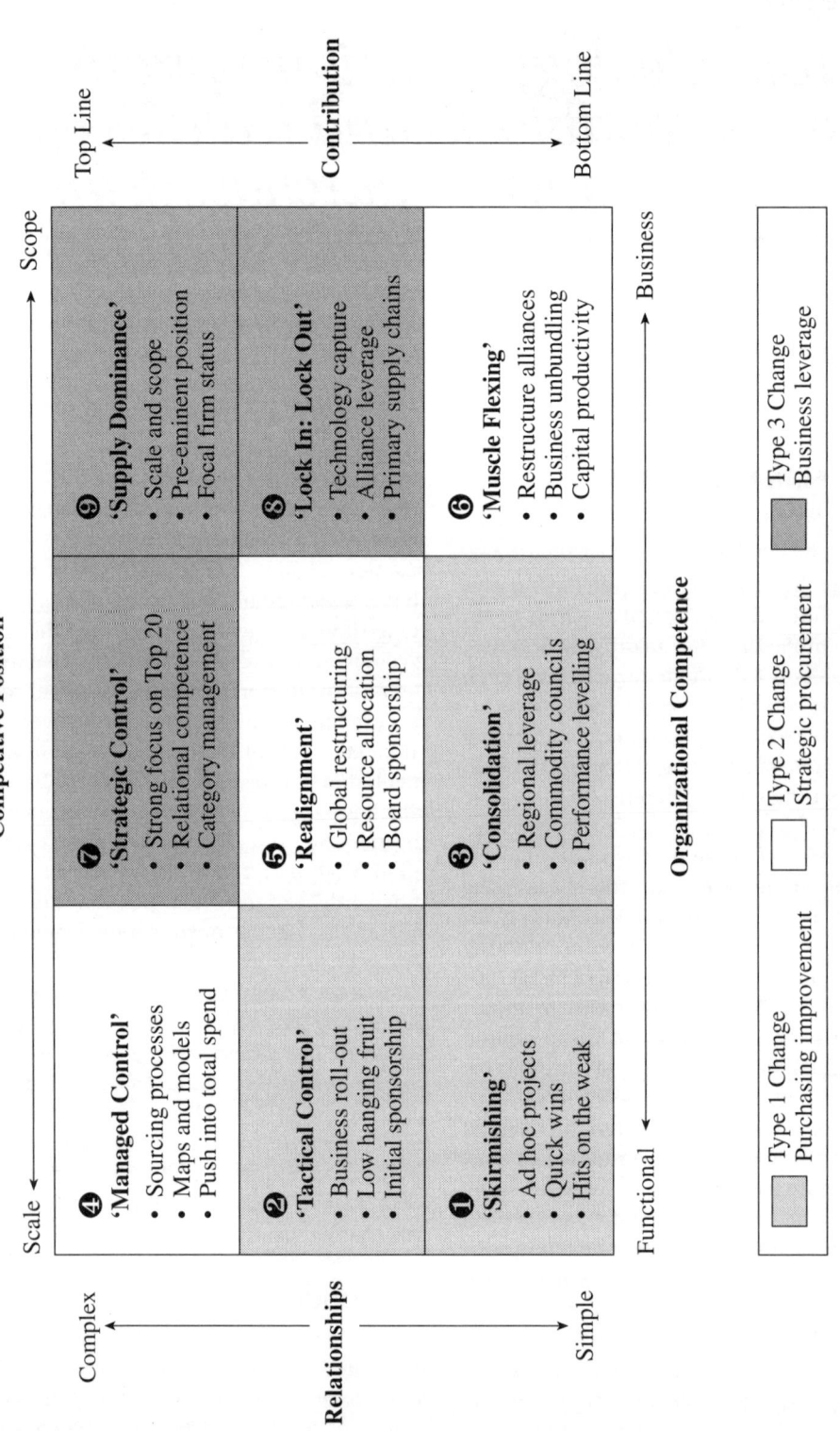

Figure 11.1 Three types of change across purchasing and the supply chain

© The Windsor Foundation for Business Development, September 1999.

Hughes et al. 1998) evaluating potential linkages between different change drivers and the types of business interventions being considered. This segmented change into three broad types:

1. Functionally driven change concentrating on purchasing improvement and the strengthening of undervalued purchasing processes.
2. A progression to more strategic procurement involving the restructuring and realignment of broader based business supply processes.
3. Radical, transformational change leveraging the whole organization and the positioning of a business in its various supply chains.

Second, a questionnaire was sent to 348 UK based companies, agencies and major government departments. Of these, 150 were designated 'exemplar organizations' by virtue of their profile within the professional community. 119 practitioners chose to participate in the study. Third, both quantifiable data and qualitative responses were analysed. Fourth, ongoing research is still underway and will be published shortly (Hughes 2000).

INFORMATION ON SURVEY RESPONDENTS

Seventy-three per cent of the selected respondents were at senior management level, with typical job titles being head of procurement, strategic purchasing manager, group purchasing director, head of contracts and vice president procurement. There were also some broader-based roles such as director of business integration and director of procurement effectiveness. It was striking to observe the relatively brief job tenure of many of these respondents. Only 15 per cent had been in post for more than four years; 64 per cent had been in post for under two years and 43 per cent for less than one year. Many companies worldwide are putting considerable emphasis on the restructuring and restaffing of their purchasing resources with consequent impact on job role definition, realignment of accountabilities and reassessment of required commercial competencies. Organizational demand for experienced

purchasing and supply change agents is high. Not surprisingly, this has caused a human resources merry-go-round, with suitably qualified and experienced purchasing professionals able to transfer readily from one long-term change initiative to another. This may have implications for the sustainability of such programmes and the processes supporting them, as well as organizational continuity.

DURATION OF CHANGE MANAGEMENT INITIATIVES

Only 30 per cent of respondents stated that their organizations had been trying to bring about change in purchasing for under two years. Twenty-six per cent reported that concerted organizational efforts had been under way between two and four years while 44 per cent commented that this had been the case for five or more years.

Clearly, the transformation of purchasing in an organization is a long-haul task. Equally, in view of the high staff turnover of purchasing change leaders described above, there must be some doubts about relative success in implementation. Further, throughout the survey there was an undercurrent of organizational frustration. Many respondents were external recruits appointed into roles defined along 'change agent' parameters. While executive decisions to strengthen purchasing, either as a functional activity or as a broader organizational competence, appear to have been made in many of these selected companies the level of support for such change, particularly at an operational level, was often relatively low or uncertain. This was a frequent theme throughout the qualitative responses within the survey. Survey responses will now be discussed in detail.

PERCEPTIONS OF SECTORAL LEADERSHIP

When respondents in purchasing and supply were asked to make a comparative evaluation between their organization and competitors within the same sector, their responses were as follows:

- 'We are the sector leader' (15%)
- 'Only a few organizations are better than us' (51%)
- 'We are an average performer' (29%)
- 'Most organizations are better than us' (5%)
- 'We are the sector laggards' (0%)

These responses appear to suggest perceived functional or process superiority on a sectoral basis. But it will also be seen throughout this chapter that overall progress on improving purchasing, even with a very traditional focus such as cost management, supplier reduction and structured sourcing, has been mixed in some instances. The relative gap between sectoral leader and sectoral laggard may on occasions be illusory rather than substantive.

FACTORS RATED IMPORTANT FOR ORGANIZATIONAL SUCCESS

Fourteen factors were provided in the survey questionnaire and respondents ranked them on a five point scale. The importance of those rated 'very important' or 'extremely important' was as follows:

1. Strengthening teamwork across the business (93%)
2. Speed of response to customers (84%)
3. Radically improving customer service (82%)
4. Changing the culture (81%)
5. Supply chain management (70%)
6. Product or service innovation (69%)
7. Investing in superior technology (62%)
8. Investing heavily in staff development (61%)
9. Becoming the lowest cost operator (54%)
10. Customer : supplier integration (45%)
11. Forming alliances with other companies (43%)
12. Branding of products or services (41%)
13. Mergers and acquisitions (35%)
14. Outsourcing and privatization (24%)

A number of other business drivers were identified by respondents including: speed to market, margin management, developing cross-group synergies, environmental sustainability, maintaining market share, industry consolidation, regulatory compliance, diversification, growing the franchise, multisite integration, business-to-business relationship management, boosting sales and geographic expansion. It is interesting to note the significant loading on external customer value delivery, internal culture change and teamwork. This is consistent with an operational focus on (1) and (2). Despite the high profile given in the professional press to alliances, mergers and outsourcing, they received a relatively low ranking. This may reflect actual priorities or be due to a combination of purchasing's traditional functional focus on supplier product sourcing rather than on third party capability assessment, as well as exclusion from or secondary involvement in more strategic business-to-business relational development.

IMPACT OF PURCHASING AND SUPPLY ON THE CORE BUSINESS MISSION

Responses to one of six options were as follows:

1. 'Without doubt, purchasing and supply is the core mission' (4%)
2. 'Purchasing and supply is crucial to our success' (26%)
3. 'Purchasing and supply is one of a number of drivers of success' (39%)
4. 'Other areas of the organization are probably more important' (21%)
5. 'Purchasing and supply makes a valuable but secondary contribution' (10%)
6. 'The contribution of purchasing and supply is minimal' (0%)

Taken at face value, this seems quite a realistic assessment. In many organizations the activities deemed to comprise purchasing and supply remain essentially a support activity. The selection and implementation of a suitable change programme to strengthen and then build on traditional core activities needs to reflect this. Certainly, many respondents were wary of presenting purchasing and supply as the 'business strategic driver'. However, there is a substantial minority, 30 per cent, who are well aware of the criticality and potentially strategic contribution to business success that can be delivered from active management of the supply chain and an organization's positioning within it.

INVOLVEMENT IN DIFFERENT TYPES OF CHANGE

Respondents were asked to assess their personal involvement in, and leadership of, the three broad levels of change outlined earlier in this chapter. The following percentages reflect where there is at least 'a lot of involvement/leadership' on a four point scale, ranging from no involvement through some involvement and a lot of involvement to total involvement.

1. Functionally driven purchasing improvement
   - Personal involvement (84%)
   - Personal leadership (83%)
2. Cross-business strategic procurement
   - Personal involvement (81%)
   - Personal leadership (76%)
3. Radical, business driven leverage of the supply chain
   - Personal involvement (55%)
   - Personal leadership (49%)

Even within the largest companies it seems that senior purchasing professionals remain focused primarily on their own functional and/or cross-business processes impacting the supply chain. Encouragingly, though, there appears to be some involvement in and leadership of the more radical, transformational types of change that can be detected in some organizations (Strebel 1992; Hamel 1996; Cox 1997; Taffinder 1998).

DESIGN ISSUES INVOLVED IN CHANGE IN PURCHASING AND SUPPLY

Respondents were asked to rate nine design issues involved in change on a five point scale ranging from no problem through some problem, quite difficult and very difficult to highly challenging. The following percentages reflect an assessment of where design issues have been at least 'quite difficult'.

1. Finding suitably skilled staff (77%)
2. Gaining support from other functions (66%)
3. Building understanding of the supply possibilities (65%)
4. Securing the necessary financial resources (53%)
5. Identifying the scope of the approach (46%)
6. Choosing a change methodology that works (42%)
7. Planning the overall approach (39%)
8. Gaining top management support (39%)
9. Defining the goals and the deliverables (34%)

In many of the respondents' organizations, there are important issues surrounding both the ideal role and skills profile of purchasing change agents as well as their shortage. Traditional routes of professional education and training are not necessarily meeting this demand. An array of additional or supplementary design issues was also provided by respondents in their qualitative responses, as follows, clustered around the top three design issues.

Top issue: finding suitably skilled staff

- Locating staff with the necessary analytical and interpersonal skills
- Appointing staff who can operate without a top-down mandate
- Clarifying the roles of those involved in designing purchasing change
- Planned training of purchasing professionals in change agent skills

Second issue: Gaining support from other functions

- Gaining commitment of the key business influencers on sourcing
- Achieving buy-in of functional colleagues in devolved organizations
- Finding the time needed to consult widely across the organization
- Achieving cultural acceptance of a purchasing leadership approach

Third issue: Building understanding of the supply possibilities

- Demonstrating the strategic, financial and operational benefits of change
- Integration of differing and potentially conflicting business agendas
- Closely linking purchasing and supply initiatives to business drivers
- Recognizing the gap between theory, practice and required capabilities

IMPLEMENTATION ISSUES INVOLVED IN CHANGE

An identical approach was adopted with regard to implementation issues as with the design issues highlighted above:

1. Overload from other initiatives (77%)
2. Dealing with resistance to change (64%)
3. Gaining cross-functional co-operation (63%)
4. Implementing measures of performance (62%)
5. Dealing with serious 'blockers' (individuals) (60%)
6. Responding to unrealistic expectations (50%)
7. Applying effective project management (49%)
8. Developing the skills of purchasing staff (45%)
9. Sustaining top management support (33%)

Top issue: Overload from other initiatives

● Being realistic in what can be achieved within a given time frame
● Fully recognizing the resource implications and time constraints
● Selling the benefits to keep purchasing on the business agenda
● Aligning purchasing and supply initiatives to other change programmes

Second issue: Dealing with resistance to change

● Securing and utilizing the support of high level sponsors
● Understanding the potentially valuable role that conflict plays in change
● Active involvement of potential resisters early on in the process
● Coaching of staff in process thinking and handling conflict

Third issue: Gaining cross-functional co-operation

● Using forums and steering groups to ensure a non-partisan approach
● Recognizing and responding to potentially conflicting goals and priorities
● Giving visibility to the contribution of cross-functional colleagues
● Ensuring deliverables meet the goals and needs of other functions

The organizational realities, roadblocks and resource constraints were often uppermost in respondents' minds. Sustainable change rarely proceeds in a linear and predictable fashion. Tuning in to organizational politics, understanding the nature of resistance and being prepared to embrace conflict are core skills of effective change agents (see Pascale 1990; De Dreu & Van de Vliert 1997; and Stone 1997) and are important differentiators of success.

BUSINESS DELIVERABLES REQUIRED FROM CHANGE

Content analysis of respondents' written comments produced the following ranking of valued deliverables, clustered around 10 broad themes:

1. Sustainable improvement and restructuring of supplier–customer supply processes.
2. A step change in supply performance aligned to required business goals and output measures.
3. Implementation of standardized, 'world class' purchasing processes.
4. Attainment of lowest total acquisition cost, year-on-year significant cost reduction and maximum value for money.
5. Company-wide acceptance of the importance of effective purchasing and full recognition of its contribution as a business driver.
6. Buy-in of top management and functional leaders with acceptance of, and commitment to, changes in purchasing and across the supply chain.
7. Greater penetration and managed control over all expenditure, particularly 'off-limits', non-traditional and non-inventory categories.
8. Close involvement of purchasing in strategy development, together with a repositioning of the function as a business competence.
9. Achieving 'service excellence' and high levels of efficient delivery and support to internal customers.
10. Building higher levels of purchasing competence, with all staff involved in purchas-

ing and dealing with suppliers being well trained.

The responses confirm that purchasing leaders are primarily focused on (1) and (2), particularly (1), extending them to impact on total corporate expenditure while building internal partnerships through effective management and facilitation of cross-business relationships. This is responsive change, concentrating essentially on operational improvement.

INFLUENCE OF ACADEMIC THEORY ON MANAGING CHANGE

Nine theoretical models were listed. Respondents were asked to evaluate their influence on a five point scale from no influence to a little influence, some influence, major influence and utmost influence. The ranking was as follows:

	Major/utmost influence	A little/ none
1. Value delivery	46%	23%
2. Supply chain management	41%	19%
3. Core competencies	39%	30%
4. Partnering	32%	31%
5. Supply chain alignment	29%	33%
6. Lean supply	28%	46%
7. Value appropriation	20%	38%
8. Critical asset theory	9%	70%
9. Virtual business	6%	63%

A number of other theoretical influences were listed by respondents; for example, transaction cost analysis, supply positioning, value chain analysis, centre led networks, just-in-time, efficient consumer response, cellular supply, re-engineering and market logic. It seems that academic theory has a relatively low influence on practitioners, even amongst those who are leading change agents within major UK companies. It is probably not surprising that models in customer service and value delivery are widely acknowledged since they are invariably central to supply process change. Theoretical treatments of leverage and dominance in supply chains, the restructuring of supply chains to ap-

propriate value and control critical assets and virtual businesses hardly appear to be on the practitioner agenda.

INFLUENCE OF MANAGEMENT CONSULTANTS

Sixty per cent of respondents stated that management consultants had been involved. While there is often an antipathy to external advisers in many organizations, this high figure may indicate that the potential business contribution of purchasing and supply is increasingly being recognized. If so, it may be assumed that consultants' methodological or facilitative offerings, over and above the competencies of internally appointed functional specialists, are also valued by the commissioning management. Of those who had been involved with management consultants, 46 per cent of respondents assessed their contribution favourably and as being at least 'a lot of value'. Fifty-two per cent rated them as being 'of some value', while two per cent rated them as being 'very poor'.

PERCEIVED LEVEL OF CURRENT GOAL ATTAINMENT THROUGH CHANGE INITIATIVES

No respondents believe that they have achieved 'complete goal attainment'. Sixty-eight per cent reported that 'a lot of progress had been made', 31 per cent 'some progress' and only one per cent 'little progress'. Despite the design and implementation difficulties experienced, this appears to be an encouraging response. However, respondents argue that it will take considerable time for them to achieve full strengthening and development of purchasing and supply.

THE CRITICAL SUCCESS FACTORS FOR CHANGE

Content analysis of respondents' written comments produced the following ranking of critical success factors for change in purchasing and supply:

1. Visible buy-in and a high level of support

from executive directors and top management for change in purchasing and supply.

2. The appointment of top quality staff with ongoing training and development to raise their skills to 'best practice' level.
3. Tangible business contribution through a significant reduction in the total cost of doing business within supply chains.
4. Adoption of high quality performance measurement, supported by clear objectives, timely information and better reporting systems.
5. Development of positive internal management and functional attitudes towards purchasing and high levels of cross-business co-operation.
6. Leadership and consistency of purpose from a committed head of purchasing, with sound understanding of change management.
7. Raising internal customer satisfaction through a timely, supportive and professionally delivered purchasing service.
8. Increasing the influence over all major categories of expenditure with agreed purchasing strategies developed and implemented.
9. A linked and collaborating network of 'purchasers', rather than just full-time functional staff, prepared to apply sourcing strategy frameworks.
10. A visible and well-regarded purchasing performance improvement programme delivering proven early successes and quick wins.

A noticeable theme running through these responses is the developmental, improvement-orientated nature of predominantly 'bottom-up' change. It is a strongly held view that purchasing and supply must be seen to prove itself in the eyes of both top management and the internal customer constituencies. It appears that this cannot be achieved without changing, strengthening, rebuilding, focusing and more effectively measuring purchasing team performance. Once that has been achieved a diffusion effect becomes possible with the purchasing team pushing outwards and enabling injection of, and coaching in, 'better practice' across the total expenditure.

TIME REQUIRED TO ACHIEVE MAJOR GOALS IN PURCHASING CHANGE

Eight per cent of respondents believe that it will take one year or less, 18 per cent one to two years, 42 per cent two to three years, 16 per cent three to four years and 16 per cent more than four years. Clearly, commitment to change in supply means that purchasing professionals and their organizations have to be prepared for the relatively long haul. However, as we saw in Questions 1 and 2, it may prove difficult to retain experienced change agents to see the necessary changes through.

CONCLUSIONS AND NEXT STAGE IN THE RESEARCH PROGRAMME

The reality of change in purchasing and supply lags considerably behind the conceptual vanguard of intellectual theory. Operational improvement predominates rather than strategic repositioning and business leverage, although there is evidence of a leadership group of exemplar companies making significant progress in building organizational support, strengthening internal capabilities and pushing back the boundaries of conventional functional practice. It may be several years, however, before even these 'purchasing leaders' can have an impact on the more strategic processes associated with business positioning in supply chains. Future research should concentrate on the enabling methodologies needed to accelerate such progress as well as their development and dissemination.

REFERENCES

Cox, A. (1997), *Business Success*, Boston, UK: Earlsgate Press.

Hamel, G. (1996), 'Strategy as revolution', *Harvard Business Review*, July-August, pp. 69–82.

De Dreu, C. and Van de Vliert, E. (1997), *Using Conflict in Organizations*, London: Sage.

Hughes, E.J. (1998a), 'Beyond Ideology: Get a Grip on Change Management', *Supply Management*, 19 November.

Hughes, E.J. (1998b), 'Pilgrims' Progress', *Supply Management*, 17 December.

Hughes, E.J. (1999), 'Going for Gold', *Supply Management*, 21 January.

Hughes, E.J. (2000), *Radical Change in Purchasing: A Practitioner's Manual*, The Windsor Foundation.

Hughes, E.J., Ralf, M.A. and Michels, W.L. (1998), 'Different markets, different drivers, different relationships', *Proceedings of the 7th International IPSERA Conference*, London, pp. 239–253.

Pascale, R. (1990), *Managing on the Edge*, New York: Viking Penguin.

Stone, B. (1997), *Confronting Company Politics*, London: Macmillan Press.

Strebel, P. (1992), *Breakpoints: How Managers Exploit Radical Business Change*, Cambridge, Mass: Harvard Business School Press.

Taffinder, P. (1998), *Big Change: A Route Map for Corporate Transformation*, New York: John Wiley.

CHAPTER TWELVE

Getting to the fundamentals in procurement training

Howard McCulloch

There is ample evidence from many practitioners and academics to suggest that the procurement function is a vital element in the overall strategy of getting better value for money in the public sector and in particular within Higher Education (HE) institutions. In September 1998, Tom Chadwick, Director of the Joint Procurement Policy and Strategy Group (JPPSG), reported that 'despite the great work going on at the moment within HE, some existing national agreements were characterized by a lack of consultation, lack of ownership and lack of professionalism' (Crabb 1998). This view has been supported by the National Audit Office who have recommended that procurement should be strengthened in this sector. In the private sector too, there is recognition of the importance of the purchasing function and the need for practitioners to be trained to a very high level. For example, there has been public recognition by British Oxygen Co. that purchasing personnel must develop strategic management capabilities in knowledge-based skills such as change management, financial competence and cultural awareness as well as leadership and the ability to build and influence relationships (Littlefield 1998). This view is echoed by Neil Deverill, Procurement Director of Philips, who is quoted as saying 'they (purchasers) must have drive, be innovative, and be able to deal with the multiple complexities that characterize the job' (Varley 1998). It is with these thoughts in mind that this chapter outlines a training strategy to meet these objectives.

PROCUREMENT STATUS

Procurement resources within HE tend to be spread very thinly indeed and few procurement officers get the chance to display the kind of skills outlined above, through no fault of their own. In extreme cases the staff are perceived to be of little value (Gadde and Hakansson 1993). The perception of their users can range from considering them as 'that department that never gets me what I want when I need it' through to 'they are all right for some things but you couldn't expect them to understand the technicalities of the equipment that we spend money on'. In other words, the procurement function and the work of the staff are viewed in a negative manner or at best a neutral manner. Parsons (1997) argues this point when he suggests that the purchasing department is like a drain. People have a neutral perception of a drain that is working effectively but as soon as it becomes blocked that perception changes to a negative one. So people in user departments within universities only take notice of procurement when something goes wrong. Continually viewed in this way, the importance of procurement is kept off the agenda of the important strategic meetings within institutions. As a result of this perception there is also a danger that the job may be perceived by the procurement staff as dead end, without prospects for advancement. This suggestion forces the consideration of Adams' theory of equity.

Equity theory focuses on people's feelings of how fairly they have been treated in comparison to the treatment received by others. People evaluate their social relationships in the same way as buying or selling an item. People expect certain outcomes in exchange for certain contributions or inputs (Mullins 1994). This exchange process leads people to expect greater recognition as a result of a high level of contribution (input). People within the procurement function will compare their own position within the organization with that of others, for example the finance department. If therefore a comparison of others' inputs and outcomes reveals a discrepancy, the aggrieved employee is likely to experience tension. The tension acts as a motivator within the person to take some form of action to relieve that tension. Adams lists six such actions. Two of those are easily recognized as relevant to the procurement function within HE and have been widely reported as occurring in procurement circles. The first is described as 'cognitive distortion of inputs and outcomes'. This may manifest itself in people distorting the utility of facts about themselves. This could be the relevance of a purchasing qualification to themselves in their present situation. Research suggests that this is a commonly found phenomena within organizations where the prospective candidate for training is working in a specialized area of procurement or where the function is under the direct control of another department e.g. finance or production.

CASE STUDY 1

At one large Scottish university two candidates' names had been put forward for a vocational qualification award by a well-meaning superior. The candidates argued that while they were responsible for buying in all the materials consumed within the department their principal task was to control research budgets. Despite the fact that the word 'procurement' appeared in the job title and their joint spend responsibility was considerable, they could not see the relevance of vocational qualifications in procurement. Buying was not deemed to be important and a vocational qualification award unnecessary. However, both candidates did complete Scottish Vocational Awards in Procurement at Level III and as a result designed some new practices and redesigned other existing procurement procedures. They had discovered,

when examining the procedures in order to produce evidence of competence, that they were, in fact, less than effective. This prompted the setting up of discussion groups with the users of the stores, and problems experienced by users were all too evident. As a result of these discussions, which were held over a period of several months, a comprehensive procedures manual was designed and distributed resulting in more accurate requisitioning and improved customer service levels. A significant cost benefit was also achieved during an exercise in stock analysis, something which had never been deemed important before. This arose from the need to generate evidence for the programme units 'Contribute to the optimization of inventory levels' and 'Contribute to the implementation of changes in inventory'. During the investigation it became apparent that there was a considerable cost attached to the storing of enzymes as they required special refrigerated storing facilities which in turn required continual maintenance. A detailed analysis of usage rates was carried out including future demand for the various products. Armed with this information and with the participation of the procurement department an agreement was made with a key supplier. The agreement required the supplier to provide and maintain predetermined amounts of identified product on a consignment stock basis and to supply the necessary refrigerated storage. This allowed for the disposal of the university's much older equipment and freed up much needed space due to the considerably smaller refrigerated units now installed; in addition, there were the obvious savings arising from deferred payments. In light of these successes within the stores operation the director of procurement was able to report a significant increase in the operational effectiveness of that particular unit, which was in no small part due to the increased importance awarded to the procurement aspects of the tasks carried out by these two 'financial controllers'.

The above case is by no means unusual in respect of the gulf that exists between procurement operations carried out throughout a typical higher education institution and what would be regarded as effective control of stores.

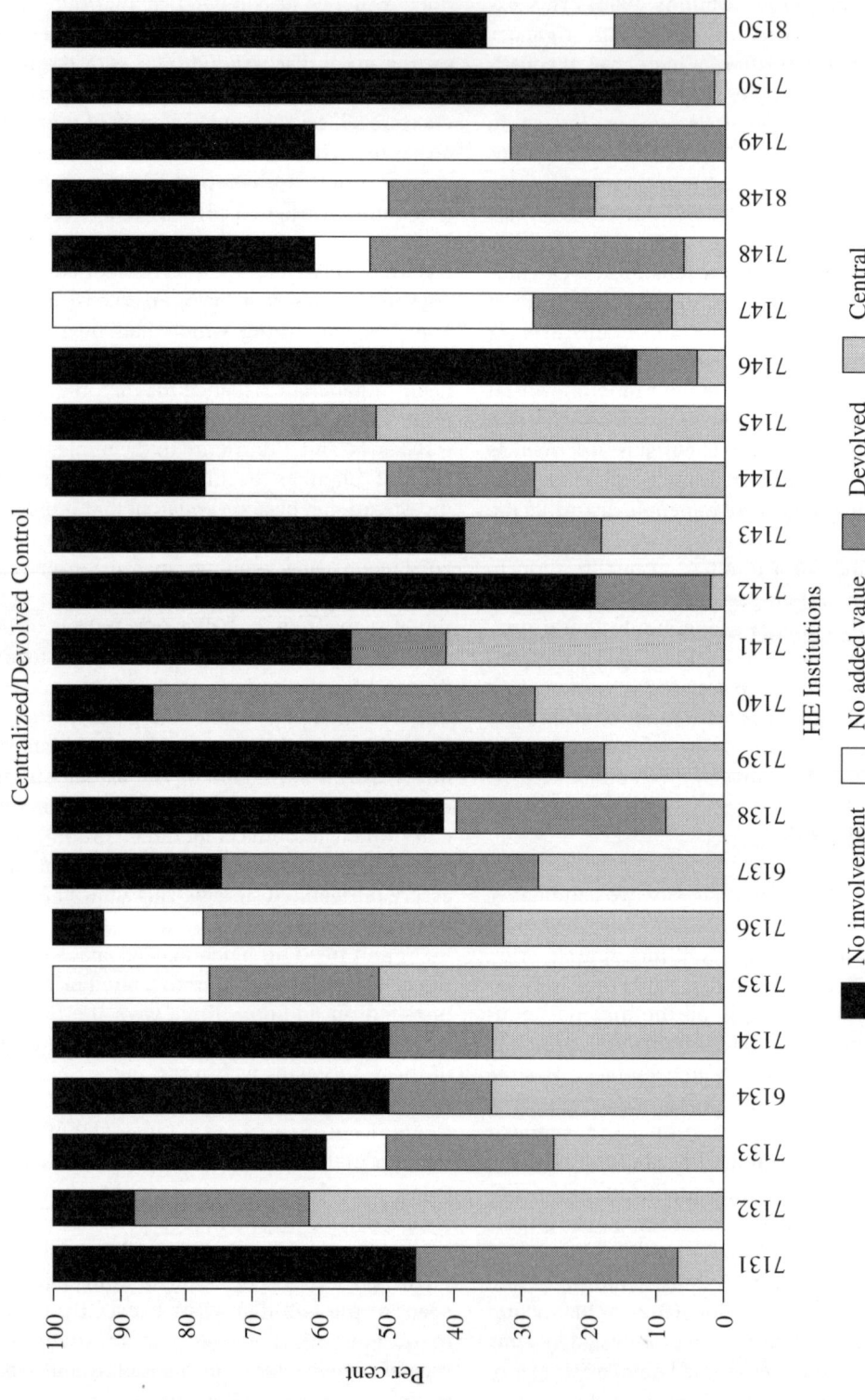

Figure 12.1 Involvement of procurement in HE institutes' spend

The key appears to be hidden somewhere in the proposition that the less the involvement, or the perceived importance, of the specialist procurement function, the less attention is paid to that particular aspect of the job of the person with spend responsibilities. It is evident that further research will be needed in order to test this proposition. Recently a survey carried out by the Joint Procurement Policy and Strategy Group (JPPSG) revealed that, on average, purchasing centrally through the institutions' procurement officers accounted for 25 per cent of non-pay spend with a further 28 per cent of non-pay spend being authorized and sanctioned by the procurement section but devolved to legitimate sources. This leaves a staggering 47 per cent of non-pay spend being consumed without the assistance or knowledge of the procurement function. It will also be noted from Figure 12.1 that in one particular institution, identified as 7138, 58 per cent of spend, representing some £7,342,732, was spent without the involvement of or input from the procurement office. A further analysis of the significance of this research and its effect on the procurement operations in HE institutions is presented in Chapter 21.

It is not the purpose of this chapter, however, to argue for more centralization of the spending activity. Indeed the whole thrust and focus of the training strategy is to encourage greater devolved authority. Nevertheless devolved buying activity can only occur when those to whom the responsibility is transferred are competent and committed, and are working with the procurement function in a culture of mutual respect and recognition of the worth of the personnel, sharing the common goal of greater value for money.

The second action classified by Adams is identified as 'leaving the field'. A person may try to find a new situation with a more favourable balance of inputs and outputs, for example, by absenteeism, requesting a transfer, resigning from a post or from an organization. Again there have been many instances of this occurring in the public sector. Indeed at an IPSERA (International Purchasing and Supply Education and Research Association) workshop held in September 1997 reports were received which claimed

that an exodus of highly trained procurement professionals was threatening to undermine government plans to implement best practice in public sector purchasing. It would be easy to point to economic considerations as the culprit for this situation but pay levels are only one factor in the equation. Brian Rigby, director of the Treasury's Procurement Group, is quoted as saying: 'It's not simply a matter of higher wages, it's a number of things, including where procurement professionals fit into the structure of government, their reporting structure and career development' (Davis 1997). This view is echoed by Theresa Nash who, at the time, was chair of the Association of University Purchasing Officers (AUPO) and purchasing manager of the University of East London. She identified major problems in recruiting and retaining procurement staff at all levels but particularly with people in the middle ranks of the organization. The suggestion is made that people from within the procurement office tend to move on following a period of training, and if this trend is going to be addressed it will have to take account of career prospects (Edwards 1998). An alternative scenario has been reported by the Boots the Chemists chain. Boots piloted retailing NVQs in 100 stores from mid-1989 to mid-1990 and reported a 14 per cent reduction in staff turnover in comparison to their other stores (Erridge and Perry 1993).

TRAINING STRATEGY

As stated above, it is not the intention of this chapter to argue for greater centralization of the authority to buy. Indeed, if it is the intention of HE institutions to seek to continually improve the productive use of physical, material and financial resources it is inevitable that greater devolution of responsibility will occur (Syson 1992). The recipients of this responsibility will however be relying on information supplied by highly trained professional businesspeople who can demonstrate awareness not just within the confines of material acquisition but of the strategic development of procurement as it relates to wider public sector procurement. The role and skills profile of the procurement officer must change to become more facilitative (van Weele and Rozemeijer 1996). This contention leads one to the conclusion that within HE institutions beyond the year 2000 two types of buyer will be found. The first is the composite business manager working closely with outside agencies in co-operative procurement strategies developing long term strategic plans to bring about long term benefits to the individual institutions by harnessing the leverage that a £3 billion plus spend can bring about. Within this first group there will be individuals with varying levels of competence and commitment ranging from the experienced senior officer to the new recruit. The second type of buyer will be found in various departments throughout every institution. This group of buyer will carry the responsibility of ensuring continuity of supply to their departments at ever increasing customer service levels. Recognized as key members of the department, they will continually analyse the effectiveness of their individual/departmental performance and stocking policies with a view to improving them, perhaps aided by closer communication with other departmental buyers. Again, there will be different people with different skill levels due to job requirements, for example the member of staff who is engaged on procurement for only part of her time or staff with senior management potential for whom a procurement job is one of several in their career progression.

Of course if the institutions are ever going to experience this utopia they have to recognize that there is a price to pay. That price is their commitment to provide meaningful, focused training tailored to individual needs and designed to bring about the precise competencies required to carry out their supply staff's identified duties. If this commitment is to be rewarded with highly skilled, committed staff, the training has to be meaningful and realistic to the individual.

> Vocational and professional qualifications are not like Olympic medals; they have value only if they are useful in the context of employment. Employees will find a qualification useful if it

is recognized and valued by employers. An employer will recognize and value a qualification if it is useful when taking human resource management and development decisions in selection, training and development, remuneration and rewards, promotion and so on (Holmes 1992 p. 37).

In order to build quality assurance into the scheme, all training has to be based on set standards of competence which will allow benchmarking to take place, both within the individual institution and across institutions. That is not to suggest that these standards are the only or the full answer to training requirements or that they are without problems in regard to the precision of language (Ramsay 1993), but they do set down a minimum level of competence which allows for valid and accurate assessment to take place.

KEY OBJECTIVES

Over the past three years much research has been carried out into the best way of training procurement staff. Having spent many years delivering training packages to a wide variety of organizations I have come to the conclusion that relying on a syllabus-based course of instruction where knowledge and understanding is tested summatively may not be the most effective use of resources for people who are already operating within a procurement environment. In addition to the cost, which can be prohibitive, the course itself is by necessity not specific to a particular individual's needs for competence enhancement. This conclusion has been reached by an analysis of candidate questionnaires carried out at the Central College of Commerce in Glasgow over a period of several years. Candidates were of mixed ability and from a variety of commercial backgrounds. In essence, they all found value in a traditional Chartered Institute of Purchasing and Supply course but few could relate their new knowledge to the practicalities of the job when they returned from the training course. Therefore the overriding consideration must be relevance to the principal duties and tasks expected of an institutional buyer or stock manager. These fundamental tasks are listed randomly below and are the product of discussions with university personnel at both senior procurement and operational levels.

1. To evaluate current procurement objectives and develop procurement operations to meet future objectives.
2. To create and maintain a purchasing research service from which strategic purchasing strategies may be developed.
3. To evaluate and monitor supplier capability and performance and to develop effective assessment tools, such as vendor rating systems.
4. To develop a user-friendly enquiry procedure system for use in the sourcing decisions of the internal customers.
5. To develop the necessary negotiating skills to act on behalf of the institution in order to achieve best value from the supplier base.

These five areas are not intended to be definitive but form the basis on which practitioners can continue to develop their purchasing and management competencies. Competence is not just about performing tasks or possessing knowledge. It also includes how individuals manage their time and work activity, how they relate to others, how they engage in planning activities and create solutions to problems as well as engaging with aspects of their work role (Warren and Reid 1996).

Examination of the available Standards of Competence published by the PSLB reveals five units which match the objectives stated above. These are as follows:

PSLB Procurement Level III

014   Monitor and evaluate supplier performance and continuity of supply
015   Contribute to the establishment and evaluation of current and future requirements for supply
016   Negotiate improvements in supplier performance

PSLB Procurement Level IV

017   Provide commercial input to decision making

018   Develop the effectiveness of procurement operations

It is suggested that individuals could use these standards as a template to match their own skills with those required by the standards. If a skill gap can be identified, the offer of professional training should be in place to rectify the situation. Using National Vocational Qualification (NVQ) Standards allows the individual to analyse how well he/she is performing in relation to the performance standard, in other words 'benchmarking' his/her competence. It is not the intention here to suggest that everyone involved within the procurement function in HE institutions would be required to prove their competence as a part of professional development, but highly skilled purchasing practitioners could, and should, be utilized as mentors to assist those less competent to improve using the standards as the catalyst. It should also be borne in mind that the primary intention is not merely to gain personal awards, although it is recognized that there is some merit in encouraging staff to complete a full award at Level III or Level IV in Procurement from an awarding body such as the Oxford and Cambridge Royal Society of Arts. Training need not be expensive if developed in a systematic manner which allows professional development to occur at a pace dictated by the individual and where support and professional guidance are always available.

THE JOINT PROCUREMENT POLICY AND STRATEGY GROUP (JPPSG) TRAINING MODEL

The JPPSG as a steering group is charged with the responsibility of improving procurement practices in further and higher educational institutions. A major part of the strategy is to encourage an increase in the competence of the procurement and supplies function through training. The JPPSG recognizes that there exists considerable variance in competence within the targeted clientele and in order to address this an equally varied programme is available. This includes the whole range of NVQs, seminars and workshops carried out by a number of highly experienced procurement practitioners and educationalists. This national programme will be reinforced by a range of advice and information pages on the JPPSG Website. As an Award Centre in its own right, the JPPSG is co-ordinating the training of procurement staff across the United Kingdom. By centralizing the function of internal verification, the group can maintain the quality of training and assessment. This is in keeping with the views expressed in the government White Paper 'Setting New Standards – a Strategy for Government Procurement' (1995) and complies with the recommendations contained within the National Audit Office Report on Higher Education Institutions in England (NAO 1999). Using the five NVQs identified above as the initial achievement point the group's aim is to encourage all procurement personnel within institutions to participate actively either by the development of portfolios of evidence that proves their competence or, in the case of suitably qualified senior procurement personnel, to assist in developing competencies in individuals under their control. Even if some potential participants feel that they are not in a position to gather sufficient evidence to complete these five units of competence, they are free to select as few as they wish. The important point is that they begin to think about self-improvement within their role.

The role of mentor is seen as being vital to the programme's success as it has two distinct purposes. First, it provides a focus that allows communication to take place within the hierarchy and assists in breaking down barriers. As communication develops, greater understanding of each others' problems is achieved and insight into the wider picture will ensue for the trainee, whilst the mentor will gain a greater depth of knowledge about the operations of the trainee's department. Second, it provides an opportunity for the mentor to think carefully about what is happening in the procurement procedures and how best to co-ordinate these procedures in light of the new knowledge gained from the trainee. Most educationalists would agree with the sentiment that one never really understands a concept until one has explained it to others. A spin-off benefit of this is that the mentor may, if he/she so wishes, apply to the JPPSG to complete a teaching qualification from the Training and Development Lead Body (TDLB) for standards D32 and D33 to become an assessor in his/her own right. In institutions where it is not possible to have a mentor, an assessor is assigned to that institution by the JPPSG. This is very much in keeping with the Chartered Institute of Purchasing and Supply philosophy of continuing professional development (CPD).

BENEFITS

Procurement training is an investment in the future of all universities and colleges. With a combined spend approaching £4 billion of what is largely public money, it is vital that the procurement function has proactive, highly skilled businesspeople planning for long term benefits. Richard Houghton, operations director for Macfarlan Smith, supported this view at a recent interview when he said that:

> …training is almost more important than savings – it is a bedrock for the future. Building these core (business skills) competencies is the key to long term success. The way you should look at it is that you have raised the profile, done the training. To borrow a phrase, you have changed the game (Edwards 1998).

Examples of the benefits accruing to individuals and organizations that have occurred over the past three years supports Houghton's views. The old saying that training the staff trains the organization is even more pertinent than ever for HE institutions.

CASE STUDY 2

John is in charge of a large chemical store that supplies one of the biggest faculties in a large university. Now in his mid-thirties, he has been in charge for several years and has built up a considerable wealth of knowledge about how the operation works. The vast majority of his spend is devolved from the procurement office agreements which had been put out to tender. This leaves John with the responsibility for ordering, inspecting and controlling the issuing. He was approached by his director of procurement who suggested that he might benefit from having a look at some of the NVQ units in procurement at Level III. John agreed to give it a try and, with assistance from his mentor, discussed suitable sources of evidence for his chosen units. One of the units that he selected was 'Monitor and evaluate supplier performance and continuity of supply', the first element of which was to assess the supplier's capability to supply. In order to do this, John realized that he would have to create some sort of checklist or vendor rating system. This he developed, with some assistance on the more technical areas of sourcing, from the procurement director. Although this particular contract was complex due to the fact that its value was a significant six-figure sum, John developed a practical checklist which he now uses to monitor other suppliers. He no longer relies on the claims of company representatives that they would have no difficulty in giving him what he ordered at an agreed delivery schedule performance. The result is that the stores operation has benefited from higher service levels to users through the correct selection of suitable suppliers.

The second element of this unit focuses on ongoing supplier performance. Here again, it had never been the practice of stores to keep such records other than some notes to ensure part-deliveries were topped up as per the original order. John started using a simple computer program into which he systematically entered all relevant details of key suppliers' performance. A hard copy of this was offered as evidence of competence in his portfolio. Some months passed before John was invited to a meeting with the director of procurement and a key supplier concerning the renewal of the contract. The supplier claimed performance levels in excess of 90 per cent based on figures supplied by his company. In the past these figures would have been accepted but John was able to produce detailed figures which indicated a significantly lower standard of performance clearly showing the discrepancies where part-

deliveries were claimed as complete deliveries. Once again the power of accurate record-keeping was being demonstrated and was rewarded by a better deal with the supplier. John admitted that he had also felt pleased to contribute in such a practical manner. In addition to this benefit, the function itself was perceived to have grown in importance to the extent that a partial organizational restructuring exercise was implemented resulting in John no longer reporting to the faculty manager but directly to the director of finance with the tangible benefit of promotion and salary increase.

CASE STUDY 3

Universities spend considerable amounts fitting out and maintaining student accommodation. In one university it was surprising to discover that the section charged with this responsibility had no trained procurement personnel on its staff. Following an offer by the procurement officer to assist in coaching a member of staff in this section towards gaining a Level III award, Liz volunteered although she feared that she might not have the abilities demanded of the standards. One of the first benefits which became apparent to the assessor was the increased confidence with which she discussed her portfolio and, as the assessor observed, the positive approach that she now used when dealing with her internal customers. Whilst in the past she would accept a requisition from a hall of residence supervisor without question, she now began to ask for clarification and make alternative suggestions. A case in point was when she was requested to purchase an ice-making machine by brand for the sum of £599 plus VAT. Liz contacted the supervisor to clarify the precise details, such as why this brand and why had the supplier been identified? The answer lay with historical data from some two years ago when the supervisor had need of such a machine in another hall. He had noted in a recent catalogue the details and had copied them out onto the requisition. Liz had been working on unit 'Contribute to the establishment and evaluation of current and future requirements for supply', and so used this opportunity to gather evidence of good sourcing practice. She collated information on a few machines basing her selection on the specification outlined in the 'branded' item and presented the supervisor with a choice of three machines together with a recommendation for a particular one which carried with it an extended free warranty. In due course the user agreed with the recommendation and a similar machine was purchased which had all the features of the original choice but cost £422 including VAT. Liz is now investigating further reductions by carrying out a standardization programme on this type of product. Admittedly the savings to the university are small in an individual case but when one considers the wider picture, savings could be considerable, as even this example demonstrates a 30 per cent reduction in material cost.

Both these cases involved employees at major universities at a Level III standard. John, however, has now completed his award and is now working towards a full Level IV award and a CIPS Diploma. Level IV operates at a strategic level and many sceptics claim that this level is inappropriate to HE institutions. However, many large corporations in the private sector have similar hierarchical organizational structures. Consider the following case.

CASE STUDY 4

David works as a purchaser at a power station and has been with the company for a number of years. His organization is split into three autonomous divisions and operates a centralized purchasing policy for strategic issues from its headquarters in the west of Scotland. David completed a Level III award in early 1998 and was keen to build a portfolio of evidence for a Level IV award. The assessor discussed ways in which this would be possible utilizing a forthcoming rationalization programme of the procurement function within the whole division. The unit 'Develop the effectiveness of procurement operations' requires the candidate to establish key objectives such as cost-saving targets and to review and improve the effectiveness of procurement operations. David was being asked to reduce the cost of ongoing maintenance at

the time and decided to focus on ongoing maintenance contracts as there was a significant spend attached to this area. He discovered that subcontractors were buying components from suppliers and then passing on this expense to his company. Obviously there was little incentive to seek low prices as the contract was of a cost plus nature. David identified the components being used and sent out an enquiry to his own suppliers to establish if they held the type of goods required by the subcontractors. He negotiated an agreement that the subcontractors would get the same discounts as his own company if they were working for his company. Copies of invoices were to be sent to him direct as a check that the correct pricing system was in operation. He then informed the subcontractors of his discovery and persuaded them to buy from his company's suppliers or to use them as a benchmark. The cost of the next contract was several thousand pounds lower as a consequence. His company has now formally adopted this strategy into its purchasing procedures.

CONCLUSION

The report on HE procurement by the National Audit Office (NAO 1999) acknowledged that universities were improving their procurement operations but that the pace of change was unacceptably slow. It is suggested that a principal driver for change is a systematic and comprehensive method of training that will meet the challenge of effective procurement in universities in the new millennium. Specifically there are three areas which will be addressed by the training initiative discussed above. These are cost reduction, improved customer service levels and supplier development.

We have seen from the case studies why it is important to train the personnel on the ground who are actually spending the money, and also why the purchasing specialist should be closely involved at the earliest stages of developing both the systems and the person, in order that greater understanding and mutual respect may be allowed to develop. One of the principal recommendations made by the NAO was 'All institutions should ensure that they have the right skills to procure goods and services effectively by identifying and assessing the training needs of staff with procurement responsibilities and developing a training programme ... to address their needs'. It is therefore argued that the close interaction between NVQ trainee and mentor allows the trainee to develop the precise skills required to develop tailor-made solutions to problems within his/her own working environment.

The case studies all show that improvements were made in at least one of the areas. In case study 4 it was the need for evidence of strategic development that produced a new approach and developed the supplier relationship. This approach, now rolled out across the entire company, has had a significant impact on ongoing maintenance costs. In case study 1, customer service levels improved through the need to communicate properly with customers and thoroughly understand their requirements. A cost saving was achieved through using consignment stocking which came from a suggestion made by the director of procurement who was acting as mentor. An additional benefit was that the two operatives changed their perspective of procurement and realized that it was a critical part of the job which could bring benefits if carried out properly. John, in case study 2, also achieved a great deal by analysing supplier performance and in common with Liz, in case study 3, not only reduced costs but developed a greater sense of self-esteem and confidence. They both now regard themselves as professional people working in a commercial environment.

All the above cases demonstrate that using NVQs brings tangible benefits to both the individual and the organization. Some of these benefits to institutions can be measured in cash terms but, just as importantly, they will also bring other benefits. Even if institutions do not wish their employees to complete a full award, it is still possible for employers to select units, from the 54 available, which provide a comprehensive definition of the jobs individuals hold and the competencies they need. This forms the basis of a training strategy tailored to the individual as well as providing the means to measure competence throughout the life of the programme.

The overall mission of the JPPSG is to make procurement more effective by encouraging more efficient use of existing resources. These resources include supply staff, who should be well trained and highly motivated. Whether the staff involved in procurement are dealing with million pound contracts in conjunction with other universities and groups of universities, and have strong career ambitions, or whether they are to be found operating and controlling a fast-moving store within an institution, they will share a common need. That need is to be valued, respected and, perhaps above all, to be 'seen' by the organization. Only then will staff realize that their efforts to improve have been worthwhile.

REFERENCES

Chadwick, T. and Rajagopal, S. (1995), *Strategic Supply Management*, Oxford: Butterworth Heinemann.

Crabb, S. (1998), 'Higher education faces qualification shake-up', *Supply Management*, 24 September, p. 12.

Davis, P. (1997), 'PPD to plug brain drain', *Supply Management*, 16 October, p. 10.

Edwards, N. (1998), 'Preventative medicine', *Supply Management*, 10 September, p. 30.

Edwards. N. (1998), 'Is there a skills shortage', *Supply Management*, 15 January, p. 37.

Erridge, A. and Perry, S. (1993), 'The validity and value of vocational qualification in purchasing', *Proceedings of the 2nd PSERG Conference*, Bath, pp. 257–267.

Gadde, L-E and Hakansson, H. (1993), *Professional Purchasing*, London: Routledge.

Holmes, L. (1992), 'Taking the lead on professional standards', *Personnel Management*, November, pp. 36-39.

Littlefield, D. (1998), 'H.R. within purchasing', *Supply Management*, 2 July, p. 24.

Mullins, L.J. (1994), *Management and Organizational Behaviour*, London: Pitman.

National Audit Office (1999), *Procurement in the English Higher Education Sector*, London: Stationery Office.

Parsons, W. (1997), 'Flushed with success', *Supply Management*, 17 July, p. 40.

Ramsay, J. (1993), 'Competencies: the threat to the purchasing profession', *Proceedings of the 2nd PSERG Conference*, Bath, pp. 287–297.

Syson, R. (1992), *Improving Purchasing Performance*, London: Pitman.

Treasury (1995), *Setting New Standards – a Strategy for Government Procurement*, London: HMSO.

Varley, P. (1998), 'What's the story?, *Supply Management*, 22 October, p. 36.

Warren, G. and Reid, W. (1996), *National Standards of Competence – Procurement*, Purchasing and Supply Lead Body.

van Weele, A.J. and Rozemeijer, F.A. (1996), *Revolution in Purchasing*, Eindhoven: Eindhoven University of Technology/Philips Electronics, Corporate Purchasing.

CHAPTER THIRTEEN

A cross-sector comparison of purchasing team use

P. Fraser Johnson, Michiel R. Leenders, Robert D. Klassen and Harold E. Fearon

Many companies are moving away from organization structures based on functional silos, rethinking their traditional approaches toward organizational design (Rahul 1995). These companies have compressed their organizational structures and made them more cross-functional in an effort to streamline decision-making, lower overheads and improve responsiveness. Part of the process of rethinking corporate organizational approaches has included new people-management philosophies. A consequence of these changes has been that the role of purchasing has moved more closely in line with key business processes, facilitated by expanding the use of teams (Ellram and Pearson 1993; Trent 1996). For example, some organizations are using cross-functional teams as a means of involving purchasing personnel in key business activities such as product development and customer service.

Based on a sample of 269 large North American supply organizations, this chapter examines the use of seven different approaches to team-based purchasing: purchasing councils, supplier councils, commodity teams, cross-functional teams, teams involving suppliers, teams involving customers, and teams involving both suppliers and customers. It examines whether certain combinations of teams tend to be more common and whether certain types of teams are used more frequently in the service, process and discrete goods industries. In doing so, the following research questions are addressed:

1. Are there patterns of use for different forms of purchasing teams?

2. What differences exist between service, discrete goods and process industries with respect to purchasing team use?
3. Does firm size influence the use of purchasing teams?
4. Does organizational structure influence the use of purchasing teams?

It was hoped that by addressing the research questions information could be learned about how firms use purchasing teams.

CONCEPTUAL DEVELOPMENT

This section will discuss the concept of purchasing teams and their usage, along with related issues.

PURCHASING TEAMS

The motivation to use purchasing teams is well established. First, teams can combine the skills and resources of several stakeholders, spanning multiple functions or sub-units, to facilitate the timely completion of a project. Purchasing teams therefore promote inter-functional co-operation and offer benefits as a result of the range of skills, knowledge and capabilities of their members (Ellram and Pearson 1993). Second, purchasing teams may only be assembled temporarily, and their members might have commitments elsewhere (Ancona 1990). Third, teams are frequently created to focus resources and energy on the completion of a particular assignment with the expressed motivation to produce a specific outcome that will benefit the organization, such as managing a new product launch or implementing a reduction in cycle times (Denison et al. 1996). Previous research has suggested a trend towards greater use of purchasing teams in the future (Ellram and Pearson 1993).

Much of the research on purchasing teams has tended to focus on factors related to cross-functional team performance. However, there are a number of other team-based approaches that organizations can use for purchasing. For example, teams may be inter-functional, as opposed to cross-functional, such as purchasing councils. Many firms use purchasing councils as a means of sharing information among de-centralized units or co-ordinating activities focused on a specific problem which impacts on several supply groups. Purchasing councils are usually composed of purchasing managers and buyers, and only involve staff from other areas as needed (Leenders and Fearon 1997).

Purchasing teams can also be focused externally, including other supply chain stakeholders, such as suppliers and customers, or both. The benefits of co-operative supply chain relationships include lower channel-wide inventories, increased service reliability, reduced product development times and costs, and better quality (Cooper and Ellram 1993; Birou and Fawcett 1994; Dyer 1996). There are several documented situations where firms such as Du Pont, Hewlett-Packard, Procter & Gamble and 3M have used supply chain management principles to improve their competitive position (Davis 1993; Cooper and Ellram 1993; Cottrill 1997; Lambert et al. 1998). However, the ability of firms to structure and manage long term co-operative relationships with customers and suppliers, and sometimes competitors, can influence the success of their supply chain initiative (Bechtel and Jayanth 1997).

PURCHASING TEAM USE

Much of the research, in both the supply and organizational behaviour literature, relates to factors associated with successful team implementation and effectiveness. Leadership, reward systems, conflict resolution processes, team identity and performance measurement have been identified as important determinants of successful team management (Trent and Monczka 1994; Denison, et al. 1996).

In order to conduct such research, investigators pre-select firms that use certain team-based approaches, such as cross-functional purchasing teams. As described previously, however, firms have a number of alternatives with respect to the types of team-based purchasing techniques that they can use as part of their organizational approaches. Other than research by Fearon and Leenders (1995), little attention has been paid to the extent that these purchasing teams are used. Furthermore, there has been no research that investigates how firms approach team use by combining various forms of purchasing teams as a method of influencing team or firm performance.

INDUSTRY SECTOR ISSUES

Contingency theory asserts that firm performance and survival is dependent on the fit or alignment between its organization structure, strategy and contingency variables, such as technology, size and environmental uncertainty (Powell 1992; Galunic and Eisenhardt 1994). The economics literature suggests a similar relationship based on the market structure–conduct–performance paradigm (Scherer and Ross 1990). Contingency theory would therefore suggest that organizational approaches will change depending on the contingencies faced by a firm. Furthermore, firms within industry segments will face common external contingencies.

The use of purchasing teams can be an important element of a firm's organization and its approach to supply chain management. Team use would vary across industry segments, as firms adjust their organizational practices to accommodate different contingent variables. However, previous research has not explored the relationship between industry sector and purchasing team use.

It is entirely likely, however, that firms within the same industry sectors might choose different organization structures. Internal contingencies, such as size and technology, can also influence organizational design, and ultimately the use of purchasing teams. Consequently, in addition to sector and size, organization struc- ture could also influence purchasing team use.

SAMPLE

A mail survey was used to collect data for this study from large North American organizations. In May 1995, surveys were mailed to 556 US firms, selected from the Fortune 500 list of serv- ice and manufacturing firms, together with 46 organizations selected from a list provided by the Purchasing Management Association of Canada. Overall, 21 different industry sectors were represented.

It was necessary to classify respondents in the manufacturing industry sectors as members of either process or discrete goods industries. The classification system was made on the basis of evaluations of firms in the sample by two re- searchers. Firms classified in the process indus- try group were from the paper, chemicals, petroleum, primary metal, lumber, rubber and stone sectors. Firms classified in the discrete goods group were from the electronic, trans- portation products, aerospace, apparel, furni- ture, fabricated metal, industrial machinery and instruments sectors. The final sample included 70 service industry firms, 94 process industry firms and 105 discrete goods industry firms, for a total of 269, representing a response rate of 45 per cent.

FINDINGS

The next section of this chapter will explore the findings of the above survey.

PURCHASING TEAM USE

Most research in the organizational science and purchasing literatures focuses on a single method of team use, cross-functional sourcing teams. However, the purchasing literature in- cludes references to many different types of team-based purchasing methods (Leenders and Fearon 1997). For the purposes of this research, the seven types of team-based purchasing tech- niques as listed at the start of this chapter were identified. Firms were asked to rate their level of use of each when performing the purchasing

function on a five point scale. Table 13.1 sum- marizes the mean scores for each of the seven purchasing team methods.

The literature suggests that team-based pur- chasing is expanding – a reflection of flatter and leaner organizations and the benefits of cross- functional input into decisions (Ellram and Pearson 1993; Carter and Narasimhan 1996). However, the reported level of use of team-based purchasing techniques was lower than antici- pated, indicating that many firms are still hesi- tant to use purchasing teams extensively. The respondents cited cross-functional purchasing teams, commodity teams and purchasing coun- cils as the most frequently used team-based pur- chasing techniques. Supplier councils and teams involving both suppliers and customers had very low reported levels of use.

Table 13.1 Purchasing team use

	Mean[†]	Rank	n
Purchasing councils (purchasing managers only)	2.91	3	267
Supplier councils (primarily key suppliers)	2.32	6	267
Commodity teams (purchasing personnel only)	3.11	2	265
Cross-functional teams	3.59	1	268
Teams involving supplier(s)	2.82	4	268
Teams involving customer(s)	2.58	5	267
Teams involving both supplier(s) and customer(s)	2.11	7	267

[†] 1 = none, 2 = slight, 3 = moderate, 4 = substantial, 5 = extensive

Exploratory factor analysis was used to classify the seven team-based purchasing techniques and analyse the patterns of relationships. An oblique, Promax rotation was chosen for this analysis based on its ability to provide more meaningful analysis (Hair et al. 1995). Results from the exploratory factor analysis are provided in Table 13.2.

Based on the factor analysis, two groups of purchasing teams were identified. The first group was labelled 'internal teams' and con- sisted of purchasing councils, supplier councils, commodity teams and cross-functional teams.

Table 13.2 Results of factor analysis

Variable	Factor 1	Factor 2
Purchasing councils	0.790	−0.232
Supplier councils	0.568	0.153
Commodity teams	0.824	−0.097
Cross-functional teams	0.579	0.215
Teams involving suppliers	0.436	0.523
Teams involving customers	−0.129	0.921
Teams involving both suppliers and customers	−0.052	0.937
Cronbach Alpha	0.6604	0.7828

The second group was labelled 'external teams' and included teams involving suppliers, teams involving customers, and teams involving both suppliers and customers.

All factor loadings exceeded the 0.50 level to be considered practically significant (Hair et al. 1995). Reliability coefficients were then calculated for each factor. The reliability coefficient of 0.7828 for the external teams factor exceeded the value of 0.70 recommended for basic research (Nunnally and Berstein 1994). Although the reliability coefficient for the internal factor was 0.6604, below the recommended threshold, it was considered adequate for the purposes of exploratory research. The following discussion addresses the implications of the two factors.

INTERNAL PURCHASING TEAMS FACTOR

The internal teams factor included four team-based purchasing techniques. The common element among these team-based activities is that they are concentrated and organized within the firm. Purchasing councils are generally comprised of senior purchasing staff from within the company and are established to facilitated co-ordination among departments, divisions or plants (Leenders and Fearon 1997). Supplier councils are typically made up of 10 to 15 senior executives from the company's preferred supplier base along with six to eight of the buying firm's top management. Supplier councils usually meet two to four times per year, and deal with purchasing policy issues at the buying firm with the objective of improving supply performance and supplier communication (Dobler and Burt 1996). Commodity teams are formed

when a commodity represents a significant annual expense, its acquisition is viewed as complex, and it is regarded as critical to the firm's success. Commodity teams can be at group-, divisional- or corporate-level, and may include personnel from other departments, such as finance, quality or engineering (Leenders and Fearon 1997). Cross-functional purchasing teams consist of personnel from at least three different functional areas brought together to complete a purchasing or materials management assignment (Trent and Monczka 1994).

EXTERNAL PURCHASING TEAMS FACTOR

The external teams factor consisted of three team-based purchasing techniques. Teams involving suppliers, customers, or suppliers and customers are used when communication between the buying firm and its key supply chain partners is critical for the successful completion of an important major initiative. Such teams can be formed to promote a number of outcomes, including better supplier responsiveness or new product development (Leenders and Fearon 1997).

The techniques that made up the internal teams factor focused mainly on combining internal and external organizational resources to improve the supply performance of the buying firm. Techniques associated with the external teams factor was concerned with broader supply chain issues that also might affect the supplier and/or customer. Internal teams are useful for activities unrelated to the buying firm's external partners, such as supplier selection and evaluation. External teams are also effective at dealing with supply chain issues, such as total cost of ownership and improving responsiveness by shortening product development lead times.

INDUSTRY SECTOR AND INTERNAL TEAM USE

The second research question focused on differences between service, discrete goods and process industries with respect to purchasing team use. The moderating effects of firm sales and organization structure were also included in this analysis.

For the purposes of this research, team use was based on the two factor variables, internal teams and external teams. Firm sales was used to measure firm size, and organization structure was based on a self-reported classification of decentralized, hybrid or centralized. Since the data for each of the independent variables was categorical, the analysis of variance (ANOVA) procedure was used to test the model presented in Figure 13.1.

Table 13.3 provides the results from the analysis for internal team use and Table 13.4 provides the mean values of internal purchasing team use. The effect of industry sector and size on the use of internal teams was statistically significant. The effect of structure on firm size was not found to be statistically significant. None of the interaction effects between the independent variables was found to be statistically significant.

Service and process industry firms reported similar levels of internal team use, and discrete goods firms reported higher levels of internal team use compared to the service and process industry firms (p # 0.01). This finding supports the expectation that discrete goods firms use internal teams to a greater extent than process industry firms, due to issues associated with product life cycles and product complexity.

While process industry firms can use internal purchasing teams to help control costs, the consistency of their product base lessens the need for activities such as cross-functional sourcing teams for new products, compared to discrete goods firms.

The cost of purchased goods and services is typically much higher for discrete goods firms than for service firms. Consequently there is a stronger incentive for discrete goods firms to make use of internal teams to control the costs and quality of raw materials and services acquired from suppliers.

Contingency theory suggests that firm size can influence its organization structure. The findings from this research found that firm size affected team use. The firms in the over $5 billion sales group reported the highest level of use of internal teams, while the firms in the under $1 billion sales group reported the lowest level of internal team use. The mean difference between these two groups was statistically significant (p # 0.01). Similarly, firms in the $1 billion–$5 billion sales group reported higher levels of internal team use compared to the low sales group. This difference was also statistically significant (p # 0.01). While the high sales group reported higher marginal means for use of internal purchasing teams compared to the medium sales group, the differences were not statistically significant.

INDUSTRY SECTOR AND EXTERNAL TEAM USE

Table 13.5 shows the results from the analysis for external team use and Table 13.6 shows the means of external purchasing team use. In addition to the main effects, the statistically significant interaction effects are also reported.

Table 13.3   General linear model: internal teams

Variable	Df	Mean Square	F	Sig. F
Sector	2	7.211	12.415**	0.000
Size	2	6.199	10.673**	0.000
Structure	2	0.326	0.722	0.722

n = 258
r² = 0.152

†p # 0.10
*p # 0.05
**p # 0.01

Table 13.4   Mean values of internal purchasing team use

	Sector Marginal Means	S.E.		Size Marginal Means	S.E.		Structure Marginal Means	S.E.
Services	2.68	0.101	<$1 billion	2.57	0.092	Centralized	2.92	0.112
Process	2.76	0.088	$1–5 billion	2.99	0.087	Hybrid	2.95	0.060
Discrete	3.23	0.085	>$5 billion	3.17	0.095	Decentralized	2.83	0.134

The effect of industry sector on external team use was only marginally significant (p = 0.093) while the effect of size was found to be statistically significant (p # 0.05). Services reported the mean levels of use of external teams, while process industry firms reported the lowest levels of use. The differences between these two groups were statistically significant (p # 0.05). Service firms, which must interact with customers in the delivery of their finished product, have a strong motivation to include external partners in purchasing activities. However, many of the important purchases for process industry firms related to commodities, which are standardized. The mean level of use of external teams for discrete goods firms was not significantly different from either service or process industry firms.

Not surprisingly, firm size was found to affect external team use. As with internal teams, the means were ordered as expected. The high sales group was statistically significant from the low sales group. The differences between the means for the medium sales group and the other two sales groups were not statistically significant. Size influences both the capacity to dedicate resources to purchasing initiatives with external partners and the ability to gain the attention of

supply chain partners. Customers and suppliers are most likely to react to initiatives for teaming from their largest supply chain partners, while suggestions for better co-operation from smaller firms might not receive an enthusiastic reaction.

Two interaction effects were also found to be statistically significant; size and sector, and structure and sector. Figure 13.1 provides the plot for the interaction of size and sector. The levels of external team use are low and focused within a narrow range at the low sales level and diverge as sales increase. The reported use of external teams for service firms increases dramatically from the low to medium sales group, where it levels off. It would appear that most of the small firms in the study, regardless of industry sector, used external teams to the same extent. For the service firms in the study, increasing sales over $1 billion appears to have influenced external team use. For discrete goods firms, the increase in use of external teams was more uniform. The progression for service and process firms was similar in terms of its overall increase between the low and high sales group. This is probably due to the fact that differences exist between large service and discrete goods firms. Service firms tend to be labour intensive, while discrete goods firms depend to a greater extent on capital equipment and purchased goods and services. Consequently, service firms with sales of $1 billion to $5 billion (that is, the medium sales group) might be regarded as industry leaders, while this is less likely to be the case for firms in the discrete goods industries. Consequently, the interaction effect in Figure 13.1 can suggest that the ability to initiate supply chain teams may be dependent on industry leadership.

Table 13.5   General linear model: external teams

Variable	Df	Mean Square	F	Sig. F
Sector	2	1.689	2.403[†]	0.093
Size	2	2.672	3.801*	0.024
Structure	2	1.034	1.471	0.232
Sales × Sector	4	1.736	2.470*	0.045
Structure × Sector	4	2.113	3.006*	0.019

n = 262
r^2 = 0.178

[†]p # 0.10
*p # 0.05
**p # 0.01

Table 13.6   Mean values of external purchasing team use

	Sector Marginal Means	S.E.		Size Marginal Means	S.E.		Structure Marginal Means	S.E.
Services	2.70	0.171	<$1 billion	2.24	0.120	Centralized	2.71	0.129
Process	2.27	0.116	$1–5 billion	2.55	0.123	Hybrid	2.58	0.068
Discrete	2.55	0.115	>$5 billion	2.75	0.140	Decentralized	2.18	0.196

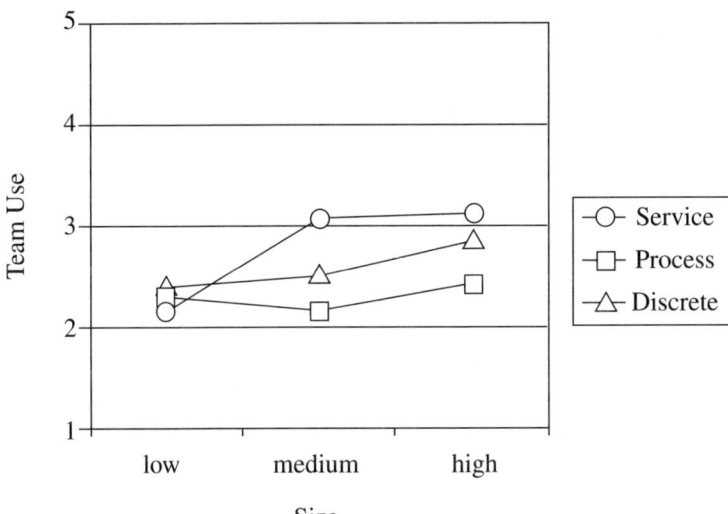

Figure 13.1 Interaction size and sector

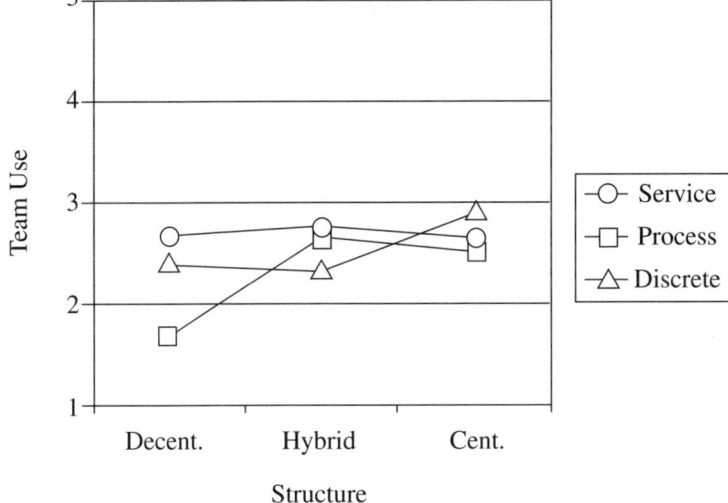

Figure 13.2 Interaction structure and industry sector

Figure 13.2 provides a plot of the interaction effect of structure and industry sector. An important observation here is the low level of use of external teams by decentralized process industry firms. It would appear that centralized co-ordination is especially important for process industry firms in order to co-ordinate purchasing teams with external supply chain partners.

CONCLUSIONS

This research has explored the influence of industry sector, organization structure and firm size on purchasing team use. Factor analysis was used to classify seven team-based purchasing techniques into two groups; internal and external teams. Analysis indicated that sector and size were important determinants of purchasing team use for both groups. A surprising finding from this research was that organizational structure did not directly influence the level of either internal or external team use. However, this was important as an interaction effect for external teams.

Firms in the discrete goods sector demonstrated higher levels of internal purchasing team use compared to service and process industry firms. However, firms in the service sector reported highest levels of external purchasing team use compared to the other two groups. Process industry firms reported low levels of both internal and external team use. Based on these results, it appears that industry sector does influence purchasing team use, which supports the contingency view that the firm's external environment influences its organization structure. The different demands placed on firms across industry sectors appear to influence approaches taken with respect to purchasing team use. Furthermore, the contingency variable, size, also influenced the approach taken by firms regarding their use of internal and external purchasing teams, with larger firms reporting higher levels of team use. Internal teams can be used in large firms as a means of internal control and co-ordination, whereas external teams may indicate greater efforts with respect to supply chain co-ordination and co-operation.

The findings presented suggest several opportunities for future research. First, while indications are that size and sector both influence purchasing team use, how and why this occurs has not been addressed. For example, an opportunity for further research includes examining how purchasing team use is influenced in reaction to changes in the competitive environment over time. Such research could investigate the influence of both supply factors, such as raw material shortages, and non-related supply factors, such as economic or political factors, on purchasing team use. Case-based research would be an appropriate methodology by which to conduct such an investigation.

Second, if size and sector influence purchasing team use, these variables are likely to influence other organization components as well. Additional research can address the influence of these variables on issues such as chief purchasing officer reporting line relationships and span of control.

REFERENCES

Ancona, D.G. (1990), 'Outward bound: strategies for team survival in an organization', *Academy of Management Journal*, **33**(2), pp. 334–365.

Bechtel, C. and Jayanth, J. (1997), 'Supply chain management: a strategic perspective', *The International Journal of Logistics Management*, **8**(1), pp. 15–34.

Birou, L.M. and Fawcett, S.E. (1994), 'Supplier involvement in integrated product development: a comparison of US and European practices', *International Journal of Physical Distribution & Logistics Management*, **24**(5), pp. 4–15.

Carter, J.R. and Narasimhan, R. (1996), 'Is purchasing really strategic?', *International Journal of Purchasing and Materials Management*, **32**(1), pp. 20–28.

Cooper, M.C., and Ellram, L.M. (1993), 'Characteristics of supply chain management and the implications for purchasing and logistics strategy', *The International Journal of Logistics Management*, **4**(2), pp. 13–24.

Cottrill, K. (1997), 'Reforging the supply chain', *Journal of Business Strategy*, **16**(6), pp. 35–39.

Davis, T. (1993), 'Effective supply chain management', *Sloan Management Review*, **34**(4), pp. 35–46.

Denison, D.R., Hart, S.L. and Kahn, J.A. (1996), 'From chimneys to cross-functional teams: developing and validating a diagnostics model', *Academy of Management Journal*, **39**(4), pp. 1005–1023.

Dobler, D.W. and Burt, D.N. (1996), *Purchasing and Supply Management*, 6th edition, New York: McGraw-Hill.

Dyer, J.H. (1996), 'How Chrysler created an American *keiretsu*', *Harvard Business Review*, **74**(4), pp. 42–56.

Ellram, L.M. and Pearson, J.N. (1993), 'The role of the purchasing function: toward team participation', *International Journal of Purchasing and Materials Management*, **29**(3), pp. 3–9.

Fearon, H.E. and Leenders, M.R. (1995), *Purchasing's Organizational Roles and Responsibilities*, Tempe, AZ: Center for Advanced Purchasing Studies.

Galunic, C.D. and Eisenhardt (1994), 'Renewing the strategy–structure–performance paradigm', in Staw, B.M. and Cummings, L.L. (Eds), *Research in Organizational Behavior*, 16, pp. 215–255.

Hair, J.F. Jr., Anderson, R.E., Tatham, R.L. and Black, W.C. (1995), *Multivariate Data Analysis With Readings*, 4th edition, New Jersey: Prentice Hall.

Lambert, D.M., Stock, J.R. and Ellram, L.M. (1998), *Fundamentals of Logistics Management*, Burr Ridge, IL: Irwin McGraw-Hill.

Leenders, M.R. and Fearon, H.E. (1997), *Purchasing and Supply Management*, 11th edition, Chicago: Irwin.

Nunnally, J.C. and Berstein, I.H. (1994), *Psychometric Theory*, 3rd edition, New York: McGraw Hill.

Powell, T.C. (1992), 'Organizational alignment as competitive advantage', *Strategic Management Journal*, **13**(2), pp. 119–134.

Rahul, R. (1995), 'The struggle to create an organization for the 21st century', *Fortune*, **131**(6), pp. 90–99.

Scherer, F.M. and Ross, D. (1990), *Industrial Market Structure and Economic Performance*, 3rd edition, Boston, MA: Houghton Mifflin Company.

Trent, R.J. and Monczka, R.M. (1994), 'Effective cross-functional sourcing teams: critical success factors', *International Journal of Purchasing and Materials Management*, **30**(4), pp. 2–11.

Trent, R.J. (1996), 'Understanding and evaluating cross-functional sourcing team leadership', *International Journal of Purchasing and Materials Management*, **32**(4), pp. 29–36.

CHAPTER FOURTEEN

A quart from a pint pot? Developing the effective use of purchasing consortia

John Ritchie and Tom Chadwick

BACKGROUND

The UK Higher Education (HE) sector comprises some 200 autonomous institutions, most of whom belong to one of seven regional purchasing consortia. Their total non-pay spend amounts to almost £4 billion annually and so represents a very considerable area in which to apply procurement expertise and to achieve best value. There are a number of influences on UK HE procurement which are relevant to developing the effective use of purchasing consortia. The national Joint Procurement Policy and Strategy Group (JPPSG) procurement strategy, first issued in September 1996, comprises a number of broad elements:

- Improve training skills and development.
- Benchmark to external standards of price and process performance.
- Improve procurement management information systems.
- Monitor and evaluate the effectiveness of procurement procedures and performances.
- Encourage standardized coding systems.
- Monitor the dissemination of good practice in procurement and outcomes from other elements of the strategy.
- Maximize the benefits to be obtained from the use and development of the purchasing consortia.

This framework has been augmented by the publication of a number of best practice/good value procurement guidance documents over the past few years. A national contract plan which will optimize procurement positioning at national, regional consortia and local institution level is currently being formulated. This is likely to mean the apportionment of product and service agreement development within procurement resources such as the purchasing consortia. A national JPPSG Website has been established as the vehicle to provide guidance documents, downloadable toolkits and consistent up-to-date information on all aspects of HE procurement. This includes: agreements being developed or available at national, regional and potentially institutional level; directory contact information for the various national and consortium purchasing groups together with other relevant bodies such as the JPPSG, the Committee of Vice Chancellors and Principals, National Audit Office (NAO) and the Funding Councils; services available including best practice guides and sources of information such as that associated with the national vendor database project.

The recently published NAO Report 'Procurement in the English Higher Education Sector' (NAO 1999) stresses the importance of greater co-operation between the purchasing consortia and of maximizing the benefits of the use and development of co-operative procurement. In developing the effective use of consortia it is essential that any direction adopted recognizes and is consistent with the current and evolving HE environment. Annual consortium business plans and annual reports should reflect this same evolutionary development process.

UK HE PURCHASING CONSORTIA – CURRENT AND FUTURE ROLES

The Centre for Advanced Purchasing Studies (CAPS) at Arizona State University defines a purchasing consortium (Hendrick 1998) as consisting of two or more independent organizations that join together, either formally, informally, or through an independent third party, for the purpose of combining their individual requirements for purchased materials, services, and capital goods to leverage more value-added pricing, service and technology from their external suppliers than could be obtained if each organization purchased goods and services alone. In the HE sector the overall aim or mission statement must be to continually maximize procurement value in all its forms. The overall direction will encompass a number of discrete areas which are expected, with a certain amount of overlap, to develop sequentially over a period of time.

The current position is, or certainly should be, that consortium agreements for goods and services incorporate total life costs. A number of publications have sought, particularly in the last 18 months, to encourage this more holistic approach to achieving best value for money. As an example, the London Universities Purchasing Consortium (LUPC) agreement for personal computers provides a total cost of ownership over three years. The first stage is to agree the specification through the consortium computing commodity group before the qualified suppliers are provided with the tender documentation. Commodity groups are made up from technical specialists, users and procurement officers representing the institutions making up the consortium. These groups are the established method of providing active involvement and assistance in the take-up of subsequent agreements (Chadwick and Rajagopal 1995). The results of the tender included delivered prices with options for delivery to store, to site, to desk including installation if required; on- and off-site service and warranty over varying time periods of up to three years, with various response times.

Once the initial price/cost based evaluation had been carried out, a number of other evaluation parameters were used: references from other customers utilizing the proposed suppliers on the tender list; quality in terms of ISO accreditation, production, post delivery and first year failure rates; comprehensive supplier appraisals encompassing some 30 areas ranging from financial performance to production, organizational culture, customer care and service performance, together with environmental considerations such as sourcing policies, disposal of packaging, and redundant equipment; technical evaluations undertaken by all member institutions represented on the commodity group to ensure robustness in the working environment including networking.

Clarification discussions with the shortlisted suppliers yielded the elimination of further unnecessary costs as well as added features such as availability of loan machines, funding options and electronic transmission of price and availability information. The evaluation of all these parameters provided the consortium with the best value agreement. It is important to remember that finalizing an agreement is really the first step in developing an ongoing commercial relationship to achieve further benefits over the lifetime of the agreement. This was achieved by the selected suppliers actively marketing their products with individual consortium members and as part of that process developing the appropriate service levels. At the consortium level the agreement was monitored, particularly in terms of business value, and developed to identify areas of further benefit such as common buying trends across institutions, and price benchmarking.

Consortium agreements do or should progressively incorporate process costs in the supply of goods and services. The potential for price/cost savings associated with goods and services typically declines over a number of years of negotiation (or agreement refinement) and could annually amount on average to, say, five per cent of the total non-pay spend (or £200 million across the sector over a five to 10 year period). These savings could be exceeded by the likely savings associated with process costs. While they are very difficult to estimate, they could yield savings of £50 per transaction. Process cost savings covering the supply chain process from order to invoice payment represent a very substantial area to influence through professional procurement. The LUPC has recently finalized a 'one stop shop' or 'managing agent' agreement for laboratory supplies.

In addition to the quality, supplier appraisal and other evaluation aspects associated with a total life costs agreement, this agreement encompassed the provision of a core list of laboratory supplies at best value prices; the ability to communicate electronically covering the full order to invoice process; the incorporation of other suppliers in the laboratory supplies market place progressively to enable the selected managing agent to develop and provide a true one stop service; consultancy services on the operation of a supply service to each member institution which could include best approaches to the supply chain process (including stores if required), goods disposal and the establishment of new laboratory sites.

The approach adopted and built on experience in the UK and US particularly, and involved both a qualitative and quantitative assessment covering the following three major steps. A request for information was issued which described the total service required and sought information on a broad range of issues to identify the potential suppliers in the market place. Each of the potential suppliers presented their views on how the one stop shop could work and benefit consortium members. The audience involved not only the consortium laboratory supplies commodity group but also, and principally, the prospective customers for the one stop shop. Thus it also served as an opportunity to further publicize our intentions beyond the commodity group members. A request for quotation was subsequently issued to the shortlisted suppliers. As the name suggests, the quantified aspects such as core list pricing and the costs for provision of waste management services were included. All these major steps were individually evaluated by each area appropriately weighted to arrive at the selected supplier.

Unlike total life cost product and service agreements, this agreement, with the exception of is-

suing the revised core list prices, has to be implemented on a site by site basis. Each institution is being provided with a bespoke service which meets its needs and this requires careful customer focus to help the institution first understand and then define its own requirements and agree how these can best be met by the service provider. This is a much more involved and sophisticated process than the previous norm of simply issuing a new set of unit prices and urging as much uptake as possible.

In parallel, third party suppliers are being contacted to join the one stop shop. While the approach to consortium one stop shop agreements and their implementation is much more complicated, the benefits are correspondingly all the more attractive. These benefits may be summarized as those associated with price/cost reduction on products and services; process cost reductions through greater single sourcing through the one stop shop including, if possible, electronic communications; the ability to analyse supplier and product ranges through the one stop shop supplier, providing much better management information to identify economies through product harmonization.

The next logical step for consortia in the drive for continuous improvement in procurement practice is through the provision of value added services. These value added services increasingly provide more indirect benefits and raise the effectiveness of purchasers or buyers, both full-time specialists and part-time buyers in organizations typically characterized by devolved budget management. The evolution and development of a consortium centre of excellence should be focused enough to develop a well articulated foresight about tomorrow's opportunities and challenge and, importantly, matched by sufficiently resourced capacity to execute the plan (Hamel and Prahalad 1994).

Such services will respond to and ideally anticipate customer needs and within the LUPC currently include:

● professional procurement advice covering, for example, EC/UK procurement legislation, sources of purchasing information/advice contained in publications such as Croner's

Purchasing and Supply Briefings, and supplier market information;

- the provision of best practice guides such as supplier appraisal, vendor rating, model terms and conditions of supply;
- advice on procurement personnel recruitment;
- an evaluation service for applicable third party agreements, particularly in terms of quality standards, best value and legal compliance; and
- the provision of training, particularly procurement and professional accreditation through a number of options to achieve best value. This includes the use of NVQs to meet the membership requirements of our principal professional association, the Chartered Institute of Purchasing and Supply.

Information should be disseminated in a number of ways to achieve maximum effect. Clearly the use of electronic communication is paramount and should continue to be encouraged.

PURCHASING CONSORTIA SUPPORT ACTIVITIES

Given the HE environment in the UK, and the overall direction proposed by the authors as a way of consortia continually achieving procurement excellence, there are a number of supporting activities or objectives. Aligning objectives, or in more modern parlance 'the development of loyal, inclusive stakeholder relationships' (Wheeler and Sillanpaa 1997) is one of the most important determinants of commercial viability and business success. The 'cycle of inclusion' of stakeholders for a consortium has the extra difficult dimension of its constituent members. Achieving these objectives may be viewed as the bedrock to achieving our aim as consortium activities develop over time.

Customer focus is the need to identify and anticipate customer service requirements through, for example, regular contact and questionnaires. The business planning process is an ideal vehicle to regularly and formally review and meet emerging customer needs. The involvement of

representatives from member institutions in the commodity group process is essential to gain commitment and potential take-up of consortium agreements. Their involvement becomes all the more important when agreements involving reviews of process costs are developed.

There must be a marketing strategy. Procurement, and particularly best value procurement, must be sold to consortium members just like any other service to meet our aim of procurement excellence. The LUPC issue regular quarterly newsletters involving both suppliers and consortium members' purchasing practitioners and has its own Website to communicate a variety of information as essential elements of its marketing strategy. It should be remembered that while the application of electronic communications is clearly the most cost effective rapid route to provide up-to-date information and is to be marketed in its own right, other non-electronic communications may be necessary to maximize effective communications with all member institutions. Other ways of highlighting LUPC agreements include seminars, supplier exhibitions and the use of the consortium logo on price lists, product packaging and so on. The marketing strategy will dovetail with customer contact and focus to promulgate and enhance the cohesiveness of the consortium as an effective procurement organization.

Benchmarking is increasingly viewed as an essential checkpoint to ensure and develop procurement effectiveness focusing typically on process or output within and outside the HE sector. An LUPC benchmarking study has been carried out on processes and latterly we have included pricing through the use of specialist consultants such as PI Pricetrak. A service group on benchmarking has been established in London to share information and selectively benchmark activities, currently including travel, and share information to raise procurement effectiveness generally.

BARRIERS TO OPTIMUM EFFECTIVENESS

There is a common perception that membership of a consortium does not bring equal benefits and large institutions may feel that their subscription plus the level of resources that they have to provide to support the various commodity groups, tender evaluation sub-committees and so on actually outweighs the benefits they receive. Certainly it can be that the net gains seem inequitable compared to those of a small institution which relies to a great extent on the consortium activities and contributes very little resource beyond basic membership fee, often because the small institution may have no real expertise to contribute. Gains will not necessarily be equal but they should be fair.

Higher education institutions can themselves be a kind of consortium as organizations with highly devolved management structures. Their constituent parts may not be prepared to become willing or active members. This may arise from a fear of losing an already established close buyer–supplier relationship. There can easily be a loss of enthusiasm from the red-hot commitment of the national working party, cooled slightly as the results are passed to the local regional consortium, further chilled as it is passed out to institutions' purchasing managers and then found to be icy cold and unpalatable when finally conveyed to the users at departmental level who, at least in theory, should benefit most. The importance of real inclusion and first class communication cannot be overstated, and even then the 'not invented here' syndrome can appear.

Insecure purchasing staff at institutions may fear a loss of status, and even face the expectation by local senior management inexperienced in purchasing that they ought to be able to beat any deal that the presumed ineffective consortium produces.

Suppliers, especially if they are unsuccessful tenderers, may be tempted to seek short term advantage by adopting the practice of divide and conquer. This is most likely to happen in the early days when effective consortium deals are not perceived as the norm by users, either because of past bad experience or because proper communication of both the evaluation process and the existence and results of contract monitoring and price benchmarking have not been communicated properly.

Tiering structures can be worrying for suppliers if they find themselves allocated to second or third tier positions and fear not only loss of contact with users, but the risk of losing market share as first tier suppliers substitute their own or other products, perhaps with the incentive of apparent price or service advantage.

PERFORMANCE

The establishment of measures of consortium procurement effectiveness is essential not only as an indicator of performance per se but also as the basis for ongoing benchmarking towards continuous improvement. The overall direction described in this paper will progressively mean more qualitative as well as quantitative measures. Performance measures will need to develop and evolve just as the purchasing consortium's activities do, to continually achieve procurement excellence over time. Current parameters such as estimated savings associated with whole life cost agreements, for example, are sometimes very difficult to establish – mostly due to lack of appropriate commodity-based information. Taking the 1997/98 LUPC annual report as an example, a number of performance measures are stated over a period of three years. In 1997/98 the principal performance measures included those in the following three paragraphs.

Estimated potential savings if all member institutions adopted LUPC agreements amounted to £4.2 million per annum. If that is factored by a 50 per cent average adoption rate by value, a more robust saving estimate would be of the order of £2.1 million per annum. On closer analysis it would be seen that 50 per cent of these savings were more robust being based on prices or values pre- and post- the respective agreements. The balance is based on educated estimates usually by the commodity group chairman, or other comparisons based for example on a fixed range of the product in question.

The difference between potential annual savings of £4.2 million and the more robust figure of £2.1 million associated with agreement take-up is in itself a target measure of effectiveness for any consortium. The LUPC in their 1997/98 annual report presented this gap graphically. Measures are being taken, including the use of questionnaires and direct member contact, to minimize this variance. These quantified savings exclude benefits associated with:

● adopted national agreements yet to be assessed;
● VAT savings associated with guidelines issued by the LUPC VAT Advisory Group;
● avoided tender costs by consortium member institutions; and
● the currently available added value services such as procurement advice and training.

Bearing in mind the extent to which savings are quantifiable, this reflects on another measure associated with the projection of total spend being influenced by consortium agreements. In London it is estimated that almost 20 per cent (£107 million) of total consortium non-pay spend could potentially be influenced by LUPC agreements.

Without due diligence in assessing benefits or savings there is a danger of belonging to 'the angler's school of benchmarking' – 'Buyers talking about price, of course, is a bit like fishermen bragging about the one that got away – always entertaining but rarely true' (Hewitt 1995). Process cost savings are even more difficult to assess – this is however an area being developed as part of the LUPC one stop shop agreement for laboratory supplies. The assessment of benefits in the future may well improve by the recent and/or forthcoming introduction of new data management systems by many HE institutions, largely in response to initiatives being undertaken by the JPPSG and previous concerns over possible millennium bug problems.

This is unlikely to assist the assessment of benefits associated with qualitative added value services. One of the outcomes of the LUPC process benchmarking study was that outside companies are often organized in such a way that the central purchasing organization only provides qualitative services and is responsible for policy rather than the development of specific supply agreements for goods and services. Their effectiveness is measured by the response to

questionnaires and in one case this exercise is carried out annually and applied to a specific number of customers.

It is very important that all consortia and indeed all their constituent member institutions use performance measures in a consistent way. One current assessment and benchmarking approach available is the JPPSG 'Financials' software toolkit. This comprises a small suite of screens to input the appropriate institution/consortium supplier spend and other financial data with a number of outputs including:

● an assessment of purchasing influence on non-pay spend. Purchasing influence levels vary from professional input to establish a competitively tendered best value agreement to local departments making their own arrangements with no purchasing involvement;
● an analysis of purchasing arrangements in place against total non-pay spend in terms of national, regional consortium, tendered or local institution agreements;
● an assessment of purchasing influence in different parts of the organization.

It provides a means of assessing consortium 'penetration' by a measure of percentage of agreement uptake.

This toolkit is described further by Florence Gregg in Chapter 21, and is part of a developing suite of benchmarking tools in use in UK HE. While this sort of approach is currently appropriate to achieve consistency, there is clearly a need for such measures to evolve in line with changes in consortium/institution procurement activities over time. Are there other measures of the benefits of consortium membership? Could some unit of procurement effectiveness be defined so that an organization could decide how many units of purchasing resource it would have to provide for itself outside or alternatively inside a consortium?

Hendrick (1998) surveyed 131 US firms and found that 28 were actively involved in at least one consortium. This ranged from one to ten with an average membership of just over two consortia. Savings reported were 13.4 per cent per annum which yielded an average annual saving of about $2.3 million for each member.

For an annual membership cost of $300,000, this meant a return on investment of over 700 per cent. In the HE sector in the UK consortia are multidimensional and multilayered with major challenges in selecting the most appropriate groupings to join or to form, and an even greater challenge in gauging how best to provide resources for them and to define ways of monitoring their continuing worth if the greatest benefits of co-operative purchasing are to be realized.

SUMMARY AND CONCLUSIONS

The thrust of this chapter has been how the proposed future direction for consortium purchasing will seek to continually achieve purchasing excellence. The quality of the output in terms of best value procurement will depend on developments in the HE procurement environment combined with consistent consortium business planning. Given the importance of the sector both in terms of high levels of expenditure, and the undeniable linkage of the quality of graduates and research output with continuing prosperity for the UK, it is crucial for procurement to make the very best contribution possible. The complexity of working with groups of institutions where individual annual expenditures might range from below £5 million to £200 million, but which have some common requirements if very different priorities, presents unusual challenges.

Success in co-operative procurement in a sector where individual choice and academic freedom are well entrenched and sometimes justified, relies on the user actually wanting to co-operate. The experiences described show that careful customer focus and the close involvement of users and specialists in commodity groups provides a start, but this must be followed up by good marketing of the measurable benefits backed by objective monitoring of supplier performance and improvement goals. As well as procurement-led groupings, it has been found that specialist affinity groups, for example librarians, can be encouraged and assisted to get together and achieve high levels of commitment to co-operative procurement given suf-

ficient and sympathetic procurement support. While first focusing on price, often against a background of reducing grant support, a properly conducted tendering process will bring attention to all aspects of the supply chain, both cost- and performance-related.

Experiences at LUPC and regional and specialist affinity consortia elsewhere are now being included in an overall review of co-operative procurement in the HE sector. There are principles to be defined and protocols and procedures needed to address the best way forward regionally and nationally, in order to avoid overlap and maximize the uptake rates and benefits gained, as quantified by the benchmarking toolkit and performance measures. This work specifically addresses the aims set out in the JPPSG strategy for the HE sector for a stakeholder inclusive version (Wheeler and Sillanpaa 1997) of the Hamel and Prahalad (1994) view of the future referred to earlier in this chapter.

Purchasing consortia have an important role to play in the UK higher education sector. However their use requires significant marketing. They must be seen to deliver a full range of benefits and they cannot escape the need for measures of effectiveness including simple savings.

REFERENCES

Chadwick T. and Rajagopal S. (1995), *Strategic Supply Management*. Oxford: Butterworth Heinemann, p. 75.

Hamel G. and Prahalad C.K. (1994), *Competing for the Future*, Cambridge, Mass: Harvard Business School Press, p. 195.

Hendrick T.E. (1998), *Purchasing Consortiums: Horizontal Alliances among Firms Buying Common Goods and Services What? Who? Why? How?*, Tempe, Az: Center for Advanced Purchasing Studies, pp. 1–4.

Hewitt D. (1995), 'The consortium option', *Purchasing and Supply Management*, January, pp. 32–3.

National Audit Office (1999), *Procurement in the English Higher Education Sector*, London: The Stationery Office.

Wheeler D. and Sillanpaa M. (1997), *The Stakeholder Corporation*, London: Pitman.

PART FOUR

ELECTRONIC COMMERCE

Introduction to electronic commerce

Ruth Fee

The advent of electronic commerce (EC) has far-reaching implications for both the public and the private sectors. Indeed, the implications of EC for procurement organizations cannot be underestimated; Fraser et al. comment in Chapter 15 that 'the use of e-commerce as a means of purchasing is on the verge of a quantum leap'. Representative aspects of EC include electronic funds transfer, electronic data interchange (EDI), fax, e-mail, remote bulletin boards and trading via the Internet. States such as the US, Canada and Australia already have well established EC and EDI networks which are private sector driven and have minimum government intervention. The US is often cited as a reliable predictor of a future European business environment; Croom indicates that business purchases conducted via Web-based media in the US will be in the order of $80 billion in 2000. Europe is at a disadvantage in comparison to the US due to disparate software systems and legal frameworks at state level but bodies such as the European Commission are now addressing this issue. Recent developments at state level also underline the growing importance of EC and consequently the need for this largely unregulated media to have a legal framework. For example, the Electronic Communications Bill in the UK announced in November 1999 aims to give the Internet legal status in UK law and clarify the legal position of electronic communications such as e-mail. The Bill would also provide a legal framework for dealing with digital signatures and allow for the setting up of a body to regulate providers of encryption services. The five chapters in this section focus on the implications of EC for the private sector in Europe, although there are also valuable lessons for the public sector.

In Chapter 15, John Fraser and his fellow authors investigate the opportunities and problems associated with the use of e-commerce systems. The infrastructure and legal problems that require solutions are outlined and a theoretical framework is provided to analyse the main factors involved in the move to e-commerce solutions. The authors provide case studies to illustrate the theoretical framework and note the implications of adopting e-commerce in the supply chain.

Chapter 15 complements Chapter 16, Simon Croom's examination of the management of maintenance, repair and operating systems (MRO) procurement through Web-based e-commerce. Based on a six-month research project, Croom examines existing research on the procurement process and notes the development of electronic links in the 1980s that conveyed important first mover advantages. Although the networks were initially hierarchical in nature, with one firm dominant, the increasing standardization of EDI and conditions may be ready for an electronic market place with larger numbers of buyers and sellers. Croom comments that the use of open information systems can provide greater levels of information to buyers, thereby opening up greater competitiveness between providers. The advantages of using the Internet over area networks and EDI are set out, as are the advantages of Web-based procurement (what Croom calls e-procurement). Among the advantages listed are expenditure control and increased procurement control. However, there are major concerns that surround the use of e-procurement; for example, the security of Websites, particularly in the financial services and legal services sectors. Croom acknowledges that the research in this chapter is exploratory in nature, intended to identify key concerns and opportunities for e-procurement, and suggests further research to examine the scale and relationships between dominant variables in the adoption of e-procurement.

Many e-procurement Websites have been established, but what really makes a site effective both for external users and for the purchasing department? In Chapter 17, Brenner and Wilking address the use of the Internet for organizational purchasing, particularly for the identification of potential suppliers as well as for associated processes. The authors use current examples to show how the publication of procurement needs on the Internet supports market-orientated activities in purchasing and, as a consequence, the work of the purchasing department. The examples used include the Brother Industry Website, the Alno Website and the Deutsche Telekom AG Website. On the basis of the examples given, a draft is developed for the step-by-step establishment of applications on the Internet. Data, functions and the organizational forms necessary for purchasing on the Internet are also detailed. This chapter should therefore be of particular benefit to practitioners who wish to establish a Website for their own company. The chapter concludes with an examination of the prospects for further development of applications towards comprehensive Internet-based solutions for decentralized supplier management.

This theme is further developed in Chapter 18, 'Making Use of Internet Technology to Achieve Lean Management in the West Midlands Automotive Supply Chain'. Diana Thompson and her colleagues developed the Autolean project with the aim of introducing Internet communications to a sample of 20 small companies in the automotive supply base, based in the West Midlands of the UK. The project examines flows between supply chain tiers and uses commercially viable Internet technologies in an attempt to enable global standards of competitiveness to be achieved. The chapter covers the salient results from the project and commences by describing the justification and perceived need for the work, continuing by briefly examining some

of the many other Internet-based 'lean communication' initiatives in the automotive supply chain. The authors identify the major outcomes, results and observations of the project and the chapter concludes with suggestions as to how these specific outcomes might be applied to the wider automotive supply chain in general.

Chapter 19, by Daniel Corsten and Michael Zagler, has links with the section on organization and management, in particular Chapter 14 by Ritchie and Chadwick. The chapter 'Purchasing Consortia and Internet Technology' reports on an Internet-based purchasing consortium for small and medium-size enterprises (SMEs) launched in 1997 in the Euregio Bodensee, the triangle of Switzerland, Germany and Austria. The chapter begins with a definition of purchasing consortia and the theoretical developments surrounding the term. The findings from the literature and the authors' own research findings on the success and failure of purchasing consortia reveal a lack of communication and communication infrastructure as one of the biggest barriers to the success of purchasing consortia. Purchasing information technology has in the past focused on operational purchasing and has neglected strategic purchasing, especially with regard to co-ordination between independent companies. Initial research by the authors revealed that software solutions to facilitate purchasing consortia did not exist. The objective therefore of the project is to provide an Internet platform to SMEs of the Euregio Bodensee where they can exchange knowledge, attract suppliers and form purchasing consortia to leverage their purchasing power. The authors identify internal and external purchasing consortium tasks and classify them as knowledge tasks, marketing tasks, pooling tasks and quotation tasks. These four categories are all related to the project and a taxonomy for purchasing consortia tasks is therefore developed. The chapter concludes by describing future research goals and the recognition that the project aims to move beyond the German-speaking horizon towards more global networks.

Overall these chapters emphasize the increasing importance of the Internet to purchasing, although the extent to which it is currently being used is revealed to be limited. Whilst there are infrastructural and legal obstacles to be overcome, the chapters provide an insight into future best practice relating to electronic linkage to customers and suppliers, Web-based tendering and submission of bids, and aggregation of requirements between members of consortia. Whilst these chapters relate principally to the private sector, they are also clearly relevant to the public sector, as demonstrated by proposals for the use of e-commerce to facilitate increased co-ordination of the procurement needs of government departments, and to establish a 'shopping mall' of goods and services covered by government contracts (Cabinet Office/Treasury 1998).

REFERENCE

Cabinet Office/Treasury (1998), *Efficiency in Civil Government Procurement*, Treasury: London.

CHAPTER FIFTEEN

The impact of electronic commerce on purchasing in the supply chain

John Fraser, Nuran Fraser and Frank McDonald

One of the biggest opportunities and challenges facing trading organizations over the coming years will be the deployment of Web-enabled technologies. As a new channel for commercial transactions, the use of e-commerce will open up fresh sources of revenue and opportunities for organizations with carefully structured strategies. Most leading UK organizations have developed an e-commerce strategy. Indeed, the top 100 UK companies believe that 20 per cent of their revenue will come from e-commerce transactions by 2000, according to the KPMG Electronic Commerce Report.

Organizations in the USA have realized the potential benefits from adopting e-commerce. The high stock market valuation of US companies such as Internet service providers America OnLine (AOL) and Yahoo!, and firms such as Amazon.com and eBay, reflect the view of the market that the Internet is set to become a very important means of conducting business activities. The UK stock market has also recently placed high values on Internet-based businesses with the flotation of companies such as Freeserve and QXL.com. These companies have few real assets, and many have not yet made an operating profit, but the markets appear to expect large returns from companies such as these as the IT revolution leads to new ways of conducting business activities. However, the share price on many e-commerce based companies fell in mid-2000, perhaps indicating that the market was reassessing the future profitability and growth potential of these companies.

The US e-commerce market was worth $26 billion in 1996/7 and is expected to be worth $330 billion by 2002 with a figure of $1000 billion by 2005. It is also estimated that by 2005 about 15 per cent of retail sales in the US will be conducted by e-commerce, as compared to a figure of 0.5 per cent in 1996/7 (OECD 1998). In the UK the total value of Internet-based purchases is expected to be £2.9 to £3.8 billion by the end of year 2000 (estimate by Sun Microsystems Ltd in 1998). It appears that the use of e-commerce as a means of purchasing is on the verge of very rapid growth.

Governments are also promoting the merits of the Internet for improving competitiveness, and the development of e-commerce is seen as being crucial to attempts by organizations to create and maintain competitiveness. Governments are also working on the development of regulatory frameworks to permit the effective use of e-commerce (European Commission 1998; DTI 1998).

Clearly, e-commerce is making an impact on the ways that purchasing activities are being conducted. Much of the early literature on this subject was speculative (Davies and Botkin 1991; Aston and Schwarz 1992; Tapscott 1995). However, the growth of e-commerce has enabled more observations to be made of its use by organizations (Cronin 1994; Tapscott 1995; Lloyd and Boyle 1998). Literature based on observation of the impact on organizations that have adopted e-commerce solutions is very enthusiastic about the benefits and excited about its future prospects.

This chapter outlines the background to e-commerce and then provides a theoretical framework that outlines the advantages and disadvantages of using this new technology. Evidence from a case study is used to illustrate the issues raised by the theoretical framework. In particular, the problems associated with being a first or second mover when adopting e-commerce solutions in purchasing systems are analysed and some tentative implications for strategy are drawn.

DEFINING E-COMMERCE

E-commerce is part of a new means of communicating that has been opened up by the development of the Internet. A useful definition of e-commerce is the use of the Internet for the exchange of valuable information and the purchase of goods and services. More specifically, orders and payments between businesses and between firms and consumers. In essence, e-commerce is the secure trading of goods, information or services. A typical e-commerce solution will have a front-end display to promote products or services, an encryption system to allow secure trading and a credit or payment authorization facility.

In the new e-commerce environment product decisions are based on on-line catalogues which can be customized to suit the needs of the viewing client. Some sales organizations are now investigating implanting Web-stores within customer intranets, enabling internal departments to place orders without having to enter the Internet. Search engines have been developed that allow customers to search the Web for opportunities to purchase online. For example, a 'bot' (robot) is a type of search engine which can search sites for the best prices for either a product or bundle of products. E-commerce systems allow buyers to conduct all, or most, of their search, ordering, monitoring and payment activities via the Internet or company intranet.

A number of questions need to be resolved if there is to be a successful transition to the 'brave new world' of e-commerce:

1. Are the high human and capital assets associated with e-commerce solutions offset by lower costs and/or expanded market opportunities?
2. Will there be customer and/or supplier resistance to the use of new technology, or will unfamiliarity with such technology require the running of expensive parallel systems that will eliminate the benefits of new e-commerce solutions?
3. Will the costs of learning by mistakes, often required with the introduction of new technology, be offset by the benefits of e-commerce solutions in the short term, the long term, the very long term or never?
4. Can learning mistakes best be avoided by waiting until the technology has been refined, when most customers and suppliers will be able and willing to make extensive use of the Internet for business purposes?
5. Which parts of business operations will not work effectively in a virtual world in the short term, the long term or in the foreseeable future?
6. Will the adoption of e-commerce solutions lead to competitive advantages that are sustainable, or is the adoption of e-commerce solutions necessary to prevent exit from the market?

These problems boil down to adopting a strategy that determines the extent and timing of the implementation of e-commerce solutions to lead to the best cost–benefit outcomes associated with using e-commerce. Whether or not the adoption of e-commerce confers sustainable competitive advantages will depend on how easy it is for competitors to replicate such solutions. Being a slow adopter of e-commerce solutions will be a problem if this strategy leads to cost disadvantages and/or the loss of market share because of inadequate provision of desired qualities.

INFRASTRUCTURE AND LEGAL ISSUES

There are a number of infrastructure and legal problems that must be solved if e-commerce is to develop into a major means of engaging in economic activity. To find solutions to these problems governments are already developing policies and introducing new legal frameworks. The federal government of the USA is the most important player in this field (Office of the Vice-

President 1999). The European Union (EU) is also important because the basis for policy and legal changes associated with e-commerce in the member states is mainly decided by the institutions of the EU (European Commission 1997 and 1999). However, each member state is also developing its own e-commerce policies (DTI 1999). International agencies such as the Organization for Economic Co-operation and Development (OECD) are also involved in looking for solutions to infrastructure and legal problems connected to the development of the Internet (OECD 1998 and 1999).

The major infrastructure problem is access, at a reasonable cost, to the Internet by most firms and households. Such access requires widespread availability of hardware (such as computers and servers), software and telecommunication systems that can connect customers to the Internet. Many households and small- and medium-sized enterprises (SMEs) do not currently have access to appropriate hardware and software systems. Furthermore, in some countries, such as the UK, connecting to the Internet is relatively expensive, compared to countries such as the US where this is free of charge. The widespread introduction of digital technology into firms and households and the expansion of Internet Service Providers (ISPs) such as AOL, Freeserve, Yahoo! and Lycos should, in the medium term, solve the hardware and software problems. However, solving the problem of securing low cost connection to the Internet is likely to be a more serious obstacle to the development of e-commerce. To solve this problem the market power of telecommunication service providers in many Asian and European countries must be tackled by regulations and/or by the opening up of these markets to increased competition.

The market power of some software firms also requires government action to prevent them from exploiting their dominance, thereby limiting the development of the Internet. Currently, the software necessary to use the Internet is available from only a few firms and Microsoft dominates this market. Moreover, Microsoft also exercises market power because many of the software programs necessary to use e-commerce

are only effective using a Microsoft operating system. However, curbing market power may undermine the spread of compatible operating systems. Such compatibility is a key requirement for an effective e-commerce system. Governments face the challenge of curbing market power by dominant Internet providers while at the same time not hindering the development of compatible and workable systems.

Even if governments can quickly solve these problems it is likely that low income households in developed countries will be excluded from the Internet. In developing countries many households and a large number of firms will be unable to connect to the Internet until these countries reach a level of development that can provide the investment for an appropriate infrastructure. Alternatively, some other means will have to be found to provide the necessary resources.

One of the main benefits of the Internet is that it allows for the low-cost gathering, processing and dissemination of information, some of which is commercially valuable, about consumers. This, however, raises new legal problems connected to privacy, intellectual property and safeguarding the interests of consumers. The EU is adopting a strong line on these issues and is planning to introduce legislation to limit the use of information obtained by electronic means. If laws on privacy restrict the use of information obtained from the Internet, one of the main benefits of using e-commerce will be restricted. Providing safe contractual conditions for Internet purchases, safeguarding payment systems and clarifying the legal status of Internet transactions involves a delicate trade-off between permitting the free flow of information while protecting the interests of consumers and owners of intellectual property. Here, however, the US tends towards a more liberal, self-regulated approach than the EU.

The use of e-commerce systems makes it easier to engage in cross-frontier transactions. However, this raises new problems on legal jurisdiction and resolving differences in national consumer protection, privacy and intellectual property laws. Increased cross-frontier transactions also raise taxation problems. It is difficult for tax authorities to verify the amount and type of transactions conducted over the Internet. This makes it hard to determine tax liability. There are also problems about which country should levy and collect taxes and how to distribute the collected revenue. The widespread use of intranet systems allows firms to hide transactions between countries and thereby perhaps evade tax liabilities. The vexed issue of taxation and the Internet is one of the most important and perhaps intractable problems that faces governments, which are reluctant to allow the widespread use of e-commerce systems that involve significant cross-frontier transactions until they find acceptable solutions to these problems.

A large number of infrastructure and legal problems require resolution before e-commerce can develop with the technology that is available today. New technological developments are likely to increase these problems. Governments face two major problems. First, how to safeguard the interests of consumers and holders of intellectual property rights without imposing undue controls that limit the potential benefits of e-commerce; and, second, how to access the information flows on the Internet for taxation purposes, but at the same time not to limit the development of cross-frontier e-commerce trade. Both of these problems require co-operation between governments to make sure that national differences in legal requirements are consistent with the development of e-commerce.

Clearly, the development of e-commerce is helped or hindered by how governments respond to the infrastructure and legal problems that arise from its growth. Furthermore, the need for co-operation between governments, especially between the US and the EU, will nearly certainly delay the introduction and development of policies and laws that affect the growth and development of cross-frontier e-commerce.

THEORETICAL FRAMEWORK

The outcome of the cost–benefit calculations of e-commerce solutions depends on a number of factors that can be analysed by means of a theoretical framework. At the core of the attractiveness of e-commerce is the ability to gain four possible sources of competitive advantage.

1. A reduction in intermediation costs associated with wholesale and retail activities.
2. The ability to lower costs associated with purchasing by curbing the time and effort involved in supply and logistics operations.
3. Improved information gathering and processing, thus permitting improved management of the supply chain.
4. The prospect of expanding market share and/or developing new markets by lowering the cost of gathering and processing information on the needs of existing and potential customers.

E-commerce may be regarded as the deployment of new resources to obtain a better performance than competitors. Hence the benefits of using e-commerce can be analysed by using a resource-based view of the firm (Wernerfelt 1984; Barney 1993; Peteraf 1993). Indeed, this view is fairly common in some of the literature (for example, Tapscott 1995) and a resource-based view is also implicit in the DTI White Paper on competitiveness (DTI 1998). However, the resource-based view depends on it being difficult for competitors to replicate successful resource allocation solutions. In the context of e-commerce this requires the early acquisition of the resources necessary for a successful e-commerce solution and the continual development of these resources to prevent competitors from catching up. First movers may also acquire a customer base that becomes locked-in to the systems of the company that develops and installs the e-commerce system. Large economies of scale may also exist for those firms that are first movers. These economies offer cost advantages that make it difficult for second movers to enter the market.

Transaction cost theory (Coase 1937; Williamson 1985) suggests that one of the main reasons for the introduction and development of e-commerce is to reduce transaction costs. This view of e-commerce regards it as a means of securing low-cost systems for managing the contractual and administrative arrangements within organizations. Transaction cost theory also highlights the incentive problem – that is, organizational structures need to ensure that contractual and administrative arrangements are low cost and also deliver desirable outcomes. Organizational systems must provide appropriate incentives to those who operate the systems such that outcomes are satisfactory in terms of the goals of the organization (Milgrom 1988). E-commerce solutions can have incentive problems because of the wide access to valuable information that emerges in many of these systems. This can lead to loss of intellectual property to those who can take advantage of their access, via e-commerce systems, to commercially valuable information. There are also problems connected to establishing effective communication that involves the subtle reading of human interactions. The analysis of human interactions to obtain subtextual information by reading and interpreting body language requires face to face human involvement until people become more accustomed to building and maintaining relationships on the Internet. Furthermore, the social interaction involved in purchasing and supplying, but not directly linked to these acts, is often a valuable part of these transactions; for example, the pleasure that some consumers obtain from going shopping. The shopping experience involves the sights, sounds and unexpected finds that cannot be replicated by virtual shopping experiences. The virtual world of the Internet is second best in these areas.

The factors involved in successfully reaping first mover advantages are illustrated in Figure 15.1.

However, there may be significant disadvantages associated with being a first mover because of the high costs of establishing the appropriate human and capital resources. New technologies such as e-commerce may have a steep learning curve and associated high learning costs, resulting particularly from possible systems failures. Furthermore, the regulatory and taxation systems associated with e-commerce are also in the process of being developed and, therefore, it is currently unclear how e-commerce transactions will be regulated,

enforced and taxed. This is a particular problem when using the Internet in cross-frontier trading. Second movers may avoid these costs and thus be able to introduce effective e-commerce solutions more cheaply and with less disruption to business operations.

Transaction cost theory indicates that, in competitive markets, organizations that do not adopt e-commerce solutions (when they provide an efficient solution) will lose competitive advantage. However, e-commerce solutions are unlikely to lead to sustainable competitive advantage, because they can normally be replicated by competitors. Only in cases where the failure to be a first mover in e-commerce solutions leads to catastrophic loss of market share, or large cost disadvantages because of economies of scale and scope to first movers, will it be dangerous to wait until the bugs have been ironed out of e-commerce solutions. If first mover advantages are available, second movers must overtake incumbent firms by introducing superior technology and/or better organizational systems.

Once e-commerce solutions have been successfully developed, it is likely that they will be quickly adopted by organizations. To secure the same outcome as first movers, second movers will have to install e-commerce technologies and organizational systems that are as least as good as those of incumbent firms. E-commerce solutions are therefore unlikely to lead to sustainable competitive advantage in the absence of clear first mover advantages. Nevertheless, e-commerce systems may be widely adopted in a short time once a workable system has been developed and when good systems are in place to supply the necessary complementary human and capital resources.

The factors influencing second mover advantages are outlined in Figure 15.2.

E-commerce solutions would appear to offer the prospect of new technological and organizational systems for purchasing activities that are potentially very beneficial for companies. However, they are unlikely to lead to sustainable competitive advantage, unless large economies of scale and the locking-in of a large customer base is available to first movers. Given

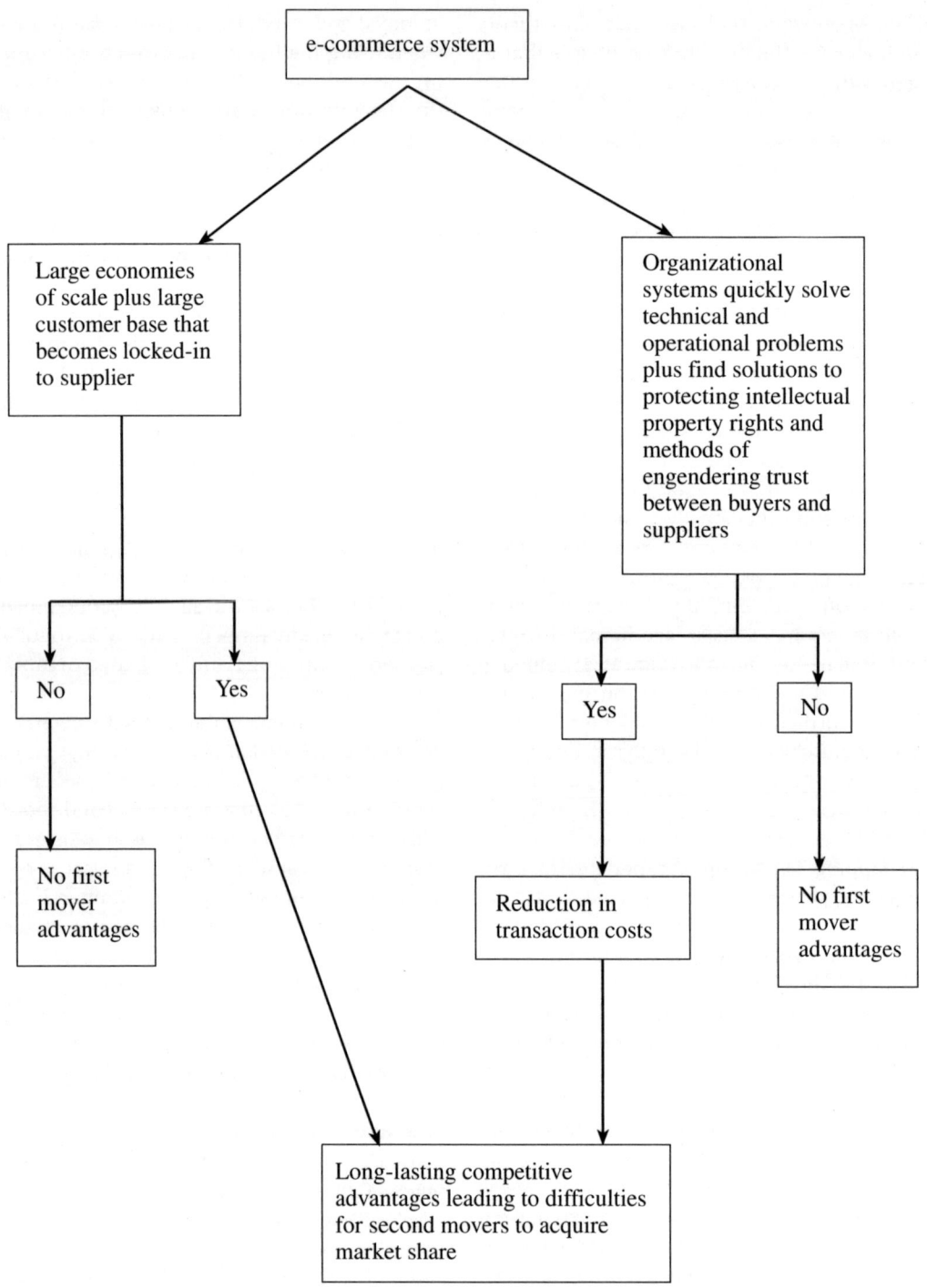

Figure 15.1 First mover advantages

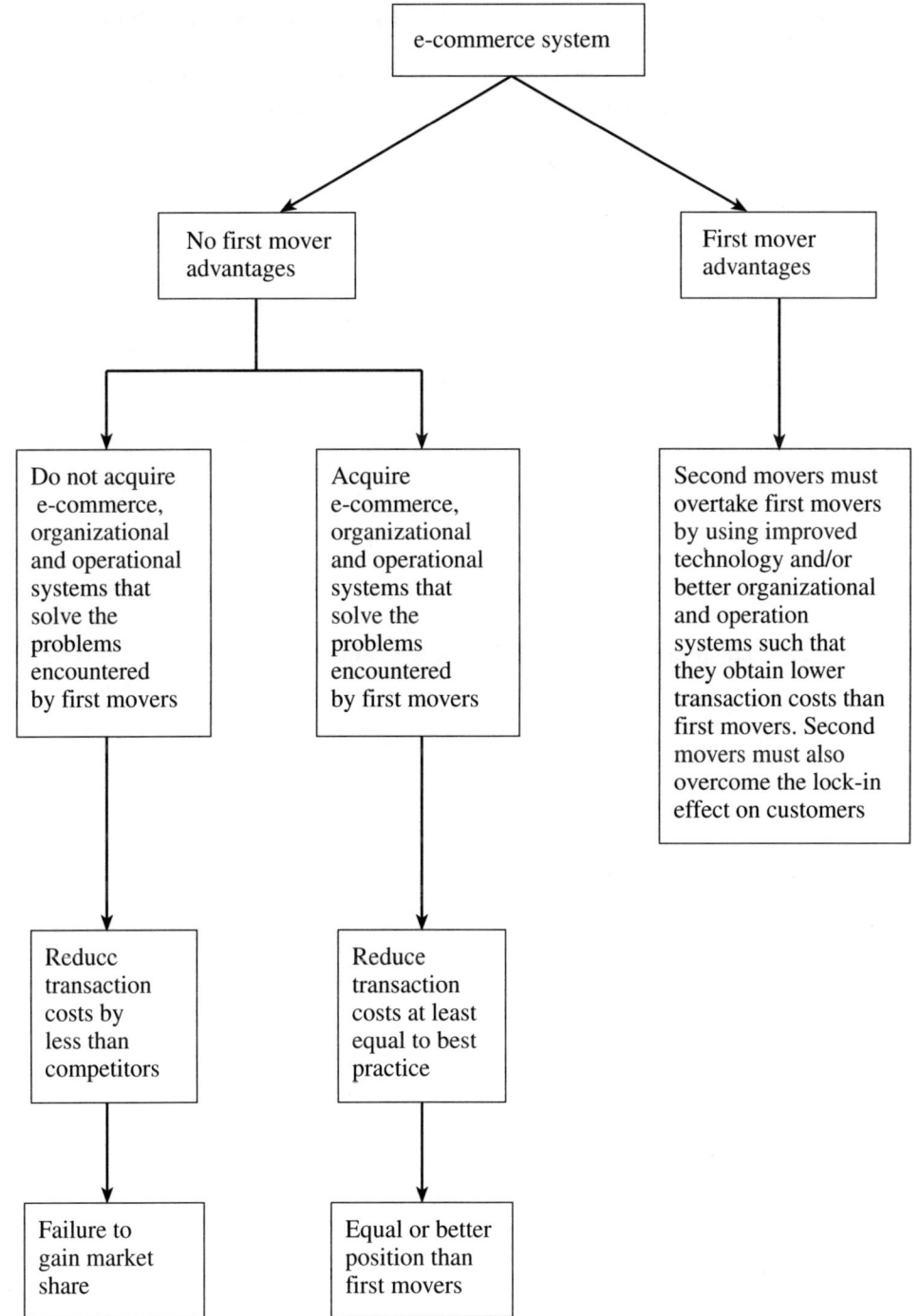

Figure 15.2 Second mover advantages

the problems that are associated with being a first mover, it is likely that they will have good IT and computing knowledge, will be used to dealing with customers at a distance and will be based in countries with large and well developed computer-based business systems. Indeed, this seems to be the case as the US is the leading country using e-commerce solutions and the main users of the Internet are information technology (IT) companies selling software and other IT products and direct mail order companies with extensive computing skills and resources. For example, over half of Internet-based sales in the US in 1996/7 were in the fields of IT software, books, CDs, videos and other related products that are often sold directly to customers by telephone (OECD 1998).

CASE STUDIES

Many case studies have been published that highlight the cost advantages and market-creating opportunities of e-commerce solutions. These studies also reveal that significant improvements in logistics systems follow from the introduction of e-commerce solutions. Part Two of Lloyd and Boyle (1998) includes 14 UK and US case studies and Tapscott (1995) provides case studies on how e-commerce has led to significant improvements in many business operations and is also leading to radical change in organizational structures. Most of the published case studies reveal that organizations that adopt e-commerce solutions are already involved in customer relationships at a distance (such as mail order, or telephone-based sales and services). These organizations also tend to have a good understanding of computer systems before they embark on e-commerce solutions and they usually do not opt for radical changes to their purchasing and customer supply systems, instead modifying and extending existing systems such as EDI or extending e-commerce options but retaining older non-computing systems. Nevertheless, the studies reveal that the pace of change once the process of adopting e-commerce solutions has begun, can be very fast.

DATRONTECH CASE STUDY

The introduction and development of an e-commerce solution in a UK company, Datrontech, has been studied by the authors. The study was based on discussions with the company and published information in Computer Weekly (January 1998). This study provides an insight into the way that e-commerce solutions can quickly alter supply systems.

Datrontech is a trade-only IT distribution firm selling components and services. It planned to give its customers a better level of service and, after considering a number of strategic options open to them, it decided that an e-commerce system would be the most effective solution to allow orders to be taken without customers having to wait on the phone. As a result of this outline planning phase, Datrontech started pulling together a three-phase e-commerce project, completing the first phase in November 1998. The contrast between this new method of ordering and the old has been significant, according to IT director Chris Michalczuk: 'The traditional method of purchasing involves phoning up, and getting frustrated on the telephone waiting for basic information. That's not really the way trading is going to go. People want information at their convenience – not at ours' (Computer Weekly, January 1998).

Datrontech began the project in spring 1997, having made the decision to work with Internet consultancy firm USWeb. Having completed a functional specification of the proposed e-commerce system, Datrontech then started to work with its key systems suppliers. More specifically, it started talking to MANCOS, author of Maginus, an Oracle-based back-end order processing system. From May to July 1998, USWeb wrote the code for the site with MANCOS and then tested the resulting solution from August to September. From October to November, the pilot site was tested against live data sets. Datrontech's internal teams were trained on the product with the site going live to customers in January 1999.

Phase two of the development ran from the end of November 1998 to April 1999. This enabled the Windows NT-based e-commerce server to write directly into the Oracle database, meaning that orders made over the Web were processed automatically. Phase three introduced a system that allowed customers to indirectly access data on the stock levels of Datrontech's suppliers, thereby creating a virtual warehouse.

Datrontech also moved its relationship with the retailer Dixons towards an e-commerce system. Dixons send orders via EDI that are then imported into Maginus. The Maginus system converts the EDI information into the new system via translation software called Intercept Plus. Dixons also transmit product-planning forecasts that give an indication of the orders that will be placed over the following week. In turn, price lists are transmitted from Datrontech to Dixons. The relentless march of e-commerce will have a significant impact on businesses and whether EDI survives in its present form is very much a moot point. However, Datrontech chose to develop its EDI system rather than adopt a totally new e-commerce system. This may reflect a desire to avoid costly mistakes that could arise from radical changes to their systems.

ANALYSIS OF THE DATRONTECH CASE STUDY

The Datrontech case demonstrates that many of the factors outlined in the theoretical framework in this chapter may be valid. The company was familiar with computing technology as this was its line of business and it was already involved in electronic purchasing using EDI with one of its main customers. Furthermore, the company did not opt for radical change and it made use of an existing and proven system (Maginus). Datrontech also used the expertise of established companies (USWeb and MANCOS) with a track record of providing workable systems. The company is planning to rapidly expand the use of e-commerce to the extent that the majority of its future business will be via the Internet and this will be directly linked to the logistics system to supply the products to customers. However, this development is basically an evolution of its previous telephone-based customer system and EDI link to Dixons. Datrontech plan to expand the use of the Maginus system to hunt for suppliers by

developing the information gathered by the Internet to develop new customer links.

The logic of its strategic approach would suggest that if the move to e-commerce is successful in reducing costs and expanding market share (that is, the organizational structure has become more efficient) it is likely that the company will follow this route. In this scenario organizations with similar problems and opportunities will also adopt such e-commerce solutions. If they do not, it is likely that recalcitrant companies will suffer a decline in competitiveness. Nevertheless, hesitant organizations (in terms of adopting e-commerce solutions) may gain if early adoption of Internet-based systems proves to be costly and to alienate large sections of the customer base. There may be advantages from being a second mover in terms of adopting e-commerce solutions. However, organizations that wait too long may find that the early movers have developed cost and quality advantages which make it difficult for late movers to take effective remedial action. Timing is very important in the adoption of e-commerce solutions.

SOME IMPLICATIONS OF ADOPTING E-COMMERCE

The purchasing activities of both firms and consumers will radically alter for buying and selling products which are amenable to e-commerce systems. Buyers and sellers may obtain a number of benefits from using e-commerce systems, as follows:

1. Reduced search costs for finding sources of supply at least cost for a given quality of products.
2. Cheap systems for exploring new sources of supply and discovering new products to meet customer needs and requirements.
3. Lower costs associated with paying for purchases.
4. Low cost of conveying needs and requirements to suppliers.
5. Reduced costs of monitoring delivery and service performance of suppliers because information on these factors can be recorded on IT systems.

These benefits permit buyers to increase their opportunities to acquire better and lower cost products and to achieve these desirable outcomes at lower cost than traditional systems. Suppliers also benefit from lower costs associated with payments as invoicing and transfer of funds can be done electronically. Moreover, suppliers will be able to build up, at low cost, profiles on the needs and buying behaviour of their customers.

Potential problems for buyers and sellers who use e-commerce systems can be summarized as follows:

1. Overcoming bugs in the technology and dealing with the problems that arise when systems crash.
2. Devising organizational systems that can effectively deal with the technical and operational problems which arise from e-commerce systems.
3. Making best use of the huge flow of information available from e-commerce systems.
4. Engendering trust between buyers and sellers who conduct business in a virtual world.
5. Dealing with different laws and policies when engaging in cross-frontier transactions.
6. Deciding to be a first or a second mover.

To benefit from the use of e-commerce systems buyers and sellers must construct new organizational systems that can overcome or at least reduce the problems associated with using these systems. The main issues to resolve are to determine if e-commerce solutions can deliver beneficial outcomes. If this is the case, organizations must decide whether these benefits will be available to first movers or if second movers can avoid the costs and problems associated with being a pioneer. Switching to an e-commerce system involves significant changes in the search, monitoring and payment activities associated with purchasing to ensure that higher quality at least cost is obtained. On-line catalogues must be constructed and updated in the light of the stated and known needs and requirements of purchasers. New logistical systems have to be developed to deliver products to customers in accordance with the stated requirements of buyers. Progress chasing systems must be altered to operate using on-line systems. Invoicing, payment and account clearing systems will have to be altered to operate with on-line systems. To take full advantage of the large flow of information on available sources of supply, quality and prices it will be necessary to introduce new procedures for processing information to enable decisions to be made on how best to proceed with future purchasing plans. Methods have to be found to protect intellectual property and to ensure that trust, or low cost recourse to the law, can be obtained in relationships between buyers and sellers in a virtual world.

CONCLUSIONS

To summarize, the key to making the most appropriate use of e-commerce is to ensure that organizational and system changes stay one step ahead of the competition; or that e-commerce solutions can be adopted when the bugs have been removed from the systems. This approach avoids the costs of learning by making mistakes. As stated earlier, being a first mover and keeping ahead of the game can be a dangerous strategy because costs of human and capital assets to effectively implement e-commerce solutions are high and the cost of learning by mistakes can also be high, while the danger with the second approach is that competitors who move first may gain cost and quality advantages thus making it impossible for late movers to compete.

Some types of business activities are more amenable to e-commerce solutions than others. Purchasing and supply activities that are already largely based on processes carried out with low levels of direct human contact such as mail order, telephone or EDI, are more amenable to develop into e-commerce solutions than those which are dependent on high levels of direct human contact. In cases where human contact is a vital part of transactions the virtual world of the Internet is unlikely to provide an attractive means of conducting purchasing and supply activities. The ability and willingness of buyers and sellers to effectively handle computer-based technology is also important in the success or failure of e-commerce solutions. It is extremely likely that the ability and willingness of people to live, work and communicate in a virtual world will grow, given the current and continuing growth in popularity of the Internet. However, there are many cultural, social, technological, economic and legal problems associated with the widespread use of virtual world technologies. These problems will not disappear quickly and in some major areas direct human interaction will continue to be very important for the foreseeable future.

Effective strategies towards the adoption of e-commerce must be based on a good understanding of the costs and benefits of using virtual world technologies. However, identifying and measuring these costs and benefits will not be easy. The costs of mistiming the introduction of e-commerce solutions, or of over- or under-using these technologies, can be very high. Nevertheless, it is likely that many purchasing and supply processes will be fundamentally changed by the introduction of e-commerce solutions and this is also likely to happen quickly. Consequently, developing and implementing the appropriate e-commerce strategies will be vital in many industries and sectors for maintaining competitiveness.

REFERENCES

Aston, R. and Schwarz, J. (1992), *Gateway to the Next Millennium*, Cambridge: AP Professional.

Barney, J. (1993), 'Firm Resources and Sustained Competitive Advantage', *Journal of Management*, 17, pp. 99–120.

Coase, R. (1937), 'The nature of the firm', *Economica*, 4, pp. 386–405.

Cronin, M. (1994), *Doing Business on the Internet; How the Electronic Highway is Transforming American Companies*, New York: Van Nostrand Reinhold.

Davis, S. and Botkin, J. (1991), *20:20 Vision: Transforming Your Business Today to Succeed in Tomorrow's Economy*, New York: Simon & Schuster.

Department of Trade and Industry White Paper (1998), *Our Competitive Future: Building the Knowledge Driven Economy-Digital Economy*, London: HMSO.

Department of Trade and Industry (1999), *Building Confidence in Electronic Commerce: A Consultation Document*, London: DTI.

European Commission (1997), *Green Paper on the Convergence of the Telecommunications, Media and IT Sectors, and Implications for the Regulation Towards an Information Society Approach*, Luxembourg.

European Commission (1998), *Community Action Plan on promoting safe use of the Internet*, Com (98), 518, Brussels: Office for the Official Publications of the EC.

Lloyd, P. and Boyle, P. (1998), *Web-Weaving: Intranets, Extranets and Strategic Alliances*, Oxford: Butterworth Heinemann.

Milgrom, P. (1988), 'Employment contracts influencing costs and the organization of economic activity', *Journal of Political Economy*, 96, pp. 42–60.

Organization for Economic Co-operation and Development (OECD) (1998), *Electronic Commerce and the Information Society*, Paris: OECD.

OECD (1999), *International Guidelines for Consumer Protection in E-commerce*, Paris: OECD.

Office of the Vice-President (1999), *Towards Digital eQuality*, Washington, DC.

Peteraf, M. (1993), 'The cornerstones of competitive advantage: a resource-based view', *Strategic Management Journal*, 14, pp. 179–191.

Tapscott, D. (1995), *The Digital Economy: Promise and Peril in the Age of Network Intelligence*, New York: McGraw-Hill.

Wernerfelt, B. (1984), 'A resource-based view of the firm', *Strategic Management Journal*, 5, pp. 171–180.

Williamson, O. (1985), *The Economic Institutions of Capitalism*, New York: Free Press.

CHAPTER SIXTEEN

The strategic contribution of e-commerce to MRO procurement

Simon R. Croom

This chapter presents the findings of a six-month research project examining the optimization of purchasing for maintenance, repair and operating (MRO) supplies through purchase process reengineering. In particular, the use and development of the Internet as a channel for procurement of MRO items was examined.

Whilst there exists a significant body of research into the area of production and primary resources procurement, such research evidence in the supporting, secondary or non-production area is poorly represented. The main research into the procurement process has been carried out in the USA by Fearon and Bales, and recently there has been research by Craig, Carter and Hendrick. A study commissioned by the National Association of Purchasing Managers into the future of purchasing and supply by Arizona State and Michigan State Universities with AT Kearney incorporates Internet-based commerce. In the Netherlands, van Weele and Telgen have explored aspects of the purchasing process, and there has been some coverage of the subject in supply chain and logistics texts.

Much of the existing data relating to the purchasing process is either single-case, self reported (for example, General Electric, Chrysler, Microsoft) or speculative. Throughout the 1980s, widely discussed case examples demonstrated how the use of telecommunications networks to link firms to their suppliers and distribution chains conveyed important first mover advantages. These cases included organizations such as Microsoft, Chrysler, Ford, General Electric, BT, Nortel, Siemens, American Hospital Supply and McKesson. From this body of literature and

reportage the benefits to the firms deploying such electronic links included:

- increased efficiency of order processing;
- reduced costs due to just-in-time inventory management;
- locking in trading partners because of the difficulties competitors faced once a network is in place; and
- greater ability to customize products and services based upon information arising from the transactions carried by the network (Cash and Konsynski 1985; Johnson and Vitale 1988).

In the past, these networks were *hierarchical*, typically put into place by a dominant firm in a value chain, and were built upon proprietary applications running over private networks. Chrysler, for example, required its parts suppliers to participate in its electronic data interchange (EDI) network. They were often implemented with the most important existing trading partners. In fact, on the upstream side, a typical goal for such applications as EDI was to reduce the total number of suppliers and enhance the quality and efficiency of the overall purchasing function (Kekre and Mudhopadhyay 1992).

The increasing standardization of such applications as EDI, as well as the availability of lower cost public network infrastructures, has convinced several researchers that inter-organizational networks will not only proliferate, but will be applied in qualitatively different ways. In particular, as the barriers to participation in such electronic transactions diminish, some researchers now believe that the conditions are ripe for the establishment of electronic market places. Rather than having networks linking existing trading partners in a tightly coupled arrangement, such new electronic markets could conceivably include larger numbers of buyers and sellers (Malone et al. 1987; Wildman and Guerin-Calvert 1991). Furthermore, Malone, Yates and Benjamin argue that the development of inter-organizational electronic networks can improve co-ordination between firms to reduce the costs of searching for appropriate goods and services (they call these electronic brokerage effects). Consequently, they claim that one of the major effects of inter-organizational networks would be a shift from hierarchical to market relationships.

TO HIERARCHIES OR MARKETS, VIA NETWORKS?

Some of the initial providers of electronic markets have attempted ... to capture customers in a system biased towards a particular supplier. We believe that, in the long run, the significant additional benefits to buyers possible from the electronic brokerage effect will drive almost all electronic markets toward being unbiased channels for products from many suppliers (Malone et al. 1987).

Thus, the use of open information systems can provide greater levels of information to buyers, thereby opening up greater competitiveness between providers. In simple terms, *electronic markets* provide conditions approaching the economic model of perfect competition. However, a converse effect is also hypothesized, whereby using electronic networks to reduce the costs of tightly integrating a particular buyer and seller, firms can achieve an *electronic integration* effect. An example would be an EDI system connecting a retailer's point of sale terminals to a supplier's delivery system, decreasing the likelihood of the retailer going out of stock on popular goods (Weber 1995). Malone et al. (1987) base their predictions about the dominance of electronic markets on the relative benefits they anticipate firms will receive from electronic brokerage and integration.

A MACRO-VIEW OF THE IMPLICATIONS FOR MARKET TRANSACTIONS OF ELECTRONIC COMMERCE

Most economists believe that, were it not for the costs of co-ordination, markets would generally be more efficient mechanisms for production than hierarchies. These costs of co-ordination relate to the planning, control, management and administration of economic activity. It is held that purchasing goods and services on the open market raises the costs of co-ordination through the additional search costs in identifying appropriate suppliers, costs of specifying and enforcing contracts, and the administration of the financial settlement (Williamson 1975). For example, customers can have difficulty specifying what they want and searching through the many alternatives to find the best suppliers and best goods, and suppliers incur costs in advertising the availability of their goods and services to potential customers (Malone et al. 1987).

Using the value chain as their framework, Malone et al. argue that the use of electronic communication links between firms can reduce both the costs of co-ordinating economic transactions and the costs of co-ordinating production. Because modern information technology lowers the costs of both communication and information processing, Malone and his colleagues hypothesize that the result of reducing co-ordination costs without changing anything else should be an increase in the proportion of economic activity co-ordinated by markets (p. 489). In other words, lowered co-ordination costs would encourage more outsourcing, enabling firms to buy goods and services less expensively than to produce them in-house (Malone 1987; Malone et al. 1987, 1989).

Empirical tests of this hypothesis are only starting, and this chapter reports on one such study. Existing evidence at the industry level indicates that increases in investment in information technology are associated with a decline in average firm size and rise in the number of firms (Brynjolffson et al. 1993). Kambil (1991) also shows that industries investing more of their capital stock in information technology (IT) also contract out more of the value of the goods and services they produce to external suppliers (that is, a higher buy-make ratio in production), with a two-year lag. As investment in information channels increases, it is therefore anticipated that firms will increase their level of outsourcing. This hypothesis is an important research topic, but is beyond the scope of this chapter.

DEVELOPMENTS IN INTERNET ELECTRONIC TRADING ACTIVITY

There have been a number of estimates of the size and scope of business-to-business Internet-based electronic commerce (e-commerce) markets. For example, IDC 1999 predicted that business purchases conducted via Web-based media in Europe would be in the order of 150 billion Euros in 2001 (see Figure 16.1). Morgan Stanley's (1997) estimate for US business-to-business e-commerce is $88 billion; Forrester Research's estimate is $100 billion per annum and the Yankee Group place the figure at around $134 billion. Although estimates for the UK are far more speculative, due to the later adoption of the Internet, 43

per cent of UK respondents in a 1997 survey indicated that they were using the Internet for some degree of inter-organizational communications.

Recent research by Forrester indicated that half of the US Fortune 1000 organizations were actively investigating the use of the Internet to reach out to their smaller suppliers. Further developments in electronic commerce have seen the establishment of a standard for acquiring MRO items on the Internet by American Express and the Internet Purchasing Roundtable. The Open Buying on the Internet (OBI) standard is intended to enable interoperability between companies.

To date, electronic business-to-business commerce can be seen to have progressed through three waves of development based upon the mediating technology: electronic data interchange (EDI), area networks (such as Value-Added Networks (VANs) and the Internet. The advantage of the Internet as an e-commerce media over VANs and EDI is undoubtedly its ubiquity. This is seen as a major driver in the adoption of electronic business-to-business commerce, largely due to the widespread accessibility of the Internet as a transaction mediator. In addition, domestic use of the Internet is raising capability across organizations. A final factor is the benefit of a non-platform de-

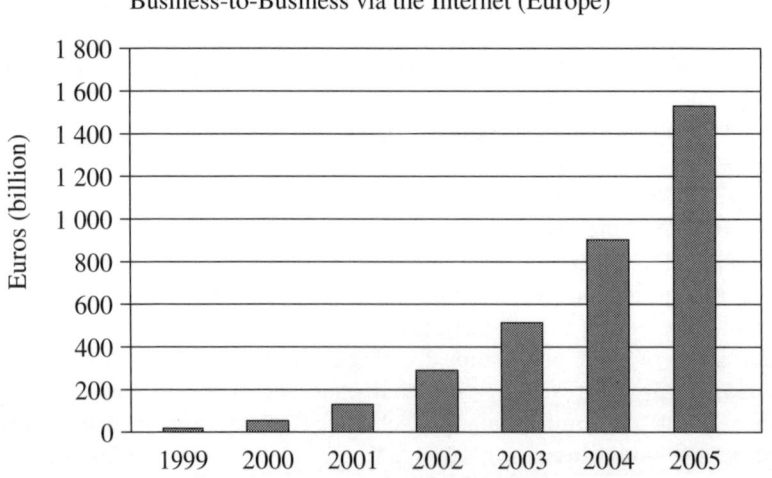

Business-to-Business via the Internet (Europe)

Euros (billion) — 1999, 2000, 2001, 2002, 2003, 2004, 2005

Figure 16.1
IDC prediction for Web-based business in Europe (based on data supplied by IDC)

pendent media, so that any level of personal computer is able, with appropriate browser software, to access the Internet.

EMPIRICAL INVESTIGATIONS OF ELECTRONIC NETWORKS AND INTER-ORGANIZATIONAL RELATIONSHIPS

In two studies, the first of McKesson Pharmaceutical's use of their network to link to independent pharmacies and the second of American Hospital Supply's system to take orders from hospitals (Keen 1988), both cases were proprietary (that is, not open) inter-organizational systems. The networks were primarily put into place with existing trading partners, and were not accessible by those not included in the system. Particularly in McKesson's case, the use of the network bound customers more tightly to the supplying firm and enhanced an already existing hierarchical relationship.

A multi-organization study by Brousseau (1990) reviewed 26 inter-organizational networks, finding that most were used to reduce production or distribution costs and served to reinforce already existing hierarchical relationships among firms. Only in two cases – from the petroleum and textiles industries – was the use of inter-organizational networks associated with buyers gaining advantage by having more suppliers from which to choose. Taken collectively, previous case study research illustrates that inter-firm networks are often used to support *electronic hierarchies*, rather than electronic market places.

One hypothesis explaining the prevalence of electronic hierarchies is that the high cost of extending private networks to trading partners encourages linkages only when a meaningful volume of transactions is expected to occur. The firm controlling the network application is further encouraged to add new types of transactions fully to load the network, justifying the dedicated capacity to each trading partner.

Thus, where data networks are proprietary and fragmented, as was the case before the growth of the Internet, electronic hierarchies are more common than electronic market places. This further suggests that when public and ubiquitous

data networks are available, the same constraints on connecting low volume trading partners, or potential partners for whom anticipated volume is uncertain, does not exist. Under such conditions, electronic market places, where more fleeting trading relationships can economically be supported by network-based transactions, should be more likely.

The review of the empirical literature shows that both electronic hierarchies and markets have been observed in practice, but the former are, in fact, more commonly observed in business-to-business networks. In general, the more extensively firms used inter-organizational networks, the more hierarchical were their relationships with trading partners, even when using highly open and ubiquitous public data network infrastructures. The relative openness of the network did not appear to predispose firms to relate to their business trading partners on a transaction-by-transaction basis, although the reduced cost of adding new partners did appear to make it easier for electronic service providers to include trading partners which only generated low volumes of transactions. Case study findings have also been consistent with the expectation that third party 'marketmakers', who provide brokerage services such as product search, comparison and evaluation, are likely to be necessary for real electronic market places to evolve.

The survey and case studies tell us little about the specific costs firms incur in their transactions, or about the costs of search and advertising, trade execution, settlement, monitoring or service after the trade. We do not know if other suppliers were available, and if there is sufficient variability in price, quality, or service to make the search for new suppliers worthwhile. We do not know if acquired goods were standard, and therefore obtainable elsewhere, or customized, and asset-specific.

RESEARCH METHODOLOGY

An exploratory study was conducted during 1998 into the level of deployment and benefits of Web-based procurement systems for the procurement of operating resources in the UK, continental Europe and the US. Participants in the study included procurement executives, information systems executives and key account sales executives. In depth semi-structured interviews were conducted with 37 individuals representing 32 organizations from industry, including national as well as multinational organizations, public sector bodies and government departments. Industrial sectors represented included fast moving consumer goods (FMCG), engineering, automotive, financial services, travel and hospitality and management services.

A quasi-Delphi method was adopted in which three rounds of interviews were conducted with the respondents at each stage reporting back the analysis from earlier rounds as well as providing the opportunity to explore issues in further detail.

ADVANTAGES OF WEB-BASED PROCUREMENT (E-PROCUREMENT)

From the study four main areas of benefit were identified, two of which are classed as 'operational' and two as 'strategic'. The operational benefits relate to the ability to reduce the administrative costs of the whole procurement process by two-thirds, and the improved audit of each transaction throughout the process. The strategic benefits include greater influence and control over expenditure by the procurement function (in many cases this was seen as a step towards raising the status and professionalism of the function) and greater opportunity to manage the total supply base. Concerns regarding Web-based transactions related to the supply of services and issues pertaining to information and data security.

PROCUREMENT PROCESS ADMINISTRATION

An initial cost analysis was conducted with a large European pharmaceutical organization (see Table 16.1). The data was adjusted and simplified to demonstrate the scale of administrative cost difference between manual and electronic procurement processes. The original analysis was then circulated to the organizations participating in round two of the Delphi study

in order to gain a wider validation of the data analysis. The resulting data represents a synthetic model agreed by the study participants.

Table 16.1 Synthetic process cost analysis for a Web-based procurement process

Process Stage	Manual Process (Adjusted Costs)	E-Procurement System (Adjusted Costs)
Requisition Generation	65.77	29.2
Requisition Distribution	6.05	0.0
Order Generation	9.87	1.5
Order Distribution	0.87	0.0
Expediting	0.91	0.3
Goods Receipt	3.83	1.5
Invoice Processing	9.40	0.7
Material	3.31	0.0
Total	100.00	33.2

Using the manual system costs as the base index (=100). Process stages with zero data entry illustrate redundant processes.

EXPENDITURE CONTROL

In the context of a typical large organization, each budget holder may be engaged in MRO procurement activity ranging from petty cash items (less than £1000) to £5000 transactions. Due to the fragmentation of budget holders in organizations it is very difficult to establish the exact size of the internal customer base (that is, those individuals who would raise requisitions). It has only been possible through this study to obtain estimated numbers. In order to represent this data a ratio of two internal customers per £1,000 of MRO procurement has been developed, excluding petty cash purchases. This serves to adjust for organizational size and variety within the sample.

AUDIT TRAIL

With a wide internal customer base and variety of transaction value a major administrative issue was the lack of clear information and consequently a weak audit trail. This was an important factor for major and/or global financial services, retail, food manufacture and automotive sector organizations. The e-procurement process provides visibility of the organization's many MRO transactions by individual budget holders, and thus offers a considerable improvement in the audit trail.

INCREASED PROCUREMENT CONTROL

The variety and variation of MRO items presented all respondents with considerable difficulty in terms of developing specialist knowledge regarding product and service technical characteristics, and supply market conditions.

The ability to consolidate and categorize suppliers, services and MRO goods is seen as an enabler in the move towards greater professional contribution to MRO procurement, without losing any level of service to internal users.

In fragmented, large organizations, procurement is carried out by numerous functions, either as local purchasing offices, or outside of the purchasing line of management (that is, with budget holders). Furthermore, purchasers may be remote from the user, often never having contact other than via telephone and requisition. The consolidation, transparency and real-time data benefits of e-procurement enable greater co-ordination between the user groups and purchasers. In addition, any centralized purchasing function was able to exert greater control over sources of supply, purchase price and inventory policy. Coupled with the enhanced status of purchasing, the ability to gain influence over MRO procurement was seen as being a critical factor in the decision to adopt an e-procurement system.

BENEFITS FOR THE MANAGEMENT OF SUPPLIERS

Greater visibility of total procurement is seen as an enabler for supply base reduction in MRO procurement. Typically, a supply base consisting of 5000+ suppliers was cited in the larger respondent organizations. A prerequisite for many e-procurement systems is a comprehensive supplier catalogue, and thus a supply base reduction strategy was seen as complementary to the adoption of e-procurement. Supply base reduction brings with it considerable benefit in terms of consolidation economies arising from the reduction in the number of supplier relationships and the ability to increase the volume of transactions with each supplier without a commensurate increase in the level of process activity.

As a result of greater visibility of the procurement expenditure and categories of MRO items, the ability to apply leverage over suppliers through centralization of procurement authority was seen as a key driver in the adoption of Internet MRO procurement by every respondent. However, there was a real concern relating to the extent of dependency on the suppliers once they are tied in to the supplier catalogue system. The distinction was made earlier in this report between electronic hierarchies and markets. The intermediating catalogue system serves to tie customers in to the chosen supplier, and at the same time serves as a barrier to entry for non-catalogue compliant suppliers. In particular this may have the effect of excluding small to medium-sized enterprises (SMEs).

DISADVANTAGES OF WEB-BASED PROCUREMENT (E-PROCUREMENT)

Following the above discussion of the advantages of e-procurement, the next section details its disadvantages.

THE MANAGEMENT OF SERVICES SUPPLY

One unresolved issue was the application of Internet systems for the more complex issue of service provision such as facilities services (for example, cleaning and catering). Means of real-time measurement of service performance were regarded as necessary for such systems in order to achieve effective supplier monitoring. Research into outsourced service provision has demonstrated considerable difficulty in service quality measurement. Although advances have been made, they are principally in people-based systems.

SECURITY

A major concern for any open protocol is that of data security. The issue of security was a major concern for all of the respondents in this study, especially in the context of electronic payments. Whilst data encryption advances appear to have secured electronic payment transfer, the level of resistance expressed was considerable. Particular anxieties were raised from organizations in the financial services and legal services sectors, primarily concerning the nature of firewalls surrounding their own systems and the potential risk from outside intrusion. Wider security issues related to funds transfer via the Internet, yet this seemed to reflect ignorance regarding existing electronic funds transfer systems rather than real concerns for the integrity of funds transfer. Secure data transfer is a major performance criterion for existing and potential users of e-procurement systems.

IMPACT ON PROCUREMENT STRATEGY

The impact of e-procurement on purchasing strategy is believed to be a major factor in the adoption of MRO systems. Currently many MRO items are managed as tactical, administrative commodities or services. As a consequence, there is considerable sub-optimization in current MRO procurement. This is largely due to the high variety and low value of many MRO items. However, improved information will enable greater consolidation and increased economies of purchase leverage. This in effect means that organizations will be able to manage their MRO low value items in a more strategic manner through such actions as the establishment of single-source arrangements, consolidation and rationalization of commodities and services, and increased buying power over the supply base.

The use of e-procurement for the management of MRO items will provide immense strategic advantage to the purchasing organization. It will be possible to manage such items with improved information, greater purchase leverage, and an increased internal service level.

A procurement matrix may be employed to illustrate the potential to reposition the procurement strategy for MRO items as a direct consequence of the informational advantages of e-procurement (see Figure 16.2). Through improved information transparency it will be possible to adopt more 'strategic' procurement approaches such as supply base reduction, lean logistics, partnership relationships and long-term supply contracts (Lamming 1993; Hines 1994).

CONCLUSIONS

This research has been exploratory in nature, intended to identify key concerns and opportunities for electronic procurement rather than examine the scale and relationships between dominant variables in the adoption of e-procurement. It is contended that such research is a useful development from the study reported here.

A number of key observations can be made regarding the impact of open Web-based trans-

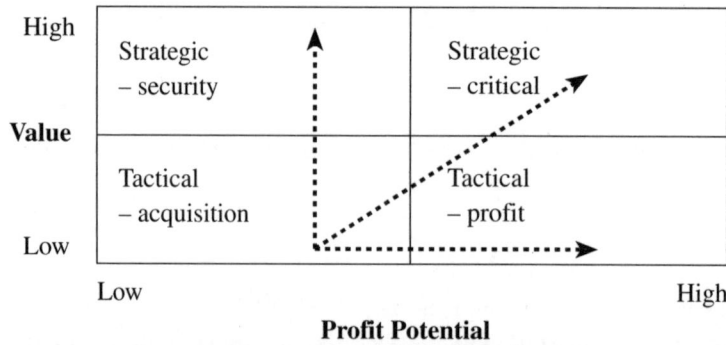

Figure 16.2 Repositioning Maintenance, Repair and Operating (MRO) procurement items as a result of information transparency (Source: Adapted from Elliot-Shircore, and Steele 1985)

actional channels on business-to-business markets:

- The forms of governance available to an organization range from markets through to hierarchies – this will not differ because of the advent of Internet-based transactions.
- E-commerce may be conducted through a range of electronic governance structures from electronic markets to hierarchies.
- According to economic theory, (electronic) markets will be more efficient mechanisms for the conduct of transactions (that is, they will achieve lower costs and higher value) than (electronic) hierarchies.
- In practice, imperfect knowledge (a consequence of imperfect information) and opportunistic behaviours serve to distort transactions and lead to less than optimal conditions.
- It is posited here that e-commerce, and especially e-procurement, improves knowledge assets, thereby leading to economic transactions near to optimal efficiencies.
- Whilst the economics of transactions may change to provide lower competitive barriers to supply, closer ties, expanded service and improved value-adding activities can tie in suppliers through the use of partnership sourcing processes.

The opportunities for strategic management of operating resources have been found so far to be important considerations in the decision to adopt e-procurement. By raising the service levels to internal customers, and by providing greatly improved and robust information relating to the procurement process, the benefits of any form of e-procurement system are far greater than the frequently cited process cost reductions. Whilst these are undoubtedly important in their own right, the ability to apply 'professional' purchasing practices and policies across the range of an organization's supply catalogue are likely to have significant benefits for profitability and the status of the purchasing function.

Such a prognosis is naturally appealing. However, many suppliers have already recognized the benefits of tie-in through their own Web-based sales systems, and thus first mover ben-

efits may drive the development of business-to-business e-commerce from the supply rather than the buyer side.

REFERENCES

Brousseau, E. (1990), 'Information technologies and inter-firm relationships: the spread of inter-organizational telematics systems and its impact on economic structure', paper presented to the *International Telecommunications Society*, Venice, June.

Brynjolffson, E., Malone, T., Gurbaxani, V. and Kambil, A. (1993), *Does Information Technology Lead To Smaller Firms?*, unpublished manuscript, Cambridge, MA: Massachusetts Institute of Technology.

Cash, J.I. and Konsynski, B.R. (1985), 'IS redraws competitive boundaries', *Harvard Business Review*, March-April, pp. 134–142.

Hines, P. (1994), *Creating World Class Suppliers. Unlocking Mutual Competitive Advantage*, London: Pitman.

Johnston, H.R. and Vitale, M.R. (1988), 'Creating competitive advantage with inter-organizational information systems', *MIS Quarterly*, June, pp. 153–165.

Kambil, A. (1991), 'Information technology and vertical integration: Evidence from the manufacturing sector', in Guerin-Calvert, M. and Wildman, S. (Eds), *Electronic Services Networks: A Business And Public Policy Challenge*, New York: Praeger, pp. 22–38.

Keen, P. (1988), *Competing in Time: Using Telecommunications for Competitive Advantage*, Cambridge, MA: Ballinger Press.

Kekre, S. and Mudhopadhyay, T. (1992), 'Impact of electronic data interchange technology on quality improvement and inventory reduction programs: A field study', *International Journal of Production Economics*, 28, pp. 265–282.

Lamming, R.C. (1993), *Beyond Partnership: Strategies for Innovation and Lean Supply*, London: Prentice Hall.

Malone, T. (1987), 'Modelling co-ordination in organizations and markets', *Management Science*, 33, pp. 1317–1332.

Malone, T., Yates, J. and Benjamin, R. (1987), 'Electronic markets and electronic hierarchies:

effects of information technology on market structure and corporate strategies', *Communications of the ACM*, **30**(6), pp. 484–497.

Malone, T., Yates, J. and Benjamin, R. (1989), 'The logic of electronic markets', *Harvard Business Review*, May-June, pp. 166–171.

Morgan Stanley (1997), *The Internet Retailing Report*, (http://www.ms.com).

Weber, J (1995), 'Just get to the stores on time', *Business Week*, March 6, pp. 66–67.

Wildman, S. and Guerin-Calvert, M. (1991), 'Electronic services networks: functions, structures, and public policy', in Guerin-Calvert, M. and Wildman, S. (Eds), *Electronic Services Networks: A Business and Public Policy Challenge*, New York: Praeger, pp. 3–21.

Williamson, O.E. (1975), *Markets and Hierarchies: Analysis and Antitrust Implications*, New York: Free Press.

CHAPTER SEVENTEEN

Supporting decentralized supplier management by publishing tenders on the Internet

W. Brenner and G. Wilking

The aim of the business process of purchasing is to place desired goods at the disposal of employees in time and with the expected functionality (Brenner 1994). Its fundamental elements can be seen in the observation of the input market as well as the cultivation of relationships with suppliers. In the 1990s, it became obvious that establishing and cultivating these relationships has an essential impact on the overall success of a company (Lamming 1993). In this situation, the Internet enables a new quality of input into market-oriented activities, as the case of Brother Industries shows.

As a corporation operating internationally, Brother have been in contact with business partners in forums for some time. The Web pages of Brother Industry have been highlighted as exemplary applications (Caffrey 1999). They are assigned to Brother's International Procurement Offices (IPOs) and support their work. The pages of Brother International Procurement (Brother 1999) can be called up either directly or via the company's home page. The 'Procurement Home Page' is clearly and strictly functionally arranged (<http://www.brother.com/E-procurement/e-procurement.html>). The single components of the page can be selected as menu items. Next to some introductory remarks about the procurement policy, a listing of the international purchasing offices and a description of the procedure for establishing business relations, under 'Suppliers Invitation' the visitor finds information relating to published procurement needs.

Altogether, the design of the Brother International Procurement Home Page is appropriate to its operational purpose, namely the establishment and cultivation of contacts with potential suppliers. The use of visual elements is reduced to a minimum, convenient user guidance being preferred. The structure of the page is clear and the reduced navigation depth based on the elimination of linked contents helps to avoid irritating the target audience. Finally, using the small icons contributes to increased design quality. Hence tenders can be intuitively identified and assigned to the product groups.

THE POTENTIAL OF THE INTERNET AND RELATED TECHNOLOGY

The example of Brother vividly illustrates reasons for using the Internet and particularly the World Wide Web (WWW) in purchasing (Brenner and Wilking 1997). The most important reason for this is the unlimited availability of information in time and space. From almost any place one always has access to data. In addition, data access can be designed intuitively and will consequently be easy to understand. In the example of Brother, it was the employment of the Web within the business-to-consumer field which created the basis for user friendly design. The private user generally speaking does not need official instructions in order to use a Website.

Tendering – as shown in the case of Brother – is a good example of the use of the Internet in purchasing. A prototype, developed by the authors at the University of Essen, shows one way in which publication of a company's needs can

Ausschr.-nummer	Kategorie	Artikelbezeichnung				Zeitraum
		ArtikelNr.:	**Kurzbezeichnung**	**Langbezeichnung**	**Menge**	
1	Büroartikel	1032	Papier	Papier DIN A4	5 Karton	18.08.2000 bis 30.08.2000
		1033	Folienstifte	Folienstifte bunt	10 Stück	
		1034	Folien	Folien für Tintenstrahldrucker	100 Stück	
		ArtikelNr.:	**Kurzbezeichnung**	**Langbezeichnung**	**Menge**	
59	Computer	1789	Bildschirm	Apple Cinema Display 22"	1 Stück	31.08.2000 bis 07.09.2000
				Apple Power Mac		

Figure 17.1   Tenders at www.beschaffung.net (beschaffung.net 2000)

be achieved. The columns in Figure 17.1 contain the following information:

- The identifying number of the tenders
- The category to which the tenders belong (i.e. stationery, computers)
- A description of the tenders
- The time during which the tenders will be valid.

Further characteristics of the Internet refer to the maturity and high standardization of the underlying technology. The wide spread of the Internet and the establishment of standards has led to high compatibility in technology and consequently to the comparatively low cost of the development and introduction of relevant systems and applications. In this way, several synergistic effects can be used, especially integration to existing data-processing landscapes. A final point concerns the immediate exchange of information. If the applications are accessible on-line, they allow the update and transfer of data in a very short time. This may happen by retrieval or delivery procedures. In addition, Web solutions based on simple e-mail systems have proven themselves successful.

A MODEL OF INTERNET-BASED PUBLICATION OF TENDERS

The next section will discuss a model of Internet-based publication.

STATE OF THE ART IN INTERNET-BASED PUBLICATION OF TENDERS

Existing purchasing-oriented pages, as mentioned above, often contain just basic components. In particular, the following points have to be considered (Caffrey 1997):

- description of the purchasing department's mission and objectives as well as purchasing policy statements;
- overview of products and services being procured by purchasing;
- supplier-related statement, concerning performance, certificates, shipment conditions and other matters; and
- information about how to get in contact with purchasing.

This information is the basis of purchasing-oriented pages. They provide information for suppliers in order that they can establish contact in the conventional way afterwards. This kind of dedicated purchasing-oriented page already represents progress. Interested visitors no longer have to infer possible procurement needs first from sales-oriented pages and then to investigate and contact the person in charge. The Internet presence of Alno AG in Germany (Alno 1999), a well-known producer of kitchens, is an example of a quite simple purchasing-oriented page. Following a reference at the company's home page, there is – in English and German – a general outline about the procurement programme and a form on which the interested supplier can register in order to make contact.

Even if some purchasing-oriented pages represent progress in comparison to established processes, because of the availability of relevant information, considerable potential still remains unused. The first point concerns the low specification of the information provided: in general with purchasing-oriented pages, one gets only general statements about purchasing needs. Detailed information, specifications and drawings are not usually presented. Consequently, conventional information and data exchange still remains necessary with all its related disadvantages such as transit time and error susceptibility.

Combined with the availability of general information, often only an address is mentioned, instead of passing on requests for quotation and tenders directly. The suppliers' enquiries and the bids themselves are sent in unstructured text, without using Internet-based forms. They have to be sorted out roughly and passed on. In this way, additional manual work is generated instead of outsourcing it to the supplier. Finally, it has to be mentioned that purchasing-oriented pages also have to fulfil the same requirements as other Websites. These requirements are access via links, search engines or appropriate addresses, questions of ergonomics and topicality, and not least the best possible connectivity to the Internet in order to enable optimal response time.

STRUCTURE OF THE INTERNET PRESENCE

Despite the evidence of publication of needs on the Internet this approach is still very new. Thus the question of an adequate cost–benefit return has to be answered. Here, a successive development of Web pages is suggested. Based on the specific characteristics of the Web, the extension should then be conducted step-by-step in the light of results already achieved. While developing an Internet presence, it is important to build on existing content, so that work does not have to be repeated for further extension of the pages (see Figure 17.2).

The first step is realizing a simple presence. It contains general remarks about purchasing and purchasing policies, an outline of the procurement programme, and contact details. The pages of Alno AG mentioned above are a good example of this (Alno 1999). Under the keyword 'Geschäftskontakte' (business contacts), general conditions and opportunities for taking up business contacts in the field of procurement with potential as well as established suppliers are explored. A simple opportunity to get in touch over

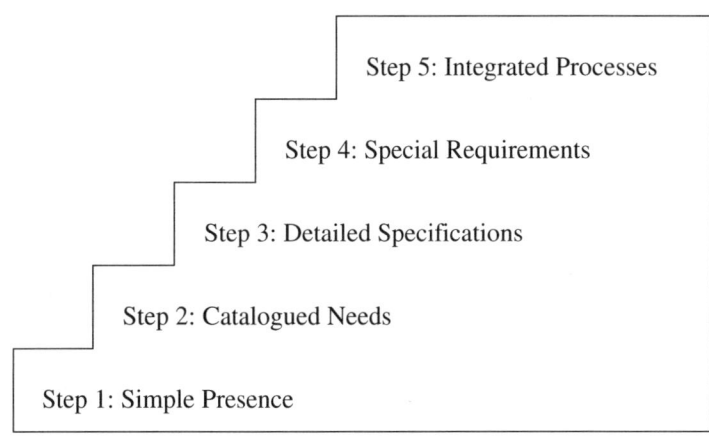

Figure 17.2 Phased model for the realization of the Internet presence of purchasing

Step 5: Integrated Processes

Step 4: Special Requirements

Step 3: Detailed Specifications

Step 2: Catalogued Needs

Step 1: Simple Presence

the Internet is provided. Entering the second step, the pages become more structured, particularly since procurement needs are no longer described in general terms, but are catalogued and split up into components. For this reason, an overview in terms of a table of contents and also a navigation aid is added to these pages. For example, the Deutsche Telekom AG, the main telecommunications provider in Germany, runs a Website, placed on a server in the United States on which representative requests for quotation are placed. They are categorized by headings and classification codes, and contain detailed information about requirements (Telekom 1998). A catalogue of procurement needs is part of the model's third step. It contains classified single products and groups of products, with detailed information and specifications. At this point, potential suppliers have the opportunity to register in a database. This supplier database plays an essential role in the operation of the pages as well as in Internet-based supplier management generally. In the next section, this will be described in more detail. ZF Friedrichshafen, a manufacturer of transmission systems, presents the procurement programme and current enquiries at great length on its purchasing-oriented page. In addition, interested suppliers are requested to fill in their data and profile in a 'Lieferanten Informations System (LIS)' (Suppliers' Information System) in order to register (ZF 1998).

At the fourth step specialized requisitions are provided; for example, technical drawings are presented, in an Internet-suited image format or as computer aided design (CAD) files for downloading. Another example is the regional distribution of requirements. The public sector in the United States publishes not only the actual needs for fuel but also the spatial distribution. Fuel generates very high transportation costs because of its bulk and weight. Thus, tenders from suppliers located far away can be excluded from the outset. In this way, manual work will be avoided by the employment of the Internet because of the implicit pre-selection of interested suppliers. As a final example, the American Priority Parts Service of the Defense Industrial Supply Center (DISC 1998) should be considered.

Here particularly urgent needs which can no longer be published in a conventional way, for example, in the paper-based *Commerce Business Daily*, are submitted via the Web. In this way the Internet enables a new form of purchasing which could not be realized by conventional means. Finally at the fifth step, a comprehensive interconnection of the pages with processes within the company is established to avoid data transfer interruptions as far as possible. These processes facilitate the publication of current and future needs as well as the resulting assessment of enquiries and tenders from interested suppliers. Thus, they enable a thorough use of dedicated purchasing-oriented pages: their realization is the subject of the following section.

THE ROLE OF A SUPPLIER DATABASE

Purchasing-oriented pages at the third or a higher stage require registration of interested suppliers. Data entered on a HTML form can be held in a supplier database. This is conducted for three reasons:

1. Contracts are evaluated in this way. Only after a positive confirmation can the supplier obtain access to restricted content. By logging in and using a password, the supplier can retrieve protected contents and CAD documents.
2. With their consent, the interested suppliers' Internet addresses are used to deliver information regularly and automatically by a push procedure. The person in charge in the company sends information to a listserver which then, based on the information contained by the database, distributes the data via e-mail.
3. The information requested from the potential supplier may be extensive and structured according to individual needs in order to increase its quality and to enable compatibility with the company's existing data structures. The required information, together with the time for the input of data onto the form, represent a hurdle for the visitors. Thus, only input from genuinely interested suppliers should be processed by the purchasing department.

Many companies move on to build up a company database, linked with the purchasing-oriented page, which is kept on an intranet – a company-run internal network, based on Internet technology. It holds centrally available supplier information, accessible to all employees. At the same time an existing infrastructure can be used. The benefits of an Internet-based supplier database may be summarized as follows:

● Information is held available and offered centrally. This ensures the avoidance of multiple task performance as well as an increase of data quality. This also applies to the evaluation of supplier performance.
● Basic data is provided by the suppliers themselves. In this way, manual and labour-intensive operations are outsourced while reaction times are reduced. The topicality of the data files increases.
● Business contacts of suppliers with different company locations become more transparent. Economies of scale established on an improved basis of negotiation and on a current exchange of experiences can be used.
● Components of the database can easily be opened for worldwide access by a third party, including by the suppliers involved. Suppliers can immediately check data concerning them, for example, for evaluation by the purchasing business units.
● Development of the site can be conducted by the employment of already existing system solutions, particularly those which are available on the Internet and possibly in the company as well. Employees and suppliers gain access via PCs provided with browsers and connected to networks.

Besides the structure of the page, questions regarding its operation and inter-connection within the company arise. Lack of connectivity is the main reason for the generation of manual work, instead of automatic processing. The processes of publishing tenders, which advertise purchasing requirements, as well as the assessment of incoming enquiries and tenders, are of special interest for the operation of purchasing-oriented pages. They are designed and carried out on the basis of strategic considerations.

THE PROCESS OF PUBLICATION

Before the introduction of the process, the structure of the request for quotation (RfQ) is of special interest. It has to be considered that not every republication of the RfQ necessitates a creative design process for layout and publication. The publication of tenders on Internet pages is instead based on templates. These are forms provided which standardize the development of a page, so that changing contents can be input for a specific screen. Requests for quotation by Hitachi show the structure of such templates (Hitachi 1999). The Hitachi Procurement Network (HPN) is an extensive application for the support of purchasing at Hitachi in Japan and other locations. The pages contain generally available information as well as content which is accessible only via a login with password protection. The 'RFQ (Request for Quotation) Item List' contains a form which helps the interested visitor to investigate specific RfQs. They are structured by product groups of first and second order, by Hitachi products and by Hitachi divisions. If the user makes a selection, a structured table with results will be shown which gives the potential suppliers information on how to proceed.

Recently, the development of templates has been supported by new Internet standards to which belong the Extensible Markup Language (XML), which is based on HyperText Markup Language (HTML), as well as Cascading Style Sheets (CSS). All of these use structures which help to separate textual content and layout on the screen (Bager 1997). In this way, content can be updated by a simple interchange within a given framework which is defined by the templates.

The publication of tenders is partially conducted in a decentralized manner. The needs are classified by required goods in an appropriate way, for example ABC-analysis. A products are of great importance for the company and put out to tender by the purchasing department in collaboration with the relevant specialist department. B-products are less important and

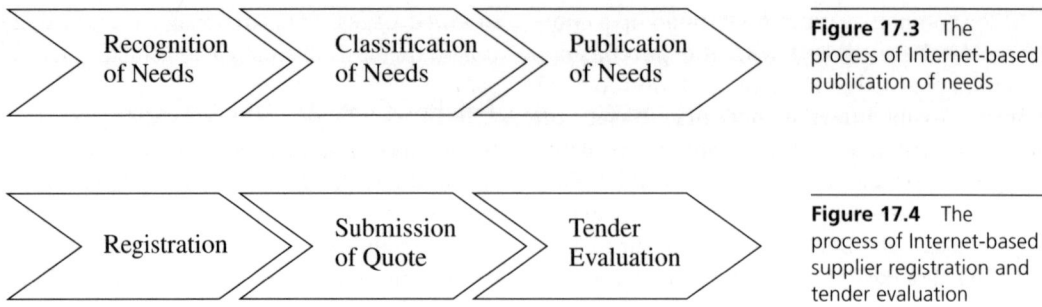

Figure 17.3 The process of Internet-based publication of needs

Figure 17.4 The process of Internet-based supplier registration and tender evaluation

can be independently purchased by the specialist department, so long as there exist general conditions and a fundamental framework for decentralized purchasing (Fearon et al. 1993). C-products, which are of little importance to the company, are not put out to tender. If the procurement of these products is based on a framework contract, this contract will be handled in the same way as A- or B-products. The pages can be put into operation after the establishment of the Internet presence and the templates as well as of the inter-connection of the specialist departments to the Internet server. This is carried out by the purchasing department in collaboration with the IT department and possibly with the specialist department involved.

The process of publication starts with the *recognition of needs* (Figure 17.3). This can be done manually or called up automatically via a manufacturing planning system. The *classification of needs* follows, since an appropriate template has to be determined according to the underlying information. The data which must be put into the template are compiled automatically or manually. Thus in the last step, the *publication of needs* can take place. This happens by filling in the templates, possibly releasing the request for quotation and finally adjusting the information which has been prepared automatically with the help of the templates on the server. From there data can be freely retrieved or password-protected as determined by the template. If active notification of potential suppliers by an e-mail-based push procedure is provided within the request for quotation, this will be invoked and carried out by the server. In order to

select the suppliers to be contacted, information from the supplier database is called up. The e-mail itself contains a reference to the pages of the RfQ which will be retrieved by the receiver of the e-mail.

THE PROCESS OF SUPPLIER REGISTRATION AND SUBMISSION OF QUOTES

The process which leads to the submission of a quote is presented in Figure 17.4. In *registration*, the interested suppliers first have the opportunity to register with the supplier database. Then they obtain access to the RfQ. The visitor carries out data input and enrolment via an Internet-based form. This form itself is structured in the same way as the established supplier database. These procedures are of great importance since the system can assign the person responsible depending on the product profile of the supplier. The person responsible evaluates the information and may approve it. In this case, the supplier is given a login name and password, and his data will be taken permanently into the database.

Following registration, the interested supplier is given the opportunity to inspect the page with the submitted needs. The *submission of quote* happens by inputting data into an Internet-based form. The structure of these forms follows the example of conventional templates (Drolshagen 1987). Furthermore, they contain a reference to the supplier's file in the supplier database; hence, the tender can be automatically sent to the appropriate person. In the final step, the processing and *evaluation of tender* will be conducted. Notification about receipt of a tender can be e-mailed, containing a hyperlink to the tender database.

Essential advantages of the employment of purchasing-oriented pages are that the form, which the interested supplier must fill in, can be designed according to the purchaser's requirements. This allows the outsourcing of data processing and data input activities to the supplier. This is particularly true for the input into the supplier database as described above. Furthermore, sufficient highly structured and specified data fields support the automatic processing of input. Examples of this kind of processing are as follows:

- automatic transmission to the officer in charge in the purchasing or in the specialist department;
- automatic assignment of bids to the tenders published; and
- comparability of the tenders based on a standardized structure – from the creation of hierarchies about all presented tenders by given data fields to an automatic pre-selection by means of agent-based systems.

EMBEDDING OF APPLICATIONS INTO A COMPREHENSIVE DECENTRALIZED SUPPLIER MANAGEMENT SYSTEM

The decentralization of activities of the purchasing department by means of Internet-based technologies can be expanded into other areas. In addition to the requests for quotation, an extensive network of suppliers can show the following components:

- information about capability and performance of suppliers, completed by existing contracts and terms of delivery, if possible completed by indices;
- commonly available and published documents from production planning for examination, CAD files for transfer from research and development to the production department as computer assisted manufacturing (CAM) files;
- logistics information, such as terms of delivery and shipping information;
- data from material requirement planning (MRP) or manufacturing resource planning (MRPII);

- information and documentation about ISO 9000 conformance; and
- internal purchaser-oriented information, for example, details of the purchasing policy and procurement planning, delivery times, new developments in the purchasing programme, news about technical trends and developments, shipping information, contracts and conditions and internal evaluation.

One example is provided by the Ford Supplier Network (FSN). Since 1996, the Ford Motor Corporation has built up a Virtual Private Network (VPN). It consists of approximately 30 000 Web pages which cover internal and purchasing-oriented information as well as information relevant to the suppliers. Currently, approximately 1900 suppliers are connected (Minahan 1998). The special benefit of an intranet and extranet, a part of the Internet with restricted access for approved partners, lies in easy connection within the company as well as in effective and efficient availability of information, which is kept and entered centrally and can therefore be kept up-to-date and consistent more easily.

SUMMARY

The sections above show that an essential part of the benefits achieved is based on the specific decentralization of purchasing activities. Not only purchasing departments but also specialist departments publish requests for quotation. For example, the research and development department has the opportunity to investigate new sources of procurement and business partners. Another dimension of decentralization lies within the outsourcing of purchasing activities to potential or existing suppliers combined with the semi-automatic preparation of processes enabled by this approach.

During the 1990s, the reorganization of purchasing processes based on appropriate information technology was often discussed in the literature (Brenner and Hamm 1996; Koppelmann and Lumbe 1994; Heinritz et al. 1991). This chapter presents a more practical overview of a new orientation of purchasing processes. At the Competence Centre for Information Technology and Purchasing at the Universities of Freiberg and Essen in Germany, a prototype is being developed, based on new procedures of purchasing to be implemented in co-operation with industrial partners (beschaffung.net 2000). It is clear that the specific IT profile of the Internet facilitates a new generation of processes which may not cover the whole purchasing spectrum but nevertheless can exploit new potential in many areas.

REFERENCES

Alno (1999), <http://www.alno.de>

Bager, J. (1997), 'HTML++, Style Sheets und XML – die Zukunft des Web?', *c't magazin für computertechnik*, **8**(97), p. 298 (in German).

beschaffung.net (2000),
<http://www.beschaffung.net>

Brenner, W. (1994), *Grundzüge des Informationsmanagements*, Berlin Heidelberg: Springer (in German).

Brenner, W. and Hamm, V. (1996), 'Information technology for purchasing in a process environment', *European Journal of Purchasing and Supply Management*, **2**(4), pp. 211–219.

Brenner, W. and Wilking, G. (1997), 'Unterstützungpotentiale des Internet im modernen Einkauf', *Der Ingenieur im Internet*, VDI Berichte 1362, Düsseldorf: VDI-Verlag (in German), pp. 151 ff.

Brother (1999), 'Welcome to Brother International Procurement Home Page!', <http://www.brother.com/E-procurement/e-procurement.html>

Caffrey, B. (1997), 'Spinning your Web', <http://purchasing.tqn.com/library/weekly/aa031297.htm>

Caffrey, B. (1999), 'Purchasing Department Sites', <http://purchasing.tqn.com/msub-corp.htm>

DISC (1998), 'Priority Parts Service', http://www.disc.dla.mil/bidboard/priority/index.html

Drolshagen, D. (1987), *Online-Einkauf mit System, Praxisbeispiel für den Einsatz von Standardsoftware*, Rationalisierungs-Kuratorium der Deutschen Wirtschaft (in German).

Fearon, H.E., Dobler, D.W. and Killen, K.H. (1993), *The Purchasing Handbook*, New York: McGraw-Hill, pp. 841–842.

Heinritz, S., Farrell, P., Giunipero, L. and Kolchin, M. (1991), *Purchasing: Principles and Applications*, New Jersey: Prentice Hall, p. 102.

Hitachi (1999), 'RFQ (Request for Quotation) Item List', <http://www3.hitachi.co.jp/HPN/owa/ hpwlcme.jmpctls>

Koppelmann, U. and Lumbe, H.-J. (Eds) (1994), *Prozeßorientierte Beschaffung*, Stuttgart: Schaeffer-Poeschel (in German), p. 38.

Lamming, R. (1993), *Beyond Partnership, Strategies for Innovation and Lean Supply*, Hemel Hempstead: Prentice Hall.

Minahan, T. (1998), 'Private Net improves talks between Ford and suppliers', *Purchasing Magazine*, 6.

Telekom (1998), 'Tender Information of Deutsche Telekom AG', <http://deutsche.telekomus.com>

ZF (1998), 'Einkauf, Werden Sie Partner von ZF', <http://www.zf-group.de/einkauf/e00_einkauf_ d.html>

Making use of Internet technology to achieve lean management in the West Midlands automotive supply chain

D.M. Thompson, G.R. Homer, P. Costello and S. Garner

INTRODUCTION – THE HYPOTHESIS

The Autolean project originated with the concept that there might be significant opportunities for improved supplier performance within the automotive supply chain through the application of Internet-technology lead communications and 'lean' business practices. The origins of lean business practices can be traced to the Toyota Production System (Monden 1983). This system assumed that business success could be achieved by the effective management of material through the supply chain, encompassing inventory management, production process, materials management and supplier development (Francis 1998).

These business processes are influenced by factors of information on timeliness, processing methods and cost. The Internet raises the opportunity of dramatically speeding up information flow across the supply chain and facilitates changes in the way companies do business with each other, that is, contributing to 'lean management'.

THE AUTOMOTIVE INDUSTRY – SOME 'LEAN' INITIATIVES

The KPMG and Harvard studies (Brown 1995) outlined the performance differences between automotive companies around the world and suggested that European manufacturers had lost much of their former leadership position. The study suggested that over 700 of the estimated 2100 West Midlands-based second tier automotive suppliers would have been deselected by their automotive suppliers by the year 2000. As a result of these studies several initiatives were established <www.ispo.cec.be> in order to redress the balance. The European Automotive Initiative Group (EAIG) was founded to help the European automotive industry regain its competitiveness by adopting lean practices. They defined lean as 'highly effective and efficient, focusing on customer value', whilst Harrison (1998) defines 'lean supply' as 'the need to support assembly processes with low cost and high quality components, yet with the capability to respond to customers' changing needs'. EAIG offers a platform for communication, experience exchange and co-operation in the form of annual congresses, seminars, ad hoc working groups and Internet forums. INTERLEAN <www.autoline.org> is an initiative undertaken by EAIG to provide a framework for supporting pilot projects for electronic commerce (e-commerce) in the automotive supply chain.

Another initiative funded by the European Commission is AUTOTRAIN, which assesses the techniques and methodologies for computer-based learning accessible via the Internet. It focuses on small companies and key participants are Rover, Ford of Spain, Volvo, Peugeot/Citroen, Lucas and Robert Bosch.

Industrial Transformation Realized via Education and Knowledge (IT REK) comprises four national projects (in the UK, France, Austria and Germany). The outcome will be a series of vocational training packages for SMEs (small to medium sized enterprises) whose employees can use them in the workplace. AUTOREG is a consortium of European Regions which provides a forum for identifying common issues and problems relating to the automotive industry.

THE ACCELERATE INITIATIVE

The Accelerate initiative was a three-year programme which began in 1995, with the objective of improving the competitiveness of the West Midlands Automotive Component Supply industry. The aim of the £29 million programme was to produce measurable and significant improvements in the key areas of cost, quality and delivery. Accelerate was targeted at 500 SMEs based in a geographical area known by the European Regional Development Fund Directorate as the Objective Two part of the West Midlands

in the UK (mainly Birmingham, Wolverhampton, Coventry, Warwickshire and the Black Country, an imprecisely defined geographic area comprising a subset of the West Midlands conurbation, which was the birthplace of traditional metal industries such as drop-forging, chainmaking and so on).

The programme proposed, through activities and services to carry out the following:

- benchmark companies against international and customer specific standards;
- identify areas of under-performance;
- implement performance improvement measures;
- build capacity in terms of expertise and management competence; and
- disseminate best practice along the whole supply chain.

The programme had the backing of some of the largest companies and organizations involved in the automotive industry, such as Jag-

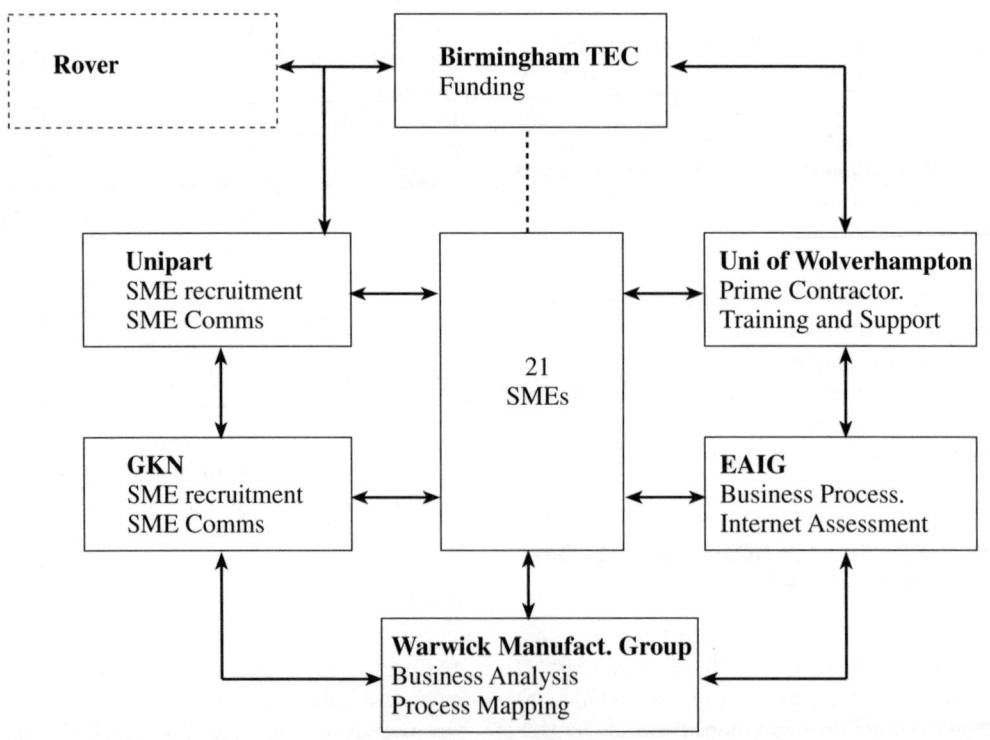

Figure 18.1 A schematic representation of the AutoLean project organization

uar, Peugeot, Rover Group and LDV (all first tier manufacturers), the Society of Motor Manufacturers and Traders (SMMT) Industry Forum, local authorities, West Midlands universities and local Training and Enterprise Councils (TECs).

THE AUTOLEAN PROJECT

The Autolean project was developed as part of the Accelerate initiative and was first conceived in September 1997. In order to fulfil the project objective of utilizing currently available information technology to enable better supply chain communication practices to be adopted, a team of academics and industrialists with sector, technology and business analysis expertise and experience was assembled. This is shown graphically in Figure 18.1.

AIMS AND OBJECTIVES

The aims of the programme include the introduction of practical Internet skills and experience into 20 West Midland SMEs in the automotive supplier chain, as a 'shop window'; and provision of overall guidance on how a particular company can use the Internet to improve their business processes. These guidelines included the:

- identification of measures of performance improvement;
- measurement and observation of any problems or weaknesses and strengths of this exercise;
- monitoring and documentation of the experiences of participating SMEs;
- development of an automotive industry pack for effective use of the Internet by SMEs;
- documentation of qualitative and quantitative benefits achieved by the use of the Internet in the supply chain;
- formulation of any lessons to be learned and reporting these to other SMEs, so that they might mimic the project's successes (and avoid the failures); and
- provision of a forum for the interchange of ideas and views via the Internet amongst the 20 participating SME and first tier companies.

IMPLEMENTATION OF THE AUTOLEAN PROJECT

The research and development approach employed for this project can be summarized in the following model:

- Select and recruit SMEs
- Install and commission Internet capability
- Train key staff in use of Internet
- Map information flows and processes
- Period of SME practice/ use of Internet within business context
- Assess impact of Internet on information flows and processes

Support in respect of technical and business-use issues

Twenty-one companies who formed some part of the supply chain that 'ended' with GKN, Rover or Unipart were recruited, initially via a roll-out seminar and, later, by targeted 'sales' techniques. Each received a high specification computer, modem, domain-name registration and connection to the Internet for one year. The system was set up in the company within a month of them enrolling on the project. A Website was designed for each company and they received technical support for the duration of the project via e-mail, telephone and Web-based materials. Training was an important component of the project: each company received three days' training, in two sessions, delivered on-site for up to five employees. Training materials (both paper- and Web-based) were also provided. All of the above activities were carried out by the School of Computing at the University of Wolverhampton.

In addition to the implementation and training associated with the introduction of Internet facilities into each SME, Warwick Manufacturing Group and EAIG performed a process mapping exercise. This involved a detailed study of information flows within the SME prior to the implementation of Internet facilities. The process mapping exercise was then repeated following the successful installation and period of use of the Internet, to determine and measure the impact of the Internet on the quality and quantity of these information flows.

THE CURRENT SITUATION

The majority of SMEs in the auto supply chain in the UK's West Midlands have fewer than 100 employees. The use made of information technology (IT) in such SMEs has often evolved piecemeal without any clear development strategy. IT support may be provided by a small software or systems house, who may have limited knowledge of the auto supply chain 'business' and who are (understandably) driven by the need to sell systems and support for maximum profit and minimum input. Alternatively, IT guidance and support may be provided by the enthusiastic 'home computer' employee. Of the 21 participating SMEs four claimed already to have an Internet connection within the company which they were using with varying degrees of success (see later).

In the case of the 'toolmaker' group of SMEs some novel methods for transporting drawings in the absence of the Internet were discovered. For example, large A1 or A0-sized drawings were routinely cut into A4-sized portions and faxed to the recipient, where they were reassembled using adhesive tape.

THE RESULTS OF THE PROJECT

It took much longer than anticipated to recruit the SMEs into the project and train them on the use of the Internet. Some 40 SMEs attended the initial roll-out seminar which was held in order to announce the scheme to the Unipart/GKN supplier base and to enrol the target 20 SMEs onto the scheme. The response was disappointing with only 11 SMEs agreeing to participate, despite the presence of and encouragement from senior staff from Unipart, GKN and Rover. It later became necessary to adopt more direct methods of contact in order to bring the total number of participating SMEs up to 21. This involved techniques more often associated with 'sales' rather than research, that is, time-consuming personal visits to each potential

Activity	Total	Activity	Total
Customer communications	15	**Supplier communications**	9
Planned	1	Planned	1
Types of information	0	**Types of information**	0
Design	9	CAD	5
General correspondence	5	Spreadsheets	1
Quotes	3	General correspondence	2
Orders	1	Online catalogues	1
Schedules	1	**Research**	16
Parts Profiles	1	Customers	2
Attachments	9	Sources of supply	6
CAD	9	Competition	12
Digital photos	1	Technical information	1
Spreadsheets	2	New products	1
Other	1	Patent data	1
E-mails/week	213	News	1
		Other uses	5
Hrs/ week	134	Updates from account	1
		Catalogues	1
		Quotes	2
		Digital photos	1

Figure 18.2   Profile of SME Internet use

SME to explain the project, and so on. During the life of the project, there was a considerable variation in the attitude and degree of positive participation in the project by the SMEs.

The integration of communication across tiers of a common supply chain could not be demonstrated. This was due to a number of reasons. Principal amongst these were that the duration of the project (10 months) proved too short to implement the necessary changes in the companies and record their effects. Further, it was only possible to assemble limited instances of homogeneous supply chain 'clusters' due to the constraints imposed by funding considerations. Many of the SMEs, however, were able to implement a number of initiatives in respect of integrating the use of the Internet into their business activities. These are summarized in Figure 18.2.

EFFECTIVE USE OF THE INTERNET IN THE SUPPLY CHAIN – SOME ISSUES

The Autolean project exposed a number of issues that directly affected the quality and performance of the project in general, and the effective use of the Internet by the SMEs in particular.

These included the crucial selection and quality of the Internet Service Provider (ISP). The current explosion in demand for Internet services has resulted in the inability of many ISPs to maintain an acceptable level of Internet service and access. Whilst this is merely inconvenient for the domestic Internet user, it threatens to negate the potential benefits achievable by use of the Internet by SMEs in the supply chain.

Thorough training in the effective use of the Internet is crucial. Many SMEs who were already 'using' the Internet prior to the Autolean project had acquired bad habits and had an incomplete understanding of what they were doing. However, paradoxically, several SMEs assigned a very low (time) priority to being trained, regularly deferring and delaying training sessions whenever tasks arose that they deemed 'higher priority'. There were, however, some notable exceptions.

A further observation became apparent as the project progressed. The successful integration of Internet-based communications into the day-to-day operations of the 20+ SMEs was possible largely due to the degree of technical support provided by the development team. Thus, the SMEs had the comfort of knowing that there was just one point of contact (e-mail or telephone call). The authors consider that the provision of this one-stop support facility is essential in order to relieve the SMEs from the frustration of endless telephone calls to their ISP, PC supplier, modem supplier, telephone company and so on in order to identify the cause of, and hence, solutions to technical problems.

There were a number of technical issues that were found to influence the efficacy of Internet use within the SMEs. Customers need to possess the 'appropriate' software to be able to read received e-mail attachments, word-processed documents, spreadsheets and so on. Whilst suitable 'read-only' viewer software can often be downloaded from manufacturers' Websites, for novice Internet users, still struggling to acquire Internet skills and experience, this task may be a major obstacle.

Internal company e-mail is desirable in order to realize the full potential of the Internet; employees require e-mail to come to their desktop, not to the office next door. Company to company e-mail alone is not good enough; integration with the office network is essential. Employees desire automatic notification that an e-mail has arrived, they prefer not to have to call up their e-mail boxes several times a day to check for e-mail. The SMEs' e-mail client software should be configured to automatically connect to their ISP and deliver/receive mail regularly throughout the day; typically, every half-hour was considered to be appropriate.

IMPLICATIONS FOR OTHER SMEs IN THE SUPPLY CHAIN

The Autolean project has been a success from the companies' perspective for many reasons. Questionnaires were distributed towards the end of the project (November 1998) and results indicated that 90 per cent of the companies participating felt that the project had been of great benefit. Not least of which, it had raised the profile of the use of the Internet and acted as a catalyst in the process of introducing change in the communication methods employed.

Autolean has introduced the 21 participating SMEs to the concept that the use of the Internet is a practical solution for everyday business communications in the automotive supply chain. A 'blueprint' for doing business around the world in the next decade is beginning to evolve. The Internet is seen as a way of expanding the global reach of the innovative SME. For those already doing business internationally, savings in telephone and fax call charges can be substantial, but the SME should expect an increase in expenditure on local (low cost) telephone traffic. The project has raised awareness amongst companies regarding the global marketing and research possibilities, particularly the ability for companies to obtain live information from the Internet and make new contacts worldwide via e-mail. In one case during a training session the sales manager was looking for a local supplier of 'minute man broaches' (a broach is a machine tool for removing surplus material (for example, metal) from the inside surface of a manufactured component). A search was made for these and an American site found. The site had an e-mail contact address displayed at the bottom, which was used during the training session for demonstration purposes only. The question, 'Can you let me know of a Birmingham supplier?' was asked. Before the session finished, the e-mail was checked. An e-mail had been sent, containing the details of a Birmingham supplier, and the sales manager was smitten with the concept of the Web.

The development of knowledge within the participating SMEs has led to a more realistic perception of the Internet's capabilities as a business tool. The Autolean project has laid foundations that have the ability to be disseminated both vertically and horizontally within the automotive supply chain.

CONCLUSIONS

Autolean has been successful in raising awareness amongst the scheme's 21 SME, West Midlands automotive suppliers. These companies

now have an understanding of how global developments in communications technology may impact upon them and have been provided with the knowledge, experience and tools to enable them to respond to these developments.

The broad mix of companies participating in Autolean were all found to contain opportunities for performance improvement. Toolmakers emerged as having the potential for substantial 'quick return on investment' opportunities: for example, in the area of CAD drawing exchange, six of the seven Autolean toolmakers are now using the Internet to exchange CAD drawings with their customers. As a result, toolmakers were often the most proactive companies in the project.

The proactive users have applied the Internet to their day-to-day business with a range of customers and suppliers. One SME has obtained four new contracts through its Internet use. Of the others, four appear to have made no progress and eleven have shown varying degrees of interest and activity. This variability of benefits suggests that SME companies have a wide range of perceptions regarding the urgency of the inevitable changes in automotive purchasing methods and the value of the Internet as an effective business tool within that context.

The implementation of e-mail in the SMEs was found to enable:

- an overall reduction in the cost of customer communications by reducing the need for faxes, telephone calls and meetings;
- structured management and audit of customer communications;
- reductions in time and cost to resolve technical problems with customers;
- reduction in general time-wasting and 'hassle' related to communications, including:
  - faxes running out of paper;
  - illegible fax pages;
  - misplaced or lost fax pages;
  - engaged fax lines; and
  - playing voicemail phone tag.

The Autolean SMEs are now positioned to take advantage of the use of the Internet for communicating both with customers and suppliers as well as having a presence on the World Wide

Web for attracting new business. In the context of Francis's definition of 'lean management', effective management of material throughout the supply chain, or EAIG's focus on customer value, Autolean has made a significant contribution in respect of the participating SMEs.

REFERENCES

Brown, D. (1995), *The West Midlands Automotive Supply Chain Development Study*, Birmingham: West Midlands Development Agency.

Francis, M. (1988), 'Lean information and supply chain effectiveness', *International Journal of Logistics: Research and Applications*, 1(1), pp. 93–108.

Harrison, A. (1998), 'A comparative study of lean reduction metrics in an automotive assembler', *International Journal of Logistics: Research and Applications*, 1(1), pp. 27–38.

Monden, Y. (1983), *The Toyota Production System*, Atlanta, GA: Institute of Industrial Engineers.

CHAPTER NINETEEN

Purchasing consortia and Internet technology

Daniel Corsten and Michael Zagler

PURCHASING CONSORTIA

According to a study by the Centre of Advanced Purchasing Studies (CAPS) a purchasing consortium consists of the following:

> … two or more independent organizations that join together, either formally or informally, or through an independent third party, for the purpose of combining their individual requirements for purchased materials, services, and capital goods to leverage more value-added pricing, service and technology from their external suppliers than could be obtained if each firm purchased goods and services alone (Hendrick 1997 p. 7).

The CAPS study reveals that a typical purchasing consortium is formally structured and managed by the participant members although for the most part without formal written agreements. There are no penalties for withdrawing from the consortium and no minimum quantity of purchasing is required for members. Most purchasing consortia exclude competitors although the inclusion of competitors is not considered a threat, and focus is on non-strategic items such as MRO, routine services and standard capital equipment (Hendrick 1997).

A distinction can be made between co-operatives and consortia. Co-operatives have for many years been formed by non-profit organizations to maximize their buying power and usually reflect the type of business they serve, such as hospitals, farms or schools. On the contrary, consortia are formal co-operations with members participating from a variety of industries (Monczka et al. 1998). The authors identify purchasing consortia as a key trend for purchasing in the next century and forecast that a growing number of firms are becoming members of purchase consortia as a means to realize lower purchase costs (Monczka et al. 1998). Purchasing history reveals that collaborative purchasing among independent organizations is not a new idea. Farmers and grocery retailers and, more recently, health care providers and municipalities have always combined their individual needs to increase their purchasing power (Monczka et al. 1998; Hendrick 1997; Arnold and Essig 1997; Telgen 1998). However, the CAPS study of Fortune 500 firms in the US reveals that the incidence, formation and use of purchasing consortia only started in the early 1990s. Less than 20 per cent of the sample of major companies in the USA indicated that they were currently involved in at least one purchasing consortium (Hendrick 1997). However, a recent survey among 79 SMEs in the machining industry in Switzerland and Germany shows that SMEs see the highest potential for horizontal co-operation in purchasing (71 per cent), followed by sales and R&D (each 43 per cent) and production and logistics (each 36 per cent)(O.V. 1998).

An explanation for this low acceptance can be drawn from two purchasing consortia in Germany. As a synopsis of these case studies eight critical success factors can be identified: adequate partner, external moderation, professional project management, co-operative atmosphere, active participation, regular information exchange, adapted controlling and optimized cost–benefit effect (Voegele and

Schindele 1996; Arnold and Essig 1997; Hofmann 1998; Weber 1998). Subsequent discussion with members of the purchasing consortia indicated that the transaction cost of forming and managing the purchasing consortium proved to be very high and a barrier to future activities. They suggested that a purchasing consortium with a more efficient communication infrastructure could be more successful.

What is the theoretical evidence on purchasing consortia? A review of purchasing texts reveals that, traditionally, little attention has been devoted to co-operative purchasing or purchasing consortia (Heinritz et al. 1991; Dobler, Burt and Lee 1990; Baily et al. 1994). Only recently have Monczka et al. added a paragraph on purchasing consortia to their purchasing book. Other exceptions are the books by Arnold and Essig (1997) and Arnold (1998). However, with regard to purchasing consortia as a key trend for the next decade these theoretical contributions do not equal the importance of the subject. A grounded theory of collaborative purchasing and purchasing consortia is still missing. Our findings support the views of van Weele and Rozemeijer (1998) that in general 'most companies lack an effective communications and information infrastructure, which may support, enable and organize the highly complex and often changing interfaces among the disciplines and organizational entities involved in the purchasing process'; and also the view of Faes and Matthyssens (1998) who indicate that, although of high empirical evidence, purchasing theory has in general neglected research on co-operative purchasing between dependent and independent firms.

INTERNET TECHNOLOGY

According to Telgen the Internet 'could change purchasing in a revolutionary manner'. He adds that 'a large part of the purchasing process could be automated, in particular for standard goods and materials. However, automated systems are generally only used for the ordering and monitoring phase of the purchasing process' (1998). Van Weele and Rozemeijer, referring to the work of van Stekelenborg, confirm these findings:

Order-handling, expediting and accounts payable are now sufficiently supported by most standard Enterprise Resource Planning (ERP) packages. However, most of these packages do not sufficiently support initial purchasing and are not capable of providing general management with purchasing management information. Apart from vendor rating these packages do not allow for effective contract management and monitoring in organizations, and adequate product-line management and supply base management. (1998 p. 424)

New examples of Internet and intranet applications for purchasing comprise purchasing market research and supplier selection, sending requests for proposals, virtual auctions, reverse marketing, commodity buying, shipment tracking and electronic payment (van Weele and Rozemeijer 1998).

Brenner and Hamm classify information technology for procurement processes according to the dimensions of 'business horizon' and 'degree of unstructured information' (see Figure 19.1). Administration systems, decision support systems and purchasing information systems are internally focused and require structured information. They are widely used. Knowledge-sharing systems are inter-organizationally focused and work with unstructured information. Their use is not widespread (Brenner and Hamm 1996).

Due to their nature, purchasing consortia predominantly rely upon inter-organizationally focused information technology for both structured and unstructured information such as electronic markets, bidding systems, purchasing transaction systems, knowledge sharing systems and messaging systems.

RESEARCH QUESTION AND METHODOLOGY

The above findings in the literature and our own research on the success and failure of purchasing consortia reveal a lack of communication

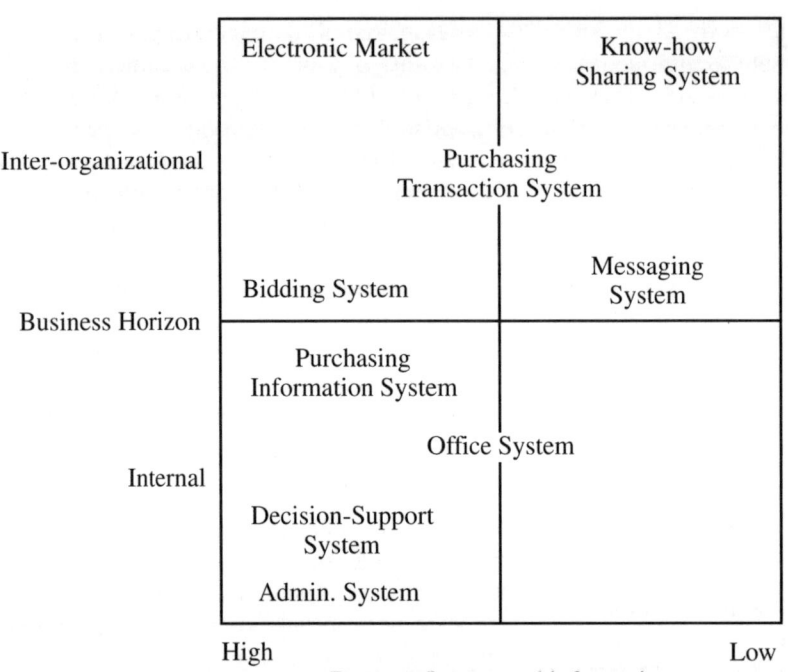

Electronic Market

Know-how
Sharing System

Inter-organizational

Purchasing
Transaction System

Bidding System

Messaging
System

Business Horizon

Purchasing
Information System

Office System

Internal

Decision-Support
System

Admin. System

High   Low

Degree of structured information

Figure 19.1
Classification of
information technology
for procurement
Source: Brenner, W. and
Hamm, V. (1996), The
role of information
technology in
reengineering procure-
ment processes, *Paper for
the 4th European
Conference on Informa-
tion Systems*, Lisbon, 2–4
July.

and communication infrastructure as one of the biggest barriers to the success of purchasing consortia. Collaborative purchasing between dependent units of a multiplant firm is already communication-intensive. Between members of purchasing consortia of independent companies that are geographically spread and have heterogeneous information systems, the existence of a common and easily accessible communication infrastructure becomes a prerequisite.

As shown above, purchasing information technology has in the past focused on operational purchasing and has neglected strategic purchasing, especially with regard to co-ordination between independent companies. However, this situation is changing. New intranet and extranet technologies are the key to providing a communication infrastructure that facilitates both strategic and initial as well as operational and routine tasks of purchasing consortia. Thus, the research question is: 'How can Internet technology help facilitate the organization of purchasing consortia in order to exploit the potentials of economies of scale without the diseconomies of increased transaction cost and communication effort?'

In order to investigate this question the Institute for Technology Management has begun a two-year research project. The project, entitled Purchasing Consortia: Co-operation and Internet has been designed and managed at the Institute for Technology Management, is financed by the Swiss Commission of Technology and Innovation (CTI) and seven participating companies, as well as being sponsored by the Swiss Association for Materials and Supply Management (SVME). Our initial research indicated that software solutions to facilitate purchasing consortia did not exist. Thus, the objective of the project is to provide an Internet platform to small and medium sized companies in the Euregio Bodensee where they can exchange knowledge, attract suppliers and form purchasing consortia to leverage their purchasing power. The first results of this project can be seen at the Website <www.buy2gether.com>.

TYPES OF PURCHASING CONSORTIUM TASKS

In order to answer the research question it is first necessary to identify relevant purchasing consortium tasks and classify them according to their implementation with Internet technology. The following types of purchasing consortium task form the backbone of the purchasing consortia and the Internet platform described in the next section. There are two types of task: project-independent or project-dependent tasks and consortium-internal or consortium-external tasks.

The activity level of a purchasing consortium can be described as 'power-on' and 'stand-by' mode. 'Power-on' comprises all project-dependent tasks that are specifically required in planning, executing and controlling a collective purchasing decision. 'Stand-by' comprises project-independent tasks that are specifically required for supporting and promoting the sourcing network outside concrete projects.

With regard to the internal and external orientation of purchasing consortium tasks we differentiate between consortium-internal and consortium-external tasks (see Table 19.1). Drawing upon earlier work on task-contingent models in marketing (Corsten 1997) we define consortium-internal tasks as dealing with internal relationships between the collaborative enterprises. This comprises all tasks necessary for the internal preparation and co-ordination of the interaction with potential and actual con-

sortium partners. On the contrary, consortium-external tasks deal with the relationships with potential and actual suppliers and comprise all tasks necessary for the external preparation and co-ordination of the interaction with potential and actual suppliers. A similar distinction has been made by van Weele and Rozemeijer who distinguish between internal and external tasks in purchasing (1998).

We can now classify purchasing consortium tasks according to these two dimensions. 'Knowledge tasks' are purchasing tasks that are project-independent and internally focused, for example, developing an intranet site for a consortium platform; facilitating general knowledge and tool exchange; developing common virtual product catalogues, standard practices and procedures for consortia (for example, contracts, rules and exit strategies).

'Marketing tasks' are purchasing tasks that are project-independent and externally focused, for example, developing an extranet site for supplier access, advertising the consortium to potential suppliers, registering and certifying potential suppliers.

'Pooling tasks' are purchasing tasks that are project-dependent and internally focused, for example, searching the platform internally for partners, forming a consortium and electing a

Table 19.1 Internal and external orientation of purchasing consortium tasks

	Project-independent Tasks	Project-dependent Tasks
Consortium-internal tasks	*Knowledge tasks* Develop an intranet site for consortium/ platform Facilitate general knowledge and tool exchange Develop common virtual product catalogues Develop standard practices and procedures for consortia (for example, contracts, rules, exit strategies)	*Pooling tasks* Search the platform internally for partners Form consortium and elect co-ordinator Facilitate specific information exchange Co-ordination of consortium Bundle demand among partners
Consortium external tasks	*Marketing tasks* Develop extranet site for supplier access Advertise consortium to potential suppliers Register potential suppliers Certify potential suppliers	*Quotation tasks* Prepare request for quotation Compare quotation and negotiate Manage contracts

co-ordinator, facilitating specific information exchange, co-ordinating the consortium, pooling demand among partners.

'Quotation tasks' are purchasing tasks that are project-dependent and externally focused, for example, preparing requests for quotation, comparing and negotiating quotations and managing contracts.

CASE STUDY: PURCHASING CONSORTIA AND THE INTERNET

This case study will report on the research project on purchasing consortia and the Internet being carried out at the Institute for Technology Management. The Internet was found to be suitable to play a vital role in the purchasing consortia and, furthermore, can offer completely new opportunities.

The starting consortium consisted of seven Swiss small and medium-sized enterprises (SMEs), mainly from the machining industry. In the first year of the project, knowledge on purchasing consortia was built up and focus was on the development of the Website <www.buy2gether.com>, which was seen as ideal for integrating buyers and suppliers as it provides perfect conditions for facilitating cooperation between SMEs for various reasons:

- the requirements for installation and support for users are low and access to a shared platform can easily be provided to many users;
- the Internet fits into the existing information infrastructure of the firms involved, while other solutions are not likely to be feasible;
- the Internet is easy to use and requires little explanation to buyers who are familiar with it; and
- a Website can attract suppliers and partners, integrate external resources and be accessed from anywhere.

The Website was also viewed as the key enabler for integrating further companies to the purchasing consortium. Together with consortium partners from the first phase more homogeneous clusters of firms with similar demands could be formed within an heterogeneous entity of companies in the consortium. Synergy in

demands would be realized while integrating a variety of competence and knowledge. The idea was to realize synergies for the participating SMEs concerning knowledge or purchasing power and establish a network of buyers. Generally, the platform was designed to cover consortium-internal and external purchasing tasks as well as project-independent and dependent purchasing tasks.

KNOWLEDGE TASKS

The participating companies faced similar problems and challenges in the field of purchasing and logistics. Knowledge exchange among cooperating supply managers therefore proved to be very powerful. The Website is designed to meet that need by providing an infrastructure to foster continuous and ongoing knowledge exchange among its members and to distribute access to all buyers within the organizations involved. It links buyers from several SMEs and creates a pool of knowledge that unites a broad variety of experience.

A special area on the Website is assigned for the exchange of general knowledge on various topics in the form of discussion groups. These are open to all buyers within the purchasing consortium. Discussion groups can be used for inter-organizational question-and-answer sessions and as a database on shared practices, procedures and tools. Using the Internet for this purpose allows the integration of external resources from the rest of the Internet and the vast wealth of information this provides. Valuable resources are being collected, classified and consolidated by buyers for buyers.

While explicit knowledge can be made directly accessible for partners in the consortium, implicit knowledge requires a different approach. Knowledge is very person-specific, therefore it is necessary to identify the right people for specific problems. The platform indicates the right people by providing information on buyers and their competence levels. Common experiences and intensified personal contacts among buyers are explicit objectives of the project.

Information exchange between suppliers is another important knowledge aspect for purchasing consortia. Suppliers are classified by the products and services they offer, as well as by their business relationship to each partner in the consortium. Benefits are expected from time reductions for supplier assessments and increased quality of individual evaluations, when suppliers have already been known to some members of the consortium. The supplier database can also help to identify opportunities for pooling as well as to improve the individual allocation of suppliers.

A central element of the Website is the information service. Partners who publish their profile of interests within their companies are automatically informed on selected topics, for example, knowledge exchange, pooling projects, newly registered suppliers or firms applying for partnership.

MARKETING TASKS

Marketing is a major external task of the Website. The main objective is to attract potential suppliers and partners by advertising the vision and concept of the site as well as all participating companies. It is a step from isolated home pages towards the formation of electronic markets in the field of purchasing.

The 'customers' of the platform are the suppliers, who are presented with many potential customers in a comprehensive and standardized way. In order to access more detailed information, links are provided to the home pages of consortium partners. In addition, names, photographs and the particular responsibilities of individual buyers are shown on the Website to allow for immediate identification and access to the right buyer.

The marketing tasks are not directed one way from the co-operating companies to the outside world. The idea is to encourage suppliers to present themselves to the consortium. Suppliers simply need to register (free of charge) via the Internet. They are given the opportunity to give their company name, address, contacts, products and references including links to their home pages. Since they are responsible for updating their data by logging in to their account, the degree to which this data is kept up to date serves as a criterion for supplier evaluation.

Critical mass is required for any Website to receive attention. Buy2gether benefits from the multiplying effect generated by the efforts of each participant of the consortium to attract their suppliers to the site, which represents the consolidated demand of the consortium. The buy2gether Website acts as a single interface between supply managers of the purchasing consortium and an open community of potential suppliers. It is designed to facilitate the process of finding and being found by potential suppliers.

POOLING TASKS

Pooling purchasing power to obtain better buying prices certainly is central to purchasing consortia. Buy2gether intends to overcome the difficulty of identifying opportunities for co-operation by making demands and opportunities clearer within the consortium.

Partners for a specific pooling project are drawn from a network of co-operating companies sharing a common infrastructure and constituting a stable platform. The starting point for any pooling activity is a project proposal filed on the Website by any buyer. The proposal will outline basic information on the project. It is then possible for all members to identify an opportunity to join the project. If necessary the scope of the project can be adapted or defined more clearly. Companies interested in a specific project then form a consortium and appoint a co-ordinator. He defines the roles and responsibilities of the participants for that specific project. The formation of a consortium also ensures exclusiveness, which means that all further activities and entries on the Internet platform concerning the project are visible to participants only. In this stage demand pooling takes place and Requests for Quotation (RFQs) are being prepared.

Pooling projects requires the co-ordination of the consortium from the initiation of the project to its conclusion. The Website is intended to improve the consortium's ability to co-ordinate projects throughout the pooling process; therefore each project is filed on the Website and follows a standard process which covers internal as well as external oriented tasks.

QUOTATION TASKS

There is a variety of external oriented tasks associated with consortium buying projects: preparing RfQs, evaluating quotations, negotiating with suppliers, managing contracts and following up projects. The Website provides the communication and co-ordination infrastructure to carry out these tasks. Buyers assigned to be co-ordinators of projects place RfQs on the Internet. Anyone on the Internet is then able to view published demands on a dedicated section of the site. As RfQs are categorized, it is possible to automatically distribute RfQs to relevant suppliers. The prerequisite is that suppliers have registered on the Website and indicated the categories they are interested in. So, whenever an RfQ is placed on the Internet, an agent will check for matches and send an e-mail to the relevant suppliers.

This information service provides potential suppliers with the necessary information to decide whether a specific RfQ is of interest. Suppliers, when interested, can download more detailed information, such as attached spreadsheets and technical drawings from the Website. If registered, suppliers can file their quotations directly via the Internet. The advantages of using the Internet to distribute RfQs is that there is virtually no time-lag between placing an RFQ and a potential supplier being notified, and there is no need for suppliers to check the consortium's Website on a regular basis, as they will be informed automatically when something comes up that might be relevant to them.

CONCLUSION

In this chapter we have developed a typology for purchasing consortia tasks and demonstrated its empirical relevance based on a research project at the Institute for Technology Management on Purchasing Consortia and Internet Technology. However, the Website <www.buy2gether.com> will have to prove the practicality of conducting pooling projects during the second year of the research project. It will be required to identify mechanisms and rules for the optimal co-ordination of projects and the management of knowledge exchange. Another goal will be to move beyond the German-speaking horizon towards more global networks. It will be interesting to see how the Website performs in attracting potential suppliers and partners, and how homogeneous clusters of firms with homogenous demands interact within a heterogeneous entity of the consortium when it comes to pooling and knowledge exchange.

REFERENCES

Arnold, U. (1998), *Erfolg durch Einkaufskooperationen*, Gabler: Wiesbaden (in German).

Arnold, U. and Essig, M. (1997), *Einkaufskooperationen in der Industrie*, Stuttgart: Poeschel (in German).

Baily, P., Farmer, D., Jessop, D. and Jones, D. (1994), *Purchasing Principles and Management*, London: Pitman.

Brenner, W. and Hamm, V. (1996), 'The role of information technology in reengineering procurement processes', *Paper for the 4th European Conference on Information Systems*, Lisbon, 2-4 July.

Corsten, D. (1997), *Gestaltungsmodelle für Marketingaufgaben*, Dissertation, University of St. Gallen (in German).

Dobler, D., Burt, D. and Lee, L. (1990), *Purchasing and Materials Management*, New York: McGraw-Hill.

Faes, W. and Matthyssens, P. (1998), 'Managing purchasing co-ordination: how to build an effective intra-company relationship', in *Proceedings of the 7th International IPSERA Conference*, London, pp. 204–215.

Heinritz, S., Farrell, P.V., Gunipero, L. and Kolchin, M. (1991), *Purchasing*, New York: Prentice Hall.

Hendrick, T.E. (1997), *Purchasing Consortia: Horizontal Alliances among Firms Buying Common Goods and Services*, Tempe, Az: Center for Advanced Purchasing Studies.

Hofmann, P. (1998),'Einkaufskooperationen mittelständischer Unternehmen in Baden-Würtemberg', in *Proceedings of the 33. Symposium Einkauf und Logistik des BME*, Berlin pp. 163–184 (in German).

Monczka, R., Trent, R. and Handfield, R. (1998),

Purchasing and Supply Chain Management, Cincinnati: South Western.

O.V. (1998), 'Zwischen Zupacken und Zaudern', *Beschaffung Aktuell*, 2, pp. 44–45 (in German).

Telgen, J. (1998), 'Revolution through electronic purchasing', *Proceedings of the 7th International IPSERA Conference*, London, pp. 499–504.

van Weele A. J. and Rozemeijer, F. (1998), 'Getting organized for purchasing and supply management in the information age; towards the virtual purchasing organization', *Proceedings of the 2nd Worldwide Research Symposium on Purchasing and Supply Chain Management*, London, pp. 421–431.

Voegele, A. and Schindele, S. (1996), 'Faktoren erfolgreicher Zusammenarbeit', *Beschaffung Aktuell*, 4, pp. 48–51 (in German).

Weber, G. (1998), 'Einkaufskooperationen mittelständischer Metallverarbeiter aus dem Raum Nürnberg', *Proceedings of the 33. Symposium Einkauf und Logistik des BME*, Berlin, pp. 185–205 (in German).

PART FIVE

PERFORMANCE EVALUATION

Introduction to performance evaluation

Andrew Erridge

Without credible and practical methods of measuring and evaluating the performance of the procurement function, we cannot know what is best practice, or how to improve existing practice. The chapters included in this section provide several perspectives on how this may be done, ranging from benchmarking of the single key measure of 'expenditure influenced by purchasing professionals' in UK universities (Chapter 21), to comprehensive methods of analysing the whole operation of the procurement function from initial identification of demand to order fulfilment in both a public sector agency (Chapter 20) and a food retail chain (Chapter 24). In addition, there is a comparison of benchmarking methods and criteria currently applied by Polish, UK and Italian manufacturing companies (Chapter 22), and an examination from Finland of how auditing methods proposed in the literature have been adapted for application in two manufacturing companies. Thus, in addition to a variety of properly validated methods of evaluation whose application is demonstrated in the chapters, a range of sectoral and national perspectives are in evidence. The extent to which methods developed in the private, manufacturing sector may be applied in the public sector is demonstrated in Chapter 20, and the extent to which the emerging Polish economy can adopt methods developed in Western economies is addressed in Chapter 22. Such transfers of knowledge and experience are vital to progress both academic study and the development of soundly based tools and techniques for practical application.

In Chapter 21, the authors undertake a comparison of the public and private sectors, illustrated by a case study of the Driver and Vehicle Licensing Agency (DVLA) Procurement Services. The authors provide an interesting example of cross-fertilization of academic and practitioner interests, with Ann Esain and Peter Hines of the Lean Enterprise Research Centre (LERC), University of Cardiff, together with Dave Griffiths, Head of Procurement Services in DVLA. The chapter focuses on the issue of performance evaluation and improvement activities (waste elimination). Building on the value stream analysis (VALSAT) approach, a series of tools and techniques are identified which help organizations visualize the 'order fulfilment' process in a cross-functional manner. The outcome of this research proves the use of these techniques for the public sector and creates a generic framework for application elsewhere.

The next two chapters examine benchmarking from different perspectives in terms of both the authors' background and sector. In Chapter 21, Florence Gregg, purchasing manager at Queen's University, Belfast, presents a practical, easy to use, benchmarking model which can help the practitioner to plot the increase in purchasing influence over non-pay expenditure and the extent of purchasing proactivity in terms of the use of local consortia and national buying arrangements, rather than merely reacting to user demands. Developed in conjunction with colleagues from other UK universities, the model will help inform future strategy, identify institutions where better, or more appropriate, practices appear to exist and, in the longer term, help the sector to improve its overall purchasing performance. The applicability of the model to other public and private sector organizations is also demonstrated.

In Chapter 22, Danuta Kisperska-Moron presents a broader empirical survey of benchmarking practices in Poland, the UK and Italy aimed at closer monitoring of superior supply chain performance. Benchmarking procedures are one way to support such long-term oriented actions focused on the identification of best practices to be followed. She argues that companies must be able to assess and compare all processes connected to procurement, including the personnel, which is a critically important factor for overall procurement success.

Hannu Vanharanta, in Chapter 23, argues that in many business enterprises, purchasing and supply is becoming a strategic activity, and finding ways to improve overall purchasing and supply performance is becoming essential. He recognizes that improving future performance must be preceded by the measurement and evaluation of present performance. With this in mind, he examines currently available textbook methods for auditing purchasing and supply management performance, but finds them to be highly theoretical in their approach. As they have not been verified or validated in practice, he uses two case studies to test some of the textbook methods on a practical level with two manufacturing companies. Audit techniques and criteria are developed in conjunction with managers in the companies studied, and the method is shown to be helpful for identifying areas of good practice, as well as those areas where improvements are necessary.

In the final chapter, Donna Samuel and Peter Hines present a further contribution from the Lean Enterprise Research Centre (LERC). Through a 'process consultation' research methodology, a case is described within the food distribution industry where an approach is currently being developed to link supply chain performance and performance measurement with the chosen strategic direction of the firm. This approach is derived from *hoshin kanri*, a Japanese method known as policy deployment, which can be translated as the method by which world-class Japanese firms cascade the company's vision to the various layers of the organization. The case applies Japanese policy deployment matrix logic to develop a balanced scorecard of strategic measures. Using process management as a model, these are then exploded down to provide measures for the primary levels of the organization. The result is a company-wide performance measurement system which offers a number of advantages over traditional methods.

Overall, therefore, these chapters provide a range of models and techniques to stimulate the interest of both academics and practitioners, and to meet the needs of both public and private sector organizations for performance evaluation of the procurement function.

CHAPTER TWENTY

Performance evaluation within the DVLA

Ann Esain, David Griffiths and Peter Hines

Survival in the new millennium is dependent on meeting customers' requirements in a flexible manner. As Kotler (1994) states 'Today's new generation of companies compete with flexible manufacturing and rapid response systems, expanding variety and increasing innovation'. It has been said that 'companies face three challenges during the 1990s – to double the productivity of their own operations, to help their suppliers double theirs, and together achieve further sustained gains through integrating all the steps down the value chain from raw material to end customer' (Jones, D., personal communication).

Customers demand products and services when they want them, at the best quality and lowest price, whilst employees want to be rewarded and recognized (Kanter 1989). All these pressures result in a focus on quality, cost, delivery, management and design. It is true to say that 'the vast majority of organizations remain uncertain about how to proceed, but they are sure that they cannot stand still' (Kennie et al. 1998).

Within the public sector and particularly in government agencies, often this pressure is not as obvious. The customer is rarely clear – is it the taxpayer, is it the government or is it those who are recipients of the service? Additionally the enthusiasm to provide services at best value is a daily requirement. But what is best value? Kotler (1994) suggests that the traditional cost based strategy for manufacturing 'require(s) managers to do whatever is necessary to drive down costs: move production to or source from a low wage country; build new facilities or consolidate old plants to gain economies of scale; or focus operations down to the most economic sub-sets of activity. These tactics reduce cost but at the expense of responsiveness.'

Generally best value in the public sector relates to cost. How to reduce the cost of delivery whilst maintaining the core principles of the Agency is therefore a key issue facing the Driver and Vehicle Licensing Agency (DVLA). This chapter attempts to answer the question: can cost and time reduction be achieved in the same way for both the private and public sector by applying so-called manufacturing methods to the DVLA (Cox 1995)? It also asks whether there are any lessons to be learnt from either community.

The chapter compares and contrasts the work undertaken in the DVLA's Procurement Services to reduce cost and the recent paper which describes similar work undertaken in the private sector, undertaken by Hines and Rich (1997). In order to keep the comparison as relevant as possible the work compares similar processes. The process chosen was 'order fulfilment' (Dimancescu et al. 1997). For the purposes of this chapter 'order fulfilment' is defined as the activities which take place from the point of receipt of a request for an item to the point at which that item has been received to the satisfaction of the customer.

The success of the Hines and Rich (1997) work has resulted in the Welsh Development Agency adopting this technique as part of the Source Wales initiative. Source Wales has two primary aims. The first is to market Welsh industry to the world and hence encourage buyers to procure from Wales; the second is to assist in the improvement of companies in Wales who do not meet the requirements of those buyers. Where lessons from the Source Wales activity are appropriate these are included.

METHOD AND STRUCTURE

The methodology selected to focus on cost reduction and time relies on the framework being sought. In this context the use of surveys as a method of analysis was considered and would have provided breadth of knowledge in the area being investigated. Breadth of knowledge was not the key insight from the research. The purpose of this work was to gain depth of understanding. The depth required was particularly in relation to personal behaviour of teams (microcosms of the organization) and between different functions and levels within the organization, highlighting issues of complexity and constraints. Hence a case study approach was selected, with structured observation and interviews (Saunders et al. 1997).

The basic components of the case study are detailed in Figure 20.1. A group briefing session initiated the case study (focusing). One-to-one interviews were undertaken to seek both qualitative and quantitative data (structured observation). These interviews were with diverse departments involved in the process. The data

was analysed and tested (systems analysis) against the observations as part of a facilitated brainstorming session (review). Finally a mandate was sought from senior management to facilitate the implementation of a standard system (standardize system).

Before improvements in a process can be considered the current state must be assessed. For order fulfilment in the private sector, a set of tools and techniques were devised (Hines and Rich 1997) and these have since been developed further (Hines et al. 1998). To ensure comparison between sectors the original tools were applied to the case study being described to test their relevance to the public sector (see Figure 20.2).

FOCUSING

The focusing part of the case study cycle brings together a team from different functions, all of which are involved, in the order fulfilment process. During the focusing exercise the commitment to structured observation is sought. There will be detailed interviews at the next stage to gain individual involvement. The focusing exercise provides a suitable platform to inform and involve, as well as allay any fears prior to interview, whilst primarily being the planning forum for the project.

Case Study Framework

Cycle	**Anticipated Outcome**
• Focusing (Plan) – Gain basic understanding, collect data at a generic level and translate to wastes • Structured Observation (Do) – Collect data which confirms or otherwise wastes established • Systems Analysis (Do) – Detailed processing of data and review of maps • Review (Check) – Present maps, key points and suggested hows for discussion • Standardized System (Act) – Translate into standard system and test on other products/projects	• Focusing (Plan) – Understand opportunities, barriers and cross functionality within the supply chain • Structured Observation (Do) – Data for maps and detailed understanding of the value stream • Systems Analysis (Do) – Presentation pack of maps plus key point from each • Review (Check) – Action plan which could include removal or reorder of value stream steps • Standardized System (Act) – Time and quality improvements with resulting cost reduction

Figure 20.1   Case study framework

Diagnostics of Public Sector Order Fulfilment

Value Stream Mapping Tools (Hines et al, 1997a & 1998)	Applicable in the Public Sector		
	Yes	No	Testing
1. Process Activity Mapping	Y		Y
2. Quality Filter	Y		Y
3. Supply Chain Response Matrix	Y		Y
4. Product Variety Funnel	Y		N
5. Value Added Time Profile	Y		N
6. Decision Point Analysis	Y		N
7. Physical Structure	Y		N
8. Demand Amplification	Y		Y
9. Relationship Mapping	Y		N
10. Overall Effectiveness Mapping	Y		N

Figure 20.2   Testing the methodology

A further purpose of the focusing stage is to describe and demonstrate the principles of value and waste. These are:

- *Value*: the activities in a process which, add value in terms of the ultimate customers' needs. Three types of value activity are defined:
  - The first is non-value adding which can be removed from a process by means of continuous improvement, for example in the private sector a company was found to be photocopying their Materials Requirement Planning (MRP) output. This was happening in order to be able to fax the suppliers their delivery schedule for the week. The MRP was being printed double-sided to save paper. However the use of the document meant that this was not at all value adding. This issue was solved within twenty-four hours of identification and saved four hours of time, and the associated cost for that activity.
  - The second is necessary but non-value adding. This activity adds no value to the end product or service but is currently necessary in the process. This type of activity requires a long-term plan to overcome the necessity of a radical change to the process. An example of this in the public sector can be the legal requirements imposed or a computer system which forces an activity that does not add value but would require investment to be changed immediately.
  - The final activity is value adding, which is often described as an activity that changes the product or service: typically within a manufacturing organization less than two per cent of activities are value adding, as has been shown by the Source Wales initiative. In the private sector this could be the assembly of two parts whereas in the public sector this could be the information which is included in a document.
- *Waste*: there are seven types of waste. Taiichi Ohno originally developed the following list of wastes. These are:
  - overproduction;
  - waiting;
  - transportation;
  - inappropriate processing;
  - unnecessary inventory;
  - unnecessary motions; and
  - defects.

The individuals from the cross functional group taken from within the DVLA and Vehicle Registration Office (VRO) were asked to rank the wastes. Ranking is determined in the following manner. The greatest probability that the waste exists in the process scores the highest value. That is, if the process is the supply of stationery, the individual may consider that waiting is the most common waste and will rank this highly (up to a maximum of 10 points). Alternatively, where the individual considers that overproduction will never occur then its score will be zero.

In order to retain an indication of scale the individual is allocated 35 points that are awarded against the seven wastes listed above (see Figure 20.3). In this figure the waste of overproduction is ranked highest. The averaging process is used to ensure that no one functional area can prejudice the outcome; in this case nine individuals from different levels in the organization and from five different functional areas were asked to rank the wastes. The focusing exercise is also used to record individual perceptions of barriers to change within the organization or supply chain (Esain 2000).

This ranking of the wastes forms the basis of the value stream analysis (VALSAT) tool. Each mapping tool (see Figure 20.4) has a relationship with the seven wastes. These are determined to be high, medium, low or no relationship. Each of these relationships is given a value and a spreadsheet is used to calculate which map will be used. The relationship between the wastes and the corresponding maps, selected for testing within the public sector, is

Waste	1	2	3	4	5	6	7	8	9	Average
1. Overproduction	5	10	8	2	10	8	10	0	7	6.67
2. Waiting	6	8	7	5	4	10	5	10	3	6.44
3. Transportation	8	4	2	10	3	9	4	0	5	5.00
4. Inappropriate processing	6	4	2	0	10	2	3	10	2	4.33
5. Unnecessary inventory	3	3	6	10	3	3	2	7	3	4.44
6. Unnecessary motion	5	1	2	0	3	2	3	6	9	3.44
7. Defects	2	5	8	8	2	1	8	2	6	4.67
Totals	35	35	35	35	35	35	35	35	35	35.00

Figure 20.3   An example of a waste ranking grid for the DVLA

	1 Process activity mapping	2 Supply chain response matrix	3 Product variety funnel	4 Quality filter mapping	5 Forrester effect mapping	6 Decision point analysis	7 Physical structure
1. Overproduction	6.67	20.00	0.00	6.67	20.00	20.00	0.00
2. Waiting	58.00	58.00	6.44	0.00	19.33	19.33	0.00
3. Transportation	45.00	0.00	0.00	0.00	0.00	0.00	5.00
4. Inappropriate processing	39.00	0.00	13.00	4.33	0.00	4.33	0.00
5. Unnecessary inventory	13.33	40.00	13.33	0.00	40.00	13.33	4.44
6. Unnecessary motion	31.00	3.44	0.00	0.00	0.00	0.00	0.00
7. Defects	4.67	0.00	0.00	42.00	0.00	0.00	0.00
Totals	197.67	121.44	32.78	53.00	79.33	57.00	9.44
Rank	1	2	6	5	3	4	7

Figure 20.4   Maps recommended by the VALSAT tool

Process Activity Map

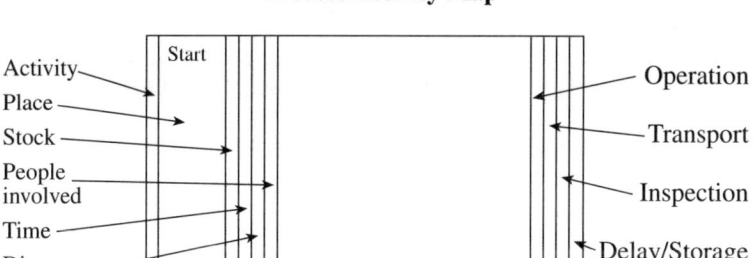

Figure 20.5 Process Activity Map (PAM)

shown in Figure 20.4. The full details of this tool are explained in Rich and Hines (1997).

At least three maps are required to ensure the triangulation of the quantified data to be collected. A degree of judgement can also be applied, hence in this case maps ranked first, second, third and fifth were selected.

STRUCTURED OBSERVATION AND SYSTEMS ANALYSIS

This section of the chapter will discuss the tools and techniques in place in the private and public sectors to reduce costs.

PROCESS ACTIVITY MAPPING

The pivotal technique applied during the interview stage is process activity mapping (Hines and Rich 1997). This map is taken from the industrial engineering discipline and applied in a different manner. It focuses on facts and detail (see Figure 20.5), which provides the information against which improvements can be made. The critical path is mapped. This is the structured observation element of the project.

During the interview process qualitative issues are recorded to help the interviewer to determine which quantitative techniques in the toolkit are applicable to the organization and/

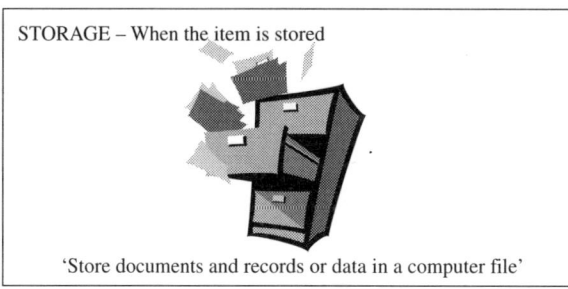

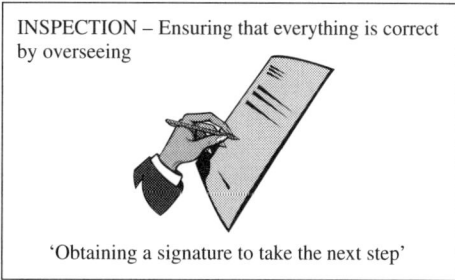

Figure 20.6 PAM terms explained in pictures

or supply chain. Hence the toolkit is designed to triangulate data gathered against perception, which has also been identified from the team, through interviews.

Since every organization has its own individual language, it is important to facilitate discussion on what these terms mean. A series of pictures was used to project the meaning in the DVLA (Figure 20.6). This ensures a localization of terminology; aids shared understanding and creates a common language for the team members who are drawn from diverse departments.

One of the key observations of the process activity map was that one product was transported 1.4 km, excluding the transport from the supplier. Additionally, the interviews established that the team had achieved significant improvements in stock and that they were actively looking for further ways of improving the stock levels.

SUPPLY CHAIN RESPONSE MATRIX

The supply chain response matrix is a means of establishing how flexible an organization can be. Having long lead times or large amounts of inventory makes an organization less responsive. The review of the process, from the annual reorder activity within the DVLA to the provision of the item to the general public via the VRO, highlighted that inventory holdings accounted for 17 weeks of product (the waste of unnecessary inventory). The lead-time itself was also a constraint on flexibility.

A similar tool applied within the private sector has shown that an attempt at inventory reduction has been taking place. Generally the private sector has been investigating this issue longer and hence inventory has reached manageable levels, using kanban (a method of holding stock which is based on the pull from the customer demand) as a means of determining sufficient stock to always provide the customer with what is required when it is required. The concept of kanban within the public sector environment is constrained by the necessary, but non-value adding, statutory requirements.

An extract from the Source Wales initiative (Figure 20.7) shows a supply chain responsiveness map, with a scale of minutes, which indicates that the supply chain is constrained by lead time – which is approximately eleven eight-hour working days against an inventory of eight days. The map itself can be used to interpret both the supply chain of a public and private sector organization.

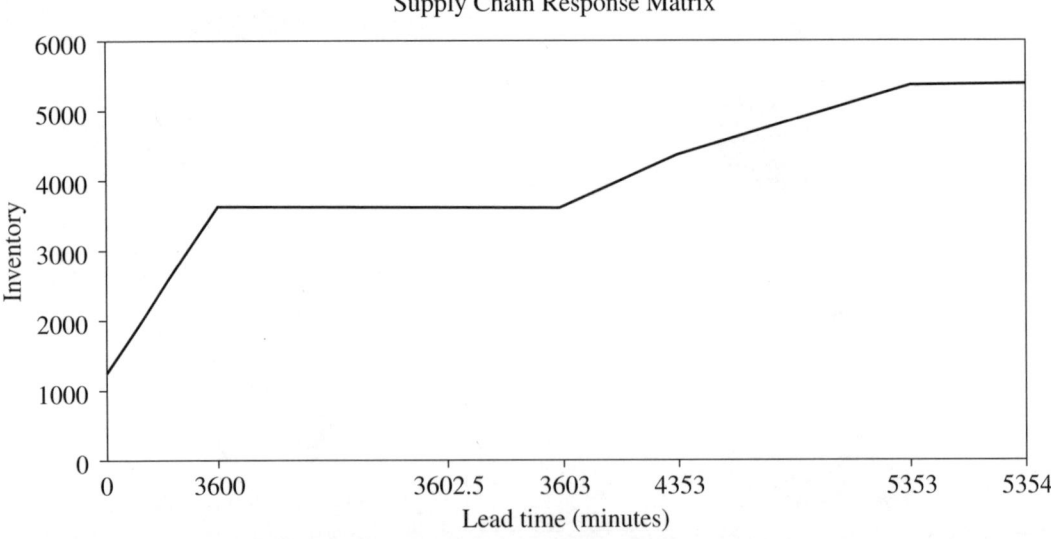

Figure 20.7   Example of the private sector supply chain response matrix

'FORRESTER' EFFECT MAPPING

This map is also known as demand amplification mapping and is based on the work of Forrester (1958) and Burbridge (1984). This map relates to the disturbance created along the supply chain due to reorder patterns. The Lean business system (Womack and Jones 1996) has evolved from the Toyota production system which focuses on making more with less. In most supply chains demand is erratic and the consequence of erratic demand is peaks and troughs in the quantity of product ordered. This can be amplified by the reordering activity that often has a standard order quantity. This is further amplified as it is passed along the supply chain through the tiers of supply. Those who are component suppliers usually feel the effects most.

This map, when applied in the public sector, highlighted that the supplier was levelling the schedule in line with capacity. The yearly forecast and issues at the supplier could have caused this. It is also noted that the data collected could have been skewed, because the period of time analysed was when a new production method was being introduced and the time period covered included December which was not typical of supply.

QUALITY FILTER MAP

The quality filter map helps the process to be viewed in respect of three types of quality: product quality, defect quality and service quality. Product quality refers to poor quality that has gone beyond the point at which the product had been made. This is the worst sort of quality defect as it could easily fall into the ultimate customer's hands. It also costs more to recover this type of quality, as further value is likely to have been added. Defect quality is a quality fault found at the point it has occurred. This quality costs the organization money and affects efficiency. The final type of quality is service quality, which relates to any issue that affects the organization's overall ability to provide the product/service to the customer. This type of defect is frequently not addressed within organizations or supply chains.

Within the public sector process the quality of delivery and product was inconsistent and hence the need for buffer stock, which in turn affected flexibility. This map identified the waste of defects and overproduction.

TRIANGULATION

Taking this into account, along with the points established from the process activity map, the supply chain responsiveness map, the Forrester effect mapping and the quality filter map the key issues were related to delivery, quality and process. The cost of the poor delivery was reflected in buffer stock and a bespoke process had been introduced to deal with the problems as they occurred. Although, in this instance, the Forrester effect mapping was inconclusive, the map is used frequently in the private sector and is particularly useful in explaining the issues between organizations. The distance travelled and the communication issues observed were due to the physical location of the individuals dealing with the process. The location of team members was within their functional area and was related to space available. Placing the individuals dealing with the process together would reduce travel and wasted time. It would also improve communication and problem resolution. This is common to both public and private sector organizations.

REVIEW

The review stage starts with feedback to the team to ensure that the charts and the interpretation of the data are supported. There should not be any skew relating to a single incident. All the data collected represents the frozen system and historic data and opinion and therefore the information may not always be representative. At this point conflicts identified between the maps are reviewed and, where appropriate, problem-solving techniques (Bicheno 1998) are used to identify the root cause(s) and generate plans to counter the problem(s):

● Pareto analysis;
● histogram and measles charts; and
● Ishikawa diagram (cause and effect).

Throughout the structured observation and systems analysis there were a number of recurring themes either emanating from the mapping or general conversation. Positive points included:

- the high quality of staff working in the areas mapped;
- the evidence of 'best practice', particularly in the despatch unit;
- the standardization of work methods within the procurement function; and
- initial action to reduce overproduction by the limiting of storage space.

There are still more wastes that can be removed and the procurement group is proactive in seeking methods to achieve this goal. Negative points included:

- the organizational structure restricting the emergence of innovative groups, supporting resistance to change and hampering progress;
- no evidence of the strategic location of departments to reduce time (lost through high transportation) and improve productivity;
- the duplication of records in all departments and processes;
- the significant level of available data underutilized for improvement purposes and the lack of a visual, customer-focused matrix;
- a perceived blame culture, accompanied by a progressive attitude towards change in areas (such as procurement), culminate in staff feeling vulnerable to external criticism. Embracing change is brave and should be rewarded; and
- no visible measures of continuous improvement.

The wastes, which were observed through the mapping, were compared against the waste matrix (see Figure 20.3) and any gaps were used to help remove barriers of perception (see Figure 20.8). This was undertaken during the review by means of a structured discussion.

STANDARDIZED SYSTEM

The quality and delivery issues that were visualized through the value stream mapping tools (see Figure 20.2) enabled the creation of a standard system. To realize the standardized system, actions to remove quality and delivery issues became a central theme of the organization. The solutions were cross-functional in nature. Teams were created and the action plans reviewed at a senior level in the organization. Therefore public sector procurement faces the same issues as private sector procurement and similar methods may be applied in spite of the different contingent natures (Hines et al. 1998).

There are constraints for both, particularly regarding the culture of organizations that do not encourage risk-taking and hence become

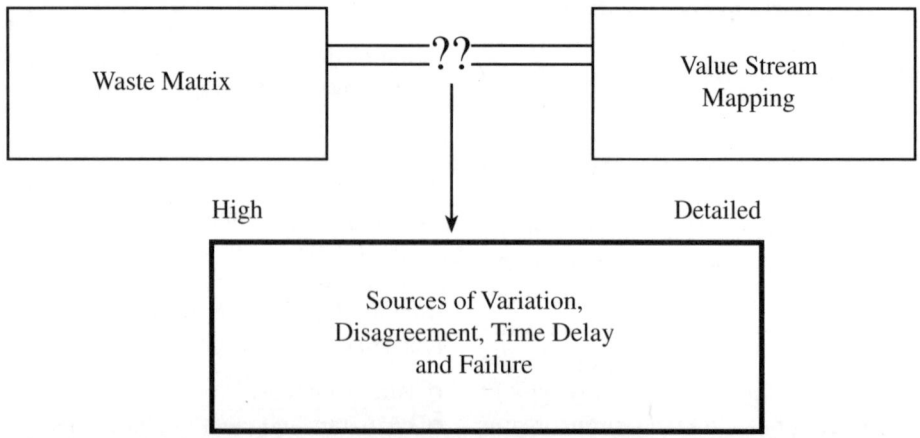

Figure 20.8 Conflicts between waste matrix and maps

'blame' organizations. The strategy of procurement must align with that of the organization (Rich and Hines 1997). Also, the skills of traditional purchasing (Hines 1994) need to be enhanced to enable suppliers to improve productivity.

The case study framework provides a mechanism to address the issues which are specific to an organization, not a sector or type of industry. The work of the DVLA has resulted in an increased focus on customer value and the activities that achieve that end. This is undertaken in a cross-functional manner and is supported by the organization.

Finally, to enact any change successfully then the fear of redundancies and restraint on career progression must be addressed. This is particularly the case in a public sector organization where the greatest cost is wages and there may be a history of cost cutting which has resulted in job losses. If jobs are to be retained then the organization needs to look at how it can take on other work, for example, the management of European driving licences. The case study framework will need to be expanded and tested to reflect this issue.

Whereas a private sector organization is encouraged to look at expanding its market, there is a perception that this is not the remit in an Agency. This is reinforced by the limited attempts made to be innovative. Whether this is a government directive is hard to establish; however those who drive the policy of the Agencies should be looking to expand their prospective work. Staff will rise to the challenge of improving efficiency if they can see how it enhances the prospect that a job will be available to them in the future. If the agencies of the UK are best in class, why should they forfeit the right to become best in class for Europe?

CONCLUSIONS

The comparison of public and private sector organizations described in this chapter and the case study framework applied in both cases has shown that organizations have individual needs; however, the methodology is applicable to both cases regardless of sector.

The methodology visualizes the process across functions and also facilitates a common language for the purposes of improvement. The structured observation drew out the perception as well as the facts relating to the process. The review encourages debate on the conflicts that become apparent (Figure 20.8) and the outcome is understanding and ownership of the improvement actions. These improvement actions address the sources of variation in the process, usually related to quality, which if resolved will improve delivery and reduce cost. Both private and public sector organizations have deployed the action plans, which has resulted in cost reduction.

There are issues that the methodology does not address, particularly the advancement of the individual (or at worst redundancies) which, need to be tackled as part of the organizational strategy. However, this is the case regardless of sector. Integral to employment is the issue of expansion of the market to take up the capacity released through improvement. The private sector can address this within their own organization and reflect this in their strategy. The public sector can address this, but their strategy is often mandated by central government. For the DVLA the improvement activity which they have initiated suggests that, for the new millennium, the government's mandate should include the ability to compete in Europe.

REFERENCES

Bicheno, J. (1998), *The Lean Tool Box*, Buckingham, PICSIE Books.

Burbidge, J. (1984), 'Automated production control with a simulation capability', *Proceedings of the IFIP Conference*, WG 5–7, Copenhagen.

Cox, A. (1995), 'Proactivity, value engineering and strategic procurement management', *Proceedings of the 1st Worldwide Symposium on Purchasing and Supply Chain Management*, Tempe, Az: Arizona State University.

Dimancescu, D., Hines, P. and Rich, N. (1997), *The Lean Enterprise, Designing and Managing Strategic Processes for Customer-Winning Performance*. New York: AMACOM.

Esain, A. (2000), 'Networks, Benchmarking and Development of the Strategic Supply Base: A Case Study', *International Journal of Logistics: Research and Application*, **3**(2), pp. 157–171.

Forrester, J. (1958), 'Industrial dynamics: a major breakthrough for decision making', *Harvard Business Review*, July-August, pp. 37–66.

Hines, P. (1994), *Creating World Class Suppliers: Unlocking Mutual Competitive Advantage*, London: Financial Times/ Pitman.

Hines, P. and Rich, N. (1997), 'The seven value stream mapping tools', *International Journal of Production and Operations Management*, **17**(1), pp. 46–64.

Hines, P., Rich, N., Bicheno, J., Brunt, D., Taylor, D., Butterworth, C. and Sullivan, J. (1998), 'Value stream management', *International Journal of Logistics Management*, **9**(1), pp. 25–42.

Kanter, R. (1989), *When Giants Learn to Dance, Master the Challenge of Strategy, Management, and Careers in the 1990s*, New York: Simon & Schuster.

Kennie, N., Hutchinson, S., Purcell, J., Rees, C., Scarborough, H. and Terry, M. (1998), *The People Management Implications of Leaner Ways of Working*, Report No 15, Institute of People Management, Issues in People Management.

Kotler, P. (1994), *Marketing Management Analysis, Planning, Implementation, and Control*, 8th edn, New Jersey: Prentice Hall.

Rich, N. and Hines, P. (1997), 'Purchasing structures, roles, processes and strategy: is it a case of the tail wagging the dog?', *Proceedings of the 6th International Annual IPSERA Conference*, T 5/3 1–17, University of Naples 'Federico II', Ischia (Naples) Italy.

Saunders, M., Lewis, P. and Thornhill, A. (1997), *Research Methods for Business Students*, London: Pitman.

Womack, J. and Jones, D. (1996), *Lean Thinking: Banish Waste and Create Wealth in your Corporation*, New York: Simon & Schuster.

CHAPTER TWENTY-ONE

Purchasing performance in the UK's Higher Education sector – functional measures to help in strategic development for the 21st century

Florence Gregg

The purpose of this chapter is to introduce a model developed by practitioners within the Higher Education (HE) sector. The model aims to help institutions make informed decisions regarding their future purchasing strategy thereby enabling a maximization of resources. The chapter will present empirical research which clearly demonstrates the ongoing, incremental improvements achieved. On the premise that the involvement of professionally trained purchasing staff will facilitate the achievement of value for money expenditure, the demonstration of an increasing involvement by such staff in universities' purchasing activities should indicate that the sector is making better use of its financial resources. The degree and quality of this value for money is, however, the subject of different studies.

This chapter will chart the increasing involvement of professional purchasing staff within the UK university sector. It will present the results of three case studies. The first will demonstrate an increasing level of influence and control within one institution over an eight-year period. Evidence will be presented of a shift from little professional purchasing involvement through a reactive approach to sourcing which has now developed into a soundly-based proactive purchasing activity. In the second, comparative data will be presented from other UK institutions. The third case study will offer comparative data

from external public and private sector organizations.

BACKGROUND

Following a visit to the two Northern Ireland universities by the Northern Ireland Audit Office in 1989 (NIAO 1990) and a later National Audit Office investigation in English universities (NAO 1993), most institutions had to re-think their approach to purchasing. In the NAO Report, it was asserted that the purchasing of goods and services accounted for some 30 per cent of an institution's total expenditure. Current research, however, indicates that this average is closer to 37 per cent. The attention of the Audit Offices resulted in determined efforts by the sector to implement more professional practices both at institutional and national level (Committee of Vice-Chancellors and Principals (CVCP) 1993, 1996). One problem faced by purchasing personnel was the difficulty in identifying what was happening in terms of supplier expenditure, historical usage patterns, forecasts and so on. These problems were exacerbated by poor, sometimes no, useful management information.

The Purchasing Consortium formed by the Scotland and Northern Ireland universities (Joint Consultative and Advisory Committee on Purchasing (JCACP)) began analysing expenditure with suppliers in the late 1980s and based its analysis on grouping suppliers into 'broad brush' categories, for example, computing, janitorial supplies and so on. It enabled members to identify where expenditure was going. Using this information the JCACP began to develop more formal arrangements. This exercise was very useful and continues today. However, in June 1996, a small group called the Scotland and Northern Ireland Benchmarking (SNIB) Group got together to further develop this analytical tool, Integrated Benchmarking Information System (IBIS 1999), one part of which is the model presented in this chapter.

RESEARCH METHODOLOGY

The methodology used in this research has been one of gradual development towards a model which would be easy to use, make use of standard, accessible information and provide outputs that could be understood by non-mathematicians. In essence, it should be simple.

Since its inception the model has been refined and extended. Completion of the model can highlight areas where there is a need to make arrangements more formal under, for example, the requirements of the EU's public procurement regulations. It will also indicate where a rationalization of the supplier base may be desirable or identify areas where a more proactive, strategic approach could be beneficial.

Performance measurement or benchmarking techniques used, not just within the sector, have tended to fall into three main areas:

- the traditional transactional type measures – number of purchase orders per 'purchasing' person, cost per order and so on (Langdon et al. 1997);
- 'unit cost' type analysis used in the NAO (1993) study; and
- the supplier analysis pioneered by JCACP.

More recently, there has been work on customer satisfaction analysis research (Mooney 1998) and the sector's own aspiration/observational-based procurement process benchmarking model (Higher Education Funding Council for England (HEFCE) 1997), each methodology having its merits which are, in the main, complementary.

The aim of SNIB was to develop a model that incorporated the most appropriate theories upon which the other techniques were based. The model is being developed so the research results presented in this chapter form the first phase of a much larger project. Some of the other measures planned for integration into the model include an assessment of the quality of the suppliers used by the institution, and work on the impact of the institution's purchasing structure on the level of influence achieved by its professional purchasing staff.

PERFORMANCE MEASUREMENT WITHIN THE HIGHER EDUCATION SECTOR

Over recent years, the popularity of benchmarking seems to have peaked and now it appears to be falling from favour. There have been examples of cross-industry benchmarking success, the two most memorable to the author being the Belfast aircraft manufacturer learning from the local bakery how to maximize the throughput of components in its ovens, or the underwear manufacturer learning from Nissan. The underlying driver behind these and other initiatives was to improve performance and the organization's competitive position (Thompson and Cox 1997) and, as these authors explained, the over-simplification of market comparisons explained the benefits and short-comings of benchmarking.

The developing SNIB model has its emphasis on performance measurement (Supply Management 1997) rather than more popular 'traditional' benchmarking. Initially, the research involved a number of institutions prepared to share with each other their collected performance measurements, this approach being preferable to one where the project became a large scale comparative exercise from which 'league' tables could be generated. The view was therefore focused, in the short term at least, on close collaboration between a small number of institutions. The use of the model is now being opened out to the Higher Education sector as well as involving a number of other public and private sector organizations.

DEVELOPMENT OF THE MODEL

The desire was that the model would not use the traditional, transactional type performance measures but rather consider how purchasing professionals influenced or controlled the purchasing activity within their respective institutions. The model needed to be able to deal with diverse purchasing structures – ranging from 'fully centralized' structures (where requisitions are created at departmental level and processed within a central purchasing office) to 'fully decentralized' structures where there was no 'formal' professional presence within the institution.

The starting point was therefore to assess the level of influence exerted by an institution's professional purchasing personnel (purchasing office) on their institution's non-pay expenditure. Non-pay, as the name indicates, is all expenditure not relating to pay as defined in 'Setting New Standards' (Treasury 1995). Four levels of influence were identified (see Table 21.1).

Each SNIB member assessed his/her own institution's non-pay expenditure for the 1993–94 financial year, allocating to each supplier one of the influence levels listed above. The results are given in Figure 21.1.

The results clearly demonstrated that each institution had some professional purchasing involvement in its non-pay expenditure, that is, Level 1 and Level 2 influences; however, the degree of influence varied between the institut-

Table 21.1 Influence level definitions

Level 1 **Adds Value**	The goods/services obtained where the purchasing office has a value-adding, active role such as providing or having involvement in a formalized purchasing exercise with, or on behalf of, staff of the institution.
Level 2 **Indirect Influence**	Purchases of goods/services made by using arrangements, such as call-off contracts prepared by other appropriate bodies, for example, national or consortia, without referral to the purchasing office.
Level 3 **No Value Added**	Purchases that are processed though the purchasing office but to which no professional purchasing value is added. For example, low value orders where central involvement is necessary to enable validation and preparation of data for input to computer systems and so on, or where sourcing work is completed at departmental level and the purchasing office authorizes the purchase, that is, validates (audits) the supporting paperwork.
Level 4 **No Involvement**	Goods/services that are obtained by the institution and for which there is no formal purchasing office involvement.

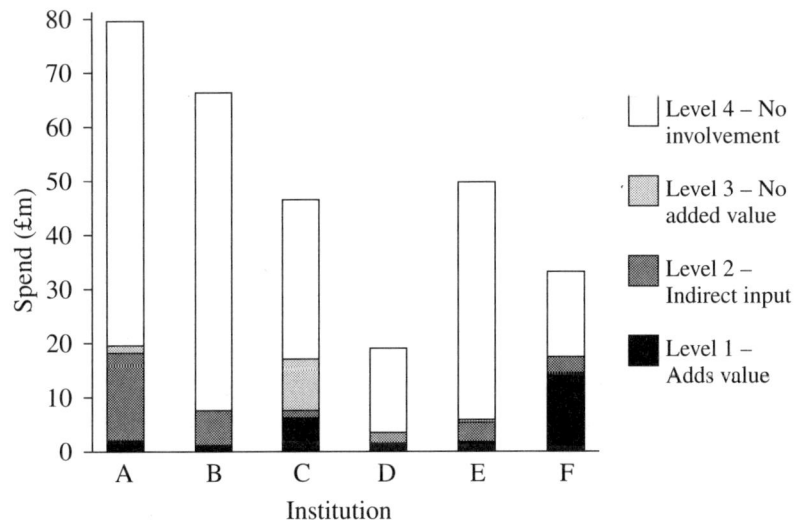

Figure 21.1 Level of influence analysis for the original SNIB universities 1993–94

Level 4 – No involvement

Level 3 – No added value

Level 2 – Indirect input

Level 1 – Adds value

ions (see Table 21.2). Of further interest is the fact that institutions A, D and, in particular, C reported 'No Added Value' activity. This indicated that staff in these offices were involved in the transactional processing of purchase orders, providing an audit rather than purchasing function. Table 21.2 below provides an indication of the diversity, in percentage terms, of the six institutions' involvement at each of the four influence levels.

Table 21.2 Minimum, maximum and average levels of influence in percentage terms of original SNIB universities (1993–94)

Influence Level	Minimum %	Maximum %	Average %
4.　No Involvement	47.17	87.80	73.97
3.　No Added Value	0	19.66	3.84
2.　Indirect Input	4.41	20.52	9.6
1.　Adds Value	1.50	44.07	12.6

Completion of this analysis highlighted one problem – the high number of suppliers used by universities. Numbers in excess of 15 000 were not unusual, making the task of allocating influence levels impractical. A review of the participating institutions' supplier profile suggested that their 'Top 100' highest paid suppliers represented approximately 40 per cent of that spend. This finding has now been confirmed by the data in case study two from 15 universities, where the 'Top 100' suppliers accounted for on average 50 per cent of their non-pay spend (the minimum representation was 34 per cent, and the maximum was 79 per cent).

Further consideration of the results, demonstrated in Figure 21.1 and Table 21.2, posed several questions, for example: What types of purchasing arrangements were being used in the institutions? How did the structure within an institution (centralized or decentralized) affect the influence level? What, if anything, was actually happening within the 'No Involvement' portion of the expenditure? It was felt that the introduction of strategic purchasing practices within an institution should result in an increase in the proportion of purchases falling within Levels 1 and 2. Further, the institutions should aim to reduce Level 3 influences and seek to gain access to the Level 4 areas. It was on this issue that the group decided to concentrate its efforts.

The first decision was to redesign the model to enable a two-dimensional analysis, that is, by influence level and type of purchase arrangement(s) in place with each supplier. It was also felt that the model should be:

- more flexible, enabling suppliers to be classified in different ways, for example, by the commodity supplied, suppliers used by individual user area, the institution's highest spend suppliers;
- able to analyse up to 100 suppliers, with the size of sample being selected by the user; and
- capable of creating graphical outputs and tables suitable for presentation to senior management as well as helping to inform the professional purchaser's developing strategies.

The type of arrangement analysis was defined into five categories (see Table 21.3).

Table 21.3 Arrangement type definitions

National	The institution is using available national contracts, for example, for fuel oil, or university sector arrangements available to all institutions.
Consortia	The UK universities have formed seven purchasing consortia which prepare, along with other services, purchasing arrangements on behalf of its members.
Local	Strategic purchasing arrangements made by the purchasing office, such as call-off contracts, framework agreements and so on for use within the institution.
Tender/Quote	One-off purchases made after the completion of a competitive exercise. In some instances the competition may be without any reference to the purchasing office.
Other	Purchases with which the purchasing office has no involvement.

The use of national consortia and local purchasing arrangements provides evidence of strategic purchasing, whilst the purchasing office preparing arrangements on behalf of its own and other institutions is viewed as proactive. Although the use of tender/quote arrangements is viewed as reactive, it is recognized that there will always be a need for this form of purchasing. The lack of available historical data and less than perfect forward planning makes the provision of proactive, local, arrangements difficult. For example, many large equipment purchases within universities are funded by external research grants, and in such cases the institution does not know which of its many grant applications will be successful. Forward planning is therefore not possible.

The influence levels (Table 21.1) were renamed to reflect a more structural approach to the analysis. Levels 1 and 2 were changed to 'central' and 'devolved' control respectively, the latter indicating the move to empowering users to get on with the transactional processes without the need to pass everything through the central purchasing office.

CASE STUDY ONE

In 1989 the Northern Ireland Audit Office visited the Northern Ireland universities (NIAO 1990): as a result these institutions reviewed their purchasing procedures and practices. This case study charts activity within one institution, University A, following its purchasing function's transition from a clerical to supportive/strategic structure (CVCP 1993).

The analysis is based upon the institution's 'Top 100' suppliers in terms of expenditure during the financial year. The figures for 1989–90 have been estimated based upon purchasing practices in place at that time (see Figures 21.2a and b).

In response to the criticisms from the NIAO (1990) the university began a process aimed at bringing the management of its non-pay expenditure onto a more professional footing. Ini-

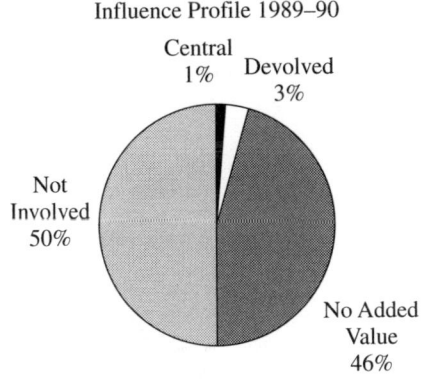

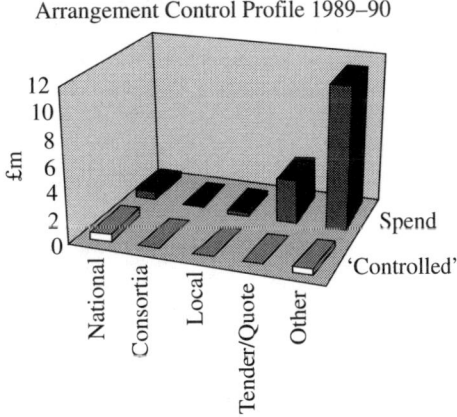

Figures 21.2a and b   Arrangement/control by value and influence profiles for University A based upon the 'Top 100' suppliers during 1989–90 (estimated)

COMMENTARY

The analysed expenditure (non-pay spend) is estimated at 40 per cent of the institution's total expenditure. In 1989–90, University A operated a transactional, audit-based purchasing structure where (apart from the estates office which had its own formal tendering procedures in operation) the purchasing office's influence, at only four per cent of the analysed expenditure, was minimal. The only proactive purchasing activity was where users purchased from a number of national arrangements for fuel oil and electronic components.

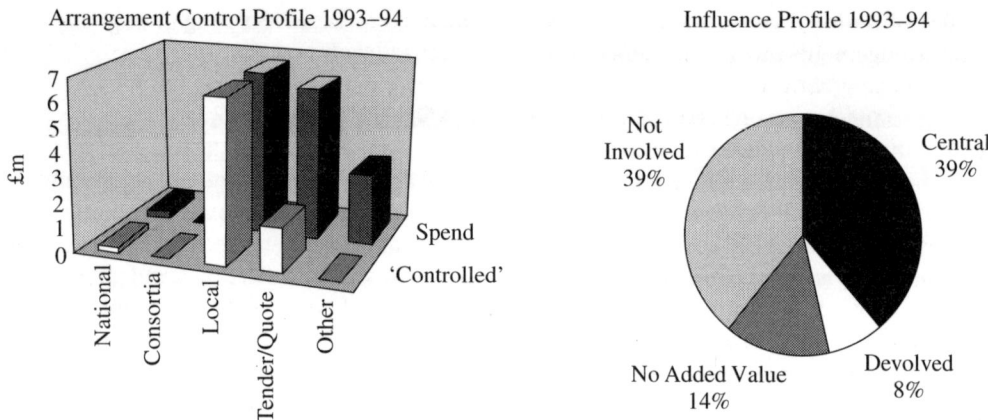

Figures 21.3a and b   Arrangement/control by value profile for University A based upon the 'Top 100' suppliers during 1993–94

COMMENTARY

The 'Top 100' suppliers accounted for 42 per cent of non-pay expenditure, and several major framework arrangements were introduced for the purchase of stationery, personal computers, and so on. There was a significant increase in the level of proactive, local contracts but the use of consortia and national arrangements was very low and nearly 20 per cent of the analysed expenditure remained outside the influence of the purchasing office. The increased level of proactive purchasing reflected the increased central and devolved influence levels, now accounting for 45 per cent of analysed expenditure.

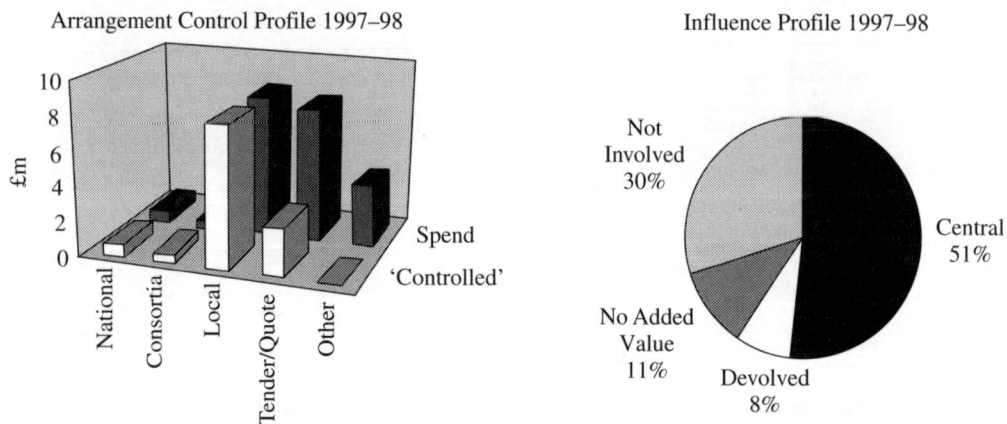

Figures 21.4a and b   Arrangement/control by value profile for University A based upon the 'Top 100' suppliers during 1997–98

COMMENTARY

The 'Top 100' accounted for 42 per cent of non-pay expenditure during 1997–98. The degree of central influence continued to rise while the devolved element appears to have remained static. The No Added Value proportion also remains, but with the planned implementation of a new integrated financial system it is envisaged that the level of devolved and transactional work will reduce.

tially, thresholds were introduced above which formal competition would be undertaken. Basic supplier analysis was undertaken and areas identified where it would be possible to introduce more formal purchasing arrangements. By 1993-94, the financial year upon which the SNIB Group carried out its first analysis, the expenditure/control profile of University A was showing significant improvement (see Figures 21.3a and b opposite).

The latest figures for University A (1997–98) indicate that the level of influence continues to increase gradually. This is in keeping with Quinn (1980) who suggested that change is managed slowly in an incremental fashion. The university slowly continues to improve the management of its suppliers and the formalization of its purchasing arrangements (see Figures 21.4a and b opposite). However, the analysis suggests that it should now extend its scope beyond the 'Top 100', iden-

tifying other areas which will lend themselves to a formalization of purchasing practices.

University A's purchasing office provides the focus for the recording of its purchasing activities and as such retains an involvement in processing paper which is a necessary, but not a value-adding, process. It is envisaged that this transactional-based approach will cease whenever the institution's new integrated financial system is introduced.

Using detailed analysis available for the last five financial years 1993–94 to 1997–98, it is possible to see the gradual increase in the purchasing office's impact on the University's purchasing practice. Figure 21.5 presents the institution's non-pay expenditure analysed in terms of:

● 'centrally' controlled/influenced purchases (that is, national, consortia, local or tender/quote arrangements) with the 'Top 100' sup-

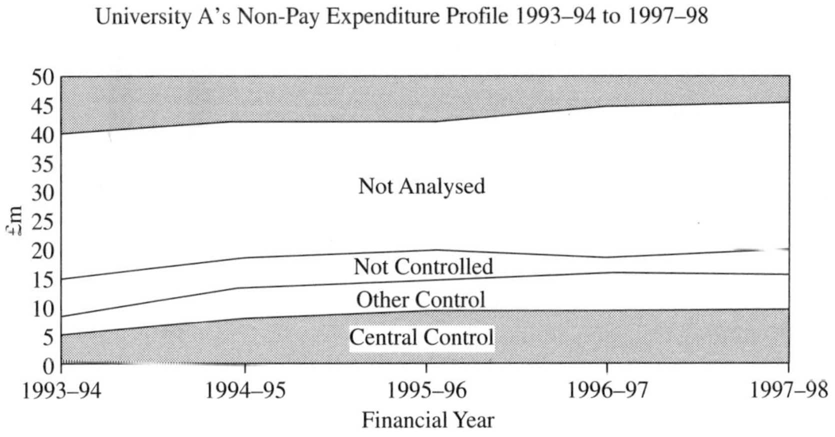

University A's Non-Pay Expenditure Profile 1993–94 to 1997–98

Figure 21.5   University A's non-pay expenditure displayed in terms of control by the purchasing office, by other offices, not controlled or not analysed. Period: 1993–94 to 1997–98 (five financial years)

COMMENTARY

This chart demonstrates the fluctuations in the proportion of non-pay spend represented by the 'Top 100' suppliers. Over the five-year period these suppliers accounted for, in monetary terms, between 41.6 per cent and 45.7 per cent of the institution's non-pay expenditure. Varying success, year on year, in obtaining research contracts involving the purchase of large, expensive pieces of equipment and major works contracts are both factors which impact expenditure levels with firms falling into the 'Top 100' sample analysed using the SNIB model.

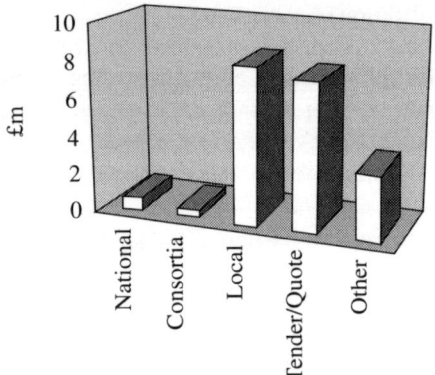

Consortia Arrangements JCACP only

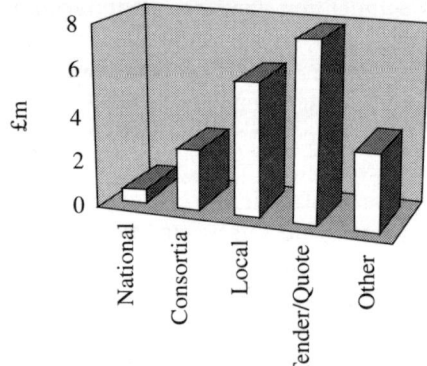

Consortia Including Northern Ireland Arrangements

Figures 21.6a and b   Charts showing the re-profiling of expenditure using local and consortia arrangements when Northern Ireland-based arrangements are classified as consortia rather than local (University A, 1997–98)

pliers and managed by the purchasing office;

● 'other' controlled purchases with the 'Top 100' suppliers. These are primarily those managed by the estates office without recourse to the purchasing office;

● expenditure with the 'Top 100' suppliers where there was no apparent formal procedures; and

● the balance of the non-pay spend with the remaining suppliers.

The use of national and consortia arrangements remains low, however, due to the geographical location of the institution. There is evidence that the Northern Ireland universities are actively working to aggregate requirements and a proportion of the local expenditure identified by University A is, in fact, joint strategic arrangements with its fellow institutions and not simply exclusive to itself. Figures 21.6a and b present a revised version of the arrangement/control profile contained in Figure 21.5.

The first case study has presented evidence of an evolving strategic approach to purchasing within one university, the same approach being reflected to varying degrees in many universities throughout the UK. The second case study presents current data from 15 other UK institutions.

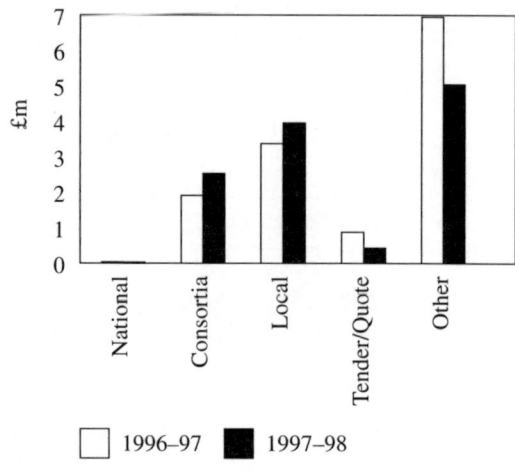

Purchasing Arrangements 1996–97 and 1997–98

☐ 1996–97   ■ 1997–98

Figure 21.7   Purchasing arrangement for University B based upon the 'Top 100' suppliers during 1996–97 and 1997–98

COMMENTARY

The chart shows an increase in proactive purchasing activities with increasing expenditure under consortia and local arrangements. There has been a reduction in the value of tenders/quotes which could be explained by the increased activity on consortia and/ or local arrangements or, possibly, a lower number of large research-based purchases to be tendered. The decrease in other expenditure should also be noted.

CASE STUDY TWO

The model has been available to the UK university sector for a number of months. Fifteen institutions have analysed their 1997–98 non-pay expenditure and provided the data to the sector's director of procurement development. Summary data has been forwarded to the author for inclusion in this chapter.

One institution, University B, provided data for two years, 1996–97 and 1997–98. This information (see Figure 21.7 opposite) confirms the incremental improvements illustrated in case study one. It should be noted, of course, that conclusions cannot be drawn using only two years' data, but the data does suggest that University B is aiming for a more strategic approach to its purchasing activities.

For purposes of comparison, Figures 21.8a and b present the average arrangement and influ-ence analyses for the 15 institutions. Where individual institutions are performing better than the average, further investigations will be carried out, examples of good practice identified and this information disseminated throughout the sector.

Based on the findings of the NAO (1993) that there was a need to improve purchasing practices throughout the sector, the data presented in this study supports the conclusions drawn in case study one. There now exists a professional approach to purchasing within the participating institutions which appears to be more devolved than in University A. On average, however, the total influence exerted by the purchasing professionals on their institution's 'Top 100' suppliers is similar to that of the institution in case study one. The next question is, therefore, how does the sector's performance compare with external bodies, both public and private?

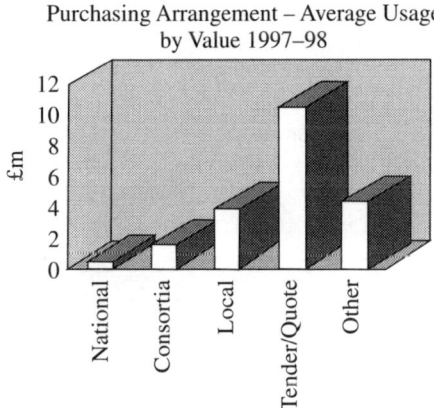

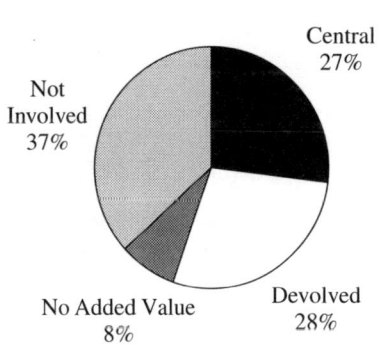

Figures 21.8a and b   Charts showing the average expenditure processed by arrangement type and average influence profile of 15 UK universities for 1997–98

COMMENTARY

These average results suggest that overall the main purchasing activity is reactive (tender/quotation) rather than proactive (national, consortia or local). They do, however, indicate that, in terms of their 'Top 100' suppliers, some 80 per cent of the expenditure falls under either proactive or reactive purchasing arrangement. In terms of influence, 45 per cent of the institutions' analysed non-pay expenditure remains outside the control of the professional purchasing staff. This may relate, in part, to expenditure committed by the institutions' estates departments where one or two major building projects can account for a significant proportion of the organization's non-pay spend for the financial year under consideration. This is an area where further investigation is merited.

CASE STUDY THREE

Limited comparative data has been obtained from outside the UK university sector. The profiles of three different types of organizations are presented based upon data from each organization for the financial year 1997–98. The first data set relates to the averaged responses from two Northern Ireland local councils, each of which is responsible for large city-based communities (Figures 21.9a and b).

The second set of external data relates to a number of Northern Ireland Health Service hospitals trusts (see Figures 21.10a and b opposite). Summary, rather than complete, data was provided by the respondents. Like the university sector, the trusts would appear to still have a high number of suppliers providing their goods and services. Also, their major building works requirements tend to be managed under competitive procedures by professional engineers rather than purchasers.

The final set of data comes from a multinational, private sector manufacturing company. In this case, the term 'global' maps to 'national' and 'European' relates to 'consortia' as used previously in this chapter (see Figures 21.11a and b opposite). The average expenditure of the 15 universities presented in case study two is equivalent to 20 per cent of the total annual expenditure of this company. The private sector differs significantly from the public sector contributors in that they have a much more focused supplier base, perhaps with only 100–150 key suppliers. Again, the sector's director of procurement development provided this data and full analytical detail was unavailable.

The external public and private sector data provides an opportunity for comparison with the university sector. Having now made these initial contracts it is hoped that there will be the opportunity to conduct more in-depth data collection and analyses, leading to further collaborative research.

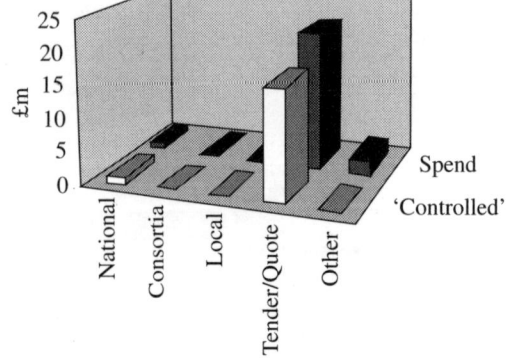

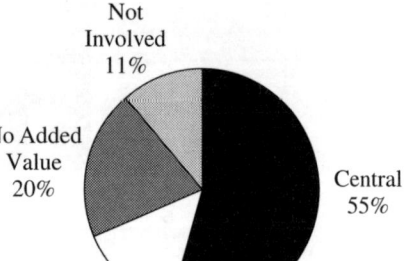

Figures 21.9a and b   Arrangement/control by value and influence profiles based upon averaged data from two Northern Ireland local councils

COMMENTARY

The arrangement/control profile indicates that the councils have a good degree of input to their organizations' non-pay expenditure. It would appear, however, that there is scope to move from a reactive, tender/quotation based purchasing style towards the introduction of more proactive local or consortia type arrangements with other councils or similar public bodies. Like University A in case study one, there appears to be a significant proportion of transactional, non-value added work undertaken.

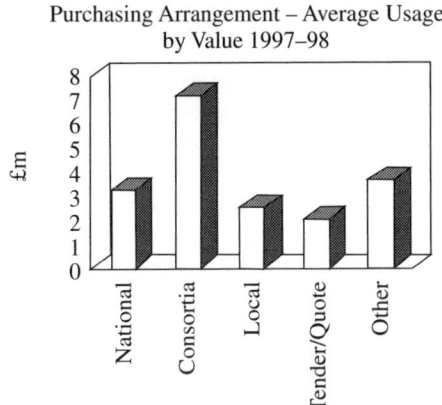

Purchasing Arrangement – Average Usage by Value 1997–98

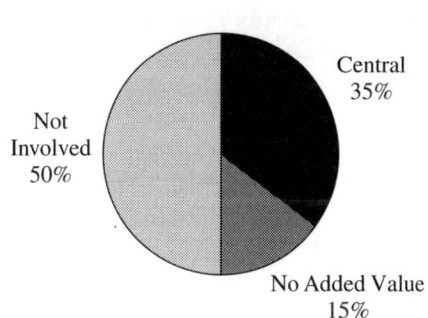

Average Influence Profile 1997–98

Figures 21.10a and b   Arrangements by value and influence profiles based upon averaged data from three Northern Ireland hospital trusts

COMMENTARY

These results demonstrate a high usage of national and consortia type purchasing arrangements which is not unexpected given the work of the regional supplies service which prepares many high value contracts on behalf of the Hospital Trusts within Northern Ireland. Perhaps more significant is the influence profile which clearly demonstrates the very centralized nature of purchasing within the sector.

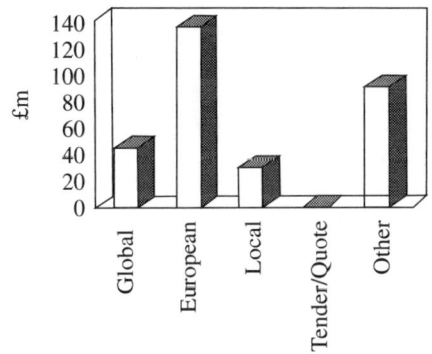

Purchasing Arrangement by Value 1997–98

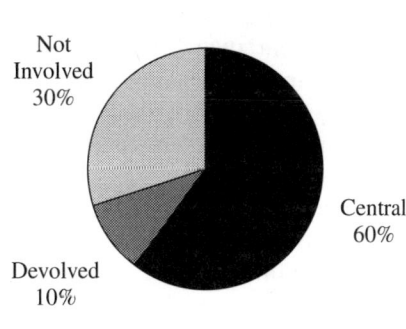

Influence Profile 1997–98

Figures 21.11a and b   Charts showing the purchasing arrangement and influence profiles of a private sector company for 1997–98

COMMENTARY

The most interesting observation from the purchasing arrangement chart is that the firm appears to deal proactively with some 70 per cent of its annual expenditure managed under global, European and local arrangements. This will be due in part to its much smaller supplier base and is, no doubt, helped by its core function (manufacturing) and its ability to plan production, raw materials requirements, and so on. The firm also appears to operate a much more centralized purchasing structure than has been found in either the Higher Education sector or the other public sector comparators presented in this chapter.

CONCLUSION

Since the visit of the NIAO in 1989, University A has made steady progress in respect of its professional purchasing practice and in the formalization of arrangements with its key suppliers. Initially, the progress was caused by a crisis, that is, the criticisms contained in the NIAO Report, and activity was in line with the thinking of Chandler (1962). After the first two years the rate of change slowed, becoming much more incremental, akin to the theories of Quinn (1980) and the university began to introduce a more strategic approach to its purchasing activity. There was a shift towards the introduction of proactive arrangements rather than reactive tenders/quotations which formed its main activity in the early 1990s. However, as thinking changed between the merits of centralized versus decentralized purchasing structures, the analogy that the way forward is similar to a marathon run in a succession of 400 metre sprints is very apt (Narayanan and Fahey 1982).

The evidence presented in case study two supports the conclusions drawn in case study one. The other universities represented in this study are currently implementing changes brought about after the 1993 NAO visit and, having started to implement change several years later than the two Northern Ireland institutions, should expect the incremental improvements to continue.

Case study three presented external comparators, the two public sector comparators evidencing profiles similar to those of the university sector. In each case, the bodies appear to be moving towards more proactive styles of purchasing with a shift towards more devolved purchasing by empowering the departmental users through the creation of strategic purchasing arrangements at either local, consortia or national level. The private sector multinational firm, on the other hand, operated with much more central control with a significant proportion of its expenditure managed by strategic contracts.

Hence, data collected using the SNIB model provides evidence that in the UK university sec-
tor there is a real shift towards proactive, strategic arrangements formed at local, consortia and national levels. Referring back to the premise proffered in the opening paragraph, which related the belief that the involvement of professionally trained purchasing staff facilitates the achievement of value for money, the research clearly demonstrates that there has been a move towards increased professionalization within the sector. These professional staff are not only improving purchasing by extending their, demonstrated, influence on their institution's 'Top 100' suppliers, but have also developed and laid down strategies, policies and frameworks of guidance and manuals for the use of departmental part-time buyers. This devolution, empowering these part-time buyers to get on with routine ordering, using proactive purchasing arrangements, enables the professional staff to exert a passive influence, improving the quality of purchasing in areas where they are not directly involved on a daily basis.

The evidence presented in this chapter comes from the use, by institutions, of the first part of an integrated performance measurement model (IBIS 1999) which is under development within the UK university sector. IBIS will be used to assess the continuing professionalization of the sector's purchasing function.

REFERENCES

Chandler, A.D. (1962), *Strategy and Structure: Chapters in the History of the Industrial Enterprise*, Cambridge, Mass: MIT Press.

Committee of Vice-Chancellors and Principals (1993), *Good Management of Purchasing*, London: CVCP.

Committee of Vice-Chancellors and Principals (1996), *Procurement Strategy for Higher Education*, London: CVCP.

Higher Education Funding Council for England (1997), *Process Procurement Benchmarking*.

IBIS (1999), Joint Consultative and Advisory Committee on Purchasing, 34 Buccleugh Place, Edinburgh.

Langdon, D.S., Schwerman, T. and Allen, S. (1997), *Purchasing Performance Benchmarks for Higher Education,* Tempe, Az: Center for Advanced Purchasing Studies.

Mooney, R.L. (1998), *A Model Purchasing Department for Creating High Customer Satisfaction,* National Association of Educational Buyers, Inc. (unpublished).

National Audit Office (1993), *University Purchasing in England,* London: HMSO.

Narayanan, V.K. and Fahey, L. (1982), 'The micropolicitics of strategy formulation', *Academy of Management Review,* 70, pp. 25–34.

Northern Ireland Audit Office (1990), *Report by the Comptroller and Auditor General for Northern Ireland: Economy, Efficient and Effectiveness Examinations of Certain Matters,* HMSO: Belfast.

Quinn, J.B. (1980), *Strategies for Change: Logical Incrementalism,* Homewood IL: Irwin.

Supply Management (1997), 'News: NAO set to return to campus', *Supply Management,* September, pp. 9–10.

Thompson, I. and Cox, A. (1997), 'Don't imitate, innovate', *Supply Management,* October, pp. 40–43.

Treasury (1995), *Setting New Standards: The Government's Procurement Strategy,* HMSO: London.

CHAPTER TWENTY-TWO

Benchmarking for strategic procurement: practices of Polish companies in an international context

Danuta Kisperska-Moron

BENCHMARKING IN SUPPLY CHAIN MANAGEMENT

While many companies view purchasing as a functional overhead centre, leading edge companies have demonstrated that this essential activity can be a dynamic force in overall business performance. The main condition is to approach procurement strategically, focusing on the overall procurement process, and not being limited to individual purchasing activities (for some authors the term 'procurement' could be identified with the general term 'supply' (Schary and Larsen 1995)). In fact, integration of procurement requires more holistic thinking, that is, looking beyond short term price-related reductions toward longer term supply improvements in both cost and quality (Christopher 1992).

Basically, that approach would aim at the creation of an integrated procurement system which, in turn, would constitute a part of the whole integrated logistics system of a single company or, as is very often the case, a subsystem of a more complex supply chain (Copacino 1997). The second approach of supply chain-centric companies helps them to become successful in today's business environment (Walker 1998). Therefore there have been many initiatives originating in the industry itself and also in academic circles for closer monitoring of superior supply chain performance. The Supply Chain Council, which was launched in 1996 in the USA is an example of such activities (Of Interest to Members 1997). One way of getting support for such long-term oriented actions is to identify best practices and patterns to be followed or developed through benchmarking and comparative analysis procedures (Rolstadas 1995).

The development process of the benchmarking concept allows us to indicate several generations of benchmarking (Watson 1993) as shown in Figure 22.1. *Reverse engineering*, as the first generation, has been based on comparisons of the product characteristics, functionality, and performance with similar products or services from competitors. *Competitive benchmarking* has moved beyond product-oriented comparison to include comparison of processes with those of competitors. *Process benchmarking* brings indirect competitors together to learn from the information they share beyond the natural boundaries of their businesses. The level of detail of information depends on their ability to share process information. *Strategic benchmarking* is a systematic process of evaluating alternatives, implementing strategies and improving performance by understanding and adopting successful strategies from external partners. It can be described as 'using benchmarking to fundamentally change the business, not just to tweak processes' (Biesada 1992). *Global benchmarking* seems to be the future generation of benchmarking where international trade, cultural and business process distinctions among the companies are bridged and their

Sophistication

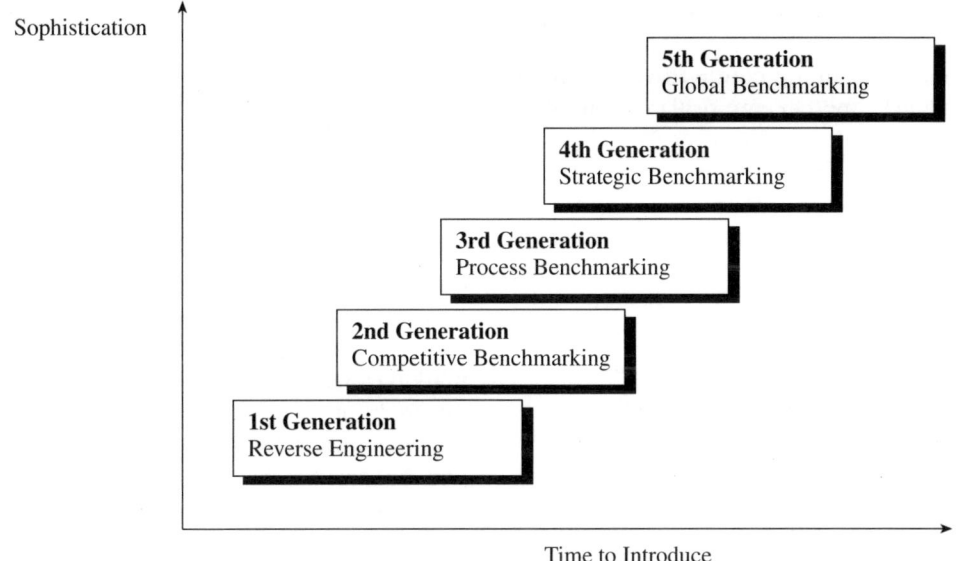

Time to Introduce

Figure 22.1 Development of benchmarking concept
Source: Watson, G.H. (1993), *Strategic Benchmarking: How to Rate Your Company's Performance Against the World's Best*, New York: John Wiley & Sons. © 1993 John Wiley and Sons Limited. Reproduced with permission.

implications for business process improvement understood.

While operating in the era of strategic and global benchmarking, we also have to be able to assess and compare all processes connected to procurement as well as to personnel, which is an important factor in the overall procurement success. Moreover, supply chain-centric firms should also drive their business with global performance measures, which would have some implications for the overall procurement process.

There have been several attempts to benchmark logistics and supply chain processes in the USA, for example, the Global Procurement and Supply Chain Benchmarking Initiative at Michigan State University (Monczka 1997a), activities of the International Benchmarking Clearinghouse (Made to Measure 1997) and several others. The Council of Benchmarking at the Strategic Planning Institute in the USA has devised a special code of conduct for these procedures. It is publicly available on the Internet at www.spinet.org (Made to Measure 1997). Some supply chain and purchasing benchmarking initiatives have also been launched in the UK, for

example, the Chartered Institute of Purchasing and Supply and its partners in the UK organized the procurement benchmarking service (Mark of Distinction 1997).

The benchmarking initiative may contain areas of study such as Monczka (1997b):

- strategic supplier alliance/partnerships;
- best commodity/purchase family strategies;
- supplier integration into new product/process/service development;
- procurement strategy development and company-wide integration (current and future assessment);
- integrated supply chain management;
- procurement and supply chain performance;
- procurement and supply chain globalization strategies;
- procurement and supply chain organization;
- supplier development and quality management;
- information systems and technology;
- human resources development; and
- indirect purchases.

Transportation is the most popular logistics process benchmarked, with more than 80 per cent of benchmarking focusing on outbound transportation and a common gain from benchmarking being competitive advantage (Foster 1992). Another empirical example (Stank et al. 1994) indicates that over 60 per cent of their respondents perform routine benchmarking on cost, customer service and warehouse operations. Hence the general conclusion is that procurement processes and purchasing are not the most popular fields on which benchmarking is carried out.

SCOPE OF BENCHMARKING IN PURCHASING AND PROCUREMENT

The purchasing function is probably one of the most difficult to evaluate. The following are the major problems in purchasing benchmarking (van Weele 1994):

● lack of definition of certain terms such as purchasing performance, purchasing effectiveness or even basic purchasing/procurement;
● lack of formal objectives and performance standards;
● problems of accurate measurement, since purchasing is not an isolated function and its performance is a result of many activities, often difficult to evaluate; and
● difference in scope of purchasing between various companies which precludes the development of broadly based uniform benchmarking systems.

Purchasing is the activity associated with the outside acquisition of goods and services, and can be divided into three categories (Byrne and Markham 1991):

1. Sourcing, that is, establishing the requirements and purchase specifications for vendors, locating, interviewing and generally negotiating with vendors, qualifying vendors.
2. Procurement, that is, buying the goods or services required by the company from the approved vendors' listing.
3. Cost control, that is, reviewing present and future requirements in search of alternative sources of supply, alternative materials and many other types of value analyses aiming at

cost reduction and increased value of purchased products.

Probably the most obvious area to benchmark within the framework of the supply chain is the suppliers themselves. For any purchasing manager, it is quite obvious that while selecting the lowest priced supplier is easy, it is much more difficult to decide on the 'right' supplier taking other reasons into account. Much work has been done in the field of suppliers' benchmarking, sometimes referred to as 'supplier benchmarking analysis'. At this point, however, it is of utmost importance to remember that the question of finding the right suppliers is not the only one that secures the correct strategic positioning of the procurement process. There are several other important issues for successful strategic procurement.

This chapter does not address the problems of supplier benchmarking, as there has been much discussion and practical action in that field. It has also been very popular among Polish companies, particularly car and spare part manufacturers, to create elaborate systems for supplier evaluation (for example, Ellram 1990; Weber et al. 1991; Weber and Ellram 1993; Ellram 1995; Roodhooft and Konings 1995; Choi and Hartley 1996; Vokurka et al. 1996 and many others). Instead, this chapter discusses some ideas for benchmarking the strategic procurement process viewed as one of the main business processes of any company and/or supply chain. In this sense, benchmarking might be used as a strategic management tool by inexperienced organizations as they start the benchmarking process, in Poland and many other successful transition economies.

BENCHMARKING MEASUREMENTS IN THE PURCHASING PROCESS

Since benchmarking is about measurement (Camp 1989; Camp 1995), this chapter will try to suggest the best ways of measuring performance in the procurement process at that initial step, assuming that a given performance level is a result of certain management processes and that it is a starting point for further analysis of factors contributing to or limiting continuous improvements in purchasing. Defining proper measures is a key step in the whole process, especially as these measures may vary according to conditions and circumstances in a particular country or even within an industry sector.

Direct measurement of the activities associated with purchasing is often neither possible nor desirable. Very often measurement of these activities may be more accurate through measuring the result of the activity, that is, purchasing performance. There are several different opinions on which precise aspects of purchasing performance should and could be measured.

Traditionally purchasing performance is considered to be the result of two elements (van Weele 1994):

● purchasing effectiveness, connected to the extent to which the purchasing function is able to realize its goals; and
● purchasing efficiency, understood as the relationship between resources engaged in the realization of a certain set of effects, that is, purchasing goals.

In other words, purchasing effectiveness can be described in terms of the quality of the output of the purchasing process, or how effectively the purchasing function is meeting requirements. Purchasing efficiency is tracked by productivity measures, sometimes accompanied by utilization measures. Improvements in effectiveness are usually connected to improvements in efficiency (productivity), for example, if the percentage of certified suppliers who check their own quality grows then the efficiency of the company's operation is also higher since less time is spent on inspecting incoming shipments.

Hence, the potential measures for the management of purchasing consist of the set of measures reflecting such major aspects of purchasing processes as identified by Byrne and Markham (1991):

1. Quality measures evaluating the quality of the purchasing management process, from the point of view of:
   – incoming product quality/service measures;

– supplier quality measures; and
– purchase order quality measures, including such potential measures as:
– measures of results (what is required);
– diagnostics (why requirements are not satisfied); and
– impact (effect of not meeting requirements)

2. Productivity measures, related to resource inputs such as labour, equipment and other inputs in purchasing activities such as sourcing, procurement, cost control and overall purchasing performance.

3. Other purchasing measures of the effectiveness of the purchasing process, indicating how well various components of the purchasing process are performing.

Each group of measures listed above may consist of detailed indicators reflecting various aspects of the particular heading. The actual mix of these indicators will depend on the nature of the business and the goals and requirements of the measurement and benchmarking exercise.

However, it is worth underlining that the measures from the third group listed above are general indicators of good and poor practices in purchasing, and they could be used as benchmarks. They may be used to measure by vendors and/or by commodity. Examples of benchmark measures are presented in Table 22.1.

Due to their universal character, these indicators may serve as a good basis for inter-company comparisons of the following:

● to measure the results of management: share of departments rating the purchasing department as an 'excellent' supplier;
● to diagnose problems: percentage of departments in a company rating the purchasing department as an 'average' or 'poor' supplier, along with reasons (for example, over-long lead time requirements, poor delivery performance, errors, damaged materials or parts, poor communication, low quality of purchasing personnel, poor response to problems and so on);
● to measure the impact of purchasing management: estimate costs of being rated lower

Table 22.1   Basic purchasing benchmark measures

Activities	Overall Activity	Labour
Sourcing	● % of total vendors qualified ● % of purchases from qualified vendors ● % of vendors located locally ● % of old parts on which price quotes are received per period ● % of new parts on which price quotes are received per period ● % of vendors providing backup stock ● % of purchased parts that are single sourced ● % of newly qualified vendors qualified on price, lead times, and quality	● number and % of vendors' facilities visited per period ● number and % of vendors interviewed per period
Procurement	● % of total purchase orders changed ● % of total purchase orders issued as blanket purchase orders ● no. of expedites processed as a % of total purchase orders issued ● no. of receipts per purchase order ● % of orders received on time ● % of line items received completed ● % of purchase orders received complete ● % of receipts rejected ● $ value rejected as a % of $ value received ● $ value returned as a % of $ value received ● expedites fulfilled as a % of expedites processed ● no. of acknowledgements received with delivery date as requested as % of acknowledgements received ● $ value reworked as a % of $ value received ● part stockouts due to late delivery as a % of total part stockouts ● quotes received with both FOB vendor plant and FOB receiving location prices as a % of total quotes received ● % of purchase orders issued with incomplete data	● % of advantageous price breaks taken ● % of purchase orders issued in error ● % of vendor acknowledgements received that match purchase order time ● % of procurement labour hours devoted to the purchase of 'A' items
Cost Control	● material cost increases as a % of competitor's or general inflation index material cost increases ● % of 'A' items subject to value analysis ● total cost savings as a % of total $ value purchased	
Overall Purchasing Management	● material cost as % of total standard product cost ● % of vendors for whom capacity is known ● % of vendor shipments over or under quantity ordered ● % of vendor invoices containing errors ● % of purchases made without purchase orders	

Source: Based on Byrne, P.M. and Markham, W.J. (1991), *Improving Quality and Productivity in the Logistics Process. Achieving Customer Satisfaction Breakthroughs,* Council of Logistics Management.

than 'excellent' (for example, revenue decline, downtime in production or lost sales, costs of providing additional service, costs of re-scheduling, lost customers, and so on).

While considering purchasing management productivity, cost analyses and indicators usually play an essential role; particularly relative indicators. Often, year to year trend analysis of these measures provides better information than single year figures. Finally, performance of purchasing management could generally be evaluated on the basis of budget performance where budget might be expressed in terms of currency units, man-hours or other appropriate measures.

BENCHMARKING PRACTICES IN PURCHASING IN POLISH COMPANIES: AN INTERNATIONAL CONTEXT

There has been relatively little recorded empirical research on purchasing performance in Poland since the economy shifted towards a market orientation. There has been no serious benchmarking performed in the general fields of logistics, supply chain management or purchasing. Therefore this research project has been undertaken to partially fill that gap, and to evaluate the potential for future benchmarking. This chapter presents some of the results of a research project on benchmarking in manufacturing and logistics which was carried out by the author at the Centre for Logistics and Transportation at Cranfield University and supported by the European Union's Phare ACE Programme of 1996. The focus of the project was to provide measurement guidelines for benchmarking logistics and supply chain (and also purchasing, as part of the concept of logistics and supply chain management).

The survey was designed to investigate which performance measures are used most commonly in Polish companies. Purchasing, as a very important element of the logistics process and the essential phase in supply chain management, has been of a particular interest. Some of the findings of the survey would probably also be true for many companies in other coun-

tries, even those with well developed market economies.

In the Polish companies surveyed by the author there were no formal and structured benchmarking projects, either in the field of manufacturing and logistics or in general business performance. However, surveys carried out by researchers from the University of Manchester suggest that benchmarking practices have become more frequent in the UK, although examples are still very limited (Davies and Kochhar 1999). The findings of that research were as follows:

1. There was a limited use of benchmark metrics due to the lack of precise performance evaluation systems at different levels in the organization.
2. There was a lack of implementation of best practices due to a short-term view of performance and the perception that existing gaps were too large to be reduced in the short term.
3. There was no formal benchmarking strategy, checklist or definition.
4. Business plan targets did not reflect many of the aspects discussed and learnt as a result of benchmarking.

Many Polish companies are currently in the process of seeking certification for ISO 9000 standards, particularly ISO 9001 and ISO 9002. This requires a very thorough analysis of all a company's procedures. During the certification process many companies rediscovered their purchasing function, and it serves as a starting point for further improvements in that area. These procedures, for example, virtually force companies to segment and evaluate their suppliers, hence that type of benchmarking might be considered quite common in Polish companies.

However, a more profound examination of the problem resulted in the following hypotheses describing the status quo of benchmarking in Polish companies:

● the general awareness of performance benchmarking is low among purchasing managers, but is higher in firms that are quality certified or foreign-owned;
● a low level of awareness of benchmarking

significantly affects the practice of benchmarking, and therefore it is only practised by a few companies;

- those companies which have programmes designed to promote quality are more likely to initiate benchmarking procedures in many areas, possibly also in purchasing;
- a low level of knowledge about benchmarking and lack of expertise to perform benchmarking narrows the potential size of benchmarking exercises in companies;
- purchasing is perceived as an extremely complex field for benchmarking, much more complicated than, for example, customer service or transportation;
- there might be a stronger drive towards industry and competitive benchmarking although at present information is treated as highly confidential and this prevents large-scale comparative inter-company purchasing benchmarking projects; and for the same reason it might be very difficult to indicate sources of benchmarking; and
- top management is most likely to initiate benchmarking.

On the basis of the survey, forms of benchmarking in the field of general procurement and purchasing were found mostly in manufacturing companies, in companies with mixed activities (manufacturing/commercial/service) and occasionally in service companies. It seems that commercial companies concentrate more on customer service, that is, outgoing streams of products, while manufacturers seem to pay more attention to warehousing and purchasing, that is, incoming streams of products and materials. However, there is no one clear tendency in this area.

Companies that measure performance in the area of general procurement and purchasing use the following indicators (listed in the order of frequency of use):

- share or number of prompt deliveries from suppliers with, for instance, a standard of 95 per cent of promptly delivered orders;
- share or number of late deliveries from suppliers, for example, number of late deliveries in relation to total number of suppliers;

- share of claims in all deliveries from suppliers;
- share of damaged products in the total number of delivered products in a specific time period;
- number of returned products;
- supplier performance evaluation;
- minimum value of the order in relation to unit price of the product;
- volume of a single order: total requirements for warehouse space in relation to daily number of orders; and
- average time of deliveries from suppliers, for example for a car servicing company, seven days for parts with hard to forecast demand.

The benchmarking indicators for purchasing and procurement listed above seem to be more typical for Polish companies. For example, comparisons with the practices of UK companies (Medori 1999 in Mufato and Pawar; Douglas 1993) show that in both Polish and UK companies the focus of logistics measurement depends on the type of company. Manufacturers focus more on the procurement and co-ordination of purchasing and sales with production schedules, while other companies put greater emphasis on customer service and quality of distribution systems. However it seems that there is a substantial difference between Polish and UK companies concerning the precision of measurement, with UK companies using more varied indicators in a more systematic way.

Italian research in the field of overall logistics performance measurement shows that most Italian companies surveyed have systems that are largely incomplete and do not cover all the phases of the supply chain (Gianesin and Agostinacchio 1999). In Italian companies the external phases of the supply chain, that is, supplier assessment and customer service levels, are the least controlled areas, whilst internal phases are more controlled.

Comparing the results of Polish and UK surveys with Italian research, a paradoxical discrepancy can be noticed: despite a commonly shared opinion that logistics measures are of the utmost importance for company competitiveness, these measures still have limited practical application. The quality and completeness of the measurement systems in logistics (and, within that, purchasing) are not significantly influenced by the size, industry or type of business of the company, but seem to depend mainly on the culture, sensitivity and previous experience of the managers.

CONCLUSIONS

It is important for companies to know the exact stage of development of their operational areas. Performance measures are one way of determining that stage. Moreover, these measures should facilitate widely understood benchmarking practices, so that companies can offer better services to customers and better integrate their logistics processes. In purchasing functions, improvements in everyday practices are essential to meet the increasingly demanding requirements of internal customers in the areas of operations management and/or distribution and sales.

In conclusion, a true measure of purchasing management and the purchasing process itself is the level of long-term internal customer satisfaction achieved for the total logistics costs incurred. Most Polish companies still have to develop such measures because of the following reasons:

● they have not yet defined the concept of the 'internal customer' and its long-term satisfaction; as a result companies cannot precisely measure that process due to a lack of defined benchmarks; and
● companies do not accurately and completely identify purchasing and logistics costs since traditional accounting methods do not support such calculations.

The results of the procurement process and purchasing performance depend greatly on the qualities of the personnel involved in supply chain decision-making. Even preliminary studies of the level of qualifications of purchasing personnel in Polish companies suggest that there is a general lack of highly qualified people who would be able to secure a satisfactory level of purchasing management. Such a low level of

qualifications remains even after the centrally planned economy has been abandoned. Whilst there is a strong tendency to learn new skills and raise the level of qualifications, the following phenomena still prevail (Dudzik 1998):

● lack of command of foreign languages;
● lack of professional negotiating skills;
● lack of basic knowledge in the fields of economics, finance, export and import and marketing; and
● occasional failure of moral and ethical rules when large amounts of money are involved.

The statements presented above concerning human resources probably reflect the reality of companies in various countries. As many companies in Poland and worldwide are in the process of improving their purchasing function, the focus of the benchmarking process should be on the managerial aspects of purchasing. Management output is less quantifiable because managers only have an indirect effect on output. Therefore it is often more important to evaluate management capability to achieve results effectively than to evaluate management's personal productivity.

There is therefore a need to evaluate purchasing managers on the basis of the following:

● line management ability, that is, their ability to manage day-to-day purchasing operations and meet goals established in terms of quality, productivity and budgeting;
● problem solving ability, that is, their ability to anticipate and diagnose problems as well as to develop and apply new strategies for cost savings, service improvement and increased return on investment;
● project management ability, that is, their ability to structure and manage projects designed to improve the purchasing process; and
● people management ability, that is, their ability to develop and motivate their employees' technical and management skills.

This chapter has argued that a benchmarking exercise in any field of logistics or the supply chain management process, not only in purchasing, could be very helpful in achieving significant improvements in these areas.

REFERENCES

Biesada, A. (1992), 'Strategic benchmarking', *Financial World*, 29, September, p. 31.

Byrne, P.M. and Markham, W.J. (1991), *Improving Quality and Productivity in the Logistics Process. Achieving Customer Satisfaction Breakthroughs*, Oak Brook: Council of Logistics Management.

Camp, R.C. (1989), *Benchmarking. The Search for Industry Best Practices that Lead to Superior Performance*, Milwaukee: ASQC Quality Press.

Camp, R.C. (1995), *Business Process Benchmarking. Finding and Implementing Best Practices*, Milwaukee: ASQC Quality Press.

Choi, T.Y. and Hartley, J.L. (1996), 'An exploration of supplier selection practices across the supply chain', *Journal of Operations Management*, 14, pp. 333–343.

Christopher, M. (1992), *Logistics and Supply Chain Management*, London: Pitman.

Copacino, W.C. (1997), *Supply Chain Management. The Basics and Beyond*, Boca Raton: St. Lucie Press.

Davies, A.J. and Kochhar, A.K. (1999), 'Why British companies don't do effective benchmarking', *Integrated Manufacturing Systems*, 10(1).

Douglas, J.M. (1993), *Benchmarking of UK Engine Manufacturing Plants' Performance*, Cranfield University, thesis.

Dudzik, T.M. (1998), 'Sytuacja sluzby zaopatrzenia materialowego w przedsiebiorstwach krajowych', Gospodarka Materialowa i Logistyka, 10, p. 207 (in Polish).

Ellram, L.M. (1990), 'The supplier selection decision in strategic partnership, *Journal of Purchasing and Materials Management*, Fall, pp. 8–14.

Ellram, L.M. (1995), 'A managerial guideline for the development and implementation of purchasing partnerships', *International Journal of Purchasing and Materials Management*, Summer, pp. 10–16.

Foster, T.A. (1992), 'Searching of the Best', *Distribution*, 91(3), pp. 31–36.

Gianesin, N. and Agostinacchio, A. (1999), 'Logistic performance assessment', in Mufato, M. and Pawar, K.S. (Eds), *Logistics in the Information Age*, SG Editoriali, Padova, pp. 678–679.

Made to Measure (1997), *Supply Management*, 3 July, p. 18.

Mark of Distinction (1997), *Supply Management*, 3 July, p. 22.

Medori, D. (1999), 'Performance measures in supply chain management', in Mufato, M. and Pawar, K.S. (Eds), *Logistics in the Information Age*, SG Editoriali, Padova, pp. 644–645.

Monczka, R.M. (1997a), 'The marks of success', *Supply Management*, 27 February, p. 49.

Monczka, R.M. (1997b), 'Marking out strategies', *Supply Management*, 10 April, p. 41.

Of Interest to Members (1997), *Logistics Focus*, June, p. 36.

Rolstadas, A. (Ed.) (1995), *Performance Measurement. A Business Process Benchmarking Approach*, London: Chapman & Hall.

Roodhooft, F. and Konings, J. (1995), 'Vendor selection and evaluation: an activity based costing approach', *European Journal of Operational Research*, 96, pp. 97–102.

Schary, Ph.B. and Larsen, T.S. (1995), *Managing the Global Supply Chain*, Copenhagen: Handelshojskolens Forlag.

Stank, T.P., Rogers, D.S. and Daugherty, P.J. (1994), 'Benchmarking: applications by third party warehousing firms', *Logistics and Transportation Review*, 30(1), pp. 55–72.

Vokurka, R., Choobineh, J. and Vada, L. (1996), 'A prototype expert system for the evaluation and selection of potential suppliers', *International Journal of Operations and Production Management*, 12, pp. 106–127.

Walker, W.T. (1998), 'The supply chain-centric enterprise', *Supply Chain Management Review*, Summer, pp. 36–44.

Watson, G.H. (1993), *Strategic Benchmarking. How to Rate Your Company's Performance Against the World's Best*, New York: John Wiley & Sons.

Weber, C., Current, J. and Benton, W. (1991), 'Vendor selection criteria and methods', *Eu-*

ropean Journal of Operational Research, 50, pp. 2–18.

Weber, C. and Ellram L.M. (1993), 'Supplier selection using multi-objective programming: a decision support system approach', *Inter-*

national Journal of Physical Distribution and Logistics Management, 2, pp. 3–13.

van Weele, A.J. (1994), *Purchasing Management. Analysis, Planning and Practice*, London: Chapman & Hall, pp. 202–203.

CHAPTER TWENTY-THREE

Textbook methods for auditing purchasing and supply management: do they work in practice?

Hannu Vanharanta

Purchasing and supply management is increasingly becoming a strategic weapon in industrial rivalry. Ensuring the overall efficiency and effectiveness of purchasing and supply operations is thus also becoming increasingly important. Purchasing and supply managers are nowadays often required to answer the following key questions: What is the current overall performance of our purchasing and supply operations? What are the parameters behind this overall performance, and how can we improve them?

Current textbooks on purchasing and supply management advocate the use of purchasing and supply auditing to answer these questions. However, most of the auditing methods recommended in the textbooks are highly theoretical in their approach, and have neither been verified nor validated in practice. This chapter uses two case studies to test some of these textbook methods. The aim is to answer the question: Do they work in practice?

The subjects of the case study audits are two manufacturing corporations. The methodology chosen for the audits was adapted and improved to meet the practical needs of each corporation. It was found that the textbook methods as such did not meet these practical needs, and it was necessary to develop a combination of several different methods. The auditing process itself delimited specific concepts and constructs, both internal and external to the corporations, that could then be used to improve purchasing

efficiency and purchasing effectiveness in each corporation.

Experiences gained from the case studies show clearly that there is a gap between the theory and the practice of purchasing and supply management auditing. Narrowing this gap will be a worthwhile objective for future research.

METHODOLOGY

The next section of this chapter presents a short literature review, and then describes the methodology chosen. The following section presents the research results, and the final section discusses the possibilities for future research.

EXISTING TEXTBOOK METHODS

The idea behind this research was to retrieve from current literature the principles and methods currently available for purchasing and supply management auditing. Since purchasing and supply research is a relatively new field of research, the main methods and ideas on the subject were readily available. This chapter begins with a review of some key elements of the literature, and goes on to describe the mix of methods chosen.

The Total Recognition of Environmental and Numerical Development (TREND) method (1966) was created with the aim of developing a holistic view of purchasing and supply operations and management, and '... to sort out the measurement confusion' which existed at that time (Pooler 1992). TREND is a three-step method for purchasing performance measurement. It was developed from an earlier concept, Indicators of Purchasing Performance (IPPs).

The first measurement step in TREND is conceptual. It covers buyer performance review, departmental objectives and individual reviews in an attempt to find out 'how well the purchasing manager [has] achieved an understanding of efficient buying with his buyers, and how well he [has] studied what makes his buyers want to buy well'. These concepts are evaluated by measuring achieved objectives. The second measurement step is behavioural. It attempts to answer the question: How have the achieved objectives been accomplished? It tries to find out what buyers do and what buyers say that they are doing. These behaviours are measured using sub-methods such as value analysis, cost analysis, learning curves and so on. The third measurement in TREND attempts to discover the outcome, that is, what has actually happened. The third step gives hard data results: statistical data, budgets, savings, standard costs, price index, purchasing profits and so on. TREND can be used to obtain an holistic view of overall performance, but it is difficult to use in a normal auditing process in which the outcome, the specific recommendations, are important.

In *Strategic Proactive Procurement*, Burt and Pinkerton (1996) state that companies often search for proactive approaches in their procurement planning, but that, although the planning process has its specific 'macro' and 'micro' plans, the process itself always has four separate phases:

1. The current situation analysis.
2. The objective development.
3. The creative action steps (new plans).
4. The implementation-monitoring-revision phase.

According to the authors, the first phase, the current situation analysis, can be likened to an audit, a purchasing system review or a diagnostic phase. To conduct this situation analysis, Burt and Pinkerton cover a long list of activities and company characteristics through which it is possible to understand where the company is and

whether or not it is successfully reaching its targets and objectives. They also give tools and action steps for creating a new procurement plan. At the end of their book they also give a sample audit-situational questionnaire, using which it is possible to measure quantitatively the standards met by a purchasing and supply department. This method contains questions concerning profit contribution, relations with other departments, supplier relations and general questions on purchasing and supply activities.

In *Purchasing Management*, van Weele (1994) devotes the whole of Chapter 12 to purchasing performance measurement and evaluation. He describes the factors that influence the way performance measurement is executed and evaluated; the key areas that should be considered when measuring and evaluating purchasing performance; the methods, techniques and performance measures that can be used; and how to conduct a purchasing audit as a tool for improving purchasing performance. According to van Weele, purchasing performance is considered to be the result of two factors: purchasing effectiveness and purchasing efficiency. Through the purchasing audit, he states, management may assess the extent to which the goals and objectives of the purchasing department are balanced with its resources; that is, the auditing should look at both the effectiveness dimension and the efficiency dimension. In spite of this general view of purchasing performance breakdown, action-specific auditing should also pay attention to the internal interfaces between the stakeholders (demand side) and the purchasing department (supply side) as well as to the external interfaces between the supply markets and the internal customer satisfaction. How a company is behaving in these respects can be measured through quantitative and qualitative yardsticks. Van Weele gives some of these qualitative and quantitative variables for performing purchasing audits via the use of examples of key data and qualitative concepts.

Leenders and Fearon (1997) state that periodic appraisal of the performance of the purchasing function is very important. According to these authors the appraisal itself – the auditing – leads to savings, which have an immediate profit impact. They state also that the supply function provides many opportunities for adding value to the firm's products and services through its internal interactions and external involvement. This is actually the same notion as that brought forward by van Weele. Leenders and Fearon, however, describe the concept from another important viewpoint: added value. This added value perspective changes the focus from cost savings and efficiency to the creation of value, that is, towards a proactive purchasing and supply approach.

This approach, in turn, implies that the concept of effectiveness also includes other important variables and indicators to which attention should be paid and which should be measured. The discussion at this point touches on several questions and concepts that are also relevant to other parts and functions of the company: How do different company activities add value? What are the various objectives to be achieved? How should those objectives be prioritized? Many of the company objectives may contradict each other, and thus render the measurement of performance more difficult. Measurements are, however, needed and Leenders and Fearon list the top 20 purchasing measurements (variables), their main groups (higher concepts) and their mutual ranking importance to be used in the overall performance evaluation.

Fearon et al.'s *The Purchasing Handbook* (1992) uses a framework to divide purchasing measurement and evaluation into three different groups according to scope, complexity and time interval. These three groups are: purchasing measurement and reporting against purchasing operating objectives (low scope and complexity/ happens weekly or monthly); purchasing policy and procedure audits (medium scope and complexity/happens quarterly or annually); purchasing functional reviews (high scope and complexity/multiyear basis). The functional review contains a situational analysis and tries to answer the following main questions: Where are we today? Where do we want to be tomorrow? Fearon et al. give a schematic layout of the functional review process, which contains situational analysis, performance standards, actual performance compared to performance standards and

recommendations. They also describe in detail how such a review process should be conducted.

CHOOSING A MIX OF METHODS

As we can see from above, the evolution from the TREND method to the modern perception of purchasing and supply performance is quite clear. TREND contained the basic ideas of a holistic approach, but did not describe in detail how to conduct an evaluation or situation analysis. The newest textbooks describe the content in detail and present many suggestions regarding what should be included and what may be important. They even describe the process for achieving the perception of current performance. The base, however, is the same for both past and current literature: to measure the present overall performance with efficiency and effectiveness in mind.

In the context of the present research it became evident that if the theoretical content of purchasing and supply performance were broken down and highly fragmented, the auditing work would become more difficult to conduct in practice. First, the test subjects may not understand all the vocabulary involved and, second, there might be too many constructs, some of which are not in use in the corporations being audited or in the research companies performing the audit. Therefore it was important to create a methodology which could be readily adapted by all parties on a practical level.

During the initial phase of the project an overall methodology was developed for this type of research. Then, on the basis of the literature reviewed above, and in the specific context of the present research task, a more precise methodology was devised. This methodology utilizes three separate methods: quantitative, qualitative and so-called other methods.

QUANTITATIVE METHODS

Quantitative methods can be used to position the company with the aid of specific parameters, and to see clearly how different characteristics have changed and developed. In the present research the content of the quantitative auditing was divided into four separate data categories: past performance data for the years

1995 and 1996; latest performance data concerning the year 1997; budgeted performance data concerning the year 1998; and planned future performance data covering the coming years 1999 and 2000. The data itself was grouped into two different data sets: general company performance data and specific purchasing and supply data. The construct of the data categories was gathered from textbooks and covered the main key figures in purchasing and supply management. The purpose of gathering this data was to answer the following questions: What are the parameters behind the overall performance? What are the measures or benchmarks for comparison? What 'gaps' exist that need to be closed? What future objectives should be achieved?

QUALITATIVE METHODS

In the present research, qualitative analysis was conducted using two separate methods: the questionnaire method and the open question method.

Questionnaire Method

The qualitative questionnaire method used in the present research is based on Burt and Pinkerton (1996). In this method qualitative auditing is performed as self-auditing by the purchasing and supply management group. The method itself is divided into four separate parts, each with its own questionnaire:

1. General (GEN) questionnaire
The objective of this questionnaire is to obtain a general view of purchasing and supply management. The questionnaire contains 16 questions to be answered by the purchasing and supply management executives or managers, who act as test subjects.

2. Relationships with other departments (REL) questionnaire
This questionnaire focuses on the internal relationships of the purchasing and supply department. There are 15 questions.

3. Supplier relations (SUP) questionnaire
This questionnaire attempts to discover how well the company has created relations with its suppliers. There are 22 questions.

4. Profit contribution (PRO) questionnaire
These questions try to find answers to the overall question: How has purchasing and supply management impacted on the profit generation of the company? There are 14 questions.

The scoring system proposed by Burt and Pinkerton (1996) was then used to value and weight the purchasing and supply management audit results, as follows:

Give an absolute 'YES'	5	for an excellent performance.
Give	1 2 3 4	as you think appropriate.
Give an absolute 'NO'	0	when you consider that your company has not at all managed this kind of statement.

The resulting total score then roughly indicated the level and position of the purchasing and supply management of the unit under research.

Generally this method tries to answer the question: What is the current overall performance of our purchasing and supply operations? The method does not give the exact performance level. It merely gives the test subjects' perceptions of how things are, that is, their subjective, collective opinion regarding the current state and overall performance of the unit.

Open Questions Method

In order to widen the background of the present research and to facilitate the current state analysis of the corporations, 13 general questions were also asked during the self-auditing work. The questions dealt with the following issues: organization, reporting relationships, computer systems, purchasing and supply strategy, global co-ordination activities, logistics, purchasing co-operation inside the corporation and traffic service co-operation.

OTHER METHODS

The other methods will now be discussed below.

Teaching and Lecturing Method

This research was totally new for the personnel of both corporations, and therefore it was launched by the managing directors of each corporation. The request to conduct the research was given by the managing directors to the plant managers and to the purchasing and supply managers. Managing directors were first taught the methodology in detail, and were given the opportunity to influence the content and methodology according to their individual wishes. To minimize problems in comprehension it was agreed that the purchasing and supply management test groups would undergo a one-day workshop in qualitative analysis before answering the questions and doing the 'homework', the qualitative and quantitative parts of the research.

Help-Desk Method

During the teaching sessions it became clear that some kind of opportunity should be provided for the test subjects to ask questions regarding the test material. Therefore it was arranged that the test subjects could call on the researchers for help at any time during the self-auditing process.

Commitment

It was clear that commitment was the most important success factor in the auditing work. By organizing the audit from 'top-down' it was possible to obtain a high level of commitment for the whole research project from the test subjects. Also, the self-auditing nature of some of the methods used served to increase future commitment to specific development projects.

TEST SUBJECTS

In this research study two purchasing and supply units were individually tested. Each of them had six test subjects. The response rate was 100 per cent.

RESEARCH RESULTS

The auditing work yielded empirical data and information. The results were computed and grouped according to the mix of methods described in the previous section. The following is a summary of the main research results.

METHODOLOGICAL RESULTS

The basic mix of methods developed for the initial phase of the present research provided a clear framework which was easy to follow. However, as the research progressed from theoretical to practical considerations, the developed mix of methods proved to be too narrow and too superficial. The management of each corporation required that the methodology should be widened to include a recommendation phase, and this recommendation phase be derived directly from the research results. Analysis of the qualitative questionnaire results revealed the existence of concepts that could be grouped into 17 separate constructs. These constructs could then be used as input for the required recommendation phase. The new constructs were:

Forecasting	Supply markets
Strategy making	Sources and sourcing
Education and training	Added value
Team-building	Cost reductions
Information technology	Contracting
Measurement	Communication
Internal efficiency	Co-operation
Internal effectiveness	Negotiation and
Internal networking	decision-making

All the questions and answers were then regrouped under these new constructs. It was then possible to rank the constructs to obtain an overall perception of which were the most important, and which were well served and maintained in the opinions of the members of the purchasing and supply group. With the help of the new constructs, it was also possible to make specific recommendations on how to improve overall performance. More detailed results are given in the following sections.

QUANTITATIVE AUDITING RESULTS

A formal spreadsheet-type questionnaire was used to ask the purchasing and supply professionals at each of the two corporations about past, present and future performance indicators. This type of information reporting appeared to be new to both corporations. The spreadsheets were only partially completed, and therefore the results could not be used for setting new objectives, targets or detailed benchmarks.

Quantitative analysis of purchasing performance revealed that the purchasing and supply data available in both of the corporations was not well defined, it was difficult to access, and much of the data was incomplete. It would appear that, on the whole, more time and effort should be invested in data mining and knowledge generation. Amongst other data categories, the following were found to need much development in both corporations:

- benchmarks
- projections
- forecasts
- specific key figures.

QUALITATIVE AUDITING RESULTS: SELF-AUDITING QUESTIONNAIRES

The scoring system used below follows that recommended by Burt and Pinkerton (1997).

Results for Corporation 1

Qualitative auditing results show clearly that Corporation 1 has not yet reached a high level of performance in purchasing and supply, such as would have been indicated by, for example, a score of 'Outstanding Performance (250-225)'. The total average performance level for Corporation 1 was 185 credit points, indicating 'Fair Performance (200-175)'. This score was closer to 'Low Performance (175-0)' than it was to 'Good Performance (225-200)'. The total number of zero answers was three, which may indicate a relatively high level of activity in purchasing and supply issues.

Regrouping according to the constructs presented in the methodological results, together with a simple ranking analysis extracted from the questionnaire, revealed that the most important issues to be developed at Corporation 1 are as follows:

	Importance Ratio (reciprocal of percentile)
1. Education and training	3.00
2. Cost reduction	2.50
3. Negotiation and decision-making	2.50

4. Forecasting	2.17
5. Information technology	2.13
6. Co-operation	2.00 (1:50%)

The specific questionnaire results for Corporation 1 are as follows:

Table 23.1 Qualitative results of Corporation 1

Corporation 1							
GEN 1	3	REL 1	4	SUP 1	1	PRO 1	3
GEN 2	3	REL 2	3	SUP 2	2	PRO 2	2
GEN 3	1	REL 3	4	SUP 3	2	PRO 3	3
GEN 4	3	REL 4	3	SUP 4	4	PRO 4	2
GEN 5	1	REL 5	4	SUP 5	5	PRO 5	0
GEN 6	2	REL 6	1	SUP 6	3	PRO 6	1
GEN 7	4	REL 7	4	SUP 7	3	PRO 7	1
GEN 8	3	REL 8	4	SUP 8	3	PRO 8	2
GEN 9	5	REL 9	3	SUP 9	2	PRO 9	3
GEN 10	3	REL 10	5	SUP 10	4	PRO 10	3
GEN 11	3	REL 11	2	SUP 11	2	PRO 11	5
GEN 12	4	REL 12	1	SUP 12	1	PRO 12	2
GEN 13	1	REL 13	3	SUP 13	1	PRO 13	0
GEN 14	1	REL 14	2	SUP 14	5	PRO 14	3
GEN 15	5	REL 15	4	SUP 15	1		
GEN 16	4			SUP 16	5		
				SUP 17	2		
				SUP 18	3		
				SUP 19	2		
				SUP 20	5		
				SUP 21	4		
				SUP 22	4		

Number of Qs total	67
Total score	185
Mean	2.76
Number of zero answers	3
Average performance	Fair

Results for Corporation 2

Qualitative auditing shows clearly that, as was the case in Corporation 1, Corporation 2 has not yet reached a high level in purchasing and supply performance. The total average performance level for Corporation 2 was 202 credit points, indicating 'Good Performance (225-200)'. This score is very close to 'Fair Performance (200-175)'. The number of zero answers (11) is, however, high which indicates low activity in those purchasing and supply issues.

Regrouping as in the previous case, together with a simple ranking analysis extracted from the questionnaire, revealed that the most important issues to be developed at Corporation 2 are as follows:

		Importance Ratio (reciprocal of percentile)
1.	Supply markets	7.69
2.	Information technology	3.03
3.	Cost reduction	2.50
4.	Forecasting	2.50
5.	Internal networking	2.00 (1:50%)

The specific questionnaire results for Corporation 2 are as follows:

Table 23.2 Qualitative results of Corporation 2

Corporation 2

GEN 1	3	REL 1	5	SUP 1	1	PRO 1	3
GEN 2	3	REL 2	3	SUP 2	4	PRO 2	0
GEN 3	0	REL 3	3	SUP 3	2	PRO 3	0
GEN 4	5	REL 4	3	SUP 4	5	PRO 4	2
GEN 5	3	REL 5	5	SUP 5	5	PRO 5	0
GEN 6	5	REL 6	0	SUP 6	3	PRO 6	5
GEN 7	5	REL 7	5	SUP 7	2	PRO 7	3
GEN 8	1	REL 8	0	SUP 8	3	PRO 8	5
GEN 9	4	REL 9	3	SUP 9	4	PRO 9	3
GEN 10	2	REL 10	3	SUP 10	0	PRO 10	3
GEN 11	3	REL 11	5	SUP 11	4	PRO 11	3
GEN 12	5	REL 12	0	SUP 12	3	PRO 12	4
GEN 13	4	REL 13	5	SUP 13	3	PRO 13	0
GEN 14	3	REL 14	2	SUP 14	4	PRO 14	5
GEN 15	4	REL 15	3	SUP 15	3		
GEN 16	4			SUP 16	1		
				SUP 17	0		
				SUP 18	0		
				SUP 19	5		
				SUP 20	5		
				SUP 21	5		
				SUP 22	5		

Number of Qs total	67
Total score	202
Mean	3.01
Number of zero answers	11
Average performance	Good

OTHER RESULTS

Although all of the purchasing and supply department professionals seemed to be well motivated to answer both the qualitative and the quantitative questionnaires, it was found that more internal discussions will be needed. The open questionnaire section on 'Other Information' revealed that either the groups did not have enough time to answer the questions, or that the questions were too general in nature. The opportunity to use the help-desk was not taken up by any of the test subjects although, afterwards, they said that the questions were not clear.

CONCLUSION

The auditing work itself has shown very clearly how an audit can help in evaluating purchasing and supply performance in separate manufacturing units. The methodology used for the audit was developed in co-operation with each of the manufacturing corporations involved and was applied in accordance with the specific wishes of each managing director. The methodology, however, was not changed and so the methods used were the same for each organization. Auditing work consisted of two parallel methods, quantitative analysis and qualitative analysis, for each of which questionnaires were prepared to be answered by key personnel. This new extended methodology proved to be effective. The auditing process itself has defined certain concepts and constructs, both internal and external, that can be used to improve purchasing efficiency and purchasing effectiveness. Many concepts arose from the lectures and open discussions organized in connection with the audits. It is recommended that the analysis work be continued by regrouping some of the defined constructs into still larger units. This would be a useful method for defining projects for implementation.

FUTURE RESEARCH

The research has shown that the textbook auditing methods examined provide a good basis for purchasing and supply auditing work. However, all of the textbook methods proved to have relatively theoretical frameworks, which would have to be applied selectively to improve their practicability. The research has also shown that purchasing practitioners are not generally familiar with the indicators, variables, concepts and constructs often applied in the textbook methods. It will therefore be an important future task to develop a new, wide-ranging methodology for auditing purchasing and supply operations, which will be coherent to the average practitioner and will meet the needs of the modern business world.

This analysis of purchasing and supply auditing has revealed new research areas for the future. It is evident that companies generally do not plan their auditing very carefully: they do not commit sufficient resources to the development and implementation phases of their auditing, and they do not follow up performance improvement intensively.

Future research should concentrate on the development of the auditing process; that is, the development of better methodology and a more careful analysis of the implementation phase. Another important objective is to gather more empirical data using the above methods and to motivate companies to perform more self-auditing.

REFERENCES

Burt, D. and Pinkerton, R. (1996), *A Purchasing Manager's Guide to Strategic Proactive Procurement*, New York: AMACOM.

Fearon, H., Dobler, D. and Killen, K. (1992), *The Purchasing Handbook*, New York: McGraw-Hill.

Leenders, M. and Fearon, H. (1997), *Purchasing and Supply Management*, Chicago: Irwin.

Pooler, V. (1992), *Global Purchasing Reaching for the World*, New York: Chapman & Hall.

van Weele, A.J. (1994), *Purchasing Management Analysis Planning and Practice*, London: Chapman & Hall.

CHAPTER TWENTY-FOUR

Process management and performance measurement in the supply chain: a food distribution case

Donna Samuel and Peter Hines

This chapter describes work currently underway at Capper and Co., a distributor of convenience food to retail outlets. This work is one of the products of a three-year joint project between Capper and the Lean Enterprise Research Centre (LERC) which began in May 1997. The overall aim of the project is to find and implement ways of improving Capper's supply chain operations, integration and effectiveness. The initial stages of work with Capper led to the development of a comprehensive, time-phased, staged improvement plan, details of which have been reported elsewhere (Samuel and Hines 1998). Within this plan, performance measurement was targeted as a key area for immediate investigation and action in order to drive improvement. This chapter reports the progress of this performance measurement work, one element of Capper's overall improvement plan, which has been carried out so far.

PROJECT BACKGROUND

Capper and Co. distribute convenience food under the Spar franchise in South Wales, along the M4 corridor to Southern England. Their headquarters and main depot are in Talbot Green, South Wales, and they have a satellite depot in Hastings, Southern England. Capper own some of its 500 retail outlets but the vast majority are independently owned. These retail outlets, then, form Capper's customer base. The fact that they do not own their retail outlets is a significant factor differentiating Capper from other food retailers such as the major supermarket chains. In recent years, Capper has identified a need to become more 'retail focused' and participation in a three-year supply chain improvement project with LERC may be seen as a key part of that overall strategy.

In 1996, the chairman of the company became convinced that adopting a supply chain, process management approach would greatly enhance his company's efforts to be more 'retail focused'. The supply chain or, more accurately, the value chain represents all the things that take place within the firm to create value to the customer (Christopher 1997). Processes are the fundamental way by which value is created. Examples of processes include: order fulfilment, new product development, customer management and supplier management. 'To achieve real integration in the supply chain requires ideally that these processes also be integrated – upstream with suppliers and downstream with customers' (Christopher 1997). Convinced of the logic underlying supply chain and process management, the chairman of Capper and Co. contacted LERC.

Following a series of discussions and as a result of mapping Capper's value streams (Hines and Rich 1997), Capper embarked on a three year project with LERC. Mapping refers to the suite of tools used to establish an organization's current state in terms of quality, productivity and time compression issues. The nature of the relationship between LERC and Capper might best be described as 'process consultation' (McKenna 1994; Schein 1969 and 1987), in that it is 'concerned with improving organizational effectiveness through involving people'.

Fairly conventional in their practices, the adoption of a supply chain approach would involve a considerable cultural change for Capper. Key to the success of the new vision would be the performance measures that underpin and guide the company's behaviour. The performance measurement project became known as 'KPIs' (Key Performance Indicators)'. This chapter describes the output of the KPI project so far.

PROCESS MANAGEMENT AND PERFORMANCE MEASUREMENT

The 1980s saw business practitioners bombarded with management jargon often encapsulated in three letter acronyms (TLAs) designed to capture new ideas, practices, approaches and concepts such as Total Quality Management (TQM), Just in Time (JIT) and Supply Chain Management (SCM) (Cox 1996). All are striving to achieve the same end via slightly different means. The common theme that binds them together is that they attempt an holistic solution to the organizational problem of managing uncertainty. They were all, in fact, attempts to re-

construct the management solution in response to the previous prevailing logic that had advocated a process of problem deconstruction. At some time during the early 1990s, the word *process* became part of mainstream management language. Now general agreement is beginning to emerge that it is, in fact, well-defined and well-controlled processes that drive superior organizational performance (Kurogane 1993). Many companies are beginning to adopt a competitive strategy of aligning organizational competencies around a few vital processes.

Christopher (1997) identifies five characteristics of business processes: they have customers for whom they create value, they typically have cross-functional boundaries, they draw on functional resources, they are team-based and they have strategic goals. He defines a process as 'any activity or group of activities that takes an input, adds value to it and provides an output to an internal or external customer'.

Dimancescu et al. (1997) (see also Hines and Rich 1998) also acknowledge the importance of processes in world-class companies. They identify the four key elements of an organizational system as being strategy (a response to external information on competitors), processes (patterns of interconnected value-adding relationships designed to meet business goals and objectives), roles and responsibilities (which are determined

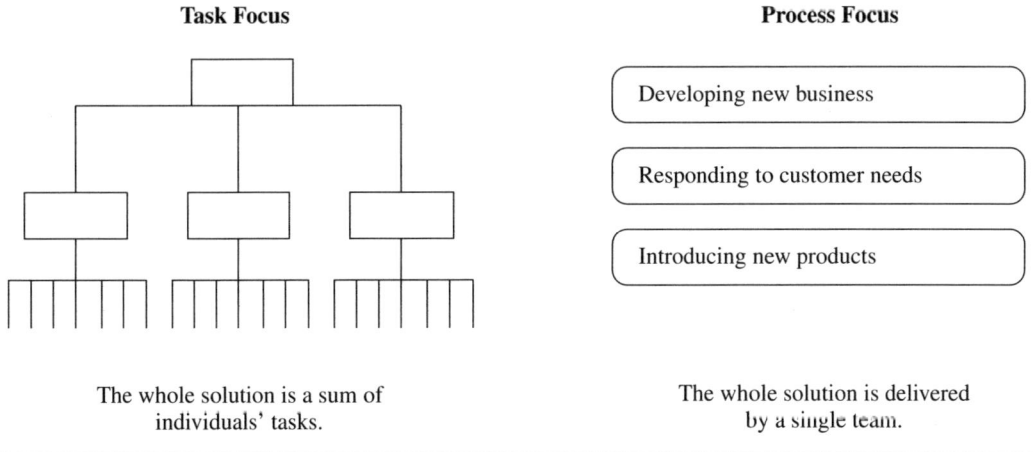

Task Focus

Process Focus

Developing new business

Responding to customer needs

Introducing new products

The whole solution is a sum of individuals' tasks.

The whole solution is delivered by a single team.

Figure 24.1   Task-focused versus process-focused strategies
Source: Reproduced from *The Lean Enterprise* (p.7). Copyright © 1997 Dan Dimancescu, Peter Hines and Nick Rich. Published by AMACOM, a division of American Management Association International, New York, NY. Used with the permission of the publisher. All rights reserved. <http://www.amacombooks.org>.

in such a way as to carry out key processes) and structure (which reflects the intended strategy and process orientation of an organization). Figure 24.1 illustrates the difference between traditional task-based management and contemporary process-based management.

Figure 24.2 shows how the two approaches relate differently to the key elements of an organizational system. This represents a significant departure from the traditional view suggested by the long-standing strategy/structure debate (Chandler 1962). Here, organizational structure is considered only after strategy, business processes and related roles and responsibilities have been clearly determined.

The full extent and implication of process management thinking is, as yet, not fully understood and will doubtless continue to occupy the minds of both practitioners and academics into the new millennium. The same can also be said of performance measurement. As Rich and Francis (1998) point out: 'the setting of performance measures ... is a contentious issue which has become increasingly problematic as the rate of market change accelerates'.

The importance of performance measurement cannot be overstated. Authors from a range of disciplines have recognized the causal relationship between performance measurement and human behaviour:

Senior executives understand that their organization's measurement system strongly affects the behaviour of managers and employees (Kaplan and Norton 1992).

There is a saying that 'what gets measured, gets managed', implying that it is through the choice of performance measurement that behaviour is determined (Christopher 1997).

Tell me how you will measure me and I'll tell you how I'll behave (Goldratt 1991).

... performance measures, which inform the manner in which employees interact and behave ... (Rich and Francis 1998).

It is commonly recognized that measurement influences behaviour in a certain direction ... (Lamming et al. 1996).

In spite of the recognition of its importance, performance measurement is still an undeveloped art. Holloway et al. (1991) identify the general pitfalls associated with the development of measures as being: lack of participation of individuals in the firm, an informal approach, poor communication and, most notably, a lack of

THE OLD
Task-based command and control system: strategy *to* structure *to* process tasks *to* roles

THE NEW
Process-based lean system: strategy *to* process *to* roles *to* structure

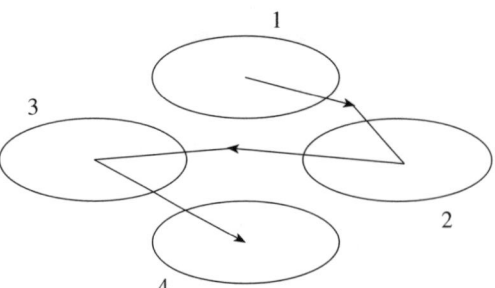
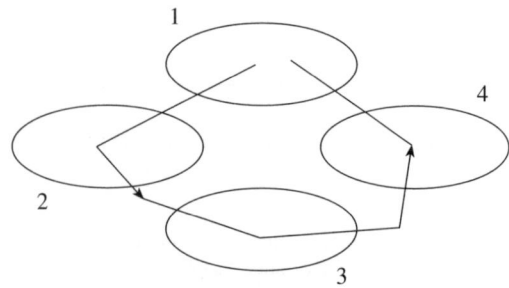

Figure 24.2   Task-based versus process-based management

alignment between the measures placed on the individual and the organization.

Kaplan (1990) is also critical of traditional methods of performance evaluation and summarizes the problems associated with them as follows:

1. The measures provide irrelevant or misleading information, or worse, provoke behaviour that undermines the achievement of strategic objectives.
2. Measures that track each dimension of performance in isolation distort management's understanding of how effectively the organization as a whole is implementing the company's strategy.
3. Traditional performance measures do not take into account the requirements and perspective of customers, both internal and external.
4. Bottom-line financial measures come too late (monthly) for mid-course corrections or remedial actions.

Within a supply chain management context, Lambert and Sock (1993) identify the following five common reasons for inventory build-up in a manufacturing environment: purchasing management being rewarded for low unit costs; production management being compensated for achieving low unit costs; salespeople wanting a market presence by positioning large inventories close to the customer; transport management having incentives towards large shipments; and, finally, both consumers and intermediaries attempting to push inventories back onto the manufacturer. It is noteworthy that three of these reasons are directly related to inappropriate performance measurement.

What is measured not only provides data that can inform judgements about standards of performance achieved but also provides signals about what is important (Saunders 1994). A number of authors offer a checklist for designing a performance measurement system (Ghobadian and Ashworth 1994; Lynch and Cross 1991; Lamming et al. 1996). In summary measurement systems should:

1. be linked to corporate objectives, and make 'fuzzy' strategic goals concrete;

2. combine different measures to meet the requirements of different organizational levels;
3. capture the essence of both efficiency and effectiveness;
4. allow the identification of trade-offs between different dimensions of performance;
5. include a balanced mixture of both quantitative and qualitative measures, with common definitions of each;
6. be recognized as an ongoing, evolving process;
7. be incapable of manipulation;
8. recognize that the measures should not become ends in themselves;
9. enable management to plan as well as to control;
10. not be entirely concerned with measuring in a 'negative' way, to facilitate correction;
11. instil the confidence in managers to empower fully the teams;
12. allow measures to be collected systematically and analysed over time;
13. permit the identification of critical situations, and cause a corresponding change in behaviour;
14. differentiate between incremental/control measures, and radical objectives;
15. track performance against customer expectations;
16. encourage cross-functionalism; and
17. limit the amount of measures used, to a few key variables, in order to maximize simplicity.

This list will be revisited in the conclusion to this chapter to determine how this project addressed each design element.

A watershed in performance measurement thinking arrived with the 'balanced scorecard':

> The balanced scorecard includes financial measures that tell the results of actions already taken. And it complements the financial measures with operational measures on customer satisfaction, internal processes, and the organization's innovation and improvement activities – operational measures that are the drivers of future

financial performance (Kaplan and Norton 1992).

Offering a fundamental change in the underlying assumptions about performance measures, the scorecard approach has two main benefits: first, it brings together, in a single management report, many of the seemingly disparate elements of a company's competitive agenda; second, it guards against sub-optimization (where an improvement in one area is at the expense of another).

The case presented in this chapter attempts to combine a balanced scorecard approach with Japanese matrix management derived from *hoshin kanri*, otherwise known as policy deployment. To give it its literal meaning, *hoshin* means compass or pointing the direction and *kanri* means control or management. The combination of these two activities is the establishment of key competitive policies, the target, means and support systems to achieve these goals (Hines and Rich 1998). In essence, policy deployment is about integrating an entire organization's daily activities with its long-term goal (Akao 1991). The benefits of Japanese matrix techniques are many, and are well documented elsewhere (Samuel and Hines 1998; Hines et al. 1998; Rich 1995a, 1995b; Hines and Rich 1998), but undoubtedly the main advantage is alignment between strategy and operational activity.

The case presented applies Japanese matrix logic, derived from policy deployment, to develop a balanced scorecard of measures which are then translated into a set of key process metrics. These process metrics can then, in turn, be translated into action team metrics designed to facilitate both the delivery and improvement of each key process.

THE CASE: THE CAPPER KPI PROJECT

The project aim was to design a measurement system that incorporated all the contemporary ideas that the company was seeking to embrace over the coming years, including process management, supply chain management and continuous improvement. The three-tier management system, shown in Figure 24.3, was used as a base model.

This model was highly appropriate for Capper since the company clearly has three primary organizational layers: the senior management team (board of directors); middle management; and the workforce itself. Within this model, strategy is translated into key processes which in turn translate into control and improvement actions. The strategic organizational level is primarily static since most measures, such as profitability or market share, have a long time lag between an action and a measured result. The process organizational level is motivational in that it provides a clear line of sight on the scale of improvement needed. Finally the operational level of the organization provides real time dynamic information on an ongoing basis.

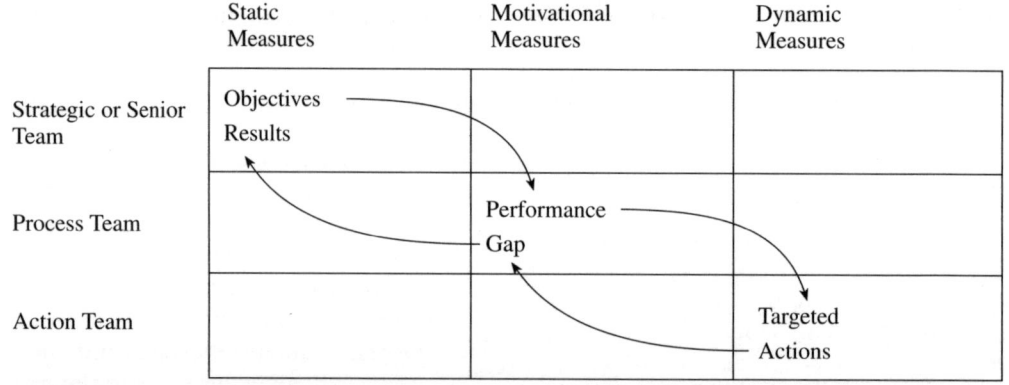

Figure 24.3 The three-tier management system

Crucially, the lower level measures (process or action) are clearly derived and provide information to the level above so that the system can continually readjust.

STAGE 1: STRATEGIC KPIs

The first action was to define Capper's key processes. After a multi-stage iterative process over a number of months, the following four were chosen:

1. Creating Spar's customer proposition (that is, having the right product).
2. Operating Spar stores (that is, serving the customer).
3. Spar stores order fulfilment (that is, getting it there).
4. Store expansion and development (that is, improving current and acquiring new stores).

The next stage (see Table 24.1), which again required a multi-stage iterative process with the board members, was to draw up a scorecard of strategic measures which, when combined, would give a balanced picture of how the organization was faring.

These key measures are divided into three segments. The first two (entitled retail stream: company stores and retail stream: independents respectively) relate to the two separate value streams (Womack and Jones 1996) identified by the company, one serving their own stores and the other serving independently owned stores. The third segment (entitled retail distribution centres) relates primarily to the company's two warehouses and their supply chain and customer service competencies. These issues had not previously been regarded as strategic, whilst now they occupied around one-quarter of the total suite of measures. Items 15, 17 and 18, for example, combine in item 19 to produce a perfect order measure (Christopher 1997). Item 5, on time delivery, was to be reported in forms A and B. A represents the half day delivery window currently measured; whilst B represents the half hour window which the company intends to measure against once certain change initiatives have been carried out.

Another radical change is represented by items 8 and 23 which are concerned with employment satisfaction issues. At present the company does not measure employee satisfaction in a systematic manner. Its inclusion within the suite of strategic measures heralds the renewed importance the company places on its staff. Whilst this measure is likely to remain relatively static on a regular basis, any trend changes will provide the senior management team with an early warning system. This is a marked improvement over the 'grapevine' and anecdotal methods previously relied upon.

Amongst the more familiar financial measures contained within the suite, the main change was the teasing out of company growth as a result of acquisition as compared to growth as a result of effective management (see items 1, 2 and 9). To a considerable degree, the traditional financial measures (1–7, 9–14, 20–22) were viewed as measuring the success of *past* strategies and their implementation, measures 15–19 represented customers' *present* perceptions of performance (and an indicator of future medium-term financial performance), with the human measures (8 and 23) reflecting a good indicator of *long-term health.*

Once the strategic KPIs had been agreed, they could be analysed against the four key business processes that had been identified. This is shown in Table 24.1.

Each of the four processes was considered in terms of the importance of its relationship to the 23 strategic measures. A simple scoring system was used:

Strong relationship	9 points
Relationship	3 points
No relationship	0 points

The matrix in Table 24.1 shows *how* each of the key processes delivers value to the strategic goals of the company.

The second matrix, shown in Table 24.2, considers the current structure of the company in terms of the key business processes. The functional divisions that currently exist are listed on the left hand side of the matrix and the four processes along the top. Each of the current departments was considered in terms of its role within each process. Again a simple scoring system was applied:

Table 24.1   Strategic KPIs and key processes

MEASURE	Creating Spar's Consumer Proposition	Operating Spar Stores	Spar Stores Order Fulfilment	Store Expansion and Development
RETAIL STREAM – COMPANY STORES				
1. Net retail sales (£M excluding VAT)(excl. commission based sales)	9	9	0	9
2. Retail % growth yr/yr like for like	9	9	3	3
3. Gross profit % (inc. W/S profit generated by own stores & other income)	9	3	0	3
4. Wages % (wages as % of net sales)(incl. RDC wages attibuted to own stores)	0	9	9	0
5. Other costs % (costs as % of net sales) (including RDC costs attributed to own stores)	0	9	9	0
6. Net profit % (including RDC profit generated by own stores)	9	9	9	3
7. Stock at stores (weeks)	3	9	0	0
8. Employee satisfaction survey	0	9	0	0
RETAIL STREAM – INDEPENDENTS				
9. RDC sales to independents (£M)(excl. VAT) (excl. drop shipment)	9	9	0	9
10. Gross profit % of RDC sales to independents including other income	9	0	0	0
11. RDC wages % (wages as % of RDC sales to independents)	0	0	9	0
12. RDC other costs %	0	0	9	0
13. Net profit % of RDC sales to independents	9	0	9	0
14. Debtors days (independents)(weeks)	0	0	3	0
RDCs – TALBOT GREEN AND HASTINGS				
15. On time delivery (A) % right ½ day	0	3	9	0
(B) % +/– ½ hour	0	3	9	0
16. % line fill vs. original order (excl. all subs)	3	0	9	0
17. % total orders with 100% fill as ordered	0	0	9	0
18. % customer order without complaint	3	0	9	0
19. Total delivery service (15A×17×18)	–	–	–	–
20. Retail G.P.% (recommended) for total guild (all stores)	9	0	0	0
21. Stock at RDCs (weeks)	3	0	9	0
22. Creditor days	0	0	3	0
23. Employee satisfaction survey	9	0	9	9

Key player	9 points
Major support	3 points
Minor support	1 point
No support	0 points

This matrix proved very revealing for Capper, suggesting to them that their current structure was not as conducive to the management of processes as it should be. In general terms, we

Table 24.2 Current structure and key processes

MEASURE	Creating Spar's Consumer Proposition	Operating Spar Stores	Spar Stores Order Fulfilment	Store Expansion and Development
Store acquisition and development	1	0	0	9
Accounts	3	3	3	9
I.T.	1	3	3	1
H.R.	1	3	3	1
Own stores	1	9	3	3
Sales (to independents)	1	3	1	9
Operations	0	3	9	0
Trading	9	1	3	0
Spar Central	3	0	1	1

would expect to have at least one 9 determined for each business process. If there were not, this would suggest that no one in the current departmental structure assumes clear ownership of that process. However, too many 9s within any given process suggests that ownership of the process is split, which may lead to 'passing the buck' behaviour. Too many 3s within a given process might suggest that too many people are involved, slowing decision-making and perhaps reducing responsiveness. The matrix is very useful in sparking debates about the current roles of various departments and what they should be.

STAGE 2: THE PROCESS KPIs

From the strategic KPIs a set of measures was developed for each of the key processes, capturing the key information for the people responsible for delivering and improving them. This is shown in Table 24.3.

Each measure directly relates to at least one of the 23 strategic measures (given on the right). Within each process there are a few key measures (the real process drivers and their raison d'être) together with some others which management at this level will need to be informed of for control purposes and a balanced view. These process measures either have been taken directly from, or are derived from, the strategic KPIs. Where appropriate, the measures have been reworked to offer greater detail for the staff at this level of the organization. However, the linkage to company strategy is clear so that

everyone understands *why* the measure exists and *where* it comes from.

STAGE 3: THE ACTION LEVEL

The next stage is to develop a set of action level measures in the same way, clearly derived from the process measures which, in turn, are clearly derived from the strategic measures. This stage has not yet been carried out. The measurement system represents such a radical departure for the company that it was decided to trial the first stage for six months before applying stage 2, and then wait for a period before applying stage 3. It was felt that the system would be more easily accepted by a process of consultation and consensus and by phasing it in, rather than to be lacking such acceptance and implementing it in one step.

CONCLUSIONS

This chapter presented a company-wide performance measurement system using Japanese policy deployment matrix logic to present a balanced scorecard. This system is being conducted as part of the work being carried out by the Lean Enterprise Research Centre and Capper, a convenience food distributor. The company is currently grappling with the best way in which to implement and cascade the proposed measurement system. However, it is too early to pass meaningful comment on the success of their efforts. Whilst the work is

Table 24.3 The process KPIs

Creating Spar's Consumer Proposition		Strat. KPI	Operating Spar Stores		Strat. KPI
1.	Net retail sales (£m excl. VAT)	1	1.	Net retail sales (£m excl. VAT)	1
2.	Retail growth yr/yr like for like	2	2.	Retail % growth yr/yr like for like	2
3a.	Gross profit % for promotions	3	3.	Gross profit %	3
3b.	Gross profit % for products introduced in first 12m of sales	3	4.	Wages at Capper stores	4
3c.	Gross profit % for other	3	5.	Other costs at Capper stores	5
4.	Net profit %	6	6.	Net profit %	6
5a.	Cost of delisted stock	7	7.	Stock at stores	7
5b.	Cost of non-delisted stock	7	8.	Employee satisfaction for Capper stores staff	8
6.	RDC sales to independents (£m excl. VAT)	9	9.	RDC sales to independents	9
7a.	Gross profit for promotions	10	10.	On time order placement	10
7b.	Gross profit for products introduced in first 12m of sales	10			
8.	Net profit of RDC sales to independents	13			
9.	% on time order placement	16			
10.	% customer orders without complaint due to NPI product retirement	18			
11.	Retail gross profit % for total guild	20			
12.	Stock at RDC relating to NPI at promotions	21			
13.	Employee satisfaction for employees involved in creating Spar's consumer proposition	23			

Spar Stores Order Fulfilment		Strat. KPI	Store Expansion and Development		Strat. KPI
1.	Retail % growth yr/yr like for like	2	1a.	% total sales from Capper stores less than 12m old	1/2
2.	Wages at RDC (for Capper stores only)	4	1b.	% increase in sales from Capper stores refurbished in last 12m	1/2
3.	Other costs at RDC (for Capper stores only)	5	2a.	Gross profit for new Capper stores	3
4.	Net profit %	6	2b.	Gross profit for refurbished Capper stores	3
5.	RDC wages %	11	3a.	Net profit for new Capper stores	6
6.	RDC other costs %	12	3b.	Net profit for refurbished Capper stores	6
7.	Net profit % of RDC sales to independents	13	4a.	% total sales from new independents	9
8.	Debtor days	14	4b.	% uplift in sales from refurbished independents	9
9.	On time delivery a) % right to half day	15a	5.	Employee satisfaction for RDC staff involved in store expansion and development	23
	b) % right to half hour	15b			
10.	% line fill vs. original order	16			
11.	% total orders with 100% fill as ordered	17			
12.	% customer order without complaint	18			
13.	Stock	21			
14.	Creditor days	22			
15.	Employee satisfaction for RDC staff involved in order fulfilment	23			

incomplete, it is the belief of the authors that the system proposed has a number of benefits and improvements over traditional methods of performance evaluation. First, the system addresses many, if not all of the pitfalls, problems and shortcomings that have been identified by a number of authors in the past. In addition, the system proposed addresses all 17 of the design suggestions given earlier. This is shown in Table 24.4.

The main benefits of the proposed company-wide measurement system can be summarized as follows:

SUPPLY CHAIN MANAGEMENT AND CUSTOMER SERVICE ARE GIVEN DUE STRATEGIC ATTENTION

Logistics and supply chain management capability has been identified as a key source of customer satisfaction. Customer satisfaction,

Table 24.4 Design checklist

Design Checklist	Addressed by Project	How Addressed
1. Linked to corporate objectives	Yes	Strategy integral to system
2. Combines measures for different organizational levels	Yes	Underlying model used (three tier management system) accommodates different organizational layers
3. Captures both efficiency and effectiveness	Yes	Efficiency and effectiveness measures embedded at all organizational levels
4. Identification of trade-offs	Yes	Clear definition and management of key business processes that should deliver strategic goals of company
5. Mixture of qualitative and quantitative measures	Yes	Primarily quantitative but some qualitative measures such as customer and employee satisfaction
6. Be recognized as evolving process	Yes	System to be disseminated as 'fluid' and always subject to improvement
7. Incapable of manipulation	Maybe	Uncertain until fully implemented but system is very transparent
8. Measures not seen as ends but means	Yes	Having the 'right' measures matters *because* they determine behaviour
9. Enable management to plan and control	Yes	By providing management at all levels with 'good' information to be able to plan and control
10. Not measures in 'negative' way	Yes	System focuses on process management
11. Instil confidence in managers to empower teams	Yes	By focusing on the management of key business process
12. Measures to be collected systematically and analysed over time	Yes	Although system not fully implemented as yet
13. Identify critical situations	Yes	Transparency fundamental purpose of system
14. Differentiate between control and radical objectives	Yes	The system is carefully balanced between control and improvement
15. Track performance against customer expectations	Yes	Through the customer satisfaction measures
16. Encourage cross-functionalism	Yes	Through focus on process rather than task
17. Limit measures for simplicity	Yes	The system is simple and cohesive

expressed through service measures, differentiate superior company performance. Focusing on performance will, in turn, lead to greater profitability (Christopher 1997). It is apt, then, that these key issues are given due representation within the strategic planning process of the organization.

STRATEGIC AND OPERATIONAL ALIGNMENT

Lack of alignment has been identified as a major failing of traditional methods (Holloway et al. 1991; Kaplan 1990; Kaplan and Norton 1992). The use of Japanese policy deployment matrix logic assures that strategic and operational objectives remain aligned. This has the intangible yet immense advantage that everyone within the organization understands how their particular activities contribute to the strategic vision of the company. When people understand how and why measures exist, they are far more likely to accept and adhere to them.

INCORPORATION OF PROCESS MANAGEMENT

Process management cuts across the functional boundaries that have, in the past, led to total system sub-optimization (Kaplan and Norton 1992; Rich 1995a, 1995b; Dimancescu 1994; Dimancescu et al. 1997). This means that improvement activity in one area of the organization will not be at the expense of another. Organizational improvement will be both facilitated and clearly visible.

SIMPLICITY

A significant advantage of the system proposed lies in its simplicity. Simple solutions are invariably the most effective since they are more easily understood by those who need to understand them.

FUTURE MODEL DEVELOPMENT

During the research, the research team has found that the potential of the three-tier management system is considerable and that, with further development, work could be extended to a fourth (individual employees) and fifth (skills and competencies) level. However, the

theoretical development and empirical testing of this will be reserved for a future research project.

TIME-BASED MEASURES

The multilayer measurement approach can be applied at differing timescales appropriate to the responsibility levels of the people involved, ranging from long-term at strategic level to real-time at the action level. In addition, at the strategic levels, the financial measures show past performance, the supply chain measures suggest future financial performance and the human measures are a longer term gauge of company success.

In conclusion, the authors believe that although the performance measurement system described is incomplete and has not yet been fully implemented, other academics and practitioners may find the work conducted so far to be of value.

REFERENCES

Akao, Y. (1991), *Hoshin Kanri: Policy Deployment for Successful TQM*, Massachusetts: Productivity Press.

Chandler, A. D. (1962), *Strategy and Structure*, Cambridge, Mass: MIT Press.

Christopher, M. (1997), *Marketing Logistics*, Oxford: Butterworth Heinemann.

Cox, A. (1996), 'Relational competencies and strategic procurement management: towards an empirical and contractual theory of the firm', *European Journal of Purchasing and Supply Management*, 2(1), pp. 57–70.

Dimancescu, D. (1994), *The Seamless Enterprise: Making Cross-Function Management Work*, New York: John Wiley & Sons.

Dimancescu, D., Hines, P. and Rich, N. (1997), *The Lean Enterprise*, New York: AMACOM.

Ghobadian, A. and Ashworth, J. (1994), 'Performance measurement in local government: concept and practice', *International Journal of Operations and Production Management*, 14(5), pp. 35–51.

Goldratt, E. (1991), *Theory of Constraints*, lecture at seminar, unpublished.

Hines, P. and Rich, N. (1997), 'The seven value stream mapping tools', *International Journal of Operations and Production Management,* **17**(1), pp. 46–64.

Hines P. and Rich, N. (1998), 'Purchasing structures, processes and strategy: is it a case of the tail wagging the dog?', *European Journal of Purchasing and Supply Management,* **4**(1), pp. 51–61.

Hines, P., Rich, N., and Esain, A. (1998), 'Creating a lean supplier network: a distribution industry case', *European Journal of Purchasing and Supply Management,* **4**(4), pp. 235–246.

Holloway, J., Lewis, J. and Mallory, G. (1991), *Performance Measurement and Evaluation,* Buckingham: OU Press.

Kaplan, R. (1990), *Measures for Manufacturing Excellence,* Boston, Mass: Harvard Business School Press.

Kaplan, R. and Norton, D. (1992), 'The balanced scorecard: measures that drive performance', *Harvard Business Review,* Jan-Feb.

Kurogane, K. (1993), *Cross-Functional Management: Principal Applications,* Tokyo: Asian Productivity Organization.

Lambert, D. and Stock, J. (1993), *Strategic Logistics Management,* Boston, Mass: Irwin.

Lamming R., Cousins P. and Hampson J. (1996), *Performance Measurement in Purchasing: Report to the Supply Chain Development Group,* Bath: Centre for Research in Strategic Purchasing and Supply.

Lynch, R. and Cross, K. (1991), 'Performance measurement systems', in Brinker B., *Handbook of Cost Management,* Warren, Gorham and Lamont.

McKenna E. (1994), *Business Psychology and Organizational Behaviour: A Student's Handbook,* Hillsdale: Lawrence Erlbaum Associates.

Rich, N. (1995a), 'Partner, associate or enemy?: The use of Quality Function Deployment for supplier evaluation', *Proceedings of the 4th IPSERA Conference,* University of Birmingham, UK.

Rich, N. (1995b), 'Quality Function Deployment: a decision support matrix for location determination, *Proceedings of the 2nd International Symposium on Logistics,* University of Nottingham, UK.

Rich, N. and Francis, M. (1998), 'Overall supply chain performance measurement: focusing improvements and stimulating change', *Proceedings of the Logistics Research Network Conference,* Cranfield University: Institute of Logistics.

Samuel, D. and Hines, P. (1998), 'Designing a supply chain change process: a food distribution case', *Proceedings of the Logistics Research Network Conference,* Cranfield University: Institute of Logistics.

Saunders, M. (1994), *Strategic Purchasing and Supply Chain Management,* London: Pitman.

Schein, E.H. (1969), *Process Consultation: Its Role in Organizational Development,* Reading MA: Addison-Wesley.

Schein, E.H. (1987), *Process Consultation Volume II: Lessons for Managers and Consultants,* Reading MA: Addison-Wesley.

Womack, J. and Jones D. (1996), *Lean Thinking,* New York: Simon and Schuster.

Index

eCommerce: A Practical Guide to the Law

Susan Singleton

eCommerce: A Practical Guide to the Law is an essential tool for both businesses and lawyers involved in electronic commerce. It includes checklists and practical advice on the principal pitfalls relating to the internet and email and how to exploit the new technologies to advantage. Written by a solicitor who advises on these issues on a daily basis, it seeks to provide a simple summary of the relevant legal issues. Importantly it is fully up-to-date and includes details of the Electronic Communications Act 2000, the EU Electronic Commerce Directive and distance selling regulations as well as other, more established, relevant statutes. All areas of ecommerce law - from shopping on the internet to trade mark and domain name disputes and employment law to contract terms - are covered. Vitally, Susan Singleton avoids jargon and writes in an authoritative and yet accessible style, making this an invaluable resource for everyone facing the challenge of working in the new electronic environment.

Gower

50 Essential Management Techniques

Michael Ward

Are you familiar with the concept of product life-cycle? Of course you are! Does the prospect of a SWOT analysis bring you out in a cold sweat? Probably not. But what about the Johari Window? Or Zipf's Law?

Michael Ward's book brings together a formidable array of tools designed to improve managerial performance. For each entry he introduces the technique in question, explains how it works, then goes on to show, with the aid of an entertaining case study, how it can be used to solve an actual problem. The 50 techniques, including some never before published, are grouped into 11 subject areas, ranging from strategy to learning.

For managers in every type of organization and at any level, as well as for students and consultants, *50 Essential Management Techniques* is likely to become an indispensable source.

Gower

The Excellent Manager's Companion

Philip Holden

This is for every manager who aspires to excellence in everything they do, but wonders how they'll ever find the time ...

With *The Excellent Manager's Companion* in your desk drawer, you'll be equipped with succinct guidance on today's most talked-about business issues. And you'll be able to pepper your conversation with pertinent quotations, and even know which books to turn to when you really do need more detailed guidance on a specific topic.

Twenty-one chapters look at key topics, ranging from corporate culture to customer orientation, and from innovation to influencing people. Each chapter is organized around standard sections, which makes 'dipping' into the book quick, easy, and rewarding.

Sections are:

• questions for self-analysis
• a step-by-step guide to best practice
• the ten 'don'ts'
• pertinent quotations
• summaries of key books and articles
• a case study
• a glossary of terms.

Philip Holden's lively *Companion* combines expertise with entertainment, with a supporting cast that ranges from Walt Disney to Confucius, and from Dilbert to Drucker. This book is guaranteed to appeal to busy managers in all sectors.

Gower

Gower Handbook of Management Skills

Third Edition

Edited by Dorothy M Stewart

'This is the book I wish I'd had in my desk drawer when I was first a manager. When you need the information, you'll find a chapter to help; no fancy models or useless theories. This is a practical book for real managers, aimed at helping you manage more effectively in the real world of business today. You'll find enough background information, but no overwhelming detail. This is material you can trust. It is tried and tested.'

So writes Dorothy Stewart, describing in the Preface the unifying theme behind the Third Edition of this bestselling *Handbook*. This puts at your disposal the expertise of 25 specialists, each a recognized authority in their particular field. Together, this adds up to an impressive 'one stop library' for the manager determined to make a mark.

Chapters are organized within three parts: Managing Yourself, Managing Other People, and Managing the Business. Part I deals with personal skills and includes chapters on self-development and information technology. Part II covers people skills such as listening, influencing and communication. Part III looks at finance, project management, decision-making, negotiating and creativity. A total of 12 chapters are completely new, and the rest have been rigorously updated to fully reflect the rapidly changing world in which we work.

Each chapter focuses on detailed practical guidance, and ends with a checklist of key points and suggestions for further reading.

Gower

Outsourcing IT - The Legal Aspects

Rachel Burnett

Information technology is one of the most common management functions to be outsourced. It is also one of the most complex.

Whether you are a supplier or a customer, it is vital to have a properly negotiated formal contract between yourself and the other party if you are entering into an outsourcing arrangement. A good contract needs careful planning and this book provides a comprehensive guide to the whole process.

It starts with structuring the contract and then covers services required, staff, location, software, costs, management liaison, allowing for change, security, duration, termination and other vital provisions. There is also advice relating to public procurement and choosing a supplier.

All parties involved in outsourcing contracts need access to well informed and competent legal advice. Rachel Burnett's book offers just that.

Gower

feld (Leinefelde) zum Kloster herein geritten, als er aber die gesehen, hätte er zweien der Nonnen, „pfrundtner mit namen (und?) goltman genennet", gesagt: Was gilts, die werden das Kloster anstecken? Denn der Haufe zieht daher. Diese zwei wären ins Kloster geritten und erstlich auf der Nonnen Schlafhaus gegangen, da noch Stroh in den Betten lag, das hätten die zwei alle angezündet und gebrannt. Alsbald kam der Haufen bei dem Dorfe Beuren her, und liefen wohl hundert Personen aus dem Haufen auch ins Kloster und steckten die Scheune an und sind demnach im Kloster hin und wieder gelaufen und haben den ersten zweien geholfen, das allenthalben anzuzünden und zu verbrennen. Das hätte er, Zeuge, gesehen. Gleich alsbald habe er, Zeuge, auch gesehen, daß Reifenstein und Scharfenstein die selbst auch gebrannt." Ein anderer Zeuge (S. 174), der Hofmeister von Kloster Reifenstein (in Hoppenstedt), berichtet: „Hätten der Zeit auch Eichsfelder etlich viel Schweine und Schafe gen Hoppenstedt (Hüpstedt), da er seine Wohnung habe, gebracht, die hätte er hören sagen, sie hättens aus dem Kloster Beuren genommen."

Ob der Haufe von Orsla aus direkt über Leinefelde auf Beuren zog oder einen kleinen Umweg über Reifenstein machte, etwa auf dem Wege, wo heute die Chaussee zieht, läßt sich nicht sagen; vielleicht zog nur eine sich abtrennende Schar dorthin, jedenfalls brannten, wie wir eben schon sahen, beide Klöster an demselben Tage. Auch über das Schicksal Reifensteins bieten unsere Akten mancherlei Auskunft. S. 168 erzählt ein Zeuge: „Zuvor und ehe die Prädikanten mit ihrem Anhang auf das Eichsfeld gekommen, seien die eichsfeldischen Dörfer und Nachbarn, um Reifenstein gelegen, nämlich Hoppenstedt (Hüpstedt), Beberstedt, Birkungen, Lenckenfeld (Leinefeld), Zella, Helmsdorf, Bernrode (Gernrode), Stadtworbis, Kirchworbis, Breitenworbis und kein Fremder in das Kloster Reifenstein gefallen, hätten gefressen und gesoffen und, was sie nicht gesoffen, die Böden ausgeschlagen und alles

was im Kloster gewesen, Orgeln und anderes, zerbrochen
und mit Füßen getreten, dazu die Glocken zerschlagen und
samt dem Vieh hinweggeführt und übel in diesem Kloster
gehandelt, daß nichts dageblieben wäre. Das habe er als
der Zeit ein Mönch im Kloster gesehen. Aber im Zuge
nach Heiligenstadt, da sei das Kloster Reifenstein gebrannt
worden." — Der schon erwähnte Hofmeister des Klosters
in Hoppenstedt sagt ferner aus: „Er habe gesehen, daß
die Eichsfelder das Kloster Reifenstein, ehe der Haufe
dahin gekommen 3 oder 4 Tage, geplündert haben und
alle Dinge zerschlagen und verwüstet; aber das Brennen
der Schlösser und Klöster habe er gesehen, als der Haufe
von Orsla nach Heiligenstadt zu gezogen; wer das getan,
hätte er nicht Wissen. Es sei noch ein Ziegelhüttlein dagestanden, sei ein Mönch im Gerücht gewesen, Bernhard
genannt, der soll es verbrannt haben. Der Abt zu Reifenstein habe seine Kleinode, Kirchengezierde, Silber, Brief
und Siegel geflüchtet; er, Zeuge, habe es mit 3 Wagen gen
Heiligenstadt helfen führen." S. 141 sagt der Zeuge: „Als
das Kloster zu Reifenstein angebrannt, sei der Abt und er,
Zeuge, auf Rustenberg zur Erhaltung ihres Leibes und
Nahrung geflohen, auf welchem Schloß die Edelleute auf
dem Eichsfeld versammelt gewesen, und wäre Hans von
Minnigerode derselben Versammelten Hauptmann gewesen."
Das bestätigt Zeuge S. 169: „Der Abt zu Reifenstein habe
des Klosters Kleinode, Kirchengezierde, dergleichen Brief
und Siegel gen Heiligenstadt geflüchtet, er habe es helfen
einpacken samt anderen Mönchen im Kloster; seien 2 Wagen
voll gewesen." Zeuge S. 180 gibt an: „Zuvor der Haufe
gezogen, habe er von etlichen von Hoppenstedt gehört, daß
sie sollten die Glocken zu Reifenstein aus dem Kloster
genommen, zerschlagen und Büchsen daraus gegossen haben.
Auch wären der Zeit etliche Bauern von Beberstedt zu
ihm gekommen, hätten viel Eisens gebracht und ihm zum
Kaufe zum Teil gegeben, hätte er ihnen gesagt, das Eisen
wäre zu Reifenstein aus dem Kloster genommen, darauf

sie bekannt, sie hätten daselbst genommen und geplündert, und im Zuge auf das Eichsfeld nach Heiligenstadt zu, ehe der Haufe hinan kommen, hätten Schlösser und Klöster gebrannt." — S. 182b wird ausgesagt: „Hätte einer eine ziemliche Glocke, die in 3 Stücke geschlagen, samt anderem Kirchengezeuge mit ihnen gen Hoppenstedt gebracht, daselbst auf einen Anger gelegt und das mit anderen geteilt. Es hätte auch einer derselben eine ziemliche Pfeife aus der Orgel zu Reifenstein gehabt und vorher gepfiffen, und seien nach der Teilung gen Mühlhausen gekommen und hätten die Glocke um Handrohr verwechselt, das habe er gesehen." — Zeuge S. 141 berichtet: „Es haben einige von Birkungen dem Abt zu Reifenstein gesagt, daß Hans Creutzeburg und ein Zimmermann, beide Bürger zu Mühlhausen, die hätten das Kloster Reifenstein angesteckt und ausgebrannt." — Der Zeuge S. 145b „hat solches von Michel dem Zimmermann, so der Zeit, ehe er das Kloster Reifenstein angezündet, bei einem zu Stadtworbis, Hans Demut, gedient, gehört sagen, als er und andere im Kloster nichts gefunden, und es geplündert gewesen, hat er Feuer geholt und das Kloster angezündet und verbrennen lassen". Auch unsere Chronik erzählt: „— wie auch einer das Kloster Reifenstein, Michel Zimmermann genannt, angesteckt und das Feuer zu Bartlof dazu geholet hatte." Zeuge S. 167 sagt aus, „er könne nicht glauben, daß Reifenstein vor 3 Tagen vor dem Zuge verbrannt, sondern im Zuge sei es verbrannt worden, das habe er gesehen". — Über die Zeit dieses Brandes gibt Zeuge S. 170b an: „Gleich alsbald als Beuren gebrannt, hat er gesehen, daß Reifenstein auch gebrannt." Das läßt noch mehr vermuten, daß nur eine Abteilung nach dem etwas seitab gelegenen Reifenstein zog, nicht der ganze Haufe.

In jenen Dresdener Akten liegt nun auch die Beschwerde vor, mit der der Abt von Reifenstein seinen Schaden anmeldete: „Wir Matthes abt des stiffts zu Reiffenstein beclagen unns sampt unserem convent, das unns in der ietzigenn vorgangenen auffruhr unsre kirchenn sampt anderen ubir zenn (? subiczenn 17 ?) gebeuwen groß unnd cleyn in grundt vorterbt unnd vorbrandt, daczu alle alteren unnd alle geschmeyde, messegewandt, altartücher, leuchter, orgeln nidergeschlagen unnd hynweg genommen, das wir uffs wenigst achtenn auf dritthalb tausend gulden, do mit wir solch gebew unnd vorrot nicht getrauwen mit auffzurichten oder in vorigen stant widder zu bringen. Auch sind unns funff teiche ausgestochen unnd gefischt, welchen schaden wir achten nuffs wenigst auff drey hundert gulden. Es haben uns auch die menner zu Lengefeldt im Molschen gericht unser schaff entfrempt, die sie noch bey sich haben unnd die woln abgenommen und der selbigen etlich geschlacht, welchen schaden wir achten uff sechzigk gulden.

Note. Es haben die vonn Molhaußen sampt dem mutwillige anhange vonn Glichisteyn hundert drey stücke rinth vyhes, darunder fuffzig funff milchkuwe sampt virzigk acht rinder gewest ungeverlich im andre unnd dryhundert unnd zwelff zeigen on einige fede unnd verwarnunge genommen und ubir Molhaußen getriben, welch ich der vogt[1] gemelts schloß zum Glichensteyn vor mich außerhalb meins gnedigsten hern vonn Mentz churfursten oder andere (?) ch. f. g. rethe oder amptman des Eysfeldes beuelich nicht angezeigt haben wyl, sundern vor mich E. f. f. g. verordnethen rethen untirthenig angezeigt haben. Von obgemelter vyhe hab ich von den Molhaußen acht melcke kuw unnd ein rind widder krigen."

Gegenüber von Kloster Beuren erhob sich auf dem Abhange des Dün Schloß Scharfenstein, das an jenem Tage gleiches Geschick mit ihm teilte. Ein Zeuge (S. 183) erzählt: „Als der Haufe von Orsla aufgebrochen und nach Heiligenstadt gezogen, wäre er und wohl 60 Männer mit ihm von dem Haufen auf das Schloß Scharfenstein gegangen,

---

1) Matthes Huneborn.

hätten sie nichts mehr da oben gefunden, weder Essen
noch Trinken, denn ein wenig Korn, noch nicht ausge-
droschen; hätte er gesehen, daß es die Nachbarn unten im
Dorf genommen und geteilt hätten, wären er und die mit
ihm wieder hinweggegangen und gen Heiligenstadt mit
dem Haufen gezogen. Alsbald sie also herabgekommen,
hätte er gesehen das Feuer um das Schloß samt andern
Schlössern und Klöstern brennen. Wer nun die Schlösser
und Klöster angesteckt habe, davon habe er gar kein
Wissen." — Daneben stelle ich das Zeugnis S. 167: „Zuvor
und ehe die Prädikanten aufs Eichsfeld gen Heiligenstadt
zu gezogen, seien durch die Eichsfelder Scharfenstein,
Horburg, Reifenstein, Kloster Worbis, Beuren und
Teistungenburg geplündert worden. Aber als der Haufe
im Zug gen Heiligenstadt zu gezogen, seien vorgemeldete
Schlösser und Klöster gebrannt worden, wer aber das
Brennen gethan, weiß er nicht. Und er, Zeuge, habe gesehen, daß die Eichsfelder die Schlösser und Klöster geplündert haben." — Auch über den Brand des Schlosses
erfahren wir näheres. Zeuge S. 166b erzählt: „Da man mit
dem Haufen bei Beuren gekommen, hätte der Pfeifer, der
auf einem kleinen Pferdlein (gesessen) voller Schellen ge-
hangen, mit der Hand gedeutet auf Scharfenstein [1]) und
gesagt: „Seht ihr dort das Dinglein?" Scharfenstein
meinend, und schwieg damit. „Neher" denn $\frac{1}{2}$ Stunde
hätte das Schloß in alle Höhe gebrannt, das hätte er, Zeuge,
selbst gesehen und gehört. Wer aber die Klöster und
das Schloß angezündet und geplündert, davon habe er nicht
Wissens." — Auch diese letzte Frage läßt sich beantworten
nach dem Zeugnis S. 188: „sie hätten — danach die
4 Klöster, auch das Schloß Scharfenstein und Horburg
durch ihre verordneten Brandmeister, nämlich Hans Hern,
Clasen Frosch, Christoffel Schmidt und Tiel Guttern ausgebrannt und geplündert". Zeuge S. 190 bestätigt die

---

1) Wir erinnern uns, daß er auf diesem Schlosse bei dem Junker
Hans v. Enzenberg gewohnt hatte. Heft 1, S. 5.

Namen dieser Brandmeister (Hans Heer), desgl. S. 134 (Clasen Krosch).

Der „Dialogus oder Gesprächbüchlein zwischen einem Müntzerischen Schwärmer und einem Evangelischen frommen Bauern" weiß noch mehr zu berichten (Duval, Das Eichsfeld, S. 232). „Da wir vor den Scharfenstein kamen, war die Zugbrücke aufgezogen, und war niemand darin. Da stiegen wir hinein über die Gräben und über die Mauern und kamen in einen Weinkeller, da dürstete uns sehr, fanden darin wohl 20 Faß Wein, der war gar vergiftet, und tranken etliche eilends davon und starben unter unseren Händen. Da wir das sahen, nahmen wir Messer und Hellebarten und hieben die Fässer zu Stücken und ließen den Wein in den Keller laufen; wir nahmen Schafe, fraßen sie zum Teil und die andern verkauften wir, das Stück zu 5 Groschen. Der mehrste Raub wurde dem Rat überliefert, um im Fall der Not etwas zu haben." Diese Giftgeschichte, die Duval aus Wolf, Denkwürdigkeiten der Stadt Worbis, S. 96 entlehnte, verdient natürlich nicht mehr Glauben als andere ähnlicher Art; sehon Wolf spricht sein Bedenken aus (vgl. Seidemann, Thomas Münzer S. 75).

Auf halbem Wege zwischen Scharfenstein und Heiligenstadt liegt Westhausen; da „der frawen von Westhusen" 57 1/2 Fl. Ersatz gezahlt werden mußten (Chronik, S. 209), so muß auch dort eine Plünderung stattgefunden haben, über die ich Weiteres nicht nachweisen kann, als daß ich in den Dresdener Akten die Forderung fand von „Ursula Reinharth von Westhusen selig Wittfrau".

Besondere Mühe gab man sich in den hier benutzten Akten, festzustellen was vor und in Heiligenstadt geschehen ist, leider ohne uns einen sicheren Einblick in die Ereignisse zu gewähren. So wurde bestimmt (S. 144): „Bei dem XX. und XXI. Punkte soll gefragt werden, ob nicht die von Mühlhausen die Stadt Heiligenstadt bei nächtlicher Weile überfallen und unversehens erobert, eingenommen und also mit Gewalt gehandelt haben. Item, ob Zeuge nicht

gehört habe oder sonst wisse, daß der Rat zu Heiligenstadt
mit ihnen eines füglichen Abzuges halber Sprache und Unter-
handlung gehabt. Item ob nicht Allstedter, als die Stadt
erobert, sich selbst in die Kirche gedrängt, nur einmal un-
geheißen des Befehls eines Rates und sonst keiner mehr
gepredigt hat." Es fällt auf, daß von diesen Ereignissen
keine sichere Kunde vorlag, über die sich aus den Zeugenaussagen folgendes ergibt. S. 150b wird erzählt: „Als
der aufrührerische Haufe vor Heiligenstadt gekommen, sei
Pfeifer samt dem Hauptmann Jost Hamwurg (Homberg)
des Nachts zwischen 10 und 11 Uhr eingelassen, desgleichen
sei der Allstedter des Morgens an einem Mittwoch nach
Walpurgis (3. Mai) auch eingekommen, habe nicht vernommen, daß sie bei einem Rate zu Heiligenstadt will-
kommen oder empfangen worden seien." Eine um 8 Tage
abweichende Angabe des Tages bietet Zeuge S. 148: „Allstedter sei mit dem gewaltigen Haufen vor die Stadt
Heiligenstadt Dienstags nach Quasimodogeniti (25. April)
gegen Abend gekommen, sich davor gelagert, folgenden
Mittwoch morgens in die Stadt vor den Rat daselbst getreten." Aus beiden Aussagen ergibt sich, daß der Haufe
Dienstag abends vor Heiligenstadt eintraf; da der Zug erst
Sonnabend, 29. April, sich nach Ebeleben wandte, so kann das
nur Dienstag, 2. Mai[1]), gewesen sein. Wenn dann unsere
Chronik (S. 189) berichtet: „Da wurden die Prädikanten
vor den Rat gelassen, und begehrte Münzer, einen Sermon
zu tun, der ist ihm verstattet worden in der Kirche
Mariae", so wird das durch die Zeugen bestätigt. So erzählt Zeuge S. 148: „Allstedter sei vor den Rat daselbst
getreten und habe begehrt, einen Sermon zu tun; das habe
ein Rat mit großer Beschwerde zulassen müssen." Genaueres berichtet Zeuge S. 149: „Als der aufrührerische
Haufe sich vor Heiligenstadt gelegt, sei Allstedter an einem

---

1) Also ist die Angabe unserer Chronik, der Haufe sei an
diesem Tage nach Mühlhausen zurückgekehrt, nicht richtig.

Morgen auf das Rathaus vor den Rat gekommen und habe
begehrt, ihm zu vergönnen, das Wort Gottes zu predigen,
darauf habe ihm der Rat sagen lassen, sie erlaubten es
nicht, so verböten sie es ihm auch nicht. Darauf ist er,
Allstedter, aufgestanden und hat in Unser Frauen Kirche
einmal geprediget." Ähnlich erzählt Zeuge S. 152: „Als
die Prädikanten und der Haufe gen Heiligenstadt gekommen,
sind des anderen Tages Pfeifer und Allstedter mit Personen, deren er, Zeuge, einer gewesen, eingelassen; sind die
Prädikanten mit einander auf das Rathaus gegangen, haben
ein Gespräch gehabt, was dasselbe gewesen, sei ihm verborgen." Münzers Predigt bestätigt der Zeuge S. 150b: „Allstedter habe zu Heiligenstadt in der Pfarrkirche zu Unser
L. Frauen geprediget, wer es aber erlaubt und zugelassen,
wisse er nicht." Auch Zeuge S. 16b sagt aus: „Münzer
habe zu Heiligenstadt geprediget, das habe er gehört", und
Zeuge S. 148b: „Allstedter habe dem Rate angezeigt,
ihm zu vergönnen, eine Predigt zu halten; das haben sie
gestattet." Ferner verdanke ich H. Pfarrer Nebelsieck
noch folgende Aussagen aus Mühlhäuser Akten: Bürgermeister Strecker (von Heiligenstadt): „Es hätte mit großer
Beschwerde zugelassen werden müssen" (daß Münzer in der
Marienkirche predigte). Hans Hersch, Verweser des
Schultheißenamtes in Heiligenstadt, sagte aus, der Rat habe
Münzer sagen lassen, „sie erlauben es yhm nicht, so ver-
bietten sie ihme es nicht"; darauf habe er einmal in der
Marienkirche gepredigt. Diese Nachrichten lauten so bestimmt, daß andere dahinter zurücktreten müssen, wie die Aussage S. 146: „Seines Wissens seien Pfeifer und Allstedter
von einem Rat zu Heiligenstadt gar nicht empfangen, viel
weniger sei ein Gespräch mit ihnen gehalten, denn ein Rat
hätte wohl leiden mögen, daß sie gar nicht zu ihm gekommen wären", oder S. 149: „daß ein Rat dieselben
empfangen oder ein heimlich Gespräch mit ihnen gehabt,
oder gefordert, das glaube er nicht."

Von einer feindlichen Behandlung der Stadt ist keine

Rede; der Haufe blieb vor den Mauern liegen, nur wenige
wurden eingelassen. Zeuge S. 148b sagt ausdrücklich:
„Heiligenstadt sei nicht mit Gewalt erobert", ein anderer
S. 146b: „Darauf soll auch der Haufe abgezogen sein
und die von Heiligenstadt nicht viel beschädigt haben",
endlich S. 152: „Der Haufe sei zu Heiligenstadt gekommen
und draußen geblieben, bis sie wieder weggezogen seien;
er wisse von keiner Eroberung." Daneben ist die Angabe
S. 134, der Haufe habe „bei nächtlicher Weile Heiligenstadt eingenommen", ohne Bedeutung. — Daß die Prädikanten eingelassen wurden, berichten ganz genau folgende Zeugen, S. 165: „Er sei mit Pfeifer und anderen an
einem Abend spät in Heiligenstadt eingelassen und in die
Herberge gekommen; wäre der Pfeifer mit etlichen Bürgern
— wer die gewesen, wisse er nicht — hinweggegangen
und bald wiedergekommen, wäre das Essen bereit gewesen,
hätten sie gegessen und getrunken und seien fröhlich gewesen. Auch hätten die von Heiligenstadt ihnen 2 Faß
Eimbeckisch und Heiligenstädter Bier in die Herberge
führen lassen, das sie getrunken. Den andern Morgen seien
sie wieder herausgeritten." Ein ebenso guter Zeuge berichtet S. 166: „Die 2 Prädikanten seien gen Heiligenstadt
an einem Abend eingelassen, er sei mit geritten und in
die Herberge, des Bürgermeisters Listomann Haus, gewiesen,
habe da gegessen, getrunken, sei 2 Nächte geblieben."
Zeuge S. 175 weiß dann noch anzugeben: „Die Prädikanten
wären ungefähr mit 30 Pferden eingelassen und der Wein
geschenkt." Wenn Zeuge S. 148b berichtet: „Anders
oder weiter sei nicht mit ihnen gehandelt, denn daß der
Haufe denen von Heiligenstadt (gegen) Geistliche und
Adelspersonen, wo sie etwas verwirkt, ihnen die Strafe
heimstelle; das sei also geschehen, und der Haufe darauf wieder abgezogen" — so ist das vielleicht nur eine
Erinnerung an den oben erwähnten Brief (S. 54), wenn es
natürlich auch möglich ist, daß jene Forderung nochmals
mündlich erörtert wurde.

Vor Heiligenstadt erhielt der Haufe Verstärkung
und Verpflegung. Zeuge S. 146b berichtet: „Er habe
einen Haufen der Zeit sehen ziehen den Reiser Grund
naeh Heiligenstadt; habe man gesagt, es seien etliche von
Mühlhausen zu Fuß und Roß darunter." — Andere hatten sich
wohl schon früher angeschlossen; S. 177b wird berichtet:
„Wäre ein Haufe Eichsfelder zwischen Zaunröden und
Orsla zu dem Haufen von Mühlhausen gekommen, und
wären als beide Haufen auf Heiligenstadt gezogen." Der
Zeuge S. 154b gibt an, „er habe 9 Fässer Bier in das
Lager vor Heiligenstadt geführt, das sei ihm durch die
Bauern ausgetrunken, und nicht viel dafür gegeben worden".
Auch Zeuge S. 159b berichtet, „er habe Bier gen Heiligen-
stadt geführt, das hätten ihm etliche Bürger geheißen,
nämlich Michael Koth (was doch sicher Koch heißen soll)
und Dietrich Weißmüller, Goldschmidt", also 2 der Achtmänner (Chronik, S. 173). Zeuge S. 159b erzählt, „der
Haufe habe vor Heiligenstadt gelegen; er, Zeuge, habe einen
Wagen und 2 Karren Brod ins Lager geführt, auf des
ewigen Rats Befehl". S. 131 wird dann angegeben, es
seien 2 Viertelsmeister, die des neuen Regiments gewesen,
mitgezogen, mit Namen Hans Schmidt und Klaus Fulstich.
Diese beiden finden wir bereits in der Liste der Achtmänner des Jahres 1523 (Chronik S. 173); sie müssen also
auch 1525 dies Amt bekleidet haben, denn mit dem „neuen
Regiment" wird der ewige Rat bezeichnet; ähnlich heißt
es Zur Gesch. d. Stadt Mühlhausen, Heft 3, S. 24 „des
newen Radts achtmann". Georg Pfeifer sagte aus (Heft 1
S. 24): „Als die von Mühlhausen ausgezogen seien vor
Ebeleben, Schlotheim und andere Flecken in der Pürsten
Lande, die Schlösser zu stürmen, da ist Reinhard Lamhart
ein Kriegsmeister und Bock, jetzt ein Ratsherr zu Mühlhausen, auf die Zeit ein Rottmeister gewesen." Lamhart
ist aus dem Bauernliede (Chronik S. 224) bekannt; Bock
ist vielleicht Heinrich Boy in der Liste Chronik S. 197.
Dem Einfluß dieser Männer wird es auch zuzuschreiben

sein, daß Geschütz dem Haufen zur Verfügung stand, wenigstens sagt Hans Ditmar aus (S. 59—61), „Michael Koch, ebenfalls einer der Achtmänner, habe ihn im Lärm erstechen wollen, daß er die Büchsen nicht habe führen wollen"; ferner „er habe aus Gehorsam die Büchsen nach Heiligenstadt, Ebeleben und Schlotheim geführt" (als Fuhrmann); „er sei also an die Büchsen gebunden gewesen", daß er nicht habe plündern können.

Was in Heiligenstadt damals geschehen, ist, so viel ich weiß, bisher nicht genauer bekannt geworden. Wolf, Eichsfelder Kirchengeschichte, S. 148 weiß zu berichten: „Nach ihrer Ankunft zu Heiligenstadt mußte sich der Rat versammeln und ihren Vortrag anhören, der hauptsächlich, wie es scheint, dahin ging, den bisherigen Gottesdienst zu ändern, die alten Zeremonien abzuschaffen und den Stiftsgeistlichen ihre Privilegien zu nehmen. Nicht genug damit, Münzer ließ sich nach geendigtem Ratssitze eine Kanzel auf dem Kirchhofe u. l. Frau errichten und hielt nach seiner Bibel eine Predigt, nicht ohne heftige Rührung der zuhörenden Bürger und Bauern. Denn von dem Kirchhofe liefen sie auf das Stift, fielen wütend in die Curien, raubten das Hausgerät, zerschlugen die Braupfanne und schleppten aus der Kirche die Kleinodien mit sich fort." Auch in seiner Geschichte von Heiligenstadt S. 55 berichtet er nicht mehr. Es fällt auf, daß die Zeugen in unseren Akten Münzer in der Liebfrauenkirche predigen lassen, von einer Predigt auf dem Kirchhofe nichts erwähnen. War der Zudrang so stark, daß die Kirche nicht ausreichte? Oder ist mit Absicht eine Änderung in der Überlieferung eingetreten? Vermutlich wird sich in Heiligenstadt Genaueres feststellen lassen. Die von Wolf erwähnten Bauern gehörten jedenfalls nicht zum Haufen, dem ja die Tore geschlossen blieben; Wolf freilich scheint angenommen zu haben, der Haufe sei in die Stadt gedrungen. Wichtig ist die von ihm (Politische Geschichte des Eichsfeldes II, Urk.-Buch S. 74) veröffentlichte Urkunde:

„Wie sich die von Heiligenstadt ihrer Empörung halber
verschrieben haben. Wir burgermeister, rat und gemeinheit
der stadt Heiligenstadt bekennen . . ᾿ , nachdem als die
aufrührige bauernschafft des Eichßfeldes verschienener weil
anher in diese stadt sich begeben und davor gelagert, und
wir wieder dieselben wie feind uns nit, sondern freundlich
gehalten, dadurch zwischen uns allen derselbigen aufruhr
und empörung in dieser stadt sich erhebet und erstanden
ist" etc. Zu beachten ist, daß hier nur die Bauernschaft
des Eichsfeldes erwähnt wird; von Pfeifer und Münzer
oder ihrem Haufen ist keine Rede.

Knieb (Gesch. der Reformation und Gegenreformation auf
dem Eichsfelde, S. 23) berichtet (nach Wolf): „Treulos öffneten
die Bürger die Tore. Auf Geheiß Münzers und Pfeifers mußte
der Rat zusammentreten und deren Forderungen entgegen-
nehmen, die wahrscheinlich auf Abänderung des bisherigen
Gottesdienstes, Abschaffung der alten Ceremonien und Privilegien der alten Stiftsherren lauteten. Darauf hielt Münzer
auf dem Kirchhofe bei der Liebfrauenkirche eine seiner
gewohnten Brandreden mit dem Erfolge, daß die Zuhörer
sofort die Häuser der Stiftsherren und die Kirchen erstürmten
und plünderten, die Braupfannen zerschlugen, die Privilegien-
briefe der Stiftsherren wegnahmen und letztere zu allen
öffentlichen Lasten zwangen." Vergebens habe ich nach
der Quelle dieser Angaben geforscht, halte es auch für
keinen Beweis, wenn noch 1564 ein steinerner Predigtstuhl
auf dem erwähnten Kirchhofe stand; hätte den Münzer benutzt, so dürfte man eher annehmen, daß man ihn eben
deswegen bald entfernt haben würde. Ebenso vermisse ich
eine Begründung für die von Knieb aus Janssen II, S. 524
übernommene Angabe, daß „selbst etliche Grafen und
Edelleute mit Gewalt gedungen wurden, ihnen anzuhangen;
wer solches nicht tun wollte, hat müssen durch den Spieß
laufen". Münzer ließ, was doch wohl betont werden darf,
kein Blut vergießen, auch das Urteil über Matern von Gehofen und die anderen Diener des Grafen von Mansfeld hat

er „aus dem Munde der gemeyne" verkündigt und hat das
„auß forcht gethan" (Seidemann, Th. Münzer, S. 154). Freilich würden seine leidenschaftlichen Worte, die er an seine
Anhänger richtete, bei längerer Dauer der Bewegung ohne
Zweifel zu blutigen Scenen geführt haben; so aber ist in
dem bekanntlich sehr kurzen Thüringer Bauernkriege von
Scenen, wie sie sich vor Weinsberg oder an anderen Orten
in dem viel blutigeren, aber auch großartigeren Bauernkriege
Oberdeutschlands abspielten, keine Rede.

Die Schriften von Wolf sind nun 100 Jahre alt oder
werden es bald sein; es wird doch wohl Zeit, daß wir in
der Kenntnis jener Ereignisse weiterzukommen suchen als
der fleißige und tüchtige Kanonikus zu Northeim. Sollten
nicht die von mainzischer Seite geführten Akten noch vorhanden sein? Sie würden eine willkommene Ergänzung
bieten, selbst wenn ich dadurch des Irrtums überführt
werden sollte.

In sehr auffallender Weise lassen uns, nachdem der
Haufe Heiligenstadt erreicht hatte, unsere Nachrichten im
Stich; schon was in dieser Stadt geschehen ist, läßt sich,
wie wir eben sahen, nicht genauer angeben, noch viel
weniger aber erfahren wir, wenn wir den Zug weiter zu begleiten suchen.

Man fragt sich unwillkürlich, woran das liegt, ohne
die Möglichkeit, eine auch nur einigermaßen sichere Antwort
zu finden. Vermuten kann man ja, daß die Mühlhäuser im
Haufen, als der Zug sich nun nordwärts in das untere
Eichsfeld wandte, zurückblieben und umkehrten, um sich
nicht zu weit von der Heimat zu entfernen; das gäbe
wenigstens die Möglichkeit, es zu erklären, daß in unseren
Zeugenaussagen, so reichlich sie auch vorliegen, über die
weiteren Ereignisse so gut wie nichts zu finden ist. Ein
Beweis kann dafür in keiner Weise geboten werden, vielmehr sind auch die weiteren Verwüstungen Mühlhausen in
Rechnung gestellt. Münzer und Pfeifer sind, wie wir sehen
werden, auch weiter mitgezogen, aber außer in Duderstadt

tritt ihre Tätigkeit fast nirgends hervor. Dennoch soll hier
alles . zusammengestellt werden, schon um eben dadurch
vielleicht zu weiterer Forschung anzuregen.

Unsere Chronik bietet über alle die folgenden Ereignisse nur die magere Notiz: „Danach zogen sie gen
Duderstadt, die machten einen Bund mit ihnen, daß sie
wieder abzogen." Wer damit gemeint ist, bleibt unbe-
stimmt; man wird doch zunächst an Münzer und Pfeifer
denken; mit dem Bunde kann dann die Verbrüderung mit
den Bauern gemeint sein, oder auch der besondere „Bund",
wie ihn Münzer weithin ausgedehnt hatte, dessen Beispiel
auch Pfeifer [1]) in Mühlhausen gefolgt war. Daß Pfeifer
mit nach Duderstadt zog, ergibt sich aus einer Zeugen-
aussage (St. A. 151): „Pfeifer habe ihn vor Duderstadt gefänglich annehmen lassen." Hier mögen auch gleich die
weiteren Aussagen folgen: (S. 147) „Der Mühlhäuser Haufe
sei von Heiligenstadt nach Duderstadt gezogen, in dem sei
das Kloster Teistungenburg geplündert und ausgebrannt
worden". Ein anderer Zeuge ist etwas genauer (S. 170b):
„Als sie nun vor Heiligenstadt gekommen, und wieder abgezogen und den andern Tag gen Duderstadt gerückt, habe
er gesehen, daß Teistungenburg gebrannt, und daß sie daselbst zu Duderstadt auch einen Tag still gelegen, demnach
wieder aufgebrochen und sich nach dem Bodenstein gewandt."

Georg Scharf von Nordhausen bekannte (Förstemann
Kl. Schr. S. 88), er sei mit vor Heiligenstadt gewesen und
darauf auf dem Wege nach Duderstadt bei der Plünderung
des Schlosses Westernhagen und des Jungfrauenklosters
Teistungenburg, welches ganz verbrannt sei; darauf sei
auch das Haus Berlts von Westernhagen zu Berlingerode
zerstört worden und das Haus Thilos von Hagen zu
Teistungen, auch sei er mit dem Haufen nach Gerblingerode
und vor Duderstadt gezogen.

---

1) Zur Gesch. d. St. Mühlh. 2, S. 33.

Wir gewinnen daraus zunächst die Möglichkeit, die Richtung des weiteren Zuges festzustellen. Der Haufe wird vermutlich seinen Weg genommen haben, wo jetzt die Chaussee von Heiligenstadt nach Duderstadt führt. „Auf dem Marsche nach Duderstadt wandte er sich gegen die Herren von Westernhagen, zerstörte das Schloß dieses Namens, die Häuser Berlts von Westernhagen in Berlingerode, Tilens von Hagen in Teistungen nebst dem Kloster Teistungenburg" [1]). Duval [2]) weiß folgende etwas romantische Sage zu erzählen: „Als die Bauern das Schloß Westernhagen zu zerstören beschlossen hatten, sannen sie auf eine List und schickten an die von Westernhagen einen Boten, der denselben einen Gruß von denen von Hanstein bringen und sie dringend bitten mußte, nach dem Hanstein zu kommen und denselben gegen die eben anrückenden Bauern verteidigen zu helfen; sie, die von Hanstein, wollten denen von Westernhagen ebenfalls beistehen, wenn auch sie etwa später von dem Bauernheere gefährdet werden sollten. Infolge dieser Aufforderung machten sich die von Westernhagen mit ihren Knechten sogleich auf den Weg, indem sie nur eine geringe Besatzung auf der Veste zurückließen.

Kaum aber waren sie fort, so rückten die im Hinterhalte lauernden Bauern herbei, griffen die Veste an, eroberten und zerstörten sie und hieben alles nieder, was sich nicht schleunig durch die Flucht zu retten vermochte. Eine Amme mit einem zarten Knaben des Geschlechts von Westernhagen auf dem Arme, rettete des Kindes Leben einzig und allein dadurch, daß sie dasselbe für ihr eigenes ausgab. Sie brachte es nach Teistungenburg, wo sich die Klosterfrauen seiner eifrig annahmen, unter deren Pflege es fröhlich aufwuchs. Die Sage fügt noch hinzu, daß, da alle des Namens Westernhagen im Bauernkriege umge-

1) Wolf, Eichsfeldische Kirchengeschichte 149.
2) Das Eichsfeld, S. 589.

kommen seien, dieser Säugling der letzte Sproß des ganzen
Stammes gewesen, — dem ist nicht so." Wir haben hier
also eine Übertragung der Erzählung von der Rettung
Volkmars von Berlepsch in Langensalza. Nüchterner lauten
die Summen in unserer Chronik (209), die von Mühlhausen
für diese Verwüstungen gezahlt werden mußten: „Hansen
vom Hayne 1578$\frac{1}{2}$ Fl., Tyelen (Thilo) von Westernhagen
150 Fl., Arnolten von West. 35 Fl., Bernharten von W.
70 Fl., Ernsten von W. 130 Fl., Otten von W. 15 Fl.,
allen von W. des Hauses W. 1200 Fl." In den oben erwähnten Akten des Dresdener Archivs (9135 No. 127)
liegen Verzeichnisse der erlittenen Verluste vor von Berlt
von W., Ernst von W., Berlts Sohn, Thilo von W.

Auf dem weiteren Zuge bereitete der Haufe dem
Kloster Teistungenburg dasselbe Schicksal wie dem Mutter-
kloster Beuren. Auch hier liegen sehr geringe Nachrichten
vor. Duval (S. 322) weiß nichts weiter zu berichten als:
„Die Bauern verwüsteten bei dieser Gelegenheit Teistungenburg, wodurch ein großer Teil der Klosterschriften verloren
ging." Einer aus dem Bauernheere, Georg Scharf, hat
nachher bekannt: „daß das Jungfrawen-Closter Teistingenburg
geplündert, beraubet und bis in den Grund verbrannt, er
habe aber für seine Person nichts dazu gethan." Diese
Aussagen bietet auch Förstemann, Kl. Schriften, S. 88.
In den Dresdener Akten [1] fand ich folgende Klage der Vor-
gesetzten des Klosters: „Wir Steffanus Hogenius probst,
Osanna Nesselroder eptisthen, Margrita Mollers priorin
unnd gantz convent gemeltes closters beclagen uns, das wir
durch die mutwillige uberfahrunge uund gewaltige emporunge
der von Molhaußen unser closter sampt der kirchen unnd
eyngebewe in grunde verbrandt, auch alle cleynoth unnd
hausroth sampt allen kirchen geschmeyde unnd glocken

---

1) Die Beschwerden der Klöster liegen dort nur in Kopie vor,
von einer Hand und machen fast den Eindruck aufgenommener
Protokolle.

auch andir das in einer eyl nicht erzelt mag werden hinweg genommen, darzu etliche vyhe szo vyl das do bifunden
auch enpfromt, welchen schaden wie oben angezeygt auffs
geringst veranschlagen auff funffczehen hundert gulden, do
mit obgemelt closter nit vermochtenn in vorigenn stande zu
bringen."

Der Zug ging dann weiter auf Duderstadt, wo der
Haufe, trotzdem die Stadt gegen einen derartigen Überfall
durch ihre Befestigungen gesichert war, wie es scheint,
unter ähnlichen Verhältnissen, wie sie in Heiligenstadt ge-
herrscht haben können, Aufnahme fand, ohne daß sich genaueres darüber und über den Bund, den man mit den
Bauern schloß sagen ließe. Wolf (Eichsfelder Kirchengeschichte S. 149) sagt: „Was die Bauern in Duderstadt
getrieben, weiß man nicht; es ist aber bekannt, daß die
dasigen Bürger sich wegen ihres Verhaltens, wie die
Heiligenstädter, eine schwere Strafe von ihrem Landesherrn
zugezogen haben." In der Geschichte der Stadt Duderstadt
(S. 154) bringt er nur die knappe Meldung unserer Chronik
und setzt hinzu: ‚Einen mächtigen Feind sich in Gutem
vom Halse schaffen, ist Klugheit und kein Staatsverbrechen.
Die Duderstädter müssen mehr als dieses gethan haben,
sonst würde sie der Herzog von Braunschweig nicht ebenso
strenge als die Heiligenstädter, ja noch strenger behandelt
haben." Das ist ganz richtig geschlossen, wenn wir auch
leider tatsächliches dadurch nicht erfahren, auch nicht
vergessen dürfen, daß die wachsende Fürstenmacht die gute
Gelegenheit benutzte, die alten Freiheiten der Städte zu
mindern; das mußten Mühlhausen, Heiligenstadt wie Duderstadt empfinden. In Münzers „Bund" hatten sich auch
adlige Herren aufnehmen lassen; man hört nicht, daß sie
dafür in gleicher Weise hätten büßen müssen. Vom Felde
vor Duderstadt schrieb Münzer an den Grafen Günther
von Schwarzburg am Donnerstag nach Walpurgis (Förstemann, Kl. Schr. S. 79, der das angegebene Datum [Mai 4]
bezweifelt).

Von Duderstadt aus wird sich der Zug zum alten
Benediktinerkloster Gerode gewandt haben, wobei es unsicher bleiben muß, ob der gesamte Haufe mit Pfeifer und
Münzer dorthin zog, oder ob nur eine kleine Schar bis an
die nordöstliche Grenze des Eichsfeldes vordrang. Jedenfalls ist der Ausdruck Förstemanns „die Benediktinerabtei
Gerode verwüsteten sie, wie scheint, auf ihrem Rückzuge
nach Mühlhausen", nach der örtlichen Lage des Klosters
bemessen, kein richtiger.

Über die Zerstörung des Klosters klagt der Abt:
„Wir Petrus abt des stifftes zu Gerode beclagen uns sampt
unserem convent, das uns in dissem uncristlichem auffruhr
unsere kirchen verbrandt mit allen gebyltnys, gestöle, auch
acht glockenn und die orgel entfromt und hynweg gefiret,
dergleichen bucher, meßbucher, meßgewandt, kannen, ampelen,
handtfesser, altartücher, handzwelen, lichte und kerzen,
darczu alle alteren inschlagen darczu das ganze closter
sampt allen eingebew zu grunde vorbrandt, alle keßel,
topffe, bette sampt alle was yn closter gewest, in . . . .
(Fleck und Loch!) closter hynweg genomen unnd gefiret,
der gleichen schweine, kuwe, pferde, schaffe, wagen, geschir
unnd was zum ackerwergk gehört alles hinweg genomen
sampt allem vorrate, was im closter gewest. Des gleichen
weyne, byr alles ausgedrungken unnd dye fesser zerschlagen,
auch die teiche ausgestochen unnd gefischt worden, das dann
uns (?) denen des Eysfeldes vom adell wol bewost, welche
beschedunge wyr auffs aller gerings auff funffthalber taußent
gulden ermessen, do mit wir unßer closter im vorigen
standt nit mugen adir können bringken und widder auff-
richten."

Duval (S. 253) berichtet: „Im Bauernkriege. hausten
die wilden Rotten hier ebenso zügellos als anderwärts.
Die Mönche, welche glücklicher Weise noch zeitig genug
vernommen hatten, daß die Bauern nach Gerode zu ziehen
gesonnen seien, beschlossen den ungebetenen Gästen aus
dem Wege zu gehen, rafften zusammen, was sie in der

Angst und Hast erraffen konnten, und flohen von dannen, um nur das Leben zu retten. Ein Mehreres blieb ihnen aber auch wirklich fast nicht übrig, denn als sie nach dem Abzuge der Bauern zu der geliebten Stätte zurückkehrten, fanden sie dieselbe leergebrannt und von allem, was ehedem hier vorhanden, nichts als ein Marienbild, ein Pult und drei Glocken." Auch Wolf, Eichsf. Kirchengesch., S. 149 weiß nicht mehr zu berichten, ebenso Kegel in dem Sammelwerke Thüringen und der Harz VIII, S. 59. Am betrübtesten waren die Mönche über den Verlust ihrer Bibliothek und Abt Nicolaus (? Petrus) sagt in einem Briefe vom 31. August 1525: „Imo quod sanguineis quoque deplorandum est lacrymis bibliothecam monasterii nostri instructissimam simul cum Gramato phylacio, archivis, imaginibus, tabulis sacris et profanis tam foede lacerarunt, consciderunt et depraedati sunt non modo raptores illi facinorosi verum etiam, ut fama fert (Knieb, S. 25), vicinorum pagi rustici, adeo ut, si quid reliquum reperiatur, illud ipsum tamen sit laceratum, mutilum vel pedibus conculcatum." Mehr weiß Duval nicht zu erzählen, obgleich er ein seiner Zeit in Duderstadt aufbewahrtes Chronicon Monasterii Gerodensis ab anno 1124—1618 kannte. War der altbewährte wissenschaftliche Sinn der Benediktiner wirklich so weit geschwunden, daß niemand das traurige Geschick des Klosters aufzeichnen mochte?

Von Gerode aus zog der mit Beute beladene Haufe wohl schwerlich über das damals vermutlich wenig wegsame Ohmgebirge; er wird sich nach Duderstadt zurückgewandt haben und von dort aus auf Worbis gezogen sein. Unterwegs stieß man auf den Bodenstein, bei dem nach bisheriger Erzählung der Angriff gescheitert sein sollte. Duval (S. 522) weiß folgendes zu berichten: „Die Bauern rückten auch endlich vor den Bodenstein, der damalige Besitzer des Schlosses aber, Barthold von Winzingerode, war fest entschlossen, lieber das Leben mit dem Schwerte in der Hand zu verlieren, als dem elenden Haufen lebendig

in die Hände zu fallen. Alle Versuche, welche Thomas
Münzers Banden machten, die Feste zu erobern, blieben
erfolglos, und der wilde Haufe faßte daher den Entschluß,
den kühnen Ritter zur Übergabe zu zwingen. Die tobenden
Feinde lagerten sich deshalb auf das nächste, südliche
Vorgebirge, welches noch bis heute von ihnen die „Mühlhäuser Burg" genannt wird, aber die Belagerer mußten
unverrichteter Sache wieder abziehen, zerstörten aber aus
Wut die Dörfer Wintzingerode und Kaltohmfeld, weshalb
später die Mühlhäuser an Friedrich und Georg von
Wintzingerode als Entschädigung 2039 Gulden und außerdem den ‚Frawen von Wintzingerode' 150 Gulden zahlen
sollten." Diese Angaben stimmen mit denen in der
Chronik I, S. 209 überein, doch kommen da noch „Heinrichs
von Wintzingerode gelassene Erben" dazu.

So bestimmt diese Erzählung lautet, so kann doch kein
Zweifel sein, daß die Burg ebenfalls zerstört wurde; so sagt ein
Zeuge (St.A. 170b), der Haufe habe „sich nach dem Bodenstein gewandt, der auch verbrannt", ebenso will Zeuge (St.A.
188b) gesehen haben, daß Bodenstein brannte. Auch Lant-
greffer (S. 75b) wird befragt, warum er habe den „budenstein"
helfen anstecken, und sagt, er habe ihn nicht helfen anstecken, er sei sonst letztlich dazugekommen. In den
Dresdener Akten finde ich: „Georgen Wissingerode sampt
seines bruders vnd wittfrauen empfangenen schadens an-
schlagk, Friederich von Wissingerode, Heinrichs selig von
Wissingerode nachgelassene wittwe"; darin heißt es: „Item
wir wolten lieber dreytausent gulden den den baw und
schloß Bodenstein das mit zweyen scheffereyen in grunt
verbrant verloren haben." Danach wird die Summe des
erlittenen Schadens auf 4677 Gulden berechnet, während
in der Chronik (S. 209) für Friedrich und Georg von
Wissingerode und Heinrichs gelassene Erben nur 2039 Fl.
angesetzt sind; der Unterschied erklärt sich dadurch, daß
in der ersten Summe noch die Hälfte des Scharfensteins
eingerechnet ist („Bau unsers teils des Scharfensteins"),

der den · Herren von Wintzingerode oft verpfändet war·
(Duval S. 231). Die andere Hälfte hatte Hans von Enzenberg
inne. (In den Dresdener Akten findet sich: Georg v. W.
Verlust zum Scharfenstein, Heinrichs v. W. Witwe desgl.
Enzenberg: Hälfte des Scharfensteins verbrannt.) Die
Verwüstung der Dörfer ist nicht ganz sicher; Wolf, Denkwürdigkeiten der Stadt Worbis, sagt darüber: „Denen von
Winzingerode sind vielleicht auch die 2 Dörfer Winzingerode
und Kaltenohmfeld von den Bauern vernichtet worden,
weil sich die von Bülzingsleben 1539 darüber beklagen,
daß man ihrem Gerichte zu Worbis, das sie pfandweise
besäßen, jene Orte entziehen wolle, da sie doch vor der
Verwüstung dabei erschienen wären."

Der Zug ging dann weiter auf Worbis, wo das Kloster
geplündert wurde. In den Dresdener Akten liegt darüber
folgendes Schreiben vor: „Wir Jost probst [1]), Anna priorin
und gantz convent gemeltes closter beclagen uns das wir
inn itzigen vorgangenen áuffruhr durch die von Molhaußen
geplundert unnd kirchenn sampt allenn eyngebew des
closters gebrant auch alle cleynoth unnd geschmeyde der
kirchenn sampt allem hausrath unnd sunderlich vyl kelche
auch zwey monstrancz hyn weg genommen, darzu hundert
sechzig sechs schafe uund ander vyhe sampt allen geschirr,
so zoum acker gehört, gewaltiglichen enteussert,· welchen
schaden wir auffs geringst uff zwelff hundert gulden ermessen, do mit obgemelt closter in vorigen standt uund
zcu zcurichten nicht moglich."

Duval (S. 187) berichtet: „Müntzer und Pfeiffer, als
sie auf dem Eichsfelde wüteten, fielen mit ihren Scharen,
zu denen sich viele Eichsfelder gesellt hatten, auch über
das Kloster Worbis her, plünderten es und steckten es
nachher in Brand"; Genaueres hat auch er offenbar nicht
gewußt. Da Nickel Heise nur 30 fl. zu zahlen waren
(Chronik, S. 209), so werden die vor Worbis und Breitenworbis

---

[1]) Jodocus Stowffenbuel; Förstemann, Kl. Schr., S. 100.

gelegenen „Heisengüter" nicht viel gelitten haben. (Wolf, Denkwürdigkeiten der Stadt Worbis, S. 87—88; über den Zug der Bauern weiß auch er nichts weiter zu berichten). Daß Pfeifer — wohl auch Münzer — ·hier noch bei dem Haufen war, ergibt sich aus der Aussage in St.A. S. 151: „Pfeifer habe ihn vor Duderstadt gefänglich annehmen und mit dem Haufen vor Breiten-Worbis geschraubt und ge- bunden führen lassen, daselbst ihn vor dem Haufen für Recht stellen und beklagen lassen. Da habe er, Zeuge, um Gottes willen gebeten, ihn ledig zu lassen, angesehen seine Unschuld, darauf der Haufe ihn ledig erkannt und gelassen." Von Worbis aus wandten sich später (Förstemann, Kl. Schr., S. 100) 8 Brüder und Vettern von Bülzingsleben an den Rat von Nordhausen. Sie hatten die Güter der dorthin geflüchteten, aus Worbis ausgetretenen Männer in Beschlag genommen, den „langen Jacoff" erwischt und hin- richten lassen. Am 23. Mai 1526 forderten „Alle von Bülzingsleben" die Kirchenkleinodien zurück, die sie im Bauernaufruhr dem Rat zu Nordhausen in Verwahrung ge- geben hatten; da der Propst zu Worbis und 2 Kirchen- vormunde die Quittung über den Empfang der Monstranzen und des übrigen ausstellten, so werden diese Kleinodien wohl aus Worbis gestammt haben.

Mit Worbis hatte Pfeifer ältere Beziehungen, vgl. Heft 1, 48; auch berichtet Sittich v. Berlepsch (Forschungen XI, 385) aus früherer Zeit: „Es haben etliche zu Stadt- worbis in der von Bolzingsleben. Gebieten einen Priester gestürmt und noch einen Priester die andere Nacht auch stürmen wollen, deshalb die von Bolzingsleben sich fast beschwert und Leute dabei gelegt. Als die Stürmer ge- kommen, haben sie zu ihnen einfallen und sie annehmen lassen. Da haben derselben Freundschaft zu Worbis sich etliche versammelt und dieselben angenommenen entwehrt, daß ihnen also zusammen 25 entlaufen; die haben die von Mühlhausen in ihre Stadt gelassen, ihnen Geleit gegeben und der deutschen Pfarrhöfe einen eingethan."

Weiter östlich wandte sich der Haufe zur **Zerstörung** der Harburg (Horburg). Auch hier fehlt es fast ganz an Nachrichten. Duval (S. 310) schreibt: „1525, als der Bauernkrieg wütete, kam der tobende Haufe auch in diese Gegend, rückte vor die Harburg, nahm sie ein, plünderte sie aus und zündete sie an. Die hier und auf dem Scharfensteine gemachte Beute wurde auf 9 Wagen von dannen geführt". In den Dresdener Akten liegen auch hier die Verzeichnisse des erlittenen Schadens: „Dis sint die verluste, so wir Henrich und Rudolff von Butzigsleben die jungern zur Horborgk von den von Molhusen und yrim anhang gelitten. Erstlich ist das haus Horborgk uns der helffte gewest, darauff wir haus gehaltenn, das zimlich und zum Teil newerlich durch unsern vater seligk Erbawet gewesen, das von den von Molhusen rein aus gebranth samt der vorborgk und unser solch hauß des stifftes Mentz eygentum und unser pfanth." — „Nach folgende bescheddigunge haben dy von Molhusen mit irem anhangk Heinrich von Bulzingsleben amptman zum Glichenstein zugefügt. Erstlich mynen teyll an der Horborgk samt myner vettern behusunge yst Mentzsch pfantschafft ausgebranth. — Rudolf der ältere v. B.: myn teil zur Horborgk — der schade am hauße zu Heigenrode [Haynrode] — das hauß in Gernrode ist abgebrandt." In dem „Schadegeldt nach dem Bawrenlerm" (Chronik, S. 208) mußte Mühlhausen zahlen an Seiffart von B. 500 fl., „darin der brandschaden des schloßes Horburg, so allen von Bultzingisleben zustendig, dweil ehs mentzisch pfant, nicht gezogen". Rudolf v. B. der Ältere erhielt 500 fl., Heinrich der Ältere 200 fl., Heinrich und Rudolf die Jüngeren 1000 fl. Wenn Duval, dem die in der Chronik benutzten Akten bekannt gewesen sind — mittelbar? — hinzusetzt, daß die adligen Herren diese Summen „wahrscheinlich niemals erhalten haben", so hat er dabei schwerlich das dicke Bündel der Abrechnungen durchstudiert, das leider noch ungeordnet in unserem Archive ruht. — Georg Scharf (vgl. S. 72) bekannte, daß er aus Siegfrieds (Seiffarts) v. B.

Hause einen Scheffel Korn bekommen, mit seiner Gesellschaft die Pfanne zu Heygenrode gelanget und nach Worbis gebracht habe (Duval S. 311, Förstemann, Kl. Schr., S. 86). Einiges der Güter, die Rudolf von Bülzingsleben in „Heigenrode" geraubt waren, war nach Nordhausen gekommen, wo später die Auslieferung verlangt wurde (Förstemann, Kl. Schr., S. 100).

Auch hier erwecken die Zeugenaussagen Zweifel, ob alle diese Zerstörung dem heranziehenden Haufen zuzuschreiben ist. Ein Zeuge berichtet (St.A. S. 68, 145), „er habe von seinem Junker Seifart von Bulzingsleben sagen gehört, daß das Schloß Horburg und Kloster Worbis zuvor und ehe der große Haufe dahin gekommen, ausgebrannt gewesen sein sollen". Ein anderer sagt aus (S. 147), „er habe hören sagen, daß Worbis und Horburg durch ihre eigenen Leute verbrannt worden; ob es also sei, oder nicht sei, davon weiß er nichts zu sagen". Weiter gibt ein Zeuge (S. 167) an, Horburg sei vor dem Zuge geplündert worden, dagegen erklärt ein anderer (S. 149), „das wisse er wohl, daß Pfeifer und Münzer samt ihren Anhängern solch Kloster und Schloß (Worbis, Horburg) verbrannt und geplündert haben". Schließlich erzählt ein Zeuge (S. 170), Bodenstein, Kloster Worbis und Horburg, diese drei wären auf einen Tag und Stunde verbrannt worden, das habe er gesehen.

„Dienstages nach Misericordias Domini [2. Mai][1]) sprach Münzer, ihm wäre im Traum angezeigt, er sollte nach Aufgang der Sonne ziehen, darum sprach er: Wer nicht gern will, der mag heimziehen. Da verliefen sich etliche Hessen und Eichsfelder, er aber mit den andern zog wieder gen Mühlhausen" (Chronik, S. 189).

Die Rechnung, die man Mühlhausen machte, erstreckte sich noch weiter. In den Dresdener Akten findet sich auch ein Verzeichnis „us der Graffschafft Hoenstein geystlicher

---

1) Daß das Datum falsch ist, haben wir schon oben (S. 65) gesehen.

und der vom adell empfangener schadenn"; unter der Auf-
schrift steht „Mulhaußen". Wir finden hier verzeichnet:
„Wolff Schmidt zu Bleichenrode pfarrer, er Johann Schmidt
(desgl.), er adam Korber vicarius (desgl.), er Nicolaus
vicarius (desgl.), er Johan Wihemut zu Elende vicarius, er
Valentin Eckenbrecht vicarius zu Elende, schaden der kirchen
zu Elende, er Heinrich Hartung vicarius zu Elendt, er
Heinrich Haydorn vicarius in exilio, Hermann Haydorn
bruder zu S. Annen zu Hauroden, Grethe Spiegels, Grethe
Spiegels tochter, die von Bursfelde, er Johann Schnetteler
zu Blicherode. Item vorzeichnus des schadens, so an den
zweien geistlichen jungfraw closter zu Monchenlohra und
Dittenborn in der Grafschaft Lohra gelegen gescheen, Ernst
Windolt, Heinrich Meysse, Nickel Heysse." — Die 3 letzten
finden sich in der Chronik S. 209. Kloster Dietenborn
wurde von den Landleuten der Umgegend ausgeplündert.
(Duval in „Thüringen und der Harz" VIII, S. 271.) Dann
folgen noch Hans von Entzenberg, Ursula Reinhardt von
Westhusen selig Wittfrau (Chronik S. 209, vgl. oben
S. 64).

Der Zug fand noch ein Nachspiel, das wir doch an
dieser Stelle nicht vergessen wollen. Unsere Chronik
(S. 198—199) berichtet: „Da nun solches alles geschehen, ließen
die Kur- und Fürsten durch einen von Schonberg[1]) in der
ganzen Stadt öffentlich einen Frieden und Sicherheit allen
Bürgern und Untertanen ausrufen, darauf dann viele Untertanen von den Dörfern mit dem, was sie in die Stadt geflohen, wiederum zu Haus zogen. Denselben wurden auch
Friedebriefe gegeben, daran der Fürsten Wappen gemalet,
die sie öffentlich anschlugen an ihre Tore, verhofften, sie
wollten also ferner unbeschädiget bleiben. Aber dessen
allen ungeachtet haben die eichsfeldischen Edelleute und
andere, so auf Schloß Rusteberg gelegen, deren Hauptmann
Hans von Mingerode gewesen (vgl. oben S. 44), item mit

---

1) Wolf von Schönberg.

ihm die Vögte Matthes Huneborn und der Propst zu Anroda,
Arnold Luckart, auch der geistliche Mönch und Daniel, der
schwarze Mönch, Matthias zu Reifenstein den armen Leuten
ihren Jammer gemehret und großen Mutwillen mit ihnen
getrieben. Denn erstlich haben sie dem Rate zu Mühlhausen
zwo Warten, als den Ziegenrain und Eichel, ausgebrannt
und zerstöret; danach haben sie das Vieh zu Dörna, Hollenbach und Lengefeld alle genommen und hinweggetrieben,
die Kirchen beraubt, die Häuser geplündert, letztlich die
Dörfer angezündet und dergestalt erbärmlich verbrannt, daß
zu Dörna nicht mehr zwei, zu Lengefeld drei und die Kirche,
zu Hollenbach gar wenig Häuser geblieben sind. Der Vogt
Matthes Huneborn auf dem Scharfenstein (Gleichenstein vgl.
oben S. 62) sagte zu Lengefeld zu den armen Leuten, als sie
auf dem Kirchhofe saßen: ‚Seid ihr noch Martinisch? Wir wollen euch Lutherischen Buben jetzt lehren', und ist darauf in
die Kirche gefallen, hat dieselbe beraubt und das Dorf angesteckt. Dieser Schade, von den Eichsfeldischen den Tag
geschehen, ist an 21 000 fl. allein geachtet worden. So
hatten zuvor Kersten von Schmalstieg und der von Benne-
burg[1]) mit dem einen Auge und die Hessischen das Dorf
Eigenrieden geplündert und gar in Grund hinweggebrannt,
daß nicht ein Haus geblieben. Als nun die letzten Feuer
zu Dörna, Lengefeld und Hollenbach von den Türmen in
der Stadt gemeldet wurden, und es die im Lager gesehen,
haben sie etliche Reiter zu den Eichsfeldischen abgefertigt,
die ihnen angezeigt, es wäre ein Friede bedingt, sie sollten
nicht mehr brennen; darauf sie miteinander ins Lager
geritten. Da nun die armen Leute solchen großen Schaden,
der ihnen im Friedestande zugefüget, weinend geklagt, tat
der Herzog von Braunschweig die gnädige Bitte für sie,
daß ihnen die Eichsfelder etlich Vieh wieder gaben.“

   Dieser Erzählung läßt sich aus den Akten noch mancherlei hinzufügen, besonders aus denen, die wir dem

---

   1) Boyneburg.

Rechtsstreit „Mühlhausen gegen Mainz" verdanken (K. 3, Nr. 18). S. 134b. Es soll gefragt werden: „Ob nicht die Kur- und Fürsten vor Mühlhausen gezogen sind und die obgemeldeten auf dem Hause Rustenberg gelegenen zu sich erfordert haben, ... sie darauf dahingezogen und etliche Wagen mit Proviant mit sich genommen, daß der gemeldete Abt, auch der Vogt zu Rustenberg und Mathes Hindeborn mit denselbigen Proviantwagen gezogen und dabei auch bis ins Lager geblieben seien." Zeuge erzählt, er sei als ein reisiger Knecht der Junker von Winzingeroda mit in das Lager gezogen, und hat gesehen, daß des andern Tags [27. Mai] Pfeifer samt etlichen Bürgern und Bauern gerichtet worden. Drei Stunden, ehe der Haufe (der Adligen) ins Lager gekommen, sei der Abt (von Reifenstein?) ins Lager bei Nacht mit Kuntze Gutghar zu Rustenberg — Zeuge S. 141 setzt noch den Amtmann auf dem Eichsfelde, Bernhard von Hartungen dazu — vorgeritten. Der Vogt zu Rustenberg, der Abt und Wolf Zeisig, diese 3 seien mit den Proviantwagen vor ihrem Haufen (gezogen).

Auf diesem Zuge in das Lager der Fürsten kamen die Adligen, etwa über Bickenriede, in das mühlhäusische Gebiet, das sie sofort als feindliches behandelten, um an ihm die Verwüstung der eigenen Schlösser und Klöster zu sühnen. In den Akten wird nun festzustellen gesucht, ob bei ihrem Einrücken in das städtische Gebiet der Friede, wie ihn im Namen der Fürsten Wolf von Schönberg verkündigt hatte, bereits in den Dörfern bekannt, die Friedebriefe angeschlagen waren. Darüber finden sich mancherlei Aussagen, aus denen hier einige hervorgehoben werden mögen. So berichtet Zeuge S. 135: „Die vom Adel seien durch die Bauernschaft von dem Ihrigen, Weib und Kind verjagt worden und auf Rustenberg zusammengekommen, sich daselbst zu rüsten, daselbst den bäurischen Haufen zu erwarten, Leib und Leben bei einander zu lassen. Als nun Gott Glüek gegeben, daß die Fürsten den bäurischen Haufen

geschlagen und auch vor Mühlhausen gelegen, hätten sich
diese Edelleute auf Rustenberg zu Hauf getan und zu den
Fürsten vor Mühlhausen kommen wollen, wie denn geschehen; damit er, Zeuge, als ein reisiger Knecht seines
Junkers von Winzingerode mitgezogen." Weiterer Bericht
lautet (S. 135): „Kunz Gutjahr, der Vogt, und der Abt
zu Reifenstein seien zuvor, ehe der Haufe von Rustenberg
gezogen, mit den Proviantwagen in das Lager vor Mühlhausen gekommen. Als dann die vom Adel, so auf Rustenberg gelegen, zu den Fürsten ins Lager gen Mühlhausen
hätten ziehen wollen und zwischen die 3 Dörfer gekommen
wären, habe er, Zeuge, gesehen, daß die 3 Dörfer gebrannt.
Indem wären auf die 200 Pferde von den Fürsten von
Mühlhausen ihnen entgegengekommen, also, daß nicht weit
gewesen wäre, daß die beiden Haufen einander geschlagen,
und jede Partei hätte schon ihren Vorteil genommen und
geschickt zu schlagen gehalten. — Dazwischen hätte man
Sprache gehalten, und sei also der Sachen eins geworden,
daß beide Haufen zufrieden und nach dem Lager gezogen
seien." Genaueres über die Absendung dieser Reiterschar
aus dem Lager der Fürsten erfahren wir S. 136b: „Als
die Dörfer gebrannt und alle Dinge hinweggenommen, wären
die Nachbarn aus diesem Dorfe zu den 3 Fürsten, so vor
Mühlhausen gelegen, gekommen, hätten solchen ihren Schaden,
der ihnen über den ausgerufenen Stillstand geschehen, geklagt, hätten sie wohl bei 600 Pferden dem Haufen in den
Dörfern, so gebrannt, entgegen geschickt. Wären die beiden
Haufen mit einander in der Fürsten Lager gezogen, das
hätte er gesehen."

Genaueres erfahren wir über die Zerstörung von Dörna.
Zeuge S. 137b erzählt: „Als er vor seiner Herrschaft von
dem Eichsfelde geflohen, wäre er zu Dörna gewesen und
hätte sich heimlich daselbst aufgehalten, wären die Nachbarn aus der Stadt gen Dörna heimgekommen, hätten zum
Teil das Ihre mitgebracht, hätten sie ihm gesagt, wie die
Fürsten auf denselbigen Tag, der da war Ascensionis Do-

mini [1]) einen Frieden ausgerufen, daß jedermann sollte heimziehen und sicher sein, und hätten Friedebriefe mit sich
gebracht und dieselben Briefe denselben Tag oder den
nächsten Morgen an die 2 Tore [2]) angeschlagen, das habe
er gesehen; das Wappen der Fürsten habe an den Briefen
gestanden. — — Als er bei den Nachbarn auf dem Kirch-
turme den nächsten Freitag nach Ascensionis Domini gewesen, hätte er samt den andern droben gesehen, daß ein
Haufe zu Roß und zu Fuß vom Eichsfelde her den Warten
zugezogen, wären dieselben Warten angesteckt und verbrannt. Derselbe Haufe hätte sich zerteilt, ein Teil still
gehalten, auf 7 oder 8 Reiter sich gen Dörna vor das Tor
getan und hätten hinein gewollt; hätten die Nachbarn auf
dem Kirchturm 2 aus ihnen zu denselben an das Tor geschickt, zu fragen, was sie wollten. Hätten dieselbigen
Reiter ihnen zweien zu Antwort gegeben, sie suchten 2
Eichsfelder, deren er, Zeuge, einer und sein Gesell von
Bickenriede der andere. Also wären die 2 Gesandten zu
ihnen auf den Kirchturm gekommen, hätten solches an-
gesagt und sie zwei nicht mehr bei ihnen haben wol'ən;
also hätten sie seinem Gesellen Weibskleider gebracht, die
er angetan und also davongekommen, und er, Zeuge, sei
über die Kirchhofsmauer hinausgefallen und habe sich in
Hecken und Genicke [3]) gesteckt und verborgen. Als demnach sie zwei hinweggekommen wären die Tore geöffnet,
und das Dorf Dörna angesteckt." Diese Erzählung ergänzt
ein anderer Zeuge (136—137): „Als er und seine Nachbarn
zu Dörna auf dem Kirchturm gewesen, hätten er und
andere da oben gesehen, daß Reiter und Fußgänger auf

---

1) Bekanntlich zogen an diesem Tage (25. Mai) die Fürsten in
Mühlhausen ein.

2) Das Dorf war durch den „Dorfhagen", einen mit Holz be-
standenen Wall, befestigt (Sommer, Bau- und Kunstdenkmäler des
Kreises Mühlhausen S. 15).

3) Vgl. das „Geneige" unseres Gebietes. Chronik I, 17.

dem Felde gehalten und sich gegen das Dorf gewendet hätten. Hätten die von Dörna 2 aus ihnen zu demselbigen Haufen geschickt, zu erforschen, was sie wollten, darauf ihnen aus demselbigen Haufen geantwortet sei, sie wollten 2 Eichsfelder bei ihnen suchen; wäre der eine sein Bruder gewesen, den sie suchten, also wäre er mit seinem Bruder ab dem Turme gestiegen und hätte ihm davon wollen helfen, da wären etliche von dem Haufen vor dem Tore gestanden, unter denen er Lukarden und den schwarzen Daniel, so ein Reifensteiner Mönch gewesen, und Liborius Thonhose, der Zeit ein Obervogt zu Rustenberg, gekannt hätte, welcher ihm und andern zu Dörna, so auf dem Tor (Turm?) gewesen, gerufen, zu ihnen zu kommen, sie sollten Leibes und Lebens sicher sein, ihnen sollte nichts geschehen, und hätten von ihm, seinem Bruder und anderen die Gelübde genommen von wegen des Bischofs zu Mainz. So wäre die Kirche geöffnet von etlichen, die geflohen aus der Kirche und über die Mauer gefallen wären. (?) Wären dieselben, auch Mathes Hundeborn und etliche vom Haufen, so vorm Tore gehalten, Reiter und Fußgänger in die Kirche gelangt, hätten geplündert und genommen, was sie gefunden, hin und wieder im Dorfe gelaufen, das Feuer angesteckt und brennen lassen und demnach dem Lager des Fürsten zu Mühlhausen zugezogen, und wäre ihnen ein Haufe von Mühlhausen entgegen gekommen und sie als miteinander in das Lager der Fürsten gezogen." Weiter erzählt ein Zeuge: „Als der Friede zu Mühlhausen ausgerufen, derzeit er, Zeuge, noch zu Mühlhausen gewesen, hätte der Wächter auf dem Turme 3 Feuer geblasen, darauf man gefraget, wo das wäre, hätte der Türmer gesagt, es wäre Dörna, da er, Zeuge, wohnhaftig, Lengefeld und Hollenbach. Hätte der Freiherr von Schönberg den Nachbarn gesagt, sie sollten hinlaufen und löschen. Wäre er, Zeuge, gen Dörna seinem Hause zu gelaufen, hätte das Dorf Dörna in aller Höhe gebrannt, dabei hätte er gesehen Mathes Hundeborn,

Vogt auf Gleichenstein, und Lukharden, jetzt Propst zu
Anrode, auch hätte Lukhard selbst ein Haus angezündet,
das hätte er gesehen. Auch wäre Mathes Hundeborn auf
einem Pferde im Dorfe hin und wieder gerannt, hätte
diesen und jenen geschlagen, Kühe, Pferde und anderes,
was er bekommen, hinweggeführt und andere hinwegzu-
führen angewiesen, und wären sonst viel Reiter, auf
80 Pferde, und Fußgänger im Dorfe gewesen, die er nicht
gekannt. Nachdem die Häuser angesteckt, wären sie vor
den Kirchhof gekommen, hätten sie die Bauern gezwungen,
die Kirche zu öffnen. Das wäre geschehen, wären diese Leute,
Reisige und Fußgänger, in die Kirche gelaufen und hätten
genommen alles, was sie darin gefunden, und mit sich
hinweggenommen. Auch hätte er gesehen, daß der Lukhard nach einem auf dem Kirchtor (Turm?) geschossen, der
hätte das Tor öffnen müssen."

Weitere Aussagen ergeben nun aber, daß die Dörfer
schon vorher (vgl. S. 84) von anderer Seite geplündert waren
(S. 138): „Da die Fürsten vor Mühlhausen gelegen, haben die
Hessischen und ihr Hauptmann Kersten Schmalstich (Schmal-
steygk) von Treffurt auf Ascensionis Domini um den Mittag
ungefähr in das Dorf Dörna gefallen und etwa die Hälfte
abgebrannt, auch die Schafe und Kleinvieh hinweggetrieben;
und folgenden Freitags naeh Ascensionis um den Mittag sei
es angesteckt worden durch den Haufen vom Eichsfeld"
S. 138b: „Außer dem, so an dem Dorf Junker Schmal-
stich samt seinen Reitern gebrannt, sei des andern Tages
durch den Haufen, so vom Eichsfelde gezogen, das Dorf
Dörna bis auf 2 Häuser und die Pfarre verbrannt." —
Noch genauer erzählt ein weiterer Zeuge (138b): „Als der
Friede ausgerufen, wären er und sein Vater der Zeit zu
Mühlhausen gewesen. Hätte der Vater zu ihm gesagt, der
Friede wäre von den 3 Fürsten ausgerufen, es sollte nun
jedermann sicher sein, und niemand nichts mehr geschehen.
Darauf habe Zeuge seinen Wagen geladen und, was er

hätte führen mögen mit 4 Pferden, wieder gen Dörna ge-
fahren· und abgeladen. Er wisse nicht, ob die Friedens-
briefe angeschlagen seien desselben Tages. Darauf desselbigen Tages wären etliche niederländische Reiter gekommen, hätten das Dorf Dörna angesteckt und zum Teil
verbrannt, dazu etlich Vieh auch genommen. Des andern
Tages hernach wäre ein Haufe vom Eichsfeld gekommen und
hätte das übrige geplündert und verbrannt; doch wären desselben Tages die Briefe an den Toren angeschlagen." Auch
ein weiterer Zeuge sagt, Dörna und Hollenbach seien zweimal in 2 Tagen nacheinander gebrannt. Auch die Plünderung des Dorfes Eigenrieden, wie sie unsere Chronik
erwähnt, bestätigt ein Zeuge: „Auf Ascensionis Domini sei
ein Haufe aus dem hessischen Lande dem Lager vor Mühlhausen zugezogen, der sei in Eigerode — in Dörna gefallen". — Einiges wichtige bietet dann folgende Aussage:
„Als auf Ascensionis Domini der Friede ausgerufen und
er, Zeuge, von seinem Vater mit den Wagen und Pferden
wieder gen Dörna geschickt, und er den Freitag danach
auch gen Dörna gekommen, wäre geboten worden zu
Dörna, welcher noch nicht den Fürsten gelobet, daß derselbige in das Lager der Fürsten käme und daselbst an-
gelobte. Also wären viele aus den Dörfern gen Mühlhausen in das Lager gekommen, den Fürsten zu Fuß gefallen und hätten um Gnade bitten müssen". Schließlich bietet
eine Aussage (S. 140) auch genaue Bestätigung der Erzählung in der Chronik: „Als der Haufe vom Eichsfeld
bei Dörna gekommen, wären 4 Reiter an das Tor zu Dörna
geritten und hätten hinein gewollt. Hätten die Bauern,
die auf dem Kirchturm versammelt, 2 aus ihnen zu denselbigen 4 geschickt, sie fragen lassen, was sie wollten.
Darauf dieselbigen zur Antwort gegeben, sie suchten zwei
ihrer Männer, darauf die ihnen wieder geantwortet, sie
wären der Fürsten und Friede sei ausgerufen, ihre Nachbarn wären im Lager und wollten deshalb Briefe

bringen. Dagegen habe Mathes Hundeborn gesagt, so sollten sie die Tore auftun und mit ihm in das Lager der Fürsten ziehn; meinten die Nachbarn, es sollte Glauben sein, und werden die Tore des Dorfes und Kirchhofes geöffnet. Hätte Zeuge gesehen, daß Mathes Hundeborn und einer, genannt Luckart, wären die vordersten gewesen, wären auf den Kirchhoff gekommen und hätten gesagt, ob sie Martinisch wären, hätte ihm ein Bauer geantwortet: Ja. Hätte er wieder gesagt: Seit ihr noch Martinisch und haltet deutsche [1]) Messen! Ich will euch eine deutsche Messe halten! und habe zu den andern gesagt: Steckt das Dorf an! und übel geflucht. — Auch hätte ihn, Zeugen, derselbige Matthes und noch einer mit einem Auge (vgl. S. 84; v. Beuneburg) gezwungen, das genommene Vieh zu helfen, mit ihnen zu treiben, und sie seien damit der Fürsten Lager zugerückt. Indem wären etliche Reiter aus der Fürsten Lager diesem eichsfeldischen Haufen entgegengeschickt, um das Brennen zu wehren, hätten sie die Bauern, so ihnen das Vieh hätten helfen treiben müssen, von sich gejagt und den Nachbarn gar nichts wiedergegeben." Eine besondere Nachricht gibt dann noch der Zeuge S. 141: „Als der Hauptmann der Edelen auf dem Rustenberge, Hans v. Minnigerode, mit seinem Haufen zum Ziegenrain, der Warte (Chronik S. 16), gekommen, hätte er den Matthes Hundeborn und seinen Untervogt gerufen, zu ihm zu kommen, hätte ihnen befohlen samt andern noch fünfen, daß sie das Dorf Dörna plündern und ausbrennen sollten; das wär also geschehen, und hätte er, Zeuge, auf einem Pferdlein gehalten und zugesehen." Nach diesen Ereignissen standen in Eigenrieden noch 3 Häuser, in Dörna etwa noch 6, in Hollenbach waren 4 Höfe abgebrannt, in Lengefeld standen noch 4 Häuser (N. M. 14, 407 vgl. S. 84). Die Gemeinde zu Dörna klagte am 3. Juni schriftlich bei Dr. v. Otthera, dem neuernannten Schultheißen,

---

1) Die hatte Münzer eingeführt. (Chronik 182, 186.)

daß sie an ihrer Behausung und ihren Gütern, ohne Ursache
am Aufruhr gewesen zu sein, merklichen Schaden durch
Feuer erlitten hätten, und baten um seine Vermittelung bei
Herzog Georg, dem Otthera die Klage alsbald übersandte.

Es ist ein reiches Detail, das unsere Akten bieten,
oft in recht lebhafter Färbung, der Schluß aber, der sich
daraus ergibt, ist doch nur ein einfacher, und es darf
wohl nun ausgesprochen werden, daß „denen von Mühlhausen" mancherlei zugeschoben ist, an dem sie nicht oder
nur wenig schuld waren. Ausgeplündert sind die Klöster
und Schlösser größtenteils von den Eichsfelder Bauern, doch
wohl den umwohnenden; als der Haufe heranzog, sind die
geplünderten und verlassenen Klöster und Schlösser angezündet worden, vielleicht aus Ärger, daß es nichts mehr
zu plündern gab. Das gilt freilich mit einiger Sicherheit
nur bis Heiligenstadt hin; darüber hinaus hört ja unsere
genauere Kunde auf.

Einige allgemeine, diese Auffassung bestätigende Zeugnisse stelle ich hier noch zusammen. S. 146b gibt ein
Zeuge an, „die Feldnachbaren hätten das Kloster (Name
fehlt) geplündert, ungefähr gleich nach Ostern Ursach seines
Wissens, denn Bernhard von Honten (Hartungen), gemeiner
Amtmann auf dem Eichsfelde, des Schreiber der Zeuge gewesen, der hätte samt seinen Reisigen etliche Bürger von
Heiligenstadt zu ihm gefordert, dieselben, so das Kloster
geplündert, schlagen (?!). — Das Kloster sei noch nicht
verbrannt gewesen, sondern nachmals geschehen." Dies letztere wird dann genauer wiederholt: „Als das obgemeldete
Kloster geplündert wäre, wäre über 3 oder 4 Tage ungefähr hernach der große Haufe, so man den Mühlhäusischen
genannt, vor Heiligenstadt gekommen; sei in demselben
Zuge seines Wissens das Kloster verbrannt worden."
S. 152: „Als die Prädikanten und der aufrührerische Haufe
von Orsla gen Heiligenstadt gezogen, seien die Schlösser

und Klöster geplündert gewesen, aber im Zuge gen Heiligenstadt seien sie durch diejenigen, so von dem Haufen
gelaufen, verbrannt worden, solch' Brennen habe er selbst
gesehen." S. 163: „Als der Haufe von Orsla auf Heiligenstadt zu gezogen sei, seien zuvor Schlösser und Klöster
geplündert und ausgebrannt, denn er von Gebelhausen
(vgl. S. 49), als er und die Eichsfelder zu ihnen gen Urbach gekommen, gehört, er und sein Anhang und der
Schlösser und Klöster Untertanen, hätten die Klöster und
Schlösser geplündert und verbrannt." S. 167: „Zuvor und
ehe die Prädikanten aufs Eichsfeld gen Heiligenstadt gezogen, seien durch die Eichsfelder Scharfenstein, Horburg,
Reifenstein, Kloster Worbis, Beuren und Teistungenburg
geplündert worden. Aber als der Haufe im Zuge gegen
Heiligenstadt gezogen, seien vermeldete Schlösser und
Klöster verbrannt worden. Er, Zeuge, habe gesehen, daß
die Eichsfelder die Schlösser und Klöster geplündert haben."
S. 178: „Er habe hören sagen, die Schlösser und Klöster
seien vorhin geplündert gewesen, ehe der Haufe gezogen;
als aber der Haufe zu Orsla gezogen nach Heiligenstadt,
hätten Schlösser und Klöster gebrannt."

Es wird ferner der Mühe wert sein, zu fragen, wer
denn eigentlich den Mühlhäuser Haufen gebildet hat. Früh,
schon im Beginne der Bewegung haben sich fremde Elemente in unsere Stadt gedrängt, deren Einfluß in anderem
Zusammenhange erörtert werden muß; hier muß doch
darauf aufmerksam gemacht werden, daß die kleine Stadt,
an deren Volkszählung vom Jahre 1525 (Chronik S. 215)
immer wieder erinnert werden möge, zu dem Haufen wirklich nicht viele ihrer Bürger oder Mitwohner entsenden
konnte. In den Akten liegen ja genug Aussagen vor über
die, welche mitgezogen waren, aber ihre Zahl ist doch
in Summa klein, wenn man an den großen Haufen denkt,
der gen Heiligenstadt zog. Fremde in Menge sind darin
vertreten gewesen, worüber ebenfalls Zeugnisse vorliegen.

So heißt es S. 151: „er sei mit dem aufrührerischen Haufen
der Zeit im Feldlager gezogen, in welchem Hessen, Mühlhäuser, Eichsfelder, vom Harze und sonst aus anderen
Orten gewesen." S. 178 erzählt ein Zeuge: „Vielerlei Volks,
als Sachsen, Hessen, Eichsfelder, Franken, Meißner und
andere seien mitgezogen, die alle gern reich und frei hätten
werden wollen." Zeuge S. 154b erzählt: „Die Prediger
sollen allenthalben hin geschrieben haben, also sind aus
Hessen, Sachsen, Eichsfeld viel zu ihnen gelaufen." Ein
anderer berichtet S. 155: „Hernach aus Hessen haben sich
von der Werra und allenthalben viel zu Pfeifer gen Mühlhausen getan, also daß der Anhang der Ausländer und der
Bürger so groß geworden, daß der Rat ihrem Mutwillen
nicht mehr hat vorkommen mögen." S. 161 heißt es,
Pfeifer habe sich einen großen Anhang gemacht von
Bürgern und ausländischen Bauern, und S. 172: „sei das
Volk allenthalben her Bürger, Eichsfelder und Sachsen in
ihre Predigt gelaufen." Leider ist keine Hoffnung vorhanden, daß wir über Pfeifers Bund, dessen Liste ich Heft 2,
S. 33—35 veröffentlicht habe, jemals genaueres erfahren.
Schließlich verweise ich noch auf das dort S. 36—37 ver-
öffentlichte Verzeichnis: „Disse Dorffe wye hernach folgendt
sint auch vf der Beschedigungk des Adels mit gewest."

„Alle Welt wollte von Mühlhausen entschädigt sein",
schrieb schon Seidemann, N. M. 14, 412. Herzog Georg,
der doch wahrlich Mühlhausen nicht freundlich gesinnt war,
ließ bei einer Tagung der Räte anbringen (N. M. 14, 417):
„Ernsten Windolt hätten der von Honstein Leute mehr
Schaden getan, als die von Mühlhausen", dennoch mußte
die Stadt Ernst und Hans Windolt 1200 Fl. zahlen (Chronik, S. 209). Der Erzbischof von Mainz forderte zunächst als
Entschädigung für die Klöster 18000 Fl. (N. M. 14, 423),
begnügte sich aber 1550 bei einem Vergleiche mit 3000 Fl.,
immerhin ein Beweis, daß der Schaden der Stadt nur zu
einem kleinen Teile zugeschoben werde konnte.

Schon in unserer Chronik tritt an einzelnen Stellen ein Streben hervor, die gegen die Stadt gerichteten Anklagen zurückzuweisen, wie ich denn auch nicht Stephan zustimmen kann, der für „die Beschreibung des Bauernkrieges" annahm, wahrscheinlich habe der Verfasser die Vorgänge selbst mitangesehen (Stofflieferungen II, S. 145). Vielmehr habe ich immer mehr den Eindruck gewonnen, daß unsere Akten dem Verfasser bei der Niederschrift nicht fremd gewesen sind. Man behauptete, der Haufe sei „mit der Stadt aufgerichtetem Fähnlein" ausgezogen (vgl. oben S. 56); daß das unmöglich war, soll die genaue Erzählung zeigen, wie der Stadt Fähnlein von Rodemann und Wettich entführt wurde; deshalb wird auch genau das weiße Fähnlein, „darin ein Regenbogen stund", beschrieben, mit dem Pfeifer und Münzer auszogen, ebenso das gelbgrüne Fähnlein des Eichsfelder Haufens. Absichtlich betont die Chronik (S. 187): „Bei diesem Haufen und Zuge sind wenig Bürger und kein Ratsherr von Mühlhausen gewesen" außer dem berühmten Jobst Homberg; war doch Klage erhoben, Mitglieder des Rates hätten den Haufen geführt. Auch was ich zuletzt zusammengestellt habe, faßt die Chronik dahin zusammen: „Das andere ist alles zusammengelaufen Volk gewesen." Genaueres Studium wird diesen Grundton der Darstellung in der Chronik wohl noch deutlicher nachweisen können. Ob sie damit recht hat, wird die vorliegende Untersuchung erkennen lassen; vielleicht dient sie dazu, daß man in Zukunft mit „denen von Mühlhausen" etwas gnädiger ins Gericht geht. Man vergleiche mit unserer Darstellung Mühlh. Gesch.-Bl. III, S. 64: „So singt Bernardus Americanus von Thomas Münzer und seinem ‚Speerarme‘, der noch rauchte von dem Blut der Edelleute"; hoffentlich wird man dann uns zustimmen, daß es Zeit ist, diese Dinge etwas genauer zu prüfen. Vielleicht vergißt man dabei auch folgende Stelle aus Münzers letztem Briefe (Seidemann S. 146) nicht, wohl dem einzigen Schreiben aus seinen letzten Jahren, in dem aufrichtiges

Gefühl nicht durch übertriebene Phrasen verhüllt ist: „Ich weyß das ewer der mehrer theyl in Molhoußen dysser uffrurischen und eygenutzigen emporung nihe anhengig gewest, szondern das allewege gerne gewerth und vorkomen" [1]).

---

[1]) Das kürzlich erschienene Werk von v. Wintzingeroda-Knorr, „Die Wüstungen des Eichsfeldes etc." konnte ich leider zu dieser Studie nicht mehr durcharbeiten (1060 Seiten!), doch möge wenigstens folgende Notiz zu S. 78 hier Platz finden: „Der jetzige Name Mühlhäuser Burg ist erst im 18. Jahrhundert gebräuchlich geworden" (S. 691). — Das S. 1020 für die Zerstörung des Schlosses Westernhagen gegebene Datum (1. Mai) wird kaum richtig sein, da der Haufe Dienstag den 2. Mai erst vor Heiligenstadt eintraf (vgl. oben S. 65). Die Sage von der Vernichtung der Familie v. Westernhagen bis auf einen Knaben wird auch hier als irrig bezeichnet, wie sie ja auch neben den von den Herrn v. W. erhobenen Forderungen (vgl. S. 74) lächerlich genug erscheint. Ich finde aber, selbst in der Sage, sonst keine weitere Gelegenheit, bei der das „Blut der Edelleute" vergossen sein könnte.

III.

Die vor- und frühgeschichtlichen Funde der Grafschaft Camburg.

Von

Dr. Gustav Eichhorn in Jena.

Mit 79 Abbildungen im Text.

Die vorliegende Arbeit ist das Resultat einer mehrjährigen Sammlung aller vor- und frühgeschichtlichen Funde, die im Saalegebiet in der Grafschaft Camburg gemacht worden sind. Das umfangreiche Material ist weit verstreut worden. Es sind Funde nach Berlin gekommen in das Museum für Völkerkunde, nach Meiningen in das Henneberger Haus, nach Jena in das Germanische Museum, nach Weimar in das städtische Museum, nach Coburg in die Sammlung des Anthropologischen Vereins; eine größere Sammlung vorgeschichtlicher Altertümer besitzt die Schule zu Eckolstedt, Herr Gutsbesitzer Becker in Schinditz, einige Stücke Herr Pfarrer Schröder in Hainichen, Herr Rittergutsbesitzer von Schönberg in Kreipitzsch, und heute noch gehen Fundobjekte in reichlicher Menge dem unermüdlichen Sammler Herrn Straßenbauverwalter Heim in Camburg zu. Ich habe die einzelnen Gegenstände genau gebucht, gezeichnet und beschrieben. Beim Abschluß der Arbeit bin ich nun lange unschlüssig gewesen, wie der umfangreiche Stoff am besten zu sondern und zu gruppieren wäre, ob ich die Funde aufzählen sollte nach den Fundorten oder

XXII.   7

nach dem jetzigen Verbleib in den genannten Sammlungen, oder ob ich eine zusammenhängende Darstellung der Vorgeschichte der Grafschaft Camburg geben und die hier gemachten Funde einflechten sollte. Schließlich bin ich zu dem Entschluß gekommen, die Funde zunächst n a c h   d e n F u n d o r t e n zusammenzustellen, jeden Fundgegenstand einzeln zu beschreiben und erst in einem Schlußkapitel einen Überblick der vor- und frühgeschichtlichen Entwickelung der Grafschaft Camburg auf Grund dieses Materials zu geben. Es wird auf diese Weise zwar der flüchtige Leser leicht ermüden, wenn er die trockene Aufzählung ganzer Serien von gleichartigen Steingeräten oder Schädelbeschreibungen durchmustert, doch geschieht damit dem Prähistoriker sowohl, wie der Landeskunde ein Gefalle, das weit verstreute Material dieser Gegend wenigstens in einer katalogartigen Zusammenstellung beieinander zu finden.

Die Fundgegenstände sind in ihrem Wert, d. h. in ihrer wissenschaftlichen Verwertbarkeit sehr verschieden. Wird ein Steinbeil z. B. eingeliefert ohne nähere Angabe der Fundstelle und der begleitenden Fundumstände, so hat es einen verhältnismäßig geringen Wert. Wir können nicht einmal mit Sicherheit sagen, ob es der Steinzeit angehört, da Steinbeile auch in der späteren metallischen Zeit noch häufig im Gebrauch waren. Wir bezeichnen ein derartiges Fundstück als „**Einzelfund**".

Wird uns aber z. B. glaubwürdig mitgeteilt, daß das Steinbeil innerhalb einer schwarzen Schicht Branderde auf einem sonst lehmfarbenen Acker beim Pflügen neben ornamentierten Gefäßscherben, Feuersteinmesserchen und Reibsteinen zu Tage gefördert worden ist, so läßt sich mit Sicherheit annehmen, daß es einer steinzeitlichen Wohnstätte entstammt. Wie hieraus erhellt, macht ein genauer Fundbericht, der präzise Angaben hinsichtlich des Fundortes und der begleitenden Fundumstände bringt, den Fund für das wissenschaftliche Studium zu einem bedeutend wertvolleren. Im Gegensatz zu den oben erwähnten Einzelfunden nennen wir derartige gleichzeitig an gleichem Orte zusammen gemachte Funde „**Gesamt-** oder **Gruppenfunde**".

Als Gesamtfunde sind dementsprechend anzuführen:

1) die Funde aus einer Wohnstätte „W o h n s t ä t t e n - f u n d e,

2) die Funde aus einem Grab, die „G r a b f u n d e",

3) die sogenannten „D e p o t f u n d e", d. h. Funde von Gegenständen, die in vorgeschichtlicher Zeit an einer Stelle in der Erde, z. B. unter einem großen Stein, in der Nähe eines Baumes oder im Wasser niedergelegt worden sind, sei es von einem fahrenden Händler, der in Zeiten der Gefahr diese Schätze vergrub, sei es von einem heimkehrenden Krieger, der dankerfüllt diese kostbaren Stücke nach glücklich bestandenem Kampfe seinen Göttern weihte.

Bei allen Gesamtfunden gilt es aber, genau zu beobachten. Es ist nicht immer richtig, alle an einem Wohnplatz, in einer Herdgrube gemachten Funde e i n e r Epoche zuzuteilen, da die Wohnplätze oft lange Zeit hindurch benutzt worden sind, und die unteren Schichten der Abfallgruben einer viel früheren Epoche angehören können als die oberen.

Ebenso sind auch die Grabhügel oft in zeitlich ganz getrennten vorgeschichtlichen Epochen als Bestattungsstellen benutzt worden. Es sind z. B. Grabhügel eröffnet worden, in welchen das Hauptgrab im Zentrum bereits in der Steinzeit angelegt worden war, während die oberen Hügelschichten Bestattungen aus der slavischen Zeit enthalten.

In der vorliegenden Arbeit sind diese äußerst wichtigen Gruppenfunde bei den betreffenden Fundorten vorangestellt.

Die Einzelfunde sind ihnen angereiht worden. Die Zeitschriften, Tageszeitungen, Abbildungen, die schriftlichen Notizen, welche die Funde schon in irgend einer Weise behandeln, sind quellenmäßig angegeben, ebenso wie der jetzige Aufbewahrungsort der Fundgegenstände bei jedem Stück verzeichnet ist.

7*

I. Die auf dem linken Ufer der Saale gelegenen Fundorte in der Grafschaft Kamburg.

1. Eckolstedt.

Steinzeitliche Wohnstätten.

Im Germanischen Museum zu Jena liegen eine große Anzahl von Tongefäßscherben, welche Herr Landwirt Carl Kunze aus Hirschroda bei Eckolstedt gesammelt und unserem Museum zu Klopfleischs Zeiten übergeben hat. Die Gefäßreste sind zumeist der Bandkeramik angehörig und stammen aus sogenannten Herdgruben steinzeitlicher Siedelungen. Im vergangenen Sommer habe ich mit Herrn Kunze eine Reihe derartiger Anlagen untersucht und neues Material derselben Art gesammelt.

Auf derartige Reste vorgeschichtlicher Wohnstätten wird man aufmerksam durch eine auffällige, schwarze Bodenfärbung, die ein meist kreisförmiges Stück auf dem sonst lehmfarbenen Ackerboden deutlich heraushebt. Besonders nach einem Regen sind die Stellen auf den frisch geackerten Feldern deutlich sichtbar. An senkrecht angeschnittenen Herdgruben sieht man, daß dieselben ursprünglich als cylinderförmige Gruben aus dem Boden ausgehoben worden sind mit senkrechten Wandungen, ihr Durchmesser schwankt von 1—2 m, ihre Tiefe beträgt $1/2$—1 m. Untersucht man derartige Stellen genauer, so findet man in der schwarzen Erde eine große Zahl Gefäßbruchstücke, die zunächst leicht zerbrechen, aber, lufttrocken gemacht, sehr rasch wieder erhärten, vereinzelt Holzkohle, Feuersteinsplitterchen oder -messerchen, Flintpfeilspitzen, Knochen von Tieren, zuweilen Steinbeile, Steinhacken, Reibsteine, Klopfer. Nach meiner Ansicht sind diese schwarzen Stellen auf den Äckern, die sogenannten Herdgruben, nicht Feuerstätten, d. h. Stellen, wo sich der Herd der primitiven Siedelung befunden hat, sondern Abfallgruben, die in der Nähe der leicht gebauten Wohnhütten, in den Boden vertieft, angelegt worden sind. Man bedurfte ihrer, um die Reste des Herdfeuers, die glühende Asche, aus der leicht brennbaren Hütte zu entfernen und sie unschädlich zu machen. Schließlich warf man auch alle Küchenabfälle, Tierknochen naeh der Mahlzeit, zerbrochene Töpfe, unbrauchbar gewordene Werkzeuge mit in die Grube.

Die Wohnstätten dieser steinzeitlichen Besiedler der Eckolstedter Flur lagen auf dem nord- und südöstlichen Hochplateau, zwischen denen sich das heutige Dorf ins Tal hinabzieht.

Die mir vorliegenden **Gefäßscherben** aus diesen Fundstellen gehören, wie eingangs erwähnt, in die Periode

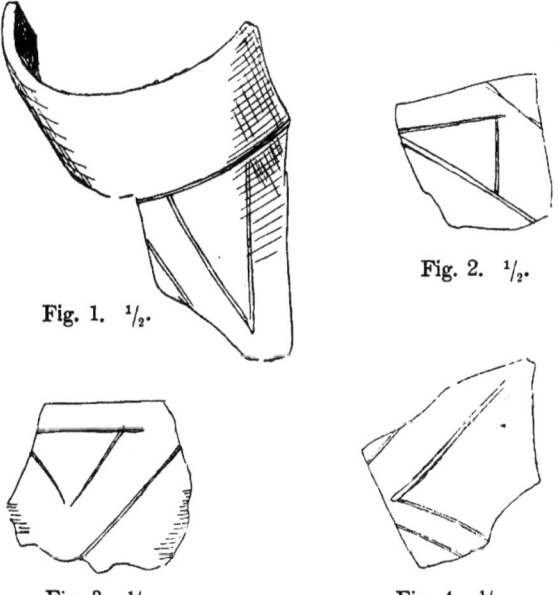

Fig. 1. ¹/₂.

Fig. 2. ¹/₂.

Fig. 3. ¹/₂.

Fig. 4. ¹/₂.

der Bandkeramik, also den letzten Abschnitt der jüngeren Steinzeit. Bekanntlich hat dieser Abschnitt der Vorgeschichte von der Verzierungsweise der Gefäße seinen Namen. Eingeritzte Linien umziehen geradlinig, in Winkeln

gebrochen, oder bogen-(spiral-)linig das ganze Gefäß.
Die Linien verlaufen zumeist parallel, zu Bändern geordnet. Klopfleisch führte daher die Namen „Winkelband" und „Bogenband" für diese Ornamentierung in
die Literatur ein. Zur ersten Gruppe gehören die Gefäßscherben, Fig. 1, 2, 3, 4, zur Bogenbandverzierung
Fig. 5, 6, 7. Wir wissen, daß die Bandkeramik aus Süd-

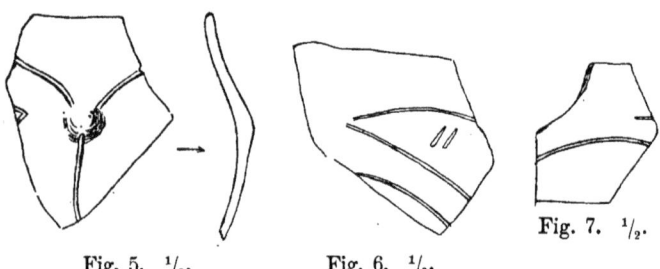

Fig. 5. ¹/₂.   Fig. 6. ¹/₂.   Fig. 7. ¹/₂.

deutschland zu uns nach Thüringen gekommen ist. Eine
neuerdings erschienene Arbeit von Dr. Schliz, „Das steinzeitliche Dorf Großgartach", bringt eine große Anzahl von
abgebildeten Gefäßbruchstücken, die in Ornamentierung,
Form und, wie die Beschreibung ergänzt, auch in der Masse
genau übereinstimmen mit den bandverzierten Gefäßresten
Eckolstedts.

Die uns erhaltenen Gefäßscherben sind R a n d-,
B a u c h-, B o d e n- und H e n k e l s t ü c k e. Ihrem Material,
ihrer Form, ihrer Verzierungsweise nach sind mit Sicherheit zwei Arten zu unterscheiden: 1) blaugraue, bräunlichgelbe
oder schwarze, hartgebrannte, d ü n n w a n d i g e Gefäße,
deren Masse mit feinem Sand versetzt ist, so daß sich dieselben feinsandkörnig anfühlen, und 2) schmutzig-ziegel-
farbene, grobgearbeitete, d i c k w a n d i g e, poröse Gefäße,
mit gröberen Quarzkörnern in der Tonmasse eingebettet.
Die ersteren sind kleinere, h a l b k u g e l f ö r m i g e Gefäße
mit weiter Mündung, gerad abgeschnittenem Rand, oder
größere, a m p h o r e n a r t i g e o d e r k u g e l f ö r m i g e Gefäße

mit engem, kurzem Hals, kugeligem Bauch und Boden. Die dickwandigen Gefäße sind groß, topfförmig. Auch hinsichtlich der Henkelbildung sind beide Gruppen wesentlich verschieden. Bei der ersten Sorte fehlen eigentliche Henkel. Von andern Fundstellen Thüringens wissen wir, daß derartige Kugelgefäße nur kleine Schnurösen

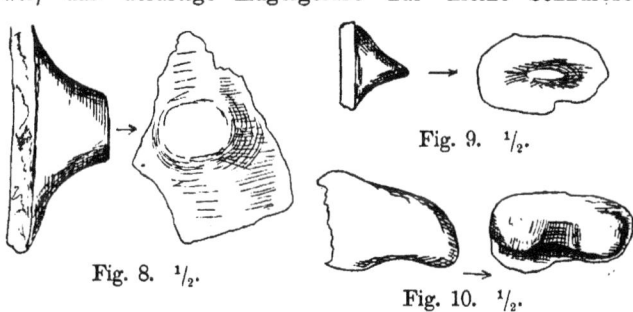

Fig. 9. ¹/₂.

Fig. 8. ¹/₂.

Fig. 10. ¹/₂.

haben. Auf den hierher gehörigen Eckolstedter Gefäßscherben haben wir nur runde, kleine, Warzen, die mehr zum Schmuck, z. B. als Abschluß eines linearen Bandmusters, angebracht sind (Fig. 5). An den größeren Gefäßen sind größere, undurchlochte Handhaben angebracht,

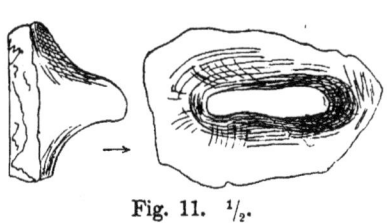

Fig. 11. ¹/₂.

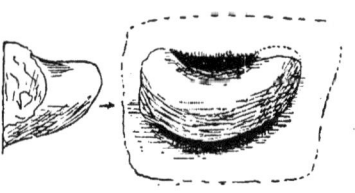

Fig. 12. ¹/₂.

kegelförmig mit plattgedrückter Spitze (Fig. 8), oder breitgedrückt, in ein oder zwei Spitzen auslaufend (Fig. 9, 10, 11), senkrecht aufsitzend auf der Wandung oder leicht nach abwärts gebogen. Daneben kommen quersitzende Bogenhenkel vor, zum Durchziehen einer Schnur berechnet,

(Fig. 12), mit geradflächiger oder schwach ausgemuldeter Ober- und gewölbter Unterseite. Die blaugrauen, bräunlichgelben und schwarzen, dünnwandigen Gefäße sind, wie erwähnt, mit der charakteristischen Linearzeichnung versehen (Fig. 1, 2, 3, 4 und 5, 6, 7). Vereinzelt ist der Bandcharakter der Verzierung durch eine ·Ausfüllung mit Tupfenstichen erhöht (Fig. 6). Von den Scherben der großen, grobwandigen Gefäße ist einer mit tiefen Fingerspitzen- und Nageleindrücken verziert, die in einer einfachen Reihe den Gefäßhals umzogen haben.

Auf ein eigentümlich verziertes, verhältnismäßig dickwandiges amphorenartiges Gefäß läßt ein Randstück schließen mit daranhängendem oberen Bauchteil (Fig. 13).

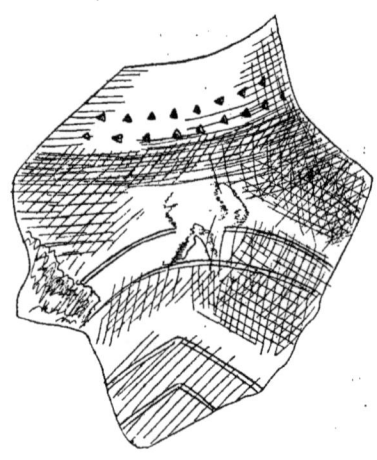

Das Gefäß hatte einen kurzen, gerad aufsteigenden Hals, eine enge Mündung. Der Mündungsrand ist glatt gestrichen, abgerundet, der Bauch kugelförmig. Den Hals umziehen am Grunde 2 parallele Reihen von tiefen Stichen, die mit einem dreieckigen Pfriemen ausgeführt sind. Den oberen Bauchteil zieren parallele, im Winkel gebrochene Linien, den Winkel überdacht ·ein

Fig. 13. ¹/₂.

Bogenband, dessen Gipfel sich dem Halse nähert. Abwechselnd mit diesem Bogen tritt daneben ein Winkelband an den Gefäßhals. Die Bandverzierung ist seitlich begleitet von kräftigen Wulsten, welche die Ornamentierung stark hervortreten machen. Das Gefäß ist aus schwarzem,

mit Kohle gemischtem Ton hergestellt, Wandung am Hals-
grund 9 mm stark; oberer Durchmesser 8 cm circa, Innen-
und Außenfläche schwarzglänzend.

Ein 7 mm wandstarker Gefäßscherben aus schwarzem
Ton ist mit Quarzstückchen in Stecknadelkopfgröße durchsetzt, Außen- und Innenfläche geglättet, die Außenfläche
mit kleinen, getupften Ovalen verziert (Fig. 14).

Die gleiche Verzierung zeigt der Bauchteil eines Rand-
stückes, das einem größeren Napf angehört, mit glattgestrichenem Rand. Das Material ist dasselbe.

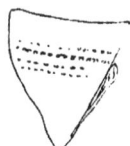

Fig. 14. ¹/₂.   Fig. 15. ¹/₂.

Zwei kleinere Gefäßbruchstücke: ein dünnwandiges
Randstück aus graublauem Ton und ein innen graues, an
der Außenfläche schmutzig-ziegelfarbenes Gefäßbruchstück
sind mit schmalem Furchenstich verziert nach Art der
Monsheimer Gefäße (Fig. 15, 16).

Fig. 16. ¹/₂.   Fig. 17. ¹/₂.

Aus der steinzeitlichen Ansiedelung stammen eine Anzahl **Wandbewurfstücke** aus Lehm im Jenaer Museum.
Ferner ein spitzer **Knochenpfriemen** (Fig. 17).

Einzelfunde.

Die S c h u l e in E c k o l s t e d t bewahrt eine reiche
Sammlung von Steingeräten. Die meisten Fundobjekte sind
— mineralogisch betrachtet — Diabase, kommen im Saale-

schotter vor und treten im Fichtelgebirge auf. Aus Feuerstein ist bisher nur e in Steinbeil auf Eckolstedter Flur
gefunden worden. An einen Kampf auf der Höhe Eckolstedts während der Steinzeit ist nicht zu denken, wie vermutungsweise zur Erklärung der großen Zahl von ganzen
und zerbrochenen Steinwaffen ausgesprochen worden ist.
Es sind vielmehr einzeln aufgelesene Funde aus jenen oben
erwähnten steinzeitlichen Wohnstätten. Wie die Menge
der gesammelten Steingeräte beweist, muß das steinzeitliche
Dorf ein großes gewesen sein. Die Bewohner haben sich
auch sicherlich mit der Massenfabrikation der Steinwerkzeuge beschäftigt, da eine Reihe halbvollendeter Beile, an-
gebohrte Steinäxte, Bohrzapfen als unbrauchbar wegge-
worfene Bruchstücke aufgefunden worden sind.

Die Eckolstedter Schulsammlung bietet mir Gelegenheit, gleich von vornherein, bestimmte

Typen der Steinwerkzeuge

aufzustellen, die immer wiederkehren und mit deren voraus-
genommener Charakterisierung ermüdende Wiederholungen
vermieden werden können.

I. Steinbeile.

Wir sehen Steingeräte in Keilform (S t e i n k e i l e), die,
hochkant, d. h. auf die Schmalseiten gestellt, mit ihrer gut
geschliffenen S c h n e i d e, den zwei symmetrischen S e i t e n -
w a n g e n, dem Rücken oder B a h n e n d e.im ganzen unseren
Beilen gleichen und wie diese zum Zerspalten weicherer
Objekte verwendet wurden. Diese Steinbeile wurden
in einen oben gespaltenen Knüttel mit dem Bahnende hin-
eingezwängt und durch umgewickelte Lederstreifen oder
Schnuren festgehalten. Das Bahnende wurde im ganzen
bei der Herstellung, bei der Glättung der Steinbeile, da
es im Holz stak, weniger sorgfältig bearbeitet als Schneide
und Seitenwangen. Auch die Schmalseiten blieben oft unbearbeitet. Es deutet schon auf eine bessere Kunstfertig-

keit, wenn wir ein Steinbeil vor uns liegen sehen mit gut geglätteten Schmalseiten und sorgfältig gearbeitetem Bahnende. Die Steinbeile sind undurchlocht. Ihrem Querschnitt nach unterscheiden wir v i e r k a n t i g e und b i k o n - v e x e, nach der gegenseitigen Richtung der Schmalseiten Steinbeile m i t p a r a l l e l v e r l a u f e n d e n S c h m a l - s e i t e n, mit k o n v e r g i e r e n d e n S c h m a l s e i t e n, mit v e r j ü n g t e m, mit s p i t z e m B a h n e n d e. Bei der Beschreibung und Messung denken wir uns das Steinbeil hochkant gestellt: infolgedessen reden wir von einer S c h n e i d e n h ö h e, von einer g r ö ß t e n B r e i t e des Beils, von links nach rechts gemessen, von einer B e i l l ä n g e, von vorn nach hinten gemessen.

Bei der Mehrzahl der Steinbeile verjüngt sich der Körper des Beils allmählich naeh dem Bahnende zu, sehr selten ist die a b s a t z w e i s e V e r l ä n g e r u n g d e s S c h n e i d e n t e i l s n a c h u n t e n.

Einzig in seiner Art unter den Steinbeilen der Grafschaft Camburg ist ein Steinbeil mit dünnem, breitem Schneidenteil und s c h a r f a b g e s e t z t e m, s c h m ä l e r e m, abgerundetem Bahnendenteil. Es erinnert in seiner Form an die Absatzcelte, eine Bronzebeilform, die einen Quersteg zwischen Schaftteil und Schneidenteil haben, damit das Beil beim Schlag nach hinten nicht ausweichen kann. Entsprechend diesem bronzenen Absatzcelt können wir es A b s a t z b e i l nennen.

Zur größeren Festigung der Steinbeile am Schaft und zur hammerartigen Verwendung des stumpfen Bahnendes versah man die Steinbeile mit einer quer über die Mitte des Beilkörpers verlaufenden R i l l e. In diese Rille hätte man die Griffgabel stecken und die Kreuzstelle mit Schnuren fest umwickeln können. Die mir bisher bekannten q u e r - g e r i l l t e n S t e i n b e i l e haben aber alle eine geradflächige Schmalseite und eine gewölbte, und diese Eigentümlichkeit gibt uns einen Anhalt für die Art der Befestigung mit dem Griff. Das Beil wurde nämlich mit dieser geradflächigen

Schmalseite auf den einen Arm eines rechtwinklig gebogenen Holzgriffes mit Lederriemen fest aufgeschnürt, die ihrerseits in der Rille ihren Halt fanden. Diese Form der Steinbeile ist selten.

A. Vierkantige Steinbeile mit breitem Bahnende, Schneiden- höhe gleich oder wenig höher als mittlere Beilhöhe, **deutliche Schmalseiten, Seitenwangen flach gewölbt oder gerade.** (Fig. 18, 19) [1]).

Steinbeil, mittelgroß, schön geschliffen, Seitenwangen flach gewölbt, Schmalseiten geradflächig, Schneidenhöhe gleich der Höhe des Bahnendes, Schneide gebogen; aus Diabas. Länge 11 cm, Schneidenhöhe 4 cm, Schwere 227 g. (ES 58.)

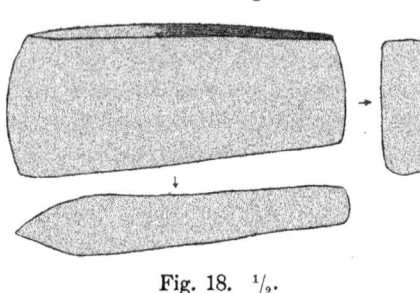

Fig. 18. $^1/_2$.

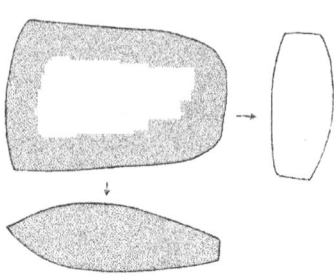

Fig. 19. $^1/_2$.

Steinbeil mittelgroß (Fig. 18), schön geschliffen an der Schneide und den geradflächigen Schmalseiten, nach dem Bahnende sich kaum verjüngend. Seitenwangen roh, Schneide gebogen, Bahnende abgerundet; aus Grauwacke, Länge 9,5 cm, Schneidenhöhe 4 cm, Schwere 121 g. (ES 31.)

Mittelgroßes, dickes Steinbeil, geschliffene Schneide und Schmalseiten, Seitenwangen flach gewölbt, nach dem Bahnende sich kaum verjüngend, Schneide gebogen, Bahnende roh; aus kristall. Schiefer. Länge 11,2 cm, Schneidenhöhe 4 cm, Schwere 215 g. (ES 57.)

Kleines Steinbeil, gut erhalten, leicht gewölbte Seitenwangen, nach dem Bahnende zu sich etwas verjüngend, geradflächige Schmalseiten, geglättetes Bahnende; aus Diabas. Länge 6,3, Schneidenhöhe 3,5, Schwere 70 g. (ES 15.)

Schön erhaltenes, gut poliertes, vierkantiges, geschliffenes Stein-

---

1) In den folgenden Aufzählungen sind die Funde, welche im Berliner Völkermuseum aufbewahrt werden, mit BV, die des Germanischen Museums zu Jena mit GMJ, die der Schule zu Eckolstedt mit ES bezeichnet, die des Henneberger Hauses in Meiningen mit HH, die in Heims Privatsammlung mit HPS.

beil mit scharfer, gebogener Schneide, flach gewölbten Seitenwangen; Schmalseiten flach gewölbt, nach dem Bahnende zu sich leicht verjüngend, Bahnende geschliffen; aus Diabas. L. 7,0, Schneidehöhe 4,6, Gewicht 88 g. (ES 28.)

Kleines, gut erhaltenes, vierkantiges Steinbeil mit flach gewölbten Seitenflächen, Schneide gebogen, nach dem Bahnende sich etwas verjüngend, geradflächige Schmalseiten; aus Diabas. L. 5,2, Schneidenhöhe 3,1, Gewicht 38 g. (ES 29.)

Schön erhaltenes, gut poliertes, vierkantiges Steinbeil aus Diabas, nach dem Bahnende sich leicht verjüngend, mit flach gewölbten Seitenwangen, halbmondförmig angeschliffeuer, gebogener Schneide; Bahnende abgerundet, Schmalseiten geradflächig. L. 5,8, Schneidenhöhe 4,2, Gewicht 62 g. (ES 49.)

Schön erhaltenes, geschliffenes Steinbeil (Fig. 19) aus Diabas, vierkantig, nach dem Bahnende sich leicht verjüngend, mit flach gewölbten Seitenwangen, halbmondförmig angeschliffener, gebogener Schneide, Schmalseiten geradflächig; Bahnende geschliffen. L. 6,3, Schneidenhöhe 4,2, Gewicht 82 g. (ES 40.)

Vierkantiges, geschliffenes Steinbeil aus Diabas, nach dem Bahnende zu sich kaum verjüngend, Seitenwangen flach gewölbt, zum Teil unbearbeitet, Bahnende roh, Schneide gebogen. L. 6,6, Schneidenhöhe 4,0. (ES 12.)

Gut erhaltenes, geschliffenes, vierkantiges Steinbeil aus kristall. Schiefer mit scharfer, gebogener Schneide, nach dem Bahnende sich etwas verjüngend, Seitenwangen gewölbt, Schmalseiten geradflächig, Bahnende abgerundet. L. 5,7, Schneidenhöhe 4,7, Gewicht 96 g. (ES 46.)

Geschliffenes, vierkantiges Steinbeil aus Diabas, nach dem Bahnende sich wenig verjüngend, Schmalseiten abgerundet, Seitenwangen flach gewölbt, Schneide gebogen. L. 6,0, Schneidenhöhe 4,3, Gewicht 82 g. (ES 38.)

Geschliffenes, vierkantiges Steinbeil aus Diabas, nach dem Bahnende zu sich etwas verjüngend, Schmalseiten abgerundet, Schneide gebogen, Seitenwangen flach gewölbt. L. 6,0, Schneidenhöhe 4,8, Gewicht 75 g. (ES 39.)

Großes, schön geschliffenes, vierkantiges Steinbeil aus feinkörniger Grauwacke, nach dem Bahnende zu sich etwas verjüngend, mit geradflächigen Schmalseiten und geradflächigen Seitenwangen, Schneide gebogen, Bahnende abgebrochen. Schneidenhöhe 6,0. (ES 13.)

Grosses, geschliffenes, vierkantiges Steinbeil aus Diabas, nach dem Bahnende zu sich etwas verjüngend, Schmalseiten geradflächig, Seitenwangen kaum gewölbt, Schneide gebogen, Bahnende fehlt. Schneidenhöhe 6,5. (ES 54.)

Mittelgroßes, geschliffenes, dickes Steinbeil aus Buntsandstein, nach dem Bahnende zu sich kaum verjüngend, Schmalseiten geradflächig, Seitenwangen flach gewölbt, Schneide fehlt, Bahnende abgerundet. Mittlere Höhe 4,7. (ES 89.)

Schneidenteil eines großen, vierkantigen Steinbeils aus Quarzit, mit geradflächigen Schmalseiten und geradflächigen Seitenwangen, Schneide gebogen. Schneidenhöhe über 5,0. (ES 26.)

Schneidenteil eines mittelgroßen, vierkantigen Steinbeils aus kristall. Schiefer mit leicht gewölbten Seitenwangen, Schneide gebogen. Schneidenhöhe 5,0. (ES 41.)

Schneidenteil eines abgerundet vierkantigen Steinbeils aus

Diabas mit flachgewölbten Seitenwangen, Schneide gebogen. Schneidenhöhe ca. 5,5 cm.   (ES 48.)
     Hierzu kommen von derartigen Steinbeilen im Völker-
museum zu Berlin: \
     Ein sehr kleines Steinbeil aus grünem Gestein, L. 5,0,
Schneidenhöhe 3,0.   (BV II b. 1102.)
     Eins aus grauem Gestein, L. 6,0, Schneidenhöhe 4,0. (BV 1103.)
     Eins aus grünlichem Gestein, L. 10,0, Schneidenhöhe 5,1. (BV 1225.)
     Eins aus grauem Gestein, L. 7,5, Schneidenhöhe 5,0. (BV 1529.)
     Eins aus grauem Gestein, L. 23,0, Schneidenhöhe 10,5. (BV 2344.)
     Eins 8,5 cm lang, Schneidenhöhe 6,5.   (BV 2618.)
     Ein flaches Feuersteinbeil, 10 cm lang, verjüngt sich nach
dem Bahnende zu stärker. Bemerkenswert ist das Stück als eins
der wenigen aus Feuerstein gefertigten.   (BV 2423.)
     Im Henneberger Haus in Meiningen ein Steinbeil mit
abgestumpfter Schneide.

     **B. Vierkantige Steinbeile, nach dem Bahnende sich ver-
jüngend**, Schneide gebogen, Schmalseiten geradflächig, Seitenwangen gewölbt, nach dem Bahnende zu stark konvergierend.

     Schön erhaltenes, mittelgroßes, geschliffenes, vierkantiges Stein-
beil aus kristall. Schiefer, nach dem Bahnende zu sich verjüngend,
Schneide gebogen, Schmalseiten geradflächig, Seitenwangen gewölbt,
nach dem Bahnende zu stark konvergierend. L. 9,2, Schneidenhöhe
7,2, gr. Dicke 3,6, Gewicht 315 g.   (ES 45.)
     Geschliffenes, vierkantiges Steinbeil aus Diabas, nach dem
Bahnende zu sich verjüngend, Schmalseiten geradflächig, Seitenwangen gewölbt, nach dem Bahnende zu stark konvergierend. L. 7,0,
Schneidenhöhe 6,0, gr. Dicke 2,2, Gewicht 130 g.   (ES 35.)
     Schön erhaltenes, fein poliertes, vierkantiges Steinbeil aus Diabas,
nach dem Bahnende sich verjüngend; Schneide gebogen, halbmondförmig angeschliffen, Schmalseiten geradflächig, Seitenwangen gewölbt, nach dem Bahnende zu ziemlich stark konvergierend. L. 5,5,
Schneidenhöhe 5,5, gr. Dicke 2,2, Gewicht 88 g.   (ES 37.)
     Schön erhaltenes, kleines, fein poliertes, undeutlich vierkantiges
Steinbeil aus Diabas, nach dem Bahnende zu sich verjüngend, Schneide
kaum gebogen, Schmalseiten geradflächig, Seitenwangen flach gewölbt, nach dem Bahnende zu konvergierend. L. 4,0, Schneidenhöhe
3,8, gr. Dicke 1,1, Gewicht 25 g.   (ES 25.)
     Kleines, vierkantiges Steinbeil aus Diabas, nach dem Bahnende
zu sich verjüngend, Schneide gebogen, Schmalseiten geradflächig,
Seitenwangen kaum gewölbt. L. 4,5, Schneidenhöhe 3,5, gr. Dicke 1,1,
Gewicht 25 g.   (ES 52.)
     Kleines, vierkantiges Steinbeil aus Diabas, nach dem Bahnende
zu sich verjüngend, Schneide gebogen, Schmalseiten geradflächig,
Seitenwangen flach gewölbt. L. 5,0, Schneidenhöhe 4,5, gr. Dicke 1,5.
                                                       (ES 21.)
     Kleines, vierkantiges Steinbeil aus Diabas, beschädigt, nach
dem Bahnende zu sich verjüngend, Schneide gebogen, Schmalseiten
geradflächig, Seitenwangen flach gewölbt. L. 6,0, Schneidenhöhe 5,0,
gr. Dicke 2,3.   (ES 42.)
     Gleichartiges aus Diabas, klein, beschädigt. L. 5,0, Schneiden-
höhe 4,0.   (ES 11.)

Mittelgroßes, geschliffenes, vierkantiges Steinbeil aus Diabas, nach dem Bahnende sich stark verjüngend, Schmalseiten geradflächig. L. 9,3, Schneidenhöhe 4,0, Gewicht 120 g. (ES 47.)

Kleines, gut poliertes Steinbeil aus Diabas, nach dem abgeschrägten Bahnende zu sich verjüngend; eine Schmalseite geradflächig, an der anderen stoßen die Seitenwangen in einer scharfen Kante zusammen. Seitenwangen sehr flach gewölbt. L. 5,8, Schneidenhöhe 3,8, gr, Dicke 1,3, Gewicht 37 g. (ES 51.)

Ein Bruchstück eines derartigen Steinbeils von mittlerer Größe aus grünlichem Gestein mit feinen dunkleren Sprenkeln ist im Jenaer Museum.

Zu diesen Steinbeilen mit sich stark verjüngendem Bahnende kommen im Berliner Völkermuseum:

Eins, 7 cm lang. (BV 1411.)

Eins aus grauem Gestein, 6,5 cm lang, 6 cm Schneidenhöhe. (BV 1530.)

Eins aus grauem Gestein, 8 cm lang, 6^1/$_2$ cm Schneidenhöhe. (BV 2103.)

Eins, 8 cm lang, 7 cm Schneidenhöhe. (BV 2619.)

C. Steinbeile mit spitzem Bahnende, flach gewölbten Seitenwangen, die an Stelle der Schmalseiten oben und unten in einer mehr oder weniger scharfen Kante zusammenlaufen, Schneide gebogen. (Fig. 20.)

Kleines derartiges Steinbeil (Fig. 20) mit breit-halbmondförmig angeschliffener Schneide, aus Diabas. Seitenwangen in abgerundeter Kante aneinander stoßend, nach dem Bahnende zu stark konvergierend. L. 6,6, Schneidenhöhe 5,6, gr. Dicke 1,9, Gewicht 67 g. (ES 36.)

Mittelgroßes, gleichartiges Steinbeil aus Diabas. Seitenwangen in abgerundeter oberer und unterer Kante aneinander stoßend, nach dem Bahnende konvergierend. L. 8,0 cm, Schneidenhöhe 4,0, gr. Dicke 2,0, Gewicht 129 g. (ES 44.)

Mittelgroßes, gleichartiges Steinbeil aus Diabas, stark beschädigt. Schneidenhöhe 5,1. (ES 34.)

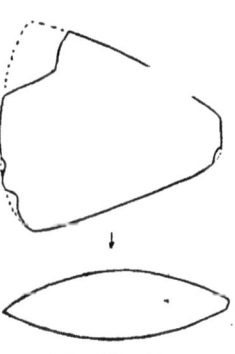

Fig. 20. ^{1}/$_2$.

D. Steinbeile vierkantig mit breitem Bahnende, Schneidenhöhe geringer als mittlere Beilhöhe, deutliche geradflächige Schmalseiten; Seitenwangen gewölbt. (Fig. 21.)

Mittelgroßes Steinbeil dieser Art aus Diabas, Bahnende fehlt; Seitenwangen flach gewölbt. Schneidenhöhe 3,2, mittlere Beilhöhe 4,5, gr. Dicke 1,8. (ES 27.)

Mittelgroßes Steinbeil dieser Art aus Diabas, Seitenwangen gewölbt. L. 8,0, Schneidenhöhe 3,0, mittlere Beilhöhe 4,0, gr. Dicke 2,3, Gewicht 151 g. (ES 19.)

Mittelgroßes Steinbeil dieser Art (Fig. 21)' aus Diabas. Seitenwangen gewölbt. L. 10,0 Schneidenhöhe 4,0, gr. Höhe am Bahnende 5,5, gr. Dicke 2,3.   (ES 20.)

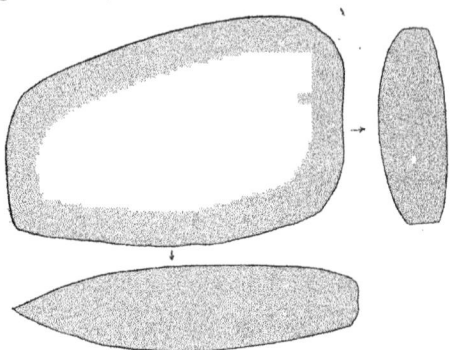

Fig. 21. ¹/₂.

Mittelgroßes Steinbeil dieser Art aus Variolit, mit flach gewölbten Seitenwangen, beschädigt. L. 7,5, Schneidenhöhe 3,5, gr. Höhe am Bahnende ca. 6,5, gr. Dicke 2,5.   (ES 24.)

E. Ein Steinbeil mit absatzweise nach unten verlängerter Schneide.
(Fig. 22.)

In Schröders Sammlung von Eckolstedt. L. 12,6, Schneidenhöhe 7,2, gr. Dicke 2,5.

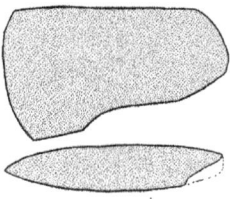

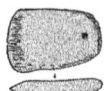

Fig. 23. ¹/₄.

Fig. 22. ¹/₄.

Originell in seiner Form ist ein kleines, zierliches Steinbeil (Fig. 23) aus schwarzem Kieselschiefer. Schneide gebogen, scharf, Seitenwangen geradflächig, in abgerundeter Kante oben und unten aneinander stoßend, nach dem Bahnende zu sich etwas verjüngend; kleines Schnurloch am Bahnende. Gewicht 20 g· Vielleicht ist es als Amulet getragen worden. Als Beil hat es bei der Weichheit des Materials sicher nicht Verwendung gefunden.   (ES 50.)

II. Steinäxte.

Diesen undurchlochten Steinbeilen stehen die wuchtigeren Steinäxte gegenüber mit Schaftloch. Ein gewaltiger

Fortschritt in der Technik der Steinwerkzeuge! Die Schaft-
löcher wurden in der Mehrzahl mit einem Hohlbohrer
hergestellt, selten mit einem Vollbohrer. Als Hohlbohrer
diente ein querdurchbrochener Röhrenknochen, ein quer-
durchsägter Holunderast. Nach den vielen Bruchstücken
zu urteilen, die uns in den verschiedensten Stadien der
Bearbeitung vorliegen, verlief die Herstellung einer Steinaxt mit Schaftloch folgendermaßen. Man schlug den ge-
wählton passenden Stein grob zu, so daß er im ganzen die
Axtform bekam. Dann begann man mit der Bohrung. Der
Hohlbohrer wurde auf die obere Fläche aufgesetzt, die an der
Bohrstelle mit angefeuchtetem Sand bedeckt war. Mit
einem halbkugelförmigen Stein drückte man den senkrecht
stehenden Bohrer an und brachte ihn durch eine umgelegte
Schnur, die bald nach rechts, bald nach links gezogen
wurde zur Drehung, wie einen Kreisel. Die Bohrlöcher
sind meist konisch, nach unten stärker werdend, kreisrund.
Dementsprechend auch die ausfallenden Bohrzapfen.
Bei genauer Betrachtung lassen sich unschwer die vom
Bohren erzeugten spiralförmigen Kritzel am Zapfen und im
Bohrloch erkennen. Das Schaftloch sitzt bei der großen
Mehrzahl der Äxte mehr nach dem Bahnende zu, oft an
der Grenze zwischen vorderen zwei und hinterem ein Drittel.
War nun die Durchbohrung gelungen, so wurde die Axt
sorgfältig geglättet und geschärft. — Die Schneide
steht wie bei den Steinbeilen senkrecht. Die Seiten-
wangen sind meist symmetrisch, das Bahnende geradflächig angeschliffen oder abgerundet.

Beim Schlag war die links und rechts vom Schaftloch
befindliche, Schneiden- und Bahnendenteil verbindende
Brücke die gefährdeteste für den Bruch des Gerätes. Und
in der Tat zeigen die meisten Bruchstücke zerbrochener
Steinäxte hier die Bruchfläche. Diesem Mangel half man
durch Verstärkung dieser seitlich vom Schaftloch gelegenen
brückenförmigen Seitenwangenpartie ab. Aus der ursprüng-
licheren dreieckigen Form des Horizontaldurchschnitts wird

XXII.   8

ein Rhombus. Die Seitenwangen sind nicht mehr einfache, zur. Schneide konvergierende Flächen, sondern stumpfwinklig gebrochene.

III. Axthämmer.

Den Abschluß dieser Entwickelungsreihe bilden schließlich die Axthämmer, bei welchen, wie der Name sagt, das sorgfältig bearbeitete Bahnende als Hammer verwendet wurde, die Schneide als Axt. Wahre Prunkstücke sind die polygonal facettierten Axthämmer, bei denen eine Reihe von angeschliffenen Längsflächen die Seitenwangen zieren.

Steinäxte von dreieckiger Grundfläche.

Sehr gut erhaltene Steinaxt dieser Art: Fig. 24 von oben, Fig. 24a seitlich gesehen. Die Steinaxt ist schön poliert, aus grauem Gestein, das Bahnende abgerundet, unregelmäßig, die Schneide scharf, senkrecht. Das Schaftloch ist an der Grenze des hinteren und mittleren Drittels der ganzen Axtlänge angebracht. Es ist oben enger als unten (2,3 : 2,5 cm), verläuft von oben etwas nach rechts hinten unten. Der obere Lochrand ist abgestumpft, der untere

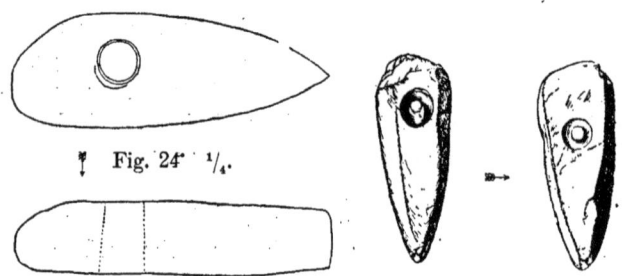

↕ Fig. 24 ¹/₄.

Fig. 24a. ¹/₄.   Fig. 25. ¹/₄.   Fig. 25a. ¹/₄.

Lochrand scharf. Im Bohrloch sind an der hinteren Wand fünf parallele, 1 mm weit voneinander entfernte Kratzlinien sichtbar; sonstige Wandung des Lochs spiegelglatt poliert, ganz vereinzelt kaum merkliche Glättkritzel von oben nach unten. L. 18 cm, gr. Breite in der Ebene des Bohrlochs 6,5 cm, gr. Höhe 4,0, Gewicht 828 g. (ES 3.)

Gleichartige Steinaxt, Fig. 25 von oben, Fig. 25a von unten, aus grauem Gestein, mit geradflächigen Schmalseiten und nach der stumpfen Schneide zu allmählich konvergierenden Seitenwangen. Das Exemplar ist besonders wertvoll und lehrreich, da hier die Schaftlochbohrung an der Grenze des hinteren und mittleren Drittels angefangen und nicht vollendet ist. Der Bohrzapfen steht noch im Bohrloch. Bohrung 14 mm tief, Bohrloch 16 mm Durchmesser, Bohrzapfen oben 8 mm. Nach links hinten ist die Umgebung des Bohrlochs durch falsche Bohrung erweitert. Richtung des Bohrlochs von hinten oben nach vorn unten. Ein zweiter Bohrversuch wurde auf der Unterseite gemacht, 2 mm tief, 17 mm im Durchmesser. Bohrzapfen oben 10 mm. L. 11,5, gr. Breite in der Querebene des Schaftlochs 4,1 cm, Höhe 2,5 cm, Gewicht 225 g. (ES 105.)

Bruchstück einer gleichartigen S t e i n a x t. Das grünliche Gesteinstück ist auf allen Seiten noch rauh, nur eine Schmalseite zeigt Sägekritzel. Auf der zur Oberseite bestimmten Fläche ist das Schaftloch halb gebohrt, der Bohrzapfen zur Hälfte noch fest im Bohrloch, Bohrkritzel stellenweise parallel laufend, 1 mm voneinander entfernt. Das Stück beweist, daß man die Bohrung vor der feineren Glättung an nur roh axtförmig zubehauenen Stücken vornahm. (ES 103.)

Bruchstück einer mittelgroßen, durchbohrten Steinaxt, aus grauem Gestein mit grünlichen Streifen, gut poliert. Lochwandung fein glattpoliert. Unter- und Oberfläche eben, Schmalseiten zur Schneide konvergierend, Bahnende breit. L. ca. 12,5, Loch zwischen 3,5—6 cm der Länge, Höhe des Bohrlochs 4,6 cm. (ES 4.)

Hier einzureihen sind 3 Steinäxte von dreieckiger Grundfläche aus dem Völkermuseum in Berlin:

Schmale Steinaxt aus schwarzem Gestein, mit langer, scharfer, senkrecht gebogener Schneide, breitem, abgerundetem Bahnende. L. 14,0, gr. Br. 3,5. (BV 2346.)

Dickere Steinaxt aus schwarzem Gestein, mit senkrecht gebogener Schneide, breitem, abgerundetem Bahnende. L. 13,2, gr. Br. 6,0. (BV 2347.)

Eine ebensolche aus schwarzem Gestein. L. 12,0, gr. Br. 5,0. (BV 2348.)

Axthämmer von rhombischer Grundfläche.

A x t h a m m e r dieser Form mit kreisrundem Bohrloch und einem zweiten Bohrversuch auf der Oberfläche, Fig. 26 von oben; die Seitenansicht, Fig. 26a, zeigt eine Reihe angeschliffener Facetten. L. 13,0, Schneidenhöhe 3,0, gr. Br. 5 cm. Privatsammlung von Schröder in Hainichen.

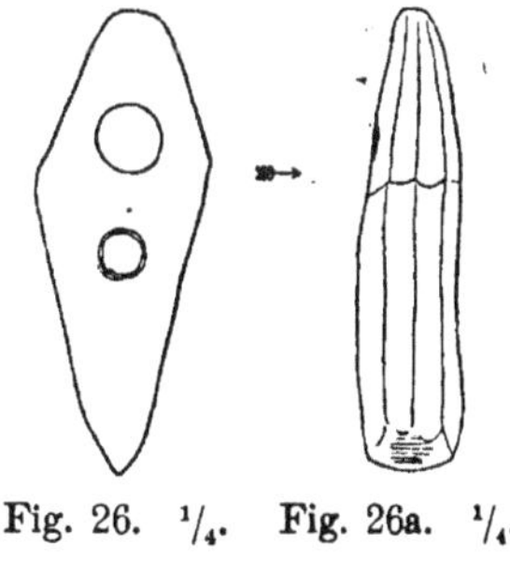

Bruchstück eines mittelgroßen, durchbohrten A x t h a m m e r s aus grauem Gestein, Schneide bis Hälfte Bohrloch 7 cm, Höhe des Bohrlochs 5 cm, Schneidenhöhe 4,5 cm, Schneide stumpf. Im Inneren des Bohrlochs ca. 57 Bohrkritzel quer, fast parallel laufend. (ES 107.)

Bruchstück eines mittelgroßen, durchbohrten Axthammers aus graugrünem Gestein. Höhe im Bohrloch 4,5 cm, Bohrloch spiegelglatt innen

Fig. 26. $^{1}/_{4}$. Fig. 26a. $^{1}/_{4}$.

poliert, berechnete, ungefähre Hammerlänge $10^{1}/_{2}$ cm. (ES 5.)

8*

Hintere Hälfte eines großen, breiten Axthammers mit größtem Teil des Bohrlochs, aus schwarzgrauem Gestein. Bohrloch oben 18 mm, unten 22 mm. Im Innern parallele, 1 mm voneinander entfernte Bohrkritzel, seichtere Bohrversuche rechts und links vom unteren Bohrloch; Höhe des Hammers im Bohrloch 4 cm, ungefähre Breite 8,5 cm, Länge ca. 15 cm. (ES 106.)

Schneidenteil eines großen Axthammers aus grünlichgrauem Gestein. Schneide abgestumpft, Schneide bis vorderen Bohrlochrand 11 cm, Bohrlochdurchmesser 2,2, Breite in der Querebene des Bohrlochs ca. 6,5, Höhe des Bohrlochs 5 cm. (ES 10.)

Bruchstück eines mittelgroßen Axthammers mit halbem Schaftloch, aus grünem Gestein. Durchmesser des Schaftlochs 2,3 cm. (ES 9.)

Ebensolches aus grünem Gestein, Lochdurchmesser 2,5 cm. (ES. 8.)

Breites Bahnende eines großen Axthammers mit halbem Bohrloch, aus grünlichgrauem Gestein. Bohrloch 2,4 cm im Durchmesser, viel senkrechte Glättkritzel in der Bohrlochwandung. (ES. 7.)

Ebensolches aus grauem Gestein mit Bohrlochhälfte. Bohrlochdurchmesser 2,4 cm. (ES 109.)

Scharfe Schneide eines großen Axthammers, hellgrau mit dunkleren Flecken. (ES 110.)

Bruchstück eines Axthammers mit ³/₄ Bohrloch, aus grünem Gestein. Bohrkritzel in der Bohrlochwandung. Kreisbogenkritzel an der Oberfläche um das Loch. Durchmesser des Schaftlochs 2,4 cm. (ES 104.)

Ein Prachtstück der Sammlung ist ein polygonal facettierter Axthammer (Fig. 27 von der Seite, Fig. 27a von unten) aus

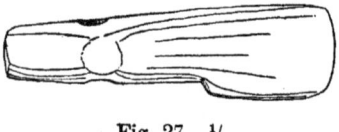

Fig. 27. ¹/₄.

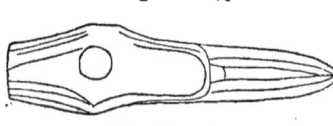

Fig. 27a. ¹/₄.

grauem Gestein, sehr fein poliert. Die Schneidenhöhe ist absatzweise nach unten verlängert, die Seiten, wangen zu beiden Seiten des Bohrlochs verstärkt. Die Schneidenhälfte zählt 17 Facetten, das Bahnende ist ein Sechzehneck. Das Schaftloch ist unten und oben gleich weit im Durchmesser 1,9 cm. Wandung innen gut poliert, man sieht nur Glättkritzel von oben nach unten. L. 18,8, Schneidenhöhe 5,0, Schaftlochhöhe 3,3, Breite in der Schaftlochquerebene 5,0, Gewicht 522 g. (ES 2.)

Bruchstück (Bahnende mit ³/₄ Schaftloch) eines polygonal facettierten Axthammers aus grünlichgrauem Gestein, 12 Facetten, Bohrlochdurchmesser 2,2 cm, Höhe des Bohrlochs 4,4 cm. (ES 6.)

Ein polygonal facettierter Hammer aus schwarzem Gestein, 13 cm lang, mit zur Seite des Schaftlochs verstärkten Seitenwangen, nach unten allmählich verstärkter Schneide, liegt im Berliner Völkermuseum aus Eckolstedt. (BV II b 2607.)

Bohrzapfen.

Bohrzapfen (Fig. 28), kegelförmig, unten am Rand glockenförmig umbiegend, Oberfläche rauh, Durchmesser unten 18 mm, oben 9 mm, Höhe 2,5 cm.

Fig. 28. ¹/₄.   Fig. 28a. ¹/₄.

Bohrzapfen (Fig. 28a), aus schwarzgrauem Gestein, Achse schräg, oberer Durchmesser 13 mm, unterer 18 mm, Höhe 2 cm. (ES 114.)

IV. Hacken.

Diesen Steinbeilen, Steinäxten und Axthämmern steht eine Form von Steinwerkzeugen gegenüber, die als **Hacken** verwendet worden sind. Wir sehen an einer derartigen Steinhaeke eine gut geglättete, g e r a d f l ä c h i g e U n t e r f l ä c h e und eine g e w ö l b t e O b e r f l ä c h e, wiederum das Gerät im Gebrauch gedacht, in diesem Falle quer gelegt. Die Schneide ist bogenförmig nach rechts und links abgerundet und nach oben schnabelnd; bei der Beschreibung reden wir selbstverständlich hier von einer S c h n e i d e n b r e i t e. Bei sorgfältig gearbeiteten Exemplaren sind schmale S e i t e n - w a n g e n angeschliffen. Das Bahnende ist auch hier, weil es im Holzgriff stak, mit weniger Sorgfalt behandelt als die Schneidenhälfte, und nach ihm zu verjüngt sich die Hacke. Dadurch wird das Bahnende beim Hacken fester in den Griff eingekeilt. Selbstverständlich mußte der Griff eines derartigen Werkzeuges ein zweiarmiges, ungefähr im rechten Winkel aneinander stoßendes Holzstück sein.

Wir unterscheiden zwei Sorten der Steinhacken:

1) b r e i t e, f l a c h e und
2) l a n g e, s c h m a l e, h o c h g e w ö l b t e (s c h u h - l e i s t e n f ö r m i g e).

Die ersteren sind die häufigeren. Eine Durchbohrung der Hacken, um dieselben an einen Stiel zu befestigen, ist äußerst selten.

A. Steinhacken: flach, breit. (Fig. 29.)

Groß, aus Diabas, gut erhalten, nach dem Bahnende zu sich etwas verjüngend. L. 10,2, Schneidenbreite ‚4,2, mittl. Dicke 1,5, Gewicht 101 g. (ES 79.)

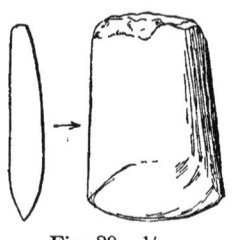

Mittelgroß, aus Diabas, gut erhalten. L. 6,5, Schneidenbreite 4,0, mittl. Dicke 1,1, Gewicht 42 g. (ES 84.)

Klein, aus Diabas, gut erhalten, nach dem Bahnende zu sich verjüngend. L. 5,3, Schneidenbreite 3,6, mittl. Dicke 1,0, Gewicht 22 g. (ES 74.)

Klein, aus Diabas, naeh dem Bahnende zu sich verjüngend. L. 5,7, Schneidenbreite 4,5, mittl. Dicke 1,2, Gewicht 49 g. (ES 83.)

Mittelgroß, aus Diabas, nach dem

Fig. 29. ¹/₂.

Bahnende zu sich etwas verjüngend, gut erhalten. L. 7,1, Schneidenbreite 4,0, mittl. Dicke 1,2, Gewicht 61 g. (ES 32.)

Mittelgroß, aus Diabas, sehr gut erhalten. L. 6,5, Schneidenbreite 3,8, mittl. Dicke 1,2, Gewicht 50 g. (ES 33.)

Mittelgroß, aus Diabas, gut erhalten. L. 6,0, Schneidenbreite 4,2, mittl. Dicke 1,5, Gewicht 67 g. (ES 65.)

Mittelgroß, aus Diabas, Bahnende roh, sonst gut erhalten. L. 5,0, Schneidenbreite 4,3, mittl. Dicke 1,4, Gewicht 46 g. (ES. 66.)

Mittelgroß, aus Diabas, schönes Exemplar (Fig. 29), halbmondförmiger Schliff der Oberfläche naeh der Schneide zu. L. 5,6, Schneidenbreite 4,0, mittl. Dicke 1,0, Gewicht 39 g. (ES 67.)

Mittelgroß, aus Diabas, Schneide etwas beschädigt. L. 7,2, Schneidenbreite 5,0, mittl. Dicke 1,1, Gewicht 75 g. (ES 81.)

Mittelgroß, aus Diabas, vollständig, eine angeschliffene, geradflächige Seitenwange. L. 6,3, Schneidenbreite 4,5, mittl. Dicke 1,0, Gewicht 51 g. (ES 85.)

Klein, aus Diabas, vollständig, angeschliffene, geradflächige Seitenwangen. L. 5,0, Schneidenbreite 3,7, mittl. Dicke 0,8, Gewicht 29 g. (ES 70.)

Klein, aus Diabas, beschädigt, angeschliffene Seitenwangen. L. 6,0, Schneidenbreite 4,0, mittl. Dicke 1,0, Gewicht 38 g. (ES 71.)

Zierlich, dünn, gut erhalten, aus Diabas, angeschliffene Seitenwangen. L. 5,7, Schneidenbreite 2,5, mittl. Dicke 0,7, Gewicht 22 g. (ES 72.)

Klein, etwas beschädigt, aus Kieselschiefer. L. 4,5, Schneidenbreite 3,2, mittl. Dicke 0,7. (ES 73.)

Mittelgroß, aus Diabas, angeschliffene, geradflächige Seitenwangen. L. 7,0, Schneidenbreite 4,5, mittl. Dicke 1,0, Gewicht 63 g. (ES 86.)

Mittelgroß, aus Diabas. L. 6,8, Schneidenbreite 5,3, mittl. Dicke 1,8, Gewicht 102 g. (ES 87.)

Mittelgroß, aus Diabas, sehr glattpoliert, angeschliffene, geradflächige Seitenwangen. L. 6,5, Schneidenbreite 5,0, Gewicht 72 g. (ES 88.)

Schneidenteil einer größeren derartigen Hacke, aus Diabas, Schneidenbreite 5,7, mittl. Dicke 2,2. (ES 18.)

Schneidenteil einer größeren derartigen Hacke, aus Diabas,. Schneidenbreite 7,0, mittl. Dicke 1,5. (ES 60.)

Bruchstück einer größeren derartigen Hacke aus Diabas. Breite 6,6, Dicke 1,4. (ES 78.)

Bahnende einer kleinen, derartigen Hacke aus Diabas. (ES 68.)

Vollständige, geschliffene derartige Hacke aus Diabas; scharfkantiges, seitliches Aneinanderstoßen von Ober- und Unterfläche. L. 6,8, Schneidenbreite 4,2, mittl. Dicke 1,1. (ES 102.)

Kleinere, dicke derartige Hacke aus Diabas, mit angeschliffenen Seitenwangen. L. 7,0, Schneidenbreite 4,7, mittl. Dicke 2,2! Gewicht 127 g. (ES 96.)

Schneidenteil einer großen, breiten derartigen Hacke aus Diabas, geradflächige Seitenwangen angeschliffen. Gr. Breite 5,3, mittl. Dicke 2,4. (ES 16.)

Hierzu kommen aus dem Berliner Völkermuseum: Steinhacke aus granem Gestein, mit angeschliffenen Seitenwangen, 6,2 cm lang, 3 cm Schneidenbreite und beinahe spitzem Bahnende. (BV 2104.)

Eine dergleichen aus dunkelgrauem Gestein, mit angeschliffenen Seitenwangen, 8 cm lang, 4,5 cm Schneidenbreite. (BV 2105.)

Aus dem Jenaer Museum: Steinhacke aus grünlichem Gestein, Schneide abgesprungen, nach dem Bahnende zu sich wenig verjüngend; gefunden auf der steinzeitlichen Ansiedelung. an der Hirschrodaer Grenze.

Eine gleiche, sehr beschädigt.

Eine flache Hacke von Eckolstedt besitzt Pastor Schröder (Hainichen), 7,5 cm lang, Schneidenbreite 3,5.

B. Steinhacken: lang, schmal, hochgewölbt, schuhleistenförmig.
(Fig. 30.)

Größere, schön erhaltene derartige Hacke aus feinkörnigem, hartem, einfarbig hellgrauem Sandstein. L. 13,5, größte Breite 3,7, mittl Dicke 2,5, Gewicht 255 g. (ES 94.)

Mittelgroße, gut erhaltene derartige Hacke (Fig. 30) aus Diabas. L. 10,6, gr. Breite 4 cm, mittl. Dicke 2,2, Gewicht 177 g. (ES 97.)

Mittelgroße, gut erhaltene derartige Hacke aus Diabas. L. 10,3, gr. Breite 3,0, mittl. Dicke 3,0 cm, Gewicht 157 g. (ES 93.)

Kleinere, etwas beschädigte derartige Hacke aus Diabas. L. 8 cm, gr. Breite 1,8, gr. Dicke 1,5. (ES 99.)

Ebensolche. L. 7,3, gr. Breite 2,0, gr. Dicke 1,5. (ES 98.)

Ebensolche, klein, sehr gut erhalten. L. 6,5, gr. Breite 1,8, gr. Dicke 1,4, Gewicht 25 g. (ES 102.)

Ebensolche. L. 7,0, gr. Breite 1,3, gr. Dicke 1,6, Gewicht 24 g. (ES 101.)

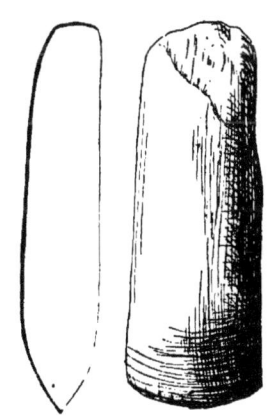

Fig. 30. $^1/_2$.

Schneidenteil einer großen derartigen Hacke aus Diabas. Gr. Breite 4,7. (ES 95.)
Schneidenteil einer größeren derartigen Hacke aus Diabas. Gr. Breite 3,8, gr. Dicke 3,0. (ES 30.)
Schneidenteil einer größeren derartigen Hacke aus Diabas. Gr. Breite 4,0. (ES 100.)
Eine hochgewölbte, schuhleistenförmige Steinhacke, 9,5 cm lang, 3,3 cm Schneidenbreite, 2,3 cm gr. Dicke, in Pastor Schröders Sammlung (in Hainichen).
zu Sehr große, langgestreckte, hochgewölbte, nach dem Bahnende sich etwas verjüngende, schuhleistenförmige Hacke (Fig. 31) aus

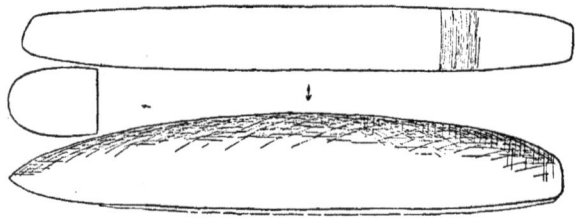

Fig. 31. $^1/_4$.

Diabas. L. 31,3 cm, gr. Höhe 5,1 cm, gr. Breite 3,8, Gewicht 1146 g. 5,5—7,5 cm vom Bahnende entfernt sind auffällig ca. 25—30 quer über die Unterfläche verlaufende Kritzel (vielleicht von der Befestigung?). (ES 2.)

Sehr großes, langgestrecktes, spitz-schuhleistenförmiges, hochgewölbtes Steingerät (Fig. 32), sehr schön poliert, aus

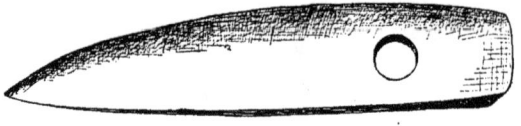

Fig. 32. $^1/_4$.

Diabas. Unterfläche glatt, Schneide wenig aufbiegend, ebenso Bahnende. Quer durchbohrtes Loch an der Grenze der vorderen $^3/_4$ und hinteren $^1/_4$ der ganzen Länge, auf der einen Seite 3 cm im Durchmesser, nach der anderen sich verjüngend zu 2,5 cm Durchmesser, kreisrund. Im Innern des Bohrlochs circa 50 im ganzen spiralig verlaufende Kratzfurchen des bohrenden Instruments sichtbar. Beim Bohren ist auf der einen Seite die Umgebung des Bohrlochs leicht abgesprengt, auch ist der Bohrer einmal ausgeglitten und hat einen scharfen Kratzer erzeugt. Das Loch verläuft etwas schräg. L. 28,9, gr. Breite 5,1, höchste Höhe 5,7, Gewicht 1552 g. (ES 1.)

Ein interessantes Stück ist eine **senkrecht durchbohrte**, breite, flache Hacke (Fig. 33) aus schwarzgrauem Kieselschiefer, mit angeschliffenen Seitenwangen, gerader Unter-, flachgewölbter Oberfläche. Das Bohrloch ist von 2 Seiten hergestellt, das obere hat nicht genau auf das untere getroffen. Das Bahnende fehlt. Lochweite oben 10 mm, unten 12 mm. L. ca. 7,0, gr. Breite 3,3, Höhe 1,2. (ES 112.)

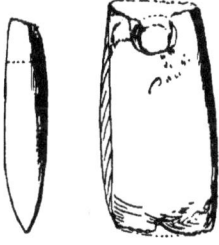

Von sonstigem Gerät, das mit jenen Steinwaffen und Werkzeugen auf Eckolstedter Boden gefunden worden ist, sind zu nennen:

Fig. 33. $^{1}/_{2}$.

V. Feuersteinmesser.

Im Jenaer Museum haben wir von da: ein sehr schmales (Fig. 34), 4,2 cm langes, 1,1 cm breites. Es ist flach dachförmig.

Ebenso ein kürzeres, aber etwas breiteres, 3,8 cm lang, 1,8 cm breit.

Ebenso ein dickeres von 2,6 Länge, 1,5 Breite.

Ebenso ein kleines von stumpf-dreieckigem Querschnitt, 2,3 cm lang, 0,8 cm breit.

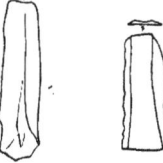

Fig. 34. $^{1}/_{2}$.   Fig. 35. $^{1}/_{2}$.

Ein 3,3 cm langes, 1,3 cm breites, feinklingiges (Fig. 35) hat trapezförmigen Querschnitt.

Ebenso ein 2 cm langes, 1,1 cm breites, etwas kräftigeres.

VI. Feuersteinpfeilspitzen.

Im Völkermuseum wird aus Eckolstedt eine **Feuersteinpfeilspitze mit Widerhaken** (Fig. 36) bewahrt, Höhe 5,6; gut erhalten. (BV II b 2420.)

Fig. 36. $^{1}/_{2}$.

In Jena eine 3,2 cm lange, 1,2 cm breite **ohne Widerhaken**.

VII. Steinsäge.

Eine **Steinsäge** aus Kieselschiefer, von Dreiecksform (Fig. 37), ein sehr seltenes Stück. Nach der Schneide

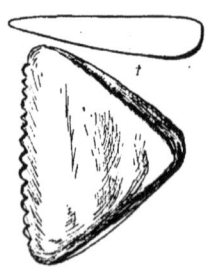

zu verdünnt sich das an der Rückseite starke Sägeblatt keilförmig und trägt 15 Zähne. Höhe des dreieckigen Sägeblattes 3,5 cm, Rückenbreite 1,2. Auf der Rückenkante verläuft ein 1,1 cm langer Einschnitt (zur Befestigung?). (ES 118.)

Fig. 37. ¹/₂.

VIII. Steinmeißel.

Ein kleiner grauer **Steinmeißel**, 5,5 cm lang, 2,5 gr. Breite, vierkantig, mit gerader Schneide ist im Berliner Völkermuseum (BV IIb. 1531.)

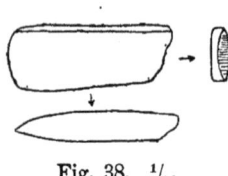

Fig. 38. ¹/₂.

Ein ebensolcher im Jenaer Museum aus blaugrauem Schiefer, 4 cm lang, 2,5 cm breit. Fo. am Lohholz.

Als **Hohlmeißel** verwendet werden konnte ein kleines, vierkantiges Steingerät (Fig. 38) aus Diabas mit scharfer hohlgeschliffener Schneide, 11 g schwer, L. 4,7, Breite 1 7, Dicke 0,8 cm. (ES 55.)

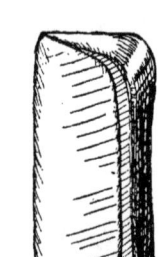

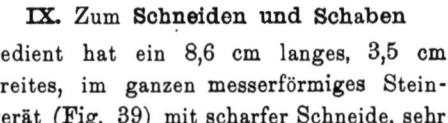

IX. Zum **Schneiden und Schaben** gedient hat ein 8,6 cm langes, 3,5 cm breites, im ganzen messerförmiges Steingerät (Fig. 39) mit scharfer Schneide, sehr starkem (1,6 cm) Rücken. (ES 117.)

X. Als **Wetzstein** kennzeichnet sich ein langes, rechteckiges Steingerät aus grünlichgrauem Diabas.

Fig. 39. ¹/₂. L. 9,2, Breite 3,0, Dicke 1,5. (ES 80.)

Bruchstück eines ebensolchen, 2,6 cm breiten, lang-gestreckten, rechteckigen Wetzsteins aus Kieselschiefer.
(ES 76.)

Ebenso ein 9 cm langes, 2,2 cm breites Stück aus Kieselschiefer (Fig. 40), mit trichter-förmigem, kleinem Schnurloch an dem einen Ende und vielen Kritzeln. (ES 64.)

Oberes Ende eines ebensolchen aus Kieselschiefer, mit zwei seitlichen, einander gegenüberliegenden Grübchen zum Einklemmen eines federnden Metallbogens. In der Tiefe des einen gewahrt man eine grünliche Ver-färbung (Bronze?). Breite 2 cm, Dicke 1,4 cm.
(ES 82.)

Ein Schleifstein von vierseitiger Prisma-form mit ausgemuldeter Schleiffläche ist aus Quarzit, 12 cm lang, 3 cm breit. (ES 62.)

Fig. 40. $^1/_2$.

XI. Reibkolben.

Unter den gesammelten Steinwerkzeugen findet man allenthalben ein Gerät in Zigarrenetuiform, im ganzen rechteckig, mit abgerundeter oberer und unterer Schmalseite. Die glatte, gerad-flächige Unterseite, die gewölbte Ober-fläche erinnern an die Steinhacken, so daß der Gedanke naheliegt, daß man diese Art Steingeräte durch Abschleifen der Bruchfläche unbrauchbar gewordener Exemplare hergestellt hat. Zum Polieren, Glätten, Reiben haben derartige Stein-geräte gut dienen können.

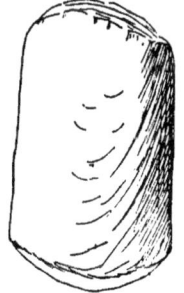

Fig. 41. $^1/_2$.

Ein derartiges schön geschliffenes, gut erhaltenes Exemplar (Fig. 41) ist in der Eckolstedter Sammlung aus Diabas, 12$^1/_2$ cm lang, 5 cm breit, 3,3 cm hoch, 335 g schwer. (ES 63.)
Ein ebensolches, kleineres aus Diabas. L. 8,0, Breite 4,5, Dicke 2,0, 147 g schwer. (ES 91.)
Ein ebensolches aus Diabas. L. 6,6, Breite 6,0, Dicke 2,0, 159 g schwer. (ES 92.)

Ein noch wenig abgeriebenes, derartiges aus Diabas. L. 6,5, Breite 4,0, Dicke 2,0. (ES 61.)

Ein gleiches, hergestellt aus einer breiten, flachen Hacke aus grünlichem, schwarzgesprenkeltem Gestein im Jenaer Museum. Fo.: zwischen Lohholz und Eckolstedt.

Beweisend für die Verwendung unbrauchbarer Steinbeile, Hämmer und Hacken zu derartigen Reibsteinen ist das Bruchstück einer durchlochten Steinaxt. Das Stück ist mitten durch das Schaftloch zersprungen, die entstandenen Bruchflächen durch Reiben abgerundet und glatt geschliffen. (ES 111.)

XII. Reibplatten.

Zum Zerreiben der Getreidekörner bediente man sich fußlanger, ovaler Platten, meist aus einem harten Sandstein, als Unterlage und faustgroßer Reibkugeln. Diese ovalen Reibplatten wurden durch längeren Gebrauch auf der Reibfläche ausgemuldet, und dies ist das Kennzeichen, an dem man sie auch in Bruchstücken erkennen kann. Meist sind die übrigen Flächen roh zugehauen.

Reibplatten sind häufige Funde auf den Eckolstedter steinzeitlichen Wohnplätzen.

Fig. 42. ¹/₁₀.

Ein schönes Exemplar (Fig. 42, links von oben gesehen, daneben im Querschnitt) besitzt das Jenaer Museum. Es ist 30 cm lang, gr. Breite 18 cm.

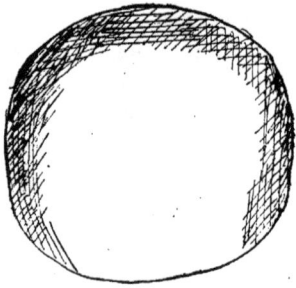

Fig. 43. ¹/₂.

XIII. Reibkugeln.

Große, schwere Reibkugel (Fig. 43) von 8 cm Durchmesser, aus graurötlichem Gestein, mit einer fast geraden Fläche. 648 g schwer. (ES 124.)

Eine ebensolche, etwas plattgedrückt, von 9 cm Durchmesser, aus Braunkohlenquarzit, 780 g schwer. (ES 123.)

Eine ebensolche, halbkugelförmig, aus Porphyr, von 6,8 cm Durchmesser, 165 g schwer. (ES 122.)

XIV.

Von besonderem Interesse sind 2 halbkugelförmige Steingeräte, die vermutlich **zum Aufdrücken des Trillbohrers** auf den zu durchbohrenden Steinhammer gedient haben: Eine 258 g schwere, grausteinerne Halbkugel (Fig. 44),

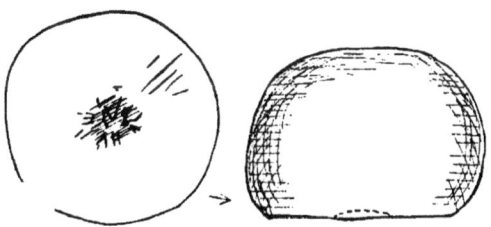

Fig. 44. $^1/_2$.

mit glatter Unterfläche, Durchmesser 6,7, Höhe 4,7. In der Mitte [derselben seichte, 1,5 cm große Aushöhlung mit vielen Kritzeln, die strahlenförmig vom Zentrum nach außen gehen. (ES. 125.)

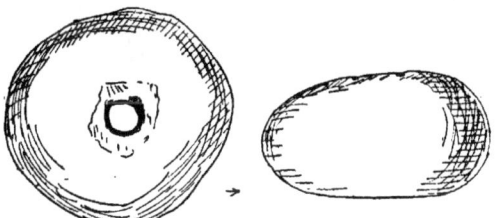

Fig. 45. $^1/_2$.

Ein 167 g schwerer, breit-ovaler Kiesel (Fig. 45) mit seichter, zentraler Anbohrung eines Trepanbohrers auf der Oberfläche. Die Umgebung des gebohrten Kreises ist durch Absprengen der Oberfläche gerauht. Durchmesser 6,5, Höhe 3,5. (ES 126.)

XV.

Bei der Töpferei könnte ein kleines, zugespitztes, prismatisches Steingerät aus Kieselschiefer **zum Ziehen der Ornamentlinien** gedient háben.   (ES 53.)

XVI. Spinnwirtel.

Als Einzelfunde sind auch eine Reihe von Spinnwirteln in der Eckolstedter Flur gemacht worden (Fig. 46—51).

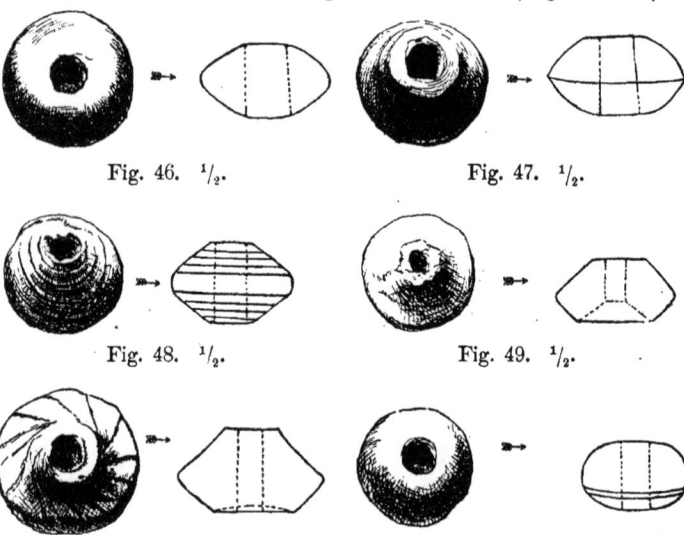

Fig. 46. $^1/_2$.   Fig. 47. $^1/_2$.

Fig. 48. $^1/_2$.   Fig. 49. $^1/_2$.

Fig. 50. $^1/_2$.   Fig. 51. $^1/_2$.

Sie haben die Gestalt von großen Perlen. In das zentrale Loch wurde ein Stab fest hineingesteckt, so daß das Ganze nun eine Spindel darstellte, die mit der Hand nach Art einer Torl in rotierende Bewegung versetzt wurde und den gesponnenen Flachsfaden auf sich wickelte. Diese Spinnwirtel sind zumeist aus Ton, einige wenige aus Stein. Auf der Außenfläche sind viele ornamentiert. Ihre Zeitstellung ist unsicher, da sie selbst noch im Mittelalter im Gebrauch blieben.

Tonwirtel aus schwarzgrauem Stein (Fig. 46), doppeltkonisch, unverziert, abgerundete Mittelkante. D. 3,7, Höhe 2,1, 28 g schwer, Lochweite oben 12,0, unten 11 mm. (ES 128.)

Tonwirtel (Fig. 47), doppeltkonisch, unverziert, scharfe Mittelkante, schmutzig-ziegelrot. D. 4,0, Höhe 2,2, 29 g schwer, Lochweite oben 11,0, unten 10,0 mm. (ES 129.)

Tonwirtel, doppeltkonisch, Andeutung von Querfurchen um die Außenfläche, schwarzgrau, abgerundete Mittelkante. D. 4,0, Höhe 2,2, 42 g schwer, Lochweite 13 mm oben, 11 unten. (ES 130.)

Tonwirtel (Fig. 48), doppeltkonisch, mit 4 parallelen Streifen oberhalb und 4 parallelen Streifen unterhalb des Umbruchs, weißgrau. D. 3,5, H. 2,2, 21 g schwer, Lochweite oben und unten 9 mm. (ES 131.)

Tonwirtel, doppeltkonisch, unverziert, gelblich. D. 3,2, Höhe 1,9, 17 g schwer, Lochweite oben und unten 9 mm. (ES 132.)

Tonwirtel, doppeltkonisch, weißlich, an einer Stelle orangefarben, 4 obere parallele Streifen, 3 untere. D. 2,4, Höhe 1,6, 8 g schwer, Lochweite oben 6 mm, unten 5 mm. (ES 137.)

Tonwirtel (Fig. 49), doppeltkonisch, mit scharfer Kante, unverziert, schwarzgrau, triehterförmige Einsenkung der Oberfläche zum Loch. Obere Breite des Trichters 21 mm, Lochdurchmesser 6 mm, Durchmesser der Unterfläche 1,6, gr. D. 3,5, Höhe 1,7, Gewicht 16 g. (ES 136.)

Tonwirtel (Fig. 50), doppeltkonisch, mit scharfer Kante; seichte Einsenkung der Oberfläche zum Loch, schmutzig-ziegelrot, mit 14 speichenartig vom Zentrum nach der Peripherie verlaufenden Schnitten. D. 4,1, Höhe 2,2, Gewicht 21 g, Lochweite oben und unten 8 mm, Durchmesser der Oberfläche 2,2, der Unterfläche 1,5 cm. (ES 127.)

Tonwirtel (Fig. 51) von ovalem Längsschnitt, verwaschene Oberfläche, an einer Stelle 2 parallele Kreislinien um das zentrale Loch des Wirtels sichtbar. Dieselben sind rötlichgelb gefärbt. D. 3,2, Höhe 1,9, Schwere 16 g, Lochweite oben und unten 8 mm. (ES 135.)

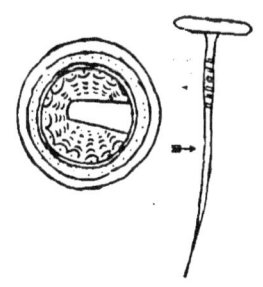

Wirtel aus bläulichgrauem Stein, im Längsschnitt trapezförmig; an einer intakten Stelle sieht man einen gelblichweißen, glasurähnlichen Belag mit 2 Paar um den Wirtel verlaufenden Linien. D. oben 3,3, unten 2,2, Höhe 1,5, Schwere 18 g, Lochweite unten 10 mm, oben 12 mm. (ES 133.)

Der jüngeren Bronzezeit gehört eine auf Eckolstedter Flur gefundene Bronzenadel (Fig. 52) an, mit reich verzierter, querstehender Kopfscheibe, 10 cm lang, der Hals der Nadel ist quergerillt. Im BV. II b 2421.

Fig. 52. $\frac{1}{3}$.

Auf der Flur Eckolstedt liegt im Norden des jetzigen Dorfes eine Wüstung Obergosserstedt. Hier wurden **slavische Scherben** mit Kammornament gefunden. Dieselben befinden sich jetzt im Jenaer Museum (Fig. 53). Es ist ein

Fig. 53. ¹/₄.

Randstück eines großen Topfes mit glattgestrichenem, leicht ausladendem Rand und 2 Halsbruchstücke. Das eine System Wellenlinien bricht auf dem einen Stück (in der Figur auf dem rechten) einmal spitzwinklig um, darüber verläuft es in niederen Kämmen; auf dem anderen Stück in der Mitte ist der Kamm nur kurz in die noch weiche Tonmasse eingetupft, so dass in bestimmten Zwischenräumen die Punkte übereinander stehen. Die Tonmasse dieser Gefäße ist grau, sehr hart gebrannt. Die Wandung der Gefäße ist 1 cm stark.

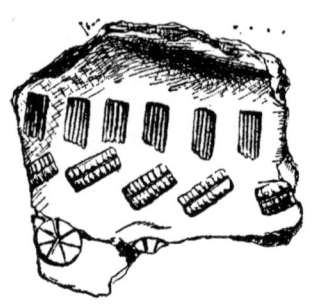

Fig. 54. ¹/₂.

Einen slavischen Gefäßscherben mit Wellenornament besitzt auch die Schule zu Eckolstedt. Das Gefäßstück ist grau, gut gebrannt, die Masse mit Sand reichlich gemengt, Gefäßwandung 9 mm stark.

Ebenda wird auch ein Gefäßbruchstück aufbewahrt (Fig. 54), welches auf seiner Außenfläche mit 3 Reihen gestempelter Ornamente verziert ist. Jede Stempelreihe ist mit einem anderen Stempel ausgeführt. Die oberste, dem Halsübergang nächste Reihe ist mit einem **rechteckigen,** mit 5 parallelen Leisten versehenen Stempel hervorgebracht, die mittlere mit einem etwas größeren, ebenfalls **rechteckigen** Stempel, der durch eine Längsleiste in zwei Hälften, jede Hälfte wieder in 9 Rechteckchen geteilt ist. In der dritten

Reihe sind Stempeleindrücke eines achtspeichigen Rades. Der Scherben gehört zu einem großen, terrinenartigen, henkellosen Tongefäß von grauer Farbe. Die Masse ist gleichmäßig durchsetzt mit rötlichen und weißlichen Quarzstückchen. Die Gefäßwand hat am oberen Bauchteil 9 mm Durchmesser.

Aehnliche Gefäße mit fast denselben rechteckigen Stempeln finden sich unter den **merovingischen** Altertümern, die den Reihengräbern bei Nordendorf in Schwaben entnommen sind.

2. Münchengosserstedt.

Von Münchengosserstedt liegen nur Einzelfunde vor: Steinbeile, Steinäxte, Hammeräxte, breite und hochgewölbte Hacken, Reibsteine, Topfscherben. Interessant ist ein Steinbeil mit Andeutung von Absatz hinter der Schneidenhälfte an der unteren Schmalseite und ein Axthammer mit sehr weitem Bohrloch, quadratischem Bahnende und sehr langer, dünner Schneide. Funde von Münchengosserstedt besitzt das Berliner Völkermuseum, das Henneberger Haus in Meiningen, das Germanische Museum zu Jena, Herr Heim in Camburg, das städtische Museum in Weimar. Näher bezeichnet wird eine Münchengosserstedter Fundstelle als „am Fußweg nach Camburg"; eine zweite als: „am Ort Münchengosserstedt".

Meiner früheren Einteilung folgend, haben wir
I. an vierkantigen Steinbeilen mit breitem Bahnende, leicht gewölbten Seitenwangen, gebogener Schneide:
Ein mittelgroßes Exemplar im HH.
Ein etwas kleineres, ebenda, aus Hornblendeschiefer.
Ein gleichartiges aus Hornblendeschiefer, mit halbmondförmig angeschliffener Schneide, ebenda.
Ein gleichartiges, ca 8,0 cm lang, ebenda.
Ein mittelgroßes aus grauem Gestein im BV 1416. Länge 7,0 cm, Schneidenhöhe 3,0 cm.
Ein desgl. mit geradflächig geschliffenen Schmalseiten, in H.P.S. Länge 10,0 cm, Breite 2,0 cm, Schneidenhöhe 5,0 cm.
Ein breites, flaches Steinbeil dieser Art im BV 1030, aus graubraunem Gestein, Länge 12,0 cm, Schneidenhöhe 6,0 cm.
Ein ebensolches im BV 2032, aus grauem Gestein. Länge 7,0 cm, Schneidenhöhe 5,5 cm.
Ein sehr langes, meißelartiges, ca. 15,0 cm lang, im HH.

II. Von vierkantigen Steinbeilen, die sich stark nach dem Bahnende zu verjüngen, bewahrt das BV ein Exemplar (1900) aus grauem Gestein, Länge 8,5, Schneidenhöhe 6,5.

III. Bikonvexe Steinbeile mit spitzem Bahnende gibt es aus Münchengosserstedt 3:

Ein schönes Exemplar in H.P.S., aus Kieselschiefer, grau mit schwarzen Flecken, Länge 9,5 cm, Schneidenhöhe 5,0 cm.

Ein gleichartiges aus schwarzem Kieselschiefer im HH.

Ein sehr langes dieser Art (Länge 16,0 cm) im BV 2652.

IV. Ein Steinbeil, vierkantig, mit geradflächiger oberer Schmalseite und hinter der Schneidenhälfte durch eine Querrille eingebogter unterer Schmalseite, in H.P.S., Länge 8,0 cm, gr. Breite 1,5, Schneidenhöhe 4,5 cm.

Steinäxte von dreieckiger Grundform mit Schaftloch:

Ein ca. 8,0 cm langes im HH., gut erhalten.

Die vordere lange Hälfte einer Steinaxt, mitten durch das Schaftloch gebrochen, mit einer zweiten unvollendeten Schaftlochbohrung aus dunkelgrauem Gestein im BV 2101. Länge 12,0 cm, gr. Breite 4,0 cm.

Ein Bruchstück: Schneidenhälfte eines ebensolchen mit spitzbogiger Vereinigung der Seitenwangen, mitten durch das Schaftloch zerbrochen, im HH.

Ein ebensolches ebenda, Schneidenhälfte.

Ein ebensolches Bruchstück mit rundlich abgeschliffenen Bruchflächen, wohl als Reiber benutzt, ebenda.

Eine sehr interessante Hammeraxt im St.M.W. (Fig. 55), von sehr schmaler Form, mit gebogener Schneide, quadratischem

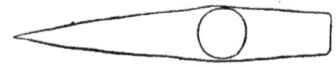

Fig. 55. $^1/_4$.

Bahnende und sehr großem Schaftloch. Die Hammerende und Schneidenteil verbindende Brücke ist kaum 1 mm dick. Länge 18 cm, Schneidenhöhe 3,5, gr. Breite in der Gegend des Bohrlochs 3,0 cm.

Steinhacken, breit, flach:

Eine mittelgroße im HH, „vom Fußweg nach Camburg".

Eine mittelgroße mit angeschliffenen Seitenwangen, Schneide abgebrochen im G.M.J., aus grünlichgrauem, schiefrigem Gestein.

Eine 11,0 cm lange, 4,5 cm breite im BV (1147), von grünlichem Gestein.

Eine 7,5 cm lange, 4,25 breite, aus grauem, schiefrigem Gestein, gut erhalten im BV 586.

Eine 8,5 cm lange, gut erhaltene im BV 2653.

Bemerkenswert ist eine ca. 10,0 cm lange, breite Hacke mit abgerundeter Schneide, breiterem Bahnende und Schaftloch, im HH.

Schuhleistenförmige Steinhacken, hochgewölbt, schmal:

Eine mittelgroße im HH.

Eine 10,0 cm lange, 2,0 cm breite aus schwarzem Gestein, im BV 2102.

Eine mittelgroße, verhältnismäßig breite, in H.P.S. aus Kieselschiefer, Länge 9,0 cm, gr. Höhe (Dicke) 2½ cm, Schneidenbreite 4,0 cm.

Eine ca. 15,0 cm lange, meißelartig geformte im HH.

Ein großes, langes, hochgewölbtes, schuhleistenförmiges Stein - gerät mit querdurchbohrtem Schaftloch, planer Unter - fläche, geglättetem Bahnende, im HH.

Als Reibkolben benutztes dickes, nach dem Bahnende zu sich verjüngendes Steinbeil mit abgebrochener Schneide im G.M.J., 8,5 cm lang, gr. Breite 5,6, an der Bruchstelle glatt gerieben.

Ein zigarrenetuiförmiger Reibkolben im BV 1415, aus schwarzem Gestein, 10,0 cm lang, 4,5 gr. Breite, mit 2 auf beiden Breitseiten angefangenen, cylindrischen Bohrungen.

Ein kugelförmiges Steingerät mit näpfchenartiger zen- traler Vertiefung, im HH., faustgroß.

Ein Bruchstück einer roten Sandsteinreibplatte mit Fo.: „Fußweg nach Camburg", im HH.

Thonscherben eines großen Gefäßes, schwarzbräunlich, dar- unter ein Randstück mit torquierter Verzierung. Als Fundort für letzteres ist angegeben „am Ort Münchengosserstedt". HH.

3. Schmiedehausen.

Im Juli 1882 berichtet Klopfleisch in der Weimarischen Zeitung von einer Fundstätte am Schmiedehäuser Weg.

Dieselbe war klein. Es fanden sich:

Knochen dort vom Schaf, ein vollständiges Gebiß des- selben,

und Getreidereibsteine, meist bläuliche Kieselsteine.

Die Klopfleischschen Fundstücke im Germanischen Museum zu Jena tragen die Signatur „Schmiedehausen zwischen Ziegelei und Dorf". Es sind Knochen vom Rind. Ein Kästchen ist gefüllt mit harzigen Körnchen und sig- niert: „Schmiedehausen vom Altare mit den vielen runden Gruben".

Die Fundobjekte sprechen dafür, daß es sich hier um Reste alter **Niederlassungen** handelt. Die Zeitstellung derselben ist unmöglich.

Eine zweite Fundstelle: „im Gelände" und eine dritte: „am oberen Lindenberg" beutete Heim aus.

9*

Beide liegen am Südwestende des Dorfes. Auch die Fundobjekte dieser beiden lassen auf alte **Wohnstätten** schließen.
Es wurden gefunden:

Scherben rohgearbeiteter Töpfe, mit Quarzkörnchen
reichlich vermengt,

ein abgebrochenes Henkelstück,

ein breiter Henkel,

ein kleiner, ausgebauchter Becher aus Ton mit ausladendem Rande, zeitlich der Bronzezeit angehörig,

3 Knochenpfriemen, von denen der längste ein zugespitzter Pferdefußzehenknochen, der mittelgroße ein feder-
artig zugespitzter zarter Röhrenknochen ist,

ein Lehmbewurfstück,

ein kegelförmiger, ein doppeltkonischer Wirtel, mit senkrechten Einkerbungen am Umkreis.

Zeitlich sicherzustellen sind die Funde einer **H e r d -
g r u b e** auf Schmiedehäuser Flur, die nach Berlin in das
Völkermuseum gekommen sind. Die Funde gehören in die
Zeit der **B a n d k e r a m i k.** Unter II b 2750 sind als aus
e i n e r Herdgrube stammend angegeben:

a) 1 Tonscherben der Bandkeramik (Bogenband);

b) 1 schuhleistenförmige, hochgewölbte Steinhacke,
L. 7,5; 1 Bruchstück einer solchen;

d) 2 Flintmesser, flach, dreikantig;

f) 1 Klopfstein in Kugelform (L. 8);

g) 1 ausgemuldeter Mahlstein, L. 25, gr. Breite 25 cm.

Südwestlich vom Dorfe „a n d e r Z i e g e l e i" hat H e i m
eine **Grabstätte aus der Bronzezeit** ausgegraben. In einer
schwarzen Brandaschenschicht, umgeben von einem Kreis
hochkant gestellter Steine, wurden

Tierknochen,

Urnenscherben in reichlicher Menge,

das Kinnstück eines menschlichen Unterkiefers mit
3 wagrecht abgekauten Zähnen zu Tage gefördert neben
einer Anzahl gut erhaltener Bronzen (Fig. 56—61):

1) Ein großer Halsring (Fig. 56), massiv, oval, offen, von rundem Querschnitt, nach rechts schnurförmig gedreht, mit wenig sich verjüngenden, glatten Enden, die etwas übereinander stehen. Weite ca. 17 cm.

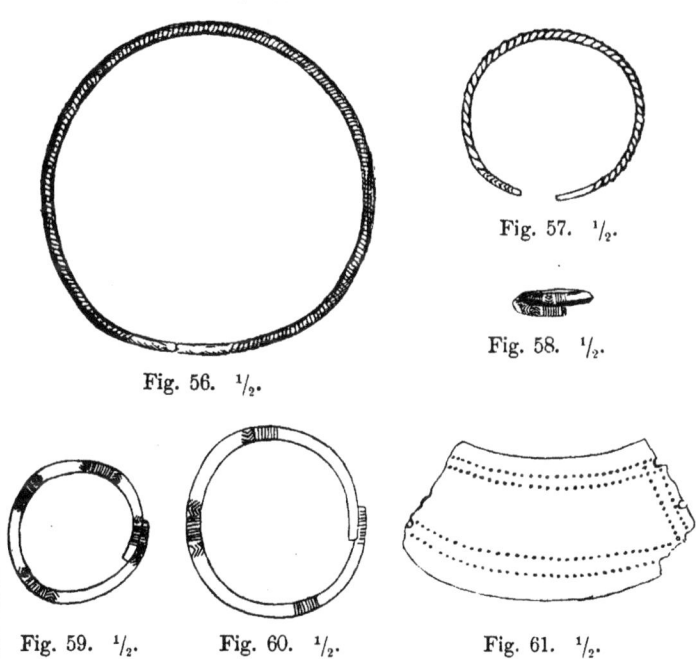

Fig. 57. ¹/₂.

Fig. 58. ¹/₂.

Fig. 56. ¹/₂.

Fig. 59. ¹/₂.   Fig. 60. ¹/₂.   Fig. 61. ¹/₂.

2) Ein Oberarmring (Fig. 57), massiv, oval, weit offen, von rundem Querschnitt, nach rechts schnurförmig gedreht, naeh den Enden sich etwas verjüngend; die ungedrehten Enden mit längs verlaufendem Grätenmuster verziert. Weite ca. 11 cm.

3) Ein Unterarmring (Fig. 58), massiv, oval, offen, mit übereinander liegenden Enden, vierkantig im Querschnitt; längs der oberen und unteren Kante verläuft ein fortlaufendes, kleinästiges Grätenmuster, quer um die Enden ein von einem System paralleler Linien beiderseits eingefaßtes, größeres Grätenmuster. Das äußerste Ende schließen kurze,

in der Längsachse des Armbandes verlaufende parallele Striche. Weite ca. 6 cm.

4) Ein Unterarmring (Fig. 59), massiv, oval, mit übereinander liegenden Enden, schön glänzender Patina; Querschnitt rund, innen glatt. An den Enden und an 3 gleich weit voneinander entfernten Stellen mit einem System paralleler, um die Außenfläche des Ringes verlaufenden Linien verziert. An den Enden sind diese einseitig, in der Ringmitte beiderseits von entgegengesetzt verlaufenden Fischgrätenmustern begleitet. Weite ca. 7,5 cm.

5) Ein Unterarmring (Fig. 60), massiv, breit-oval, offen, mit übereinander gelegten Enden, Enden etwas verjüngt, Querschnitt rund, innen abgeplattet, Ober- und Unterseite durch Scheuern an einem anderen beim Tragen stellenweise plattgeschliffen, an den Enden und 3 anderen Stellen mit einem System parallel um den Ring verlaufender Linien ornamentiert, die in der Ringmitte jederseits von einem Fischgrätenmuster begleitet werden. Dicker als vorheriger. Weite ca. 8,5.

6) Ein bronzenes Zierstück (Fig. 61), leicht schalenförmig gemuldetes Blechband, 14 cm lang, 5 cm breit ungefähr, beschädigt, mit 2 den Rändern parallel verlaufenden, eingepunzten Punktreihen, an den Schmalseiten je 2 zum Teil ausgebrochene größere Löcher.

Die genannten Funde sind in das Henneberger Haus nach Meiningen gekommen[1]).

Außerdem sind eine große Reihe von **Einzelfunden** auf Schmiedehäuser Gebiet gemacht worden, besonders auffällig viel Spinnwirtel, wenig Steinbeile und Steinhacken. Die meisten Einzelfunde sind steinzeitliche, einige slavische.

---

1) In E. Eichhorn, Die Grafschaft Camburg (im 20. Heft der Schriften des Vereins für S.-Meiningische Geschichte und Landeskunde) sind die Ringe auf Tafel III ohne Nennung des Fundortes abgebildet, Fig. 6, 2, 8, 5, 4.

Ein kleines, vierkantiges Steinbeil mit breitem Bahnende im HH.

Ein größeres ebensolches im HH.

Ein ebensolches mit gebogener Schneide im HH.

Ein vierkantiges Steinbeil, beschädigt, L. 9,5, im BV 2793.

Ein desgl., naeh dem Bahnende zu sich verjüngend, im BV 2794. L. 7,0 cm.

Ein desgl. im BV 2748. L. 5,0 cm.

Ein Steinbeil mit spitzem Bahnende im HH.

Ein desgl. mit ovalem Querschnitt, die Schneide nach Art der Hacken gekrümmt, aus grauem Gestein. L. 10,0, Schneidenhöhe 5,5. Im BV IIb 1224.

Eine durchlochte Steinaxt von dreieckiger Grundfläche im HH, mit abgerundetem Bahnende.

Eine desgl. mit ungleich langen Seitenwangen, in Pastor Schröders Besitz, hat eine Länge von 17,0 cm, Schneidenhöhe 2,0, Bahnendehöhe 3,0 cm, gr. Breite 6,7 cm.

Ein durchlochter Axthammer von rhombischer Grundfläche, L. 10,0 cm, die eine Hälfte fehlt, im BV 2749.

Bruchstück einer durchlochten Steinaxt (Schneidenteil) im HH.

Ein desgl., Axthammerende, im HH.

Ein sehr flacher Axthammer von rhombischer Grundfläche, mit abgerundeter Schneide, 24,0 cm lang, 2,8 Schneidenhöhe, 7,0 cm gr. Breite, in P. Schröders Besitz.

Ein längliches Steingerät, wohl das roh zugehauene Stück zu einem Axthammer, mit näpfchenartiger, angebohrter Vertiefung, graubraunes Gestein, im BV 1097. L. 16,5, gr. Breite 3,5.

Ein polygonal facettierter Axthammer aus grauem, schwarzgesprenkeltem Gestein, mit scharf vorspringender, senkrechter Kante zu beiden Seiten des Schaftlochs, L. 13,5, Breite 5,0, Schneidenhöhe 3,5 cm, in Heims Privatsammlung.

Eine flache, breite Steinhacke, gut erhalten, in H.P.S., 8,5 cm lang, 5,0 cm Schneidenbreite, 1,5 cm dick.

Eine breite, verhältnismäßig dicke Steinhacke, Oberfläche beschädigt, aus Kieselschiefer, L. 8,5, Schneidenbreite 5,0, in H.P.S.

3 Feuersteinmesser im HH.

2 Flintmesser im BV 2752. L. 4,5 resp. 6 cm.

1 Wetzstein aus Schiefer im HH.

1 Reibstein im HH.

1 durchlochtes, webegewichtartiges Gerät im HH.

1 Tonwirtel, doppeltkonisch, die niedere Hälfte leicht ausgemuldet, im BV 2756, mittlerer Durchmesser 3,5.

1 Steinwirtel, doppeltkonisch, Durchm. 2,9, im BV 2757.

1 Steinwirtel, breit-oval, mit konzentrischen Linien um die Außenfläche, Bruchstück, in H.P.S. Durchm. 3,5.

1 Tonwirtel, doppeltkonisch, die niedere Hälfte ausgemuldet, Außenfläche mit je 2 parallelen Furchen auf jedem Quadrant, in H.P.S. Durchm. 2,6.

1 Tonwirtel, doppeltkonisch, in H.P.S. Auf der niederen Hälfte senkt sich das Stabloch trichterförmig ein.

1 Tonwirtel, breit-oval, mit abgeplatteter mittlerer Zone, in H.P.S. Durchm. 4,0 cm, Höhe 2,5 cm.

10 weitere Spinnwirtel im HH.

1 Bernsteinperle, hell, doppeltkonisch, kirschengroß, im HH.

2 Stück Wandbewurf im BV 2753.

5 Tonscherben älterer Art, davon eine ornamentiert mit Reihen von kleinen Spitzovalen (Fig. 62), eine andere mit gestichelten Dreiecken (Fig. 63), im BV 2755.

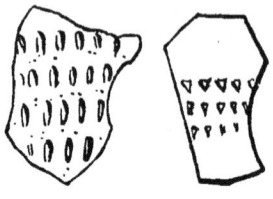

4 slavische Topfscherben mit Wellenornament, mit 7-zinkigem Kamm gezogen, im BV 2751.

2 Tiergehörne, das Geweih ziemlich gut erhalten.

Fig. 62.   Fig. 63.

4. Stöben.

Im Mai 1882 wurden auf einem frischgeackerten Felde in der Stöbener Flur vom Lehrer A. Sorge in Camburg schwarze Stellen entdeckt, die bei näherer Untersuchung Knochen, Urnenreste, eigentümliche Kieselsteine enthielten. Klopfleisch wurde hiervon benachrichtigt. Am 12. Juli 1882 wurden Ausgrabungen in der Nähe von Stöben veranstaltet. Die von Klopfleisch hierüber gemachten Tagebuchnotizen und Skizzen beweisen, daß man auf **vorgeschichtliche Abfallgruben** gestoßen war, in deren Nähe einstens menschliche Niederlassungen gelegen hatten.

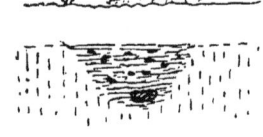

Fundstelle 1: „In der unteren Trift", an dem Feldraine beim Dorfe (Besitzer Albert Hauemann) wurden trichterförmige Herdstellen freigelegt.

Fig. 64.

Unter der Ackererde senkte sich in den lehmigen, natürlichen Boden trichterförmig eine Grube (Fig. 64), die ausgefüllt war mit schwärzlicher, aschenartiger Erde. In dieser lagen zerstreut bunt durcheinander:

viele Tierknochen,

viele Urnenscherben, die meist schön geglättet, schwarz gefärbt, teilweise mit hübschen Randleisten versehen sind,

Reste von Reibern,

größere Reibplatten aus Sandstein, eine von ihnen: 19 cm lang, 12$^1/_2$ cm breit, 5 cm dick,

kleinere Handreiber,

Holzkohlen.

Fundstelle 2: „a u f d e r H e i d e“ (Fig. 65), auch noch auf Schmiedehäuser Flur, Besitzer Albert Hanemann.

40 cm unterhalb des lehmigen Bodens stieß man auf einen großen, mit kleinen Steinen eingefaßten Kreis von 2,80 m Durchmesser. Innerhalb desselben fand sich melierte

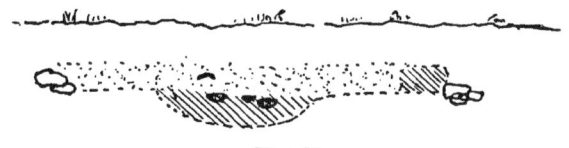

Fig. 65.

Branderde mit Tierknochen. An der Nordseite der Peripherie, innerhalb des Kreises, war eine kleinere, runde Stelle von 50 cm Durchmesser als Brandstelle deutlich zu unterscheiden. Das Zentrum der steinumgrenzten Fläche bildete eine in den Boden flach eingesenkte, kreisrunde Vertiefung, die mit Branderde ausgefüllt war und ziemlich viel Tierknochen und einzelne Tonscherben enthielt. Weiterhin wurde ein kleiner Bronzerest gefunden, daneben eine zerquetschte, sehr weiche Urne von Schalenform, Reste eines etwas härteren Gefäßes und eines töpfernen Napfes mit hohem Rande.

Fundstelle 3: „a u f d e r H e i d e“, südwestlich der Fundstelle 2, von ähnlicher Anlage.

Hier war eine rautenförmige Steinumgrenzung unter der Lehmdecke zu Tage gekommen. An der Nordecke Reste eines sehr starken, großen Tongefäßes innerhalb der umgrenzten Stelle. Die Mitte der Fundstelle war, wie bei der vorigen Fundstelle, tiefer in den Lehmboden eingesenkt und mit vereinzelten Tierknochen durchsetzt. Am Grunde der Senke lag ein Stein. Im Profil wie Stelle 2.

Fundstelle 4: „a u f d e r H e i d e“, südwestlich hinter Stelle 3, in einer Linie mit 2, bereits in der Mitte durchwühlt. Die Anlage war im ganzen so wie die der anderen, ein kreisförmiger Fleck mit schwarzer Branderde ausgefüllt. In derselben lagen Tierknochen, Tierzähne zerstreut und ein besonders nennenswertes zertrümmertes Gefäß von roter Farbe, durch Feuer nachträglich gehärtet, klingend.

Fundstelle 5: „auf der Heide", schon angegraben. Anlage ebenso, schwarze Branderde mit zahlreichen Tierknochen und Urnenresten, darunter ein sehr starkes, großes Gefäß und ein Bruchstück eines Henkelgefäßes.

Ein in der Weimarischen Zeitung noch im Juli 1882 erschienener kurzer Bericht bezeichnet diese Stellen als Opferstätten unserer Vorfahren und gibt ihr Alter auf 2—3000 Jahre an.

Am 21. August 1889 suchte Klopfleisch neue Fundstellen in der Nähe von Stöben auf. Ein an der Ausgrabung damals mitbeteiligter Herr, der Landwirt Carl Kunze in Hirschroda, schilderte diese Ausgrabung in einem schriftlichen Bericht, dem wir folgendes entnehmen:

Hanemann war wiederum beim Ackern auf vorgeschichtliche Fundobjekte gestoßen. Die Stellen waren an der Oberfläche nicht sichtbar, höchstens beim frischen Ackern fielen sie durch eine dunklere Färbung des Ackerbodens auf.

Die erste Stelle lag am Fahrweg nach Schmiedehausen. In schwarzer Erde fand man einige Urnenscherben.

Eine etwas erhöht gelegene zweite Stelle war von circa 4 m Durchmesser und $1/_2$ m Tiefe. Dieser Raum war angefüllt mit Branderde. Der Boden im Mittelraum war mit Steinen besetzt; ein mit Branderde gefülltes Loch ging noch über 1 m unter den Boden. Gefunden wurden: ziemlich viel Urnenscherben und ein ziemlich gut erhaltener Unterkiefer eines Hirsches.

Die dritte ausgegrabene Stelle hatte einen Durchmesser von ca. $1^1/_2$ m und eine Tiefe von über 2 m. In diesem Raum war der oberste Teil angefüllt mit Branderde. Diese lag auf einer Schicht Estrich, einer rot aussehenden gebrannten Lehmschicht, die nach Art einer Tenne behandelt und gebrannt wurde. Unter dieser Estrichschicht befand sich wieder ein kleiner Raum, angefüllt mit Branderde. In dem oberen Raum lagen zahlreiche Knochen und

Scherben von Urnen, im unteren ein vollständiges, gut erhaltenes Skelett einer jungen Ziege, umgeben von Scherben und anderen Knochen.

Weitere Fundstellen wurden am 24. August 1889 ebenfalls auf Hanemannschen Grundstücken a u f d e r H ö h e n a c h L a c h s t e d t z u ausgebeutet. Die **erste Stelle** war 3 m im Durchmesser, 1 m tief, mit Branderde ausgefüllt, die mit Knochen und Scherben vermengt war. In der Mitte des Bodens waren eine ziemliche Anzahl von Steinen gelegt.

Die **zweite Stelle**, ziemlich so groß, mit Branderde gefüllt, bot eine große Zahl sehr mürber Tierknochen, darunter 2 Kinnladen, Rippen, Zähne vom Rind. Der Boden war stellenweise mit Estrich belegt.

Die **dritte Fundstelle** war die ergiebigste: $1^1/_2$ m breit, 70 cm tief. Gleich von Anfang an wimmelte es von Scherben. Die mächtigen Scherben mit Fingertupfeneindrücken auf einem $1^1/_2$ cm unter dem Rand um das Gefäß herumlaufenden Wulst ermöglichten eine ungefähre Zeitbestimmung.

In einer ähnlichen, etwas kleineren Stelle mit Branderde fand man 2 noch zusammenhängende Kinnladen von einem Hausrind.

Auch hier handelte es sich also — wie wir sehen — um eine Anzahl von **Abfallgruben** im Bereiche vorgeschichtlicher Siedelungen.

D i e i n d i e s e n A b f a l l g r u b e n v o r g e f u n d e n e n p r ä h i s t o r i s c h e n F u n d e sind ihrerzeit in das Germanische Museum zu Jena gekommen. Die hier aufbewahrten Scherben sind meist Reste grobgearbeiteter Gefäße. Die Masse der meisten ist mit Quarzkörnchen durchsetzt von Sandkorn- bis Hirsekorngröße. Die hartgebrannten sind geringer an Zahl und haben meist eine schmutzig-ziegelrote Farbe. Die meisten sind dickwandig, bis über 1 cm stark, hell-lehmfarben, braun, bis schwarzgrau. Die größeren sind oberflächlich geglättet, die dünnwandigeren besser.

Als besonders interessant seien genannt:

Das Bruchstück eines großen, dickwandigen Gefäßes mit geglätteter Oberfläche, schwarzgrau, die Masse mit bräunlichen und weißen zerkleinerten Steinchen reichlich durchsetzt, ist besonders interessant, weil am Halsübergang zum oberen Bauchteil eine nicht verstrichene Furche sichtbar, die beweist, daß der Hals extra auf das Gefäß aufgesetzt ist, nachdem der Bauch fertiggestellt war. Der Durchmesser der Urne an dieser Übergangsstelle beträgt 14 cm. Hals und oberer Bauchteil bilden einen Winkel von 110°.

Auf eine beträchtliche Größe läßt ein Gefäßrandstück schließen mit oberem Bauchteil. Der Durchmesser des Gefäßes an der Halswurzel beträgt 28 cm, der Winkel, den Hals und oberer Bauchteil miteinander bilden, 120°. Der Rand ist abgerundet, ohne verstärkenden Wulst. Die Substanz des Gefäßes durchweg grau, mit Quarzstückchen vermengt, die Oberfläche geglättet. Die Wandungsstärke 6—8 mm.

Ein Bodenstück mit teilweise erhaltener, anschließender Gefäßwand, äußerlich gut geglättet, schmutzig-braun, die Masse im Bruch schwarzgrau, mit vielen bis hanfkorngroßen Quarzkörnchen durchsetzt, die Wandung 10 mm stark. Bodenfläche und Wandung bilden einen Winkel von 125°. Der Bodendurchmesser 12 cm.

Ein anderes Bodenstück eines ebenfalls dickwandigen, großen Gefäßes mißt im Durchmesser 14 cm, die Wandung steht auf ihm im Winkel von 125°.

Ein Bodenstück eines kleineren Gefäßes hat nur einen Durchmesser von 4,5 cm.

Der **Rand** der aufgefundenen Gefäße ist entweder dadurch hergestellt, daß die Gefäßwandung oben einfach glattgestrichen ist, ohne Ausladung, ohne besondere wulstförmige Verstärkung, so besonders bei den großen Gefäßen, deren Masse mit Quarzkörnchen reichlich durchsetzt ist, oder der Rand ist leicht wulstig umgebogen oder er ist von einer krauselförmig gefalteten Tonleiste begleitet, die man, den oberen Gefäßhals verstärkend, aufgelegt und in bestimmten Zwischenräumen mit der Fingerkuppe ein- und angedrückt, das verdrängte Stück nach unten geschoben hat. Randstücke dieser Art finden sich eine ganze Anzahl (Fig. 66—69). Sie gehören zu großen Gefäßen mit dicken Wandungen.

An der Halswurzel hat das eine (Fig. 66) einen Durchmesser von 22 cm. Es ist schmutzig-backsteinrot auf der Außenfläche und Innenfläche gefärbt, die Masse innen grau, mit Quarzstückchen reichlich vermengt, 7 mm starke Wandung.

Bei einem gleichartigen (Fig. 67) liegt über der Leiste ein verstärkender Randwulst. Dies Gefäß ist dunkelziegelrot, die Masse in der Mitte schwarzgrau, mit Quarzkörnchen vermengt, Wandstärke 10 mm, Dm. am Hals 24 cm.

Bei einem weiteren derartigen Gefäß (Fig. 68) sieht man besonders gut, wie das verdrängte Stück nach unten geschoben worden ist. Dm. des Mündungsrandes 22 cm.

Schließlich sieht man bei einem kleineren Randstück (Fig. 69), wie die Fingerkuppen zweier nebeneinander gelegten und eingedrückten **Finger** den aufquellenden kleinen Kamm noch einmal von beiden Seiten eingedrückt haben.

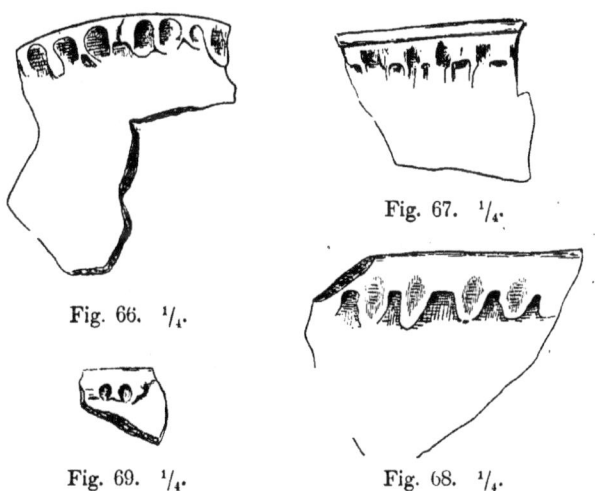

Fig. 67. $^1/_4$.

Fig. 66. $^1/_4$.

Fig. 69. $^1/_4$.　　　　　Fig. 68. $^1/_4$.

Diese Tupfenleiste tragen einige Gefäße am Hals, nicht mit dem Rande zusammenhängend, als besonderes Ornament (Fig. 70).

Auch eine abgesprungene derartige Leiste wurde gefunden (Fig. 71).

Zwei hell-ziegelrote, hart gebrannte Randstücke (Fig. 72) demselben Gefäß angehörig, sind in einiger Entfernung vom

Fig. 70. $^1/_4$.　　　　Fig. 71. $^1/_4$.　　　　Fig. 72. $^1/_4$.

Rand durch eine Kette von oben nach unten ausgehobener, lanzettförmiger Stiche verziert. Der obere Durchmesser dieses Gefäßes betrug 10 cm nach Berechnung.

Die gefundenen **Henkel** (Fig. 73—76) sind alle breit, das Henkelloch für einen Finger passierbar. Sie sitzen am Halse, gehen mit ihrem einen Bogenansatz unmittelbar in den Gefäßrand über, mit dem anderen unmerklich in die Wandung des Topfes (Fig. 73, 74) oder sie sitzen am Um-

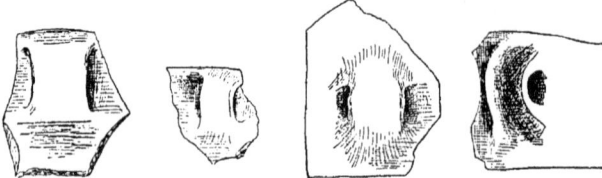

Fig. 73. $^1/_4$. Fig. 74. $^1/_4$. Fig. 75. $^1/_4$. Fig. 76. $^1/_4$.

bruch des Bauches (Fig. 75, 76). Der eine ist im Querschnitt plankonvex, er gehört zu einem Gefäß von 28 cm weitestem Durchmesser, der andere, plankonkav, zu einem Gefäß von 24 cm Durchmesser zwischen den Henkeln.

Nur wenige Gefäße sind in ihrer ganzen Form rekonstruierbar: Ein napfförmiges, hartgebranntes, ziemlich dünnwandiges, ziegelrotes (Fig. 77). Der Boden, $6^1/_2$ cm

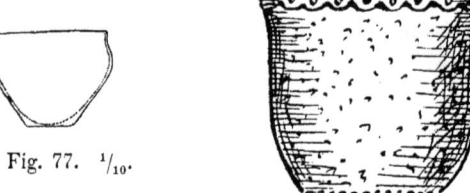

Fig. 77. $^1/_{10}$.

Fig. 78. $^1/_{10}$.

im Durchmesser, größter Durchmesser $17^1/_2$ cm in $8^1/_2$ cm Höhe, ganze Höhe 13 cm. Nach dem Rande zu biegt die Wandung sanft nach innen, Durchmesser hier 16 cm, um 1 cm vom Gefäßrand wieder wenig auszuladen. Der Rand ist ohne Wulstverstärkung, scharf. Die Bodenfurche innen ist ausgefüllt; auf dem oberen Bauchteil hüben und drüben je ein brustwarzenförmiger Buckel.

Ein großes, im ganzen kugelförmiges Gefäß, am Halse sich leicht verjüngend, der Rand dann wieder ausladend, einfach glatt abgerundet; Wandstärke 12 mm, größter Durchmesser 30 cm, oberer Durchmesser 26 cm, Hals im Lichten 24 cm.

Ein sehr großes, glockenförmiges Gefäß mit Tupfenleiste unter dem Rande; 29 cm oberer Durchmesser, 28 cm Höhe, sehr dickwandig (Fig. 78).

Von weiteren Fundobjekten aus den Herdgruben sind zu nennen:

14 teils kugel-, teils eierförmige Körper, die einen künstlich hergestellt aus Ton, die anderen abgeschliffene, feine Sandsteingebilde.

Eine kleine Anzahl Feuersteinspäne,

ein großes Webegewicht, aus rötlichgrauem Lehm, schwach gebrannt, 4 Längsseiten, Unterseite beschädigt durchgehendes Loch von $1^{1}/_{2}$ Durchmesser;

eine hochgewölbte schuhleistenförmige Steinhacke 16,0 cm lang, 3,5 cm breit, 4,0 cm hoch, 410 g schwer;

eine kleine Steinhacke, flach, breit.

Fundort „an der Schweinsbrücke", ausgebeutet von Heim. Hier fanden sich Urnenreste ohne Verzierungen, ein kleines, henkelloses, napfartiges Gefäß aus Ton mit 4 bronzenen, vierkantigen Stückchen im Innern (Reste einer Nadel).

Als Einzelfunde von Stöben liegen im Henneberger Haus in Meiningen:

Eine Steinaxt aus Grünstein, Schaftloch im Zentrum der Axt, was besonders zu bemerken[1]), 15 cm lang, im Horizontalschnitt dreieckig, mit langer Schneide, Bahnende seitlich abgerundet.

Eine Steinhaeke, flach, breit, mit gebogener Schneide, geradem Bahnende, aus Kieselschiefer, mit Schaftloch, eine Seltenheit[2])!

Ein Bruchstück: der Schneidenteil einer Steinaxt aus grünhchem Gestein.

Heim in Camburg besitzt zur Zeit ebendaher eine durchlochte Steinaxt von unregelmäßig-dreieckiger Grundfläche, mit ge-

---

1) Vgl. E. Eichhorn, Die Grafschaft Camburg, Heft 20 der Schriften des Ver. f. S.-Mein. Gesch. u. Landeskunde, Taf. IV, Fig. 7.
2) Vgl. ebenda Taf. IV, Fig. 7.

bogener Schneide, schiefem Bahnende, aus graugrünem Gestein; auch hier befindet sich das Schaftloch mehr nach dem Zentrum zu.

Im Berliner Völkermuseum:

Ein vierkantiges Steinbeil aus grauem Gestein, mit gebogener Schneide, breitem Bahnende, flach gewölbten Seitenwangen. L. 8,5, Schneidenhöhe 4,0 cm. (BV II b 1611.)

Ein Steinhammer, durchlocht, im Horizontalschnitt unregelmäßig-dreieckig, Ober- und Unterseite flach gewölbt. L. 11,5 cm. (BV II b 2641.)

Ein Klopfstein von länglicher Gestalt, aus grauem Gestein. L. 8,5, gr. Br. 3,0. (BV II b 1612.)

In einer **Lehmgrube zwischen Stöben und Camburg** fand Klopfleisch eine steinzeitliche Abfallgrube, die Tonscherben waren gut gebrannt, grau, mit feinem Sand gemengt, mit Bandverzierung (gerade Linien und Tupfen von unten nach oben aus der Tonmasse ausgehoben).

Dabei ein stark gebrannter, ziegelroter Gefäßscherben, 3 mm stark, ein Randstück mit einer Kette von ausgestochenen lanzettförmigen Gruben unterhalb des glatten Gefäßrandes.

Andere Scherben waren unverziert. Diese Fundobjekte liegen im Germanischen Museum zu Jena.

Es sei hier ein prachtvoller Bronzekelt (Fig. 79) erwähnt, der in Stöbens Nachbarschaft auf Lachstedter

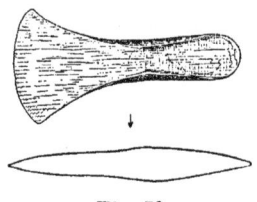

Flur bei Großheringen gefunden worden ist neben menschlichen Skeletten. Nähere Fundberichte fehlen. Der Kelt befindet sich im G.M.J.

Er ist 269 g schwer, mit niederen Randleisten versehen, nach der Schneide zu kräftig ausladend, Schneide gebogen, Bahnende abgerundet, grün patiniert. Länge 13,0 cm, Schneidenhöhe 6,0 cm, in der Mitte 2,3 cm hoch, Dicke 14 mm, Höhe der Randleisten 2 mm. In der Schaftrille ist an der bräunlichen Verfärbung der Patina die Holzschäftungsform noch erkennbar.

Fig. 79.

(Fortsetzung folgt.)

Miszellen.

I.

Landmesserordnung und Holzordnung im Amt Keula aus den Jahren 1567 und 1572.

Mitgeteilt von Pfarrer Fleischhauer in Oberspier.

Die nachstehenden zwei Ordnungen, eine Ordnung im Landmessen zur Feststellung der Grenzen und Beilegung der Grenzstreitigkeiten zwischen Flurnachbarn und eine Ordnung für die Nutzung der Gemeindewaldungen, sind entnommen der Gemeindelade von Großbrüchter, einem Dorfe des früheren Amtes Keula, das den Viergrafen des Reiches von Schwarzburg gehörte.

Das Amt Keula, jetzt der westliche Teil der Schwarzburg-Sondershausenschen Unterherrschaft und dem Landratsamt, Amtsgerichtsbezirk und der Superintendentur Ebeleben zugeteilt, kam durch Erbvertrag zwischen den Grafen von Honstein und Schwarzburg um die Mitte des 14. Jahrhunderts an die letzteren.

Im Jahre 1421 nahm Graf Heinrich von Schwarzburg Keula nebst Straußberg vom Erzbischof zu Mainz zu Lehen, wogegen der Erzbischof seinen Ansprüchen auf Heringen entsagte.

Im Jahre 1437 kam durch Tausch gegen das Dorf Blankenburg Kleinkeula (jetzt zu Gotha gehörig) und halb Urbach, die beide bisher im Besitz der Landgrafen von Thüringen gewesen waren, an das Amt.

Um 1540 führte Graf Günther XL. die Reformation in-seinen Landen ein.

1670—1681 residierte als Herr des Amtes Graf Anton Günther II. in Kenla.

·1682--1716 bestand ein Unterkonsistorium daselbst.

Im Jahre 1852 ist der Sitz des Justizamtes nach dem Marktflecken Ebeleben verlegt worden.

Zum Amt Keula gehörten die Ortschaften Keula, Holzthaleben, Großbrüchter, Kleinbrüchter, Urbach, Toba, Wiedermuth, Rockensußra, Großmehlra.

Zur „Holtzordnung“, die einige Hauptbestimmungen der jetzt in den Ortschaften Keula, Holzthaleben, Großbrüchter und Urbach (sog. obere Pflege des Landratsamtes Ebeleben) geltenden Waldordnung enthält, ist zunächst zu bemerken, daß sie wohl der erste bekannte Versuch ist (vergl. auch Art. 6), den vorbenannten Orten die Nutznießung des ihnen gehörigen Waldes zu ordnen und ein Gemeindevermögen zu erhalten, das noch heute als die vorzüglichste Ursache ihrer Wohlhabenheit zu gelten hat. Besonders sind in dieser Richtung Artikel 1 und 2 bedeutsam. Nach den Bestimmungen der neuesten Zeit sind die politischen Gemeinden Besitzer der Interessentenwaldungen, so z. B. Keula, das 748 ha 22 a 38 qm Wald besitzt, durch endgültiges Urteil des Revisionskollegiums für Landeskultursachen in Berlin vom 10. Juli 1868 und durch Zuschreibungsurkunde des Fürstlichen Justizamtes in Ebeleben aus demselben Jahre.

Art. 1 ist selbstverständlich nicht mehr gültig. Dagegen besteht Art. 2 seinem Inhalt nach noch jetzt zu Recht. Die Besitzer von Holzgerechtigkeiten (im genannten Orte 95 an der Zahl) sind Hausbesitzer oder Besitzer von Hausstätten (Grundstücke, auf denen ein Haus gestanden hat), zu denen die Holzgerechtigkeiten untrennbare Pertinenzen sind.

Art. 6 hat in den neuesten Bestimmungen dahin eine Abänderung gefunden, daß sämtlichen Ortsangehörigen, so lange sie im Ort ihren bleibenden Wohnsitz haben, also auch zugezogenen Heimatsberechtigten, die Ausübung folgender Nebenberechtigungen zusteht:

1) Die Nutzung der Stämme (Stocken), der beim Fällen stehen gebliebenen Schaftenden, deren Höhe mindestens 2 Fuß von der Erde ab betragen muß, nebst Wurzeln. Ausgenommen von der Nutzungsberechtigung sind der Pächter der fürstlichen Domänen, der Pfarrer, die Lehrer, Alimentanden, die nicht eigene Wirtschaft führen, und Witwen, die keinen über 14 Jahre alten Sohn haben.

Zu dieser Bestimmung kann Einsender von einer ihm mitgeteilten Sitte berichten, die noch in den 30er und 40er Jahren des vorigen Jahrhunderts bestand (1846 abgeschafft). An einem festgesetzten Frühlingstage nach Beendigung der Schlagzeit versammelten sich die erwachsenen männlichen Bewohner Keulas an einer bestimmten Stelle des Dorfes. Beim Glockenschlag begannen sämtliche Teilnehmer zum Walde zu laufen, um dort die Stocken, die ein jeder zuerst erreichen konnte, für sich in Besitz zu nehmen. Wer am frühesten am Ziele war, hatte die Auswahl unter den besten Stocken bis zu einer gewissen Anzahl. Die Besitzergreifung bestand zu Recht.

2) Das Recht der Gräserei mit gewissen Einschränkungen.

3) Das Sammeln von Raff- und Leseholz für den Hausbedarf.

4) Die Nutzung der Laubstreu. Ausgeschlossen bleiben die drei jüngsten Schläge.

5) Die Nutzung der Bucheckern. Nur das Auflesen, resp. Zusammenkehren der Eckern, nicht aber das Anschlagen und Klopfen der Bäume ist gestattet.

Wegen dieser Einschränkung entstand im 3. Jahrzehnt des 19. Jahrhunderts ein Streit zwischen der Gemeinde Keula und der Regierung. Die Gemeinde nahm das Recht des Bucheckerschlagens für sich in Anspruch. Im Interesse der Waldverjüngung und des Nationalwohlstandes konnte die Regierung das Recht nicht gelten lassen. Als die Ortsbewohner trotz mehrfacher Verwarnung und Strafen nicht von der Ausübung ihres vermeintlichen Rechtes abließen, mußte eine Abteilung Soldaten des Schwarzburger Kontingents in den Ort gelegt werden. Es kam sogar im Walde zum Kampf, bei dem Blut geflossen sein soll. Die Begebenheit wurde im Volksmund der Bucheckerkrieg genannt.

Art. 9 bestimmt, daß bis zum Walpurgistag das gefällte Holz aus der Maße geschafft sein sollte. Nach den jetzt geltenden Statuten (§ 13—15) muß das Fällen der Bäume spätestens bis 1. Mai, die Aufbereitung des Holzes bis 24. Juni, die Abräumung der Maßen durch Abfuhr bis spätestens den 1. Dezember beendet sein.

Zum Schluß ist zu bemerken, daß, wie heute dem Staate (Fürstl. Ministerium, Abt. des Innern), zur Zeit der Aufstellung der Holzordnung die Oberaufsicht den Grafen von Schwarzburg (den gräfl. Räten zu Keula) zustand. Sie bestimmten die Strafen, setzten die Holzförster ein, wie sie auch Urheber der hier wiedergegebenen Holzordnung gewesen sind. So heißt es am Ende: „Es soll auch unser gnädiger herr diese ordnung jederzeit zu mehren, zu mindern oder abzuthun macht haben".

1. Ordnung im landtmessen des ambts Keula.
Anno 1567.

Erstlichen.

Wer befindet, daß ihm von seinen nachbar etwas aus unbilligkeit abgepflüget, der soll denselben gütlich bereden, oder mit zween mann beschicken und begehren ihm sein abgepflügtes landt in der güthe wieder zu geben, und wo er ihm an früchten schaden gethan, denselben auf billige wege erstatten und wenn sie sich unter einander nicht vergleichen können, ein jeder zween unpartheyische männer zu sich bitten;

2) Wenn aber diese güthl. handlung der sachen nicht helffen will, soll der kläger den bürgermeister oder heimbürger bitten, den geschwohren männern zu befehlen, einen gelegenen tag zu ernennen, und den gebrechen abhelffen.

3) Soll der kläger verpflichtet seyn, denen meßer 4 gr., ehe sie hinausgehen, zu erlegen.

4) Wenn nun beyde theile hinaus beschieden, sollen die meßer beyder partheyen bericht nothdürftig hören und mahl-steine, steine, alte gewende fleißig besehen, auch wo es noth, andere leuthe befragen und nach des oder derselben anzeigunge, bey ihren pflichten vertheilen, den nicht an allen orthen der ruthe meisterin seyn kann.

5) Sollen auch die meßer, wo siehs ohne verrückung anderer gewende leiden will, all ende, so sie verglichen, alsobalden versteinigen, damit gezänke, so viel möglichen, abgeschaffet werden mögen.

6) Soll der beklagte, so er in wenigen oder vielen unrecht befunden, den klägern die ausgelegten 4 gr. alsobalden wieder erstatten, und den meßer von jeder forche (:doch unbegeben gnädiger herrschafft strafe:) 3 gr., ist aber der acker bestellt, 7 gr. erlegen und den kläger seinen schaden nach erkänndtnüß obgenanndter messer entrichten.

7) Weiln es aber gleichwohl an deme, daß die gesetzten mahlsteine heyden theilen zu guthe gerichtet, soll jeder parth von jeglichen steine, welche auch kläger und beklagte zugleich schaffen sollen, den messer 6 ₰. vergnügen, und ob wohl 4 ruthen breit und 30 lang und also auf und zurichten einen gemeinen acker, da (?) die ruthe 14. sehue lang seyn sollen, so soll es doch (?) um die ruthen und größe der acker, wie es an einem jeglichem orthe von alter hergebracht, gehalten werden und bleiben.

8) Sollen auch beyde partheyn verbunden seyn, wenn sie den meßer ihre notdurfft angezeigt, auf begehren von der irrung ahzuweichen, damit sich die meßer desto freyer zu unterreden und die handlung fürzunehmen haben.

9) Würde eine oder beyde partheyen, in ausführen oder erscheinen, sie die meßer mit losen worttem angreiffen, oder gegen dieselben sich ungehohrsamb erzeigen, so sollen die ungehohrsamen, so oft es geschieht, den meßer 5 gr. zur straffe verfallen seyn, doch unbegeben unser gnädigen herrn straffe.

10) Sollen die meßer bey ihren geschwohren eyde hirinnen vorsichtig, fleißig, auch unpartheyisch handeln, im fall aber da es von ihnen anderst vermerckt, sollen sie um gestalte sachen u. g. herrn strafffällig seyu, obgleich nicht vermuthl., daß die meßer jemand wißendtlich unrecht thun, derowegen ihnen auch von den partheyen gefolget werden soll, so soll doch eine oder heyden theilen, so sich beschwerth befunden, weilu am meßen geirrt werden kann frey stehen, wenn sie den meßer wie gehöret, ihre gebühr zuvor erlegt, das ambt zu besuchen, da aber nach besichtigung befunden, daß er die meßer zur unbilligkeit beklaget, so soll er Mgfl. 4 . . (?) uuabläßig zur straffe verfallen seyn, würde aber daß er seine suchens ursach gehabt, erkandt, so soll die irrung naeh weisung des ambts gerichtet und sein erlittener schaden nach erkändtnüß deßelbigen erstattet werden.

11) Soll ein jeglicher, der eine langweilige irrung zu haben vermeinet, zur zeit, wann das feldt offen und unbestellt ist, sonder in der braache, solche suchen und rechtfertigen laßen, würde er aber zur zeit bestellter felder derentwegen ansuchen, so sollen die messer nicht verbunden seyu, dazumahl die meßunge für die handt zu nehmen, aber in neuen abpflügen sonderl. in der brache soll kein verzug geschehen.

12) Sollen die meßer an allen orthen der fluhr uf die mahlsteine fleißig achtung geben und wo sie befunden, daß jemand dieselbigen verrückt, umbgeworffen oder verändert, solches alsobalde bey ihren pflichten im ambte anzeigen und bescheides gewarten.

13) Würde eine gemeine fluhr irrung zu rechtfertigen von nöthen seyn, daran sollen sich die meßer ohne vorwissen des ambts nicht unterstehen, auf daß niemanden darinnen zu kurtz geschehe.

2. Geschwohren- oder stein-setzer eydt.

Demnach ihr bey der gemeinde NN zum ältesten und geschwohrenen außerlesen und vorgeschlagen worden und anitzo darzu bestätiget werden sollet, als sollet ihr zu der heil. dreyfaltigk. geloben und schwehren.

Daß ihr zuförderst gnster herrschafft unsern gnsten graffen und herrn, dero hochlöbl regierung und ambte treu, hold, und gewärtig seyn, nutzen fördern, schaden und nachtheil aber hüten und warnen, sodann 2) auf richtig maaß, gewichte, schue und ruthen sehen und halten, und nicht zugeben, daß darinnen unterschleiff vorgenommen werde. — 3) Auf die gräntze genaue aufsicht mit halten, und da was guster herrschafft dem ambte oder der gemeinde nachteiliges vorfiele, oder unternommen würde, sofort gehörigen orths berichten. 4) So irrungen zwischen reinen (Rainen?) und steinen geschehen, solches auf erhaltenen ambts-befehl euren besten wißen und gewißen nach mit anbescheiden helffen, auch auf erfordern zu versteinen und uhrkunden zu machen, mit den maß-ruthen richtig anschlagen und darinnen niemand so viel oder zu wenig geschehen lassen, auch 5) dafern von dem ambte bey Be-sichtigung von baustädten, feuerstädten und dergl. it. Executionen, immissionen oder Taxationen häuser, acker und wiesen erfordert werden, solts euch darbey willig finden und auch in allen als wie treuen, rechtschaffenen geschwohrenen zustehet, verhalten, und da-bey nicht ansehen wollet freundtschafft oder feindschafft, geschenke oder gabe, haß, furcht, gunst oder ungunst, oder wie es nahmen haben möge. So wahr euch gott belffe.

3. Copia der holtzordnung im amte Keüla aufgerichtet anno 1572.

Art. 1.

Welcher einwohner seine holtzmaßen verkauffet und nicht zu seinem haushalt gebraucht, derselbige soll meinem gnäd. herrn ein fuder bier und der gemeind ein faß zur straffe geben.

Art. 2.

Es soll keine holtzmaßen von den häusern verkaufft werden, sondern eine jede maße soll bey dem hause, darzu sie gegeben, bleiben; wer daß über treten wird, soll obenangezogen straffe geben; da aber jemand über seinen hauß halt etwas zu verkauffen übrig hat, daß soll ihm hier mit nicht verbothen seyn.

Art. 3.

Wer im holtze mit hauen oder fahren schaden thut oder sonsten an schaden betroffen wirt, derselbe soll meinem gnäd. hern 2 fl. und der gemeinde 1 fl. straffe geben und sich mit dem förster abfinden und verdragen.

Art. 4.

Wer ohne erlaubnis des holtzförsters in seinem übergebenen forst eigenmächtig einen reiß stock hauen würde, derselbe soll meinen gnäd. herrn 2 fl. zur straffe geben und sich mit der gemeind und förster abfinden.

Art. 5.

Alle hauungen sollen mit hüten und treiben von hirtten und schäffern, desgl. mit den pferden, sieben jahr lang geheget und nicht betrieben noch behütet werden bey straffe 3 fl., so offt einer dar-über begriffen und befunden wirt.

Art. 6.

Dieweil befunden wird, daß sich viel mithlinge in die dörffer um daß holtzes und feuerwerckes willen begeben, dem selben soll nicht mehr, wie wohl geschen, holtz gegeben werden, sondern wer die einnimmt und aus dem amte sie einzunehmen vergünstigung und laube hat, der soll sie mit feuerwercke aus seiner holzmaßen mit versehen, wer aber daß nicht thun kan oder will, der mag ihrer müßig gehen und aus dem seinen laßen bey straffe 5 gfl.

Art. 7.

Sollen alle heegereiser so geschlagen und gemarcket sein be-
neben den haubtstämmen, sie sein gleich jung oder alt, abzuhauen
verbothen seyu bey straffe 5 gfl. meinen gnädig herrn, und der gemeinden isre straffe unbenommen.

Art. 8.

Verbothene und unnöthige wege im holtze soll niemand fahren;
wer das thut und darüber begriffen, der soll der hérrschaft 2 fl. zur
straffe geben und den förstern ihr pfandgeld.

Art. 9.

Ein jeder soll sein holtz wintters zeit und im frühlinge auß der
maßen schaffen, also daß die gehölze von groben holtze und vom
reisich auf den tag Walburgis gantz ledig und gereümet sein, bey
verlust des holtzes und gäntzlicher enthaltung des selben, wie denn
auch nach dem tage Walburgis keiner mehr holtz führen soll bey
straffe 2 fl. auf jede fuhre. Es würde den in ansehung der hohen
nothurfft und gelegenheit der vorgefallenen verhinderungen auff ansuchen und bitten, aus dem amte einem insonderheit oder ingemein
nach Walburgis auf ein oder mehr tage gunst und verlaubnis gegeben.

Es soll auch unser gnädiger herr diese ordnung jederzeit zu
mehren, zu mindern oder abzuthun macht haben.

Hiernach wolle sich ein jeder halten und zu richten wissen,
und sich vor schaden selbst hüten, den ein jeder soll hiermit ge-
nungsam vor der straffe gewarnt seyn.

Literatur.

I.

Dr. Eduard Böhl, Beiträge zur Geschichte der Reformation in Österreich, hauptsächlich nach bisher unbenutzten Aktenstücken des Regensburger Stadtarchivs. Jena, G. Fischer 1902.

Das Böhlsche Buch hat für die Thüringer Geschichte eine speziellere Bedeutung, indem die von hier vertriebenen Anhänger des Flacins gutenteils in Österreich Aufnahme gefunden und auf die Weiterentwickelung des dortigen Protestantismus entscheidenden Einfluß ausgeübt haben. Ein aus Österreich gebürtiger Referent im kirchenhistorischen Seminar (der in der Darstellung der dogmatischen Streitfragen den Verfasser möglichst in dessen eigenen Worten anführt, somit zugleich auch ein klares Bild von dem Standpunkt seines Werkes gibt) stellt die hierauf bezüglichen Tatsachen folgendermaßen zusammen.

Von außerordentlicher Bedeutung für die Entwickelung und Verbreitung der protestantischen Lehre in Österreich sind die mehrmaligen Vertreibungen evangelischer Prediger und Lehrer aus Thüringen.

Im vorliegenden Buche werden diese Ausweisungen in dem historischen Überblick behandelt. Der Verfasser beginnt mit den Ereignissen nach Luthers Tod. Nach Gegenüberstellung der entgegengesetzten Ansichten Maurenbrechers und Wolfs über den Charakter des Kurfürsten Moritz geht er auf das Augsburger Interim über, das 1548 auf dem Reichstag zu Augsburg vom Kaiser erlassen, auch als Reichsgesetz proklamiert, jedoch nicht allgemein durchgeführt werden konnte.

Seit Flacius und Gallus und überhaupt die Magdeburger 1549 euergisch für die Interessen des Protestantismus eintreten, werden die Klagen über das Interim allgemein, infolgedessen die Opposition immer stärker. Im Frühjahr 1549 läßt Moritz von Sachsen, um den verschiedenen Klagen gerecht zu werden, von Vertretern beider Parteien das Augsburger zum Leipziger Interim umarbeiten, das den Protestanten wohl mehr zusicherte, die katholische Kirche aber immer noch so weit bevorzugte, daß ein großer Teil der Protestanten, im Gegensatz zu dem Mitarbeiter am Interim Melanchthon, erklärte, das Interim nicht annehmen zu können.

Gleichermaßen erklärten die strengen Katholiken, das Interim benachteiligte sie, und deshalb könnten sie es nicht annehmen. So war denn die Folge dieser Einheitsbestrebungen, daß die protestan-

tischen und katholischen Kirchen keinesfalls einander näher getreten
waren, und daß es von nun an innerhalb des protestantischen Lagers
zwei feindlich sich gegenüberstehende Parteien gab, die der Orthodoxen (Flacius, Amsdorf, Wigand u. s. w.) und die der Paktierer
mit der katholischen Kirche (Melanchthon und die Wittenberger
überhaupt). Im Anschluß an das Interim folgen nun jene erbitterten,
gehässigen Kämpfe um die Adiaphora, den Synergismus und Majo-
rismus, die immer mehr persönlichen Charakter annahmen, vor allem
weil Melanchthon in den den Adiaphorismus betreffenden Fragen
privatim wohl Schuld bekannte, nicht aber öffentlich, weil er be-
fürchtete, sich selbst bloßzustellen und viele Anhänger von sich ab-
zuwenden.

Es ist leicht zu begreifen, daß bei einem solchen Stand der
Dinge das Wormser Kolloquium ergebnislos sein mußte, das auf
dem Regensburger Reichstag beschlossen worden war.

„Erst der Naumburger Fürstentag 1561 brachte größere Klarheit in die Situation." Nach Melanchthons Tod hörte die Nach-
giebigkeit gegen seine Schule auf, und die strenge Richtung Jenas,
wo seit Jahren schon Flacius und seine Freunde lehrten, drang
durch. 1574 geht auch Kursachsen in das Lager der strengen
Lutheraner über, nachdem dem Kurfürsten August „über die schon
anfänglich durch Melanchthons Beispiel genährte Unaufrichtigkeit
von Männern wie Peucer, Cracov, Stößel, Schütz die Augen geöffnet" worden.

Während der adiaphoristische Streit im Sinne der strengen
Lutheraner seinen Abschluß fand, endete der synergistische Streit, der
bald nachher entstanden war, mit dem ersten Exodus thüringischer
Pfarrer und Professoren, die auf Luthers Standpunkt im Streite
über die Erbsünde verharrten.

Eingeleitet wurde der Streit durch ein Vorgefecht zwischen
dem Leipziger Pfaffinger und Amsdorf nebst Flacius. Gegen den
Frankfurter Rezeß vom Jahre 1558 ließ Herzog Johann Friedrich
auf Rat des Flacius das Konfutationsbuch ausgeben, verfaßt von
Strigel und Stößel und von Flacius durchgesehen. Dasselbe war
keineswegs dazu angetan, die Kluft zwischen den Jenaern und
Wittenbergern zu überbrücken, im Gegenteil, es erweiterte die Tren-
nung. Nun ereignete sich das Unerwartete, daß Strigel, der Mit-
verfasser der Confutatio, der erste Prorektor der neugegründeten
orthodoxen Universität, bald im Sinne der Synergisten zu lehren begann. Flacius bekämpfte ihn, erzielte jedoch nur so viel, daß er am
10. Dezember 1561 aus Jena ausgewiesen wurde. Herzog Johann
Friedrich, der bisher ganz und gar von der orthodoxen Partei geleitet worden war, konnte so weit umgestimmt werden, daß er das
Urteil unterschrieb. Man kann diesen Umschwung ins gerade Gegenteil vielleicht zu beschönigen suchen durch die Vorfälle am Hofe,
sowie den Fall Wesenbeck und die Behandlung der reformierten
Kurfürstin Marie v. d. Pfalz, die ja tatsächlich den Beweis brachten,
daß die Orthodoxen doch zu weit gingen; aber trotzdem ist es ein
Zeichen der Charakterschwäche des Herzogs. Der Herzog war offenbar der Spielball jener Leute, die sein Ohr hatten, besonders des
(jüngeren) Kanzlers Brück. Genug, das Urteil war gefällt: Flacius
nebst 40 anderen Predigern und Pfarrern, unter denen auch der
spätere österreichische Prädikator Magdeburgius war, mußten das
Land räumen.

„1562 wurde durch eine Visitation den Predigern zwangsweise auferlegt, sich des Zankes über den Synergismus zu enthalten." Damit fand der erste Exodus seinen Abschluß.

In den Jahren 1571—73 fand eine zweite Massenvertreibung statt, die durch den Erbsündestreit veranlaßt wurde. Flacius lehrte in Übereinstimmung mit Luther, daß der Mensch sich in der Bekehrung nicht nur rein passiv verhalte und zum Guten völlig erstorben sei, sondern daß er sogar nur widerstreben könne. Anfangs, auf dem Kolloquium zu Weimar, wich sein Gegner Strigel dem Flacius beständig aus, und letzterer blieb im Recht. Doch als Heshus infolge eines Mißverständnisses dem Placius Dinge aufbürdete, die Flacius gar nicht behauptet hatte, und als es den Gegnern gelang, Flacius' Lehre vom Boden der Augsburgischen Konfession zu verdrängen, da hatten sie gesiegt.

Die folgenden Blätter sind der Geschichte der Flacianer und ihrer Bebandlung in den thüringischen Ländern gewidmet. Überall ließ man dem Haß gegen den Verfolgten und seinen Anhänger frei die Zügel schießen, weil er die Erbsünde als Substanz definierte. Dieser Haß ward bald auch in Österreich allgemein. Kaiser Maximilian schloß sich schon aus politischen Gründen dem Kurfürsten August an. Und demnach sind gerade hier in Österreich die Flacianer fast die einzigen Stützpfeiler des Evangeliums gewesen dadurch, daß sie für Luthers Lehre von dem „unfreien Willen" sich von Stadt zu Stadt, von Land zu Land verfolgen ließen — aber aufrichtig treue Lutheraner blieben. „Sie widerstanden aufs heftigste dem ihnen vom Kaiser und den Papisten gelegten Fallstrick, daß man Ceremonien, wie sie die Adiaphoristen zuließen, in die neue Agende nehmen solle, und perhorreszierten Leute, wie Camerarius, Eber, kurz die Melanchthonianer, die sich zu solchen Kompromissen hergaben."

Die nennenswertesten der flacianischen Prediger in Österreich sind wohl Mathias Klombner, der in Krain wirkte, Sebastian Krell, mit Flacius aus Jena geflohen, und Primus Truber.

Es tritt in dieser Übersicht deutlich zu Tage, daß Professor Böhl seinen aus früheren Veröffentlichungen bekannten dogmatischen Standpunkt auch in der Darstellung der den alten Protestantismus innerlich zerfleischenden Gegensätze zur Geltung gebracht hat. Es ist hier aber nicht der Ort, diese Gegensätze selber genauer zu zeichnen bezw. an der Böhlschen Urteilsweise Kritik zu üben. Es wird genügen, neben den bekannten zusammenfassenden Geschichtswerken, zumal von Hase und Kurtz, die bei dem Jenaer Jubiläum von 1858 erschienene Schwarzsche Geschichte der ersten 10 Jahre der dortigen Universität in Erinnerung zu rufen, wo begreiflicherweise sowohl die Strigelsche wie die Flaciussche Tragödie im Mittelpunkt stehen. Ebenso zeichnet sich die Einleitung zu der Loebeschen Geschichte der Kirchen und Schulen im Herzogtum Sachsen-Altenburg durch ihre objektive Zeichnung der gegenseitigen Verfolgungen aus, deren Opfer hüben und drüben so zahlreiche Pfarrer- und Lehrerfamilien geworden sind.

Mit den Beziehungen zwischen den Thüringer Exulanten und der österreichischen Kirche ist jedoch nur ein kleiner Ausschnitt aus dem Böhlschen Werke gegeben. Sein übriger Inhalt wird in dem schon erwähnten Referat folgendermaßen gekennzeichnet.

Die Bedeutung der „Beiträge" ist, wie der Verfasser in der

Vorrede bemerkt, darin zu suchen, daß er bei seiner Arbeit der Mehrzahl naeh bisher unbekannte Quellen benutzte. Es sind dieses Akten und Briefe aus dem Regensburger Stadtarchiv, die bis in die mittleren Jabre des 16. Jahrhunderts zurückreichen und interessante Daten zur Reformationsgeschichte überhaupt, wie speziell zu derjenigen Österreichs bieten. Sie werfen ein helles Licht auf die dogmatischen Streitigkeiten innerhalb der protestantischen Kirchen, die naeh Luthers Tode die Gemüter in Aufregung hielten, und reinigen zugleich die Reformationsgeschichte Österreichs von mannigfachen Irrtümern.

Dem eigentlichen Thema schickt der Verfasser einen theologischen und einen politischen Überblick voraus.

Der theologische Überblick hat es mit den dogmatischen Streitigkeiten zu tun, deren wir schon oben gedachten. Spezieller hebt sich die Schilderung der Folgen des Leipziger Interim S. 38 herans.

In dem historischen Überblick finden die Vertreibungen evangelischer Professoren und Pfarrer aus Thüringen eine eingehende Behandlung, weil sie auf die österreichischen Verhältnisse und den Gang der Reformationsbewegung in den habsburgischen Erbländern einen nicht zu unterschätzenden Einfluß ausgeübt haben.

Dem ersten Exodus von 1561 folgte zu Anfang des nächsten Jahrzents der zweite 1571—73, der direkt durch die Parteinahme für Flacins im Erbsündestreit verursacht war. Dieser zweite Naehschub fand in Österreich abermals bereitwillige Aufnahme.

1573 fand eine dritte Vertreibung statt, als Kurfürst August mit Hilfe des Kaisers die Vormundschaft in den durch Johann Wilhelms Tod verwaisten sächsischen Herzogtümern erhalten und nun aus Rache alle Gegner seiner Richtung — damals der melanchthonischen — auch Wigand und Heshusius, fortschaffen ließ, wobei so viele Prediger das Land räumen mußten, daß großer Mangel an Kandidaten eintrat.

Während der Verfasser im bisherigen besonders die Beziehungen Thüringens zu dem evangelischen Österreich erläutert, tritt er jetzt auf österreichischen Boden über. Zunächst untersucht er auf Grund des vorliegenden Quellenmaterials die Stellungnahme der vier Herrscher Ferdinand I., Maximilian II., Rudolf II. und Mathias zur Reformationsbewegung. Keiner der vier Kaiser hat sich absolut feindselig zu den Evangelischen gestellt und — abgesehen von der ersten Regierungszeit Ferdinands — dieselben blutig verfolgt. Wenn sich der Protestantismus trotzdem für die Dauer nicht befestigen konnte, so lag das an den protestantischen Fürsten selbst, die gerade in entscheidenden Augenblicken am meisten entgegen arbeiteten, unter ihnen besonders August von Sachsen (1553—86).

Unter den leitenden Persönlichkeiten des Jahrhunderts kommt zunächst König Ferdinand I. in Betracht. Er war für seine Person dem alten Glauben ergeben und sah mit Schmerz, wie ein Teil seiner Untertanen, besonders der Adel, sich dem neuen Bekenntnis zuwandte. Er duldete aber die Verbreitung des protestantischen Gottesdienstes trotz aller Mandate dagegen und gab selbst seinem Sohn Maximilian einen Lehrer von protestantischer Richtung.

Die Verderbtheit und Unwissenheit des Klerus hatte auch in Österreich die Reformation vorbereitet, und als die Bewegung einmal im Gange war, konnte Ferdinand sie nicht mehr hemmen. Er mußte trachten, die protestantischen Stände für sich zu gewinnen, weil er ihre Hilfe im Kriege gegen die Türken unbedingt brauchte. 1546 ändert sich die Sachlage. Es wird für österreichische Theologen nicht bloß das Studium in Wien und Freiburg obligatorisch gemacht und die Universität Wittenberg verboten, sondern bald bringt der Bischof von Laibach, Urban Textor, auch die Jesuiten ins Land. Nach den Regensburger Akten scheint im Jahre 1554 die Verfolgung der Protestanten ihren Höhepunkt erreicht zu haben. Perkheim, Herr von Wirting und Roseneck, klagt in einem Brief an den Juristen Hiltner in Regensburg: „Und werdn nun theglich mehr gefenklich eingezogen, wellns alles auff das pabstumb pringen." Weiter berichtet er über einen Hofkaplan Paulus: „Redt frei heraus trefflich und thut den sachen recht; ist schon einmal von der K. M. selbst und zwier vor dem Herrn Hofmarschall im Capitl gebest, hart angeredt wordn."

In einem zweiten Brief berichtet er, wie man sich vom Hofe aus bestrebe, die Protestanten zu entzweien und gegeneinander aufzuhetzen.

28. August 1554 schreibt er an Gallus: „Vor verrugkhung der Ro. K. M. in Wien sein abermal 3 arm pfarherr gefangen wordn, allain, das sy das sacrament des altars In bederlaj gestaldt gehn hahn, di lign noch gefangen."

Nach Karls V. Rücktritt von der Regierung 1556 eröffneten sich für Ferdinand die Aussichten auf die deutsche Kaiserkrone, und er mußte bestrebt sein, den Religionsfrieden aufrecht zu erhalten und die Protestanten für sich zu gewinnen, zumal da der Papst sich in einer Anklageschrift offen gegen seine Nachfolge erklärte. In diesem Zusammenhang führt der Verfasser eine Reihe von Briefen an, die deutlich beweisen, wie sich die Politik Ferdinands zu Gunsten der Protestanten geändert hatte. Diese Umwandlung in Ferdinands Verhalten den Protestanten gegenüber ging so weit, daß er noch in seinem Todesjahre sich ernstlich bestrebte, eine Union zwischen Protestanten und Katholiken zu erwirken und auf dem Tridentiner Konzil energisch die Gewährung des Laienkelches forderte.

1564 kommt Maximilian II. zur Regierung. Er ist eine durchaus unberechenbare Persönlichkeit. Faßt man seine Jugendjahre ins Auge, so ist es schwer verständlich, wie er, der der Protestanten halber von seinem Vater viel hatte leiden müssen, es so weit kommen ließ, daß er gegen seine innere Überzeugung zu Zeiten die Protestanten in ihrem Rechte einschränkte. Er lavierte zwischen den streitenden Parteien hindurch, bald dieser, bald jener etwas zur Beruhigung nachlassend. So behandelte er die Jesuiten äußerst streng und ließ sich dann doch wieder von ihnen leiten, wenn sie sich schmeichelnd an ihn heranmachten. Er wollte allem Anschein nach Vermittler zwischen den Parteien sein. Doch war die einzige Folge seiner Bestrebungen die, daß bei seinem Tod niemand wußte, ob er als Protestant oder Katholik gestorben.

So ist es auch erklärlich, daß die zeitgenössischen Schriften nur ein unklares, verschwommenes Bild seiner Person geben können. Unter den Regensburger Dokumenten finden sich mehrere Briefe Reuters, Perkheims u. s. f., aus denen man deutlich herauslesen kann, wie die Protestanten auf Maximilian bei seinem Regierungsantritt die größten Hoffnungen setzten, wie sie später immer mehr an seiner Aufrichtigkeit zu zweifeln beginnen, bis sie ihm schließlich nicht selten mit offenem Mißtrauen entgegentreten. Und dennoch müssen wir einen Maximilian hochschätzen, wenn wir seine Regierung mit der seines Sohnes und Nachfolgers Rudolfs II. vergleichen. Persönlich ist auch er den Protestanten nicht feindlich gesinnt gewesen. Obgleich in Spanien von Jesuiten erzogen, zeigte er in politischen wie in religiösen Dingen eine auffallende Gleichgültigkeit. Er war nicht der Mann, um mit dem System seines Vaters plötzlich zu brechen, und rührte nicht an die Privilegien und Freiheiten der protestantischen Stände. Das Verhängnisvolle seiner Regierung war, daß er die Verwaltung des Erzherzogtums Österreich seinem Bruder, Erzherzog Ernst, übertrug, der an Entschlossenheit und Willensstärke Rudolf weit überragte. Von seiner Zeit datiert die Gegenreformation in Österreich. Obgleich die Protestanten ursprünglich noch an Zahl bedeutend stärker waren als die Römisch-Katholischen, gelang es der Regierung bald, der evangelischen Kirche ihre Rechte und Privilegien zu entziehen, und damit war der Anfang zur vollständigen Unterdrückung der evangelischen Bewegung gegeben.

Unter Mathias wurde die Gegenreformation allgemein durchgeführt, hier gewaltsam, wie in Oberösterreich, dort auf Umwegen, wie in Niederösterreich.

Es ist eine auffallende Erscheinung, daß im Regensburger Stadtarchiv keine einschlägigen Schriften erhalten sind, als ob die Beziehungen der Protestanten Österreichs zum Beginn der Gegenreformation zu denen des Reiches mit einem Schlage aufgehört hätten.

„Die evangelische Bewegung ist in Österreich so mit dem Adel verwachsen, daß, wer eine vollständige Geschichte derselben geben wollte, die Geschichte der vornehmsten Adelsgeschlechter schreiben müßte." Daß bei der Gegenreformation trotzdem auch von dieser Seite nur verhältnismäßig schwacher Widerstand geleistet werden konnte, hat seinen Grund darin, daß die Jesuiten es von jeher gründlich verstanden, die Protestanten in ewigem Streit und Hader zu erhalten.

Die Hauptfaktoren bei der Ausbreitung des Evangeliums waren die Prädikanten. An diesen war Österreich nicht arm; es erhielt sie vom Reiche, besaß aber auch unter den eigenen Landeskindern Prediger und Lehrer, die als kühne Streiter für ihren Glauben eintraten. Der größte Teil der einheimischen Prädikanten bestand aus Mitgliedern alter Adelsfamilien und vor allen Dingen aus ehemaligen katholischen Geistlichen oder Mönchen. Die Visitation der Klöster vom Jahre 1528, veranlaßt durch Faber, den Bischof von Wien, zeigte, daß die Reformation in den Klöstern Ober- und Niederösterreichs zahlreiche Anhänger hatte. Und wenn der Kampf gegen das Luthertum auch von den Kanzeln organisiert wurde, so blieben solche Verteidigungsmaßregeln ähnlichen Erscheinungen gegenüber doch wirkungslos.

Von allen Prädikanten verdient an erster Stelle genannt zu werden Nikolaus Gallus.

1516 war er in Köthen in Anhalt geboren. Frühzeitig, nachdem er seine Studien in Wittenberg vollendet und daselbst magistriert hatte, wurde er als Diakonus an die Marienkirche in Regensburg berufen. Beim Ausbruch der theologischen Streitigkeiten zwischen Melanchthon und Jena bekennt er sich als entschiedener Anhänger des Flacius. Später wurde er in Regensburg Superintendent, und

als solcher entfaltet er eine außergewöhnlich umfangreiche Tätigkeit.
Für Österreich hat er insoweit eine große Bedeutung, als er, lange
bevor durch die Agende ein mehr geordnetes Kirchenwesen zu stande
kam, für Österreich eingehend sorgte. David Chyträus rühmt ihm
nach, daß er „totins vicinae, Austriae et Stiriae ecclesias emendavit,
doctrina et consiliis suis pie et fideliter erudiit et gubernavit".
Grenzenlos war das Vertrauen der Herren vom Adel, gewisser
Magistrate und vieler Prädikanten zu ihm; unter letzteren besonders
Reuter. Gallus war unermüdlich, allen an ihn gerichteten Gesuchen
um Prüfung und Ordination zu entsprechen. Nur die von ihm Ordinierten seien gut, so lautete das Urteil eines Pfarrers aus Österreich. Groß und unermüdlich war er auch auf literarischem Gebiet.
54 Jahre alt starb er im Zellerbad in Württemberg 1570, wohin er
sich begeben hatte, um Linderung von Steinbeschwerden und Podagra
zu suchen.

Zu den bedeutenderen Prädikanten gehören weiterhin Wolfgang
Waldner, Christoph Reuter und Joachim Magdeburgius.

Wolfgang Waldner, etwa 1520 in Tulln bei Wien geboren, war
der Sohn eines Bauern. Seit 1545 war er Geistlicher zu Steyr und
lebte als solcher, wie viele seiner Zeit, im Konkubinat, das er später
in eine Ehe umwandelte. Diese Ehe, wie auch der Umstand, daß
er zuerst und allein evangelisch wirkte, machte ihn in Steyr unmöglich. Er ging zunächst nach Augsburg, von da nach Nürnberg
und beteiligte sich lebhaft an den späteren Lehrkämpfen. Er stand
entschieden zu der Partei, die Melanchthon und die Wittenberger
überhaupt scharf verurteilte. Als Prediger am Dominikanerkloster
zu Nürnberg erhält er von Steyr aus mehrere Ansuchen, in die
Heimat zurückzukehren, doch kann er sich nicht entschließen, seine
feste Stellung in Nürnberg für die unsicheren Verhältnisse Österreichs umzutauschen. Doch verfolgt er auch später von Regensburg
aus die Vorgänge im Nachbarlande mit aufmerksamem Auge und
ist stets bereit, die Evangelischen mit seinem Rat zu unterstützen.

Im Anschlusse an die Charakteristik dieses Mannes gibt der
Verfasser eine Auswahl der Briefe, die der alte Hans Waldner mit
seinem berühmten Sohn Wolfgang wechselte, und die uns tief in
die intime Gesinnung der österreichischen Landbevölkerung blicken
lassen.

Unter den in Österreich selbst wirkenden Prädikanten war der
bedeutendste Christoph Reuter. Derselbe war etwa im 4. Jahrzehnt
des Jahrhunderts in der Oberpfalz geboren. 1555 kam er nach
Österreich und lebte anfangs zu Spitz in Niederösterreich. Dann
ward er als Schloßprediger nach Rosenberg versetzt. Einige seiner
Briefe aus Rosenberg teilt der Verfasser im Anschluß mit, aus denen
wir sehr Wertvolles über die damaligen Zustände in Österreich erfahren. Man begegnete ihm allgemein mit solchem Vertrauen, daß er
aufgefordert wurde, ein Bekenntnis aufzustellen, welches er 1562 im
Druck erscheinen ließ. Wegen dieses Bekenntnisses mußte er im
folgenden Jahr aus Österreich weichen, doch durfte er schon 1564
wieder in Wien erscheinen, und bald lernte ihn Kaiser Maximilian
so hoch schätzen, daß er sich oft bei ihm Rat holte. Es war ein
ernster Lutheraner, dem es auf die Seelsorge und nicht auf dogmatische
Distinktionen ankam. In seiner Bescheidenheit konnte er es nicht
verstehen, daß ihn die Stände und der Kaiser als eine Art Beirat in
allen kirchlichen Fragen betrachteten.

Das letzte Lebenszeichen, das wir von ihm haben, ist ein Brief an Backmeister, in welchen er von demselben Abschied nimmt.

Nach dem Tode Ferdinands I. erhielt dessen Sohn Erzherzog Karl bei der Erbteilung Innerösterreich. Anfangs tolerant, machte er den Protestanten immer größere Zugeständnisse, blieb aber selbst streng katholisch. Die Jesuiten und seine Gemahlin, eine bayerische Prinzessin setzten es aber bald durch, daß er gegen die Protestanten strenger auftrat. Es wurde dem gewaltig vordringenden Protestantismus dadurch ein Damm entgegengesetzt, daß 1573 in Graz eine Jesuitenschule gegründet wurde, die schon 1578 den Charakter einer Universität annahm. Bald darauf erfolgte die entscheidende Verordnung Karls, daß die ihm untergebenen Städte und Märkte die Jugend auf keine andere als die Jesuitenschule schicken dürften. Ebenso wurde den Bürgern der Stadt Graz der Besuch des evangelischen Gottesdienstes in der Stiftskirche verboten. So war denn an Stelle der Toleranz in kurzer Zeit Gewalt getreten, besonders seitdem sich der Bischof Martin Brenner als Haupt der Gegenreformation an die Seite Karls stellte. Aus den Schriften dieser Zeit können wir die große Gefahr erkennen, die den Bestand der evangelischen Kirche bedrohte, obgleich sieh die Protestanten nach Kräften gegen solche Gewaltmaßregeln wehrten. So wurde 1574 an die Reformierung der Landschaftsschule in Graz geschritten, damit dieselbe nicht hinter der 1573 eröffneten Jesuitenschule zurückbleibe. Gleichzeitig sollte auch eine neue Kirchenordnung aufgestellt werden. Hierbei kam es aber zwischen den beiden Hauptpersonen, Khun und Chyträus, zu Zwistigkeiten, welche das Gelingen des ganzen Werkes nicht wenig gefährdeten. Endlich entschied man sich dahin, daß die heilige Schrift, die altkirchlichen Symbole, Luthers Katechismus und die Konfession hinzugenommen werden sollen, und die Declaratio (Norm der Lehre) auf Grund dieser Schriften insgesamt verfaßt werde. Luthers Schriften durften unter keinen Umständen ausgeschlossen werden. Endlich wurde auch noch über die Ordination der Kirchendiener und die Ceremonien verhandelt; bezüglich der letzteren sollten keine lateinischen Gesänge und überhaupt weniger Ceremonien gebraucht werden. Der letzte Punkt betraf die Bestellung des Predigeramtes, die Einsetzung eines Kirchenvaters, die Visitation und Aufsicht über Kirche und Schule, die Aufstellung nützlicher Synoden u. s. w.

Der Einfluß dieser neuen innerösterreichischen Kirchenordnung auf die Nachbarländer (Steiermark, Kärnten, Krain) kann nicht gerade günstig genannt werden. Überhaupt gibt der ganze Fortschritt der Reformationsbewegung reichlich Anlaß zu Enttäuschungen. Der Grund dafür lag darin, daß die beteiligten Prädikanten nicht geeignet waren, um dem gewaltigen Vorstoß des mit den Jesuiten verbündeten Hofes erfolgreich Widerstand zu leisten. Dieser, oder besser die Jesuiten scheuten sich nicht, das Volk zu vergewaltigen. Tortur, öffentliche Hinrichtungen und Kerker waren in Graz nichts Ungewöhnliches.

So wurde die Gegenreformation in diesen gut evangelischen Ländern durchgeführt. Sie übte mit ihren Gewalttätigkeiten auf den Geist der Bevölkerung eine niederschmetternde Wirkung, die bis heute noch in ihren Folgen nicht überwunden ist.

Auch der Streit um die Erbsünde war mit den aus Sachsen Vertriebenen nach Österreich verpflanzt und konnte nicht so bald beigelegt werden. Ebenso schieden sich in der Frage um das Abendmahl die Philippisten von den Antiphilippisten. Das Interesse des einen an Melanchthons Namen sich hängenden Teiles lag nunmehr darin, die Streitfrage möglichst unentschieden zu lassen. Sie hofften auf Ausgleichung und Abstumpfung der Gegensätze im Laufe der Zeit. Diese Partei, die augenblicklich noch die Oberhand hatte, betrieb eifrigst die Vertreibung der Pfarrer der Gegenpartei. Es begann überhaupt auf der ganzen Linie ein Vorstoß zur Unterdrückug der strengen Lutheraner, dessen Opfer ohne ihr Vorwissen Opitz und seine Freunde in Regensburg wurden. „Man entledigte sich der Klamanten und Schreier, wie es hieß, um soviel Ruhe als möglich zu bekommen und konform mit den benachbarten Städten vorzuziehen. Ja, man bediente sich der Gutachten von orthodoxer Seite, um nur unter einem guten Schein die Partei des Flacius tunlichst zu schwächen. In diesem Zusammenhang fügt sich nun der Erbsündestreit der 70er Jahre in Österreich ein. Es war nur die Fortsetzung des Kampfes im Reiche und wurde von manchen herzlich beklagt. So schreibt Philipp Barbatus 1573 an Waldner in Regensburg: „Nicht mit wenigen Schmertzen erfahre ich auch, daß es albereidt unter den Predigern und Lehrern Eurer Kirchen und Schulen über dem Zank De peccato originis zu splittern anfahe. Ach der bösen, jammerlichen Zeith. Blibe man bey Gottes Wortt und der Lehre D. Luthers, welcher an vielen Ortten seiner Bücher, wie auch in Schmalkaldischen Artikeln klar zeuget . . . “.

Innerhalb der evangelischen Stände selbst war Zwiespalt anläßlich der bevorstehenden Berufung eines Landschaftspredigers in Wien. Die Bestellung eines Superintendenten war nämlich nicht gestattet. Nach längeren Parteiumtrieben wurde Opitz, der aus Regensburg hatte flüchten müssen, zum Landschaftsprediger in der Hauptstadt gewählt. In dieser Stellung wirkte er nun 4 Jahre, dann wegen seiner als flacianisch verschrienen Lehre wurde er bald verleumdet und war seinen Gegnern ein Dorn im Auge. Wenn dieser erst 32-jährige hochgewachsene Mann rücksichtslos predigte, in seinem Feuereifer selbst ärgerliche Dinge auf der Kanzel vorzubringen sich nicht scheute, so darf ihm das nicht als Schuld angerechnet werden. Seine schweren Erlebnisse hatten ihn nicht entmutigt und nicht die Überzeugung bei ihm bewirkt, daß er, weil er verfolgt wurde, eine ungerechte Sache vertrete. Die große Stadt Wien lag vor ihm offen, die Ernte reif zum Schnitte. Schon gaben die Römischen ihre Sache verloren. Ein Brief aus dieser Zeit gibt ein gutes Bild von der Stimmung, die in katholischen Kreisen herrschte: „Das Religionswesen ist allhie in 20 Jahren nicht übler eingestanden, als eben jetzo. Außer des Hauffleins so die frummen heiligen Vatter der societas Jesu bis anhero auffgehalten, ist es alles gefallen. Die sacramenta werden nicht mehr bei der haupt- und pfarrkirchen, sondern alle im landhaus gesucht und prophaniert. Auch Skt. Stephan werde in kurzem zu einer Wüste werden, und niemand nehme sie zu Herzen.“ — Die Erregung wurde aufs höchste gesteigert, als Opitz die Erzählung von etlichen tausend Kindsköpfen, die in Klöstern gefunden sein sollten, auf die Kanzel brachte. Der Jesuit Georg Scherer schrieb gegen diese das katholische Gefühl verletzende, doch allgemein verbreitete Erzählung, ließ aber außer acht, daß es Opitz nicht auf die Zahl der Köpfe ankam, sondern daß er das System treffen wollte, das Cölibat, das solche Früchte notwendig tragen mußte.

Die Aufrüttelung der Gemüter durch Opitz und seine Mitprädikanten war eine gewaltige; sie griff tief in die Bürger- und Handwerkerkreise ein, die angewiesen wurden, keine Gemeinschaft mehr mit den Katholiken zu pflegen.

Da aber schon die überwiegende Mehrheit des Adels, nun der der Bürger der Augsburger Konfession angehörten, mußten wieder Gewaltmittel helfen. Nach einer Verordnung vom 7. Juni 1578 sollte allen Verhandlungen über die evangelischen Angelegenheiten die Ausweisung der Prädikanten und Schulmeister aus Wien vorausgehen. Trotzdem nun die Verordneten Rudolfs den Evangelischen Zugeständnisse machten, verlangten die letzteren, Regendorf an der Spitze, freie Verfügung über ihre Prediger; besonders wollten sie von einer Ausweisung des Opitz nichts wissen. Als die kaiserlichen Abgeordneten darauf bestanden, wurden die Verhandlungen abgebrochen, und die Resolution trat in Kraft. Am 21. Juni erhielten Opitz und die übrigen evangelischen Lehrer und Prediger den Ausweisungsbefehl zugestellt. Opitz, offenbar schon vorbereitet, empfing die Nachricht mit größter Ruhe; dagegen in der Stadt gärte es. Zur befürchteten Revolte kam es aber nicht.

Wie wohlberechnet dieser Schachzug war, zeigt nicht bloß der Triumph der römischen Partei, die soeben noch verzweifelt dagestanden, sondern mehr noch die Folgen der Ausweisung: in der Hauptstadt war der evangelische Gottesdienst mit einem Schlag allgemein eingestellt; es gelang nicht wieder, die Schließung der Landhauskirche und -schule rückgängig zu machen, sogar der Gottesdienst war untersagt.

Der augenblickliche Erfolg der römischen Partei in Wien hatte keineswegs eine Entmutigung der Evangelischen außerhalb Wiens zur Folge; diese verdoppelten ihre Kräfte, und namentlich die geschlossene Partei der Flacianer war für ihre Sache außerordentlich tätig. Wollte aber auf protestantischer Seite ein Sieg errungen werden, so war dazu einheitliches Vorgehen der Parteien unbedingt nötig. Diese Einigkeit konnte nur durch eine Austragung der protestantischen Dogmenstreitigkeiten erzielt werden, und hierzu war eine Synode nötig, die von den Flacianern auch gefordert wurde. Statt der Synode wurde aber 1580 die von den Ständen dekretierte Visitation durchgeführt. Diese Visitation hatte ein strengeres Vorgehen gegen die „beständigen" Lutheraner zur Folge. Letztere spalteten sich später in zwei Parteien, bekämpften sich gegenseitig, und so kam es, daß sie in den 80er Jahren gänzlich verschwanden.

So sind also eine Reihe bedeutsamer Momente in der Geschichte der österreichischen Reformation und Gegenreformation, welche durch die von Böhl herangezogenen Regensburger Quellen mannigfach genauer illustriert werden. Zur vollen Verwertung derselben kommt es aber zugleich darauf an, die letzteren mit der einschlägigen Literatur in die rechte Verbindung zu setzen. Es ist dies um so leichter möglich, weil gerade die österreichische Reformationsgeschichte neuerdings in überaus fruchtbringender Weise archivalisch gefördert worden ist. Schon die formlose, aber stoffreiche Wiedemannsche Aktensammlung zur Geschichte der österreichischen Gegenreformation verdient trotz der römisch-katholischen Tendenz des Verfassers nach wie vor gründliche Beachtung. In noch höherem

Grade gilt dies von den bahnbrechenden Untersuchungen Loserths, sowohl über die hussitische Vorreformation wie über die Reformation selber und die verschiedenen Stadien ihrer Unterdrückung. Und wie wir dem Grazer Professor Loserth eine Fülle der überraschendsten neuen Einblicke speziell in die steiermärkische Geschichte verdanken, so hat der unermüdliche Wiener Kirchenhistoriker Loesche schon durch seine gründliche Mathesiusforschung die gesamte österreichische Reformationsgeschichte bedeutsam gefördert, überdies aber zugleich dem „Jahrbuch für die Geschichte des österreichischen Protestantismus" einen gewichtigen Aufschwung gegeben. An das Jahrbuch haben sich dann noch zahlreiche Einzelarbeiten angeschlossen, deren Aufzählung hier zu weit führen würde. Wir erinnern nur an die (aus dem an gut gesichtetem Quellenmaterial überreichen Archiv des C.V. geschöpften) Darstellungen der von dem G.A.V. unterstützten Gemeinden, zumal in den Berichten für die große Liebesgabe, aber auch in den provinziellen Veröffentlichungen. Das besondere Verdienst des Böhlschen Werkes liegt somit darin, daß es über eine überaus fleißig bearbeitete Periode trotzdem · viel neues Licht verbreitet. Zugleich aber darf vor so vielseitig geweckte historische Forschungstrieb als ein besonders bedeutsames Symptom für die Zeit der österreichischen Los-von-Rom-Bewegung bezeichnet werden. Nippold.

II.

Hessische Landtagsakten, herausgegeben von Dr. Hans Glagau, Privatdozenten an der Universität Marburg. Erster Band, 1508 bis 1521. Marburg 1901. XV, 593 SS. M. 14.—.

In Bd. XX, S. 318 f. dieser Zeitschrift ist Glagaus Monographie über Anna von Hessen angezeigt worden. Der jetzt vorliegende Band bildet gewissermaßen das Urkundenbuch dazu, denn er enthält mehr, als man nach dem Titel erwarten sollte. Doch wird man dem Herausgeber dankbar dafür sein dürfen, daß er sich keine allzu strenge Beschränkung bei der Auswahl der Akten auferlegt hat.

An der Hand der mitgeteilten, bisher mit ganz wenigen Ausnahmen ungedruckten Akten können wir nun die Darstellung des Herausgebers in seinem Buche über die Landgräfin genauer nachprüfen und feststellen, wie weit seine Auffassung von seiner Heldin in den Quellen begründet ist. Von anderer Seite[1]) hat man demgegenüber jetzt eine andere Anschauung vertreten; nicht als eine Vorkämpferin landesherrlicher Macht, sondern als eine Fürstin, die nur von persönlicher Herrschsucht und egoistischer Bestrebungen bestimmt war, hat man Anna auffassen wollen. Ihren einheitlichen und großartigen Charakter würde ihre Politik auch dann behalten, an allgemeinem Interesse aber würde sie bedeutend verlieren. Nun läßt sich allerdings die Richtigkeit der Auffassung Glagaus aus den vorhandenen Quellen nicht strikt beweisen, Referent möchte ihr aber auf Grund seiner Durchsicht der Akten doch eine größere Berechtigung zugestehen, als das durch Wolf geschieht.

Für uns kommt auch die vorliegende Publikation Glagaus wieder vor allem in Betracht wegen der Bedeutung, die sie für die

---

1) Vgl. G. Wolf in den G.G.A., Bd. 164, S. 465—480 (Juni 1902).

thüringische Geschichte hat, doch brauchen wir hier auf die sachlichen Ergebnisse der Forschungen Glagaus nicht noch einmal hinzuweisen. Man wird es thüringischerseits mit Freuden begrüßen
dürfen, daß uns der Herausgeber auch das Material zur Beurteilung
der wettinischen Politik in der hessischen Frage nicht vorenthalten
hat, an einigen Punkten berührt und ergänzt sich seine Publikation
mit Burkhardts inzwischen erschienenen Ernestinischen Landtagsakten, ohne aber durch diese überflüssig gemacht zu werden. Für
jeden, der die wettinische Geschichte von 1509—21 studiert, wird
jedenfalls auch Glagaus Publikation von höchster Wichtigkeit sein.

Äußerlich hat Gl. seine Ausgabe nach dem Muster der Below-
schen Ausgabe der Landtagsakten von Jülich-Berg gestaltet und
verweist auf diese. Vielleicht hätte er sich für solche Benutzer,
denen Belows Publikation nicht zur Hand ist, aber doch etwas ausführlicher über die befolgten Grundsätze aussprechen können. Die
Einleitungen zu den 8 Abschnitten des Buches sind präzis und übersichtlich, die Inhaltsangaben am Kopfe der einzelnen Aktenstücke
von genügender Gründlichkeit, was besonders bei den zum Teil sehr
umfangreichen Protokollen der Landtagsverhandlungen die Benutzung
sehr erleichtert, das Register macht einen sehr genauen Eindruck
und scheint auch praktisch eingerichtet zu sein.

An Einzelheiten sei bemerkt, daß auf S. 111 doch wohl dieselbe Landgräfin Elisabeth gemeint ist wie auf S. 103, als pfälzische
Prinzessin konnte sie sehr wohl als „aus dem Fürstenstamm Bayern"
gebürtig bezeichnet werden. tebten auf S. 81 möchte Referent
als Tapeten oder Teppiche deuten. Eine Erklärung ungebräuch-
licher Ausdrücke wäre auch sonst hie und da erwünscht gewesen.
Was bedeutet z. B. erne auf S. 544? Mancher wird auch Mitteilungen über den äußeren Hergang der Landtagsverhandlungen ver-
missen. Man darf wohl vermuten, daß der Herausgeber sich in dem
versprochenen Einleitungsbande, der die Zeit vor 1509 darstellend
behandeln soll, auch darüber aussprechen wird.   G. Mentz.

III.

Ermisch, H., Codex diplomaticus Saxoniae regiae. Im
    Auftrage der Königlich Sächsischen Staatsregierung herausgeg.
    von Otto Posse und Hubert Ermisch. Erster Hauptteil.
    Abteilung B. Zweiter Band. Urkunden der Markgrafen von
    Meißen und Landgrafen von Thüringen 1396—1406. Leipzig,
    Giesecke und Devrient, 1902. XV und 597 SS. 4º.

Der erste Hauptteil des Codex dipl. Saxoniae regiae hat für alle
unter der Herrschaft der Wettiner stehenden oder einst von diesem
Geschlechte beherrschten Länder die größte Bedeutung, denn in
dieser Abteilung der groß angelegten Publikation sollen ja alle Urkunden zur Geschichte des Gesamthauses bis zu der folgenreichen
Teilung vom Jahre 1485 und bis zu deren Bestätigung durch Kaiser
Friedrich III. vom 24. Februar 1486 ediert werden. Darum ist von
allen Interessenten auf das lebhafteste bedauert worden, daß gegenüber dem rüstigen Fortschreiten der Arbeit an den Urkundenbüchern des zweiten Hauptteiles, der die Urkunden zur Geschichte
der einzelnen Stifter und größeren Städte umfassen soll (s. O. Posse,
Cod. dipl. Sax. regiae. Seine bisherige Herausgabe und seine
Weiterführung. Leipzig, Giesecke und Devrient, 1876, S. 5), die

Arbeit an dem ersten Hauptteil nicht recht von der Stelle rücken wollte. Daß in einem Zeitraume von mehr denn 20 Jahren nur drei schwache Bände mit insgesamt 1301 Nummern erschienen, konnte nicht verwundern, da bekannt war, daß die Bearbeitung dieser Abteilung, trotzdem sie bei weitem schwieriger und zeitraubender als die für die Urkundenbücher des zweiten Hauptteils ist, lange Zeit im wesentlichen auf den Schultern eines Mannes ruhte, der überdies durch andere mit dem Cod. d. Sax. r. in inniger Verbindung stehende wissenschaftliche Unternehmungen abgehalten worden war, sich der Aufgabe ausschließlich zu widmen.

Mit Freuden begrüßte man daher den Entschluß, die bewährte Kraft eines Ermisch, der schon für den zweiten Hauptteil das Beste geleistet hat, für den ersten Hauptteil mit heranzuziehen. Mit außerordentlichem Fleiße hat er sich seiner Aufgabe angenommen, die Abteilung B des ersten Hauptteiles, die die Urkunden der Wettiner des späteren Mittelalters, zunächst von dem Tode des Markgrafen Friedrich III. (1381) bringen wird, zur Drucklegung zu fördern. Dank seiner Rührigkeit und seiner Sachkunde konnten in verhältnismäßig kurzer Zeit zwei stattliche Bände dieser Abteilung veröffentlicht werden. Dem 1899 erschienenen ersten Bande mit 637 Nummern für die Jahre 1381—1395 folgte schon 1902 der 2. Band, der nicht weniger als 719 Urkunden und Regesten für die Zeit von 1396—1406, d. h. bis zum Ende der Regierung Balthasars und Wilhelms I. der Forschung erschließt.

Ueber das bei der Publikation beobachtete Verfahren, das von dem von Gersdorf einst aufgestellten Plane nicht unerheblich abweicht, hat sich Ermisch im Vorbericht zum 1. Bande, S. XX geäußert. Er hat es mit Rücksicht auf den gewaltigen Umfang des Urkundenvorrates des späteren Mittelalters für nötig gehalten, für die Drucklegung eine Auswahl unter den Urkunden zu treffen, hat dabei aber in den Anmerkungen zu den Urkunden wenigstens kurze Verweise auf viele ausgelassene Stücke gegeben. Im 1. Bande sind so ca. 400 Urkunden, die in dankenswerter Weise am Schlusse S. 519—521 zusammengestellt worden sind, nur in den Anmerkungen erwähnt worden, eine große Anzahl nach dem subjektiven Ermessen des Herausgebers unbedeutender Urkunden, z. B. Bestallungen untergeordneter Personen, Verschreibungen über geringfügige Schulden, Lehn-, Leibgeding- und Gunstbriefe, desgleichen Verschreibungen der Land- und Markgrafen für Städte und Ortschaften, die in dem zweiten und dritten Hauptteile Aufnahme finden, oder soweit — was uns im besonderen angeht — Thüringen in Frage kommt, thüringischen lokal- oder familiengeschichtlichen Urkundenbüchern überlassen bleiben sollen, sind überhaupt von der Aufnahme ausgeschlossen worden. Man kann aus mehr denn einem Grunde bedauern, daß Vollständigkeit das gebotenen diplomatischen Apparates somit nicht gewährleistet werden kann, man würde aber ungerecht sein, wenn man darüber mit dem Herausgeber rechten wollte. Mir will sogar scheinen, als ob die Arbeit des Editors bei dem beobachteten Verfahren schwieriger gewesen sei, als wenn er alles, was an urkundlichem Material für die Geschichte der Markgrafen und Landgrafen vorhanden ist, ohne Auswahl hätte publizieren können. Tatsächlich läßt sich für das spätere Mittelalter mit seinem reichen Urkundenvorrat und seinen in vielen Fällen zu Akten auswachsenden Diplomen ebensowenig alles dem Drucke übergeben als bei den

Aktenpublikationen zur neueren und neuesten Geschichte. Selbstverständlich mußte überdies bei den meisten Urkunden die Regestenform an Stelle des vollständigen Druckes treten.

In eigenartiger Weise hat Ermisch aber die Gesamtheit der von Wettinern ausgestellten Urkunden skizzenhaft angedeutet in der Uebersicht über die Wettinerurkunden im 1. Bande für die Zeit von 1381—1395, im 2. Bande für die Jahre 1396—1406. Diese Listen dienen zugleich als Itinerare. Es ist dabei alles so wohl durchdacht und so exakt ausgeführt, daß man diese Uebersichten zur Nachahmung empfehlen kann. Nur in einem Punkte muß man mehr wünschen. Ich halte es für nötig, daß bei Stücken, die in den Codex nicht aufgenommen werden, ein Wort über die eigentliche Disposition gesagt wird, natürlich so präzis wie möglich, so daß in jedem Falle nur einige Worte dazu kommen. Anzuerkennen ist, daß für solche Urkunden die Zeugenreihen nicht unterdrückt worden sind. Von größter Wichtigkeit ist auch, daß er zahlreiche Rechnungen zur Erklärung der Urkunden und zur Vervollständigung des Itinerars verwertet hat. Man sieht, Ermisch ist in verschiedenen wichtigen Punkten seine eigenen Wege gegangen, und man muß ihm dafür Anerkennung zollen; es sind Wege, die nur ein gewiegter Praktiker finden und weisen konnte.

In beiden Bänden sind eine Menge inedita enthalten, die über die Geschichte der Wettiner und ihre Lande neues Licht verbreiten und die nicht zum wenigsten gerade für Thüringens Geschichte von Bedeutung sind. Ermisch verspricht, die Ergebnisse seiner Publikation in einer darstellenden Arbeit zusammenzufassen, sobald das Material bis zum Tode Friedrichs des Streitbaren (4. Jan. 1428) gesammelt vorliegen wird. Dann wird man die Bedeutung seiner Publikation erst recht würdigen lernen.

Die Behandlung der Texte, die Regesten, die Bemerkungen über die handschriftliche Ueberlieferung, die Anmerkungen zur Erklärung der Texte und die Indices sind so vortrefflich, wie wir es bei Ermischs Publikationen längst gewöhnt sind, nur in den Drucknachweisen ist Vollständigkeit nicht erreicht, wohl auch nicht erstrebt worden.

Möge die Fortsetzung dieser mustergiltigen Publikation in dem Tempo, das sie bis jetzt eingehalten hat, erfolgen!

O. Dobenecker.

Berichtigung.

S. 94, Z. 3 v. u. ist zu lesen: 7000 Fl.

Zur Nachricht.

Eine Anzahl Rezensionen und die Literaturübersicht können erst im nächsten Hefte zum Abdruck kommen.

IV.

Studien zur Geschichte des Unterganges des alten Thüringischen Königreichs im Jahre 531 n. Chr.

Von

Dr. Wilhelm Pelka.

Teil I. Grundlegung.

Seit Gloëls klassischer Abhandlung[1]) durfte man es wohl als nutzlos bezeichnen, den Thüringerkrieg des Jahres 531 noch einmal zum Gegenstande einer Untersuchung zu machen[2]). Erst neuerdings haben Lorenz[3]) und Größler[4]) die Frage wieder aufgenommen, und dabei hat sich doch herausgestellt, daß noch immer nicht, selbst nicht in den Hauptpunkten, eine Einigung erzielt ist.

Auffallend, welch helles Licht unsere Überlieferung gerade auf den Untergang des Thüringerreichs wirft; merkwürdig, wie tief das Dunkel, in dem die Vorgeschichte des Reiches für uns liegt. Trojas Geschick scheint hier erneut; wo ist aber der Homer, der uns den Heldenkampf dieses untergehenden Volkes geschildert hätte?

---

1) A. Gloël, Zur Gesch. der alten Thüringer. Forsch. zur Deutsch. Gesch. IV, S. 195 ff. Die Litteratur vor Gloël habe ich nicht benutzt, sie ist am besten zu finden bei Lorenz, vergl. unter Anm. 3.

2) H. W. Lippert, Zeitschrift des Vereins für thüring. Geschichte Bd. 15, S. 5.

3) E. Lorenz, Die thüring. Katastrophe vom Jahre 531. Z. d. V. f. th. G. Bd. 15, S. 335 ff.

4) H. Größler, Der Sturz des thür. Königreichs im Jahre 531. Z. d. V. f. th. G. Bd. 19, S. 1 ff.

Wohl erhebt Venantius Fortunatus kaum vierzig Jahre
später klagend seine Stimme:

Condicio belli tristis, sors invida rerum!
quam subito lapsu regna superba cadunt!
quae steterant longo felicia culmina tractu
victa sub ingenti clade cremata iacent.
aula palatino quae floruit antea cultu
hanc modo pro cameris maesta favilla tegit
ardua quae rutilo nituere ornata metallo
pallidus oppresit fulgida teeta cinis

Wohl mögen später auch im Munde des Volkes Lieder
und Sagen umgelaufen sein, aber bis auf unsere Zeit ist
nichts davon hinübergerettet.

Wie großartig muß es daher um die historische Überlieferung bestellt sein, wenn die neueren Forscher im
stande sind, die Plätze der verschiedenen Schlachten zu
bezeichnen, in denen die thüringische Streitmacht vernichtet
wurde, wenn Größler[1]) sogar die Furt zeigen kann, über
die vor nunmehr fast 1400 Jahren die Sachsen zogen,
ehe sie den letzten Sturm auf Burgscheidungen unter-
nahmen. Sieht man jedoch genauer zu, so ergibt sich,
daß es mit der Überlieferung nicht so sehr gut bestellt sein
kann. Gewiß können neuere Forscher die verschiedenen
Schlachtorte angeben, aber eine Übereinstimmung ist nicht
erzielt; der eine[2]) behauptet, alles habe sich im Verlauf
von wenigen Stunden ereignet, ein anderer[3]) braucht
Wochen, ja Monate dazu; der eine[4]) nimmt drei, der
andere[5]) vier Schlachten an; auch darüber, wo man die

---

1) a. a. O. S. 51 ff. Größler läßt alle 3 Furten, die sich heutzutage in der Nähe von Burgscheidungen befinden, benutzt werden,
die eine von den Franken, die andere von dem thüringischen Abge-
sandten, die dritte von den Sachsen. Daß Furten sieh im Lauf
der Zeit ändern können, berücksichtigt Größler nicht, wiewohl er
selbst davon spricht. Vergl. a. a. O. S. 52.

2) Lorenz, a. a. O. S. 387.

3) Größler, a. a. O. S. 21 ff.

4) Lorenz, a. a. O. S. 391.

5) Größler, a. a. O. S. 35.

benannten Orte, Runibergun u. s. w., eigentlich zu suchen hat, herrscht keine Klarheit. Die Verwirrung ist eine vollständige, und zwar, wie wir gleich sehen werden, vor allem deshalb, weil man es bisher nicht für nötig gehalten hat, mit den Quellen eine reinliche Scheidung vorzunehmen.

Unter den Quellen zur Geschichte des Untergangs des Thüringerreichs lassen sich zwei große Gruppen unterscheiden.

I. Die fränkischen Quellen:
  1) Venantius Fortunatus [1])
  2) Gregor v. Tours [2])
  3) Der Scholasticus Fredegar [3])
  4) Der liber historiae Francorum [4])
  5) Die Gesta Theoderici [5]),

wozu man auch noch Aimoin [6]) rechnen kann, die mit Ausnahme des letzteren sämtlich vor 750 geschrieben haben, Venantius sogar nur wenig mehr als 30 Jahre, Gregor etwa 60 Jahre später [7]).

Vorweg sei bemerkt, daß diese fränkischen Quellen, auch Aimoin, von sächsischer Hilfe gegen die Thüringer nicht das mindeste wissen, einige erwähnen außerdem die Verwandtschaft Amalabergas mit den Ostgoten, während die anderen nichts darüber melden.

---

1) M. G. Auct. antiqu. IV, 1, S. 271 ff.
2) M. G. SS. rerum Merov. I, S. 111—116.
3) M. G. SS. rerum Merov. II, S. 103 f.
4) M. G. SS. rerum Merov. II, S. 277 f.
5) M. G. SS. rerum Merov. II, S. 206.
6) Bouquet, Recueil des historiens des Gaules et de la France. III, 50.
7) Das betreffende Gedicht des Venantius muß nach 565 geschrieben sein, weil er erst von da an in Gallien sich aufhält und erst von da an seine Beziehungen zu Radegunde datieren. Gregors historia eccl. Francorum ist zwar erst nach 591 ganz fertig gestellt, die ersten Bücher jedoch (in denen sich auch die Erzählung vom Thüringerkrieg findet) sind bereits um 577 entstanden. Vergl. Teuffel, Gesch. d. römisch. Litteratur II [5], S. 1261. 1278. Wattenbach, Geschichtsquellen I [6], S. 91. 100.

Auf der anderen Seite stehen II. die sächsischen Quellen, die uns von sächsischer Hilfe berichten **und die** Amalaberga zu einer Schwester des Merowingers Theuderich machen:

1) Ruodolfi translatio S. Alexandri [1]
2) Widukind [2]
3) Die Annales Quedlinburgenses [3].

Scheinbar beeinflußt von den sächsischen **Quellen,** in Wahrheit aber unabhängig von ihnen [4]), ist

4) Der Anonymus de origine Suevorum [5]).

Ganz abseits steht

5) Procop v. Caesarea [6]) (um 550) mit **einigen** Nachrichten.

---

1) M. G. SS. II, 674 f.
2) M. G. SS. III, 420—424.
3) M. G. SS. III, 31 f.
Ist die den Thüringerkrieg behandelnde Stelle in den **Annal...** Quedlinburgenses echt? Nach dem Vorgang von L. **Hoffmann** (Jahresbericht über die höhere Bürgerschule in Rathenow 1872) **ha...** sie auch Wattenbach (sowohl: Geschichtsquellen I[6], 342 f. **als: G...** schichtsschreiber der deutschen Vorzeit [Widukind[2], 1882; S. **XIV f.**] für interpoliert erklärt. Im Gegensatz zu Hoffmann jedoch, d... den Bericht für eine Zutat des 13. Jahrhunderts hält, **glaub...** Wattenbach, die Erzählung sei bereits im 12. Jahrhundert **vorhand...** gewesen.

H. Lorenz (Germania XXXI, S. 137 ff.) hat gegen die **Au...** fassung dieser Stelle als interpoliert erhebliche Bedenken **gelten...** gemacht.

P. Rajna, le origini dell' epopea francese. Firenze 1884, **S. 16...** n. 1 hält es für wahrscheinlich, daß die Erzählung vom **Thüring...** krieg in den Ann. Quedl. auch vom Verfasser der **Chronik ...** schrieben ist. Der Verfasser habe wahrscheinlich die **Erzähl...** in sein eigenes Werk eingefügt, als es schon geschrieben **war. ...** lasse diese Frage unentschieden, bemerke jedoch, daß wenn **m...** die Stelle als Interpolation auffaßt, man diese **Interpolation ...** zu den Worten: ...... „cultello perfossus, interiit" **reich...** lassen muß.

4) siehe weiter unten.
5) Zeitschrift für deutsches Altertum XVII, S. 59—61.
6) ex. recens. Dindorf. Bonn 1833 (corp. scr. hist. Byz.).

Diese sächsischen Quellen sind mit Ausnahme der translatio S. Alexandri sämtlich nach 900 geschrieben, verdienen also, wie man annehmen sollte, von vornherein geringeren Glauben. Trotzdem hat man sie von verschiedenen Seiten in beträchtlichem Umfange mit zur Darstellung verwertet, ein „gemischtes Verfahren" beliebt, wie sich Größler ausdrückt[1]), andererseits steht man ihnen jedoch wieder mißtrauisch gegenüber[2]). Die Hauptvertreter des „gemischten Verfahrens" sind Lorenz und Größler. Letzterer nimmt z. B. aus den sächsischen Quellen all das heraus, was nur einigermaßen zu den fränkischen paßt[3]), und erklärt dies für richtig, alles andere für falsch.

---

1) a. a. O. S. 3.

2) Gloël a. a. O. S. 189 ff. nimmt eine Art Mittelstellung ein. Den Nachrichten, welche sich auf Hauptbegebenheiten beziehen, ist er geneigt Glauben zu schenken, insbesondere tritt er warm für die Quedlinburger Annalen ein. Lippert spricht sich in seinen „Beiträgen zur ältesten Geschichte der Thüringer" über Widukind aus: „bei letzterem sind alle diese Begebenheiten von dichtem Sagengewebe umrankt" (Z. d. V. f. th. G. Bd. 15, S. 12).

3) Ein Beispiel dafür findet sich gleich im Anfang (a. a. O. S. 4 f). Größler stellt die Quellenstellen über den ersten Zusammenstoß der Franken und Thüringer zusammen. Zuerst Gregor: venientibus Francis dolos praeparant. Dazu bemerkt Größler ganz richtig: Die Handlung beginnt also für ihn (d. h. Gregor) bereits beim Anrücken der Franken. Aimoins Bericht: „Profectus itaque Theodericus in Thoringam obvium habuit Hermenofredum cum innumera multitudine hostium" legt er dann dahin aus, daß Irminfried dem Merowinger entgegengezogen sei. Obvium habere aliquem heißt aber: jemandem begegnen, also muß die Stelle übersetzt werden: Theuderich begegnete dem Hermanfried. Weiter zieht Größler noch die Stellen Widukinds und der Ann. Quedlinburgenses heran (appropinquans terminis Thuringorum invenit .... generum suum se expectantem in loco, qui dicitur Runibergun und venit in regionem Maerstem vocatam et Irminfridum illic sibi bello occurentem vicit et fugavit) und schließt dann: Also sowohl die sächsischen als auch die fränkischen Quellen behaupten übereinstimmend, daß Irminfried den Franken entgegengezogen und daß es außerhalb Thüringens zur ersten Schlacht gekommen sei." Von einem Entgegenziehen Irminfrieds wissen nur

Lorenz verfährt fast genau ebenso, kommt aber doch dabei zu vollständig entgegengesetzten Resultaten. Gerade dieser Umstand aber ist ein deutlicher Beweis, daß die beiden Forscher sich entweder einer falschen Methode bedient haben oder in der Beurteilung der Quellen fehl gegangen sind. Sehen wir uns daher zum mindesten die sächsischen Quellen etwas genauer an.

Wir beginnen mit dem Anonymus de origine Suevorum, der von Müllenhoff herausgegeben ist und dem 13. bez. 12. Jahrhundert zugeschrieben wird [1]). Alles, was in den andern Quellen von den Sachsen erzählt wird, wird hier auf die Schwaben übertragen.

Nach einer Einleitung, die für uns nicht in Betracht kommt, berichtet der Anonymus von dem Kriege zwischen Theuderich und Irminfried. Gleich zu Anfang dieses Berichtes heißt es: causa vero congressionis in hystoria Saxonum describitur talis. Müllenhoff sieht in dieser hystoria Saxonum eine Ableitung von Ekkehards Weltchronik [2]). Zwar ließe es sich nicht leugnen, daß eine wörtliche Benutzung der Vorlage, wenn man Ekkehard vergleicht, überhaupt nicht oder nur in sehr geringem Maße stattgefunden zu haben scheint, aber es wird das Werk des Ekkehard vorausgesetzt [3]). Worauf stützt aber Müllenhoff seine Behauptung? Er schließt folgendermaßen [4]). Der betreffende Abschnitt in Ekkehards Chronik ist aus Widukind geschöpft, er wird jedoch eingeleitet durch einen Bericht über die Verteilung des Franken-

---

die Annalen etwas; daß es außerhalb Thüringens zur ersten Schlacht gekommen sei, behaupten allerdings die Annalen und scheint Widukind anzudeuten. Die fränkischen Quellen lassen alles unentschieden.

1) Müllenhoff, Von der Herkunft der Schwaben. Zeitschrift für deutsches Altertum Bd. XVII, S. 63 f.

2) Müllenhoff a. a. O. S. 63. Dümmler, Zeitschr. für deutsch. Alt., XIX, S. 131 f. hält Ekkehard selbst für die Vorlage.

3) Müllenhoff a. a. O. S. 63.

4) Müllenhoff a. a. O. S. 63.

reiches nach dem Tode Chlodwigs unter dessen vier Söhne, einen Bericht, der, aus dem liber historiae Francorum abgeleitet, sich bei Widukind nicht findet, wohl aber in den Anonymus übergegangen ist. Letzterer kann daher nicht Widukind benutzt haben, sondern schon eine Vorlage, in der die Erzählung des Korveyer Mönches mit dem Bericht über die Verteilung des Reiches verbunden war. Erst Ekkehard[1]) verbindet diese Nachrichten, aber auch er kann nicht die Vorlage gewesen sein, sondern nur eine daraus abgeleitete jüngere sächsische Chronik[2]). Ist diese Hypothese richtig? Sehen wir im einzelnen zu, wie sich der Anonymus zu Widukind-Ekkehard verhält[3]). Die sachliche Uebereinstimmung zwischen den beiden Berichten des Anonymus und des Widukind-Ekkehard beginnt etwa mit den Worten des Anonymus: Quo (sc. Theuderico) regnante misit legatos ad Irminfridum. Beide Berichte erzählen übereinstimmend, daß Theuderichs Gesandtschaft von dem Thüringerkönig gut aufgenommen, daß der Zweck der Gesandtschaft aber von Amalaberga mit Irings Hilfe hintertrieben wird. Die Gesandten kehren zurück (der Anonymus ist hier im Verhältnis zu Widukind sehr kurz), es kommt zum Kriege.

Und hier findet sich der erste große Unterschied zwischen beiden Quellen. Der Anonymus weiß nichts von der Schlacht bei Runibergun und den sich daran anschließenden Beratungen im Frankenlager, bei ihm verwüstet Theuderich nur das Land und verbindet sich dann mit den Sachsen, nicht etwa in der Absicht, sich durch sie zu verstärken (Widukind), sondern in der Absicht, den Thüringerkönig

---

1) Ich setze trotz Bresslau's berühmter Abhandlung (N. A. XXI, 1896. „Bamberger Studien") hier immer den Namen Ekkehard anstatt Frutolf, einerseits weil ich hier über M's. Ansicht referiere, und dieser noch keinen Frutolf kannte, andererseits weil der Name Ekkehard sich einmal eingebürgert hat.

2) Man sieht nicht recht, weshalb Müllenhoff eine Ableitung Ekkehard's annimmt und nicht vielmehr Ekkehard selbst, wie Dümmler (a. a. O.).

3) Ekkehard ist hier nur Abschrift von Widukind.

ihrer etwaigen Unterstützung zu berauben. Man erkennt hier deutlich, wie konsequent der Anonymus verfährt. Er erwähnt keine Schlacht (d. h. bis zur Ankunft der Sachsen), er weiß daher von keinen Verlusten des Theuderich, für ihn wird somit die Angabe Widukinds, Theuderich habe sich durch die Sachsen verstärken wollen, überflüssig; er muß sich nach einem andern Grunde umsehen. Was liegt da wohl näher als die Vermutung, Theuderich habe aus Furcht, Irminfried möchte die Hilfe der Sachsen erlangen, selbst seinerseits mit den Sachsen angeknüpft, zumal der Anonymus merkwürdigerweise die Erklärung Widukinds: Saxones, qui iam olim erant Thuringis acerrimi hostes nicht beachtet? Man könnte vielleicht einwenden, der Anonymus berücksichtige diese Worte doch, indem er die Sachsen als so eminent bündnisfähig hinstellt, aber dem steht entgegen, daß die Sachsen nach dieser Ueberlieferung soeben erst von Norden her die Elbe überschritten haben daß Theuderich nur aus Furcht vor einer Verbindung der Thüringer und der Sachsen mit letzterem abschließt.

Im folgenden ist der Anonymus wieder reicher als Widukind.

Widukind.	Anonymus.
si quidem vincerent Irminfridum urbemque caperent, terram eis in possessionem aeternam traderet.	(Theudericus) spopondit eis terram illam in proprietatem traditurum, quam fluvius Salza per decursum suum cingeret defluendo in flumen Sala.

Aehnlich wie der Anonymus berichten die Ann. Quedlinburg.: si Thuringos sibi adversantes vincerent, omnem illis eorum terram daturum, usque ad confluentiam Salae et Unstradae fluviorum [1].

Interessant ist ferner, daß bei dem einen Schriftsteller die Reiterei der Schwaben (= Sachsen) den Franken zu Hilfe kommt, ja es wird noch erwähnt: Das Fußvolk wird zu-

---

1) Eine Abhängigkeit des Anon. von den Ann. ist hier natürlich ausgeschlossen.

rückgelassen (relicto pedestrali exercitu), während es bei
dem andern (Widukind) unverkennbar Fußtruppen sind, die
den Sturm auf Burg-Scheidungen unternehmen. Kurz, wir
sehen, der Anonymus unterscheidet sich doch nicht unbe-
trächtlich von Widukind-Ekkehard. Ich übergehe die nächsten
Ereignisse, obwohl sich auch hier sehr starke Unterschiede
zwischen den beiden Quellen zeigen[1]), und komme gleich zur
sogenannten Jagdanekdote. Zur Orientierung diene, daß
die Thüringer sich nach Burg-Scheidungen zurückgezogen
und somit die Unstrut zwischen sich und ihre Feinde gelegt
haben[2]). Nun geht es bei Widukind-Ekkehard folgendermaßen weiter[3]): Interea urbe ex pace promissa securiore
reddita, egressus est quidam cum accipitre, victum quaeritans[4]) supra litus fluvii supradicti. Emisso vero volucre,
quidam ex Saxonibus in ulteriore ripa ilico eum suscepit.
Quo rogante, ut remitteretur, Saxo dare negavit. Ille autem:
„Da", inquit, „et secretum tibi sociisque utile prodam".
Saxo econtra: „Dic, ut accipias, quod quaeris". „Reges",
inquit, „inter se pace facta decretum tenent, si cras invenia-
mini in castris, capiamini aut certe occidamini". Ad haec
ille: „Serione haec an ludo ais?" — „Secunda hora, ait,
sequentis diei probabit, quia vos oporteat sine Iudis agere.
Quapropter consulite vobis ipsis et fuga salutem quaerite".
Saxo statim emittens accipitrem, sociis retulit quae audivit.
Illi satis commoti, in promptu non inveniebant, quid super
hoc agere debuissent.

Es kommt zu Beratungen im Sachsenlager, und am
nächsten Tage früh stürmen sie Burg-Scheidungen.

---

1) Auf einen sehr wichtigen Unterschied komme ich noch später
zurück.

2) Vergl. die Karte bei Größler, a. a. O., S. 54.

3) Widukind I, 10, Separatausgabe (Waitz 1882, S. 11).

4) Der Reiher (ardea. Vergl. den Bericht des Anonymus) ist
zwar ein Jagdvogel (Heyne, Deutsche Hausaltertümer II, S. 242, 245),
indes habe ich keinen Beleg dafür finden können, daß er auch als
Nahrung diente.

Sehr klar und verständlich ist diese Erzählung eben nicht.
Schon das „Nahrungsuchen oberhalb des Flusses" [1]) ist sehr
merkwürdig, als ob die Burg, die eben èrst eingeschlossen
ist, bereits an Nahrungsmangel litte. Auffällig ist auch
die Reiherbeize nach Sonnenuntergang — es heißt ja
kurz vorher (cap. 9): talique spectaculo tota dies illa trahitur. Wie vollends der Sachse in den Besitz des Vogels
gelangen soll, ist nicht recht zu ersehen. Vergleichen wir
jetzt dazu den Bericht des Anonymus, so wird die Sinn-
losigkeit des Berichtes bei Widukind-Ekkehard uns noch
klarer. Der betreffende Absatz beim Anonymus lautet [2]):

Praeterea forte accidit, ut quidam ex Thuringiis, Wito
vocabulo, ripam fluminis accipitrem mann gestans descen-
deret alteramque ripam Gosholdus quidam de Swevis e regione ascenderet. et mittens Wito accipitrem ad irretiendam
ardeam flumen transvolare, a Gosholdo ambe aves sunt in-
terceptae. Quem Wito imprecatus, ut si suum volatile sibi
restitueret, rem quam ignoraret, ei insinuaret. Tum demum
Gozoldus fecit eum amnem transire et accipitrem cum ardea
recipere. qui caballo vadum quoddam pernatavit atque ardeam cum accipitre recepit, Gosholdo quoque inquit: id pro
certo tibi notifico, quod reges sunt placati, et hoc quod
hactinus hereditarie possidebamus, ex Iringi [3]) superflua ra-
tionatione modo in praestationem recepimus". Haec audiens
Gozoldus ad commilitones suos rediit eisque causam pactionis
examussim exposuit. At illi confederationes regum metu-
entes, ne vel Theoderici sponsionum fraudarentur vel regum
conspiratione ex provincia propellerentur, decreverunt noctu
vadum per Gosholdum monstratum transire ac Thuringio-
rum castra ex inproviso irrumpere. Quo peracto tantam
stragem de hostibus dederunt, ut vix quingenti cum Irminfrido evaderent.

---

1) Geschichtsschreiber der deutschen Vorzeit X 6 [2], S. 18.
2) Müllenhoff a. a. O., S. 61.
3) Iring spielt am Hofe Irminfrieds die Rolle eines einfluß-
reichen Günstlings.

Auch hier bleiben innere Unwahrscheinlichkeiten. Weshalb verrät z. B. eigentlich der Thüringer das Bündnis mit den Franken? Im ganzen genommen ist dieser Bericht jedoch klarer wie der des Korveyers; wir sehen aber auch, daß Widukind die Pointe der Erzählung, die listige Auffindung der Furt, einfach weggelassen hat, falls er sie überhaupt kannte. Da sich nun der ganze Bericht über den Thüringerkrieg bei Ekkehard ebenso findet, wie bei Widukind, so kann der Anonymus in den angeführten Stellen unter keinen Umständen auf Ekkehard zurückgehen.

Müllenhoff hat aber schon bemerkt [1]), daß im Anonymus ausdrücklich gesagt wird: causa vero congressionis in hystoria Saxonum describitur talis, d. h. nur der Grund zum Kampfe wird der hyst. Sax. entlehnt. Daraus folgt aber unmittelbar, daß der Anonymus zum mindesten noch eine weitere Quelle benutzt haben muß, die sogar besser unterrichtet war, als Widukind-Ekkehard.

Wir verlassen für einen Augenblick diese Gedankenreihe und wenden uns den Quedlinburger Annalen zu. Gewisse Uebereinstimmungen zwischen ihnen und dem Anonymus finden sich wohl, doch sind sie so geringfügig, daß an eine Abhängigkeit beider Quellen von einander nicht gedacht werden kann. Andererseits findet man zwischen dem Quedlinburger und Widukind eine auffallende Uebereinstimmung, so daß man fast auf den Verdacht kommt, jener habe diesen excerpiert. Und doch ist der Quedlinburger teilweise wieder viel reichhaltiger als der Korveyer Mönch. So hat er allein die Erinnerung an eine Schlacht bewahrt, die nach der Ankunft der Sachsen geschlagen und doch der Schlacht an der Unstrut noch voraufgeht [2]). Man höre: Qui (sc. Saxones) nihil morantes venerunt ad eum et persequentes Irminfridum pugnaverunt contra eum super Unstradan fluvi-

---

1) a. a. O., S. 66.

2) Die Schlachten im Gau Maerstem und an der Ocker sind, wie ich später nachzuweisen versuchen werde, freie Erfindungen des Annalisten.

um etc. Dieses „persequentes" setzt aber schon einen
anderen Kampf voraus[1]), von dem weder in den Quedlinburger Annalen noch bei Widukind sich eine Spur findet,
nur der Anonymus hat uns einen Bericht darüber aufbewahrt: Quod ut Irminfridus rescivit (sc. daß die Sachsen
den Franken Hilfe gebracht haben), manum validam equestri-
um elegit et ad pugnandum contra Theodericum direxit,
in qua congressione Irminfridus terga vertit atque amuem
Unstruot cum suis celerius transivit et in ripa eiusdem
fluminis hostibus acrius restitit.

Der Anonymus allein hat uns diesen Bericht aufbewahrt,
in der Vorlage des Quedlinburgers muß dieser Kampf aber
auch erwähnt gewesen sein, denn sonst ist der Begriff
„persequentes" nicht recht zu verstehen. Wir geben zu,
daß dieser Schluß nicht zwingend·ist, er hat zunächst nur
eine gewisse Wahrscheinlichkeit für sich, wird aber durch
weiteres noch gestützt werden. Da der Anonymus später
geschrieben hat als der Quedlinburger, so kann jener nicht
die Quelle von diesem sein, wir müssen für beide eine
gemeinsame Quelle annehmen.

Und nur unter dieser Voraussetzung ist es uns möglich,
den Schluß des Berichts in den Ann. Quedl. zu verstehen.
Der Anonymus läßt Irminfried zu Attila ziehen, der Annalist
läßt ihn zwar von den Mauern Zülpichs herabgestürzt
werden, bringt aber merkwürdigerweise gleich im Anschluß
daran den Satz: Attila rex Hunorum et totius Europae
terror, a puella quadam, quam a patre occiso se rapuit,
cultello perfossus interiit, ein Satz, der in keinem erkennbaren Zusammenhang mit dem Bericht über Irminfrieds
Schicksal steht, zumal da Attila und Irminfried fast
100 Jahre auseinander lebten. Wir sehen uns so in der
Tat zu der Annahme gedrängt, daß beiden Autoren ge-
gemeinsam dieselbe Quelle vorgelegen haben muß.

---

1) An und für sich könnte man dies aus dem „persequentes"
nur schließen, wenn man das Wort stark preßt. Der Vergleich mit
Anonymus macht aber obigen Schluß höchst wahrscheinlich.

Wir haben oben[1]) bemerkt, daß der Unterschiède zwischen Widukind und dem Anonymus nicht wenige sind, es dürfte sich aber doch verlohnen, die Kehrseite des Verhältnisses zwischen diesen beiden Quellen aufzusuchen, die Uebereinstimmungen zwischen beiden Schriftstellern im einzelnen zu prüfen. Doch bevor wir dazu schreiten, bedarf es noch einer kleinen Digression. Die Quedlinburger Annalen stimmen teilweise auffallend mit Widukind überein[2]), doch hat Widukind durchaus nicht alles, was jene haben; so fehlt bei ihm z. B. die Erwähnung jener Schlacht, von der uns der Anonymus allein einen Bericht aufbewahrt hat, und die die Annalen wenigstens andeuten; daher können die Annalen zum mindesten hier nicht Widukind zur Vorlage gehabt haben. Da aber der den Annalen und dem Anonymus gemeinsam vorliegende Bericht sehr reichhaltig, vielleicht allerdings nur stellenweise, gewesen sein muß (er brachte ja Tatsachen, die Widukind in seiner recht ausführlichen Erzählung nicht bot), die merkwürdige Uebereinstimmung zwischen Widukind und den Annalen aber nicht aus der Welt zu schaffen ist, so dürfen wir zunächst wohl vermuten, dem Korveyer Mönch habe dieselbe Quelle vorgelegen, die wir als gemeinsame Vorlage des Anonymus und der Ann. Quedlinb. erkannt haben.

Und in der Tat läßt diese Vermutung sich wahrscheinlich machen. Wir haben ja ein Mittel, diese Frage weiter zu verfolgen, — eben jene Vergleichung zwischen Widukind und dem Anonymus, die wir oben für einen Augenblick ausgesetzt haben.

Ich setze die wichtigsten Stellen zum bequemeren Vergleich neben einander:

Widukind.	Anonymus.
Ad haec Irminfridus iuxta quod regalem decuit dignitatem clementer legato respondit, pla-	Cuius legationem Irminfridus benigne quidem suscepit et iure pacem concordiamque cum eo

<hr />

1) S. 171 ff.
2) Wattenbach, Geschichtsquellen I⁶, S. 342.

cita sibi placere populi Francorum, ab eorum concordia non
discordare, pace omnimodis indigere, super negotio vero regni
responsionem suam in amicorum
praesentiam velle differre.

habere asseruit, quod sororem
suam sibi in matrimonium copu-
laverit, super regni vero stabili-
tate nil ei posse respondere nisi
principum suorum assentatione.

Die Uebereinstimmung ist hier schon auffallend, noch
mehr aber in Folgendem:

Widukind.

Audiens autem regina, lega-
tum fratris supervenisse et locu-
tum cum rege super negotio regni, suasit Iringo, ut pariter per-
suaderent viro, quia sibi regnum
cessisset iure hereditario, utpote
quae filia regis erat et filia regi-
nae, Thiadricum vero suum servum tanquam ex concubina na-
tum, et ideo indecens fore, pro-
prio servo umquam manus dare.

Anonymus.

Soror itaque regis Theoderici
indignum ducens, ipsum regem
constitutum affirmabat, illum non
iure sibi regnum vendicasse, set
potins ex paterna hereditate se
debere attinere, ascitoque Iringo
Irminfridi consiliario egit cum
eo, quatinus in auribus principum ac fratris veredariorum con-
ferret, Theodericum patris sui con-
cubine filium fore et ideo merito
sibi servum, non debere regnum
invadere, quod eam attingeret
ex paterna successione.

Auch hier die Verwandtschaft, aber — nur die in-
haltliche, in der Struktur des Satzes und in der Stilistik
weichen beide Berichte beträchtlich von einander ab.

Wir gehen zur Hauptstelle über:

Widukind.

Et haec dicens (sc. legatus)
reversus est ad Thiadricum, quae
audivit non eelat. Thiadricus autem nimiam iram vultu eclans
sereno: Oportet nos, inquit, ad
servitium Irminfridi festinare,
quatinus qui libertate privamur,
inani saltem vita fruamur.

Anonymus.

legati … ad dominum su-
um rediere sibique huiusmodi
verba intulere. Qui furorem ani-
mi simulans statuit, quia Irminfridus se pro servo haberet, quantocius ei ad obsequendum occur-
reret.

Nach der Lektüre dieser Stelle dürfte wohl niemand
mehr zweifeln, daß beide, Widukind wie der Anonymus,
auf dieselbe Quelle zurückgehen. Wenn dies aber der
Fall ist, so ist naeh dem oben (S. 177) Gesagten höchst

wahrscheinlich, daß allen drei Berichten dieselbe Urquelle
zu Grunde liegt.

Aber die eben angeführten drei Stellen lehren uns
noch etwas Anderes, nicht minder wichtiges. Dieselbe
Quelle liegt dem Anonymus und dem Korveyer Mönche
zu Grunde, und doch ist es uns unmöglich, durch Vergleichung beider den Wortlaut jener Urquelle zu rekon-
struieren. Der Inhalt ist — fast möchte man sagen, satz-
weise — übereinstimmend, der Ausdruck ganz verschieden,
wie sich aus den mitgeteilten Stellen, besonders der letzten,
zur Evidenz ergibt. Wäre es zu kühn, daraus zu folgern,
daß die gemeinsame Quelle keine lateinische gewesen sein
kann, daß sie vielmehr eine deutsche gewesen sein[1] muß,
selbstverständlich, da deutsche Prosa in jener Zeit völlig
ausgeschlossen ist, ein deutsches Heldenlied, das den Untergang des Thüringerreichs behandelte, wo nicht zum Vorwurf
hatte[2]?

Bisher hatte man eine Zusammensetzung des Quedlinburger Berichts aus Widukind und der Volkssage[3], eine
Zusammensetzung des Berichtes des Anonymus aus Widukind,
den Ann. Quedlinb. und der Volkssage[4] angenommen. Nur

---

1) Besonders klar wird dies bei der Betrachtung der letzten
Stelle, wo einerseits die (wahrscheinlich) direkte Rede des Heldenliedes
in das Lateinische hinübergenommen ist, während der Anonymus
den Inhalt der Worte Theuderichs durch einen Nebensatz mit quia
wiedergibt, wo andererseits ein Begriff, der etwa unserm heutigen
„sich beeilen" entspräche, von beiden verschieden übersetzt wird,
von dem einen mit „festinare", von dem andern mit „quantocius
occurrere". Daß Widukind hier auf Volkssagen bez. Heldenlieder
zurückgeht, ist längst erkannt worden, er ahmt sogar die Allitteration
nach; z. B. cap. 9: Indecorum est victoribus, victis vincendi locum
dare oder vincere velle aut certe vivere nolle.

2) Es ist mir nicht sicher, ob die betreffende gemeinsame Quelle
nur den Untergang des Thüringerreichs behandelte, oder ob auch
die Vorgeschichte der Sachsen darin poetisch dargestellt wurde. In
letzterem Falle würden wohl auch die ersten Kapitel des Widukind
auf diese poetische „origo Saxonum" zurückgehen.

3) Wattenbach, Geschichtsquellen I⁶, S. 342.

4) Wattenbach a. a. O. I⁶, S. 333. Müllenhoff a. a. O. S. 67.

Könnecke[1]) sprach gelegentlich von der Wahrscheinlichkeit einer gemeinsamen Quelle für Widukind und die Quedlinburger Annalen, ohne aber einen Beweis dafür zu erbringen. Wir müssen, wie gesagt, eine gemeinsame Quelle annehmen, ein sächsisches Heldenlied[2]).

Und doch! Werden wir uns dazu entschließen, eine schriftliche Quelle anzunehmen? Wohl sind wir durch Verfolgung der Uebereinstimmungen zu unserem Resultat gelangt, aber vergessen wir doch nicht, daß unsere Arbeit von den kleinen Unterschieden zwischen den einzelnen Autoren ihren Ausgang nahm. Berücksichtigen wir dies, so können wir ruhig einen Schritt weiter tun, indem wir sagen: Das Lied hat sich wahrscheinlich zunächst nur mündlich fortgepflanzt. Manche[3]) Abweichungen der Autoren von einander verdanken ihren Ursprung lokalen Varianten.

Wenn in der Geschichtsliteratur neue Quellen auftauchen, so pflegt man zuerst nach der Zeit der Entstehung und nach dem Verfasser zu fragen. Es dürfte sich hier vielleicht doch verlohnen, wenigstens nach jener zu forschen. Man wird es möglicher Weise als widersinnig bezeichnen, die Entstehungszeit eines Liedes feststellen zu wollen, das nur im Volksmunde lebt, und das sich daher sozusagen in stetem Fluß befindet. Aber so war jene Frage auch nicht gemeint. Es kann doch nur heißen: Können wir feststellen, innerhalb welcher Zeitgrenze das Lied so gestaltet wurde, wie Widukind es gekannt, oder falls es gestattet ist, diese

---

1) Könnecke, Das alte Thüringische Königreich und sein Untergang. Querfurt 1893, S. 26.

2) Daß das Lied ein sächsisches gewesen ist, ist ohne weiteres klar. Der ganze Inhalt ist ad maiorem gloriam Saxonum zugeschnitten.

3) Nicht etwa alle! Ich werde unten zeigen, daß der Quedlinburger Annalist die Schlacht an der Ocker z. B. frei erfunden hat. Daß der Bericht über die Teilung des Reiches (in den Ann. Quedl.) auf eine echte historische Quelle zurückgeht, ist ebenfalls klar. Auch der Umstand, daß in den Ann. Quedlinb. die Leichenbrücke erwähnt wird, wie bei Gregor v. Tours, läßt auf Benutzung einer echten Quelle schließen.

„Gestaltung" als Recension zu bezeichnen, innerhalb welcher
Zeitgrenzen kann die von Widukind benutzte Recension
des Liedes nur zu stande gekommen sein? · Der terminus
ad quem ist natürlich das Jahr 967, das Jahr, in dem
Widukind sein Werk vollendete [1]). Schwieriger ist es, den
terminus a quo zu bestimmen. Hier gibt uns aber glücklicher-
weise Widukind selbst einen Fingerzeig.

Nicht mit Unrecht ist seine Schilderung der Sachsen
(I 9) so berühmt. „Ihm geht das Herz auf [2])", wenn er
von diesen Kriegern spricht, die durch Körperkraft und
Mut hervorragend, bewaffnet mit langen Lanzen, auf ihre
Schilde gestützt dastehen, bewundert und angestaunt von
den Franken. Mit naivem Stolz erzählt er, wie bereits damals manche Franken sich hätten vernehmen lassen: tantis
ac talibus amicis Francos non indigere; indomitum genus
hominum fore, et si presentem terram inhabitarent, eos
procul dubio esse, qui Francorum imperium quandoque
destruerent [3]). Ist dies etwa keine vaticinatio post eventum?
Und wenn es eine ist, so kommen wir auf das Jahr 919,
in welchem die Herrschaft endgültig von den Franken auf
die Sachsen überging.

Man wird einwenden: Diese ganze Stelle sei erst von
Widukind seiner Quelle eingefügt worden und habe daher
für die chronologische Festsetzung des Liedes durchaus
keinen Wert. Es läßt sich zeigen, daß dem nicht so ist.

Als Iring in Irminfrieds Auftrage zu Theuderich geht,
um den Frieden zu erbitten, da bietet der schlaue Thüringer
dem Merowingerkönig ein Bündnis gegen die Sachsen an:
utilius esse, eum in fide suscipere, quem iam superatum
haberet tamque contritum, ut numquam se contra eum possit
levare quam illud genus hominum indomabile et ad omnem

---

1) Wattenbach, Geschichtsquellen I [6], S. 328.
2) Köpke, Widukind von Korvey S. 5.
3) Widukind I, 9, Separatausgabe von Waitz, 1882, S. 9 f.

laborem perdurabile, a quo nichil expectaret Francorum. imperium nisi solum periculum [1]).

Theuderich geht auf den Vorschlag ein, den Sachsen wird das Bündnis verraten, sie stürmen, um ihm zuvor zu kommen, am nächsten Tage früh Burg Scheidungen.

Man sieht hier deutlich, wie der Gedanke, den Franken drohe von den Sachsen nur Gefahr, zum forttreibenden Motiv der Handlung wird. Daher muß der Gedanke dem Heldenlied entstammen, und er ist wohl verwertbar zur, chronologischen Fixierung [2]).

So stellen wir denn als bisheriges Resultat unserer Untersuchung nochmals fest.

Für die Darstellung des Thüringerkrieges von 531 haben Widukind, die Annales Quedlinburgenses und der Anonymus de origine Suevorum ein jetzt verlorenes, in der von Widukind benutzten Recension zwischen 919 und 967 entstandenes sächsisches Heldenlied benutzt, in dem der Krieg zwischen Theuderich und Irminfried ausführlich geschildert, wo nicht zum Vorwurf gemacht war. In diesem Heldenlied verschob sich das Verwandtschaftsverhältnis Amalabergas insofern, als man ihre Person im Gegensatz zu den echten historischen Quellen an die Merowinger statt an die Ostgoten anknüpfte, wodurch sich allmählich eine Verschmelzung der Persönlichkeiten der beiden Theoderiche vollziehen mußte. Diese Verschmelzung mußte logischer Weise dazu führen, die Irminfriedsagen mit dem Sagen: kreise Dietrichs von Bern (des Ostgoten Theoderich), d. h.

---

1) Das „periculum" wird man am ehesten doch auf den Ueber-gang der Krone von den Franken an die Sachsen beziehen können. Etwa an den großen Sieg der Sachsen über Chlotar I. zu denken, geht nicht an, weil dieser Erfolg nur ein ganz vorübergehender war.

2) Ueber die Persönlichkeit des Verfassers wage ich kein Urteil. Auffällig sind allerdings die zahlreichen Anklänge an angelsächsische Sagen. Der Ausdruck Huga für Franke, der bei Widukind und den Ann. Quedl. erscheint, kommt bereits im Beowulf v. 2195 und v. 2503 vor. Vergl. Kurth histoire poétique des Méroving. 1893, S. 338, n. 2.

auch mit dem Hunnenkönig in Verbindung zu bringen; und
wirklich finden wir im Nibelungenliede Irminfried und Iring
am Hofe Etzels lebend[1]). Aber auch schon unser Gedicht
wirft Irminfried, Iring und Attila zusammen: Der Anonymus
läßt Irminfried mit Iring an Etzels Hof kommen, der
Quedlinburger schließt einen Kompromiß mit den historischen
Quellen, indem er den Thüringerkönig von Theuderich zwar
töten läßt, daran jedoch jenen Satz über Attila anschließt,
der in diesen Zusammenhang gar nicht hineinpaßt; Widukind erwähnt Attila überhaupt nicht und hat über den
Tod des Irminfried eine vom Quedlinburger abweichende
Version. Daraus folgt, daß sowohl der Quedlinburger als
Widukind mindestens noch je eine Quelle benutzt haben.

Aber des Quedlinburgers Bericht ist nur ein Anklang
an die echten historischen Quellen: Post haec Theodericus
data fide Irminfrido in Zulpiaco civitate illum dolo perimi
iussit, ein Satz, der sich ebensowohl mit Gregor von Tours[2])
als mit Widukind verträgt. Wie jedoch der Korveyer zu
seiner Nachricht kommt, Iring habe den Irminfried auf
Befehl des Theuderich erschlagen und dann Theuderich
selbst getötet, ist nicht mehr zu erkennen. Vielleicht war
es die ursprüngliche Sagenfassung[3]), und Widukind mag
diese aus Furcht, einen Anachronismus zu begehen, wenn
er in einem Geschichtswerk die Person Irminfrieds mit

---

1) Nibelungenlied, übersetzt von K. Simrock 1893, 22. Abenteuer
Str. 1286, 35. Abenteuer Str. 1965 ff.

2) III, 8. Idem vero regressus (sc. Theud.) ad propria, Hermenefredum ad se data fidem securum praecipit venire, quem et honorificis
ditavit muneribus. Factum est autem, dum quadam die per murum
civitatis Tulpiacensis confabularentur, a nescio quo impulsus, de
altitudine muri ad terram corruit ibique spiritum exalavit. Sed quis
eum exinde deiecerit ignoramus; multi tamen adserunt Theudorici
in hoc dolum manifestissime patuisse.

3) Dies ist wohl das Wahrscheinlichste. Man wolle übrigens
bemerken, daß Widukind die Erzählung vom Tode Irminfrieds scharf
von der vorhergehenden sondert (Qui autem finis reges secutus sit,
quia memorabilis fama est, prodere non negligo).

13*

Attila verband, vorgezogen haben. Auch der Quedlinburger
scheint diesen Anachronismus gescheut zu haben, verrät
uns aber doch durch jenen Satz über Attila wieder die gemeinsame Quelle. Erst der Anonymus, der mehr die Sagen
aufzeichnete als Geschichte schrieb, konnte ohne Bedenken
seiner Vorlage folgen.

Auf Grund unserer bisherigen Untersuchung können wir
jetzt in die Verhandlung darüber eintreten, ob den sächsischen Quellen irgend welche historische Glaubwürdigkeit
beizumessen ist oder nicht.

Teil II. Kritik der Sage.

Schon Ephoros[1]) hat im Wesentlichen das Princip
ausgesprochen, dessen man sich in diesen und ähnlichen
Fällen bedienen muß:

περὶ μὲν γὰρ τῶν καθ᾽ ἡμᾶς γεγενημένων τοὺς ἀκριβέστατα
λέγοντας πιστοτάτους ἡγούμεθα, περὶ δὲ τῶν παλαιῶν τοὺς
οὕτω διεξιόντας ἀπιθανωτάτους εἶναι νομίζομεν, ὑπολαμβάνον-
τες οὔτε τὰς πράξεις ἁπάσας οὔτε τῶν λόγων τοὺς πλείστους
εἰκὸς εἶναι μνημονεύεσθαι διὰ τοσούτων.

Streng genommen müßten wir also über die sächsischen
Quellen (Widukind, die Ann. Quedlinburg., den Anonymus
de origine Suevorum) in Bausch und Bogen das Verdammungsurteil aussprechen; aber ist ein so völlig absprechendes Urteil auch wirklich gerechtfertigt? In einem
Punkte wohl sicher nicht. Erinnern wir uns daran, daß
historisch bedeutsame Örtlichkeiten nicht so leicht vom
Volke vergessen werden. Die homerischen Epen nimmt
heutzutage niemand mehr für Geschichte, und doch hätte
Schliemann ohne ihre Existenz wohl schwerlich jene
epochemachenden Ausgrabungen auf Hissarlik vorgenommen.
Die Nutzanwendung auf unser Gebiet liegt nahe. Wir
werden die in unserm Heldenlied vorkommenden Örtlich-

---

1) Ephoros bei Harpokration u. ἀρχαίως (Harpokration ed. Bekker,
1833, S. 36).

keiten und Schlachten bis auf Weiteres als historisch betrachten, aber auch hier werden wir das Lied nur als bestätigende, nicht als grundlegende Quelle verwenden dürfen.

Manchem wird es schwer fallen, den ihm lieb gewordenen Glauben an die Verwendbarkeit des Details der sächsischen Quellen aufgeben zu müssen; es wird daher nicht nutzlos sein, den Inhalt des Liedes einer sachlichen Kritik zu unterziehen.

Ist diese Forderung aber überhaupt durchführbar?

Nicht als ob die sachliche Kritik an sich großen Schwierigkeiten begegnete, die Schwierigkeit liegt in der erforderlichen Rekonstruktion des Liedes.

Es giebt dazu nur einen Weg.

Wir müssen nach den Ausführungen von Teil I. die drei uns bereits bekannten sächsischen Quellen als verschiedene Ableitungen ein und derselben Urquelle betrachten. Die Abweichungen der Quellen von einander schrieben wir schon oben (S. 180) teilweise lokalen Varianten zu; an manchen Stellen genügt dies jedoch nicht. Daher kann man als dem Liede angehörig alle diejenigen Stellen bestimmt annehmen, die mit dem Berichte der anderen Quellen übereinstimmen, oder wenigstens sich gegenseitig nicht völlig ausschließen. Es wird demnach am einfachsten sein, bei einer Kritik der Sage von Widukind auszugehen und nötigenfalls die Stellen der anderen Quellen zum Vergleich, resp. zur Ergänzung heranzuziehen.

Im Anfang ist bei Widukind Sage und Geschichte in wirrem Durcheinander gemischt. Erst etwa von den Worten „Thiadricus autem designatus rex" an scheint Widukind ganz der Sage zu folgen, wie ein Vergleich mit dem Anonymus lehrt. (Quo regnante misit legatos etc.).

Der von Theuderich an Irminfried „pro pace atque concordia" abgesandte Bote hält vor dem Thüringerkönig eine bemerkenswerte Rede. „Mortalium optimus maximus, dominus mens Thiadricus misit me ad te, exoptans te

bene valere et lato magnoque diu imperio vigere seque
tibi non dominum sed amicum, non impera-
torem, sed propinquum, propinquitatisque iura in-
violabiliter tibi fine tenus velle servare demandat; tantum
ut a populi Francorum concordia non discordes rogat;
ipsum namque sibi regem sequuntur constitutum."

Auf was für Voraussetzungen fußt denn diese Rede?
Weist sie nicht deutlich auf ein Abhängigkeitsverhältnis
Irminfrieds von Theuderich hin? Man sage nicht etwa
die Ausdrücke dominus und imperator seien nur eine
rhetorische Phrase im Munde des Gesandten; ein Ge-
sandter, der pro pace atque concordia zu einem fremden
Herrscher hingeht, wird sich hüten, diesen grundlos zu
beleidigen. Zum Überfluß aber ergänzen hier die Ann.
Quedlinb. den Korveyer Mönch auf das vortrefflichste.
Es wird von der Teilung des fränkischen Reiches unter
die Söhne Chlodwigs gesprochen und dann heißt es:
Cuius (sc. Theoderici) parti cum Thuringia cessisset, Irminfridus, gener eius, hortatu uxoris suae
Amelburgae invitationem regis respuit (vorhin war schon
erwähnt worden: Theodericus rex . . . . . . ad electionem
suam Irminfridum regem Thuringorum honorifice invitavit).
Wir sehen: die Worte dominus und imperator stehen
nicht zufällig bei Widukind. Die ganze Notiz ist aber so
absurd, keine der fränkischen Quellen bestätigt sie, obwohl
diese doch am ehesten davon etwas wissen mußten; wir
sind daher gezwungen diese Nachricht als unhistorisch zu
verwerfen.

Bei der folgenden Entgegnung Irminfrieds ist nur der
Anonymus außer Widukind zum Vergleich heranzuziehen;
beide Berichte sind inhaltlich fast identisch, nur fehlt beim
Anonymus die Beteuerung des Thüringers: pace omnimodis
indigere. Man wäre fast versucht, diese Worte als nichts-
sagende Phrase aufzufassen; aber der weitere Bericht des
Korveyers steht dieser Auffassung unter allen Umständen
im Wege. Denn bei der Versammlung der Großen, die

Irminfried einberuft, raten diese ihm: quae pacis atque côn-
cordiae sunt, eum sentire, quia impetus Francorum ferre
non posset, maxime qui acrioribus hostium armis ex alia
parte premeretur. Und trotz dieses Rates schenkt Irminfried seinem Vertrauten Iring Gehör, der ihm rät, er dürfe
den Franken nicht nachgeben! Wer sind denn diese Feinde,
um derentwillen Irminfried „gar sehr des Friedens bedarf",
mit denen er jetzt bereits im Kampf ist und deren Waffen
noch schärfer sind als die der Franken? Sind es etwa die
Sachsen, qui iam olim erant Thuringis acerrimi hostes?
Aber diese kommen ja selbst erst auf den Ruf Theuderichs
(nach dem Liede) den Franken zu Hilfe, wir. erfahren
nichts davon, daß sie schon zu Beginn des fränkischen
Feldzuges mit den Thüringern in Fehde liegen! Und trotz
dieses bedeutenden Krieges gegen unbekannte Feinde fühlt
sich Irminfried doch veranlaßt, noch einen Krieg gegen
die Franken einzugehen! Sowie dieser Krieg aber beginnt,
verschwinden die anderen Feinde plötzlich, wir erfahren
nichts mehr von ihnen! Auch die Gründe, die Iring anführt, um Irminfried zum Kriege fortzureißen, sind dazu
angetan, das ganze Verhalten des Königs in ein recht
merkwürdiges Licht zu rücken. Zwar was Iring zuerst
sagt, läßt sich hören: Die Sache Irminfrieds sei die gerechtere;
aber gleich darauf heißt es: latum praeterea imperium, mili-
tum manus et arma caeterasque belli copias sibi ac· Thia-
drico parum procedere.

   Hier wird es klar ausgesprochen: Die Macht Irminfrieds
reicht nicht an die Theuderichs heran; wenn der Unterschied
auch nur klein ist, er ist aber doch eben da. Irminfried
übernimmt also den Kampf gegen die Franken, deren Macht
·bedeutender als die seinige ist, zu dem Kampf gegen eine
andere Nation, deren Macht noch bedeutender als die der
·Franken sein soll! Wohin wir uns wenden, lauter Widersprüche, lauter Unmöglichkeiten!

   Sehen wir uns den Inhalt des Liedes weiter an.

   Es kommt zum Kriege, die erste Schlacht findet „an

den Grenzen der Thüringer" statt, in loco qui dicitur Runibergun [1]). Wo diese Schlacht eigentlich stattgefunden hat,
kann hier noch unerörtert bleiben. Genug, die Thüringer
werden in die Flucht geschlagen, aber auch die Franken
erleiden solche Verluste, daß in dem Kriegsrat, der s o f o r t
abgehalten wird, man den Gedanken in Erwägung zieht, unge-
säumt nach Hause zurückzukehren. Dieser Kriegsrat muß
unmittelbar nach der Schlacht abgehalten sein, denn noch sind
die Toden nicht bestattet, noch ist kein Lager von den
Franken aufgeschlagen [2]). Trotzdem daß also dieser Kriegsrat anch „an den Grenzen der Thüringer" stattfinden muß,
behauptet der Sklave des Theuderich: Nunc terra in nostra
est potetaste (!), und, damit noch nicht genug: Num singulis
urbibus administranda sufficimus presidia? Et eas omnes
perdimus, dum imus et redimus.

Kann man sich einen größeren Widerspruch denken?
Der Kriegsrat findet sofort nach der ersten Schlacht an
der Grenze des Landes statt, und doch soll das Land bereits
in der Gewalt der Franken sein, und doch können diese
die Befürchtung. aussprechen, sie würden die Burgen verlieren, wenn sie abziehen würden.

Während Theuderich zu den Sachsen schickt, muß das
fränkische Heer (nach dem Liede) weiter gezogen sein,
denn die Sachsen treffen im Lager Theuderichs vor Burg-
Scheidungen ein. Neun Scharen zu je tausend Mann sind
es, die den Kampf gegen die Thüringer wagen wollen.
Möglich, daß dies noch eine Erinnerung an die alten
Tausendschaften ist, in diesem Falle müßten die Elemente
des Liedes bis weit in die fränkische Zeit hinaufreichen.
Die neuen Bundesgenossen begrüßen den Frankenkönig verbis
pacificis. Ist dieser Zusatz nicht selbstverständlich? Fast

---

1) Ueber die Lage dieses Ortes vergl. weiter unten im Teil III.
2) Walderich sagt im Kriegsrat: Censeo causa caesos sepeliendi
. . . . patriam remeandum. Der Sklave Theuderichs sagt im selben
Kriegsrat: castrorum esto labor. (Widukind I, 9, Sep.-Ausg. 1882,
S. 8 und 9.

scheint es nicht, denn Theuderich nimmt den Gruß hilarior
auf. Hat etwa eine Spannung zwischen Sachsen und Franken
bestanden, die jetzt durch den Vertrag beseitigt ist? Wir
wissen es nicht; über die Vorgeschichte des Vertrages
meldet nicht einmal unser Lied etwas. Die Sachsen schlagen
nun ein Lager auf ad meridianam plagam urbis in pratis
fluvio contiguis d. h. im Süden der Burg auf den dem Fluß
benachbarten Wiesen. Da sie bei dem ersten Sturm am
nächsten Tage aber den Fluß nicht zu überschreiten brauchen,
so muß man sich das Lager zwischen Burg und Fluß denken.
Damit ist nun wieder die Jagdanekdote nicht vereinbar,
die ja von der Voraussetzung ausgeht, daß Sachsen und
Thüringer durch den Fluß getrennt sind. Ich gebe zu, daß
die Auffassung Größler's [1]), daß die Sachsen ihr Lager
südlich vom Flusse gehabt hätten, sich allenfalls halten
läßt; auffallend muß dann aber die Stellung der Jagdanekdote bleiben. Diese Anekdote gipfelt doch (in der Urquelle),
wie wir gesehen haben, in der listigen Auffindung der Furt,
sie ist eingeschoben zwischen dem ersten und zweiten Sturm
der Sachsen. Wie kommt es nun (immer unter der Voraussetzung, daß der Fluß Sachsen und Thüringer trennt),
daß die Sachsen, um den zweiten Sturm machen zu können,
erst die Furt auffinden müssen, während sie doch bereits den
ersten Sturm gemacht haben, ohne die Furt zu kennen?
Diese heikle Frage hat Größler völlig übersehen. Auch hier
liegen wieder unlösbare Widersprüche vor.

Die Sachsen sind im Lager Theuderichs eingetroffen
und haben dann selbst ihr Lager aufgeschlagen. Am nächsten
Tage beginnen sie in aller Frühe den Kampf, stürmen die
Vorburg und stecken sie in Brand. Die in der Burg befindlichen Thüringer machen einen Ausfall, es kommt zu
einem fürchterlichen Handgemenge, talique spectaculo tota
dies illa trahitur. Erst die Nacht macht dem Treffen ein

---

1) a. a. O. S. 36. Größler hält übrigens die Schilderung des
Angriffs für historisch.

Ende: Cum neuter agmen loco cessisset, iam tardior hora prelium diremit. Dann wird Iring der Friedensunterhandlungen wegen zu Theuderich geschickt, Theuderich verspricht am nächsten Tage mit den Thüringern vereint die Sachsen anzugreifen, es folgt die Jagdanekdote, die Beratung im Sachsenlager, und dann plötzlich heißt es: Quod supererat diei in reficiendis suis corporibus expendebant, während wir doch vorhin schon gehört hatten, daß erst die Nacht dem Treffen ein Ende macht. Bereits in der ersten Nachtwache unternehmen sie den Sturm [1]). Ich frage, wie ist das chronologisch denkbar? Man könnte versucht sein, sich zu helfen, indem man zwischen den ersten und zweiten Sturm einen ganzen Tag einschiebt und an diesem die Friedensverhandlungen spielen läßt, aber in den sächsischen Quellen steht davon nichts [2]).

Was sollen wie noch das ganze Detail im Einzelnen nachprüfen? Längst ist erkannt worden, daß das sächsische Löwen- und Drachenbanner der Sage angehört [3]), und der Umstand, daß es teilweise doch zur Schilderung der Ereignisse mit verwendet wird [4]), ändert daran nicht das mindeste. Ehe wir aber diesen Teil abschließen, müssen wir noch eine Stelle besprechen, die von Größler zum Ausgangspunkt seiner Hypothese gemacht wird, das der Krieg „den ganzen Sommer hindurch" gedauert habe [5]). Wir meinen die Datierung von Burg-Scheidungens Einnahme auf den 1. Oktober [6]).

---

1) Die erste Vigilie tritt bekanntlich gleich nach Sonnenuntergang ein.

2). Damit erledigt sich die Ansicht Koennecke's (a. a. O. S. 47): „Der Sturm der Sachsen auf die Vorburg und der verzweifelte Ausfall der Thüringer können also recht wohl geschichtlich sein", ebenso wie die Auffassung Größler's, der (a. a. O. S. 46 ff.) eine detaillierte Schilderung der letzten Ereignisse um Burg-Scheidungen giebt.

3) Geschichtsschreiber d. deutschen Vorzeit X, 6 [2], S. 19 n.

4) Kirchhoff, Thüringen doch Hermundurenland. 1882, S. 34.

5) Größler, a. a. O. S. 22.

6) Widukind, I, 12, Separatausgabe 1882, S. 13. Giesebrecht, Gesch. der deutschen Kaiserzeit I, 812 hält die Notiz W. für ein-

Eins ist von vornherein klar: dem Heldenlied kann
dieses Datum nicht entstammen. Es muß Widukinds
eigene Zutat sein, der auf die Datierung folgende Satz
läßt darüber keinen Zweifel: Acta sunt autem haec omnia,
ut memoria maiorum prodit, die Kal. Octobris. Qui dies
erroris religiosorum sanctione virorum mutati sunt in
ieiunia et orationes, oblationes quoque omnium nos prece-
dentium christianorum [1]). Auch darüber, daß unter den
erwähnten Festtagen die sog. „gemeine Woche" verstanden
ist, ist man einig [2]). Ist aber die Ableitung selbst richtig?
Homeyer [3]) nimmt es an und Grotefend [4]) scheint ebenfalls
keine andere zu kennen. Und doch giebt es noch eine
andere, freilich wohl auch nur lokalen Ursprungs. Trotz
Wattenbach's [5]) Zitat scheint sie so gut wie unbekannt
geblieben zu sein, selbst Grotefend erwähnt sie nicht.
In einem Sammelbande der Bibliothek der Ritter-

---

geschoben, da sie sinnstörend sei; er glaubt allerdings, daß Widukind
die Notiz nachträglich selbst eingeschoben habe. Die Cronica du-
cum de Brunswick (M. G. deutsche Chronicken II. 1877, S. 581),
die auf die Nienburger Annalen, deren Quellen hier wieder Ekkehard
und die Ann. Quedlinb. sind, zurückgeht (a. a. O. S. 574), läßt die
Eroberung Burg-Scheidungen am 25. September 534 vor sich gehen.
Die Jahreszahl ist sicher falsch, vgl. Richter „Annalen der
deutschen Geschichte" unter dem Jahre 531. Wie die Chronik zu dem
von Widukind um 6 Tage abweichenden Datum kommt, vermag ich
nicht zu sagen.

1) Herr Professor Rühl macht mich darauf aufmerksam, daß
der Text an dieser Stelle völlig korrumpiert sein muß. Das „die
Kal. Oct." giebt keinen Sinn, weil es ja nachher heißt: qui dies
mutati sunt. Vielleicht hat es ursprünglich „circa diem" oder ähnlich geheißen.

2) Waitz, in s. Widukindausgabe, 1882, S. 13 n. 3. Wattenbach
in den „Geschichtschreiber der deutschen Vorzeit" X, 6[2], S. 21, n. 1.
G. Homeyer, Stadtbücher des Mittelalters, 1860, S. 71 f.

3) Homeyer, a. a. O.

4) Grotefend, Zeitrechnung des deutschen Mittelalters und der
Neuzeit I, 72 unter „gemeine Woche".

5) Wattenbach, Geschichtschreiber der deutschen Vorzeit X, 6[2],
S. 21, n. 1.

akademie zu Brandenburg[1]) steht eine „Commemoracio sancti episcopi Borchardi et confessoris". Dieser Burchard, ein ungebildeter Priester, nesciens aliam missam quam pro defunctis, wird, als ein Bischofswechsel eingetreten ist, de ignorancia sui officii bei dem neuen Bischof verklagt.

---

1) Mitteilungen aus den Handschriften der Ritter-Akademie zu Brandenburg a. H. I. Johannes von Hildesheim, beigegeben dem 22. Jahresbericht über die Ritter-Akademie von E. Köpke, Brandenburg 1878. Der für uns in Betracht kommende Passus findet sich S. 2 f. Commemoracio sancti episcopi Borchardi et confessoris. Elapso tempore hic Borchardus fuit illiteratissimus et sacerdotum simplicissimus, nesciens aliam missam quam pro defunctis, quam devotissime, cum ab affine episcopo suo fuit beneficiatus, celebravit. unde per eum multe anime fuerunt salvate. postea aliquo tempore moritur collator et episcopus sue ecclesie, et dos eius cum villa funditus fuit exusta. Novo episcopo superveniente et villico alio succedente Beatus Borchardus de ignorancia sui officii apud novum episcopum accusatur, et quomodo ecclesiam possideret citatur et interrogatur. Ille affirmans a mortuo episcopo esse curam, cui novus episcopus respondit: Si infra quindenam autenticum literarum vestre eure a primo (?) unius testis non adhibueritis, privabo vos beneficio et officio. Beatus Borchardus abiit flens et iterum flendo se super tumulum defuncti episcopi locavit auxilium accusacionis ab eo petens. Mortuus vero episcopus divina ordinacione illum consolatus est dicens: Breviter tuus episcopus consilium generale habebit cum omnibus suis prelatis et clericis. Tune vadas et compareas oboedienter, et sequor te. Et secutus est eum sicud cum infula sua fuit usque ad kathedralem suam sedem, ubi visus est ab omnibus cum episcopo sedentibus. Qui dum mortuum viderunt, omnes fugierunt. Quibus precepit sub virtute sancte oboediencie ut resideremt et eum in negocio suo audirent. Episcopus vero et alii audientes obedienciam nominare, se reposuerunt ipsumque audierunt. Tune mortuus episcopus affatur episcopo vivo dicens: Cur sanctum Borchardum beneficio suo et officio privare intendetis? preferens eis, quod quamdiu ecclesie sue prefuisset omnium anime sub sua cura defunctorum essent salvate, et adiecit: si privaveritis sanctum Borchardum beneficio et officio, vos privabimus regno celorum. His dictis mortuus episcopus, dimittens se ab omnibus, redivit ad sepulchrum. Sanctus Borchardus adhuc stans ante suum presulem graciam exspectans, cui episcopus: „Borcharde, vis nobis in omnibus oboedire?" Cui ille: „Volo." „Precipio ergo tibi in vice

Dieser droht ihn abzusetzen, falls er innerhalb 14 Tagen kein authentisches Zeugnis dafür schaffen könne, daß er seine Kirche zu Recht besäße. Burchard entfernt sich weinend und klagt am Grabe des alten Bischofs diesem sein Leid. Der Verstorbene ist bereit, ihm zu helfen, er erscheint mit ihm in einer Versammlung, die der Bischof mit seinen Prälaten und Klerikern abhält, und befiehlt ihnen, den heiligen Burchard in seinem Amte zu belassen, widrigenfalls sie des Himmelreichs verlustig gehen würden. Dann kehrt der Verstorbene zu seinem Grabe zurück. Der neue Bischof tritt, erschüttert durch diesen Vorfall, seine Würde an den Heiligen ab, und man feiert die Begebenheit mit einem Gastmahl. „Daher rührt die Sitte der Kleriker, jährlich an St. Burchardstag ein Gastmahl zu halten. Et ex isto miraculo communis septimana sanctis patribus solempniter pro defunctis in memoria habeatur. Tandem sanctus Borchardus obdormivit in domino".

Die Identificierung dieses Burchard macht nicht geringe Schwierigkeiten, vornehmlich aus zwei Gründen. Einmal läßt sich die Geschichte, wie sie hier erzählt wird, von keinem der bekannten Heiligen dieses Namens nachweisen[1], und sodann fallen die Tage, an denen man die

---

sancte obediencie, ut capias locum mee dignitatis; et mei miserere." Et provolutus pedibus eum episcopus cum aliis digne et alta voce in sede sua collocavit omnibusque grande convivium fecit. Exinde inolevit mos clericorum omni anno in die Sancti Borchardi habere convivium. Et ex isto miraculo communis septimana sanctis patribus solempniter pro defunctis in memoria habeatur. Tandem sanctus Borchardus obdormivit in domino.

1) Die verschiedenen Heiligenverzeichnisse führen an: 1. S. Burchardus, Graf von Melun (Acta SS. Boll. 26. Febr.) 2. S. Burchardus, Abt von St. Gallen. (Mabillon Acta SS. ord. S. Benedicti saec. VI, 1. von Mas Latrie im „trésor de Chronologie" Paris 1889, S. 694 als S. bezeichnet, während Potthast Bibliotheca II², 1227 und Grotefend a. a. O. II, 2, 75 ihn als v. (venerabilis) bezeichnen). Festtag: 4. März. 3. S. Burchardus, Erzbischof von

Feste dieser Heiligen gewöhnlich feiert, nicht in die „gemeine Woche [1]“. Diese Schwierigkeit wird noch dadurch
erhöbt, daß weder in der Diöcese Brandenburg noch bei
den Prämonstratensern („Die Bischöfe und Kapitularen des
Hochstifts Brandenburg waren bis zum Jahre 1506 sämtlich regulierte Chorherren des Prämonstratenser-Ordens [2]“.
Die Handschriften des Hochstifts sind zum Teil in die
Bibliothek der Ritter-Akademie hinübergerettet, und einer
dieser Handschriften entstammt die obige Erzählung) die
Verehrung eines Heiligen Namens Burchard sieh nachweisen läßt [3]). In Betracht kommt für uns eigentlich
nur Bischof Burchard von Würzburg, da dieser sein Fest
meistenteils am 14. Oktober hat. Wenn nun auch der
vierzehnte Oktober nicht mehr in die „gemeine Woche"
fällt, so erinnern wir uns daran, daß die Feste der Heiligen
örtlich verschieden gefeiert werden. Da nun in der Diöcese Lebus, die der Diöcese Brandenburg benachbart ist [4]),
der Tag des heiligen Burchard am 6. Oktober, also genau eine Woche nach Michaelis, gefeiert wird, ferner der
Heilige im Lebuser Diöcesankalender als cf. (= confessor)

Vienne. (Acta SS. Boll. 19. August, nur Mas Latrie führt ihn
auf, bei Potthast und Grotefend fehlt er.) 4. B. Burchardus, Presbyter in der Schweiz. (Acta SS. Boll. 20. August. Mas Latrie
bezeichnet ihn a. a. O. als prêtre et conf. en Suisse. 5. S. Burchardus, Bischof von Worms (Mas Latrie bezeichnet ihn fälschlich als
S.; nach Grotefend a. a. O. II, 2, 75 ist er nie kanonisiert worden.
In den Acta SS. Boll. fehlt seine Vita). 6. S. Burchardus, Bischof
von Würzburg. (Acta SS. Boll. 14. Oktober).

1) Grotefend erklärt a. a. O. I, 72 die „gemeine Woche" als
„meist die volle Woche nach dem Michaelisfeste" (29. Sept.) Der
Halberstädter ordo divinus versteht unter der gemeinen Woche die
Woche nach Remigius (1. October), vgl. die Nachweise bei Grotefend a. a. O.

2) E. Köpke, a. a. O. S. 1.

3) Vgl. die entsprechenden Diöcesan- und Ordenskalender bei
Grotefend a. a. O. II, 1, 14 ff. II, 2, 48 ff.

4) Spruner-Menke, Handatlas 1880, Karte no. 42.

auftritt [1]), so dürfte, zumal da der heilige Burchard in der Überschrift unserer Erzählung auch als confessor erscheint, die Ableitung der „gemeinen Woche" von dem heiligen Burchard ein geistiges Produkt der Lebuser Diöcese sein.

Wir haben jetzt die Wahl zwischen beiden Erklärungen, derjenigen Widukinds und derjenigen der Brandenburger Handschrift. Aber gerade der Umstand, daß beide Erklärungen rein lokaler Natur sind, führt auf die Vermutung, daß auch Widukinds Ableitung erfunden ist. Die „gemeine Woche", die sich in einem großen Teil von Deutschland, und nicht bloß auf sächsischem Stammesboden nachweisen läßt [2]), sollte ihren Ursprung einem lokalen Ereignis verdanken, mag es nun die Eroberung von Burg-Scheidungen durch die Sachsen oder die wunderbare Erhebung des heiligen Burchard auf den Bischofsstuhl sein? Wie sagt doch der Halberstädter ordo divinus? In illa septimana erunt communes orationes tam pro vivis quam pro defunctis. Und ähnlich heißt es in der Brandenburger Handschrift: Et ex isto miraculo communis septimana sanctis patribus solempniter pro defunctis in memoria habeatur. Die gemeine Woche ist also eine Gedächtniswoche für die Toten, sie vertritt die Stelle des späteren Festes Allerseelen [3]), ja, zuweilen werden bestimmte Tage in ihr als „aller selentag" oder „seledago" bezeichnet, auch lateinische Bezeichnungen finden sich: commemoratio omnium animarum, memoria omnium animarum [4]). Und hier drängt sich uns eine neue Frage auf: hängt vielleicht die gemeine Woche mit dem Feste Allerseelen zusammen, und inwiefern hängt sie zusammen?

---

1) Grotefend, a. a. O. II, 1, 101. II, 2, 75.

2) Vgl. die Nachweise bei Grotefend a. a. O. I. S. 72 f. er führt Beispiele an aus: Halberstadt, Duderstadt, Frankfurt a. M., Bremen, Mecklenburg, Stolberg, Oldenburg, Braunschweig, Verden, Jena, Niederrhein.

3) „Die Feier des 2. November als Allerseelen-Tag drang in Norddeutschland erst spät ein". Grotefend a. a. O. I, S. 73.

4) Die Nachweise bei Grotefend a. a. O. I, S. 73.

Naeh Widukinds Bericht (er hat im Jahre 967 geschrieben) bleibt es 300 Jahre lang still, in keiner Quelle finden wir die „gemeine Woche" erwähnt, bis sie 1243 plötzlich in dem sog. scriptum super Apocalypsim auftaucht [1]. Urkundlich erscheint sie selbst in jener Zeit noch nicht, erst vom Jahre 1304 an kommt sie in Diplomen vor, zuerst (d. h. 1304) auf thüringischem Boden in einer Urkunde der Herren von Heldrungen [2]. Von da ab erscheint sie öfter und läßt sich bis zum 16. Jahrhundert einschließlich — das letzte uns bekannte Beispiel stammt aus dem Jahre 1536 und fiudet sich in den Schmalkaldischen Artikeln (art. 2 de Missa) [3] — nachweisen; im 17. Jahrhundert scheint sie nicht mehr vorzukommen. Wahrscheinlich wird sie um diese Zeit durch die Feier des 2. November als Allerseelentag verdrängt. „Diese drang in Norddeutschland erst spät ein, die liturgischen Bücher der Diöcesen Verden, Paderborn, Osnabrück und Minden aus der ersten Hälfte des 16. Jahrhunderts führen dieselbe noch nicht im Kalender auf [4]". Muß es schon eigentümlich berühren, daß wir nach Widukind fast 300 Jahre lang von der „gemeinen Woche" nichts hören, so muß es noch mehr überraschen, daß zu Widukinds Zeiten die Feier eines Gedächtnistages für die Verstorbenen überhaupt noch nicht gesetzlich geregelt war. Erst Abt Odilo von Cluny (994—1048) hat, angeblich durch die Vision eines Pilgers bewogen, das Fest Allerseelen eingeführt.

Man pflegt sieh auf eine Stelle Sigeberts von Gembloux [5] zu stützen, wenn man, wie es gewöhnlich geschieht, die Einführung des Festes Allerseelen im Jahre 998 stattfinden läßt, da eben bei diesem Jahre Sigebert die Legende bringt, im Anschluß an die Thronerhebung Papst Agapits.

---

1) Vgl. Wattenbach, Geschichtsquellen II[6], S. 254.
2) Haltaus, calendarium medii aevi etc. Lipsiae 1729, S. 136.
3) Haltaus a. a. O. S. 136.
4) Grotefend a. a. O. I, S. 73.
5) M. G. SS. VI, S. 353.

Ernst Sackur hat neuerdings diese Auffassung in ihren Grundfesten erschüttert[1]). Er zeigt, daß Sigebert in völlig unberechtigter Weise zwei Nachrichten, den Bericht über den sagenhaften Papst mit der Erzählung über die Einführung des Allerseelentages (Marianus Scotus und die Vita Odilonis von Jotsald) verbunden hat. Er setzt vermutungsweise die Einführung des Festes Allerseelen in den Anfang der dreißiger Jahre des 11. Jahrhunderts, ohne jedoch den Beweis hierfür antreten zu können. So viel steht immerhin fest: unter Abt Odilo von Cluny ist die Einführung des Festes erfolgt, zunächst jedoch nur innerhalb des Cluniacenserordens, erst Papst Leo IX. (1048—1054) soll, einer Angabe der Vita S. Bertulfi zufolge, den neuen Festtag in die gesamte Kirche eingeführt haben[2]).

Aber nun wird die Stelle Widukinds noch unverständlicher. Wer sind denn diese „religiosi viri", durch deren sanctio „diese Tage des Irrtums verwandelt sind in Fasten und Gebetstage und in Opfergaben für alle Christen, die vor uns gelebt haben"? Widukind spricht davon, wie von etwas ganz Bekanntem, wir aber finden in der gesamten Litteratur des Mittelalters vor 1243 keinen weiteren Beleg für seine Angaben. Man kommt unwillkürlich auf den Verdacht, daß die Stelle erst später eingeschoben sei, aber diesen Verdacht müssen wir in etwas gleich einschränken.

Abgesehen von der ersten Ausgabe Widukinds, die 1532 von Martin Freeht nach einem jetzt verlorenen Ebersbacher Kodex veröffentlicht ward, ist uns das Geschichtswerk des Korveyer Mönches in drei Handschriften überliefert[3]). Alle drei gehören dem 12. Jahrhundert an, die eine vielleicht sogar schon dem ausgehenden 11. Jahrhundert, alle drei bringen jenen in Frage stehenden Satz, also muß jene Erwähnung der gemeinen Woche sicherlich dem 11. Jahrhundert

1) E. Sackur, Die Cluniacenser, 1894, II, S. 475 ff.
2) E. Sackur a. a. O. II, S. 231.
3) Vgl. hierzu und zum Folgenden die Separatausgabe Widukinds von Waitz, 1882, S. XII f.

angehören, vielleicht hat sie gar schon 'als Randglosse im
Archetypus gestanden. Daß wir es hier mit einer Randglosse zu tun haben, ergibt sich mit 'hoher Wahrscheinlichkeit aus dem folgenden: His itaque omnibus peractis
reversi sunt ad Thiadricum in castra, wo das Subjekt aus
der Erzählung der Sachsenfeier (sc. Saxones) ergänzt werden
muß. Am wahrscheinlichsten bleibt es immer, daß diese
Glosse bereits im Archetypus gestanden hat, denn die drei
Handschriften, die uns vorliegen, sind völlig unabhängig
von einander und geben doch alle drei das Datum und
den Erläuterungssatz an.

Wie schade, daß wir nicht jene Notiz Sigeberts ver-
werten dürfen! Möglich, daß der Schreiber der Glosse —
daß es Widukind selbst ist, ist nach dem Stil sehr wahrscheinlich — tatsächlich die Einführung des Festes Allerseelen im Auge gehabt hat, daß mit den religiosi viri die
Cluniacenser gemeint sind. In diesem Falle müßte Widukind — immer unter der Voraussetzung, daß Sigebert die
richtige Jahreszahl hat — noch nach dem Jahre 998 gelebt
haben. Aber mit dem Nachweis, daß Sigeberts Verfahren
ungerechtfertigt ist, müssen wir uns aller Kombinationen
enthalten.

Und vielleicht läßt sich doch etwas gegen den Zusammenhang der „gemeinen Woche" mit dem Feste Allerseelen
geltend machen, der Umstand nämlich, daß in manchen
Diöcesen mehrere Gedenktage für die Verstorbenen im Jahre
stattzufinden pflegten. Nur eine einzige Urkunde ist es,
die hierüber Aufschluß erteilt. In einer Verordnung des
Willehadkapitels zu Bremen über die Verteilung der an
gewissen Tagen bei den Altären dargebrachten frommen
Gaben und über die Feier der Leichenbegängnisse — die
Urkunde stammt wahrscheinlich aus dem Jahre 1308 —
heißt es[1]): Sed sacerdos cuius est prior missa in die nativi-
tatis domini, habebit de oblationibus huiusmodi dimidium

---

1) Bremer Urkundenbuch II, 91, S. 97.

fertonem, in pasche XV solidos, in die pentecostes unum
lotonem, in tribus autem diebus animarum ebdo-
medarius recipiat oblationes prioris misse. Und weiter: Nota
quod constitutum est a canonicis ecclesiae beati Willehadi,
quod in octava pentecostes dictis vesperis maiores vigilie
sollempniter dicantur pro animabus fidelium defunctorum
..... et simile debet fieri post festum beati Michaelis in septimana beati Dyonisii martiris, quan-
do agitur memoria fidelium defunctorum.

Wir sehen, es wird nicht nur einmal im Jahre für die
Seelen der Verstorbenen von der Kirche gebetet.

Die Bestimmung, die memoria defunctorum falle post
festum beati Michaelis in septimana beati Dionysii martiris,
paßt, wenigstens auf das Jahr 1308, dem die Urkunde
wahrscheinlich angehört, vortrefflich. Die „gemeine Woche"
ist doch, wie wir gesehen haben, die volle Woche nach
Remigius [1]); da der 1. Oktober 1308 aber ein Dienstag war,
so muß die „gemeine Woche" in diesem Jahre von Sonntag
den 6. Oktober bis Sonnabend den 12. Oktober gereicht
haben.

Das Fest des heiligen Dionysius fällt aber auf den
9. Oktober. Man wird zur näheren Fixierung der „gemeinen
Woche" diesen Tag gewählt haben, weil Dionysius der
bekannteste der Heiligen war, die in der Zeit vom 6. bis
12. Oktober ihr Fest haben. Zugleich geht aber aus dieser
Tatsache, daß man zur Fixierung einen Tag wählte, der
nicht unter allen Umständen in die „gemeine Woche" fiel,
hervor, daß dieser Erlaß nur für das betreffende Jahr bestimmt sein konnte.

Wir kehren zu Widukind zurück. Wir haben gesehen,
daß die Notiz über die „gemeine Woche" wahrscheinlich
eine Glosse ist, die vielleicht schon von Widukind selbst
geschrieben, jedenfalls im 11. Jahrhundert bereits vorhanden
war. Aber die Frage, von der wir ausgingen, haben wir

---

1) vergl. oben S. 194, n. 1.

noch nicht beantwortet: ist die Ableitung der „gemeinen Woche"˙ von der Eroberung Burg-Scheidungens richtig?

Ein naheliegender Gedanke ist, daß ursprünglich in heidnischer Zeit um den 1. Oktober herum ein Götterfest gefeiert wurde, das die katholische Kirche später in ein christliches Fest umwandelte. Schon Widukind deutet das an [1]), wenn er sagt: (Saxones) secundum errorem paternum sacra sua propria veneratione venerati sunt; nomine Martem, effigie columpnarum imitantes Herculem, loco Solem, quem Graeci appellant Apollinem. Ex hoc apparet aestimationem illorum utcumque probabilem, qui Saxones originem duxisse putant de Graecis, quia H i r m i n vel Hermis Graece Mars dicitur.

Daß hier Ares und Hermes verwechselt sind, darüber besteht kein Zweifel. Wir sehen aber: die Sachsen ver-ehren zur Feier ihres Sieges ihr Heiligtum, das „dem Namen nach den Mars vorstellt", — eine Feier. zu Ehren ihres Kriegsgottes. „Das Fest fand dem I r m i n zu Ehren statt, der durch seinen Namen an Hermes-Mars erinnert [2])". Das Fest ist dreitägig, acta sunt autem haec omnia, ut maiorum memoria prodit, die Kalendis Octobris, also muß es entweder am 29. September, 30. September oder 1. Oktober begonnen haben.

Zum Vergleich ziehen wir eine Parallelüberlieferung heran. Wahrscheinlich unter den Karolingern oder Ottonen [3]) ist das sog. excerptum ex Gallica historia entstanden, das man früher wohl auf Caesar oder Velleius Paterculus zurückführte [4]).

---

1) Separatausgabe 1882, S. 12 f. (c. 12).

2) K. Koppmann, „Irmin und St. Michael" im Jahrbuch des Vereins für Niederdeutsche Sprachforschung II, 1876, S. 114. Ich folge im weiteren den Ausführungen Koppmann's, ergänze sie aber teilweise.

3) M. G. SS. XXIII, S. 387.

4) So Wolfg. Lazins, Commentariorum reipublicae Romanae libri duodecim. Basileae (1551), S. 85.

Es erzählt von einem Sieg der Schwaben über die Römer bei Augsburg [1]): Germanorum gentes, qui Retias occupaverant, non longe ab Alpibus . . . . ., ubi duo rapidissimi amnes inter se confluunt, in ipsis Noricis finibus civitatem non quidem muro, set vallo fossaque cinxerant, quam appellabant Cizarim, ex nomine deae Cizae, quam religiosissime colebant . . . . . Hane urbem (Augsburg ist gemeint) Titus Annius praetor ad arcendas barbarorum excursiones Kalendis Sextilibus exercitu circumvenit. Die Belagerungsmaßregeln werden geschildert, dann heißt es weiter: Igitur quinquagesimo nono die, quam eo ventum est, cum is dies deae Cizae apud barbaros (sc. Suevos) celeberrimus ludum et lasciviam magis quam formidinem ostentaret, immanis barbarorum (sc. Suevorum) multitudo e proximis silvis repente erumpens ex improviso castra irrupit, equitatum omnem et, quod miserius erat auxilia sociorum delevit. . . . . . Oppidani vero non minori fortuna, set maiori virtute praetorem in auxilium sociis properantem adoriuntur, Romani hand segniter resistunt. . . . . . Et inclinata iam res oppidanorum esset, ni maturassent auxilium ferre socii, in altera ripa iam victoria potiti. Denique coadunatis viribus castro irrumpunt, praetorem, qui paulo altiorem tumulum frustra ceperat, Romana vi resistentem obtruncant, legionem divinam, ut ne nuntius cladis superesset, funditus delent.

Otto von Freising nennt diesen Hügel, der später die Gebeine der Erschlagenen deckte, perleich [2]). Im Jahre 1064 sind, wie Grimm angiebt [3]), Stift und Kirche St. Peter auf dieser Anhöhe gegründet worden. „Auf dem Perlachturm war ein Bild des heiligen Michael angebracht, das am Michaelisfeste bei jedem Glockenschlage zum Vorschein kam" [4]).

Jene Augsburger Tradition berichtet nun doch, daß am Tage der Göttin Cisa, der der 29. September gewesen sein

---

1) M. G. SS. XXIII, S. 388.
2) Ottonis Fris. chronicon, III, 3. (M. G. SS. XX, S. 173.)
3) J. Grimm, Mythologie, S. 274 [2].
4) Grimm, Mythologie, S. 274 [2], n. 3.

muß — denn der 59. Tag nach den Kalenden des August ist der 29. September —, ein Siegesfest gefeiert wurde zur Erinnerung an einen errungenen Sieg. '

Wenn nun auch, wie Bachlechner gezeigt hat[1]), der Name der Göttin Cisa wahrscheinlich auf ein Mißverständnis zurückgeht, so bleibt doch die Tatsache des Siegesfestes bestehen. „Beide Erzählungen (sc. Widukind und die Augsburger Tradition) gehören offenbar zusammen, beglaubigen und erläutern einander"[2]). Am 29. September wird bei den Sachsen u n d Schwaben ein Siegesfest gefeiert, sollte es sich nicht vielleicht um ein gemeingermanisches Fest zu Ehren des Kriegsgottes (Ziu oder Irmin) handeln? Erwägen wir, daß erst 813 auf dem Konzil zu Mainz der 29. September als Tag des heiligen Michael in die deutsche Kirche eingeführt wurde[3]) erwägen wir ferner, daß St. Michael, „der Erzengel, bei dem der Sieg ist", im Muspilli dem Antichrist das Haupt spaltet, der in den Ungarnschlachten von 933 und 955 den Sachsen voranzieht[4]), so wird es in der Tat klar — wir wissen ja, daß die katholische Kirche mit Vorliebe ihre großen Feste auf heidnische Festtage verlegt hat —, daß am 29. September das Fest des germanischen Kriegsgottes war. Ein dreitägiges Fest, das mit diesem Tage beginnt, mußte also mit dem 1. Oktober schließen. „Acta sunt autem haec omnia, ut maiorum memoria prodit, die Kalendis Octobris."

Verstehen wir jetzt den Sinn dieses Satzes? Was ist natürlicher, als an das Fest des Krieggottes, das man feiert, die Erinnerung an gewonnene Siege anzuknüpfen.

---

1) Haupt's Zeitschrift für deutsches Altertum VIII, S. 587.

2) Koppmann a. a. O. S. 115.

3) Die Aachener Synode von 809 führt in ihrer Aufzählung der Feste das des heiligen Michael noch nicht auf. Zuerst erscheint es in den Akten der Mainzer Synode von 813, vgl. Mansi sacrorum conciliorum collectio XIV, S. 73, can. 36 und H. Kellner, Heortologie, 1901, S. 15.

4) Koppmann a. a. O. S. 115.

Und dazu kommt noch eins. Koppmann hat in schöner Weise darauf hingewiesen [1]). „Mit dem Siegesfeste zu Ehren Irmins war eine Totenfeier für die Verstorbenen verbunden. ..... St. Michael heißt praepositus paradisi [2]) et princeps animarum, er gilt als Empfänger und Wäger der Seelen." So konnte sich am Michaelistage eine Totenfeier ausbilden, in der man den Heiligen nicht als den siegbringenden Erzengel, sondern als den praepositus paradisi verehrte.

Warum später allerdings diese Totenfeier in der Form einer Woche erscheint, ist uns völlig verborgen; vielleicht ist schon früh das Fest des heiligen Michael mit einer Oktave versehen worden, und dies der Ursprung der „gemeinen Woche" [3]). Die Umwandlung muß ins 11., 12. oder 13. Jahrhundert fallen, denn Widukind erwähnt die „gemeine Woche" noch nicht; bei ihm sind es nur die dies erroris, die „durch die Heiligung frommer Männer", vielleicht das Konzil von 813, verwandelt sind in Fasten und Gebetstage.

Es ist ein Akt der großartigsten Volksdankbarkeit, wenn das Volk, und mit ihm Widukind, die „gemeine Woche" an die Einnahme Burg Scheidungens durch die Sachsen knüpft. In der Tat, was konnte verlockender sein, als die Feier der Woche, in der man Gebete für die Verstorbenen zum Himmel sandte, an ein Ereignis anzuknüpfen, durch das 6000 Sachsen ihr Streben, ihrem Volk neues Land zu gewinnen, mit ihrem Blut bezahlt hatten [4]), eine

---

1) Koppmann a. a. O. S. 115.

2) Vgl. den codex tradit. Wessofont. in den Monumenta Boica VIII, S. 371.

3). Heute wird die Oktave des Michaelisfestes überall begangen, und zwar am 6. Oktober. Vgl. Grotefend, Zeitrechnung II, 2, S. 143. Die oben gegebene Erklärung hat den Fehler, daß die Definition der „gemeinen Woche", wie sie der Halberstädter ordo divinus gibt, sich mit ihr nicht in Einklang bringen läßt. Ob die Halberstädter Definition erst das Produkt einer späteren Entwickelung ist?

4) Widukind I, 9, de Saxonibus vero numerati sunt sex milia caesa.

Tat zudem, durch die die Sachsen sich zum ersten Male den Franken überlegen gezeigt hatten. Und gerade bei einem Schriftsteller, wie Widukind, der durch und durch Sachse ist, mußte sich eine derartige Kombination am ehesten finden.

Und nun fragen wir nochmals: ist die Hypothese Größlers, daß der Thüringerkrieg den ganzen Sommer gedauert habe, da die Franken bereits im Frühjahr auszurücken pflegten[1]), und die Eroberung der Burg erst am 1. Oktober vor sich ging, berechtigt? Wir können diese Frage nur verneinen, da wir eben gesehen haben, auf welchen Grundlagen diese Kombination beruht. Über die Dauer des Krieges gewährt uns die Stelle Widukinds durchaus keinen Aufschluß.

Als Resultat dieses Abschnittes dürfen wir aussprechen:

Bei einer eingehenden Prüfung der sächsischen Quellen stellt sich heraus, daß sie historisch durchaus unglaubwürdig sind. Einige Tatsachen mögen vielleicht wahr sein, die Methode zeigt uns aber keinen Weg zu ihnen zu gelangen. Daher dürfen diese Quellen für eine Darstellung des Thüringerkrieges von 531 unter keinen Umständen verwendet werden. Der Grund dazu liegt in nicht wegzuschaffenden inneren Widersprüchen. Auch das Datum der Einnahme Burg-Scheidungens ist nicht historisch.

Von diesem Verdikt nicht berührt bleiben vorläufig nur die Schlachtorte.

Fast scheint es, als ob wir gezwungen sind, auch die Sachsenhilfe zu leugnen, aber diese ist, wie wir versuchen werden zu zeigen, wirklich historisch; mit der Erörterung dieser Frage verlassen wir das Gebiet der Sage und treten in das der Geschichte ein.

---

1) Es ist kein Grund vorhanden anzunehmen, daß die Franken gerade in diesem Jahre von ihrer Gewohnheit abgewichen seien. Gregor sagt zwar nichts über den Zeitpunkt ihres Ausrückens, indes spricht dieser Umstand gerade zu unsern Gunsten, da er eine Abweichung von der Regel wohl verzeichnet haben würde.

Teil III. Kritik der historischen Probleme.

Außerordentlich dürftig ist, was uns übrig bleibt. Nie wird es gelingen, jene furchtbare Katastrophe im Einzelnen aufzuhellen, nur die Umrisse der Ereignisse festzustellen, kann unsere Aufgabe sein.

An Quellen bleiben uns nur die fränkischen Autoren nebst Prokop und Rudolf von Fulda.

Rudolfs translatio S. Alexandri ist zwischen 851 und 865[1]), also rund 100 Jahre vor Widukind geschrieben. Sagenbildung ist auch bei ihm nicht zu verkennen, aber die Ausgestaltung, die die Sage durch unser Lied erhalten hat, ist ihm noch völlig fremd. Trotzdem wird man gut tun, ihm nicht zu viel Glauben zu schenken, denn die Elemente der Sage sind ihm auch vertraut. Irminfried ist der Schwager Theuderichs, er ist dux Thuringorum, wodurch natürlich das Abhängigkeitsverhältnis des Thüringerkönigs von den Franken angedeutet werden soll. Vor allem aber berichtet auch er die Hilfe der Saohsen, ihr „Herzog" heißt hier Hadugoto, bei Widukind Hathagat [2]).

Kann es als historisch richtig betrachtet werden, daß die Sachsen den Franken zu Hilfe gekommen sind? Zweifel hat, soweit wir sehen, niemand ausgesprochen. Nach Lorenz [3]) geht die Mithilfe der Sachsen „sicherlich auf historischen Kern zurück. Liefert ihm (sc. Widukind) auch die Volks-überlieferung den Stoff zur Darstellung des Gegenstandes, so ist auch zu berücksichtigen, wie fest sich dieselbe an historische Vorgänge nnd namentlich an ein so wichtiges Ereignis, wie den Feldzug von 531 klammert."

Könnecke [4]) hält es für klar, daß die Sachsenhilfe „von den sächsischen Geschichtsschreibern nicht aus der Luft gegriffen sein kann", und Größler [5]) weist sogar seinen Vor-

---

1) Wattenbach, Geschichtsquellen I [6], 238 f.
2) Bei Widukind ist Hathagat nur veteranus miles.
3) Lorenz, a. a. O. S. 374.
4) Koennecke, a. a. O. S. 26.
5) Größler, a. a. O. S. 18 f.

gänger Lorenz scharf zurecht, weil dieser „das Maß und
die Bedeutung der Sachsenhilfe in die gebührenden Schranken weisen" will [1]). Die Gründe von Lorenz und Könnecke erledigen sich aber durch den Hinweis, daß wir ebenso,
falls uns die fränkischen Quellen hier im Stich ließen, Irminfried für einen Schwager Theuderichs halten müßten.
„Wie fest klammert" sieh nicht diese „Tatsache" an
historische Vorgänge an, der ganze Krieg entspringt ja,
nach den sächsischen Quellen, aus ihr. „Daß sie nicht
aus der Luft gegriffen sein kann, ist klar."

Sehr viel schwerwiegender ist der Einwand Größler's [2]):
„Was soll es da heißen, wenn Lorenz meint, die Bedeutung
und das Maß der Sachsenhilfe müsse in die gebührenden
Schranken. gewiesen werden? Kann etwa die Tatsache
umgestoßen werden, daß seit dem Sturze des thüringischen
Königreichs durch die Franken das ganze Nordthüringer
Land Sachsenboden geworden und seitdem geblieben ist,
jene Tatsache die den Anstoß dazu gab, daß der Sachsen-
name erst auf die heutige Provinz Sachsen, dann auf das
Kurfürstentum und Königreich und die thüringischen Her-
zogtümer sich verbreitet hat? Das Vordringen des Sachsen-
namens zunächst bis an die Unstrut, die Helme und den
Sachsgraben wäre ganz unbegreiflich, wenn die Sachsen
keine entscheidende Rolle in dem thüringischen Trauer-
spiel gespielt und die Frankenkönige nicht zur Anerkennung.
ihrer Ansprüche genötigt hätten."..

Gegen den Schlußsatz dieses Beweises wird man viel-
leicht Widerspruch erheben, gegen die Anfangssätze kaum.
Sind diese aber wirklich in ihrer Allgemeinheit richtig?
Woher weiß Größler, daß „seit dem Sturze des thüringischen
Königreichs durch die Franken" das ganze Nordthüringer
Land Sachsenboden geworden ist? Direkte Belege aller-

---

1) Lorenz, a. a. O. S. 374.
2) Größler, a. a. O. S. 18 f.

dings finden sieh nicht, wohl giebt es aber Stellen, aus denen sich die angedeutete Tatsache erschließen läßt.

Im Jahre 568 ziehen 26000 Sachsen mit Alboin und seinen Langobarden nach Italien[1]); in den von ihnen verlassenen Gegenden siedelt der Merowinger Sigebert „Suavos et alias gentes“ an. Später kehren die Sachsen zurück und kämpfen mit den Schwaben um ihr früheres Land, in diesen Kämpfen kommen die meisten Sachsen um, der Rest steht vom Kriege ab.

Jede Gaukarte des Mittelalters[2]) zeigt nördlich von der Unstrut vier Gaue, die ihren Namen augenscheinlich von Volksnamen hergeleitet haben. Es sind dies (von Süden nach Norden gerechnet): Der pagus Hassegowe mit dem pagus Frisoneveld, der pagus Suevon und der pagus Nortthuringia. Hält man dazu die Nachricht der Ann. Quedlinburg.[3]), daß Theuderich den Sachsen alles Land der Thüringer bis zum Zusammenfluß der Saale und Unstrut versprochen und ihnen später wirklich alles Land im Norden des Harzes gegeben habe, so wird es allerdings sehr wahrscheinlich, daß die Sachsen bereits in sehr früher Zeit, jedenfalls vor dem Jahre 568, bis an die Unstrut gesessen haben.

Vielleicht aber läßt sich ein noch früheres Datum ermitteln.

Nach der Eroberung von Burg-Scheidungen verschwinden die Sachsen zunächst völlig aus unserer Ueberlieferung. Erst in den Jahren 555 und 556 erscheinen sie wieder in

---

1) Vgl. zu dem Folgenden: Gregor v. Tours IV, 42; V, 15; Fredegar, III, 68. 76. Paulus Diaconus II, 6; III, 7 (SS. rerum Langob. et Ital.). Vgl. auch Ann. Mett. a. 748 (M. G. SS. I, 330): fines Saxonum, quos Nordosquavos vocant.

2) Spruner-Menke, 1880, Karte no. 33.

3) Ann. Quedlinb. (M. G. SS. III, 31.) Ob die betreffende Stelle der Annalen ursprünglich zum Lied gehört hat oder nicht, tut nichts zur Sache.

den Quellen, gleichzeitig bei Gregor v. Tours[1]) und bei
Marius v. Avenches[2]).

Gregor berichtet (IV, 10): Eo anno `(555) rebellantibus
Saxonibus Chlotacharius rex, commoto contra eos exercitu,
maximam eorum partem delevit, pervagans totam Thoringiam
ac devastans, pro eo quod Saxonibus solatium praebuisset:

Marius ergänzt diesen Bericht: a. 555. 1. Hoc anno
Theudobaldus rex Francorum obiit et obtinuit regnum eius
Chlotacarius patruus patris eius . . . . 3. Eo anno Saxones
rebellantibus Chlotacharius rex cum gravi exercitu contra
ipsos dimicavit, ubi multitudo Francorum et Saxonum ceci-
derunt, Chlotacharius tamen rex victor abscessit. Und a. 556. 1.
Eo anno iterum rebellantibus Saxones Chlotacarius rex
pugnam debit ibique maxima pars Saxonum cecidit. 2. Eo
anno Franci totam Toringiam pro eo quod cum Saxonibus
coniuravit vastaverunt.

Man beachte, daß bereits in diesem Jahre die Kriege
der Sachsen gegen die Franken unter dem Gesichtspunkt
einer Empörung aufgefaßt werden. Welchen Rechtsgrund
die Franken dazu haben, erfahren wir auch von Gregor,
vier Capitel später (IV. 14)[3]): Igitur Chlotacharius post
mortem Theodovaldi cum regno Franciae suscepisset atque
eum circuiret, audivit a suis in iterata insania efferviscere
Saxonis sibique esse rebelles, et quod tributa, quae annis
singulis consueverant ministrare, contempnerent reddere.
His incitatus verbis, ad eos dirigit. Cumque iam prope
terminum illorum esset, Saxones ad eum legatus mittunt,
dicentes: „Non enim sumus contemptores tui, et ea quae
fratribus ac neputibus tuis reddere consuevimus non nega-
mus, et maiora adhuc, si quaesieris, reddimus. Unum tamen
exposcimus, ut sit pax, ne tuus exercitus et noster populus
conlidatur".

---

1) M. G. SS. rerum Merov. I, 147.
2) M. G. Auct. antiqu. XI, 236 f.
3) M. G. SS. rerum Merov. I, 151.

Wir sehen: Schon die Erhebung des vorhergehenden. Jahres (unsere Erzählung fällt in das Jahr 556) wird deshalb als Empörung aufgefaßt, weil die Sachsen gewöhnt sind, jährlich Tribut zu zahlen. Wer sind aber die „Brüder und Neffen", denen sie ursprünglich den Tribut zu zahlen pflegten?

Chlotar hatte drei Brüder: Chlodomer, der über Aquitanien herrschte und bereits 524 starb, und Childebert, der zu Paris seinen Sitz hatte, können nicht in Betracht kommen; so bleibt Theuderich übrig. Dieser, der in Austrasien herrschte, kann allein gemeint sein. Daraus folgt aber unmittelbar, daß bereits vor dem Jahre 534, dem Todesjahre Theuderichs, die Sachsen in einer Art Abhängigkeitsverhältnis von den Franken gestanden haben [1]).

Und nun wird in der Tat die Sachsenhilfe höchst wahrscheinlich. Wir werden uns die Sache so zu denken haben, daß die Sachsen für das ihnen von Theuderich überlassene Land einen Tribut bezahlen, der vielleicht aus 500 Küben bestanden hat [2]) und der ihnen dann von Dagobert erlassen wurde (632 oder 33).

Diese ganze Beweisführung beruht auf der Voraussetzung, daß zum mindesten jene vier Gaue, von denen oben

---

1) Die „Neffen" sind natürlich Theuderichs Sohn und Enkel, Theudebert und Theudebald.

2) Vergl. Fredegar IV, 74. Es muß höchst auffallend erscheinen, daß die neueren Forscher nicht das geringste von diesem Tribut der Sachsen unter Theuderich wissen, obwohl schon bei Wenck Hessische Landesgeschichte 1789, II, S. 198, das Richtige steht, freilich ohne Quellenangabe. Lorenz, a. a. O. S. 402 ist hier-in einen merkwürdigen Irrtum verfallen; er verwechselt den Schweinezins, den die Thüringer zu zahlen haben, mit diesem Tribut der Sachsen. Dieser Schweinezins der Thüringer, wie er uns aus den Ann. Quedlinb. und Thietmar von Merseburg (V, 9) bekannt ist, wird wohl nur auf die Thüringer gehen, die, zwischen Harz und Thüringer Wald sitzend, direkt unter fränkische Oberhoheit kommen; die nördlich von der Unstrut wohnenden Thüringer mußten Tribut an die Sachsen zahlen (Widukind I, 14: Saxones .... reliquias pulsae gentis tributis condempnaverunt).

die Rede war, einst noch zum thüringischen Gebiet gehört
haben. Wer bürgt uns aber dafür, daß sich das Thüringer-
reich soweit nach Norden erstreckt hat?

v. Wersebe[1]) ist, soweit wir sehen, der erste gewesen,
der die bis dahin übliche Auffassung, daß der pagus Nortthuringia seinen Namen von der einstigen Zugehörigkeit
zum thüringischen Königreich erhalten habe, angegriffen
hat. Was er vorbringt, klingt nicht unwahrscheinlich. Wie
der pagus Suevon seinen Namen von den Schwaben hat, die
dort von Sigebert angesiedelt werden, der pagus Hassegowe
von hessischen, der pagus Frisoneveld von friesischen Kolonisten, so läßt sich „dieser Name (sc. Nortthuringia) weit
natürlicher von einer dahin verpflanzten Kolonie südlicher
Thüringer, die bei dem sächsischen Heere gegen den König
Sigebert mit gefochten, als davon, daß diese entfernte
Gegend einen Teil des alten thüringischen Königreichs
ausgemacht, ableiten" [2]). Wir werden uns bei der Bedeutung
v. Wersebe's nicht der Pflicht entziehen können, unsere
abweichende Anschauung durch Gegenbeweise zu stützen.

Nur ein Gelehrter hat bis jetzt versucht, die Ansicht
v. Wersebe's zu widerlegen, der Meister mittelalterlicher
Gauforschung, Leopold v. Ledebur [3]). Leider muß diese
Widerlegung in der Hauptsache als total mißlungen bezeichnet
werden, wenn ihn allerdings auch nur teilweise die Schuld
daran trifft.

Auf einer Wundererzählung der Vita S. Emmerami

---

1) v. Wersebe, Über die Verteilung Thüringens zwischen den
alten Sachsen und Franken. Hamburg 1834, S. 13 ff. Ferner: v. Wersebe, Beschreibung der Gaue zwischen Elbe, Saale und Unstrut, Weser
und Werra etc. Hannover 1829, S. 109. Ihm folgt: Bolze, Die
Sachsen vor Karl dem Großen (Jahresbericht der Luisenstädtischen
Realschule Berlin 1861), S. 10. 18.

2) v. Wersebe, Beschreibung etc. S. 109.

3) L. v. Ledebur, Nordthüringen und die Hermunduren oder
Thüringer, 1842. Neudruck: Berlin 1852. Vgl. über ihn das Vor-
wort zu Böttger's Diöcesan und Gau-Grenzen Norddeutschlands 1875,
I, S. VIII ff.

von Arbeo [1]) baut sich der erste Beweis v. Ledebur's auf. Er giebt zunächst den Inhalt der Erzählung wieder.

1) Die Ausgabe der Acta SS. Boll. tom. VI, Sept. 22 ist ver. altet, neue Ausgabe (v. Sepp) in den Analecta Bollandiana, Band VIII, (1889), S. 211 ff. Hier ist auch die Schreibweise Arbeo, (früher Aribo) eingeführt. Die Vita ist geschrieben von Arbeo, Bischof v. Freising, zwischen 770 und 772 (a. a. O. S. 217 f.). Die in Be. tracht kommende Erzählung findet sich im Cap. IV, Absatz 39, (a. a. O. S. 249 ff.): Unde silentio praetereundum non est, quod a quodam religioso et prudenti viro me contigit audisse; aiebat enim, quia quadam die ad beati martyris ecclesiam pro suis delictis minuendis accedere voluisset. Sed contigit ei, dum solus iter carperet et venisset in solitudinem quandam, quae locutione vulgari feronifaidus appellatur, in latrones incidisse, ... extra terminum genti francorum venundant. Quidam vero, qui eum exinde redimerat, genti duringorum partibus aquilonis tradidit in confinio parahtanorum gentis, quae ignorat deum. Cumque se praedictus senex gentilium idolorumque cultoribus proximum cerneret, coepit viribus, ut potuit, domino suo temporali tam presenti, quam absenti, dignum omnino praebere famulatum. Erat enim operandi peritia instructus, ita ut molendinam domino suo perfecisset edificiorumque miro modo conpositiones, [40] et ob hoc in conspectu eius gratiam invenit. Cumque hoc continuo per triennium, prout poterat, ex pura voluntate ministraret et tamen a dei cultura et oratione minime recessisset, accidit, ut quidam de conservis eius moreretur. Qui relicta vidua iuvencula secundum huius carnis putredinem speciosa sine procreatione filiorum, quam temporalis dominus huic seni in matrimonium volebat sociare, ut demo et omnibus defuncti substantiis frueretur. Sed senex idem obtemperare huic facto nolens respondit dicens: Uxorem in cognatione mea reliqui, cum pro innumeris meis captivitati huic traderer peccatis et eo modo his locis devenirem. Nunc igitur ea vivente quomodo aliam in matrimonium ducam? Unde dominus eius asperrimis sermonibus adiunxit dicens: Haec mihi facit dominus et addat, nisi illam in matrimonio sumpseris, genti te saxonum tradam, quae tot idolorum cultibus dedita est, quia novi et didici experimento, si accipere mulierem hic rennueris, nullo modo te mecum velle commorari, sed magis fugere, ut de pretio tuo remaneam omni modo fraudatus.

Im Weiteren ist der lateinische Text zur Vergleichung nicht wesentlich, nur der Schluß mag hier noch Platz finden: [44] Peraetis itaque continuis diebus in profectione quindecim tanta prosperitate ac securitate supernus iudex eum reduxit ex itinere fatigatum, ita

„Ein frommer und verständiger Mann erzählte mir, so hebt Aribo an, er sei in einer Wildnis, die den Namen Feronifaidus führe (oder wie der spätere Bearbeiter Meginfried [1]) sagt, Verroniwaida, was er in longinqua pascua überträgt und für den Wald von Langwaid gehalten wird), von Räubern überfallen, außer Landes geführt und dem Volke der Franken verkauft worden. Diese letztern nennt Meginfried bestimmter Ostfranken, worunter also zunächst die Franken des Würzburgischen Sprengels zu verstehen sind. Einer aus diesem Volke nun verkaufte ihn wieder, wie Aribo sagt, an jemand in den nördlichen Teilen des Volkes der Thüringer [2]) an der Grenze des Volkes der Porahtanen, die Gott nicht kennen! oder, wie Meginfried sich ausdrückt [3]), an einen Thüringer an den Grenzen der Parathanen, die zu jener Zeit grausame Heiden waren. So in der Nähe von Heiden und Götzendienern, fährt Aribo fort, bemühte sich

ut in tertia hora quintae decime diei staret in monte contra radas-ponam inter danubii et imbris fluenta iuxta plantationem vinearum. Et ex eodem iugo montis urbem ' avidam videns beati etiam dei martyris ecclesiam contemplans magnas et immensas domino gratias referebat et demum ita descendens venit ad portum.

1) An dieser Stelle müssen noch einige Bemerkungen über den Text eingeschaltet werden. Der in den Analecta Boll. jetzt gebotene und hier wiedergegebene Text ist weit älter als der Text der Acta SS. Boll. Nach Sepps Ansicht sind die drei Handschriften, die er zur Rekonstruktion des Textes benutzt und die der ältere Herausgeber noch nicht gekannt hat, direkt aus dem Archetypus geflossen (Anal. Boll. VIII, S. 213). Außerdem gibt es aber noch eine Überarbeitung der Vita, von dem Magdeburger Probst (Potthast Bibliotheca etc. II, 1289) Meginfried im Jahre 1030 verfaßt, und die Monographie Arnold's v. Vochburg über die Wunder des heiligen Emmeram.

2) Quidam ex his, qui eum pretio redemerat, in partibus Aquilonis Thuringorum gentis cuidam venundavit in coniacenti confinio Porahtanorum gentis, quae ignorat Deum (so die Acta SS. Boll.)

3) v. Ledebur ist noch der Ansicht, daß sowohl die spätere Überarbeitung der Vita als auch die Schrift de miraculis S. Emmerami auf Meginfried zurückgehen, während die letztere doch von Arnold v. Vochburg verfaßt ist (Anal. Boll. VIII, S. 214). Die unter Meginfried citierten Stellen finden sich alle bei Arnold (M. G. SS. IV, 550).

derselbe, in allen Kräften seinem Herren treu und redlich zu dienen." Nach drei Jahren will ihm sein Herr eine Witwe zur Ehe geben, er weigert sich jedoch dessen. „Er habe bereits daheim ein Weib und diese zurücklassen müssen, als er, wohl seiner großen Sünden wegen, in Gefangenschaft geraten und seiner Heimat entrissen worden sei: solange aber diese Gattin lebe, dürfe er keine andere Ehe eingehen. Sein Herr aber erwiderte ihm in listigen und gebieterischen Worten: „Nun bei Gott, wenn du die´nicht zum Weibe nimmst, da überliefere ich dich dem Volke der Sachsen, das ganz dem Götzendienste ergeben ist: denn ich sehe schon aus deiner Weigerung, daß du nicht bei mir bleiben und mich durch Flucht um den Kaufpreis bringen willst[1])." — Der Diener muß schließlich, um nicht an die Sachsen verkauft zu werden, in die Heirat willigen, flieht aber gleich darauf und kommt am 15. Tage glücklich zu dem Berge, „von wo aus er über die Weinpflanzungen zwischen der Donau und dem Regen hinweg des heiligen Emmeram Kirche und die mit Mauern und Türmen prangende Stadt erblicken konnte[2])."

Der Beweis v. Ledebur's ist nun folgender. Er identifiziert die Parathaner Meginfrieds (d. h. Arnolds) mit den Barden des Bardengaus; da zwischen dem Gau Nordthüringen aber und dem Bardengau noch der Balsamgau liege, die Parathaner aber an den nördlichen Teil des Volkes der Thüringer anstießen, so müsse der Balsamgau in jener Zeit notwendig zu Nordthüringen gehört haben. Daraus ergebe sich aber wieder, daß der Begriff „Nordthüringen" umfassender sei als der pagus Nortthuringia. v. Ledebur behauptet nun, die Ausdrücke Nortthuringia und Nordthuringorum gens könnten „für das ganze nordwärts der Unstrut gelegene Sachsenland, soweit der Sprengel von Halberstadt sich erstreckte, genommen werden"[3]). Wenn aber

1) v. Ledebur a. a. O. S. 24—26.
2) ebenda S. 27.
3) a. a. O. S. 31.

dies ganze Land Nordthüringen heißt, so muß es zu Thüringen gehört haben, denn sonst wird der Name unerklärlich.

Ein auffälliger geographischer Irrtum, in den v. Ledebur hier verfallen ist! Der Balsamgau nämlich stößt nirgends an den Bardengau [1]), wohl aber ist dies beim Derlingau der Fall, der auch zum Bistum Halberstadt gehört [2]). Wir könnten also allenfalls den Balsamgau in dem Ledeburschen Beweis durch den Derlingau ersetzen; aber der Beweis selbst wird dadurch nicht besser. Mag immerhin der Begriff Nortthuringia sich in früher Zeit auch auf den Derlingau mit erstreckt haben, so könnte daraus nur geschlossen werden, daß auch im Derlingau Thüringer gesessen haben; ob das ganze Land aber von der Unstrut nordwärts bis zum Derlingau einst zu Thüringen gehört hat, ist damit nicht entschieden. Man könnte recht gut annehmen, im Jahre 568 seien nach dem Auszug der Sachsen nach Italien neben Schwaben, Friesen und Hessen auch Nordthüringer, und zwar in dem Gebiete des späteren Nordthüringgaus und des späteren Derlingaus angesiedelt worden, in einem Gebiete, das man damals als Nortthuringia bezeichnete. Erst später sei die Beschränkung dieses Namens auf den eigentlichen pagus Nortthuringia eingetreten. Und dann das Andere! Warum identifiziert v. Ledebur die parahtani mit den Barden? Er hat sich durch die Schreibweise parathani verleiten lassen, die sich aber erst in der Schrift Arnold's findet; die alten Lebensbeschreibungen lesen parahtanorum oder porahtanorum.

Grund genug jedenfalls, sie nicht mit den Barden zu

---

1) Der pagus Belesem stößt an die Gaue: Nielitizi, Liezizi, Zemzizi, Moraciani, Northuringowe und Osterwalde. Vgl. Böttger, Diöcesan- und Gaugrenzen III, S. 181 f.

2) Urkunde Ludwigs des Frommen vom 2. September 814. v. Wersebe, Beschreibung etc. S. 137 schiebt zwischen Derlingau und Bardengau noch den pagus Wittinga ein; nach Böttger Diöcesan- und Gaugrenzen III, 176 ist der pagus Witingao nur „ein Untergau des Derlingowe".

identifizieren [1]). So müssen wir diesen Beweis v. Ledébur's ablehnen; wie steht es mit dem zweiten Beweise? In einer Urkunde Karls des Großen werde die Stadt Scannige als in Nordthuringia liegend angegeben, dieses „Schöningen" aber liegt, wie sich aus sonstigen Urkunden klar ergibt, im Derlingau [2]). v. Ledebur findet es bemerkenswert, daß in der Urkunde in Nordthuringia, nicht etwa in pago Nortthuringon oder ähnliches stände [3]).

v. Ledebur bringt die Bezeichnung in Nordthuringia als gewichtigen Grund für die Echtheit des Diploms zur Sprache. Anstatt mit einem echten Diplom die Zugehörigkeit Schöningens zu Nordthüringen zu beweisen, sucht er die Echtheit des Diploms eben durch den Umstand zu beweisen, daß Schöningen zu Nordthüringen gehört hat, was eben noch bewiesen werden muß. Was würde v. Ledebur wohl sagen, wenn er wüßte, daß das Stück als eine Fälschung entlarvt ist, die womöglich erst dem 18. Jahrhundert angehört? Würde er auch dann noch die Worte in Nortthuringia „höchst beachtenswert" finden? Wir müssen auch diesen Beweis v. Ledebur's ablehnen. Wie würden wir uns aber verhalten, wenn die angezogene Urkunde echt wäre? In diesem Falle würde sich gegen sie wohl mit Recht dasselbe geltend machen lassen, was wir bereits gegen den ersten Beweis v. Ledebur's vorgebracht haben. Es möchte daher nutzlos scheinen, dieses noch einmal zu wiederholen, in der Tat werden wir dadurch jedoch ein gut Stück weiter geführt werden.

---

1) Ich verstehe nicht, wie Sepp in s. Ausgabe (Anal. Boll. VIII 249) trotz der endgültig festgestellten Schreibart parahtanorum noch immer die Barden in ihnen sehen kann. Höchst wahrscheinlich sind die Brukterer gemeint, allerdings muß man in diesem Falle dem Verfasser der Vita Unkenntnis der ethnographischen Verhältnisse zur Last legen. Für Brukterer hält die parahtani bereits: Zeuß, Die Deutschen und die Nachbarstämme, 1837, S. 352. Rudhart erklärt (Archiv für Geschichte und Altertumskunde von Oberfranken, 1842, II, 1, S. 103 ff.) die parahtani nach dem Vorgang von Mannert und v. Lang für Bayreuther.

2) v. Ledebur a. a. O. S. 30 f.

3) Vgl. Mühlbacher, Reg. der Karolinger I², 1899, no. 267 (258).

Der Derlingau liegt ungefähr im Norden des Nordthüringgaus und grenzt an diesen. Es ist nun nicht
richtig, wie wir eben gesehen haben, aus dem Umstand,
daß eine im Derlingau liegende Stadt als in Nortthuringia
bezeichnet wird, zu schließen, daß das ganze Gebiet von
der Unstrut nordwärts bis zum Derlingau einschließlich
einst zu Thüringen gehört hat. Man konnte recht gut annehmen, daß bei der gleichzeitigen Ansiedelung von vier
Kolonistengruppen durch König Sigebert im Jahre 568 der
thüringischen Kolonistengruppe das Gebiet, das später in
die Gaue Nordthüringen und Derlingau zerfiel, angewiesen
wurde, ein Gebiet, das damals zuerst und nur aus diesem
Grunde den Namen Nordthüringen erhielt, während sich die
Bezeichnung pagus Nordthuringia erst später für einen bestimmten Teil dieses Gebietes festsetzte. Diese Annahme
aber wird unmöglich, wenn sich zeigen läßt, daß irgend eine
beliebige Stadt, die in einem der 3 andern Kolonistengaue
gelegen ist, auch als in Nordthuringia gelegen bezeichnet
wird, denn die Abgrenzung der vier Gaue gegeneinander
erfolgte ja gleichzeitig, da die Kolonisten in ein und demselben Jahre (568) angesiedelt wurden. Wenn uns ein
Nachweis dieser Art gelingt, so ist zugleich damit der Beweis geführt, daß das ganze Land von der Unstrut nordwärts
bis mindestens zum Nordthüringgau einschließlich, soweit
es eben jene genannten vier Gaue umfaßt, einst tatsächlich
zum thüringischen Reiche gehört hat.

Eine einzige Urkunde gibt es [1]), die den Beweis liefert,

---

1) Zu den bei Böttger, Diöcesan- und Gaugrenzen III, S. 183 ff.
für den pagus Northuringowe angezogenen Urkunden kommen noch
folgende Urkunden hinzu:
1. Urkunde Ludwigs des Jüngeren für Drübeck. 877. 26. Januar
   (U.B. d. Klost. Drübeck, 1874, S. 1, no. 1).
2. Urkunde Ottos I. für St. Moritz in Magdeburg. 941. 23. April
   (M. G. DD. I, S. 123, no. 37).
3. Urkunde Ottos I. für St. Moritz in Magdeburg. 965. 12. April
   (M. G. DD. I, S. 397, no. 281).
4. Urkunde Ottos III. für s. Tante, die Äbtissin Mathilde. 987. 21. Mai
   (M. G. DD. II, S. 434, no. 35).

wenn auch spätere Abschrift, so doch „sachlich unver-
dächtig [1]).“ In dieser Urkunde Ludwigs des Jüngeren für das
Kloster Drübeck vom 26. Januar 877 heißt es : . . . . . Quapropter
noverit omnium . . . . . industria, qualiter Tbeti et Wikker
nostri fideles comites . . . . . tradiderunt nobis quoddam
monasterium, quod dicitur Drubiki . . . . .; ipsi autem . . . . .
quoddam monasterium sui iuris quod dicitur Hornburg in
pago North-Thuringa situm . . . . . ad idem monasterium
contradiderunt. Dieses Hornburg ist das „im Mansfelder
Seekreise, 1½ Stunden südlich von Eisleben belegene vor-
malige Kloster Holzzelle oder Hornburg-Celle, Celle Hornburg,
unter dem jetzigen Dorfe Hornburg, südwestlich vom salzigen
See“ [2]). Es hat also nicht in dem pagus Nordthuringa gelegen, sondern vielmehr im Hassago, speziell in dem unter
dem Namen Frisoneveld bezeichneten Teil desselben [3]).

Es wird somit höchst wahrscheinlich, daß das thüringische
Reich vor der Katastrophe von 531 sich über die Unstrut

5. Urkunde Heinrichs II. für Merseburg. 1021 5. Oktober (M. G.
    DD. III, S. 571, no. 449).
6. Urkunde Konrads II. für Nienburg. 1025. 8. Februar (Cod. dipl.
    Anhalt. I, S. 84, no. 106).
7. Urkunde Heinrichs III. für Nienburg. 1041. 22. Juli (Cod. dipl.
    Anhalt. I, S. 89, no. 113).
8. Urkunde Heinrichs IV. für Nienburg. 1062 5. März (Cod. dipl.
    Anhalt. I, S. 111, no. 138).
9. Urkunde Heinrichs IV. für einen gewissen Lantfried. 1068. 5. Aug.
    (Schmidt, U.B. des Hochstifts Halberstadt, S. 67, no. 92).
10. Urkunde Bischof Rudolfs von Halberstadt (über die Ansprüche
    des Klosters Hamersleben). 1144. 18. Juni (Schmidt a. a. O. I,
    S. 174 ff., no. 206).

1) Einer genauen Prüfung ist die Urkunde unterzogen von
E. Jacobs (Zeitschrift des Harzvereins XI, 1878, S. 1 ff.). Er kommt
zu dem Resultat (S. 15), daß die Urkunde zwar nicht eine „Original-
ausfertigung“, aber eine „sachlich unverdächtige Nachbildung des
jetzt verlorenen Originals“ ist. Auch E. Mühlbacher (Zeitschrift des
des Harzvereins XI, S. 25) bezeichnet die Urkunde als „sachlich un-
verdächtig“.

2) G. Bode in Zeitschrift d. Harzvereins IV, S. 24.

3) Spruner-Menke 1880 Karte no. 33.

hinaus nördlich bis mindestens zum Nordthüringgau einschließlich erstreckt hat; ob aber wirklich Nordthüringen
mit dem nachmaligen Halberstädter Sprengel zusammenfällt,
ob also der pagus Derlingowe, der pagus Belkesheim [1]) und
der pagus Hartingowe auch einst zu Thüringen gehört haben,
ist nicht mehr auszumachen [2]). Immerhin kann diese Ansicht, die von v. Ledebur eingehend — wie uns allerdings
scheinen will, in unzulänglicher Weise — begründet ist,
nicht als unmöglich bezeichnet werden. Über das Gebiet
des Halberstädter Sprengels hinaus aber hat sich Nordthüringen nicht erstreckt, das ist die Ansicht aller, die sich
mit diesem Gegenstande beschäftigt haben.

Sollte aber nicht die erste Schlacht, die Schlacht bei
Runibergun, an den Grenzen des Landes stattfinden [3])?
Was könnte uns verhindern, ihr den Platz im Gau Maerstem
anzuweisen, wie es so häufig geschehen ist [4])?

Wir haben oben gesehen, wie unglaubwürdig der Bericht des sächsischen Liedes ist: bei Runibergun „an den
Grenzen der Thüringer" findet die Schlacht statt, gleich
nach der Schlacht wird ein Kriegsrat abgehalten, in dem
davon gesprochen wird, daß das ganze Land in der Gewalt
der Franken sei u. s. w.

Sollte die Angabe des Quedlinburgers, die erste Schlacht
sei im Gau Maerstem geschlagen, richtig sein, so ständen
wir vor einer Fülle von Widersprüchen. Liegt denn das.

---

1) v. Ledebur a. a. O. S. 10 erklärt den Namen dieses Ganes
durch dort angesiedelte Belgier und scheint ihn auch zu jenen Gauen
zu rechnen, die im Jahre 568 von Sigebert neu besiedelt wurden.

2) Gesichert ist nach den obigen Ausführungen nur die Zugehörigkeit der 4 Gane: Hassigowe, Frisoneveld, Suevon und North-
thuringia zum einstigen thüringischen Reich.

3) Widukind I, 9. a. a. O. S. 8. Et cum gravi exercitu appropians terminis Thuringorum, invenit cum valida quoque manu
generum suum se expectantem in loco qui dicitur Runibergun.

4) v. Ledebur a. a. O. S. 5 f; Gloël a. a. O. S. 225; Venediger,
Das Unstrutthal und seine geschichtliche Bedeutung (Jahresbericht
des Stadtgymnasiums zu Halle a. d. S. 1886), S. 24; Größler a. a. O.
S. 10 ff.

Ronneberg im Gau Maerstem wirklich „an den Grenzen der Thüringer"? Der Gau Maerstem gehört zur Diöcese Minden [1]), wird also von dem Halberstädter Sprengel durch die ganze Breite des Hildesheimer getrennt, wie kann hier die Schlacht stattgefunden haben? Wie kann in diesem Falle, wo ein Kriegsrat abgehalten wird, um zu beraten, ob man nach Hause ziehen solle — ehe man überhaupt noch thüringischen Boden erblickt hat!, — der Sklave Theuderichs die Behauptung wagen: Nune terra in nostra est potestate, wie kann er wissen, daß „der Anführer (sc. Irminfried) selbst wie ein schwaches Tierlein durch seinen Versteck sich schützt, sich hinter den Mauern seiner Burg vergräbt?" Diese Erwägung gibt in der Tat den Ausschlag [2]). Das Lied muß ein Runibergun in der Nähe von Burg-Scheidungen gemeint haben, das Ronneberg im Gau Maerstem ist ausgeschlossen.

Interessant ist es zuzusehen, wie Größler manövriert, um dieser unabweislichen Folgerung zu entgehen. Für ihn steht es fest, daß Runibergun im Gau Maerstem gemeint sei — Widukind sagt ja: die Schlacht habe außerhalb Thüringens stattgefunden, und die Übereinstimmung Widukinds und der Quedlinburger Annalen ist doch zu merkwürdig! —, er argumentiert folgendermaßen weiter [3]): „Wenn nun aber auch der servus satis ingeniosus des Theuderich in dem von Widukind geschilderten Kriegsrate mit Beziehung auf Irminfried spöttisch bemerkt: Ipse namque dux, ut quaedam bestiola suo munitur latibulo, urbis circumdatur claustro, so setzt diese Bemerkung voraus, daß die Franken sehr lange bei Orheim gelegen haben müssen, sonst hätte ja die Kunde, daß Irminfried sich nach Scheidungen begeben habe, nicht in das dortige Lager der Franken gelangen können." Zunächst beruht es auf einer durch

---

1) Böttger, Diöcesan- und Gaugrenzen II, 113 B. glaubt übrigens auch, daß die sächsischen Quellen das „Runibergun" im Gau Maerstem meinen.

2) Es ist Könneckes Verdienst, hierauf aufmerksam gemacht zu haben a. a. O. S. 37.

3) a. a. O. S. 26.

nichts gerechtfertigten Kombination von Widukind und den
Quedlinburger Annalen[1]), wenn Größler von einem Lager
bei Orheim spricht, und sodann wird der Kriegsrat so schnell
nach der Schlacht berufen, daß man überhaupt noch kein
Lager aufgeschlagen hat[2]). Die „überzeugende Kraft der
Gründe", die Größler sich gerade in dieser Frage vindiziert[3]),
ist gewiß nicht auf seiner Seite.

Wir müssen trotz Gloël und Größler zu der Ansicht
von Joh. Gottlob Böhme zurück, die in neuerer Zeit wieder
von E. Lorenz und Koennecke aufgenommen ist: das Runibergun Widukinds sind die Ronneberge an der Unstrut
bei Nebra. Der Ausdruck Widukinds „appropians terminis
Thuringorum" läßt nur darauf schließen, daß der Verfasser
des Liedes in diesen Gegenden nicht genau Bescheid gewußt hat.

Wie ist unter dieser Voraussetzung aber die Schlacht
bei Orheim an der Ocker, von der uns der Quedlinburger
zu erzählen weiß, zu erklären?

Die Schlacht bei Ronneberg wird von dem Annalisten
in den Gau Maerstem verlegt, ohne Zweifel, weil er nur
dort ein Ronneberg[4]) kannte. Das Heldenlied wußte aber
von drei Schlachten, erstens bei Runibergun, zweitens einer
unbekannten, von der nur der Anonymus erzählt, die die Annalen aber wenigstens andeuten[5]), drittens der Schlacht an
der Unstrut. Es mochte für den Annalisten wohl etwas
Verlockendes haben, da er bereits den Ort der ersten
Schlacht genannt hatte, auch den Ort der zweiten Schlacht

---

1) Wenn eine Kombination von Widukind und dem Quedlinburger möglich wäre, so handelt Größler durchaus konsequent, indem
er den Kriegsrat erst nach der Schlacht an der Ocker stattfinden
läßt; denn erst nach dieser Schlacht wird die Sachsenhilfe in Anspruch genommen. Nach Widukind wird aber der Kriegsrat sofort
nach der Schlacht bei Runibergun gehalten, daher können beide
Berichte nicht kombiniert werden.

2) Vgl. S. 188 Anmerkung 2.

3) a. a. O. S. 6.

4) E. Lorenz a. a. O. S. 391 f. Koennecke a. a. O. S. 38.

5) S. 175 f.

näher zu bestimmen. Weshalb er aber gerade auf Orheim
an der Ocker verfallen ist, bleibt völlig rätselhaft. Vielleicht ist es indes auch nur eine lokale Abwandlung des
Liedes gewesen, die der Quedlinburger aufgezeichnet hat.
Auch das wird man nicht unerwähnt lassen dürfen, daß an
der Ocker bei Ohrum ein „Duringesrod" sich nachweisen
läßt [1]). Weitere Folgerungen hieraus wird man aber nicht
ziehen dürfen. Außerdem hat der Annalist noch die größte
Verwirrung dadurch angerichtet, daß er die Ankunft der
Sachsen erst nach der zweiten Schlacht erfolgen läßt,
während sie im Liede bereits nach der ersten Schlacht erfolgte
(vor dem Kampf, von dem der Anonymus allein berichtet,
und der in dem Liede der zweite gewesen sein muß, haben
sich die Sachsen bereits mit Theodorich verbündet). . So
viel steht in allen Fällen fest: für die Schlacht an der
Ocker ist im Thüringerkrieg von 531 kein Platz [2]).

Wir kommen jetzt zu der Frage: Wann haben die
Sachsen in die Ereignisse eingegriffen und wieviel Schlachten
haben überhaupt stattgefunden? Gregor v. Tours spricht
von zwei Schlachten [3]), einer in campo plano, auf einem
Blachfelde. Der liber historiae Francorum kennt ebenfalls
zwei [4]), die sich mit denen Gregors decken. Aimoin berichtet
auch nur von zwei [5]). Rudolf von Fulda erzählt [6]): nach zwei
Schlachten mit zweifelhaftem Ausgang und großem Blut-
vergießen (ancipiti pugna incertaque victoria miserabili
snorum caede) habe Theuderich Boten an die Sachsen um

---

1) Trad. Fuld. ed. Dronke S. 101: in terminis Darlingen novale
quod dicitur Duringesrod iuxta fluvium Oncra. Vgl. Böttger a. a. O.
III, S. 168.

2) Koennecke S. 36 f. glaubt an die Schlacht an der Ocker, setzt
sie aber vor die Schlacht bei Runibergun — ein höchst bedenkliches
Verfahren.

3) Gregor v. Tours, III, 7 a. a. O.

4) Liber hist. Franc. c. 22 a. a. O.

5) Aimoin II, 9 bei Bouquet III, 50.

6) SS. II, 67: Et cum duobus proeliis ancipiti pugna incertaque
victoria miserabili suorum caede decertassent, Thiotricus spe vincendi
frustratus, misit legatos ad Saxones.

Hilfe geschickt. Widukind weiß nur von e i n e r Feldschlacht, nach deren Verlauf die Franken bereits so sehr geschwächt sind, daß sie die Sachsen um Hilfe angehen. Der Quedlinburger spricht von drei Schlachten, bei Runibergun, bei Orheim an der Ocker und an der Unstrut. Da Widukind außerdem von der Erstürmung der Vorburg (oppidum) Burg-Scheidungens redet, so sieht sich Größler[1]) natürlich veranlaßt, damit ja alle Berichte in seinem Schema Platz haben, vier Schlachten anzunehmen; Lorenz[2]) nimmt drei Schlachten an, bei Runibergun, an der Unstrut und vor Burg-Scheidungen. Koenneckes[3]) Ansicht ist, daß „abgesehen von den Vorgängen bei Burg-Scheidungen nur zwei Schlachten im ganzen Kriege geschlagen sind", und zwar bei Ohrum an der Ocker und bei Runibergun. Alle drei Forscher stützen sich auf die fränkischen u n d sächsischen Quellen, alle drei suchen alle Berichte möglichst in Einklang miteinander zu bringen, alle drei kommen dabei zu abweichenden Resultaten.

Kein Zweifel, das Heldenlied steht in einem gewissen Widerspruch mit den fränkischen Quellen; diese wissen nur von zwei, jenes kennt drei Schlachten. Aber man wird es doch bemerkenswert finden, daß nur zwei von den drei Schlachten des Liedes lokalisiert werden; die Erinnerung an den Ort der zweiten, d. h. derjenigen Schlacht, die der an der Unstrut noch voraufgeht, scheint gänzlich aus dem Gedächtnis des Volkes geschwunden zu sein.

Es hieße die Grenzen der historischen Kritik verkennen, wollte man hieraus noch weitere Schlüsse ziehen; das jedoch wird man zugeben müssen, daß mit hoher Wahrscheinlichkeit nur zwei Schlachten in diesem Kriege geschlagen sind, eine bei Runibergun, eine an der Unstrut (abgesehen von der Eroberung Burg-Scheidungens).

Haben die Sachsen die Schlacht an der Unstrut mitgeschlagen? Mit anderen Worten: hat Widukind oder

---

1) a. a. O. S. 35.
2) a. a. O. S. 390 ff.
3) a. a. O. S. 35.

Rudolf von Fulda Recht? Jener läßt die Sachsen bereits
nach der Schlacht bei Runibergun rufen, dieser läßt zwei
Schlachten vergehen, ehe Theuderich Beistand in Anspruch
nimmt. Nach der Volksüberlieferung haben die Sachsen
an der Schlacht an der Unstrut bereits teilgenommen (sowohl die Ann. Quedlinb. als der Anonymus geben das zu),
Rudolf, der jenen Gegenden ferner stand, wenn auch früher
schrieb, läßt die Sachsen am zweiten Kampfe nicht teilnehmen
— wenn wir hier überhaupt einen Schluß machen wollen,
so werden wir die Überlieferung des Liedes vorziehen.

Schon bei der zweiten Schlacht, so will das Lied,
haben die Sachsen mitgekämpft. Sie soll an der Unstrut
geliefert worden sein, aber wo? Die Antwort dürfte hier
nicht schwer fallen.

Die erste Schlacht hat, wie wir sahen, bei Runibergun
d. h. den Ronnebergen in der Nähe von Vitzenburg stattgefunden [1]), die Thüringer haben also die Unstrut direkt im Rücken
gehabt. Irminfried flieht, und wenn auch Theuderichs Heer
zunächst noch stehen bleibt, um jenen Kriegsrat abzuhalten,
so ist es doch nicht anzunehmen, daß, nachdem die Fortsetzung des Krieges einmal beschlossen ist, er nicht über
den Fluß seinen Feinden nachgerückt sein sollte. Es ist
also von vornherein wenig wahrscheinlich, daß das zweite
Treffen etwa in unmittelbarer Nähe der ersten Wahlstatt
geschlagen worden ist [2]). Nun geht aber der Bericht der
zweiten Schlacht wieder von der Voraussetzung aus, daß die
Thüringer die Unstrut im Rücken haben, daß die Unstrut
sie von Burg-Scheidungen trennt. Daher muß der Kampf sich
in unmittelbarer Nähe von Burg-Scheidungen abgespielt
haben, vielleicht auf der Strecke Wennungen-Tröbsdorf, vielleicht auch direkt im Süden der Burg und des Flusses östlich
von Tröbsdorf. Größler nimmt merkwürdigerweise an [3]),
die Stätte des Gefechts sei bei Seigerstädt, das er für Sieger-
städt erklärt, zu suchen, also auf demselben Ufer der Unstrut,

1) vgl. Koenneckes Ausführungen a. a. O. S. 39 ff.
2) Generalstabskarte, Sektionen Querfurt und Naumburg.
3) a. a. O. S. 29 ff.

auf dem auch Burg-Scheidungen liegt. Dann läßt er die
Franken auf das andere Ufer gehen (!), nach Süden ziehen,
wo sie „nordwestlich von Tröbsdorf der Feste gegenüber
auf dem Tröbsdorfer Unterfelde unterhalb, der Neideck ihr
Lager aufschlagen." Die Sachsen beziehen ebenfalls auf
dem südlichen Ufer der Unstrut östlich (!) von Tröbsdorf
ihr Lager. Von hier aus findet der Sturm statt (man muß
also von neuem den Fluß überschreiten!) und dann folgt
die weitere Erzählung nach Widukind. Größler weiß uns
sogar den Pfad[1]) zu zeigen, auf dem Irminfried geflohen
ist. Daß der Übergang der Franken bei Carsdorf auf das
andere Ufer, in unmittelbarer Nähe der feindlichen Burg
gegen allen Kriegsgebrauch und Vorsicht verstösst, sieht
Größler selbst ein[2]). Womit motiviert er ihn denn aber? Die
Franken hätten auf der linken Seite des Flusses nicht die
Möglichkeit gehabt, sich zu verpflegen[3]), wenn eine längere
Belagerung in Aussicht stand. Aber gründet sich nicht diese
Voraussetzung wieder auf eine andere, die nämlich, daß der
Krieg erst am 1. Oktober zu Ende gegangen sei, eine Ansicht, die, wie wir oben gezeigt haben[4]), von Widukind selbst
erst kombiniert ist. Im Gegenteil, nimmt man an, daß die
erste Schlacht an den Ronnebergen bei Vitzenburg stattgefunden hat, daß die Sachsen selbst schon in der Schlacht
an der Unstrut mitgekämpft haben, so wird es höchst wahrscheinlich, daß der Krieg nicht so übermäßig lange gedauert
hat, wenn man auch nicht mit Lorenz[5]) der Ansicht sein
wird, alles hätte sich im Verlaufe von wenigen Stunden
abgespielt. Die Größler'sche Anschauung muß, wenn auch
zugegeben werden soll, daß sie höchst scharfsinnig kon-
struirt ist, zurückgewiesen werden, weil sie auf falschen
Voraussetzungen beruht[6]).

---

1) a. a. O. S. 49.
2) a. a. O. S. 30.
3) a. a. O. S. 30.
4) S. 190 ff.
5) a. a. O. S. 387.
6) Soweit ich sehe, hat außer Größler niemand versucht, die
Schlacht an der Unstrut näher zu lokalisieren.

Der Sturz des thüringischen Königreiches ist die Folge der Katastrophe. Berthachar, der Vater Radegundens, der Bruder Irminfrieds, kann erst jetzt [1]) gestorben sein; wahrscheinlich ist er in einer Schlacht gefallen; Radegunde fällt in die Hand Chlotars [2]), dessen Gemahlin sie später wird;

---

1) Gloël a. a. O. S. 208 f. hat bekanntlich zuerst darauf hingewiesen, daß die Erzählung Gregors von der Ermordung Berthachars durch Irminfried jedes realen Hintergrundes entbehrt. Er hat gleichzeitig gezeigt, daß der Tod Berthachars frühestens in die Mitte der zwanziger Jahre fallen kann (a. a. O. S. 212). Baderich, der andere Bruder Irminfrieds, ist (Lippert, Z. d. V. f. th. G. u. A. XI, S. 287) zwischen 515 und 522 geschlagen und getötet, hat also die Katastrophe nicht mehr erlebt. Andrerseits ist Berthachar vor Irminfried gestorben (Radegunde bei Venantius Fortunatus ad Artachin [Auct. antiqu. IV, 1, S. 278]: nam pater ante eadens et avunculus inde secutus). Schon der Ausdruck eadens läßt auf einen gewaltsamen Tod schließen, zum Überfluß sagt aber Theudebert I. in einem Briefe an Justinian (M. G. epistolae III, S. 132 f., no. 20): Dei nostri misericordiam feliciter subactis Thoringiis et corum provinciis adquisitis, extinctis ipsorum tunc tempore regibus. Also kann Berthachar, der neben Irminfried nur allein noch als rex bezeichnet werden kann, erst zur Zeit des Frankenkrieges gestorben sein; ob er aber in einer Schlacht gefallen oder erst später, etwa ähnlich wie sein Bruder, ums Leben gekommen ist, bleibt dunkel; jedenfalls deutet das extinctis auch auf einen gewaltsamen Tod.

2) Nach Gregor III, 7 wird Theuderich von seinem Bruder Chlotar und seinem Sohne Theudebert iu dem Thüringerkriege unterstützt. Wann und wie Radegunde in die Hände Chlotars gefallen ist, bleibt völlig dunkel. Koennecke a. a. O. S. 44 f. hält es für wahrscheinlich, daß sie in der ersten Schlacht (bei K. also in der Schlacht an der Ocker) gefangen genommen wird. Über sie geraten beide Frankenkönige in Streit miteinander. Koennecke hat im Anschluß daran eine neue Hypothese aufgestellt. Bei Gregor findet sich nämlich der Satz (III, 7): Chlotacharius vero rediens, Radegundem, filiam Bertacharii regis, secum captivam abduxit. Koennecke argumentiert nun so (a. a. O. S. 45): Zwischen der zweiten Schlacht und der Einnahme von Burg-Scheidungen liege ein so kleiner Zeitraum, daß „für die Mißhelligkeiten zwischen den beiden fränkischen Königsbrüdern kein rechter Raum mehr bleibt." Daher müßten wir die Gefangennahme Radegundes und den Streit der Brüder nach der ersten Schlacht ansetzen. Chlotar sei dann erzürnt mit seiner Beute abgezogen und Theuderich habe sich jedenfalls nach Abzug seines

Irminfried selbst entkommt, wird aber später zu Zülpich
auf Betreiben Theuderichs [1]) von der Stadtmauer hinabge-

Bruders nicht mehr stark genug gefühlt, die Thüringer zu überwinden.
So sei die Sachsenhilfe zu erklären. Aber Koennecke hat die Stelle
bei Gregor aus dem Zusammenhang gerissen; Gregor hat nämlich
bereits von der zweiten Schlacht (an der Unstrut) gesprochen und
fährt dann fort: Patratam ergo victuriam, regionem illam capessunt
et in suam redigunt potestatem. Chlotacharius vero rediens etc.
Hiernach kehrt Chlotar also erst nach Schluß des Feldzuges, nach
Unterwerfung Thüringens zurück.

1) Wohin Irminfried zunächst entkommt, wissen wir nicht. Erst
sein Tod gibt Gregor (III, 8) Veranlassung, ihn wieder zu erwähnen:
er soll von Theuderich, nachdem ihm Sicherheit verbürgt war, nach
Zülpich eingeladen und dann dort von der Stadtmauer herabgestürzt sein. Der liber historiae Francorum und Aimoin folgen der
Version Gregors. Fredegar dagegen (III, 32) erzählt: Ipsi (= Ipse =
Ermenfridus) a Theodeberto, filium Theuderici interfectus est. Hier
ist also Theuderichs Sohn, Theudebert, der 534 zur Regierung kommt,
der Mörder.

Diesem Berichte Fredegars werden wir doch nicht ohne weiteres
Glauben schenken können. Zunächst hat Fredegar später, wenn
auch nicht viel später, geschrieben als Gregor, sodann ist sein ganzer
Bericht so außerordentlich dürftig, daß man nur annehmen kann, er
sei schlecht unterrichtet gewesen. Alles, was er sagt, ist folgendes:

III, 32: Thoringorum tres fratres regnabant, Badericus, Ermenfridus et Bertharius. Ermenfridus Bertharium interfecit. Instigante
uxore Ermenfridi nequissima nomen Amalberga et Baderici, germanum
suum cum solatio Theuderici interfecit. Ipse vero a Theudeberto,
filium Theuderici interfectus est. Regnum Toringorum Francorum
dicione subactum est.

Wir werden uns entschließen müssen, der ersteren Fassung
(Gregor und liber historiae), daß Irminfried auf Betreiben Theuderichs
ermordet sei, den Vorzug zu geben. Man beachte übrigens, daß Gregor
sagt: Sed quis eum exinde deiecerit, ignoramus; multi tamen adserunt,
Theuderici in hoc dolum manifestissime patuisse, daß er mithin nur
von einem Gerücht spricht. Auch der liber historiae läßt es nur
gleichsam durchschimmern, daß Theuderich der eigentliche Urheber
des Mordes war. Wie fest und bestimmt tritt dagegen nicht die
Nachricht bei Fredegar auf: Ipsi vero a Theudeberto, filium Theuderici interfectus est. Wahrscheinlich liegt hier wieder die bekannte
Tatsache vor, daß ein unbestimmtes Gerücht sich zu einer bestimmten
Tatsache verdichtet hat.

stürzt und findet so ein elendes Ende. Amalaberga flieht. und kommt im Jahre 534 (wo sie so lange geweilt hat, wissen wir nicht) zu ihrem Bruder Theodahat, der damals bereits König der Ostgoten war[1]); ihr Sohn Amalafried und mehrere Töchter begleiten sie [2]). 540 nach der Kapitulation von Ravenna wurde Amalafried mit Witigis von Belisar nach Byzanz gebracht, wo ihn Justinian zum „Archon' machte [3]). 551 wurde ihm eine Feldherrenstelle in einem

---

Wie es jedoch hier zu einer Verwechslung Theuderichs mit Theudebert gekommen ist, können wir nicht sagen.

L. v. Ranke ist übrigens bei der Besprechung dieser Stelle Fredegars ein Versehen mit untergelaufen. Er interpungiert die Stelle falsch: Ermenfridus Bertharium interfecit instigante uxore Ermenfridi nequissima nomen Amalberga. Et Baderici etc. Auf diese Weise konstruiert er einen Gegensatz zwischen der Erzählung Gregors und der des Fredegar (Weltgeschichte IV, 2, Analekten S. 337). Daß Irminfried jedenfalls einer Treulosigkeit der Franken erlegen ist, ergibt sich mit ziemlicher Sicherheit auch aus einer Stelle bei Procob (de hello goth. II, 28). Dort verdächtigen die Franken dem Witigis bei der Belagerung von Ravenna die byzantinische Treue, worauf Belisars Gesandte erwidern : τὸ δὲ δὴ τούτων (sc. der Franken) πιστὸν, ᾧ χρῆσϑαι αὐχοῦσιν ἐς πάντας βαρβάρους, μετάγε Θορίγγους καὶ τὸ Βουργιονζιώνων ἔϑνος καὶ ἐς τοὺς ξυμμάχους ὑμᾶς παρὰ τῶν ἀνδρῶν ἐπιδέδεικται. Die hier erwähnte Treulosigkeit gegen die Thüringer wird man am ehesten auf Irminfrieds Tod beziehen, da wir die Stelle mit einem andern Ereignis nicht gut in Verbindung setzen können. Außerdem sagt Procop selbst (de hello goth. I, 13): . . . . . οἱ Φράγγοι . . . . . ἐπὶ Θορίγγους ἐστράτευσαν καὶ Ἑρμενεφρίδον τε τὸν αὐτῶν ἄρχοντα κτείνουσιν. Vgl. über den Tod Irminfrieds den Aufsatz von Lippert („Der Tod König Herminafrids" in Zeitschrift für thüring. Gesch. u. s. w. XV, N. F. VII, S. 5 ff).

1) Procop a. a. O. I, 13: ἡ δὲ τοῦ Ἑρμενεφρίδου γυνὴ ξὺν τοῖς παισὶ φυγοῦσα, παρὰ Θευδάτον τὸν ἀδελφόν, Γότϑων τηνικαῦτα ἄρχοντα ἡ ϑε.

2) Von Irminfrieds Kindern kennen wir nur einen Sohn, Amalafried mit Namen. Daß er auch Töchter gehabt hat, ergibt sich aus Venantius Fortunatus „de excidio Thoringiae", Vers 159 ff.

3) Procop a. a. O. IV, 25: . . . . . καὶ Ἀμαλαφρίδος, Γότϑος ἀνὴρ Ἀμαλαφρίδης μὲν ϑυγατριδοῦς, τῆς Θευδερίχου τοῦ Γότϑων βασιλέως ἀδελφῆς, Ἑρμενεφρίδου δὲ υἱὸς τοῦ Θορίγγων ἡγησαμένου. Ὅνπερ Βελισάριος μὲν ξὺν Οὐιττίγιδι ἐς Βυζάντιον ἤγαγε, βασιλεὺς δὲ Ῥωμαίων ἄρχοντα κατεστήσατο. καὶ τὴν αὐτοῦ ἀδελφὴν Αὐϑουίν τῷ Λαγγοβάρδων ἄρχοντι κατηγγύησε,

Krieg gegen die Gepiden übertragen [1]). Dann entschwindet
er unsern Blicken. Größler läßt ihn bald darauf sterben [2]),
ohne aber einen Beweis dafür anzutreten, Lippert hat es
wahrscheinlich gemacht [3]), daß er erst nach 561 gestorben ist.

Wir sind am Schlusse. Absichtlich haben wir darauf
verzichtet, die Vorgeschichte des Krieges in den Bereich
unserer Untersuchung zu ziehen, da besonders durch die
Arbeiten von Lippert diese, soweit es überhaupt möglich,
aufgeklärt ist. Nur der Katastrophe haben wir unser Augenmerk zugewandt. Wir fanden dabei, daß die drei sächsischen
Quellen (Widukind [4]), die Ann. Quedlinburg. und der Anonymus de origine Suevorum) auf ein jetzt verlorenes Heldenlied gemeinsam zurückgehen und stellten ihre fast völlige
historische Unglaubwürdigkeit fest. Von der so geschaffenen
Grundlage aus haben wir dann versucht, ein Bild von der
Katastrophe zu gewinnen. Wir geben uns der Hoffnung
hin, daß dieses Bild das richtige sein mag.

---

1) Procop a. a. O. IV, 25: ἡγοῦντο δὲ τῆς στρατιᾶς ταύτης (sc.,
gegen die Gepiden) . . . . . Ἀμαλαφρίδος κ.τ.λ. Vgl. hierüber noch
Lippert, Z. f. th. G. XII, S. 80 f.

2) Größler, „Radegundis". Mansfelder Blätter II, S. 69 ff.

3) Lippert, Z. d. V. f. th. G. XV, N. F. VII, S. 23 ff.

4) Größler, „Sturz des thüring. Königreichs" (Z. d. V. f. th. G.
XIX, N. F. XI, S. 3) bezeichnet Widukind als Abt (!) und Rudolf
von Fulda als Presbyter (!). Es ist mir völlig rätselhaft, woher
Größler diese Kenntnis geschöpft hat. Beide waren schlichte Mönche..

V.

Ueber ein 1525 und 1526 geplantes Religionsgespräch zur Beseitigung des Gegensatzes zwischen Ernestinern und Albertinern

Von

G. Mentz.

In Bd. IV dieser Zeitschrift hat 1885 W. Karstens über die sächsisch-hessischen Beziehungen in den Jahren 1524, 1525 und 1526 gehandelt, in demselben Jahre gab Friedensburg den Briefwechsel zwischen Herzog Georg von Sachsen und Landgraf Philipp von Hessen aus den Jahren 1525—1527 heraus [1]), vollständiger als das schon 1849 durch Seidemann [2]) geschehen war. Zu diesen Arbeiten sollen hier einige Ergänzungen gegeben werden.

Für die Ausbreitung der Reformation war der Gegensatz zwischen Ernestinern und Albertinern ein großes Hindernis, andererseits wurde aber auch wieder durch die Abneigung Herzog Georgs gegen Luther und sein Werk die Feindschaft der beiden sächsischen Linien gesteigert. Landgraf Philipp, der Freund und Bundesgenosse Johanns des Beständigen und der Schwiegersohn Georgs, schien die geeignetste Persönlichkeit, um die Vermittlung zu übernehmen. Ihm sowohl wie den Ernestinern war 1525 das gespannte Verhältnis zu dem albertinischen Vetter sehr

---

1) Neues Archiv für Sächs. Gesch. Bd. VI.
2) In Niedners Zeitschrift für die historische Theologie. N. F. XIII, 1849, S. 175 ff.

unbequem, sie benutzten gern jede Gelegenheit zu einer
Versöhnung. Die gemeinsame Aufgabe, die die Erhebung
der Bauern den benachbarten Fürsten stellte, bot einen
erwünschten Anlaß zu Verhandlungen, vor Mühlhausen
einigte man sich auf eine gemeinsame Politik den Untertanen gegenüber. Andere Fürsten sollten für den Eintritt
in diesen Bund gewonnen werden [1]). Bald aber zeigte sich,
daß man dabei von ganz verschiedenen Voraussetzungen
ausging. Die Nachrichten, die Johann und Philipp im
August 1525 zum Teil aus Georgs eigenem Munde über
seine Dessauer Verabredungen mit den Kurfürsten von Mainz
und von Brandenburg u. a. erhielten, verschafften ihnen
die unerwünschte Erkenntnis, daß Georg dem Bunde einen
antievangelischen Charakter zu geben suchte. Trotzdem
gaben sie die Hoffnung, die Einigung zu erhalten, nicht
auf. Es entstand jetzt in ihnen der Gedanke, durch ein
Religionsgespräch die religiöse Differenz zu beseitigen, und
wir dürfen wohl annehmen, daß sie dabei die Hoffnung
hegten, Georg für den neuen Glauben zu gewinnen. Längere
Zeit kamen sie immer wieder auf diesen Gedanken zurück,
und es ist dieser Punkt, den ich hier auf Grund bekannter
und unbekannter Akten verfolgen möchte.

Zuerst findet sich der Vorschlag in dem Briefe, den
Johann und Philipp am 15. Sept. 1525 aus Treffurt an
Herzog Georg richteten [2]). Es heißt darin, sie sähen für
gut an, „das die obgemelten churfursten und fursten (d. h.
die, die zu Dessau versammelt waren), auch E. L. und wir
zu allen theiln gelarte, erbare, gotsfurchtige und geschigte
personen, auch wenn von allen theilen unsern freunden und
verwanten, uf einen gelegenen platz zusamen schigten und
sich von allen misspreuchen und sachen das evangelium
und wort gottis sampt den ceremonien belangent erbarlich
und christlich zu unterreden, und was dann befunden, das

---

1) Vgl. Friedensburg, Zur Vorgeschichte des Gotha-Torgauischen
Bündnisses, S. 7 ff.

2) Friedensburg, Vorgeschichte, S. 114 ff.

am allermeisten dem wort gottis gleich were, das' man dasselbige furgehen liess, was aber am meinsten darwidder were,
das solchs nachpliebe bis auf einen mehrern christlichen und
entliehen beschlus". Auch am 25. Oktober scheinen die
beiden Fürsten ihren Vorschlag noch einmal wiederholt zu
haben [1]), sie hofften, daß nach Beilegung des Religions-
streites die Beseitigung der übrigen Differenzen der Wettiner keine großen Schwierigkeiten mehr machen würde [2]),
bei Georg aber fanden sie mit ihren Vorschlägen wenig
Anklang. Er zog sich auf seine Dessauer Verbündeten
zurück. Diese erklärten in ihrer Antwort vom 13. November,
die Georg am 12. Dezember an Johann übersandte, daß
sie sich auf dergleichen Verhandlungen nicht einlassen
könnten, weil sie den Reichstagsbeschlüssen und den Geboten des Kaisers zuwider laufen würden. Trotzdem gaben
die evangelischen Fürsten ihren Plan noch nicht auf, in
ihren Briefen vom Dezember 1525 und Januar 1526 ist
noch öfters davon die Rede, sogar in einem Briefe an
Georg berühren sie ihn noch einmal [3]), aber wohl nur, um
diesen zu nötigen, Farbe zu bekennen. Besonders der
Landgraf scheint sich keine großen Hoffnungen mehr
gemacht zu haben, daß man auf diesem Wege etwas erreichen könne [4]). Erst als ihm seine Schwester Elisabeth
im Februar 1526 meldete, der Herzog gestatte die freie
Predigt des Evangeliums, wagte Philipp einen neuen Vorstoß. Im Februar, März und April fand eine Korrespondenz
zwischen ihm und seinem Schwiegervater statt [5]), die aber
bald zeigte, daß auch diese neuen Hoffnungen eine Täu-
schung waren. Auch die Ermahnungen, die der Landgraf am

---

1) Karstens, S. 362. Vgl. auch Friedensburg, Vorgeschichte,
S. 93 ff.
2) Karstens, S. 369.
3) am 7. Jan. 1526. Vgl. Friedensburg, Vorgeschichte, S. 97.
4) ebenda S. 96.
5) Abgedruckt bei Friedensburg im Neuen Arch. f. die sächs.
Gesch., VI, 129—135.

1. April an den Kurfürsten Johann ergehen ließ, Georg gegenüber behutsam zu verfahren und besonders Luther, den er so sehr hasse, zurückzuhalten [1]), hatten nun keine weitere Bedeutung.

Man hat bisher angenommen, daß Philipp von nun an die Hoffnung auf Gewinnung seines Schwiegervaters aufgegeben habe [2]). In der Tat scheint er selbst direkt nicht weiter in Verbindung mit ihm getreten zu sein, dagegen veranlaßte er aber im Juni, daß kursächsischerseits der Gedanke des Religionsgesprächs noch einmal aufgenommen und ein letzter energischer Versuch, Georg auf diese Weise zu gewinnen, gemacht wurde. Der folgende auch in anderer Hinsicht interessante Brief belehrt uns darüber:

Landgraf Philipp an Herzog Jobaun Friedrich. Eppenberg [1526 Juni 16]. [3]).

Ich hab E. L. schreiben verstanden und will meiner swester bei eigener botschaft antwort geben. Zum andern hz. Heinrichs halben, was er zu Quedelburg gemacht hat, das hab ich E. L. vater vorhin angezeit, wie E. L. an zwiffel von im vernemen werden, desglichen so schick ich E. L. ein briff von hz. Heinrich an mich gangen, do wirt E. L. sein gemut wol in vernemen und ist darnach mein frundlich bit an E. L., als E. L. und mein gluck stet, E. L. woll sich kegen hz. Heinrich nit verhetzen lassen, das E. L. ein unfrundlich gemute zu im entpecht, wan er wert E. L. dunn, was E. L. lieb ist, das hat er mir zugesagt, so wirt es E. L. auch selbst von im horen.

---

1) ebenda S. 114.   Karstens S. 372.   Weim. Arch. Reg. A, 237.

2) Friedensburg, ebenda S. 116.

'3) eigenh. Or. Weim. Arch. Reg. N. 50. Dort ins Jahr 1525 gesetzt, doch gehört der Brief offenbar ins Jahr 1526. Es ist der Hauptbrief zu dem bekannten Briefe Philipps an Joh. Friedr. vom 17. Juni 1526 (Eppenberg am sontage nach Viti et Modesti anno XXVI. Or. von Kanzleihand Reg. H. p. 3. C. beginnend mit: Wir bitten auch E. L.), den Seckendorf II, 47 f. und Friedensburg, Speier S. 291 f. u. a. benutzt haben.

Nachdem ich nu E. L. und E. L. fater mit verwantnis und frundschaft zugetan bin, so kan ich nit underlassen; nachdem auch es dem evangelium, nach menchslicher weise zu reden, schaden tut und vil leut dardorch geergert werden, wo das also war were, nu gehet ein gemeine geschrei, wie das E. L. her vater die monch und nonnen us den clostern jag mit gewalt und in nichts geben und mit dem clostergut auch ubel gehandelt wirt und die closterleut daruber zu huren und buben werden. Wo das nu so were, das ich nit hoff, so wers mirs leit, es wer auch nit ewangelichs, es werden auch vil lut daruber geergert, ich kunt auch kein glauben do mirken, nachdem die liebe nit da wer, und darumb ist mein frundlich bit an E. L. umb Cristi willen, wo das also wer, wolt das abstellen und mit Martino und Melanthon nach laut des wort gots darin handeln, uf das unser schatz, das wort gots, durch unser hose leben nit gelestert werde.

Desglichen hore ich, das vil buberei mit ebruch und sust mit nemen einem dem andern und das sich czwei hinnemen, morn wieder von ein[ander]laufen, in E. L. vater land sei, do sich dan vil leut an ergern, das bit ich auch E. L., wo im also ist, das E. L. her vater darin ein insehen habe, das das gestrafft werde, wie dan das Sein Liebe schuldig ist zu dun, wie dan das Petrus und Paulus sagen, da sie schriben, die oberkeit trag das swert nit vergebelich, wan sie seie gots dinerin zu straffen den, der bosses tut, uf das [das] evangelium nit durch unser leben gelestert werde.

Nachdem uns auch nu Cristus gebeut und heist uns frid haben, auch Paulus sagt, wir sollen mit iederman frid haben und auch Petrus spricht, man sol dem frid nach- jagen und iderman um bitten, und ich auch gelessen hab in der schrift der geschicht der apostel, wan ein irrung gewesen ist, das sie dan zu hauf komen sein und sich nach laut des worts gots vereiniget, und ich nu mirk, das zwei- spellicheit und irrung zwischen E. L. vater und hz. Joîgen ist, und ir mir von beiden teilen verwant seit und sich zu

besorgen were, das ein funklein ain ganzen walt anstechken
wird, wo es nit in der zeit vorkomen werde, und mir nu
ein menchs [1]), dem evangelio geneit, ein anslag geben hat,
wie E. L. fater und hz. Jorg in ein entlichen vertrag komen
konten, so kan ich E. L. nit bergen, das mir angezeit worden
ist die meinung, das hz. Jorg ein halstarigen kopf habe
und wo man im auch nit ein wenig nachgibt, so bringt
man in numer davon, wan mir wirt angezeit, er sprech,
was den corforsten gut dunkt, das sol also recht sein.
Nu hat mir der menchs den weg angezeit, das er meinte,
und ich halts auch darvor, er kunt nit darvor uber und ob
ers schon nit duen wolt, so vermerk ich so vil, das er dem
son das regiment ubergeben und liß den dun, und es hat
mich glaublich angelangt, wie ich E. L. wol anzeigen wil,
wan ich einmal bei E. L. kum oder bei den corforsten.
Und das ist der weg, das sich E. L. her vater der corforst
zu hz. Jorgen schickt, wo es dan Sein Lieb haben wolt,
so wolt ich dergleichen auch dun, und lies im sagen, das
S. L. gern frundschaft und guten willen bei S. L. haben
wolt, auch gern sehen, das S. L., desglichen sein eigen
undertan in einer guten eintracht und einikeit weren, und
wolt es auch gern machen, das got gefil, und darumb wer
sein bit an S. L., das S. L. wolt etlich frome gelerte menner
us S. L. landschaft [verordnen], desglichen wolt er auch dun,
desglichen wol er mich vermogen, ich solt auch die meinen
darbei schicken, und das die das wort gots vor sich nemen
und alle cermonien und userliche sachen darnach richten.
Wie die es machen nach laut des wort gottes, so solt es im
gefallen, und nem das E. L. vater, so kunt es hz. Jorg
nit abslagen, und ich hoffe, alle sachen solten gut werden,
es wer auch recht und wer dem wort gots glich, es wirt
auch Lutern, versehe ich mich, gefallen, er und ander musten
auch darbei sein. Wan auch das geschege, su were der
paffen pratica ser gebrochen und wan man dan ein veinen

---

1) Vielleicht Herzogin Elisabeth.

wandel furet, wie ich for geschriben hab, so werden sich
vil leut bessern und nit ergern, so fer als auch got sein
gnade verleit. Ich bit, E. L. wol dis mein schriben in
geheim halten und nimant wan E. L. her vater und, wo
E. L. wil, dem Lutter sehen lassen und sich cristlich und
frundlich darin erzeigen und mein schriben nit anders dan
us getruem herzen keigen E. L. vermirken ... D. Ebpen-
berk sambstag nach Viti etc.

Johann Friedrich scheint den Wunsch des Landgrafen
bereitwillig erfüllt zu haben, denn in der Instruktion, mit
der am 4. Juli Hans v. d. Planitz und Günther von Bünau
als kursächsische Gesandte an Herzog Georg geschickt
wurden [1]), kehren die hessischen Vorschläge, allerdings in
mancher Hinsicht modifiziert und ohne Erwähnung des
Landgrafen, wieder. Nachdem der Kurfürst darin zunächst
auseinandergesetzt hat, daß ohne Beilegung der Differenzen
in Glaubenssachen auch auf eine Beseitigung der zeitlichen
Streitigkeiten nicht zu rechnen sei, betont er seine Bereit-
willigkeit, sich einem freien christlichen Konzilium oder
einer Versammlung, „so von Kais. Mt, kfen, fursten und
andern stenden des heiligen reichs, auch allen cristglaubigen
menschen furgenomen wirdet“, zu fügen und fährt dann
fort: „So aber E. f. Gn. solchs auch nit gefallen wolt, vil-
leicht darumb, das sichs darmit zu lange verziehen wurde,
ader aus andern ursachen, kounen und mogen S. kf. Gn.
wol leiden und wollen S. kf. Gn. sich auch hiemit darzu
erboten haben, das beide E. kf. und f. Gn. sich eines tags
und malstadt freuntlich vereinigen und auf denselben tag
beiderseits gelerte und ungelerte rete in gleicher anzahl
geschickt und verordent werden und das dazumal notturf-
tiglich und mit gutem bedacht aus verleihung gotlicher
gnaden von demjhenigen, so in beiderseits E. kflichen und
f. Gn. furstentumben und landen fur mißbreuchlich und
unschigklich angesehen wirdet, gehandelt und geredt werde,

---

1) Weim. Arch. Reg. A 237 Gonc. Vgl. Karstens S. 378 f.

auch mit gotlicher hulf und durch sein 'wort vereinigung
gemacht, wie es allenthalben bis auf ein frei cristlich concilium solte gehalten und gebraucht werden.

Und zu einem weitern erbieten, wo es E. f. G. nicht
gefellig, wollen S. kf. Gn. willigen und sich darzu erboten
haben, das durch gemeine landschaft und von allen stenden
beiderseits E. kf. und f. Gn., inmassen wie hiebevorhn von
den reten meldung bescheen, aus verleihung gotlicher gnaden
und durch sein heiligs wort gehandelt werde."

Die Antwort Georgs vom 19. Juli [1]) lautete rundweg
ablehnend. Er erkannte zwar an, daß Einigkeit in den das
Seelenheil berührenden Dingen erwünscht sei, empfahl im
übrigen aber, die Beschlüsse des bevorstehenden Speierer
Reichstags über die Missbräuche und über die bis zum
Konzil zu beobachtende Haltung abzuwarten, und erklärte
eine besondere Verhandlung darüber für unangebracht.

Unsere Kenntnis über die Verhandlungen der beiden
Gesandten mit Georg ist aber nicht auf die beiden erwähnten
offiziellen Aktenstücke beschränkt, wir besitzen vielmehr
darüber noch einen lebensvollen Bericht des Hans von der
Planitz an den Kurprinzen, der sich seinen berühmten
Berichten vom Reichsregiment würdig anreiht und auch
zur Charakteristik Herzog Georgs einen hübschen Beitrag
liefert. Ich denke manchem eine Freude zu machen, wenn
ich ihn hier mit anreihe:

Hans von der Planitz an Hz. Johann Friedrich. Grimma
1526 Juli 21 [2]).

Er Gunther von Bunau und ich seint am nechsten
mitwochen zu Dresden einkommen und am donerstag das
antragen. getan in gegenwertigkeit der rett Jorgen von
Karlwitz, des canzlers, Hanssen von Haubitz und Hanssen

---

1) Dresden dornstags nach Alexii 1526. Or. Reg. A. 237. Karstens S. 379. Am 26. Juli wurde Georgs Antwort von den Räten
aus Weimar dem Kfen nach Speier nachgesandt (ebenda Or.), daher
wohl das Datum bei Karstens S. 385.

2) eigenh. Or. Reg. N. pag. 68. C. No. 17.

von Schonberghs, gab uns unsser gn. herr hz. Jorge antwort desselben tages umb VII hore auf den ahent, wie E. f. Gn. befinden werden, dan wir dieselbigen unsserm gnsten. hn. dem kfen, E. f. Gn. vattern, haben zugeschigkt, und hetten gern weiter antwort gehabt, wue nichts auf disem reichstag von sulcher ordnung aufzurichten gehandelt ader beschlossen wurde, ab alsdan S. f. Gn. der erpiten eins und welchs annemen und willigen wolde, wir haben aber nichts erlangen mogen. Dan ich allein bekam von S. f. Gn. mein auspeut und also: Do wir die antwort entpfangen hetten und unssern abschidt nemen wolten, sprach ich zu m. gn. hn. hz. Jorgen, ich wolt mich auch versehen, die reichsstende wurden von einer ordnung reden, wie man es mit den ceremonien und anderen halten solde bis auf ein zukonftig concilium, wue es aber nicht beschee, als woll zu besorgen stunde, nochdem es die geistlichen nicht gern wurden nachlassen, ßo verhoffet ich doch, S. f. Gn. wurden sich mit m. gn. hn. dem kfen einer ordnung vereinigen. Darauf S. Gn. antwortet Wir haben ein gute ordnung gehabt, hett man es dobei bleiben lassen. Saget ich: Gn. her, E. f. Gn. wissen dennochst woll und haben gesehen, was unordnung die geistlichen haben mit eingefurt, dieselben alle zu dulden were auch vast beschwerlich. Antwortet er: Man soll darumb den baum mit der wurzel nicht ausreissen. Zu dem ich antwortet: Were etwas guths und cristlichs umbgestossen, gn. h., so richt man es wider auf, allein das E. beider kf. und f. Gn. darvon reden und handeln lissen, was dem evangelio gemeß ader ungemeß were, darnach hett man die ordnung aufzurichten. Do sprach er zorniglichen: Ja Ir und ich verstehen und wissen woll, was dem ewangelio gemess sei oder nicht. Darauf ich sagot: Gn. her, E. beider kf. und f. Gn. haben, gott hab lobe, vill verstendiger und redlicher leut im furstentum, die sulchs woll verstehen und wissen. Ja, sprach ehr, was itzunt ein ausgelaufener monch saget, das muß recht sein. Man kan kein besser ordnung machen, dan die, ßo hievor gewest. Und wurde also school-

lig und ungeberig, das ich mein pfeif' einzog, gab ern
Gunthern und mir ein gute nacht, zogen alßo in uusser
herbergh, und in summa, S. f. Gn. mogen ubel leiden, das
man mit im von disser sachen rede, und ßonderlich vermerk
ich, das er es von mir unliber, den von einem andern hat.
Er ist auch etwas schwach gewest am fiber und ist noch
nicht' woll geschigket, dan S. Gn. haben einen bosen husten,
sagen die erzt, es sei ein fluß, der falle S. Gn. auf die lunge.
Gott helf uns allen.

Von neuen zeitungen aus disen landen weiß E. f. Gn.
ich nichts zu schreiben, den das man saget, wie das der
kg. von Polen zu Danzig vill leut hab richten lassen, und
mussen die von Danzig alle altar und ceremonien, wie zuvor
gewest, widerumb aufrichten. Nicht wes ich, ob dem also.
Greffendorff, wen der kommet, wirt die warheit wissen.
D. Grim am XXI. tage julii anno dni XV^c und XXVI.

Die Beschlüsse des Speierer Reichstags konnten in
keiner Weise dazu dienen, die Gegensätze im Hause Wettin
zu beseitigen. Wohl aber lag es nahe, daß man von
ernestinischer Seite jetzt auf den Gedanken einer gemeinsamen Regelung der religiösen Frage wieder zurückkam.
Tatsächlich wurde in einem Briefe Johanns an Georg
vom 3. Januar 1527 [1]) an den Vorschlag vom vorigen Jahre
noch einmal erinnert. Georg ging in seiner Antwort vom
8. Jan. [2]) aber auf die Sache überhaupt nicht ein, und nun
scheint man auch auf ernestinischer Seite den Plan fallen
gelassen zu haben.

---

1) Reinentw. Reg. A. 238.
2) ebenda·

VI.

Der Diesberg (Diesburg) an der Rhön, und der Steinwall auf demselben.

Von

Landesgeometer **A. Mueller.**

(Mit einer Karte.)

Zwischen den Dörfern Wohlmuthausen, Aschenhausen (Sachs.-Weimar) und Oberkatz (Sachs.-Meiningen), erhebt sich in den östlichen Vorbergen der Rhön bis zu einer Höhe von 710 m der Baseltkegel „der Diesberg", von den benachbarten Basaltbergen Alte Mark, Hutsberg, Streufelsberg etc. durch einen breiteren, von Ost nach West laufenden Rücken sich unterscheidend. Den Gipfel umschließt ein von Basaltsteinen (sogen. Wackersteinen) aufgeführter Ringwall in elliptischer Form, der bei einer unteren Breite von 7—8 m, von außen immer noch eine Höhe von $1^1/_2$—2 m hat, während im Innern durch Anschwemmung und Humusbildung die Erhebung über den Boden nur eine geringe ist. Ein jedenfalls alter Eingang liegt auf der westlichen Seite des Rings, nach Wohlmuthausen hin, während noch drei weitere Ausgänge, nach Süden und Westen, erst in neuerer Zeit zur Abfuhr des auf der Höhe geschlagenen Holzes in den Steinwall gebrochen worden sind. Derselbe schließt eine Fläche von ca. $1^1/_2$ ha = 15000 qm ein, und hat in der Richtung von Süd nach Nord eine Länge von etwa 230 m, bei einer größten Breite von 150 m von Ost nach West; der Steinwall selbst bedeckt eine Fläche von 40 ar. Bis vor etwa 80 Jahren war der Rücken des Berges inner-

halb des Ringes nur mit einzelnen Bäumen bestanden und
diente als Viehweide; dann haben die Gemeinden, des
höheren Ertrags wegen, die eingeschlossene Fläche auf-
geforstet, wodurch natürlich die Uebersicht und Aussicht
höchlichst beeinträchtigt wird.

Auf der höchsten Stelle der Umwallung, die im Volksmunde „der Kringel" genannt wird, stoßen, wie aus dem
beigegebenen Kärtchen ersichtlich, die Grenzen der drei
genannten, ehemals hennebergischen, Flüren zusammen, die
nach Absterben dieses Hauses 1583, an Sachsen, und zwar
Aschenhausen und Wohlmuthausen an S.-Koburg — später
Eisenach (Weimar) —, Oberkatz an S.-Hildburghausen —
später Meiningen — fielen, so daß die Flurgrenze zwischen
Oberkatz und Aschenhausen-Wohlmuthausen, jetzt gleichzeitig Landesgrenze zwischen Sachsen-Weimar und Sachsen-
Meiningen, ist.

In einer Abhandlung (Programm) vom 29. Dezbr. 1709
stellte der aus Oberkatz stammende Jenaer Professor und
Rechtsgelehrte J. W. Ditmar die Behauptung auf, daß jene
Umwallung auf dem Diesberge, die er aus eigener Anschauung genau kannte, das längst gesuchte Dispargum des
Gregor von Tours, die fränkische Königsburg des Chlodio
sei, von welcher aus der Frankenkönig im Jahr 491 den
Römern nach Cambray (Cameracum) gefolgt sei und sie
geschlagen und vertrieben habe. Dieser Ansicht trat der
um die Mitte des 18. Jahrhunderts als Pfarrer in Betten-
hausen lebende Magister Johann Ludwig Heim, und nach
ihm die meisten Forscher, bei.

Wenn nun jetzt auch feststeht, daß diese Ansicht unrichtig, und das Dispargum in unserer Diesburg nicht zu
erblicken ist, so dürfte es doch ebenso irrig sein, Diestheim
bei Tongern (s. Binder, „Das ehemalige Amt Lichtenberg
v. d. Rhön", in Bd. XVI, S. 238 d. Zeitschr.) dafür anzusehen, als das Ronneberg bei Hannover für das „Runibergun" Gregors zu halten, wo im Jahre 531 der Kampf
zwischen den Thüringern und Franken stattgefunden.

Nach Ansicht der Umwohner hat allerdings den Gipfel des Diesbergs eine Königsburg gekrönt, und in der Regel wird die Umwallung, ja der ganze Berg, die „Diesburg" genannt, freilich nicht erst, wie Binder vermutet, seit Ditmars Hypothese, denn schon 1661 kommt nachweislich die Benennung „Dießburgk" vor[1]) vor. Wir kommen später darauf zurück.

Auf alle Fälle bleibt die Frage bestehen: Welchen Zwecken hat die Umwallung (der Steinring) ursprünglich gedient?

Ditmar beschreibt den Berg folgendermaßen: Est mons altissimus, longe lateque conspicuus, in cacumine magnam planitiem, raris arboribus continet, lateribus inhaerent nemora . . . und fährt dann fort: in monte hoc nulla supersunt rudera, nisi quod in superna planitie circulus ex lapidibus collectus, et lapis limitaneus tribus cochlearibus incisus notabilis appareat", und Heim setzt erläuternd hinzu: „Dieser Grenzstein ist von ziemlicher Größe oder Umfang, oben darauf ist eine Schüssel, in welcher drei Löffel liegen, gehauen; anzuzeigen, daß derselbe 3 Ämter unterscheide, als das Amt Lichtenberg, Amt Kaltennordheim und Amt Sand — (jetzt Meiningen) — und fährt scherzend fort: „sodann, wann etwa die 3 Herren Beamten bey einer Grenz-Beziehung wollten eine Suppe verzehren, ein jeder sich auf den Stein bey die Schüssel setzen und dabey seine Füße auf seinem Amts-Territorio könne ausruhen lassen."

Zu Ditmars und auch zu Heims Zeiten also war noch ein großer Stein auf der höchsten Stelle der Umwallung vorhanden, dessen Vorhandensein Binder, der in der Umwallung eine Kultus- und Opferstätte erblickt, fälschlich auch jetzt noch anzunehmen scheint. „Der Block in jenem

---

1) Man hat gegen die Ansicht, eine Burg habe den Berggipfel gekrönt, geltend gemacht, daß sich kein einziger Überrest eines Bauwerks auf dem Berge vorfinde; es ist dieser Grund deshalb hinfällig, weil noch im 4. und 5. Jahrhundert unserer Zeitrechnung die Innen-bauten der Höfe — Burgen — nur aus Holz errichtet waren.

Steinring", sagt er, „ist jedenfalls der Opferstein gewesen, und die schüsselförmige Vertiefung . . . . dürfte zum Auf- fangen des Blutes der geopferten Tiere, oder Menschen gedient haben."

Dieser große Stein auf dem höchsten Punkte der Um- wallung, von jeder Stelle derselben sichtbar, solange der Gipfel unbewaldet war, ist heutzutage nicht mehr vorhanden, und niemand ist imstande, über den Verbleib oder das Schicksal desselben Kunde zu geben, wenn sich auch die Erinnerung an den „großen Stein" bei den Umwohnern noch erhalten hat. Was aber heute von den Bewohnern der umliegenden Dörfer als „der große Stein" bezeichnet wird, ist eine zu Tage tretende Basaltfelsmasse, auf dem Ost- abhange des Berges, außerhalb des Kringels gelegen.

Jetzt befindet sich auf der höchsten Stelle der Um- wallung ein neuer Landesgrenzstein zwischen Sachsen-Mei- ningen und Sachsen-Weimar.

Der Verfasser, der 4 Jahre lang zum Zwecke der Landesvermessung in Wohlmuthausen stationiert war, kam zu der Überzeugung, daß sich in den Protokollen über frühere Landesgrenzbegehungen Aufzeichnungen über den verschwundenen Stein vorfinden würden. Herr Professor Koch in Meiningen, der mich auch später in meinen Nach- forschungen freundlichst unterstützte, verschaffte mir Ab- schriften von Begehungsprotokollen aus dem Archive des Herzoglichen Landratsamts in Meiningen, in welchen dieser sogen. große Stein erwähnt wird. In dem Protokoll vom 28. Juni 1837 heißt es: „Die Grenzbeziehung begann auf der Höhe der Duisburg am 1. Stein. Nr. 1 ein alter Stein, auf dem Kopf abgeschlagen (mit unkenntlicher Bezeichnung, und sind daran noch Spuren von Nr. 42 vorhanden), stehend am Anfang der Flurgrenze zwischen Oberkatz und Wohl- muthhausen auf dem sogen. Kringel."

In einem anderen Protokolle vom 6. Aug. 1845, in welchem auf eine frühere Grenzbegehung vom 31. Juli 1834 Bezug genommen wird, heißt es betreffs des vorerwähnten

Steins Nr. 1 „zwischen den Markungen Wohlmuthhausen,
Oberkatz und Aschenhausen": „Der Punkt wurde heute
anerkannt, der alte Stein ausgehoben und ein neuer be-
hauener, oben abgerundeter Sandstein, auf der einen Seite
S. W. E., auf der anderen S. M., eingesetzt etc.". Dieser
Stein ist der jetzt noch vorhandene.

Es ist also damals (1845) der von Ditmar und Heim
erwähnte große Stein mit ausgehauener schüsselförmiger
Vertiefung (die allerdings stark beschädigt war) entfernt
worden. Das Protokoll von 1834, dessen Abschrift mir
aus dem Archiv der Großherzoglichen Bezirksdirektion in
Dermbach mitgeteilt wurde, weist wieder auf eine im Ge-
meindearchiv in Oberkatz befindliche Abschrift einer Grenz-
beschreibung vom 18. Sept. 1669 hin. In dieser, mir ebenfalls durch die Freundlichkeit des Herrn Professor Koch,
der sich deshalb selbst nach Oberkatz begeben, zugänglichen
Abschrift heißt es S. 110: „Zum Fünfften: „Grenzet unsere
Fluhrmarkung gegen Niedergang an deß Junkern von
Speßart seine Fluhrmarkung zu Aschenhaußen, derowegen
den 4. February" Anno 1661 das erste mahl[1]), sodann den
18. Septembris Anno 1669 wiederumb begangen, vnd weilen
solche Fluhrmarkung gar Eckicht, nachfolgend nicht allein
alle Stein, so noch gestanden, sondern auch, wo Stein
gemangeldt, Neue Eingesetzet, vnd wie sie befunden vnd wo
sie stehen vfgesetzet."

„Erstlich ein gehaubener Eck-Stein, oben auf der Diß-
burgk, so nicht allein zwischen vnß, vnd dem von Speßart,
sondern auch gegen den Wohlmutheußern die Fluhrmarkung
scheidet, Zum Andern zwey Neue Stein an der Dießburgk
herab auff den Ellern Eingesetzet" etc. etc.

Es ist demnach dieser von Ditmar und Heim erwähnte
„gehaubene" Stein im Jahre 1661 schon vorhanden gewesen,
keinesfalls aber ist es, wie Binder annimmt der ursprüng-

---

1) Das erste Mal wahrscheinlich nach den Wirren und Greueln
des 30-jähr. Krieges.

liche Opferstein, der sicher ein behauener Stein nicht gewesen ist.

Durch örtliche Nachgrabungen glaubte der Verfasser einen sicheren Anhalt über den Zweck, den der Steinwall gehabt, zu gewinnen. Etwa in der Mitte desselben befindet sich eine, auch aus dem beigegebenen Kärtchen ersichtliche, Stelle ohne Baumwuchs, bloß von Moos und Pflanzen bedeckt, auf welcher der Boden feucht scheint, als ringsum, weshalb dieselbe für ehemals Sumpf oder Moor gehalten werden konnte, wie man es ja des öfteren an der Rhön trifft. Diese Stelle erschien zur Nachgrabung am günstigsten. Eine solche hat nun in Verbindung mit Herrn Professor Koch der Verfasser an gedachtem Platze vorgenommen. An fünf verschiedenen Stellen wurden Gruben in einer Breite von ca. 1 m, bei etwa 2—2^1/$_2$ m Länge und bis zu einer Tiefe von 1^1/$_2$ m ausgeworfen, ohne daß sich das Geringste vorgefunden hat. Eine nach Angabe von Bewohnern in Wohlmuthausen schon vor ungefähr 30 Jahren durch einen Ungenannten vorgenommene Nachgrabung auf dem Kringel, deren Spuren sich noch erkennen ließen, soll ebenfalls ohne Resultat verlaufen sein. Auch die in großer Anzahl vorhandenen Dachsgruben an verschiedenen Stellen der Umwallung, haben ebenfalls nie etwas an Waffen, Knochen, Scherben etc. zu Tage gefördert.

Diese negativen Resultate verstärken die Annahme, daß wir hier eine große Kultus- und Thingstätte vor uns haben. Wäre der Ringwall ein Überrest von Wohnstätten, oder hätte irgend ein Kampf auf dem Berggipfel stattgefunden, dessen Resultat die Zerstörung des Ringwalls gewesen, so würden sich wohl noch Waffen, oder Waffenstücke, oder sonstige Überreste bei den Ausgrabungen etc. vorgefunden haben. Diese Annahme erleidet auch keine Störung durch die ortsübliche Bezeichnung Diesburg. In einem Vortrage: „Ein Streifzug durch das mittelalterliche Weimar" im Wartburgs-Herold Bd. I sagt O. v. Franke: „Die Altenburg (bei Weimar) ist weiter nichts als eine hundertfach unter diesem oder

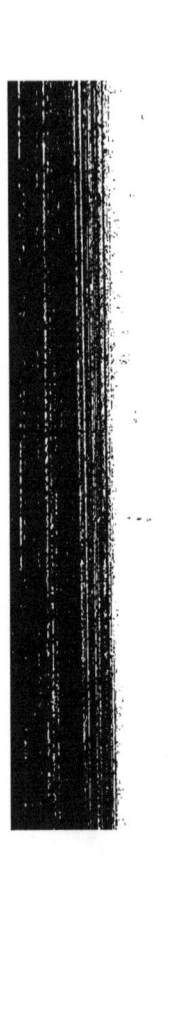

ähnlichem Namen vorkommende alte heidnische, m e i s t
b e f e s t i g t e, Kultusstätte, wie wir sie in Verbindung mit
„B u r g" beispielsweise bei Hetschburg, Oettern und Mel-
lingen, — Hainburg — als „Burg" schlechtweg bei Ober-
grunstedt finden." Die Altenburg in Merseburg, jetzt
Kirche mit Kirchhof, ist auch ohne jeden Zweifel eine alte
heidnische Kultusstätte gewesen. Auf Befestigung deutet
die Bezeichnung „Burg" unbedingt, und wir erkennen, daß
diese heiligen Stätten befestigt waren, zum Schutze des
Heiligtums selbst wie der Bewohner, die wahrscheinlich in
Zeiten der Gefahr innerhalb der Befestigung Zuflucht
suchten. Die Befestigung der heiligen Stätten hat sich
auch in die christliche Zeit hinübergetragen, wo überall
die um die Kirche herumliegenden Kirchhöfe befestigt, d. h.
wenigstens mit Mauern umgeben waren, und in Kriegszeiten gar oft die letzte Zufluchtsstätte der Bewohner, wie
nicht minder der kämpfenden Scharen, bildeten; in die
Nähe des Heiligtums flüchteten die Bewohner ihre Hab-
seligkeiten. B u r g ähnliche Befestigungen erblicken wir an
der Rhön besonders in Ostheim und in Walldorf bei Meiningen.

Wessen Dienste die Kultusstätte gewidmet gewesen,
zeigt uns der Name des Berges, der schon von Grimm als
Kultusstätte bezeichnet wird. Mannhardt: „Die Götter der
deutschen und nordischen Völker", sagt S. 262: „Der
älteste unter allen germanischen Göttern: goth. Tius, ags.
Tiw, ahd. Zio, altn. Tyr, war der Gott des lichten Himmels-
gewölbes, der Vater Himmel, welcher dem Laut und Begriffe
nach dem vedischen D y a n s, griechischen Z e u s genau
entsprach. Nach ihm führte der dritte Wochentag bei den
Angelsachsen den Namen Tiwesdag (engl. Tuesday): in
Schwaben und Bayern heißt er Ziestag (ahd. Ziwestac) und
auch unser D i e n s t ag ist aus Tag des Tiu verderbt. Das
Wenige, was wir von dem Dienste dieses Gottes wissen,
berichtet uns Tacitus. Zwischen Elbe und Oder wohnte
im ersten Jahrhundert der Hauptstamm der Sueven, Sem-

XXII.   17

nonen, d. h. Feßler, genannt. „Für die ältesten und edelsten
der Sueven", sagt der römische Geschichtsschreiber, „geben
sich die Semnonen aus. Zur festgesetzten Zeit kommen in
einem Walde, der durch der Väter Weihe und altherkömmliche Scheu geheiligt ist, alle Völkerschaften desselben
Blutes vermittelst Gesandschaften zusammen und begehen
nach barbarischem Gebrauche schauderhafte Weihen."...
Die Semnonen wanderten später nach Süden aus, und hier
finden wir sie am Ende der Völkerwanderung als Juthungen,
d. h. „die echten Abkömmlinge des Gottes", und als
Schwaben, nördlich vom Bodensee wieder. Ihren National-
gott haben sie in die neuen Sitze mitgebracht, und wir
lernen seinen Namen kennen. Es ist Zio. Denn die
Schwaben werden in Glossen des 9. und 10. Jahrhunderts
Ziuwarî, d. h. Männer des Zio, genannt, und die Stadt
Augsburg führte vom Kulte des Gottes den Namen Zies-
buro (Stadt des Zio). Ein Tiesdorf kömmt in nieder-
schlesischer Elbgegend vor, ein Ziesberg liegt im Weimarischen" [1]).

Daß diese Kultusstätte eine besonders hervorragende
gewesen sein muß, läßt sich nicht nur aus der eigentümlichen
Lage des Berges, sondern vornehmlich aus der Größe der
Umwallung erkennen, die bei ca. 15000 qm Flächengehalt
leicht bis zu 8000 Menschen zu fassen im stande war.
Gerade gegen eine solche bedeutende Kultusstätte mußte

---

1) Es ist dies unser Diesberg. Etwa 1½ Stunden von demselben entfernt liegt zwischen Kaltensundheim, Mittelsdorf uud
Reichenhausen eine Höhe, Zeunsberg oder „am Zeunsberg" genannt,
ein Diedorf ebenfalls in dortiger Gegend, im Feldagrunde, 1 Stunde
nördlich von Kaltennordheim, ein Dietlas gleichfalls im Feldagrunde.
Sollten uns diese Namen nicht vielleicht den Weg zeigen, den die
Semnonen auf ihrer Wanderung von der Elbe nach Westen und
Süden genommen? Haben nach dem Berichte des Tacitus die Semnonen noch im 1. Jahrhundert unserer Zeitrechnung an der Elbe
gesessen, so ließe sich mit einiger Wahrscheinlichkeit die Errichtung
des Heiligtums — Steinwall — auf dem Diesberge in das Ende des
ersten oder zu Anfang des zweiten Jahrhunderts setzen.

sich in besonderem Grade der Religionseifer der christlichen Missionare und Priester richten, und sie nahmen vorzüglich auf dem höchsten Punkte des Ringes, der Nordseite, auf welchem sich wohl der Opferstein befand, eine so gründliche Zerstörung vor, daß diese Seite der Umwallung wenig mehr als ein großes Trümmerfeld von Basaltsteinen zeigt; auch die übrigen Seiten des Berges, namentlich die Westseite, sind mit Basalttrümmern bedeckt. Daraus läßt sich, außer aus dem oben schon erwähnten Grunde, wohl mit Recht schließen, daß der von Ditmar und Heim beschriebene umfangreiche Stein auf dem Gipfel der Umwallung nicht mehr der ursprüngliche Opferstein gewesen sein kann, für den ihn Binder ansieht, der ebenso unrichtig, den Namen Diesberg von „dissen" (Hegedissen) ableitend, in ihm den Blocksberg der Rhön erblicken will. Wenn außerdem Binder in seinem Aufsatz über das Amt Lichtenberg einer dem Diesberg analogen Opferstätte und Umwallung im kleinen bei Urspringen Erwähnung tut, so irrt er auch darin, wie ich in einer späteren Arbeit nachweisen werde.

Auf eine andere, der auf dem Diesberg ähnliche, Umwallung machte mich Herr Professor Koch in Meiningen aufmerksam. Er schrieb: „Im Juni d. J. (1902) besuchte ich mit einigen Freunden zum erstenmal den Gangolfsberg, einen mit der hohen Rhön durch einen ziemlich flachen Sattel verbundenen Basaltberg bei Urspringen bez. Oberelsbach. Dabei entdeckte ich einen alten Basaltwall, der sich auf einem Teil des Nordrandes, sowie des westlichen Bergabhanges hinzieht. In den landläufigen Rhönbüchern ist nichts davon zu lesen, und weder der bayerische Förster, zu dessen Revier der Gangolfsberg gehört, noch der Pfarrer von Oberelsbach, der im vorigen Jahre einen kleinen Aufsatz über den Gangolfsberg veröffentlichte, hatten eine Ahnung von der Existenz dieses doch ganz ausgeprägten, dem auf der Dißburg ähnlichen Walles. Im September (1902) suchte ich denselben noch zweimal auf. Dabei stellte es sich heraus, daß die Umwallung gerade da sich findet, wo sich der Berg am leichtesten ersteigen läßt; sie diente somit augenscheinlich zum Schutze des Gipfels.

Bei einem freien Ausblick vom Nordrand des Gangolfsberggipfels nach Norden zu ergab sich die überraschende Tatsache, daß die Dißburg im ganzen Umfang ihrer Südhälfte frei in der Gesichtslinie liegt, und zwar so merkwürdig frei, als wenn ein rechts und links von mäßigen Erhebungen eingefaßtes Hochtal die beiden Berge verbände. Von der Dißburg aus wird jedenfalls nur der Gipfel des Gangolfsbergs zu sehen sein, da dem letzteren ein Ausläufer der hohen Rhön vorgelagert ist. Aber das genügte auch vollständig, um etwaige Zeichen von dem einen zum anderen Gipfel auszutauschen. Denn in Anbetracht der eigenartigen Befestigung auf dem Gangolfsberge, komme ich zu der Ansicht, daß die Gipfel, sowohl dieses Berges wie der Dißburg befestigt waren, um in erster Linie Beobachtungsposten zum Schutz zu dienen, die dort droben Umschau halten mußten, und mittels verabredeter Zeichen sich gegenseitig Nachrichten über den Stand der Dinge übermittelten."

Der Wall auf dem Gangolfsberge — nicht R i n g wall, denn er bedeckt bloß die Nord- und einen Teil der Westseite — den ich selbst in Begleitung des Herrn Professor Koch besuchte, scheint mir nicht durchaus in Bezug auf seinen Zweck mit dem auf dem Diesberge verglichen werden zu können, da er einen Abschluß nicht hat, und allerdings wohl l e d i g l i c h zu Schutz- und Verteidigungszwecken gedient haben mag. Ein ganz regelmäßiger Bauüberrest am Nordrande des Steinwalls auf dem Gangolfsberge gehört, wenn wenn er auch nicht Überrest einer Klause ist, offenbar einer späteren Zeit an.

Hoffentlich führt Herr Professor Koch die geäußerte Absicht, einen Hinweis auf diese Basaltumwallung zu veröffentlichen, recht bald aus.

VII

Neues über den Sturz des Thüringischen Königreichs.

Von

Prof. Dr. Hermann Größler
in Eisleben.

(Mit einem Kärtchen der Gegend von Runibergun.)

Die „Studien zur Geschichte des Unterganges des alten Thüringischen Königreichs im Jahre 531 n. Chr." von Herrn Dr. Pelka kann ich nicht in die Öffentlichkeit gehen lassen, ohne zu ihnen Stellung zu nehmen[1]), da ich weder seiner Methode noch seinen Ergebnissen zustimmen kann. Da mir aber durch den Herrn Herausgeber räumlich enge Schranken gezogen sind, so werde ich mich möglichst kurz fassen und nicht auf alle Einzelheiten eingehen, die Pelka an meiner Auffassung bemängelt. Es ist dies aber auch nicht nötig, da ich schon durch Erörterung der Hauptfragen zu einer hinlänglich klaren Entscheidung zu gelangen hoffe und die meisten Einwände Pelkas gegenstandslos werden, wenn die Unhaltbarkeit seines Standpunktes überhaupt erwiesen ist. Ein weiterer Grund mich kurz zu fassen, ist der, daß ich auch noch einiges Neue vorzubringen habe.

Zur Kennzeichnung meines Standpunktes bemerke ich im voraus, daß nach meiner Ansicht selbst durch noch so umständliche, ja haarspaltende Untersuchungen über Beschaffenheit, Ächtheit, Alter, Verwandtschaft und Benutzung

---

[1]) Herr Prof. Dr. Größler erhielt zu diesem Zwecke von der Redaktion die Revisionsbogen der Abhandlung Pelkas. Bem. des Herausgebers.

der „Quellen" schwerlich etwas Neues, unsere Erkenntnis
Förderndes zu ermitteln sein wird, da jede Stellungnahme
auf diesem Gebiete angreifbar ist und\ jeder, der diesen
Weg einschlägt, Gefahr läuft, unter dem Anschein der
Objektivität recht subjektiven Phantasieen zu verfallen,
denn es kommt eben darauf an, was einer für möglich,
wahrscheinlich, selbstverständlich oder unzweifelhaft hält.

Den Anlaß und die Notwendigkeit seiner „Studien etc."
findet Pelka (S. 167) in der „vollständigen Verwirrung",
die nach seiner Meinung auf diesem Forschungsgebiete
herrscht. Wenn er unter dieser Verwirrung Vielheit der
Auffassungen versteht, zu deren Vermehrung auch er das
Seinige beiträgt, so hat er recht. Versteht er aber darunter
Verwirrung aller bisher aufgestellten Auffassungen selbst,
so dürfte eine solche Behauptung als eine starke Über-
hebung bezeichnet werden, die nur durch den Nachweis,
daß er selbst volle Klarheit zu schaffen vermag, gerechtfertigt werden könnte.

Doch nun zur Sache. Die Verwirrung ist nach Pelka
deshalb eine vollständige, weil man es bisher nicht für
nötig gehalten habe, „mit den Quellen eine reinliche
Scheidung vorzunehmen". (Soll übrigens wohl heißen „eine
reinliche Scheidung der Quellen vorzunehmen"?) Diese
Behauptung ist falsch, denn es sind ja verschiedene Versuche der Art gemacht worden; die Hoffnung aber auf
einen Erfolg in dieser Richtung dürfte sich als eine eitle
erweisen, weil eine reinliche, d. h. keinen Zweifel zurück-
lassende Scheidung der Quellen unmöglich ist, oder die
erwünschte „reinliche Scheidung" doch nur in der Weise
stattfinden könnte, daß man entweder nur die fränkischen
Quellen maßgebend sein läßt, die von der Sachsenhilfe nichts
wissen oder wissen wollen, oder nur die sächsischen, die
denn doch unverkennbar gut unterrichtet sind. Um so
gespannter ist man natürlich darauf, wie denn Pelka die
von ihm in Aussicht gestellte reinliche Scheidung zu stande
bringen wird. Aber sehr bald wird man zu seinem Er-

staunen gewahr, daß dieser Anwalt einer reinlichen Scheidung nicht nur von den fränkischen, sondern auch von den
sächsischen Quellen Gebrauch macht und aus ihnen, als
hätte er den Lorenz und mir gemachten Vorwurf des
„gemischten Verfahrens" ganz vergessen, ebenfalls ganz
munter heraus nimmt, „was in sein Schema paßt"; ja
schließlich, anstatt sich mit einer Scheidung zu begnügen,
noch eine dritte Quellengruppe oder zum mindesten noch
eine neue Quelle aufstellt, nämlich den Anonymus de origine
Suevorum, beziehungsweise das dieser Schrift zu Grunde
liegende „Heldenlied".

Mit diesem Heldenliede nun hat es nach Pelka folgende
Bewandtnis: Er nimmt nämlich (S. 176) an, daß der Quedlinburger Annalist und der später schreibende Anonymus
eine gemeinsame Quelle gehabt haben, und weiter (S. 177),
daß diese Quelle auch Widukind vorgelegen habe. Also
haben nach ihm alle drei Berichte dieselbe Urquelle (S. 179
und 185), und zwar eine deutsche, da zwar der Inhalt
übereinstimmend sei, nicht aber der Wortlaut. Sei es aber
eine deutsche, so könne es nur ein sächsisches
Heldenlied gewesen sein. Im besondern sei anzunehmen,
daß alle Stellen der erwähnten drei Berichte, welche miteinander übereinstimmten oder wenigstens sich gegenseitig
nicht völlig ausschlössen, diesem Heldenliede angehörten;
die abweichenden aber seien lokale Varianten.

Neu ist der Grundgedanke dieser Behauptung nicht.
Wenigstens ist schon früher in gewissen Teilen des Widu-
kindschen Berichtes und auch der Quedlinburger Annalen
die Wiedergabe eines epischen Gedichts erblickt worden.
Die Frage ist nur, wie die mannigfachen Abweichungen
der sächsischen Berichte zu erklären sind, und welche
Glaubwürdigkeit man ihnen beimessen kann. Wenn Pelka
sagt, die Punkte, betreffs deren sie voneinander abweichen,
seien „lokale Varianten", so ist damit nichts erklärt. Läge
wirklich eine gemeinsame Quelle vor, aus der alle drei
geschöpft haben, so müßte doch wohl eine durchgängige

Übereinstimmung in allen Hauptzügen und in der Fassung
der Gedanken wahrzunehmen sein, die aber Pelka nicht
hat nachweisen können. Dagegen läßt sich die Verschieden-
heit begreifen, wenn man annimmt, daß nicht bloß Ein
Heldengedicht die für den sächsischen Stamm so wichtigen
Begebenheiten besungen hat, sondern mehrere. Aus der
Tiefe des sächsischen Volkstums heraus werden eben verschiedene selbständige Gestaltungen desselben
Stoffs an verschiedenen Orten hervorgegangen sein,
die sich im wesentlichen auf die Mitteilungen von Teil-
nehmern an den Kämpfen stützten, und deren Urgestalt
daher bis in die Zeit der in ihnen erzählten Begebenheiten
zurückreichen wird. Woran ein solcher Sänger oder seine
Gewährsmänner nicht teilgenommen, das konnte er natürlich
auch nicht besingen. Diese Volksepen aber dienten bei
dem Mangel geschichtlicher Lehrbücher und Unterrichts-
stätten den Zeitgenossen als zeitgemäßer Ersatz für unsere
heutigen Zeitungen und ihren Nachkommen als Lehrmittel
der Geschichte der Vergangenheit. Je nach dem Orte ihres
Entstehens und der Kenntnis und Urteilsfähigkeit ihres
Verfassers konnten diese Dichtungen natürlich mancher
Trübung, manchem Irrtume unterliegen, zumal sie zunächst
Jahrhunderte hindurch nur mündlich fortgepflanzt wurden.
Die sächsischen Berichterstatter können also, jeder für sich
aus einer andern epischen Urquelle geschöpft haben. In
diesem Falle wird sowohl die Übereinstimmung in den
meisten Hauptbegebenheiten, wie auch die Abweichung
in Einzelheiten (die „lokalen Varianten" Pelkas) begreiflich.

Die sodann notwendig sich erhebende Frage, welche
Glaubwürdigkeit denn nun den sächsischen Berichten beizumessen sei, wird von Pelka dahin
beantwortet, daß sie von vornherein geringeren Glauben
verdienten, eine Behauptung, die er freilich nicht begründet,
daß aber ein völlig absprechendes Verdammungsurteil doch
nicht gerechtfertigt sei. Namentlich müsse man sich erinnern, daß historisch bedeutsam gewordene Örtlichkeiten

nicht so leicht vom Volke vergessen würden, beiläufig
bemerkt, eine Tatsache, die nicht erst von Pelka entdeckt
ist, auf die vielmehr vorher ich[1]) hingewiesen hatte. Er
werde also, fährt Pelka fort, die in dem Heldenliede vorkommenden Örtlichkeiten und Schlachten bis auf weiteres
als historisch betrachten, das Lied dagegen nur als bestätigende, nicht aber als grundlegende Quelle.

Ist das nun eine reinliche Scheidung der Quellen?
Wissen wir nun, ob die sächsischen Berichte irgend welchen
geschichtlichen Wert haben? Pelka will es offenbar mit
den Franken halten, ohne aber zuvor ihre Glaubwürdigkeit,
im besonderen die Gregors von Tours, kritisch untersucht
zu haben, jenes Berichterstatters, der nicht nur bewußt die
Sachsenhilfe verschweigt, vermutlich weil er nicht wagte,
mißliebige Dinge, die dem fränkischen Nationalstolz wehe
taten, zu berichten, sondern auch zweifellose Irrtümer berichtet, wie z. B. die meuchlerische Beseitigung Berthars
durch Irminfried. Andererseits kann er sich der Bedeutung
der sächsischen Berichte nicht ganz verschließen. Aber
obwohl er wenigstens die in ihnen erwähnten Örtlichkeiten
für geschichtlich bedeutsam erklärt, bringt er es doch,
diesem seinem Zugeständnis zuwider, fertig, zu behaupten,
der Quedlinburger Annalist habe die Schlachten in pago
Maerstem und an der Ocker frei erfunden. Was bleibt
denn dann von seinem Zugeständnisse noch übrig?

Aber warum wird er dem von ihm verkündeten Grund-
satze untreu? Weil er sich von seiner irrigen Voraussetzung nicht losreißen kann, daß allein die Franken maßgebend seien, und daß auf den Ronnebergen bei Vitzenburg
die erste Schlacht stattgefunden habe, obwohl die fränkischen
Berichterstatter diesen Namen nicht einmal nennen. Ich
frage daher nochmals: Ist das eine reinliche Scheidung
der Quellen? Ist das nicht vielmehr der höchste Gipfel
der Verwirrung? Und welchen Zweck hat denn überhaupt

---

1) Zeitschr., Bd. XIX, 1897, S. 19.

Pelkas Versuch, eine gemeinsame Quelle der sächsischen Berichte nachzuweisen, wenn er weder diesen noch jener irgend welche Beweiskraft zugestehen will? Dann hätte er sich die ganze Mühe sparen können. Ich meinerseits spreche allerdings den sächsischen Berichten, die nach meiner Ansicht aus m e h r e r e n älteren Heldenliedern geflossen sind, eine gewisse Beweiskraft zu. Gewiß ist in solchen Volksepen manches frei erfunden, ja sogar Mythen können eingewebt sein; trotzdem aber können geschichtliche Tatsachen in ihnen treu überliefert sein, und zwar um so treuer, je entschiedener der Bericht a u f e i n e b e s t i m m t e Ö r t = l i c h k e i t sich bezieht. Wir haben dafür ein recht beweiskräftiges Beispiel in dem angelsächsischen Epos „Beowulf". Dort steht im zehnten Gesange folgender Bericht (nach Hans von Wolzogens Übersetzung) über den Tod des Gautenkönigs Hygelac (ahd. Hugileich):

> „Wahrlich, nicht war es das wenigst schwere
> Handgemenge, wo H u g i l e i c h sank;
> Hin gab da im Kampfe der gautische König,
> Der liebe Volksfürst, im L a n d e d e r F r i e s e n,
> Des Rodilo Erbe, den Rottrunk des Eisens,
> Vom Beile getroffen. Doch Bärwelf entrann
> Durch seine Kraft, die Sundstraße nutzend,
> Und trug noch am Arme einunddreißig
> Maschige Streithemden mit an den Strand.
> Da erwuchs den C h a t t w a r e n nur wenig Ruhm
> Aus dem Fußgefecht; die zuvor ihm die Schilde
> Entgegen gekehrt, nun entgingen nicht viele
> Dem schlagfertigen Helden, die Heimat zu schauen."

Und im zwölften Gesange spricht der Bote, der seinen Landsleuten die Nachricht vom Tode Beowulfs bringt, unter Bezugnahme auf dasselbe Ereignis die Befürchtung aus:

> „Das Land erwarte
> Blutige Zeiten, sobald da draußen
> F r a n k e n u n d F r i e s e n der Fall unsres Fürsten
> Bekannt geworden! Wir waren im Kampfe
> Fast stets mit den Hugen, seit H u g i l e i c h gesteuert
> Zum Friesenlande mit den Leuten zu Schiff,

Wo auf der Wahlstatt ihn warf der Chattwaren
Eilig bereite Übermacht,
Daß der Held in der Brünne sich beugen mußte,
Im Fußkampf gefällt. Wir empfingen nie mehr
Gaben vom Fürsten; auch gönnten uns fürder
Wenig Milde die Merowinge!"

Dagegen halte man nun folgende Stelle aus Gregors
Historia Francorum, Lib. III, cap. 3. zum Jahre etwa 515
(Mon. Germ. SS. rer. Merow. I, p. 111):

„His ita gestis Dani cum rege suo nomine Chlochi-
laichum (rectius Chochilaichum) evectu navale per mare
Gallias appetunt. Egressique ad terras, pagum unum
de regno Theudorici devastant atque captivant onera-
tisque navibus tam de captivis quam de reliquis spoliis
reverti ad patriam cupiunt; sed rex eorum in litus resedebat,
donec navis alto mare conpraehenderent, ipse deinceps secu-
turus. Quod cum Theudorico nuntiatum fuisset, quod sci-
licet regio eius fuerit ab extraneis devastata, Theudobertum
filium suum in illis partibus cum valido exercitu ac magno
armorum apparatu direxit. Qui, interfectu rege, hostibus navali proelio superatis oppraemit omnemque rapinam
terrae restituit."

Wer sähe hier nicht, daß beide, das Epos und der
Geschichtschreiber, im wesentlichen übereinstimmend, dasselbe Ereignis darstellen, daß also das Epos eine anderweit
beglaubigte Nachricht von einem geschichtlichen Ereignisse
bringt und insofern genauer bringt, als der Geschichtschreiber, als es die Erinnerung an die Gegend, in der
der feindliche Zusammenstoß stattgefunden, treuer festgehalten hat? Und wie es hier geschehen, so können, ja
werden auch in den sächsischen Heldengedichten wirklich
geschichtliche Ereignisse der Nachkommenschaft treu überliefert worden sein, so daß zwar Einzelzüge abweichen
mögen, die eigentliche Tatsache aber als fester geschichtlicher Kern gelten darf.

Was aber nun die Entstehungszeit dieser Helden-
gedichte oder des nach Pelkas Auffassung als Urquelle

der sächsischen Überlieferung benutzten einzigen Helden-
gedichts betrifft, so habe ich meine Ansicht bereits ausgesprochen; Pelka dagegen ist der Meinung, es müsse
zwischen den Jahren 919 und 967 entstanden sein. Das
Jahr 967 ist als terminus ad quem nicht anzuzweifeln,
wenn Widukind aus dem Gedichte geschöpft hat; um so
mehr aber das Jahr 919 als der terminus a quo. Schon
an sich ist es kaum denkbar, daß erst im 10. Jahrhundert es
einem Dichter eingefallen sein soll, das größte Ereignis des
6. Jahrhunderts auf sächsischem Boden zu besingen.
Gedichte, die solche geschichtliche Katastrophen behandeln,
muß man sich als unmittelbar oder bald nach jenen entstanden denken, denn nur da war das nötige Interesse
für die in ihnen erzählten Begebenheiten vorhanden, was
natürlich nicht ausschließt, daß später mit Rücksicht auf
spätere Hörer und Zustände Zutaten und Änderungen stattgefunden haben. Warum aber erst nach 919? Weil die
Äußerung Irings (nach Widukind I, 9): „eos (Saxones) procul
dubio esse, qui Francorum imperium quandoque
destruerent" nach Pelka ein vaticinium post-eventum
ist, welches die Tatsache im Auge habe, daß in diesem
Jahre die Herrschaft endgültig von den Franken auf die
Sachsen überging. Und diese Deutung gibt derselbe Pelka,
der an anderen Stellen, wenn auch nicht mit besonderem
Glück, größten Wert auf genaue Deutung des Wortsinnes
legt (vgl. die gekünstelten Erörterungen über die Bedeutung
von persequentes auf S. 175 und 176), hier aber gar nicht
zu bemerken scheint, daß imperium destruere eine höchst
unzutreffende Bezeichnung für den Übergang der Führung
von den Franken auf die Sachsen ist, da ja der Herzog
der Sachsen von einer fränkischen Gesandtschaft um Über-
nahme der Führung ersucht wird und der Übergang der
Krone von den Franken auf die Sachsen in der friedlichsten
Weise stattgefunden hat. Von einer Destruktion der fränkischen Herrschaft und einem vaticinium post eventum kann
also wirklich keine Rede sein. Alles, was Pelka auf diesem

schwachen Grunde aufbaut, hat natürlich keinen Halt. Er
selbst empfindet das, da er wenigstens erwägt, ob man
nicht an den großen Sieg der Sachsen über Chlothar I.
denken müsse, wenn Iring davon spreche, daß die Sachsen,
illud genus hominum indomabile et ad omnem laborem
durabile, zu einer Gefahr für die fränkische Herrschaft
werden könnten, ein Gedanke, den er aber alsbald nur aus
dem Grunde verwirft, weil „dieser Erfolg nur ein vorübergehender" gewesen sei. Ich halte solches Nachrechnen
überhaupt für überflüssig und ergebnislos, da mir feststeht,
daß in jener Zeit, wo es noch keine nach unverbrauchten
Stoffen suchenden Dichter gab, ein Gedicht nur geschaffen
worden ist, um gleichzeitige Ereignisse oder solche, die
nur wenig zurücklagen, zu Kenntnis weiterer Kreise zu
bringen.

Da Pelka es für nötig hält, mich auf eine nach seiner
Meinung richtigere Übersetzung des Wortlauts hinzuweisen,
so will ich gleich hier über seine mit dem Anschein philo-
logischer Akribie auftretenden Übersetzungen noch einiges
bemerken. S. 174 übersetzt er „victum quaeritans supra
litus fluvii dioti" „Nahrung suchend oberhalb des Flusses",
was gar keinen Sinn gibt, während es doch nur übersetzt
werden kann „am Ufer des Flusses, entsprechend dem fran-
zösischen sur Marne, sur Aube; S. 169 belehrt er mich
freundlichst, daß obvium habere aliquem heiße „jemandem
begegnen". Aber wer bezweifelt denn das? Und was
läßt sich daraus zu Ungunsten meiner Erklärung schließen?
Der fragliche Satz Aimoins lautet ja: „profectus itaque
(Theodoricus) in Toringiam obvium habuit Hermenefredum".
Da muß ich denn doch fragen, ob ihm die Bedeutung von
proficisci unbekannt ist. Proficisci bedeutet „sich fort-
machen, sich aufmachen, einen Marsch antreten"; also ist
der Satz zu übersetzen: „Auf dem Marsche nach Thüringen
begegnete er dem Hermenefried". Dieser Satz, welcher
also im wesentlichen dasselbe besagt, wie Widukinds „appropinquans terminis Thuringorum" und des Annalisten

„bello sibi occurentem", hätte schon aus sprachlichen Gründen ihn hindern müssen, die Ronneberge bei Nebra für den Ort des ersten Zusammenstoßes auszugeben, wozu dann freilich noch topische und psychologische Gründe kommen. Pelka bemerkt zwar spöttisch, als hätte ich etwas ganz Unerhörtes und Unhaltbares behauptet, ich .wüßte sogar die Furt zu zeigen, über die vor nunmehr fast 1400 Jahren die Franken gezogen seien, aber damit beweist er eben nur, daß er von dem Gewichte gerade solcher Beweisgründe eine recht unzulängliche Vorstellung hat. Gerade die örtlichen Verhältnisse gewähren den sichersten Anhalt für die Beurteilung geschichtlicher Fragen. Erst, wenn die Örtlichkeiten, die für eine Reihe geschichtlicher Begebenheiten in Frage kommen, festgelegt sind, kann der Verlauf der Begebenheiten selbst mit einiger Sicherheit beurteilt werden. Es gereichte mir daher zu nicht geringer Befriedigung, als ich einige Zeit nach dem Erscheinen meiner Abhandlung in der Einleitung zu Moltkes leider unvollendet gebliebenem Werke über Rom und seine Umgebung folgende, meine Forschungsmethode aufs schönste bestätigenden Bemerkungen des großen Feldherrn fand: „Geschichte und Ortskunde ergänzen sich, wie die Begriffe von Raum und Zeit. Die Örtlichkeit ist das von einer längst vergangenen Begebenheit übrig gebliebene Stück Wirklichkeit. Sie ist sehr oft der fossile Knochenrest, aus dem das Gerippe der Begebenheit sich herstellen läßt, und das Bild, welches die Geschichte in halb verwischten Zügen überliefert, tritt durch sie in klarer Anschauung hervor. Denn wenn auch die Jahrtausende nicht spurlos vorübergehen an der größten aller Ruinen, der Mutter Erde, wenn der Anbau die Oberfläche glättet, die Wälder verschwinden, die Bäche versiegen und tarpejische Felsen sich zu sanfteren Hängen ebnen, so sind doch alle diese Einwirkungen höchstens imstande, nur die Hautfarbe der alma mater zu verändern, ohne ihre Gesichtszüge unkenntlich zu machen." Und weiter: „Selbst wenn die Forschung eine Überlieferung nur noch als Fabel bestehen läßt, bezieht sich diese doch meist auf eine ganz bestimmte Örtlichkeit, welche der ursprüng- liche Erzähler im Auge hatte. Eine Erzählung kann geschichtlich unwahr und örtlieh vollkommen genau sein. . . . Die Aufgabe, welche wir uns stellen, wird nicht die sein, die Fabel von der Wirklichkeit zu scheiden, sondern beide mit derjenigen Örtlichkeit zu verbinden, auf welche sie sich jedesmal beziehen." Ganz im Geiste Moltkes, ob- wohl damals noch unbekannt mit seinen eben wieder- gegebenen Äußerungen, habe ich „aus dem fossilen Knochen- reste der Örtlichkeit" das Gerippe jener längst vergangenen Begebenheit des Thüringerkriegs herzustellen gesucht und bin der Meinung, daß diese Methode zu neuen und brauch- baren Ergebnissen geführt hat. Gewiß weiß auch ich, worauf Pelka mich aufmerksam machen zu müssen meint, daß Furten im Laufe der Zeit sich ändern können, aber doch nur, wenn die Bedingungen ihres Entstehens und ihrer Fortdauer sich geändert haben. Bei einem Plusse, der, wie das bei der Unstrut der Fall ist, zur Zeit des gewöhnlichen Wasserstandes 3—5 m Tiefe hat, können nur ganz bestimmte Stellen des Flußbettes in Frage kommen, und meine Auf- spürung eben dieser Durchgangsstellen verliert dadurch doch nicht an Beweiskraft, daß keiner vor mir auf den Gedanken gekommen ist, die Furten zu erkunden, die für die Feststellung des Ganges der Begebenheiten von aus- schlaggebender Bedeutung sind, und noch weniger dadurch, daß sie die Angaben gerade der sächsischen Quellen, auch des von Pelka bevorzugten Anonymus de origine Suevorum, in mich selbst überraschender Weise bestätigt haben.

In gleicher Weise nun, wie ich es betreffs der Furten getan, habe ich die Vereinbarkeit der verfehlten Annahme, die erste Schlacht habe auf den Ronnebergen bei Nebra stattgefunden, mit den örtlichen Verhältnissen dieses Ge- birgsstocks nachgeprüft. Ich kann allen, welche es be- zweifeln, daß jene Schlacht, in welcher die Thüringer ihre berittenen Gegner durch Anlegung von Gruben zu Falle

gebracht haben sollen, nicht auf den Ronnebergen bei
Nebra stattgefunden haben kann, und im besonderen Herrn
Dr. Pelka, nur empfehlen, diese Örtlichkeit durch den
Augenschein kennen zu lernen. Dann werden sie sehen,
daß dieser mächtige, von einer nur dünnen Erdschicht
bedeckte Sandsteinblock mit allseits steil abfallenden
Hängen als Ort einer Reiterschlacht und als geeignet zur
Anlage einer Reihe von Fallgruben überhaupt nicht in
Frage kommen kann. Gedankenlos, muß ich sagen, haben
alle Späteren die leichtfertige Behauptung des Leipziger
Professors Böhme nachgeschrieben, obwohl sich dieser mit
ganz allgemeinen Vermutungen begnügt und selbst zweifel-
haft ist, ob die ihm zugesandten Fundstücke von den
Ronnebergen der Zeit des Thüringischen Königreiches zugeschrieben werden können. Auf diesen Gewährsmann,
dessen Schrift Pelka gar nicht gelesen zu haben scheint,
sonst würde er ihm nicht solche Autorität zusprechen, und
die von ihm besehenen Funde, von denen nicht ein einziger
mehr nachweisbar vorhanden ist, darf man sich um so
weniger berufen, als die später auf den Ronnebergen und
namentlich auf ihrer südlichsten Erhebung, dem Bock,
gemachten Funde, welche ich bei Herrn Baron von Hell-
dorf auf dem Rittergute Zingst habe besichtigen können,
sämtlich teils der jüngeren Steinzeit, teils der ältesten und
mittleren Bronzezeit, also einer Zeit angehören, die von
der Schlacht bei Runibergun durch mindestens ein bis
zwei Jahrtausende getrennt ist, wie ich in meinem Führer
durch das Unstruttal (2. Aufl., S. 160, Freyburg, 1904 bei
Joh. Finke) mitgeteilt habe.

Zu den Gründen, die sich aus der Beschaffenheit der
Örtlichkeit ergeben, gesellt sich nun aber ein nicht minder
maßgebender psychologischer. Welcher unbefangene Be-
urteiler kann es wohl für möglich halten, daß der thüringische
König trotz der innumera multitudo seines Heeres stumpf-
sinnig bei Burgscheidungen gewartet hat, bis ihn die
Franken dort aufsuchten und auf den kaum 10 km in der

Luftlinie von Burgscheidungen entfernten Ronnebergeń zum Kampfe zwangen? Ein solches Verhalten wäre wohl denkbar nach einer oder mehreren verlorenen großen Schlachten, nicht aber vor irgend einer Schlacht. Das ist doch wohl so einleuchtend, daß es sich wirklich nicht verlohnt, darüber noch weitere Worte zu verlieren.

Auf die übrigen Einwände Pelkas und seine Versuche, meine Ausführungen zu erschüttern, glaube ich bei der Unhaltbarkeit der von ihm vertretenen Auffassung bezüglich der Lage von Runibergun vorläufig nicht weiter eingehen zu sollen, obwohl es nicht schwierig wäre, sie zu widerlegen, wenn ich auch seinem Fleiße meine Anerkennung nicht versagen kann. Wohl aber möchte ich nun noch Verschiedenes geltend machen, was geeignet ist, meine Behauptung, daß die erste Schlacht in der Nähe von Hannover stattgefunden haben müsse, zu bestätigen, weil schon dieser Nachweis genügt, die Unhaltbarkeit der Pelkaschen Auffassung darzutun.

Da in Deutschland eine beträchtliche Anzahl von Orten den Namen Ronneberg führt und auch bloß aus diesem Grunde ohne Rücksicht auf passende Lage viele von ihnen als die Stätte der Schlacht bei Runibergun in Anspruch genommen worden sind, so wird man fordern dürfen, daß irgend welche bedeutsamen Namen, Sagen oder Funde nachgewiesen werden, die es wahrscheinlich machen, daß an dem Orte dieses Namens eine große Völkerschlacht stattgefunden hat. Für die Ronneberge bei Nebra ist man bisher diesen Nachweis schuldig geblieben und auch Pelka wird ihn schwerlich liefern. Anders steht es, wie ich zeigen werde, um Ronnenberg südwestlich von Hannover, welches westlich der Leine und ihres Zuflusses Ihme am Nordende eines den gleichen Namen tragenden Bergrückens liegt, nördlich dessen in einer von mehreren Bergrücken umgebenen Ebene die Dörfer Empelde und Benthe liegen. Nun hat Sanitätsrat Dr. Weiß in Bückeburg-Eilsen in einem

XXII. 18

vor 3 Jahren erschienenen Aufsatze[1]) zur Erklärung des Ortsnamens Empelde folgendes bemerkt: „Das Dorf Empelde,
südwestlich von Hannover (im 9. Jahrhundert Amplithi,
1186 Emplithe, 1204 Emplethe, 1676 Empelde) ist dadurch
merkwürdig, daß in seiner Gemarkung der Sattel des un-
geheuren unterirdischen Salzgebirgs der Umgegend von
Hannover so nahe unter der Erdoberfläche liegt, wie an
keiner anderen Stelle, wie durch neue bergbauliche Untersuchungen erwiesen ist. Nun erscheinen in der Empelder
Feldmark in höchst auffälliger Weise eine ganze

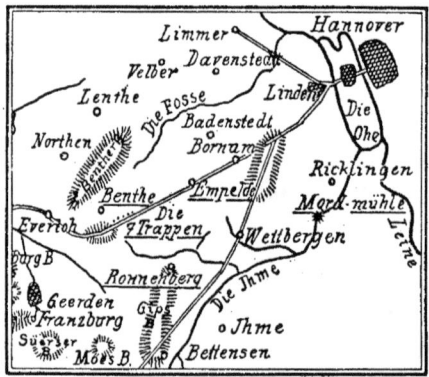

Anzahl von Bodenvertiefungen. Noch zu Menschen-
gedenken war die Flur durchsetzt mit nicht übermäßig tiefen
Erdfällen von trichterförmiger Gestalt. Die Entstehung ·
derselben ist sehr leicht erklärbar. Durch Auslaugen des
Salzbergsattels oder der Gypsdecke entstanden hier Hohl-
räume, die, weil sie oben lagen, sich nicht, wie es sonst
bei Hohlräumen im Salzlager der Fall zu sein pflegt, mit
Wasser füllten, sondern ein Nachstürzen der Decke ver-
anlaßten, welcher Vorgang wiederum an der Erdoberfläche
zur Bildung von Trichtergruben Veranlassung gab. Diese

----

1) „Neue Erklärungen der Namen von einigen wichtigen Orten
in Niedersachsen.“ Jahrgang 1900 der Zeitschrift des historischen
Vereins für Niedersachsen, Hannover, Hahn, 1900, S. 181—193.

Gruben scheinen teilweise trocken geblieben zu sein; waren
sie aber tief, so bildeten sie, jedenfalls durch einströmendes
Grundwasser, „Kölke". Solche finden sich, oft ausgezeichnet
durch ihre Tiefe und scheinbar ohne Zusammenhang mit
anderen Gewässern, gar nicht selten in dem Gelände über
dem Salz- und Gypslager. Sie führen in der Umgegend von
Hannover den besonderen Namen „Glocksee" und zwar sicher
von ihrer Gestalt. Stadtler erwähnt ausdrücklich g r o ß e
E r d f ä l l e   a m   E n d e   d e s   R o n n e b u r g e r   H o l z e s .
unmittelbar an der Empelder Mark, welche als drei etwa
7 Morgen große „Teiche" früher Glocksehe genannt wurden."
     Aus dieser Eigentümlichkeit des Geländes erklärt nun
Weiß den Ortsnamen Empelde. Die urkundlich älteste
Namensform Amplithi kann nicht etwa auf eine Wurzel
Amp— und ein Grundwort —lithi (richtiger hlîtâ! = Leite,
Bergabhang) bezogen werden, „weil w e g e n   v o l l s t ä n d i g
e b e n e r   B e s c h a f f e n h e i t   d e r   F e l d f l u r   eine Zusammensetzung mit lithi (hlîtâ) ausgeschlossen ist. Es
muß also der Name aus der bereits erweiterten Wortform
Ampl— mit dem Suffix —ithi gebildet sein, welches dem
vorangehenden Worte den Begriff der Häufigkeit verleiht
oder es verallgemeinert." Das zu Grunde liegende ampl—
führt Weiß — meines Erachtens mit Recht — auf das
(dem lateinischen ampulla entlehnte) ahd. ampullâ (amplâ),
mhd. ampel, nhd. A m p e l zurück, welches ein Gefäß von
kegel- oder trichterförmiger Gestalt bedeutet, und von der
Wurzel amb, welche Krümmung und Bogenform bezeichne,
abzuleiten sei. In dem Namen des Dorfes oder seiner Flur
komme also die auffällige Häufigkeit trichterförmiger, durch
Erdfälle entstandener Gruben zum Ausdruck.
     Da nun d i e s e   E r d f ä l l e sich ganz in der Nähe von
Runibergun in regione Maerstem zeigen, so findet es Weiß
— und man kann sagen: mit gutem Grunde — wahrscheinlich, daß sie in der dreitägigen Völkerschlacht des
Jahres 531 (Weiß setzt unrichtig 530) zwischen Franken
und Thüringern, weil nicht sehr groß, als W o l f s g r u b e n

v e r w e n d e t und der fränkischen Reiterei verderblich
geworden sind. Hierzu möchte ich bemerken, daß es kein
Bedenken zu erregen braucht, wenn die fränkischen Berichterstatter diese zu Fallgruben eingerichteten Erdfälle als
fossae oder fossata[1]) bezeichnen, da den Erdfällen, falls
sie zu flach erschienen, durch nachhelfende Ausschachtung
größere Tiefe gegeben sein kann oder auch die vereinzelten
durch Verbindungsgräben zu einer fortlaufenden Hindernis-
kette verbunden sein mögen. Darum werden auch diese Vertiefungen, wie ich bald nachweisen werde, G r u f t e n genannt.

Am Schlusse seiner Ausführungen macht Weiß darauf
aufmerksam, daß auf dem naturgemäß sehr ausgedehnten
Ronneberger Schlachtfelde bei dem Dorfe Benthe die a l t e
G e r i c h t s s t e l l e d e r „s i e b e n T r a p p e n" gelegen habe,
die noch im vorigen Jahrhundert eine Reihe von sieben
Löchern und zwar in Einer Flucht mit den bekannten,
damals an anderer Stelle als jetzt stehenden 8 Steinen, an
diese ostwärts sich unmittelbar anschließend, gebildet hätten.
Die erste Trappe war flach, jede folgende tiefer, als die
vorhergehende, so daß die letzte etwa $1^1/_2$ m (Tiefe) er-
reichte. Auf einem Hofe in Benthe aber ruhte die Verpflichtung, die Trappen in jedem Jahre aufzuräumen und
wieder herzustellen[2]). Weiß hält es nicht für unmöglich,
daß wir es hier mit einer Gedächtnisstätte und Gedächtnis-
feier in Bezug auf die Fallgruben der Schlacht bei Runibergun zu tun haben und daß die Steine vielleicht als
Grabsteine aufzufassen seien. Diese Annahme wird, woran
Weiß nicht gedacht hat, bestätigt durch mehrere S a g e n ,
welche sich an die sieben Trappen der Benther Gerichts-

---

1) Auffällig ist überdies, daß nördlich von Benthe und Empelde
ein Bach, die F o s s e , unterhalb von Linden in die Leine geht.
Ob dieser zu der lateinischen Bezeichnung fossa in irgend welcher
Beziehung steht, muß ich dahingestellt sein lassen.

2) So berichtet G. F. F i e d e l e r , Das Kirchspiel Gerden.
Zeitschrift des Historischen Vereins für Niedersachsen, Jahrg. 1862,
S. 145—242.

stätte knüpfen und welche Fiedeler in seinem Aufsatze erwähnt. Diese Sagen erzählen folgendes: „Nicht weit von
Hannover sind die sogenannten sieben Trappen oder
Gruften zu sehen, woselbst ein Brauer (!) — offenbar
ein Druckfehler für Bauer — sich verflucht, daß er seiner
Magd das Lohn gegeben, und soll darauf daselbst unter-
gesunken sein[1].“ Ausführlicher und etwas abweichend
ist folgende Fassung: „Zu Benthe unweit Hannover zeugen
noch heutiges Tages die sieben Trappen oder Fußtapfen .
von einem besondern daselbst gehaltenen Gerichte“[2]), und
namentlich folgende Fassung: „Des Weges nach Gerden
hin zwischen Eberloh und Empele (!) bemerkt man einen
Platz zwischen einem Knick, die Sieben Trappen genannt.
Die Tradition saget hiervon, daß vorzeiten hieselbst öffentlich
Landgericht gehalten worden. Als nun ein Bauer vor-
kömmt, der seinem Nachbar Land abgepflüget,
oder, wie eine andere Tradition will, seinem Knecht
das verdiente Lohn versaget, (hat er) einen falschen
Eid gethan und sich dermaßen vermaledeyet, daß ihn Gott
sollte lassen versinken, ehe er von dem Platze ginge, wenn
die Sache nicht so wäre, als er ausgesaget. Allein, wie er
kaum seinen Abtritt genommen, fänget er an zu gleiten
und in dem siebenten Schritt sinket er gar in die Erde.
Ob er nun sein Leben noch davon gebracht, ist nicht
bekannt. Indessen muß ein Bauer dasiges Orts diese sieben
Schritt oder Trappen jährlich unterhalten und erneuern[3]).

Wieder etwas abweichend lautet die Sage auf Grund
mündlicher Überlieferung bei Kuhn und Schwarz[4]).
„Bei Everloh unweit Hannover liegen am Berge sieben große
Steine, die man die sieben Trappen nennt und die auf die

---

1) P. L. Berckemeyer, Vermehrter Curieuser Antiquarius,
S. 675. Hamburg.

2) W. E. Baring, Beschreibung der Lauensteinschen Saale,
S. 73, 1744.

3) W. E. Baring, Beiträge zur Hannöverschen Kirchen- und
Schulgeschichte, S. 89 der Vorrede. 1748.

4) Norddeutsche Sagen, S. 253. Leipzig 1848.

folgende Weise ihren Namen bekommen haben sollen. Zur
Zeit, als das Gericht noch unter freiem Himmel gehalten
wurde, war mal ein Bürgermeister, der schwor
seinem Knecht das Lohn ab, sagend, er hätte es
ihm bereits gegeben, und wenn es nicht wahr sei, so wolle
er gleich in die Erde versinken. Da hat er denn nur noch
sieben Schritte gemacht, und bei dem letzten ist er in die
Erde gesunken. Zum Andenken aber hat man nachher bei
jedem Schritt, den er gethan, einen Stein gesetzt, und davon
haben diese Steine den Namen der sieben Trappen erhalten.“

Offenbar liegt in diesem Bericht insofern eine Ver-
wechselung vor, als nicht die Steine, sondern die neben
ihnen befindlichen Vertiefungen die sieben Trappen heißen.
Auch sind es nach Fiedeler nicht sieben, sondern acht
Steine. Laut einer an Ort und Stelle eingezogenen Er-
kundigung haben diese 8 Steine vor dem Jahre 1857 in
einer Reihe, und zwar ungefähr 10 Schritte von ihrem
jetzigen Standorte nach Benthe zu gestanden, sind aber
nach diesem Jahre infolge der Verkoppelung der Benther
Feldmark beim Bau des dort errichteten Müllerhauses an
ihre jetzige Stelle gesetzt worden, und vor denselben haben
sich die sieben Trappen befunden, welche jährlich auf-
geräumt und dadurch erhalten gewesen. Die erste Trappe
sei klein, die zweite größer, die folgenden immer größer
als die vorhergehende, und die siebente ein großes Loch
gewesen. Eine Lagezeichnung der Trappen und auch der
Steine sowohl nach ihrem früheren, wie auch nach ihrem
jetzigen Stand bei dem Müllerhaus dicht an der Chaussee
von Nenndorf nach Hannover ist dem Fiedelerschen Aufsatze beigegeben [1]).

Die erwähnten 8 Steine, welche a. a. O. ebenfalls nach
einer um das Jahr 1830 angefertigten Zeichnung abgebildet
sind, sind etwa 2' breit und 3—4' hoch gewesen, übrigens
mehr oder weniger beschädigt. Auf der Vorder- und Rück-

---

1) Zeitschr. des Histor. Vereins für Niedersachsen, Jahrg. 1862,
vor S. 171.

seite waren durch einfache, vertiefte Linien Kreuze von mannigfacher altertümlicher Form eingehauen, welche es wahrscheinlich machen, daß sie als Grabdenkmäler vornehmer, dort gefallener Franken dienen sollten [1]), zumal da ihre Zahl eine so beträchtliche ist.

Der eigentümlichste Zug der über die sieben Trappen überlieferten Sagen ist der, daß ein B a u e r o d e r B ü r g e r - m e i s t e r , in jener ländlichen Gegend d a s U r b i l d d e s M a c h t h a b e r s , seinem Knechte d a s v e r d i e n t e L o h n v e r s a g t oder seinem Nachbar das diesem gehörige L a n d a b g e p f l ü g t und darum seinen Untergang gefunden haben soll. Es liegt nahe, in dieser dem Volksverständnis angenäherten Darstellung eine E r i n n e r u n g a n d i e U r - s a c h e d e s f r ä n k i s c h - t h ü r i n g i s c h e n K r i e g e s , die Vorenthaltung des von Irminfried seinem Bundesgenossen und Helfer Theodorich vorenthaltenen Beuteanteils, und in dem Untergange des von der göttlichen Vergeltung ereilten Wortbrüchigen eine Erinnerung an den den Späterlebenden als ein Gottesgericht erscheinenden Untergang des Thüringerkönigs zu erblicken, eine Auffassung, die freilich den fränkischen Siegern und ihrem Einflusse ihren Ursprung verdanken wird. Denn der Unterlegene erscheint immer im Unrecht nach dem Worte des Dichters: „Denn jeder Ausgang ist ein Gottesurteil."

Machen es schon diese sagenhaften Überlieferungen wahrscheinlich, daß bei Benthe unweit Ronnenberg tatsächlich der große Völkerkampf zwischen Franken und Thüringern stattgefunden hat, so wird diese Wahrscheinlichkeit durch die Bedeutung des Namens B e n t h e zur Gewißheit erhoben. Es mag hier ganz davon abgesehen werden, daß nach einer Urkunde vom Jahre 1362 im Gogericht Gerden eine M o r d m o h l [2]) erwähnt wird, welche in ihrem

---

1) Man vergesse nicht, daß die Franken damals bereits Christen waren.

2) Nach F i e d e l e r a. a. O. S. 171 die jetzige Landwehrschenke, Amts Linden.

Namen die Erinnerung an den blutigen Zusammenstoß der feindlichen Heere bewahrt haben kann. Weit wichtiger ist der Name Benthe (urkundlich Benethe) selbst, dessen Urform Banithi gelautet haben muß. Offenbar liegt demselben die Wurzel bhan in der Bedeutung schlagen und das ahd. und as. Wort bano, mhd. bane (vgl. das griechische φονή), welches Tod und Verderben bedeutet, zu Grunde. Mit dem verallgemeinernden Suffix —ithi zusammengesetzt, welches ein häufiges Vorkommen der Wurzelbedeutung anzeigt, bezeichnet es eine Stätte oder Gegend, in welcher Todschlag und Verderben in ungewöhnlichem Maße stattgefunden hat, ist also ein durchaus passender Name für die Stätte eines großen Völkerkampfes. Faßt man alle besprochenen Umstände zusammen, so kann es wohl kaum noch einem Zweifel unterliegen, daß bei den Orten Ronneberg, Empelde und Benthe die erste große Schlacht zwischen Thüringern und Franken stattgefunden hat und daß die durch eingeritzte Kreuze ausgezeichneten Steine Denkmäler dort gefallener und begrabener, vornehmer fränkischer Krieger sind, die ebenso einmal erneuert worden sein mögen, wie man die Trappen oder Gruften neben ihnen, welche wohl die Ursache ihres Todes ad oculos demonstrieren sollten, durch stetige Erneuerung zu erhalten bemüht gewesen ist. Hat aber die erste Schlacht in dem Kriege tatsächlich bei Ronneberg unweit Hannover stattgefunden, so wird nicht nur wahrscheinlich, daß die Westgrenze des Thüringischen Königreichs sich damals (531) bis an die Leine erstreckt hat, sondern man muß dann auch zugeben, daß die sächsischen Quellen betreffs des Örtlichen weit besser, betreffs des allgemeinen Ganges der Begebenheiten aber mindestens eben so gut unterrichtet sind, als die fränkischen, und daß dann eben nichts weiter übrig bleibt, als die Anwendung des von Pelka als vollständige Verwirrung bezeichneten „gemischten Verfahrens".

Die vor- und frühgeschichtlichen Funde der Grafschaft Camburg.

Von

Dr. **Gustav Eichhorn** in Jena.

II. Stadt Camburg an der Saale.

Slavisches Gräberfeld
in der Nähe des heutigen Amtsgerichtsgebäudes.

Am 2. April 1869 teilte Dr. Bender in Camburg
Prof. Klopfleisch, der in Tierschneck mit Ausgrabungen gerade
beschäftigt war, brieflich mit, daß sich beim Ausgraben
eines Grundes in der Stadt Camburg 2 sehr alte Skelette
gefunden hätten, dabei ein Messer, ein kleiner Wetzstein von
messerähnlicher Form, an einem Ende durchlocht, und ein
Topf von schwarzer Masse. Die Sachen ständen zur Verfügung.

Mit dieser Benachrichtigung hat Dr. Bender der thüringischen Prähistorie einen großen Dienst geleistet. Klopfleisch wurde nämlich auf die Spur eines Gräberfeldes
geleitet, das sich bei den veranstalteten Ausgrabungen als
eines der größten in Thüringen erwies, dessen
Schädelmaterial unsere namhaftesten Anthropologen zu
wiederholten Malen auf den Kongressen auf das lebhafteste
beschäftigte. Der Schädel einer Jungfrau wurde schließlich
zu einer internationalen Berühmtheit.

Die Ausgrabungen wurden erst im Mai des Jahres 1872
abgeschlossen. In der Zwischenzeit waren alljährlich eine
größere Anzahl Gräber aufgedeckt worden unter spezieller
Aufsicht Klopfleischs, der, wie Virchow auf dem VII. allgemeinen Kongreß zu Jena am 9. August 1876 rühmend
sagte, „mit einer Treue und Sorgfalt, wie sie außerhalb der
Kreise der Naturforscher, einschließlich Altertumsforscher

selten gefunden wird, seit Jahren das Material, das auf diesem Boden zu haben ist, gesammelt hat." Die Funde befinden sich im germanischen Museum zu Jena.

Unter den Akten des germanischen Museums befindet sich ein Situationsplan dieser Gräber von der Hand Klopfleischs (Fig. 80).

N.

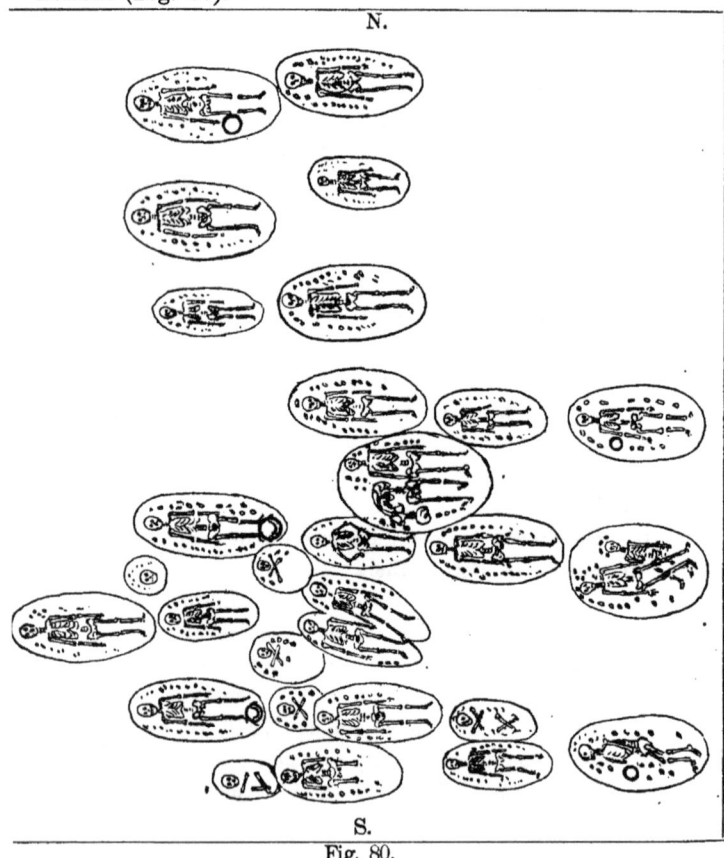

S.

Fig. 80.

Wie ich gleich vorweg nehmen will, war dieses Gräberfeld ein slavisches. Es lag auf dem westlichen Ufer der Saale ungefähr da, wo jetzt das Hotel zur Post und dessen Nebengebäude stehen. Die Ausschachtungen · beim Bau der Saaleisenbahn zerstörten es. Der Fundort ist übrigens ganz besonders zu beachten. Wir wissen, daß ganz in der Nähe dieses slavischen, also frühgeschichtlichen Gräberfeldes die älteste Burg Camburgs im frühen Mittelalter errichtet wurde, da, wo heutigen Tages das Amtsgerichtsgebäude steht.

Die Skelette lagen 0,60—1,50 m tief, meist einzeln, in ungleichmäßigen Abständen voneinander, in nicht sehr regelmäßigen Reihen, ohne jede Steinsetzung oder Spur von Holzumhüllung im Lehmboden. Fast durchgängig aber war eine dünne Schicht Asche mit Kohlen unter und neben die Toten gestreut worden, keine Scherben.

Die Toten waren derart beerdigt, daß die Füße im Osten oder Südosten, der Kopf im Westen resp. Nordwesten lag. Es sind Frauen jeden Alters, Kinder, Männer. In einzelnen Fällen waren zwei Erwachsene, oder Frau und Kind dicht beieinander beerdigt. In einem Grab lagen zwei Erwachsene nebeneinander, der eine kopfüber, wie in abwärts sitzender Stellung.

Die **Beigaben der Toten** waren im ganzen ärmlich.

Bei vier Skeletten standen zur rechten Seite halbierte **Urnen,** teils wagrecht, teils senkrecht zerschlagen. Die Urnen waren am oberen Bauchteil mit dem charakteristischen slavischen Wellenornament verziert. Die zwei · senkrecht halbierten Gefäße (Fig. 81. 82) habe ich ergänzt.

Hohes G e f ä ß von Topfform (Fig. 81), proportioniert. Der Rand schwach ausladend; unterhalb desselben laufen am Hals 2 Systeme von unregelmäßigen Wellenlinien um das Gefäß, die mit einem mehrzinkigen (5—7), kammartigen Instrumente unter mäßigem Druck in die noch weiche Tonmasse gezogen sind. Die Tonmasse ist hart gebrannt, mit Glimmer durchsetzt, rötlich grau; Außenfläche wenig sorgfältig glattgestrichen. Der Boden gerade. Wand mittelstark: 0,8 cm. Das ergänzte Gefäß hat im oberen Durchmesser 17,5 cm, im größten Durchmesser 19 cm, im Bodendurchmesser 10,5; ganze Höhe 20 cm, Umbruch in 15 cm Höhe. (No. 1538). (War 1880 mit auf der Ausstellung vorgeschichtlicher Altertümer in Berlin.)

Mittelhohes Gefäß von Topfform (Fig. 82), dem vorigen gleichartig. Der Rand ebenfalls schwach ausiadend. Unterhalb desselben umzieht ein System von Wellenlinien, mit einem 7-zinkigen Instrument erzeugt, den Gefäßhals. Eine gleichartige Wellenlinie umzieht den Umbruch des Gefäßbauches. Die Tonmasse ist hart gebrannt, mit Sandkörnchen reichlich durchsetzt, rötlich grau. Die Außenseite ist ohne große Akkuratesse glatt gestrichen, Innenfläche schwärzlich. Das ergänzte Gefäß hat einen oberen Durchmesser von 15 cm; größter Durchmesser 16 cm, Bodendurchmesser 8 cm, Höhe 15 cm; Umbruch in einer Höhe von 10 cm vom Boden. Wandstärke 1 cm. (No. 1539). (War 1880 mit auf der Ausstellung vorgeschichtlicher Altertümer in Berlin.)

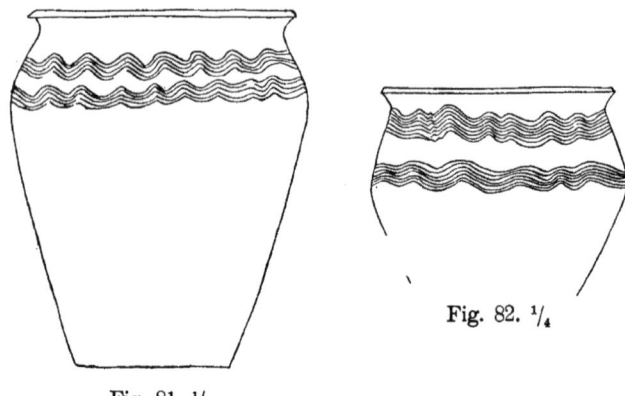

Fig. 82. $^1/_4$.

Fig. 81. $^1/_4$.

Bodenhälfte eines großen Tontopfes, aus einzelnen Bruchstücken wieder zusammengesetzt. Die Tonmasse ist hart gebrannt, mit Sandkörnchen reichlich durchsetzt, so daß sie sich anfühlt wie Sandpapier; Außenfläche gut geglättet, gelblich grau, Innenfläche geschwärzt; der Boden ist glatt und in scharfem Winkel abgesetzt von der Seitenwand. Durchmesser 13 cm. In 8 cm Höhe ist der Topfdurchmesser 18,5 cm. Wandstärke 6 mm. Auf der Kante rings um den Boden scharfe geradlinige Einschnitte, zum Teil sich spitzwinklig schneidend, wohl vom Wetzen eines metallenen Werkzeuges auf der sandigen Fläche und Kante herrührend. (No. 1540.)

Bodenstück eines mittelgroßen Tontopfes von roher Arbeit. Die unteren Partieen der Seitenwandung sitzen in stumpfem Winkel auf. Tonmasse bräunlich grau, mit klargestoßenen Steinstückchen reichlich durchsetzt. Auf der Außenfläche des Bodens im Zentrum nabelförmige Einsenkung und einige konzentrische Furchen, durch die Befestigung auf der Töpferscheibe erzeugt; periphere Furche innen am Übergang des Bodens in die Seitenwandung. Durchmesser des Bodens 11 cm, des Topfes in $4^1/_2$ cm Höhe 14 cm. Wandstärke 6 mm. (No. 1541.)

Bei 5 Skeletten wurden zu Füßen die eisernen **Reifen,** **Handhaben und Ösen von je einem Eimer** gefunden, die Holzgefäße waren natürlich vermodert.

Die eisernen H e n k e l (Fig. 83—88) sind gut erhalten, durch die Erdlast aber verbogen. Sie sind aus einem vierkantigen Eisenstab geschmiedet, der entweder als solcher halbkreisförmig gebogen, an seinen Enden zur Aufnahme der Ösen umgelegt war (Fig. 84, 85); oder der mittlere Teil des Bogens war in der Glühhitze nach rechts um seine Achse vielmal gedreht, so daß er schnurförmig aussah (Fig. 83); oder der mittlere Teil war bandförmig breit gehämmert und nach Art der noch heute gebräuchlichen Eimerhenkel halbzylinderförmig aufgebogen (Fig. 86, 88). Ein starker vierkantiger Henkel ist durch zwei längliche Knoten geziert (Fig. 87).

Die Ö s e n (Fig. 86, 87), in welchen sich die umgebogenen Henkelstücken drehten, haben die Form eines geschwungenen V. Ihre freien Enden sind rechtwinklig abgebogen, um ins Holz des Eimers nagelförmig einzugreifen. Gefunden wurden 10 Stück, von denen einzelne noch mit ihrem Henkel zusammenhängen. Bei einem Henkel (Fig. 88) hängt an dem einen Ende ein fingerlanger, gerader Eisenstab, der sich ringförmig um dasselbe legt.

Die eisernen E i m e r r e i f e n bilden einen Kreis, einige ein Oval. Ihr Querschnitt ist dreieckig, quadratisch, schmal rechteckig; einige sind bandförmig breit; ein vierkantiger ist schnurförmig, in der Glühhitze nach rechts gedreht. 4 Reifen sind vollständig, dreikantig, kreisrund, 7 ebenso, aber verzogen oder gebrochen; ein Reif hat quadratischen Querschnitt, er ist kreisrund, vollständig; 2 vierkantige waren nur in Bruchstücken erhalten; 2 sind breitbandförmig, 3 schmalbandförmig. Die Stelle, an welcher die ursprünglichen Enden aneinander geschmiedet sind, ist nur bei wenigen etwas verdickt. Bei den bandförmigen sind die Enden übereinander gelegt und vernietet.

Eiserner Henkel (Fig. 83) zu einem Holzeimer, gut erhalten, nach der einen Seite etwas auseinandergezogen, auf der anderen Seite nach innen gedrückt, verrostet. Der vierkantige Henkel ist aus einem im Querschnitt quadratischen Stab hergestellt, der im Verlauf

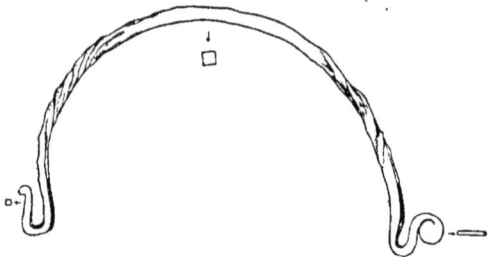

Fig. 83. ¹/₄.

des Bogens vielmal nach rechts gedreht worden ist, die zum Haken bestimmten Enden sind nicht gedreht, ? -förmig abgebogen und auf der einen Seite zu einer Spiralscheibe eingerollt. Dicke des ungedrehten Stabes 0,5 cm, in der Bogenmitte 0,7 cm. Durchmesser des Bogens von einem Haken zum andern 20 cm, Peripherie des Bogens außen 38 cm. Aus diesen Zahlen ergibt sich eine obere Peripherie des Eimers von 76 cm, vorausgesetzt, daß der Henkel auf den Eimerrand auflag, wie bei unseren jetzigen Holzeimern. Durchmesser des beigesetzten Eimers ursprünglich 21 cm. (No. 1542.)

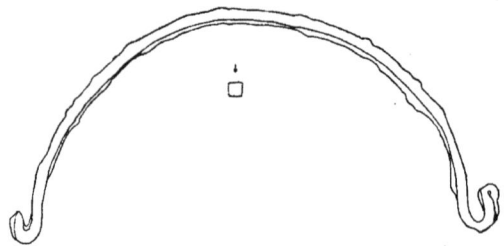

Fig. 84. ¹/₄.

Eiserner Henkel (Fig. 84) zu einem Holzeimer, gut erhalten. verrostet, vierkantig, gleichmäßig nach beiden Seiten etwas auseinander gezogen. Der Henkel ist aus einem ungedrehten Eisenstab hergestellt von quadratischem Querschnitt, die Enden zur Aufnahme der Oese umgebogen. Dicke des Stabes 0,6 cm, Peripherie des Bogens 39 cm, Durchmesser zwischen den beiden Haken 25 cm; berechnete obere Peripherie des dazugehörigen Eimers 78 cm, Durchmesser desselben 21,6. (No. 1543.)

Eiserner Henkel (Fig. 85) eines Eimers, gut erhalten, verrostet, vierkantig, aus einem bandförmigen Eisen gearbeitet, die Enden verjüngt, hakenförmig umgebogen. Bogenperipherie 31 cm, Durchmesser zwischen den Haken 20,5 cm. Größte Breite 1 cm in der Bogenmitte, Dicke 2 mm. Berechnete obere Peripherie des zugehörigen Eimers 62 cm, Durchmesser desselben 19,5 cm. (No. 1544.)

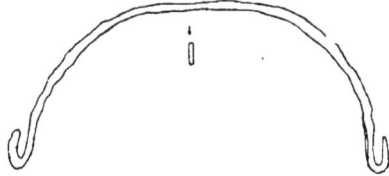

Fig. 85. ¹/₄.

Eiserner Henkel (Fig. 86) eines Eimers, in zwei Stücke gebrochen, mit den daran festgerosteten Ösen, gut erhalten. Der Henkel ist aus einem vierkantigen Stab hergestellt, von quadratischem Querschnitt; die Mitte des Bogens ist breitgehämmert und muldenförmig umgebogen, damit es besser in der Hand liegt. Die Enden sind hakenförmig umgebogen. Der Henkel hat auf dem oberen Eimerrand aufgelegen, infolge dessen sind die ankerförmigen Ösen rechtwinklig dazu angerostet. Sie lagen auf der äußeren Eimerwand nach beiden Seiten sich spreizend auf und waren — wie ein in der Mitte des einen Ankerschenkels angerosteter Nagel beweist — durch Nägel

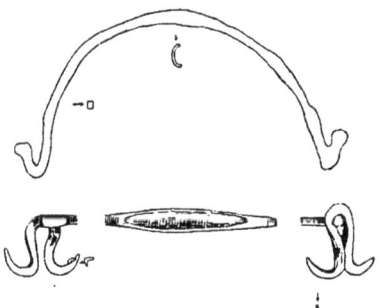

Fig. 86. ¹/₄.

befestigt. Gleichzeitig läßt die Richtung der Ösenschenkel den Schluß zu, daß die Eimer oben enger, der Boden weiter war. Bogenperipherie 26 cm. Ösenlänge 4 cm. Berechnete obere Eimerperipherie 52 cm, Durchmesser oben 13,5 cm. (No. 1545.)

Kräftiger eiserner Henkel (Fig. 87) eines großen Eimers, gut erhalten, mit dazu gehörigen, lose daran hängenden, ankerförmigen Ösen. Der Bügel ist aus einem 1 cm starken, vierkantigen Eisenstab hergestellt, von quadratischem Querschnitt; durch zwei längliche Knoten ist der Bogen in drei Drittel geteilt. Peripherie des Bogens außen 40 cm. 23,2 cm jetziger Durchmesser. Die Enden des Henkels sind rechtwinklig abgebogen und durch einen quadratischen Knopf abgeschlossen. Die anhängenden, bandförmig gehämmerten Ösen enden in divergierende Bogen, die Spitzen sind zugespitzt und nach der Eimerwand zu abgebogen, um nagelförmig ins Holz einzugreifen. Berechneter oberer Umfang des Holzeimers 80 cm. (No. 1546.)

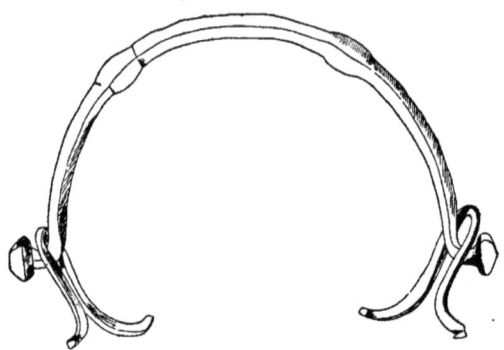

Fig. 87. ¹/₄.

Eiserner Eimerhenkel (Fig. 88) mit rechtwinklig dazu angerosteter, einarmiger Öse. Auch dieser Bügel ist hergestellt aus einem vierkantigen Eisenstab von quadratischem Querschnitt, der in

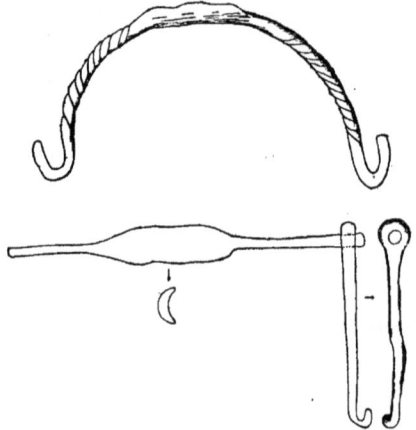

Fig. 88. ¹/₄.

kurzer Entfernung von den hakenförmigen Enden viele Male naeh rechts gedreht ist und in der Mitte für das Anlegen der Hand breit gehämmert und muldenförmig aufgebogen ist. Peripherie des Bogens 29,5 cm, Durchmesser des Bogens jetzt 17 cm. Dicke des Eisenstabes 0,6 cm, des breitesten Teiles der mittleren Mulde 1,7 cm. Berechnete obere Peripherie des Eimers 59 cm. Die anhängende Öse ist ein 11 cm langes, stabförmiges, gerades Eisen, das obere Ende legt sich kreisförmig um den Henkelhaken, das untere Ende ist nach außen abgebogen. Vermutlich lag diese Öse auf der äußeren Eimerwand auf, und ein Reif drückte dieselbe fest an. Das umgebogene Ende verhinderte das Hervorgleiten unter dem Reif. Die Öse ist in einem leicht stumpfen Winkel angerostet, so daß auf eine nach unten sich erweiternde Eimerform zu schließen wäre. Ebenso gut aber kann es auch auf eine Verschiebung des ganzen Eimers durch die drückende Erdlast zurückgeführt werden. (No. 1547.)

Eiserne Eimeröse, aus einem 7 mm breiten, bandförmigen Eisenstück hergestellt, mit gespreizten Schenkeln. Höhe 7,2 cm. (No. 1548.)

Eiserne Eimeröse, aus einem Eisenstab hergestellt von quadratischem Querschnitt. Die Schenkel auseinander gespreizt und nach der Eimerwandung zu zugespitzt und abgebogen, um ins Holz einzugreifen. Höhe 8,5 cm. (No. 1549.)

Eiserne Eimeröse, aus einem Eisenstab hergestellt von quadradischem Querschnitt, mit ebenso gespreizten Schenkeln und ins Holz eingreifenden Spitzen, aber sehr verschoben beim Zusammendrücken des Holzeimers. Jetzige Höhe 9,2 cm. (No. 1550.)

Eiserne Eimeröse — der eine gespreizte Schenkel fehlt —, ebenfalls hergestellt aus einem Eisenstab von quadratischem Querschnitt und geformt wie die anderen; auch hier ist das letzte Ende des erhaltenen Schenkels zum Eingreifen in das Holz des Eimers abgebogen. Höhe 9 cm. (No. 1551.)

Eiserne Eimeröse, die sich spreizenden Schenkel fehlen; schmal bandförmig. (No. 1552.)

Eiserner Eimerreif, vollständig, kreisrund, von dreieckigem Querschnitt, innere Peripherie 53 cm, die Seiten des gleichseitigen Dreiecks 0,6 cm breit. (No. 1553.)

Eiserner Eimerreif, vollständig, kreisrund, von dreieckigem Querschnitt, innere Peripherie 56 cm; 0,6 cm Länge der Seite des gleichseitigen Dreiecks. (No. 1554.)

Eiserner Eimerreif, vollständig, kreisrund, Querschnitt ein gleichseitiges Dreieck, jede Seite 0,6 cm, innere Peripherie 65,5 cm. (No. 1555.)

Eiserner Eimerreif, vollständig, kreisrund, im Querschnitt ein gleichschenkliges Dreieck von 0,8 cm Hypothenusen = 0,6 Seitenlänge, innere Peripherie 68,5 cm. (No. 1556.)

Eiserner Eimerreif, vollständig, zu einem unregelmäßigen Oval verzogen, im Querschnitt ein gleichseitiges Dreieck von 0,6 cm Seitenlänge, innere Peripherie 58 cm. (No. 1557.)

Eiserner Eimerreif, vollständig, breitoval, im Querschnitt ein gleichseitiges Dreieck von 0,6 cm Seitenlänge, innere Peripherie 85,5 cm. (No. 1558.)

XXII.   19

Eiserner **Eimerreif**, oval, gesprengt, die Enden stehen 3 cm auseinander, Querschnitt dreieckig, 0,6 cm breit, innere Peripherie 67 cm. (No. 1559.)

Eiserner **Eimerreif**, $^3/_4$ eines Ovals, Querschnitt dreieckig, von 0,6 cm Seitenlänge, innere Peripherie 59 cm. (No. 1560.)

Bruchstücke eines eisernen **Eimerreifs**, im Querschnitt ein Dreieck von 0,6 cm Seitenlänge; dieselben ergeben zusammen, ihren Krümmungen entsprechend, einen Reif von 75 cm innerer Peripherie. (Nr. 1561.)

Mehrere Bruchstücke eines eisernen **Eimerreifs**, in ihren Krümmungen entsprechend einem Ring von annähernd derselben Peripherie wie No. 1561. Im Querschnitt ein Dreieck von 0,6 cm Seitenlänge. (No. 1562.)

Bruchstücke eines eisernen **Eimerreifs**, im Querschnitt ein Dreieck von 0,6 cm Seitenlänge, an einer Stelle schleifenförmig (zum Einhängen des Henkels?) in die Höhe gezogen. Innere Peripherie ohne Ausbiegung zur Schleife 55,5 cm, $^3/_4$ eines Ovals in seiner vorliegenden Gestalt. (No. 1563.)

Schön erhaltener, starker, kreisrunder **Eimerreif**, hergestellt aus einem 0,8 cm starken vierkantigen Eisenstab von quadratischem Querschnitt; der Stab ist in seiner ganzen Länge um seine Achse vielmals nach rechts gedreht, die Enden hakenförmig abgebogen und übereinander gelegt. Innere Peripherie 66,5 cm. (No. 1564.)

Schwächerer, eiserner **Eimerreif**, aus 3 Bruchstücken bestehend, im Querschnitt rechteckig, die Enden hakenförmig übereinander gelegt. Innere Peripherie ca. 62 cm, das größere Bruchstück oval verzogen. (No. 1565.)

Eiserner **Eimerreif** in 3 Bruchstücken von ca. 66 cm innerer Peripherie, die Enden hakenförmig umeinander gebogen und ineinander gerostet, Querschnitt vierkantig. (No. 1566.)

Drei isolierte kleine Bruchstücke von eisernen **Reifen**, vierkantig. (No. 1567.)

Eiserner **Eimerreif** in 3 Bruchstücken, nach ihren Krümmungen zu einem Reif von ca. 82 cm innerer Peripherie gehörig, schmal bandförmig, im Querschnitt rechteckig, 0,7 cm breit. (No. 1568.)

Zwei kleine Reifenbruchstücke von rechteckigem Querschnitt aus Eisen. (No. 1569.)

Eiserner **Eimerreif**, breit bandförmig, vollständig, geschlossen, ohne erkennbaren Niet; innere Peripherie 77 cm, oval, Breite 3 cm. (No. 1570.)

Bruchstücke eines eisernen **Eimerreifen**, breit bandförmig, an dem größten eine 10 cm lange Stelle doppelter Dicke. Hier waren die Enden übereinander gelegt und genietet. (No. 1571.)*)

Bald rechts bald links in der Handgegend hatten die Toten verrostete **Messerklingen aus Eisen** liegen (Fig. 89—100), einschneidig, in langer, schmaler Form oder kürzer und breiter, die meisten mit Griffdorn, an einem

---

*) Von den eisernen Eimerhenkeln waren zwei, von den Eimerreifen einer mit auf der Ausstellung in Berlin 1880.

sogar die Spuren einer Holzverschalung (Fig. 91), im Ganzen 15 Stück.

Fig. 89. Fig. 90. Fig. 91. Fig. 92. Fig. 93. Fig. 94.

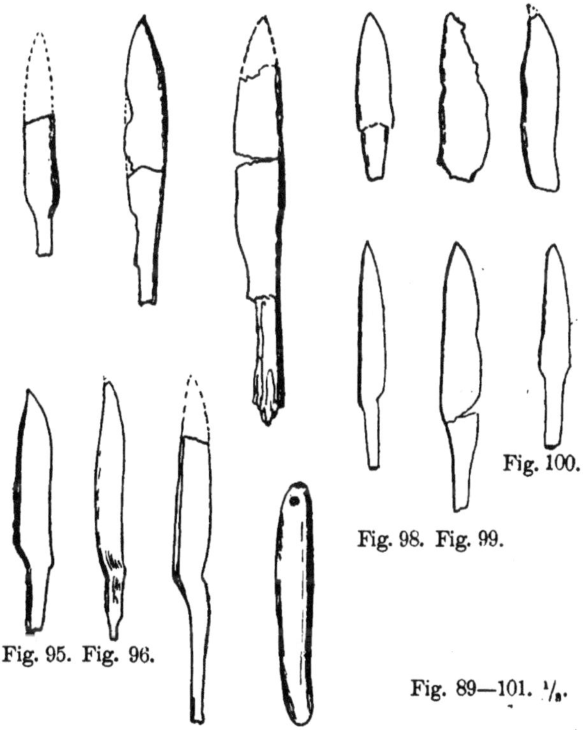

Fig. 100.

Fig. 98. Fig. 99.

Fig. 95. Fig. 96.

Fig. 89—101. ¹/₃.

Fig. 97. Fig. 101.

Lange, schmale, eiserne, einschneidige Messerklinge (Fig. 89), ein Drittteil mit der Spitze fehlt, mit Griffdorn. Länge des erhaltenen Klingenteiles 4,5 cm, des Griffdorns 3 cm, Breite 1,2 cm. Verrostet, Form deutlich. (No. 1502.)

Lange, schmale, eiserne, einschneidige Messerklinge (Fig. 90), Rücken und Schneide gleichmäßig zur Spitze sich vereinend, mit Griffdorn. Länge der Klinge 12 cm, des Griffdorns 3,5 cm, größte Breite in der Mitte 1,8 cm. Verrostet, aber mit Deutlichkeit die Form zu erkennen. (No. 1501.)

Großes, mittelbreites, eisernes Messer (Fig. 91), in drei Bruchstücken, die Spitze fehlt, Länge der Klinge 9 cm, größte Breite

19*

2 cm, in der Mitte, Griffdorn 8 cm lang, mit Resten der Holzverschalung. (No. 1503.)

Eiserne Messerklinge (Fig. 92), klein', mittelbreit, Rücken
wenig, Schneide mehr zur Spitze sich umbiegend, mit Griffdorn,
stark verrostet. Klinge 6, Griffdorn 3 cm lang, Breite der Klingenmitte 1,5 cm. (No. 1504.)

Breite, eiserne Messerklinge, in 2 Stücke zerbrochen, stark verrostet, Griffdorn fehlt, Länge 9 cm, Breite in der Mitte 2,2 cm.
(No. 1505.)

Breite, eiserne Messerklinge (Fig. 93), Rücken gerade, Schneide
allmählich zur Spitze umbiegend, Griffdorn fehlt, verrostet, Länge 9 cm,
Breite 2,2 cm. (No. 1506.)

Schmale, eiserne Messerklinge (Fig. 94), Rücken leicht,
Schneide mehr geschweift, Griffdorn fehlt, Länge 9,5 cm, Breite in
der Mitte 1,7 cm. Verrostet. (No. 1507.)

Lange, schmale, eiserne Messerklinge, Rücken gerade, Schneide
allmählich zur Spitze umbiegend, nach dem Schaft zu sich leicht
verjüngend, Griffdorn fehlt, Länge 9 cm, Breite in der Mitte 1,7 cm,
verrostet, Form aber sehr deutlich. (No. 1508.)

Langes, schmales Messer (Fig. 95), gut erhalten, mit Griffdorn,
Rücken leicht, Schneide mehr geschweift, Rücken am Griffansatz
abfallend, Länge der Klinge 10 cm, des Griffdorns 4 cm, mittlere
Breite 1,7 cm. (No. 1509.)

Ebenso geformtes, etwas schmäleres Messer (Fig. 96), gut
erhalten. Länge der Klinge 10 cm, des Griffdorns 2,5 cm, Breite
der Klingenmitte 1,3 cm. (No. 1510.)

Eisernes Messer (Fig. 97), lang, schmal, mit langem, deutlich
abgesetztem Griffdorn, ein viertel der Klinge mit der Spitze fehlt.
Rücken und Schneide gleichmäßig zur Spitze zu sich verjüngend.
Länge des Klingenrestes 8 cm, des Griffdorns 8 cm. (No. 1511.)

Besterhaltenes, schmales, spitzes Eisenmesser (Fig. 98), Rücken
und Schneide fast gleichmäßig im schwachen Bogen zur Spitze sich
vereinend. Griffdorn abgesetzt, Länge der Klinge 8 cm, Klingenbreite in der Mitte 1,2 cm, Griffdorn vollständig, 3,5 cm lang.
(No. 1512.)

Eisernes Messer (Fig. 99), gut erhalten, in 2 Stücke zerbrochen,
mit Griffdorn, mittelgroß, mittelbreit, zugespitzt. Länge der Klinge
10 cm, des Griffdorns 4,5 cm, Breite der Klingenmitte 2 cm. (No. 1513.)

Kleines, gut erhaltenes, eisernes Messer (Fig. 100), mit langem
Griffdorn, Rücken gerade, Schneide allmählich aufgebogen. Länge
der Klinge 6,5 cm, des Griffdorns 5 cm, Klingenbreite in der Mitte
1,4 cm. (No. 1514.)

Langes, schmales, stark verrostetes Messer mit breitem Griffdorn,
Länge der Klinge 9,0 cm, Breite in der Mitte 1,3 cm, Griffdorn 3,5 cm
lang. (No. 1515.)*)

Einzelne Skelette hatten auch **Schleifsteinchen** und
Flußkiesel bei sich.

Ein Schleifstein (Fig. 101) war messerförmig, aus grauem

---

*) 2 eiserne Messer davon waren 1880 auf der Ausstellung vor-
geschichtlicher Altertümer in Berlin.

Schiefer, mit beiderseits trichterförmigem, kleinem Loch nahe dem einen Ende zum Anhängen. 14 cm lang, 2 cm breit, 1 cm größte Dicke, beide Enden abgeschliffen. (No. 1516.)

In der Nähe der rechten Hand einer erwachsenen Person lag eine kleine patinierte **Bronzenadel** (Fig. 102) mit platt gehämmertem und ᒐ-förmig umgebogenem Kopf. Länge 7 cm. (No. 1518.)*)

In der Ohrgegend lagen bei einem Skelett z w ei g l ei c h - a r t i g e, g r o ß e, b r o n z e n e, p a t i n i e r t e **Schläfenringe** (Fig. 103), das eine platt gehämmerte Ende mit der charakteristischen ᒐ-förmigen Umbiegung, das andere hakenförmig im rechten Winkel abgebogen, so daß es mit der ᒐ-förmigen Schleife einen festen Verschluß bildet.

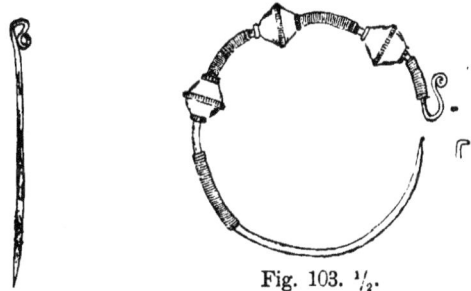

Fig. 103. ¹/₂.

Fig. 102. ¹/₂.

Auf jeden Ring sind lose aufgeschnürt drei vergoldete, kugelförmige Metallperlen mit je oinem geperlten Kranz um die Mitte und an jedem Ende dem Schnurloch vorgelegt, und vier zylinderförmige Spiralen aus feinem Silberdraht in abwechselnder Reihenfolge vom ᒐ-förmigeu Ende an. Die kleinere Halfte des Ringes ist froi. Der Haken des zweiten Ringes ist nach der entgegengesetzten Seite abgebogen, so daß der eine Ring zum Tragen für die rechte, der andere für die linke Seite berechnet worden ist. Durchmesser

---

*) War 1880 mit in Berlin auf der Ausstellung vorgeschichtlicher Altertümer.

béider Ringe gleich, 6,2 cm im Lichten. Stärke des Drahtes 2 mm, Breite der Perle 1,2 cm, Dicke 1,3 cm, Länge der Spiralen 1,1—2,1 cm. Gewicht beider Ringe gleich, je 12 Gramm. (No. 1519.)*)

Außerdem wurden 11 kleinere Schläfenringe (Fig. 104—108) gesammelt, die bekanntlich die Slaven in der Ohrgegend an einem um den Kopf gelegten, ledernen Stirnriemen trugen, einzeln oder paarweise, in größerer Zahl. 6 waren aus Silber, 5 aus Bronzedraht.

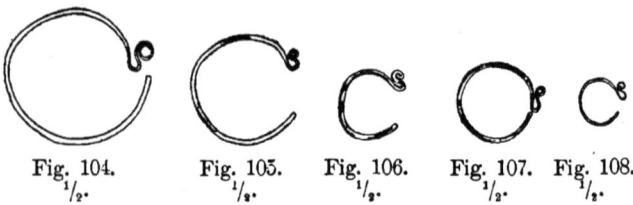

Fig. 104.   Fig. 105.   Fig. 106.   Fig. 107.   Fig. 108.
$^1/_2$. $^1/_2$. $^1/_2$. $^1/_2$. $^1/_2$.

Schläfenring (Fig. 104) aus Silberdraht, mittelgroß, Durchmesser im Lichten 3,5 cm. Drahtstärke 1,8 mm. (No. 1520.)

Schläfenring (Fig. 105) aus Bronze, mit Patina überzogen, mittelgroß, in 2 Stücke gebrochen, Durchmesser im Lichten ca. 3,0 cm. Drahtstärke 2 mm. (No. 1521.)

Schläfenring aus Silber, mittelgroß, von dem ?-förmigen Ende fehlt ein Stück. Durchmesser im Lichten 2,8 cm. Drahtstärke 2 mm. (No. 1522.)

Schläfenring aus Silber, in drei Teile zerbrochen, mittelgroß, Durchmesser im Lichten ca. 2,5 cm, Drahtstärke 1,3 mm. (No. 1523.)

Schläfenring aus Silber, in zwei Teile zerbrochen, das ?-förmigeEnde fehlt, mittelgroß. Drahtstärke 1,3 mm. (No. 1524.)

Schläfenring (Fig. 106) aus Bronzedraht, patiniert, weit offen, klein. Durchmesser im Lichten 1,5 cm. Drahtstärke 1,8 mm. (No. 1525.)

Schläfenring (Fig. 107) aus Bronzedraht, patiniert, Enden wenig übereinander liegend, klein. Durchmesser im Lichten 1,9 cm. Drahtstärke 1,5 mm. (No. 1526.)

Schläfenring aus Silber, sehr klein, Enden aneinander liegend. Von der ?-förmigen Schleife fehlt ein Stück. Durchmesser im Lichten 1,1 cm. Drahtstärke 1,3 mm. (No. 1527.)

Schläfenring (Fig. 108) aus Silber, sehr klein, in zwei Teile gebrochen, ?-förmiges Ende abgebrochen. Drahtstärke 1,1 mm. (No. 1528.)

Schläfenring aus Bronze, patiniert, mittelgroß, von der

---

*) Waren 1880 mit in Berlin auf der Ausstellung vorgeschichtlicher Altertümer.

₤ -förmigen Schleife fehlt ein Teil. Durchmesser im Lichten 2,5 cm. Drahtstärke 1,8 mm. (No. 1529.)

Sehr kleiner Schläfenring aus relativ dickem Bronzedraht, die ₤ Schleife fehlt zum großen Teil. Drahtstärke 2,9 mm. Durchmesser im Lichten 0,8 cm. (No. 1533.)

Von 5 weiteren kleineren und mittelgroßen **Ringen** ist nicht sicher mehr zu sagen, wo und wie sie getragen wurden. Von einem kleineren wissen wir, daß er in der Hüftgegend lag.

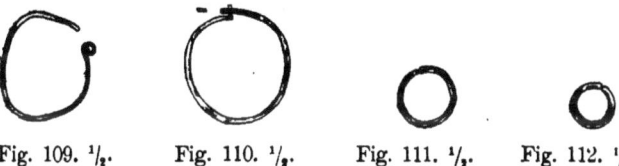

Fig. 109. ¹/₂.   Fig. 110. ¹/₂.   Fig. 111. ¹/₂.   Fig. 112. ¹/₂.

Mittelgroßer Ring (Fig. 109) aus Bronzedraht, patiniert, verbogen, das eine Ende etwas platt gehämmert und eingerollt. Durchmesser im Lichten ca. 2,5 cm. (No. 1530.)

Mittelgroßer Ring (Fig. 110) aus Bronzedraht, patiniert, vierkantig, das eine Ende zu einer Schleife umgebogen, das andere in die Schleife eingreifende Ende abgebrochen. Durchmesser im Lichten 2,5 cm. (No. 1531.)

Kleiner ovaler Ring aus Bronzedraht, patiniert, einzelne Stellen mit braunem Rost inkrustiert, die Enden übereinander gebogen. Drahtstärke 2,1 mm. (No. 1532.)

Kleiner, offener Bronzering (Fig. 111), patiniert, Durchmesser im Lichten 1,3 cm, relativ starker Draht 2,0 mm. (No. 1534.)

Sehr kleiner, offener Bronzering (Fig. 112), patiniert, von relativ starkem Draht. Durchmesser im Lichten 0,9 mm. Drahtstärke 2,0 mm. (No. 1535.)

Eine eiserne **Schnalle** (Fig. 113), in Bruchstücken, verrostet, mittelgroß (No. 1536) lag zusammen mit einem kleinen, zylinderförmig gerollten, starken Bronzeblech (Bronzeperle ? Fig. 114), 1,3 cm lang, in der Beckengegend einer erwachsenen Person. (No. 1537.)

Fig. 113. ¹/₂.   Fig. 114. ¹/₂.

In der Halsgegend wurden hier und da bei Erwachsenen und Kindern **Glasperlen** gefunden, einzeln oder mehrere Stück bei einander. Die Glasperlen hatten doppeltkonische Form (Fig. 115, 116, 117), oder sie waren breit faßförmig (Fig. 118), platt kugelförmig (Fig. 119), zylinderförmig (Fig. 120—124). Die langen, zylinderförmigen hatten im Querschnitt Sternform. Die Farbe der Perlen ist schwärzlich, grünlich, rotbraun, blau, durchsichtig oder undurchsichtig. Einige sind mehrfarbig, gefleckt, eine Perle ist mit einer zackigen Glasauflage geziert (Fig. 115).

Bei allen zylinderförmigen Glasperlen ist das Schnurloch innen ausgekleidet mit einer sehr dünnen, mit grüner Patina überzogenen Metallschicht (Bronze). Bei einzelnen durchbrochenen Stücken (Fig. 121a) ist das Glas abgesprengt und die sehr feine Blechplatte isoliert sichtbar. Bei genauer Betrachtung der Struktur der Glasschicht (Fig. 123) sieht man ferner eine Summe einzeln übereinander liegender Flächen. Diese beiden Beobachtungen geben einen Aufschluß über die Herstellung der Perlen. Man fertigte erst dünne, metallene Hohlzylinder, umwickelte diese eine Reihe mal mit einem sehr fein ausgezogenen Glasband und drückte in die noch weiche Glasmasse vier Längsfurchen.

Perlen von Halsketten. (No. 1517.)*)

Fig. 115. $^1/_1$.   Fig. 116. $^1/_1$.   Fig. 117. $^1/_1$.   Fig. 118. Fig. 119. $^1/_1$.

a) Große Perle (Fig. 115) mit weitem Schnurloch von annähernd doppelkonischer Form aus schwärzlichem, undurchsichtigem Glasfluß. Auf die Außenfläche ist ein gelblichweißes Glasstäbchen in unregelmäßige Zacken gelegt aufgeschmolzen. Durchmesser der Perle 1,5 cm, Dicke 1,0 cm, Schnurlochweite 0,6 cm.
b) Mittelgroße Perle (Fig. 116) von doppelkonischer Form aus schwärzlichem, undurchsichtigem Glasfluß. Auf der Außenfläche vier große auswendig weiße, mit hellblauen Zentren versehene,

---

*) Waren 1880 mit in Berlin zur Ausstellung vorgeschichtlicher Altertümer.

kreisförmige Flecken in unregelmäßigen Abständen. Schnurloch kreisrund, beiderseits flachtrichterförmig. Durchmesser der Perle 1,1 cm, Dicke 0,8 cm, Schnurlochweite 0,3 cm.

c) Mittelgroße doppelkonische Perle (Fig. 117) aus malachitgrünem, undurchsichtigem Glasfluß. 1,0 cm Durchmesser, 0,8 cm Dicke, Schnurloch kreisrund, 0,3 cm weit.

d) Mittelgroße, schmale Perle (Fig. 118), breit faßförmig, von rotbraunem, undurchsichtigem Glasfluß. Die Seitenflächen senken sich flach trichterförmig zum kreisrunden Schnurloch. Durchmesser 1,1 cm, Dicke 0,5 cm, Schnurlochweite 0,3 cm

e) Kleine, blaue, durchsichtige Glasperle (Fig. 119), platt kugelförmig. 0,5 cm Durchmesser, 0,25 cm Dicke, Schnurlochweite 0,1 cm.

Fig. 120. ¹/₁.   Fig. 121. ¹/₁.   Fig. 121a. ¹/₁.

f) Lange, zylinderförmige Perle (Fig. 120) von durchsichtigem, grünlichem Glas mit vier tiefen Längsfurchen, so daß die Perle aus vier um das Schnurloch gelegten Wulsten zusammengesetzt erscheint, der Querschnitt infolgedessen sternartig. Durchmesser 0,7 cm, Länge 2,1 cm, Schnurloch kreisrund, 0,2 cm Schnurlochweite.

g) Lange, zylinderförmige Perle (Fig. 121) von durchsichtigem, grünlichem Glas, durch vier Längsfurchen in vier Wülste gesondert, Querschnitt sternförmig. Durchmesser 0,9 cm, Länge 2,5 cm, Schnurloch kreisrund, 0,2 cm Schnurlochweite. Ein Bruchstück dieser Perle (Fig. 121a) zeigt die innere Auskleidung des Schnurlochs mit einer sehr dünnen Bronzeschicht.

Fig. 122. ¹/₁.   Fig. 123. ¹/₁.   Fig. 124.

h) Lange, olivenförmige Perle (Fig. 122) von durchsichtigem Glas, die eine Hälfte bläulich, die andere grünlich, durch vier Längsfurchen vierwulstig geformt. Gr. Durchmesser 1,1 cm, Länge 2,4 cm, Schnurloch kreisrund, 0,2 cm weit.

i) Hälfte einer langen, zylinderförmigen Perle (Fig. 123) von durchsichtigem, grünlichem Glas, vier tiefe Längsfurchen, Querschnitt sternförmig, kreisrundes Schnurloch, Dicke 1,1 cm. Zwei wulstförmige Bruchstücke derselben Perle angehörig.

k) Bruchstücke einer mittelgroßen, zylinderförmigen Perle (Fig. 124) aus grünlichem Glas, vier Längsfurchen mit abgerundeten Enden.

Nicht alle Skelette hatten Beigaben, einzelne dagegen mehrerlei. Die Notizen von den Ausgrabungen am 13. Oktober 1871 berichten darüber:

1 Frauenskelett mit Messer von Eisen, zur Linken neben dem Vorderarm ein paar Flußsteine.

1 Kind mit silbernen Ohrringen, Glasperle.

Die Ausgrabungen am 6. 7. 8. Mai 1872:

1 erwachsene Person mit kleinem Bronzering in der Hüftengegend, ein etwas größerer Bronzering unter dem Kopfe zur rechten Seite, in der Mitte ein Messer.

1 Kind mit zwei silbernen, kleinen Ohrringen, Bronzeperle und Bernsteinperle, kleinem Reibstein.

1 Kind, dabei länglich geteilter Schleifstein.

1 Erwachsener, Messer zur Linken.

1 alte Person, Ohrring von Bronze.

1 erwachsene Person, in der Beckengegend Reste einer eisernen Schnalle und eine lange Bronzeperle.

1 Kind, am Kopf ein Hahnenskelett, zu Füßen ein Eimer.

1 erwachsene Person, ein eisernes Messer mit Holzspuren am Griff.

1 Skelett, bei der linken Hand ein Messer.

1 Skelett, bei der rechten Hand eine Nadel; ein Eimer.

1 Skelett mit Messer in der rechten Hand.

1 Skelett mit Messer in der linken Hand, am Halse drei Perlen.

1 Skelett mit Messer in der rechten Hand.

1 Kind, beim Schädel drei Perlen.

1 Skelett, beim Schädel zwei Ohrringe; ein Eimerhenkel.

1 Skelett mit Messer in der Linken.

1 weibliches Skelett mit Perlenbruchstücken an der linken Halsseite.

1 männliches Skelett mit Messer in der Rechten.

1 Skelett mit Messer in der Linken.

Das von Klopfleisch sorgsamst gesammelte, große Material an **Skelettresten** ist bisher nur zu einem kleinen Teil wissenschaftlich verwertet worden. 1880 waren es nur 6 Schädel, die, fast unversehrt dem Boden entnommen, zur Ausstellung vorgeschichtlicher Altertümer nach Berlin gesandt wurden, und Virchow stellte auch nur an diesen bei Gelegenheit der allgemeinen Anthropologenversammlung zu Jena 1876 seine Messungen an. Im vergangenen Jahre habe ich nun das gesamte Knochenmaterial gereinigt, geordnet und die Schädel mit gütiger Unterstützung des Herrn Zahnarztes Hahn in Jena, soweit es möglich war, zusammengesetzt. Die Schädel und Schädelreste gaben die wichtigsten Anhaltepunkte zur nachträglichen, näheren Bestimmung der hier Beerdigten nach Geschlecht und Alter. Wir erinnern uns daran, daß größeres Volumen, größere Derbheit der Knochen, kräftigere Entwickelung der den Muskeln zum Anheften dienenden Knochenhöcker und Leisten besonders am Hinterhaupt, knochigeres Gesicht mit wulstigeren Umrahmungen der Augenhöhlen, tiefen Fossae caninae, größere Zähne, massiverer Unterkiefer, kräftigeres Gebiß den männlichen Schädel gegenüber den weiblichen charakterisiert. Ganz besonderen Wert lege ich auf die genaue Untersuchung der Zähne. Sie sind oft der einzige wissenschaftlich brauchbare Körperüberrest, während das übrige Skelett morsch unter unseren Händen beim Ausgraben zerfällt. Aus ihrem Erhaltungszustand, der Art ihrer Entwickelung, ihrem Bau, ihrer Stellung können eine ganze Reihe von Schlüssen gezogen werden auf das Geschlecht, auf das Alter, auf die Ernährungsweise ihrer Besitzer.

Um einem weiteren Kreise die Möglichkeit einer selbständigen Beurteilung der Schädel zu ermöglichen, habe ich in der photographischen Abteilung der Firma Zeiss in Jena Photographien derselben anfertigen lassen. Die Bilder sind alle in demselben Verhältnis 1 : 4 der natürlichen Größe mit einem sehr großen Apparat in weitem Abstand vom Original aufgenommen worden, so daß eine Verzeichnung so gut wie ausgeschlossen ist. Sie sind so scharf, daß jede

Einzelheit am Knochen auf das deutlichste hervortritt. Auf die gleichmäßige Aufstellung der Schädel beim Photographieren wurde besondere Acht gegeben. ' Sie sind allesamt in die deutsche Horizontalebene eingerichtet photographiert, d. h. in die Ebene, welche bestimmt wird durch 2 Grade, die beiderseits den tiefsten Punkt des unteren Augenhöhlenrandes mit dem senkrecht über der Mitte der Ohröffnung liegenden Punkt des oberen Randes des knöchernen Gehörganges verbinden.

Im ganzen sind es 56 Personen, die hier ausgegraben worden sind, und deren Skelettreste wir im Germanischen Museum haben, und zwar:

im ersten Kindesalter verstorbener (bis Ende des 6. Lebensjahres gerechnet): 8 (No. 16. 17. 25. 32. 33. 53. 54. 55);

im zweiten Kindesalter (vom 7. bis Ende des 13. Jahres): 1 (No. 52);

im Jugendalter (vom 14.—25. Jahr): 7 (No. 1. 2. 10. 15. 26. 41. 45);

im Greisenalter (über 60 Jahr) mit Sicherheit 1;

die übrigen 28 gehören dem kräftigen erwachsenen (25.—40. Jahr) und reifen Alter an (40.—60. Jahr). Von diesen sind weiblichen Geschlechts 22, männlichen Geschlechts 17. Die übrigen sind unbestimmbar.

Wissenschaftlich verwertbar sind heute nach der Zusammensetzung 24 Schädel. Ein flüchtiger Ueberblick sagt uns, daß es fast durchgängig Schmalgesichter sind, lange, relativ schmale und verhältnismäßig hohe Schädel. Die einen (Fig. 125) im Bau, in ihrem Profil ebenmäßig, andere (Fig. 129) starkknochig, mit kräftigen Augenbrauenwülsten, Sattelnase, hervortretenden Backenknochen und starker Prognathie, d. h. die Ober- und Unterkieferzahnreihe ist stark schnauzenartig nach vorn gezogen. Das Extrem von Prognathie zeigt der Schädel eines 14-jährigen Mädchens (Fig. 126), der international berühmt gewordenen „Camburger Jungfrau". Einige der Schädel haben sehr hohe Unterkiefer, auch ist das Mittelstück, das die Schneidezähne enthält, sehr breit. Stellenweise ist die Kinnbildung eine sehr starke, durchweg aber steht die Bildung im Gegensatz zur progenäischen Form, d. h. trotz der starken Ausbildung des Kinns schiebt sich die Kiefergegend gleichzeitig nach vorne. Das gibt einen s t a r k e i n g e b o g e n e n Unterkiefer, an dem sowohl das Kinn als die Zahngegend hervortreten. Die Differenz in der Kieferwinkeldistanz ist eine sehr große. Bei den Männern beträgt diese Distanz im Mittel 92,5 mm, bei den Frauen 94,5; in mittlerer Summe 93,8. Die Zähne sind im ganzen sehr gut, kräftig, blendend weiß; nur ausnahmsweise mit Zahnstein besetzt. Einige Personen haben allerdings Caries der Zähne, vereinzelt auch sehen wir einige Fistelöffnungen und Spuren gewaltsamer Extraktionen während des Lebens. Ein Schädel (Fig. 128) hatte f ü n f untere Schneidezähne.

Als interessant seien hier erwähnt 2 Schädel mit vollständig erhaltener S t i r n n a h t (Fig. 134, 143) und 2 Schädel, welche einen P r o c e s s u s f r o n t a l i s s q u a m a e t e m - p o r a l i s aufweisen (Fig. 144, 145), Exemplare von solcher Güte, „wie sie", nach Virchows Ausspruch „vielleicht kein anderes Museum an deutschen Schädeln zu zeigen im stande ist". Es sind dies Schädel, bei welchen die Schuppe des Schläfenbeins unmittelbar an das Stirnbein anstößt dadurch, daß die Schläfenschuppe einen Fortsatz von hinten her so weit vorschiebt, daß die Verbindung zwischen Keilbeinflügel und Seitenwandbeinwinkel unterbrochen wird, eine Eigentümlichkeit der höheren Affen. Fig. 145 ist das Bild des Schädels eines etwa 1 1/2-jährigen K i n d e s (1590). Bei Fig. 144, dem Schädel einer Erwachsenen (1591), ist ein Processus frontalis incompletus, wo die Schläfenschuppe nicht ganz an das Stirnbein reicht, aber doch einen Vorsprung bildet, der so groß ist, daß nur noch ein kleiner

Zwischenraum übrig geblieben ist. Eine zweite Eigentümlichkeit desselben ist eine ungemein starke Vorschiebung des Kiefers, ein zweites Merkmal niederer Rasse. Im ganzen ist dieser Schädel ziemlich groß und gut entwickelt.

Chirurgisch interessant ist eine einzelne linke Tibia mit geheilter F r a k t u r. Der Bruch verlief schräg, beinahe in der Mitte des Knochens. Das untere Stück ist medialwärts etwas disloziert.

Im folgenden gebe ich eine genaue Beschreibung des gesamten Camburger Skelettmaterials. Ich folge dabei den auf den Knochen mit Tinte oder Blei notierten Buchstaben und Zahlen und den kleinen Zetteln, die den einzelnen Knochen beilagen. Diese geben die Reihenfolge an, in der die Toten zu Tage gefördert wurden. Ueber die als A und B bezeichneten Ausgrabungen Klopfleischs besitzen wir keine speziellen Tagebuchnotizen. Was von den Ausgrabungen C, D, E, F an Einzelheiten in Klopfleischs Büchern angegeben worden ist, ist bei den betreffenden Nummern bemerkt.

A. Erste Ausgrabung.

1) „A." Kräftige Person unter 20 Jahren.
Nur erhalten die linke Hälfte des Stirnbeins und der kräftige Unterkiefer mit allen Zähnen. Weisheitszähne noch nicht vorhanden. Abkauung der Zähne horizontal.

2) „A." Weibliche Person.
Rechte Oberkieferhälfte des Schädels. Weisheitszahnpartie abgebrochen. Die vorhandenen Zähne klein, gut erhalten, nicht abgekaut. Fossa canina tief.

3) „A 3." Weibliche Person von 25—40 Jahren.
Sehr gut erhaltener vollständiger Schädel Fig. 125.
Unterkiefer mittelgroß, zierlich, stärkere Muskelansätze; Kieferast eher dünn, liegend, Kieferwinkel 135°. Distanz der Kieferwinkel 10,0 cm. Gelenkfortsätze klein, Gelenkachsen schräg gestellt; Proc. coronoid. klein, Incisur flach; unterer Rand des Unterkieferkörpers dick, ausgeschweift; Kinn spitz, Kinnprotuberanz stark entwickelt, Alveolarteil vollständig erhalten.
Gebiß : *)

---

*) Die arabischen Zahlen bedeuten die bleibenden Zähne und zwar :

1) 1. Schneidezahn	5) 2. Prämolar
2) 2. „	6) 1. Molar
3) Eckzahn	7) 2. „
4) 1. Prämolar	8) 3. „

die römischen die Milchgebißzähne. ⌒ = im Durchbruch begriffen.
[ ] ausgefallen. ( ) fehlt, Alveole oblitteriert.

$$\frac{8 \quad (7) \quad (6) \quad 5 \quad 4 \quad [3] \quad 2 \quad [1]}{7 \quad (6) \quad [5] \quad 4 \quad 3 \quad [2] \quad 1} \left| \frac{[1] \quad 2 \quad 3 \quad 4 \quad 5 \quad (6) \quad (7) \quad [8]}{[1] \quad [2] \quad 3 \quad 4 \quad 5 \quad 6 \quad 7} \right.$$

Zahnbogen im Oberkiefer elliptisch, im Unterkiefer ein Halbkreis, geschlossen; gerader Biß, scharf artikulierend; Zahnkronen klein, horizontal abgekaut mäßigen Grades; die relative Größe der einzelnen Zähne untereinander normal; am Weisheitszahn oben rechts Caries der Krone.

Gaumen lang, schmal, mäßig gewölbt, sehr stark höckerig, Gaumenlänge 4,6, Mittelbreite 3,5, Gaumenendbreite 3,6. Leptostaphylin

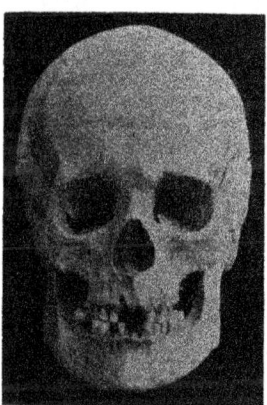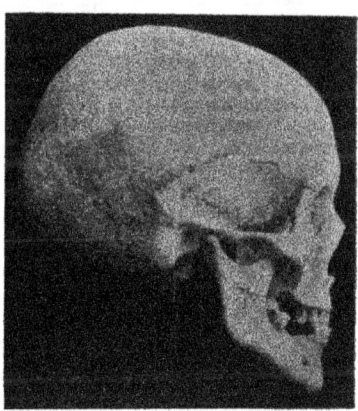

Fig. 125. $^1/_4$.

(Index 78). Alveolarfortsatz des Oberkiefers hoch, gegen die Horizontale senkrecht gestellt; Juga alveolaria im Unterkiefer stark entwickelt, oben nicht; Fossa canina flach. Wangenbein zierlich; Jochbogen leicht ausbauchend. Nasenhöhe 4,7, gr. Breite der Nasenöffnung 2,4. Platyrrhinie (51,1). Nasenbeine schmal, viereckig, Medionasalnaht geschlängelt; Nasenrücken im Seitenprofil eingesattelt, im Querschnitt hoch und schmal gewölbt; Nasenöffnung birnförmig; Nasenstachel spitz, rechte Nasenhöhlenhälfte bedeutend enger wie die linke durch schief verlaufende Nasenscheidewand, unterer Nasenrand scharf. Orbita verhältnismäßig klein, abgerundet viereckig, Querachse rechts stärker abfallend wie links. Augenhöhleneingang: gr. Breite 3,5, horizontale Breite 3,2, gr. Höhe = Vertikalhöhe 2,9, Mesoconchie (Index 82).

Gesichtsbreite (Virchow) 9,1, nach v. Hölder 10,1. Jochbreite 12,1. Gesichtshöhe 11,1, obere Gesichtshöhe 6,7, demnach im ganzen schmalgesichtig (Index 100), schmales Obergesicht (Index 66). Glabella wenig vorspringend, ebenso Arcus superciliares. Der Schädel ist dolichocephal (Index 71), orthocephal (Index 71), gerade Länge 18,4 größte Länge, Intertuberallänge 18,3. Größte Breite 13,1, kleinste Stirnbreite 8,4. Gerade Höhe 13,1 = Hilfshöhe. Ohrhöhe 10,9, Hilfsohrhöhe 11,0. Länge der Schädelbasis 9,5, Breite derselben 10,4.

Länge der Pars basilaris 2,4. Foramen magnum langoval, (gr. Länge 3,8, gr. Breite 2,8), Richtung auf Gaumen. Horizontalumfang des Schädels 50,0, Sagittalumfang 37,0, vertikaler Querumfang 29,5, Profillänge 8,8.

Koronalnaht zum größten Teil verwachsen, Pfeilnaht geschlängelt, Lambdanaht zahnreich, erscheint an der Spitze durch drei große, zusammenhängende Schaltstücke gedoppelt. Hinterhauptsschuppe ausgebaucht.

Vom übrigen Körperskelett sind erhalten:
die beiden Humeri,
die beiden Darmbeine und das Os sacrum, dessen oberste Wirbelsegmente zusammen verknöchert sind,
die beiden Femora, die beiden Tibiae und Fibulae.

Länge des Beins vom Trochanter major bis äußere Knöchelspitze 70 cm, Kniegelenkspalt bei $37\frac{1}{2}$ cm, Distanz der weitesten Stelle der Hüftbeinkämme 26,5 cm, der vorderen Darmbeinstachel 23,5 cm, gerader Durchmesser des Eingangs des kleinen Beckens 10,5 cm, querer 13 cm. Länge des Humerus vom Tuberculum majus bis Epicondylus lateralis 29 cm.

B. Zweite Ausgrabung.

4) Grab 1. „B, 1." 14-jähriges Mädchen.

Vollständiger, wieder zusammengesetzter Schädel No. 1572 mit einer affenähnlichen Prognathie Fig. 126.

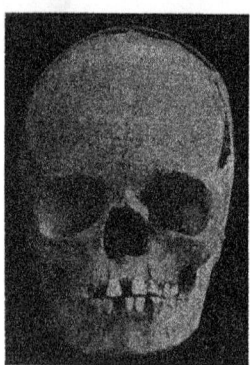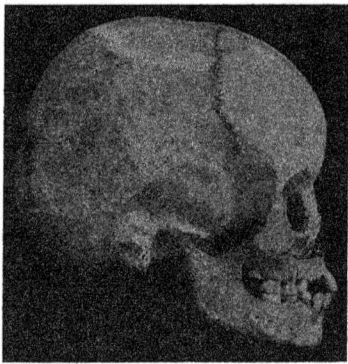

Fig. 126. $\frac{1}{4}$.

Er hat die allgemeine Aufmerksamkeit der Anthropologen erregt. Schaafhausen (Bonn) hat ihn eingehend untersucht und auf dem internationalen Kongreß in Stockholm besprochen. Herr Schaafhausen zeigte in Stockholm eine Abbildung desselben und nach dieser Abbildung künstlerich ausgeführtes Bild. „Es waren Fleisch und Haare herangezeichnet, wie sie etwa, der Schädelform entsprechend, im Leben vorhanden gewesen sein konnten." Es kam dieses Schädels wegen dann auf der Versammlung zu einer Auseinandersetzung zwischen Herrn Schaafhausen und Virchow. Der erstere erklärte die Schädelform als einen Typus einer niederen Rasse, „einer deutschen Jungfrau der Vorzeit", wie er sich ausdrückte, Virchow erklärte die Schädelbildung als eine krankhafte, die Jungfrau als ein Cretin urgermanischer Herkunft.

Der Prognathismus dieses Schädels war so hochgradig, daß er „dem Schimpansen ziemlich nahe kommt, ja daß er ihm Konkurrenz machen kann". Es ist aber bei diesem Schädel nicht bloß die ungewöhnliche Entwickelung der Kiefergegend, sondern zugleich die tiefe Lage der Nasenwurzel, die stark eingedrückte Form des Nasenrückens, die Breite der Nasenöffnung, welche ihn dem Affenschädel annähern. Trotzdem ist die Stirn ziemlich stark gewölbt. Der Schädel hat eine Kapazität von 1260 ccm; das ist allerdings keine mikrocephale Kapazität.

Auf der VII. allgemeinen Versammlung der Anthropologen zu Jena am 9.—11. August 1876 kam Virchow nochmals auf den Cretin-Schädel der Jungfrau von Camburg zu sprechen. Bei dieser Gelegenheit berichtet er von seinen Messungen der übrigen Schädel und führt an: durchschittliche Länge der Nasenwurzel bis Ohrlochlinie für die Männer 107, für die Weiber 101,8 und als Gesamtmittel 103,5 mm; dagegen bei dem Cretinkopfe nur 95 mm. Die Entfernung der Linie vom Nasenstachel bis Ohrloch beträgt bei den Männern 106,5, bei den Frauen 101,7, im Gesamtmittel 103,3, bei der Cretine 99 mm. Es ist also bei den Männern die Basis des Schädels (Nasenwurzel bis Ohrloch) etwas länger als die Entfernung vom Ohrloch bis zum Nasenstachel; bei den Frauen ist sie ein klein wenig kürzer; die Frau schiebt schon im ganzen den Nasenstachel etwas weiter vor. Gewöhnlich ist (im Mittel) die Differenz beider Linien sehr unerheblich, aber bei der Cretine erscheint auf einmal eine Differenz von 4 mm, um welche die Spina nasalis weiter nach vorn geschoben ist. Die Nasenhöhe (Linie zwischen Nasenwurzel und Nasenstachel) ist bei den Männern 51,7, bei den Frauen 51,6, als Gesamtgröße 51,65; bei der Cretine sinkt die Zahl auf einmal bis auf 38.

Bei dieser großen Differenz der Nasenhöhe und bei der relativ starken Vorschiebung der Spina nasalis mußte der untere Teil des Gesichts vorrücken. Wenn man den Schädel in die horizontale Stellung bringt, so geht die Profillinie von dem Nasenstachel an nicht gerade abwärts, sondern der Zahnfortsatz des Oberkiefers macht nach vorn einen schrägen Vorsprung, und die Zähne stehen fast horizontal nach vorn. Hier ist eine ungewöhnliche Breite der Schneidezähne vorhanden. Die Schneidezähne, namentlich die mittleren, stehen außer allem Verhältnisse zu der Größe der Prämolaren und der Backzähne. Sie sind so groß, daß die Eckzähne durch sie ganz aus der Reihe herausgedrängt und gar nicht zum Ausbruch gelangt sind. Höchst interessant ist übrigens die fast horizontale Richtung der schaufelförmigen Zähne.

Der Prognathismus, der sich bei der Cretine findet, ist derselbe, den wir bei den Cretins aller Völker antreffen. Alle Cretins werden prognath, weil ihre Zunge ganz unmäßig wächst und vor und zwischen den Zähnen liegt.

Bei der Cretine beträgt die Kieferwinkeldistanz nur 81 mm, sonst durchschnittlich bei den Camburger weiblichen Schädeln 94,5, dabei ist er am allerwenigsten progenäisch, d. h. das Kinn als solches drängt sich hier nicht heraus.

XXII.   20

Die von mir vorgenommene Untersuchung des Schädels ergibt:
Schädel im ganzen klein, dolichocephal, schmalgesichtig, mit auffällig großen Augen, sehr starker
alveolärer Prognathie, Unterkiefer dementsprechend klein,
zierlich. Distanz der Unterkieferwinkel 8,1, Kieferwinkel 130°;
Muskelansätze mäßig entwickelt; Ast liegend; Gelenkfortsätze klein,
zierlich; Axen der Gelenkköpfe etwas schräg gestellt; Coronoidfort-
satz klein, Incisur flach; unterer Rand des Unterkiefers dick, wenig
ausgeschweift; Kinn spitz, Kinnprotuberanz kräftig entwickelt.
Alveolarteil des Unterkiefers vollständig erhalten, Juga wenig hervortretend, Zahnbogen halb elliptisch, vergrößerte Peripherie der Schneide-
und Eckzähnepartie durch die starke dentale Prognathie, Lücke
zwischen Schneide- und Eckzahn, größere noch zwischen Eckzahn und
ersten Prämoloren (Diastema). Offener Biß von den Eckzähnen an,
Backzähne artikulieren scharf. Die Schneidezähne des Oberkiefers
bilden mit denen des Unterkiefers einen stumpfen Winkel von 113°.
Zahnkronen groß; im Oberkiefer erster Molar größer als der zweite,
mittlere untere Schneidezähne kleiner als die äußeren. Kaufläche der
oberen echten Molaren (1 und 2) mit vier Höckern, ein fünfter ist angedeutet (Primatentypus), untere Molaren mit fünf deutlichen Höckern;
teilweise noch Milchgebiß, keine Abnutzung, echte Karies des zweiten
Milchmolar oben rechts. Gebißformel:

$$\frac{\overline{8}\ \overline{7}\ 6\ V\ 4\ [\text{III}]\ \overline{2}\ 1\ \mid\ 1\ \overline{2}^*\ \text{III}\ 4\ V\ 6\ \overline{7}\ \overline{8}}{\overline{7}\ 6\ V\ IV\ 3\ 2\ [1]\ \mid\ 1\ 2\ [\text{III}]\ IV\ V\ 6\ \overline{7}}$$

Gaumen mesostaphylin, ziemlich flach gewölbt. Alveolarfortsatz
des Oberkiefers niedrig, gegen die Horizontale sehr schräg gestellt, Juga
alveolaria schwach ausgeprägt, Alveolarrand oben halbkreisförmig,
Fossa canina tief. Wangenbein zierlich, stark vortretend, schnell
nach hinten umbiegend, Tuberositas malaris ausgeprägt, hinterer
Rand des proc. front. des Jochbeins leicht flügelförmig ausgezogen.
Jochbogen zierlich, schwach aushauchend. Nasenbeine dreieckig,
an das Stirnbein mit einer Spitze heranreichend. Nasenrücken breit,
eingesattelt. Nasenöffnung abgerundet viereckig, Nasenstachel stumpf,
unterer Nasenrand verstrichen.
Orbita sehr groß, breit oval, im Jochbeinteil stark nach unten
aushauchend, Querachse stark nach außen abfallend, untere Ränder
stark vorspringend. Stirnbeinschuppe 12 cm hoch, 11,4 größte Breite,
steil gestellt, kugelig gewölbt, Stirnhöcker mäßig hervortretend,
Glabella glatt, keine Supraorbitalwülste, Koronalnaht wenig gezackt,
Pfeilnaht wenig gezackt; Scheitelbeinhöcker wenig ausgeprägt, Hinterhauptsbein im ganzen langoval, schalenförmig, Muskelansätze wenig
ausgeprägt, Protuberantia occipitalis mäßig entwickelt, Proc. mastoi-
deus klein, die Außen- und Unterfläche des rechten durch Patina
grün verfärbt.
Schädelmaße: Gerade Länge 17,7, größte Länge 18,00, Intertuberallänge 18,1.
Größte Breite 12,6, Kleinste Stirnbreite 9,7.
Ohrhöhe 11,5, Hülfsohrhöhe 11,5.

*) Der zweite Schneidezahn links oben im Durchbruch und stark
palatinalwärts disloziert.

Breite der Schädelbasis 10,7.
Horizontalumfang des Schädels 49,0.
Vertikaler Querumfang 30,2.
Gesichtsbreite nach Virchow 8,6, nach v. Hölder 10,3.
Ganze Gesichtshöhe 9,0, obere Gesichtshöhe 5,5.
Nasenhöhe 3,9, größte Breite der Nasenöffnung 2,6.
Augenhöhleneingang gr. Breite 4,1, horizontale Breite 3,8.
gr. Höhe 3,2, vertikale Höhe 3,2.
Gaumenlänge 4,5, Gaumenmittelbreite 3,7, Gaumen-
endbreite 3,8.

Der Schädel ist dolichocephal (70,0), schmalgesichtig (116), mit schmalem Obergesicht (64,0) mit sehr breiter Nase (66,0), Chamae-conchie (78,0).

Von weiteren Skelettresten nichts vorhanden.

5) „B neben Grab 1." Ältere Frau.

Schädel (No. 1605) ganz zertrümmert, doch läßt sich konstatieren: Sagittalnaht fast vollständig obliteriert, Proc. mastoid. beiderseits ohne Patinaverfärbung. Der Unterkiefer grazil, Kinn spitz, vor-springend. Erster Molar rechts intra vitam verloren, Alveole obiiteriert, der zweite Molar mit kariöser Krone, Weisheitszahn stark horizontal abgekaut. Zweiter Prämolar links bei Lebzeiten verloren, Alveole obliteriert. Kieferwinkel 132 ⁰.

Vom sonstigen Skelett erhalten:

Der rechte Femur, die rechte Patella, das rechte Os ileum, einzelne Fußknochen.

6) „B¹, 2—3,1." „IV B, 2—3,1." Ca. 50 Jahre alte Frau.

Vollständiger, gut erhaltener Schädel (No. 1577) Fig. 127.

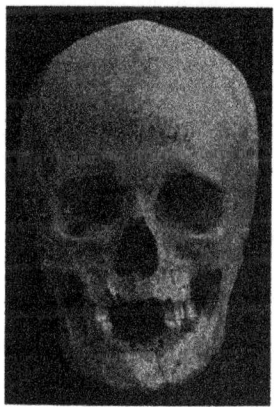
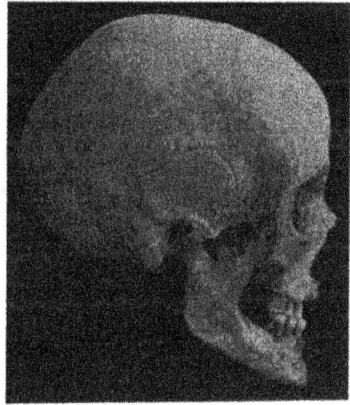

Fig. 127. ¹/₄.

Schädelmaße: Gerade Länge 18,3 = größte Länge, Intertuberallänge 18,2, größte Breite 14,0, kleinste Stirnbreite 9,6, ganze Höhe 13,8, Hilfshöhe 13,7, Ohrhöhe 11,4 = Hilfsohrhöhe, Länge der Schädelbasis

10,0, Breite derselben 10,8, Länge der Pars basilaris 3,0, Foramen magnum langoval, gr. Länge 3,8, gr. Breite 2,8, Horizontalumfang des Schädels 51,5, Sagittalumfang desselben 37,1, vertikaler Querumfang 31,2.
Der Schädel ist mesocephal (Index 76) und orthocephal (Index 74). Gesicht schmal (Index 138), schmales Obergesicht (Index 66), Gesichtsbreite nach Virchow 9,3 v. Hölder 10,8, Gesichtshöhe 11,0, obere Gesichtshöhe 6,2, Jochbreite 13,2. Stirn schmal, hoch, steil gestellt, kugelig gewölbt. Stirnhöcker mäßig entwickelt, Glabella wenig hervortretend, Arcus superciliares mäßig entwickelt, auf der linken Stirnhälfte nahe der Mittellinie kleine Exostose, Augenhöhlen abgerundet viereckig, Querachsen mäßig nach außen abfallend. Augenhöhleneingang gr. Breite 3,7 = horizontale Breite, gr. Höhe 3,2 = vertikale Höhe. Hypsiconchie (Index 86). — Nasenhöhe 5,0, gr. Breite der Nasenöffnung 2,6. Hyperplatyrrhinie (Index 52). Nasenbeine schmal, viereckig, Nasenrücken eingesattelt, flach dachförmig. Nasenöffnung langoval, rechts tiefer wie links. Unterer Nasenrand schneidend scharfkantig. Fossa canina mäßig tief. Alveolarfortsatz des Oberkiefers niedrig, gegen die Horizontale gerade gestellt.
Gebiß:

(8)	(7)	6	5	4	[3]	[2]	(1)		(1)	[2]	[3]	4	5	6	(7)	(8)
[8]	(7)	6*	5	4	[3]	[2]	[1]		[1]	[2]	[3]	4	5	(6)	7	8

Die beiden mittleren oberen Schneidezähne sind intra vitam extrahiert (selten!). An Stelle des 2. und 3. linken oberen Molaren ein großer Knochendefekt, gut verheilt, vermutlich die Folge einer Oberkieferhöhleneiterung. Am rechten, unteren ersten Molar Halscaries. An dem schlechten Gebiß außerdem auffällig starker Zahnsteinansatz. Gerader Biß, scharfe Artikulation. Zahnbogen halbkreisförmig, Zahnkronen groß, stark horizontal abgekaut. — Gaumen flach gewölbt. Am Foram. incisiv. von der Gaumennaht rechtwinklig beiderseits eine kleine Naht abgehend. Gaumenlänge 4,5, Gaumenmittelbreite 3,4, Gaumenendbreite 3,8. Der Gaumen ist mesostapylin (Index 84), Profillänge 9,3. — Unterkiefer zierlich, Distanz der Kieferwinkel 9,6, Kieferwinkel 113°, Ast ziemlich steil gestellt. Rand des Unterkieferkörpers dick, geradlinig, Kinn spitz, Protuberanz desselben stark entwickelt. — Koronalnaht zartlinig, ebenso Sagittalnaht. ⁴/₅ der letzteren verknöchert. Die Sagittalnaht tritt leicht kielartig hervor. Lambdanaht zartlinig, wenig gezahnt. Schaltstücke in beiden Schenkeln. Protuberantia occipit. und Muskelansätze kräftig entwickelt.
Vom Skelett sonst erhalten: der rechte Humerus, der rechte Radius, der linke Femur, die linke Tibia und das vollständige Becken.
7) „B ²/₁, 2." Erwachsener Mann über 40 Jahr alt.
Schädel beinahe vollständig (No. 1574). Es fehlt·rechtes Schläfenbein, Hinterhauptsbein. Fig. 128. Der Schädel ist dolichocephal (Index ca. 73,0), eben noch als schmalgesichtig zu bezeichnen (Index 91), während das Obergesicht breit ist (Index 53,0). Größte Breite des Schädels 13,8, kleinste Stirnbreite 9,7. Ohrhöhe 11,8, Hilfsohrhöhe 12,0.
Unterkiefer groß, massiv, Distanz der Kieferwinkel 10,5, kräftige Muskelansätze, Kieferwinkel wenig stumpf 112°, die zum Proc. coronoid. aufsteigende Kante sehr steil, kleiner wie im rechten Winkel, Proc. coronoid. groß, unterer Rand des Unterkieferkörpers

dick, stark ausgeschweift. Kinn stumpf, Kinnprotuberanz· mäßig entwickelt. Alveolarteil vollständig erhalten.

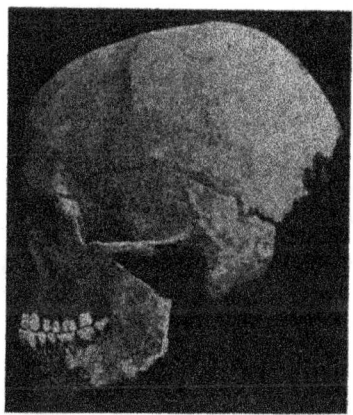

Fig. 128. ¹/₄.

Gebiß: $\dfrac{[8] \quad 7 \quad 6^* \quad 5 \quad 4 \quad 3 \quad 2 \quad 1 \mid 1 \quad 2 \quad 3 \quad 4 \quad 5 \quad 6 \quad 7}{[8] \quad 7 \quad 6 \quad 5 \quad 4 \quad 3 \quad 2 \quad [1] \mid [1] \quad 2 \quad 3 \quad 4 \quad 5 \quad 6 \quad 7 \quad 8}$

Erster Molar rechts oben durch Karies zu Grunde gegangen, nur palatinale Wurzel da. Es waren f ü n f untere Schneidezähne da in normaler Stellung. Zahnbogen im Unterkiefer halb elliptisch über die kleinere Achse hinaus fortgesetzt, im Oberkiefer halbkreisförmig, nicht eng geschlossen; normaler Biß, scharf artikulierend; Zahnkronen groß, relative Größe der einzelnen normal, mäßig horizontal abgekaut; der linke obere Weißheitszahn nicht durchgebrochen, nicht angedeutet. Gaumenmittelbreite 4,2, Gaumenendbreite 4,7, Gaumenlänge 5,1. Gaumen brachystaphylin (Index 92), mäßig gewölbt. Alveolarfortsatz des Oberkiefers hoch, gegen die Horizontale schräg gestellt (mittlerer Grad der Prognathie). Juga alveolaria stark ausgeprägt, besonders am Eckzahn des Oberkiefers. Fossa canina sehr tief. Wangenbein massiv, stark nach vorn vortretend, in weitem Bogen umbiegend, hinterer Rand des Proc. frontal. des Jochbeins flügelförmig nach oben ausgezogen. Jochbogen massiv, weit abstehend. Nasenbeine schmal, viereckig, Medionasalnaht ganz oblitteriert, Nasenrücken eingesattelt, steil dachförmig, Nasenöffnung langoval, schmal, Nasenstachel mäßig hervortretend, unterer Nasenrand scharfkantig. Nasenhöhe 4,5, gr. Breite der Nasenöffnung 2,4, Platyrrhinie (Index 53,0). Orbita verhältnismäßig klein, niedrig, viereckig, Querachse sehr wenig nach außen abfallend, Cribra in der Mitte des Orbitaldachs. Augenhöhleneingang gr. Breite 3,8, horizontale Breite 3,7, gr. Höhe 3,0, Vertikalhöhe 3,0. Chamaeconchie (Index 78). Gesichtsbreite nach Virchow 9,3, nach v. Hölder 12,0, Jochbreite 14,0. Gesichtshöhe 11,0, obere Gesichtshöhe 6,4. Stirn hoch gewölbt, relativ schmal, Glabella und Arcus superciliares kräftig. Koronalnaht zackenreich, die einzelnen Zacken stark verästelt. Die Sagittalnaht auf der Höhe des Scheitels kielartig hervortretend. Stirnbeinhöcker mäßig, Scheitelbeinhöcker gar nicht hervortretend. Im rechten Schenkel der Lambdanaht ein Schaltknochen. Proc. mastoid. groß.

Vom übrigen Skelett sind erhalten: Der linke Humerus, das rechte und linke Darmbein, der rechte Oberschenkel, die rechte Tibia.

8) „B No. 3". Frau mittleren Alters.

Fast vollständig erhaltener Schädel (No. 1595) Fig. 129. Hintere Kopfhälfte etwas nach rechts gedrückt. Gesicht sehr schmal. Kopfdurchmesser von vorn nach hinten sehr lang.

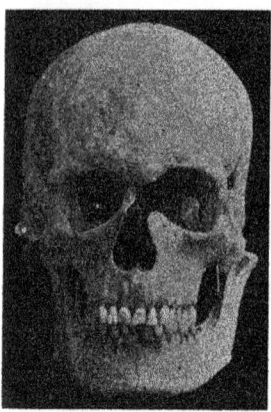 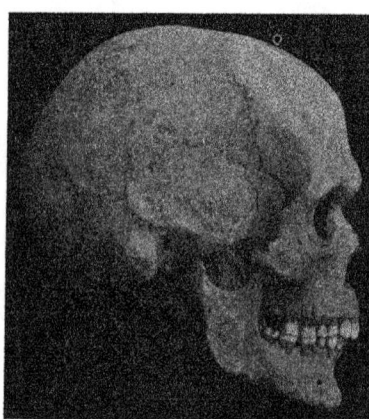

Fig. 129. ¹/₄.

Gerade Länge 19,4 = größte Länge. Intertuberallänge 18,8. Gesichtsbreite 12,9, kleinste Stirnbreite 9,3. Ohrhöhe 11,6. Hilfsohrhöhe 11,7. Breite der Schädelbasis 10,8. Horizontalumfang 51,2. Sagittalumfang 37,0. Vertikaler Querumfang 30,5. Der Schädel ist dolichocephal (Index 66).

Gesichtshöhe 11,4, Gesichtsbreite (Virchow) 9,7, nach v. Hölder 10,4; obere Gesichtshöhe 6,85. Schmalgesichtigkeit (Index 117); schmales Obergesicht (Index 70). Stirnhöcker stark entwickelt, auf dem rechten kleine Exostose. Glabella überhängend vorgewulstet, Supraorbitalwülste mittelstark. — Augenhöhleneingang breit viereckig, abgerundet, gr. Breite 4,0, horizontale Breite 3,8, gr. Höhe 3,1 == Vertikalhöhe. Chamäkonchie (Index 77). — Nasenrücken tief eingesattelt, Nasenhöhe 4,6, gr. Breite der Nasenöffnung 2,3. Mesorrhinie 50. Wangenbeine seitlich gestellt. Alveolarfortsatz des Oberkiefers lang. Gebiß:

[8]	7	6	5	4	3	2	1	1	2	3	4	5	6	7	⸗8
8	7	6	5	4	3	2	1	[1]	2	3	4	5	6	7	[8]

Keine Caries, kein Zahnstein. Zähne sehr gedrängt stehend, obere Vorderzähne fast dachziegelförmig an einander. An den Eckzähnen Gebiß oben und unten winklig umbiegend. Zahnkronen klein, mäßig schräg abgekaut. Die Vorderzähne überbeißend, Backzähne scharf, gerade aufbeißend. — Kinn breit, geradlinig, sehr stark vorspringend, eckig umbiegend. Unterer Rand des Kieferkörpers mitteldick. Kieferwinkel 124°, Distanz der beiden 10 cm. — Gaumen hochgewölbt, schmal, mittlere Breite 3,7.

Nähte feinlinig, reichlich gezackt. Sagittalnaht im letzten Teil obliteriert, zu beiden Seiten dieses Stückes zwei Foramina parietalia. Am Lambda schaltbeinförmiges Knochenstück mit der Spitze der Occipitalschuppe fest verwachsen. Muskelansätze auf der Schuppe des Hinterhaupts mäßig hervortretend.

Vom Skelett sonst erhalten:

Der linke Femur, lang, schlank; die rechte Patella, zwei Fingerknochen, der Epistropheus.

9) „B 3, 1a". Frau mittlerer Jahre.

Vom Schädel (No. 1593) ist nur erhalten die Hinterhauptsschuppe, das linke Schläfenbein, das Gesicht mit Ausnahme der Umgebung des rechten Auges, der Unterkiefer bis auf den rechten Ast. Fig. 130.

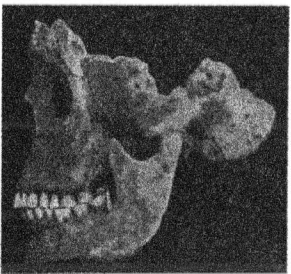

Fig. 130. ¹/₄.

Gesicht schmal (Index 13,3). Gesichtsbreite (Virchow) 8,6, ganze Gesichtshöhe 11,0, obere Gesichtshöhe 6,3, schmales Obergesicht (Index 78). Glabella flach. Nasenrücken flach konkav, Nasenbeine viereckig. Nasenhöhe 4,6, gr. Breite der Nasenöffnung 2,4. Platyrrhinie (Index 53). Augenhöhleneingang gr. Breite 3,5, horizontale Breite 3,45, gr. Höhe 3,45, Vertikalhöhe 3,5. Hypsikonchie (Index 98). Fossa canina mäßig tief, starke alveolare und dentale Prognathie. Gebiß:

[8]	7	6	5	4	3	2	1	1	2	3	4	5	6	7	[8]
8	[7]	6	5	4	3	[2]	[1]	[1]	2	3	4	5	6	7	8

Zahnbogen parabolisch, großer medianer Zwischenraum zwischen den zwei ersten oberen Schneidezähnen. Biß gerade, Vorderzähne etwas übergreifend. Zahnkronen wenig abgekaut, mittelgroß, enge Zahnhälse. Unterer Rand des Unterkieferkörpers dick, Kinn stumpf.

Unterkieferwinkel 121°, Distanz derselben ca. 10 cm. Gaumenlänge 4,9, Gaumenmittelbreite 4,2, Gaumenendbreite 3,9. Leptostaphylin (Index 79). Zwei strahlenförmig von For. incisivum schräg nach den Schneidezähnen zu verlaufende linienartige Nähte; querer Hinterhauptswulst.

Vom übrigen Skelett erhalten:

Die linke Scapula, die beiden Darmbeine, unteres Ende der Tibia und des rechten Femur.

10) „B 3, 3“. Mann mittlerer Jahre.

Schädel unvollständig. Vorhanden sind: Stirnbein größere Hälfte, beide Scheitelbeine, linkes Schläfenbein, Hinterhauptsbein, kleines Stück der rechten Hälfte des Oberkiefers ohne Zähne; sehr breiter, kräftiger Unterkiefer, links die Molaren schräg nach außen stark abgekaut, rechts hintere Molarenalveolen oblitteriert.

Vom übrigen Skelett sind erhalten: das vollständige Becken (auf dem Os sacrum sitzt der unterste Lendenwirbel mit seinem linken Fortsatz fest verwachsen auf, der rechte ist abgebrochen, nach hinten verschoben), die beiden Femora, die beiden Tibiae und Fibulae, der rechte Humerus, Ulna und Radius.

11) „B 3, 5“. Frau in mittleren Jahren.

Zusammengesetzter Schädel (No. 1581), fast vollständig. Fig. 131. Im allgemeinen betrachtet ist der Schädel grazil. Stirn schmal, Scheitelbeine in der Sagittalnaht winklig zusammenstoßend, kräftiges, wohlerhaltenes Gebiß.

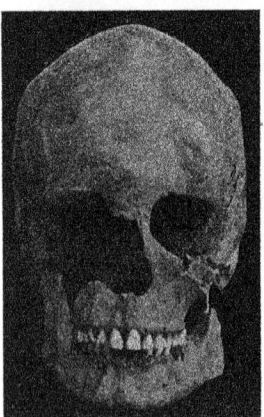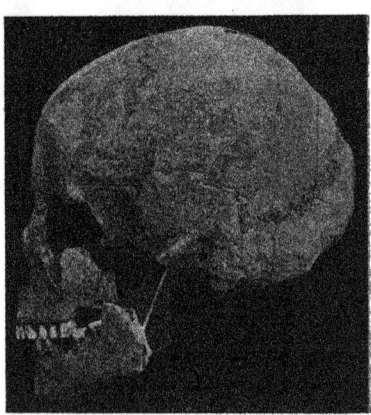

Fig. 131. ¹/₄.

Gerade Länge 18,7 = größte Länge, Intertuberallänge 18,6, größte Breite 13,4, kleinste Stirnbreite 9,65, ganze Höhe 14,3, Hilfshöhe 13,9, Ohrhöhe 11,65 = Hilfsohrhöhe. Länge der Schädelbasis 10,5, Breite der Schädelbasis 10,2. Horizontalumfang 52,0, Sagittalumfang 38,0, vertikaler Querumfang 31,5, Profillänge des Gesichts

11,0. — Der Schädel ist demnach dolichocephal (Index 71,6), orthocephal (Index 74,0).

Gesichtsbreite nach Virchow 9,0, Gesichtshöhe 10,9, obere Gesichtshöhe 7,1. Das Gesicht ist schmal (Index 121,0), schmales
Obergesicht (Index 78,0). Glabella flach, kaum angedeutete Arens
superciliares. Die Augenhöhlen waren verhältnismäßig niedrig, in
ihrer Form oval. Nasenhöhe 4,8, größte Breite der Nasenöffnung
3,0. Hyperplatyrrhinie (Index 62,0), unterer Nasenrand stumpfkantig,
Nasenstachel mittellang. Gaumenlänge 5,3, Gaumenmittelbreite 4,1,
leptostaphylin (Index 77,0). Alveolarfortsatz des Oberkiefers mittelhoch, Juga alveolaria deutlich, Fossa canina flach. Gebiß:

8	7⅜	6	5	4	3	2	1		1	2	3	4	5	6	(7)	(8)
8	7	(6)	5	4	3	2	[1]		[1]	[2]	3	4	5	[6]	7	8

Zahnstein in geringem Grade. Zahnbogen halbkreisförmig.
Überbiß, scharfe Artikulation der Backenzähne, Zahnkronen mittelgroß; Abkauung schräg palatinalwärts abfallend. Der erste Molar
links oben stark abgekaut, weil er intra vitam der einzige Molar gewesen. Unterkiefer mittelgroß, an den Kieferwinkeln nach außen
etwas ausladend, kräftige Eßmuskelansätze. Kieferwinkel 115°,
Distanz der beiden 10,5. Unterer Rand des Unterkieferkörpers mitteldick, ausgeschweift; Protuberantia mäßig stark, Kinn stumpf.

Koronalnaht zahnreich, ebenso Sagittalnaht und Lambdanaht.
Hinterhauptsschuppe mit stark entwickelten Muskelansätzen; linker
Proc. mastoid. klein, rechter groß, durch Patina grün gefärbt. Foramen
magnum langoval 2,9 breit, 3,2 lang.

Sonstige Knochenreste dieses Skeletts:

Das vollständige Becken ohne Symphysenpartie (bemerkenswert
ist, daß die rechte Darmbeinschaufel kleiner als die linke ist), der
rechte Oberarm, der rechte Oberschenkel, die rechte Tibia und Fibula.

12) „B 3, 6". Mann.

Schädel in Bruchstücken. Stirnbein mit kammartiger Erhebung
in der Medianlinie, beiderseits dachförmig abfallend, dabei noch
Becken in drei Teilen mit 12 cm geradem Durchmesser im Beckeneingang und 14 cm quer.

13) „Bei B 3, 6". Weibliche Person von 18 Jahren.

Linker Oberkiefer mit drei festsitzenden Zähnen, darunter der
Milch-Eckzahn; der Weisheitszahn noch nicht durchgebrochen. Der
Oberkiefer ist zierlich.

14) „B 3, 7". Frau von ungefähr 30 Jahren.

Schädel (No. 1583) zusammengesetzt, bis auf unwesentliche
Stücke vollständig. Im allgemeinen breites Gesicht, mehr runder Kopf.
Fig. 132.

Gerade Länge 19,3 = größte Länge, Intertuberallänge 19,4,
größte Breite 14,5; kleinste Stirnbreite 10,1. Ohrhöhe 12,2, Hilfsohrhöhe 12,3. Breite der Schädelbasis 10,8, Horizontalumfang 54,4,
Sagittalumfang 40,5, vertikaler Querumfang 34,0. Es ist der Schädel
also mesocephal (Index 75,2).

Gesichtsbreite nach v. Hölder 12,2, Jochbreite 13,3, Gesichtshöhe 11,3, obere Gesichtshöhe 6,7. Der Schädel gehört demnach immer
noch zu den Schmalgesichtern (Index 92,0) mit schmalem Obergesicht
(Index 54,0). Stirnhöcker deutlich, Glabella flach, Arc. superciliar.
wenig entwickelt. — Augenhöhleneingang abgerundet viereckig, Quer-

axe wenig nach außen geneigt. Gr. Breite 3,7 ⊥ horizontale Breite; gr. Höhe 3,1 = Vertikalhöhe. Mesokonchie (Index 83,0). — Nasenhöhe 4,5, gr. Breite der Nasenöffnung 2,6. Platyrrhinie (Index 57,0). Unterer Nasenrand verstrichen mit Andeutung von Fossa praenasalis.

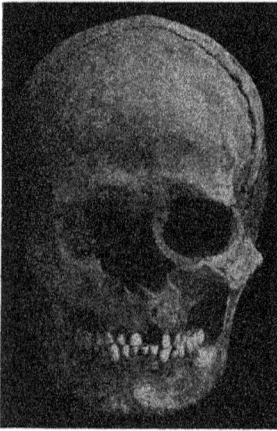 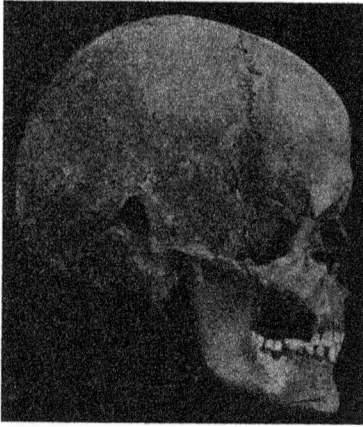

Fig. 132. ¹/₄.

Nasenseptum nicht in der Mitte, mehr nach rechts gedrückt. Nasenstachel spitz, mittellang. Wangenbeine mehr nach vorn gestellt. Alveolarfortsatz des Oberkiefers niedrig; Juga alveolaria deutlich. Gebiß:

$$\frac{8\ 7\ 6\ 5\big\}\ 4\ 3\ 2\ 1\ \big|\ [1]\ 2\ 3\ 4\ (5)\ (6)\ \big\{7\ 8}{8\ 7\ 6\ 5\ \ 4\ 3\ 2\ 1\ \big|\ 1\ 2\ 3\ 4\ 5\ \ 6\ 7\ 8}$$

Zweiter Molarzahn beiderseits im Unterkiefer mit seiner Krone tiefer stehend. Sehr gute Zähne, Zahnkronen klein, horizontal wenig abgekaut; Zahnbogen parabelförmig. Biß gerade, an Vorderzähnen Aufbiß. — Gaumen mittelbreit. — Unterkiefer hoch. Kinn breit, vorspringend, Protuberanz mittelgroß. Unterer Rand des Kieferkörpers dick, geradlinig. Unterkieferwinkel 115°, Distanz der beiden 10,6. Koronalnaht reichzackig, Sagittalnaht geschlängelt, Hinterhauptsschuppe mit mäßig stark entwickelten Muskelansätzen; Warzenfortsätze lang, relativ schmal.

Vom übrigen Skelett sind erhalten:

Das vollständige Becken, ein Lendenwirbel, der linke Femur, die linke Tibia und Fibula, der rechte und linke Humerus, der linke Radius und die halbe Ulna, das linke Schulterblatt, die rechte Clavicula, Atlas und Epistropheus.

15) „B 3, 8 (a)". Alter Mann.

Vom Schädel (No. 1594) nur erhalten Oberkiefer und Unterkiefer. Gesichtsbreite 9,3, gr. Breite der Nasenöffnung 2,4. Fossa canina mitteltief, Alveolarfortsatz des Oberkiefers hoch. Gebiß:

$$\frac{(8)\ (7)\ (6)\ 5\ [4]\ [3]\ 2\ [1]\ \big|\ [1]\ 2\ 3\ 4\ [5]\ (6)|\ [7]\ [8]}{(8)\ 7\ 6\ 5\ [4]\ [3]\ 2\ 1\ \big|\ 1\ 2\ 3\ 4\ 5\ 6\ 7\ (8)}$$

Im Unterkiefer rechts sind die Molaren 6 und 7 stark verlängert, weil Antagonisten lange fehlen. Von links unten 6 beide kariöse Wurzeln erhalten, von 7 nur die mesiale kariöse Wurzel; Aufbiß gerade; Abkauung sehr stark, teilweise bis zum Zahnhals. Zahnbogen schmale Parabel. Kinn schmal. Unterkieferwinkel 115°, Distanz der beiden 9,9. Gaumenlänge 5,5, Gaumenmittelbreite 4,4, Gaumenendbreite 4,2. Leptostaphylin (Index 76,0).
Keine weiteren Skelettreste.

16) „B 3, 8 (6)". Frau mittlerer Jahre.
Schädel in Bruchstücken: Os frontis mit deutlichen Arcus superciliares und Glabella, beide Scheitelbeine, beide Oss. temporalia, Os occipit. beschädigt; rechte Oberkieferhälfte mit 2. stark horizontal abgekautem Molar. 3. Molar einwurzelig, sehr klein. Vom Unterkiefer ist nur die Kinngegend erhalten. Der Bau des Schädels ist im ganzen grazil.

17) „B 3, 9". Erwachsene Person.
Schädel in Bruchstücken: Os frontis, Ossa parietalia in einem Stück, Oberkiefermittelstück mit Zähnen, Hinterhauptsschuppe. Auffällig ist die Schwere der Knochen. Stirnbein mit deutlich entwickelten Arcus superciliares, zwei Finger breit über dem rechten Supraorbitalwulst quer laufende Delle. Hinterhauptsschuppe und die angrenzenden Partien der Ossa parietalia höckerig uneben. Die Parietalia stoßen in der Sagittalnaht flach dachförmig aneinander. Die Zähne sind stark schräg abgekaut, erhalten bis inklusive 2. Bicuspis, haben breite Kronen, sehr engen Hals. Wurzeln schwarz gefärbt, auch die Zahnkronen auf der Innenseite.
Vom übrigen Körper ist das Mittelstück eines Oberschenkels erhalten, auch dieser Knochen fällt auf durch seine Schwere und höckerige Unebenheit.

18) „B 4, 2". Frau jüngerer Jahre.
Schädeldach vollständig erhalten (No. 1596), rechte Gesichtshälfte zum größten Teil, die rechte Unterkieferhälfte, das linke Schläfenbein. Fig. 133.
Größte Länge 19,5. Intertuberallänge 19,9, größte Breite 13,5. Hilfsohrhöhe 14,2. Horizontaler Umfang 54,3. Der Schädel ist dolichocephal (Index 69), hoch.
Von vorn betrachtet, fällt das flachdachförmige Zusammenstoßen der Scheitelbeine auf. Die Stirnhöcker wenig ausgeprägt, Supraorbitalwülste wenig hervortretend. Augenhöhleneingang niedrig. Wangenbein seitlich gestellt, eher anliegend. Fossa canina flach. Die erhaltenen Zähne:

$$\frac{7\ 6\ 5\ 4\ [3]\ \underline{\ \ \ }}{7\ 6\ 5\ [4]\ \underline{\ \ \ }}\ \Big|$$

mittelgroß, wenig abgekaut, nach schräg außen, noch kein Weisheitszahn, viel Zahnstein an den oberen Zähnen, gerader Biß. Unterkieferwinkel 124°. Nähte feinlinig gezackt. Drittes und viertes Fünftel der Sagittalnaht verwachsen.
Vom übrigen Skelett erhalten:

Rechte Tibia, schlank; rechter Femur, schlank, groß; linke Darmbeinschaufel; linkes Schienbein und Fibula; rechter Humerus.

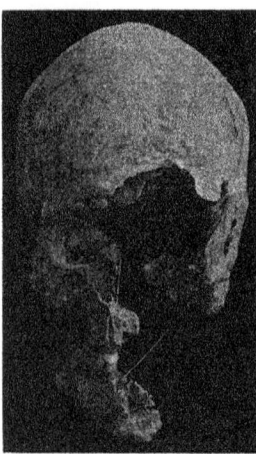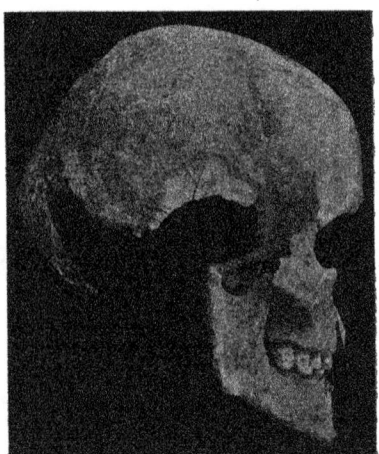

Fig. 133. $^1/_4$.

19) „B 4, 3“. Kind 6. 4 Jahr alt.

Vom Schädel erhalten: Squama occipitalis, linke Oberkieferhälfte mit Zahnbogen, Unterkieferzahnbogen, Äste desselben abgebrochen. Gebiß:

$$\frac{\text{I [II] [III] IV V}}{\text{V IV [III] II [I]}\ |\ \text{I II III IV V } \overline{6}}$$

Milchzahngebiß vollständig, hinter dem linken II. Milchmolar ist der Keim des bleibenden ersten Molar ausgefallen.

Kinn unterer Rand geradlinig, eckig umbiegend.

20) „B 4, 4“. Jüngerer Mann.

Schädel in Bruchstücken: Scheitelbeine, rechtes Schläfenbein, linke Unterkieferhälfte mit sehr starken Zähnen, 2. Prämolar, 1. und 2. Molar.

21) „B 5“. Ein Erwachsener.

Nur die Gehirnkapsel erhalten in einem Stück: Os frontis, Parietalia, Occiput, Temporalia, Wespenbein. Schädel oval, Nähte gezackt, keine Schaltknochen. Arcus superciliares nicht hervortretend, auch Glabella nicht. Auf der rechten Höhe des rechten Parietale achtförmiges Loch mit glatten Rändern. Foramen magnum breitoval. Außerdem sind Atlas und Epistropheus erhalten.

C. Dritte Ausgrabung am 13. Oktober 1871.

22) Kind 2, 8—9 Jahr alt.

Schädelreste: Os frontis in Stücken, Parietalia, Schläfenbeine,

Hinterhaupt, alle einzeln und beschädigt. Unterkiefer fast vollständig, spitzes Kinn. Gebiß:

$$\overline{6 \ V \ IV \ [III] \ 2 \ 1} \ \Big| \ \overline{[1] \ [2] \ \overset{\frown}{3} \ [IV] \ V \ 6} \\ \overset{\frown}{4}$$

In der Alveole des ausgefallenen ersten Milchmolaren links ist der erste bleibende Bicuspis sichtbar; etwas tiefer liegend als dieser in der Alveole des Eckzahns der bleibende Eckzahn; erster Milch-molar mäßig horizontal abgekaut.

23) „C 2“. Jun   14 Jahren.
   Schädel (N   ig, zusammengesetzt; im ganzen
breites Gesicht,   Kopf, mit stark ausgebauchter Hinterhauptsschuppe. Fig. 134.

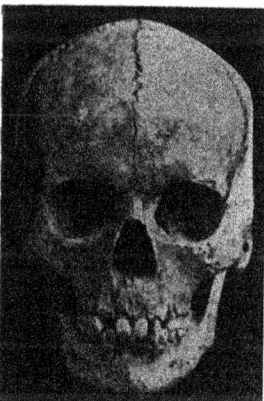 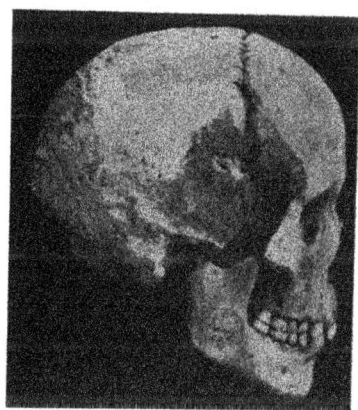

Fig. 134. $^1/_4$.

Gerade Länge 18,5, größte Länge 18,6, Intertuberallänge 18,9, größte Breite 13,9, kleinste Stirnbreite 10,15. Ganze Höhe 14,5, Hilfshöhe 14,7, Ohrhöhe 11,4, Hilfsohrhöhe 11,5, Horizontalumfang 52,3. Sagittalumfang 37,3, vertikaler Querumfang 31,7. Demnach ist der Schädel eben noch dolichocephal (Index 74), aber hart an der Grenze der Mesocephalic und chamäcephal (Index 63,0).

Gesichtsbreite nach Virchow 9,25, nach v. Hölder 11,4. Jochbreite 13,1, Gesichtshöhe 11,2, obere Gesichtshöhe 6,9, schmalgesichtig (Index 120,0), schmales Obergesicht (Index 74,0). Stirnnaht in ganzer Länge erhalten, scharfzähnig. Auf der linken Stirnbeinhälfte schwärzliche Brandflecken. Glabella wenig gewulstet, ebenso Arcus superciliares. Augenhöhleneingang abgerundet viereckig. Querachsen wenig nach außen unten geneigt. Gr. Breite 3,7 = horizontale Breite; gr. Höhe 3,1, Vertikalhöhe 3,2. Mesokonchie (Index 83,0). Nasenrücken breit, wenig eingesattelt, Nasenbeine viereckig; Nasenhöhe 4,8, größte Breite der Nasenöffnung 2,5. Plathyrrhinie (Index

52). Nasenöffnung ulmenblattförmig. Unterer Nasenrand verstrichen. Gaumenlänge 5,1, Gaumenmittelbreite 4,4, Gaumenendbreite 4,4. Brachystaphylin (Index 86). Hinter dem Foramen incisivum zwei rechtwinklig von der Gaumennaht abgehende Nähte. Alveolarfortsatz des Oberkiefers hoch. Fossa canina flach. Profillänge des Gesichts 9,2. Gebiß:

7	6	5	4	3	2	1	1	2	3̂	4	5	6	7
7	6	5	4	III	2	1	1	2	3	4	5	6	7

Zahnwurzeln der Schneidezähne und des Eckzahnes sehr lang. Zahnbogen in Form einer Parabel, breit. Vordere Zähne überbeißend, Backzähne aufbeißend. Zahnkronen mittelgroß, nicht abgekaut. — Unterkieferwinkel 118°, Distanz beider 9,5. Kinn spitz. Protuberanz mittelgroß. — Länge der Schädelbasis 10,2, Breite derselben 11,8. Länge der Pars basilaris 2,9. Foramen magnum longoval, gr. Breite 3,1, gr. Länge 3,8. Hinterhauptsschuppe kapselförmig vorspringend, Muskelansätze verhältnismäßig kräftig.

Keine weiteren Knochen vom Skelett vorhanden. Eine Notiz hierüber sagt:

„C 2, Skelett von 1,87 m Länge, ohne Beigaben. mit auffällig kurzen Armen, das Handwurzelgelenk beginnt am Skelett schon 2 Zoll unter dem Hüftknochen.“

24) „C“ (3?). Erwachsene, schmalgesichtige Frau, mit spitzem Kinn.

Schädel in Bruchstücken: Os frontis mit wenig erhabenen Supraorbitalwülsten, wenig vortretender Glabella. Kleinste Stirnbreite 9,0. Ossa parietalia. Os occipitis mit mittelstarker Protuberantia. Os temp. Ein stark schräg abgekauter 1. Oberkiefermolar mit Oberkieferbruchstück, von der linken Oberkieferhälfte ein Bruchstück mit Eckzahn und den zwei Prämolaren. Zähne gut, aber stark schräg abgekaut, klein. Vom Unterkiefer Bruchstücke der linken und rechten Außenseite und je dem 1. Molar. Kinnpartie ohne Zähne. Eine zu C 3 gehörige Notiz sagt:

„C 3, Frauenskelett, Länge 1,72 m, mit Messer von Eisen, zur Linken neben den Vorderarmen ein paar Flußsteine beigelegt.“

25) „C“ (4?). Mann in mittleren Jahren.

Schädel (No. 1582) zusammengesetzt, bis auf die mittlere Gesichtspartie vollständig, aber verschoben in der Richtung von rechts vorn nach links hinten. Schädel im allgemeinen kräftig, schwer, mit auffälliger kielartiger Leiste in der Sagittalnaht, kräftiges Gebiß. Fig. 135.

Größte Länge 19,5, Intertuberallänge 19,9, größte Breite 13,9, kleinste Stirnbreite 9,9. Hilfshöhe 16,48. Horizontalumfang 54,0, Sagittalumfang 40,0. Es ist also ein dolichocephaler Hochschädel. (Dolicocephalieindex 71,0, Hochschädelindex 84,7).

Gesicht schmal, Stirnhöcker deutlich, Glabella kräftig entwickelt, Arcus superciliares weniger. Nasenbeine viereckig, Nasenrücken stark eingesattelt. — Unterer Nasenrand stumpfkantig. Alveolarfortsatz des Oberkiefers hoch. Gebiß:

8	7	[6]	5	4	3	2	1	1	2	3	4	5	6	7	8
8	7	6	5	4	[3]	[2]	[1]	[1]	[2]	3	4	5	6	7	8

Fast an allen Zähnen Halscaries. Zahnbogen in der Form

einer Parabel, breit; Biß gerade, Vorderzähne überbeißend, schaufel. artig nach innen gestaltet, Backenzähne artikulierend, Zahnkronen mittelgroß, horizontal mäßig abgekaut. — Gaumenlänge 5,0, Gaumen. mittelbreite 4,5, Gaumenendbreite 4,4. Brachystaphylin (Index 88,0). — Unterkiefer massiv, rechter Kieferwinkel stark lateralwärts aus. ladend, kräftige Muskelansätze. Unterer Rand des Kieferkörpers

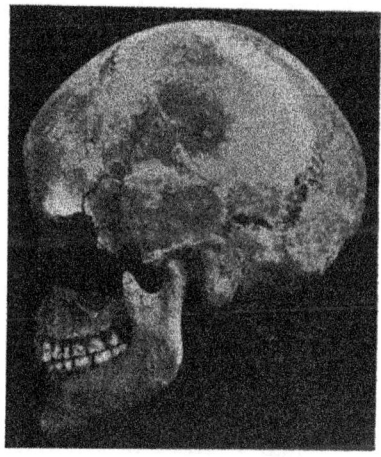

Fig. 135. .¹/₄.

dick, geradlinig. Kinn vorspringend, breit, Protuberantia mäßig ent. wickelt. Kieferwinkel 120°, Distanz der beiden 11,4. Koronalnaht zahnarm. Sagittalnaht in der mittleren Strecke verknöchert. Lambda. naht mit mehreren kleinen Schaltstücken in beiden Ästen. Hinter. hauptsschuppe mit kräftigen Muskelansätzen. Foramen magnum langoval: 3,1 breit; 4,4 lang. Breite der Schädelbasis 12,15 (ver. schoben), Länge derselben 12,0.

Keine weiteren Skelettreste jetzt vorhanden. Eine Notiz besagt: „C 4. Skelett von 1,70 m Länge, wohl erhalten."

26) Kind 4. 3—4 Jahr alt.

Vollständiges Milchzahngebiß des Unterkiefers und der linken Hälfte des Oberkiefers.

					[I]	[II]	[III]	IV	V
V	IV	[III]	[II]	[I]	[I]	[II]	[III]	IV	V

Vom sonstigen Schädel nur noch das linke Jochbein erhalten. Unterkiefer außen durch Brand schwarz gefleckt.

D. Vierte Ausgrabung Klopfleischs am 6. u. 7. Mai 1872 „bei Appler".

27) „D". Eine erwachsene Person.

Gehirnkapsel in einem Stück: Parietalia, ein Stück der Hinter. hauptsschuppe, Os frontis. Dazu lose, aber passend die Temporalia.

Es fehlen Kiefer und Gesichtsknochen. Der Schädel ist oval, die rechte Seite des Hinterhaupts ist platt gedrückt, Nähte gezähnt. Arcus superciliares, Glabella kaum hervortretend.

28) „D 2". Erwachsene Person.

Schädel in Bruchstücken, unvollständig. Os frontis, Parietalia, Os occipitis, Os temporale rechts. Gehirnkapsel mit rechter hinterer Seite stark nach links gedrückt. Vom Unterkiefer erhalten ein größeres Bruchstück der rechten Hälfte mit

$$\overline{6 \quad 5 \quad 4 \quad 3 \quad [2] \quad [1]} \mid [1] \quad [2]$$

Zähne abgekaut schräg nach unten außen, dentale Prognathie; Protub. mentalis kräftig. Eine hierher gehörige Notiz berichtet:

„D 2, am 7. Mai 1872 ausgegraben. Skelett schlecht erhalten, Schädel eingedrückt, Stirnpartie erhalten. Lage südöstlich, Länge 1,29 + 0,15 (Kopf), etwas verschoben, liegend.

In der Hüftgegend ein kleiner Bronzering, ein etwas größerer Bronzering unter dem Kopf zur rechten Seite; in der Mitte ein Messer."

29) „D 3" Kind 9. 3 Jahr alt.

Bruchstück des Stirnbeins und die Mandibula zum größten Teil.

$$\overline{6 \quad V \quad IV \quad [III] \quad [II] \quad [I]} \mid [I] \quad [II] \quad [III] \quad IV \quad V$$

Kinn spitz, einige graue Brandflecken auf der Außenseite.

„D 3. Der Kinderschädel lag ganz allein; mit zwei silbernen, kleinen Ohrringen, Bronzeperle und Bernsteinperle; kleiner Reibstein."

30) „D 4" Kind 7. 5-jährig.

Ober- und Unterkiefer. Nur Milchgebiß:

$$\frac{V \quad IV \quad III \quad II \quad I \mid I \quad II \quad III \, IV \, \frac{5}{5}V}{V \quad IV \quad III \quad [II] \quad [I] \mid [I] \, [II] \quad III \quad IV \, .V \, \overline{6}}$$

Unterkiefer breit, Kinn breit.

„D 4. Dabei ein länglich geteilter Schleifstein."

31) „D 5". Mann über 40 Jahre.

Unterkiefer (No. 1600) sehr kräftig, hoch, dickknochig. Kinn spitz, vorspringend, Außenfläche des Kiefers beiderseits schwarz gefleckt. Zähne gut, groß, stark abgekaut. Links fehlen 2. und 1. Molar, deren Alveolen sind oblitteriert; 3. Molar links nach vorn gewandert und geneigt. Kondylenachsen geradlinig verlaufend. Kieferwinkel 125°, Distanz beider 9,3, kräftige Masseterleisten.

Vom übrigen Schädel vorhanden Os frontis, Ossa parietalia, beide Ossa temporalia. Schädel langoval, rechtes Parietale glatt gedrückt, Nähte gezackt. Keine sonstigen Skelettteile.

Notiz zu D 5. „Skelett eines Erwachsenen, 1,60 lang, Schädel schief gequetscht, auf Asche liegend, kohlige Erde auch darüber, zwei Fuß tief; Messer zur Linken."

32) „D 6". Frau mittlerer Jahre.

Schädel (No. 1597) im ganzen vollständig vorhanden, zusammengesetzt aber nicht genau aneinanderpassend, der Hinterkopf verdrückt.

Der Schädel dolichocephal. Gr. Breite 12,5, kleinste Stirnbreite 9,2. Breite der Schädelbasis 10,0. Stirnhöcker deutlich. Supraorbitalwülste kräftig. Glabella vorgewulstet. Gesicht schmal. Alveoläre Prognathie, während Zähne gerade herunter stehen. Gebiß:

7	6	5	4	3	2	[1]		[1]	2	3	4	5	6	7	8
8	7	6	5	4	3	2	1	[1]	2	3	4	5	6	7	8

Der rechte obere Weisheitszahn fehlt noch. Gedrängte Stellung der Schneidezähne unten, dadurch in der Höhe unregelmäßig. Zahnkronen klein, fast nicht abgekaut. Elliptischer Zahnbogen oben, unten parabolisch. Kinn spitz. Protuberanz kräftig. Kieferwinkel 111°, Distanz beider 9,4. Gaumen mittelhoch, Gaumenlänge 4,9, Gaumenmittelbreite 4,0, Gaumenendbreite 3,8. Leptostaphylin (Index 77). Linienhafte schräg vom For. incisiv. nach dem Interstitium zwischen 1. und 2. Schneidezahn verlaufende Naht rechterseits. Nähte grobzackig, am Lambda sehr großes Schaltstück. Auf der linken und rechten Seite, besonders auf den Scheitelbeinen schwärzliche Flecken von Branderde, ebenso an beiden Proc. mast. For. magn. langoval, 3,7 zu 3,0. Protub. occipital. kräftig.

Keine weiteren Skelettreste.

Notiz zu D 6. „Gleich links neben dem vorigen, 1,71 m lang, Arm in unregelmäßiger Lage, alte Person, Ohrring von Bronze

33) „D 7". Älterer Mann.

Schädel (No. 1589) ohne Oberkiefer und Wangenbeine, unvollständige Basis, linker Unterkiefer abgebrochen. Fig. 136. Größte Länge 19,0, Intertuberallänge 18.8, größte Breite 14,3, kleinste Stirnbreite 10,1, Hilfsohrhöhe 13,5, Breite der Schädelbasis 11,5, Horizontal-

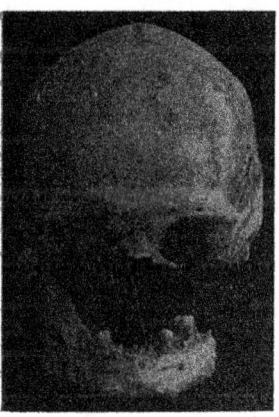 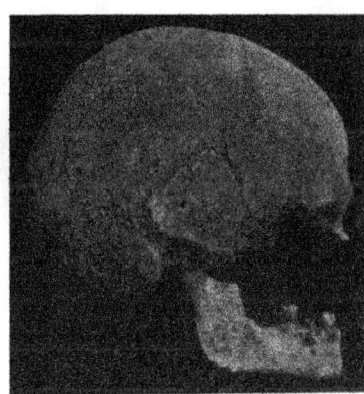

Fig. 136. $^1/_4$.

umfang 53,0, Sagittalumfang 38,6. Der Schädel ist dolichocephal (Index 75). Starke Arcus superciliares. Sattelnase, mediane Nasennaht teilweise obliteriert. Koronalnaht feinlinig, zahnreich. Sagittalnaht im hinteren $^3/_5$ verwachsen. Zwei Foramina parietalia. Lambdanaht labyrinthisch verschlungen, großer Schaltknochen am Lambda, Gegend des Lambda eingesunken, rechte Hälfte der Koronalnaht und Sagittalnaht flach dachförmig hervortretend. Kräftige Muskelinsertionsleisten auf der Hinterhauptsschuppe. Unterkieferwinkel lateralwärts ausladend, 110°. Unterer Rand des Unterkieferkörpers dick, geradlinig. Kinn sehr breit, eckig umbiegend, Spina mentalis interna gedoppelt. Zahnbogen parabolisch. Zahnkronen nicht abgekaut. Gebiß im Unterkiefer:

(8) (7) 6 [5] 4 [3] [2] [1]	[1] [2] [3] 4 [5] [6] 7 {8

Von 6 steht nur noch die kariöse mesiale Wurzel mit Fistel. Beginnende Caries des Halses des 2. linken Molaren.

Keine weiteren Skelettreste.

Notiz zu D 7. „Gut erhaltener? Schädel, Skelett 1,70 lang, ohne Beigaben, ein Scherben."

34) „D 8". Junger Mann, über 20 Jahre alt.

Vollständiger, sehr gut erhaltener Schädel (No. 1586), auffällig hoch und groß. Stirn, Wangenbeine, Unterkiefer, durch Berührung mit Branderde schwärzlich gefleckt. Fig. 137. Gerade Länge 18,9 = größte Länge. Intertuberallänge 18,5, größte Breite 13,6, kleinste

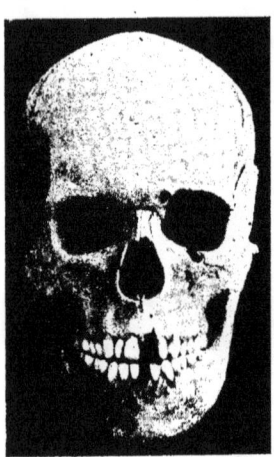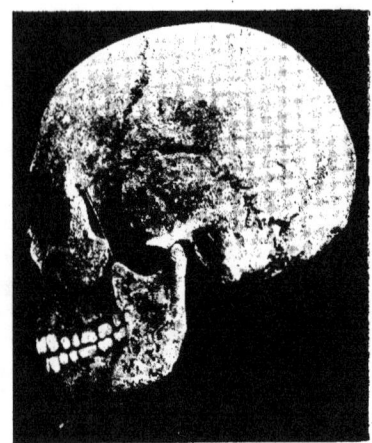

Fig. 137. $^1/_4$.

Stirnbreite 10,1. Ganze Höhe 14,5 = Hilfshöhe. Ohrhöhe 10,9 = Hilfsohrhöhe. Länge der Schädelbasis 10,4, Breite derselben 11,35. Horizontalumfang 52,5, Sagittalumfang 37,8, vertikaler Querumfang 31,6. Der Schädel ist dolichocephal (Index 71,0), ein Hochschädel (Index 76). Das Gesicht ist schmal (Index 128), Index des schmalen Obergesichts 71,5. Gesichtsbreite nach Virchow 10,0, nach v. Hölder 11,78. Jochbreite 13,4, Gesichtshöhe 12,8, obere Gesichtshöhe 7,15. Stirnbeinhöcker kaum entwickelt. Glabella mittelstark, ebenso die Supraorbitalwülste. — Nasenrücken mäßig eingesattelt, Nasenbeine viereckig, dachförmig gestellt. Nasenhöhe 5,0; gr. Breite der Nasen-öffnung 2,6, Nasenöffnung ulmenblattförmig, unterer Nasenrand scharfkantig, Stachel stumpf. — Augenhöhleneingang abgerundet viereckig, Querachsen sehr wenig schräg gestellt; gr. Breite 3,9 = horizontale Breite, gr. Höhe 3,2, vertikale Höhe 3,3. — Fossa canina flach. Wangenheine etwas nach vorn gestellt. Jochbogen leicht ausgebaucht. Alveolarfortsatz des Oberkiefers mittelhoch. Gebiß sehr gut, keine Caries, weiße Farbe, kein Zahnstein.

8	7	6	5	4	3	2	1	[1]	2	3	4	5	6	7	8
8	7	6	5	4	3	2	1	[1]	2	3	4	5	6	7	8

Der zweite obere rechte Schneidezahn um 90° gedreht. Zahnbogen in Parabelform, gerader Biß, große Zahnkronen, nicht abgekaut. Unterkiefer hoch, unterer Rand des Unterkieferkörpers sehr dick, geradlinig. Kinn vorspringend, geradlinig, eckig umbiegend. Kieferwinkel 122°, Distanz der beiden 9,8. Muskelansätze wenig hervortretend. — Gaumenlänge 5,1, Gaumenmittelbreite 4,5, Gaumenendbreite 4,8. Brachystaphylin (Index 94,0). Gaumen hochgewölbt, vom Foram. incisiv. beiderseits ausgehende ca. 1 cm lange kleine Nähte quer über das Gaumendach. — Koronalnaht mäßig gezackt, ebenso Sagittal- und Lambdanaht. Die Sagittalnaht beiderseits von je einer kammartigen Leiste begleitet. Muskelinsertionsleisten der Hinterhauptsschuppe kräftig. Hinterhauptsloch langoval; gr. Breite 3,1, gr. Länge 4,15. Länge der Pars basilaris 3,1. Profillänge 9,6.

Keine weiteren Skelettreste.

Notiz zu D 8. „Das Skelett 1,60 m lang, sehr hohe Unterkiefer. In der Beckengegend Reste einer eisernen Schnalle und eine lange Bronzeperle."

35) „D 9." Erwachsener Mann.

Unterkieferfragment mit 17 losen Zähnen. Unterer Rand des Kieferkörpers dick, Kinn stumpf. Zähne stark horizontal abgekaut, einzelne kariös.

Ein dabei liegendes linkes Schlüsselbein stark gebogen.

Notiz zu D 9. „Skelett sehr mitgenommen. Am Kopf in der Nähe des Unterkiefers lag ein Huhnskelett (Opfer). Eimer zu Füßen des Skeletts."

36) „D 10." „VII D 10." Frau, über 40 Jahre alt.

Ganz vollständig erhaltener, im ganzen kleiner Schädel (No. 1588). Fig. 138.

Gerade Länge 18,0 = größte Länge. Intertuberallänge 17,8, größte Breite 13,6, kleinste Stirnbreite 9,6. Ganze Höhe 13,6 = Hilfshöhe. Ohrhöhe 11,6, Hilfsohrhöhe 11,75. Länge der Schädelbasis 9,8, Breite der Schädelbasis 10,0, Horizontalumfang 50,5, Sagittalumfang 37,0, vertikaler Querumfang 30,7. Dolichocephalie 75, Orthocephalie 75. Stirnhöcker wenig entwickelt. Glabella breit, wulstartig. Arcus superciliares wenig entwickelt. Gesichtsbreite 9,1 (Virchow), 11,3 (v. Hölder). Jochbreite 12,5, Gesichtshöhe 10,6, obere Gesichtshöhe 6,3. Schmalgesichtig (Index 116), schmales Obergesicht (Index 69). Nasenrücken flach sattelförmig, unterer Nasenrand stumpfkantig. Nasenhöhe 3,9, gr. Breite der Nasenöffnung 2,7, Hyperplatyrrhinie (Index 71). — Augenhöhleneingang abgerundet viereckig, gr. Breite 3,6, horizontale Breite 3,5, gr. Höhe 3,1 = Vertikalhöhe. Hypsikonchie (Index 86). Fossa canina tief. Wangenheine anliegend.

Alveolarfortsatz des Oberkiefers mittelhoch, gegen die Horizontale schräg gestellt. Stellung der Zähne schräg nach vorn.

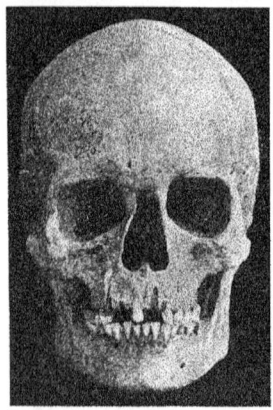 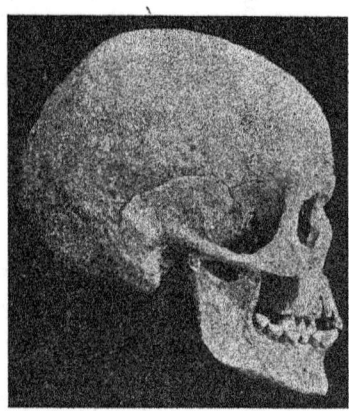

Fig. 138. $^1/_4$.

$$\frac{8\quad 7^{\underline{3}}\quad 6\quad 5\quad 4\quad [3]\quad [2]\quad 1\ \Big|\ [1]\quad 2\quad 3\quad 4\quad 5\cdot 6^{**}\ (7)\ (8)}{8\quad 7\quad 6\quad 5\quad 4\quad 3\quad 2\quad 1\ \Big|\ 1\quad 2\quad 3\quad 4\quad 5\quad 6\quad 7^*\quad 8}$$

Von 7* unten nur die distale kariöse Wurzel erhalten, bei links oben 6** Gaumenfistel. Der daneben stehende Zahn 5 kariös, durch Caries der Krone eröffnete Pulpahöhle. Zahnbogen in Form einer Ellipse über die kleine Achse fortgesetzt, Biß offen, Backzähne artikulieren scharf. Zahnkronen klein, stark abgekaut und zwar unregelmäßig, mehr schräg. — Unterkiefer mit kräftigen Muskelansätzen. Unterer Rand des Unterkieferkörpers dick. Kinn etwas vorspringend, breit, Protuberanz mäßigentwickelt. Kieferwinkel 121°, Distanz der beiden 9,7. Gaumen brachystaphylin (Index 88), Gaumenlänge 5,1, Gaumenmittelbreite 4,8, Gaumenendbreite 4,5. — Koronalnaht feinlinig, zahnreich. In der Sagittalnaht treten die Scheitelbeine flach dachförmig aneinander. Kleines For. pariet. auf dem rechten Scheitelbein, Scheitelbeinhöcker deutlich. Foramen magnum langoval, klein, 2,65 breit, 3,3 lang. Länge der Pars basilaris 2,2. Profillänge 9,8.

Keine weiteren Skelettreste.

Notiz zu D 10. „Skelett, Länge 1,30 + 0,21 = 1,51. Eisernes Messer mit Holzspuren am Griff."

37) „D 11." Cirka 40-jähriger Mann.

Schädel (No. 1585) fast vollständig erhalten, seitlich zusammengedrückt, aber auch abgesehen davon mit schmalem Gesicht, langem ovalen Kopf. Fig. 139.

Gerade Länge 19,9 = größte Länge. Intertuberallänge 19,2, größte Breite 13,4, kleinste Stirnbreite 9,8. Ohrhöhe 11,8, Hilfsohrhöhe 11,9. Horizontalumfang 53,8, vertikaler Querumfang 32,0.

Der Schädel ist dolichocephal (Index 67,0) chamäcePhal. (59). Gesichtsbreite nach Virchow 9,3, nach v. Hölder 10,9, Gesichtshöhe 12,0,
obere Gesichtshöhe 6,9. Schmalgesicht (Index 129), schmales Obergesicht (74,0). Glabella und Arc. supercil. vorgewulstet. Nasenrücken

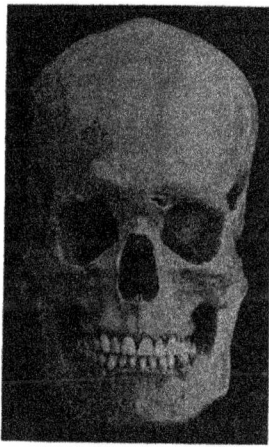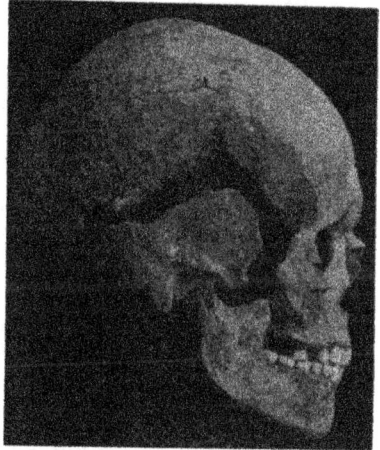

Fig. 139. ¹/₄.

tief eingesattelt, Nasenbeine viereckig, Medionasalnaht teilweise oblitteriert. Nasenhöhe 4,8, gr. Breite der Nasenöffnung 2,26. Leptorrhinie (Index 47,0). Unterer Rand der Nasenöffnung scharfkantig,
Nasenstachel spitz, lang. — Augenhöhleneingang abgerundet viereckig, gr. Breite 3,7, horizontale Breite 3,4; gr. Höhe 3,0, Vertikalhöhe 3,2. Mesokonchie (Index 81). Gaumenlänge 5,1, Gaumenmittel-
länge 4,0. Leptostaphylin (Index 78,0). Alveolarfortsatz des Oberkiefers mittelhoch. Fossa canina tief. Wangenbein anliegend. Gebiß:

[8]	[7]	6	[5]	4	3	2	1	1	2	3	4	5	6	[7]	[8]
8	7	6	5	4	3	2	1	1	2	3	4	[5]	6	(7)	8

Auffällige Verstärkung des vorderen Alveolarrandes der unteren
Schneide- und Eckzähne. Am linken unteren ersten Molaren tiefe
Caries der Krone und des Halses. Zahnbogen parabelförmig. Gerader
Biß, Vorderzähne überbeißend. Zahnkronen mittelgroß, wenig abgekaut, horizontal. Unterkiefer sehr hoch, massiv. Unterkieferwinkel
113°, Distanz beider 10,8. Kinn stumpf, Protuberanz gering. Koronalnaht feinlinig, gezackt. Zwei große Foramina parietalia in der Nähe
der Sagittalnaht. Sagittalnaht wenig gezackt, auf der Höhe des
Scheitels kielartig vorspringend. Kleines Schaltbein im rechten Ast
der Lambdanaht. Hinterhauptsschuppe mit mittelstarken Muskelansätzen.
    Dazu gehörig ein linker Femur und eine linke Tibia.
    Notiz zu D 11. „Skelett 1,80 m lang.“

E. Fortsetzung der Ausgrabung durch Schachtmeister Mayer*) am 8. Mai 1872.

38) „E." Jüngerer Mann.

Unterkiefer (No. 1599). Unterer Rand des Unterkieferkörpers dick, Kinn stumpf, Gebiß vollständig, linker Weisheitszahn noch nicht vorhanden. Zahnkronen mittelgroß, horizontal abgekaut, wenig. Außenfläche des Unterkiefers schwarz gefleckt durch Brand. Kieferwinkel 115°, Distanz beider 10,2.

Vom übrigen Schädel Os frontis, Ossa parietalia, Os occipitis und linkes Os temporale in einem Stück erhalten, von der linken Seite her durch Druck verschoben. Die Gehirnkapsel war im ganzen schmal, oval. Die Parietalia vereinigen sich in der Sagittalnaht flach dachförmig, starke Protub. occipitalis.

Keine weiteren Skelettreste.

Notiz zu E 1. „Vom Skelett nur Schädelreste vorhanden, vom Körper nichts. In der Nähe stand ein Eimer allein (eine alte schon durchgegrabene Stelle nach dem einzelnen Eimerrest."

39) „E 2." 30—40-jähriger Mann.

Wohlerhaltener Schädel (No. 1576). Fig. 140. Unterkiefer groß, massiv, mit starken Muskelansätzen; Distanz der Kieferwinkel 11,0, Kieferwinkel 135°, Kieferast dick, liegend, am scharfen Winkel lateralwärts ausgebogen; Gelenkfortsätze groß, schräg gestellt; Proc. coronoid. klein; Incisur rechts tiefer als links. Rand des Unterkieferkörpers dick, geradlinig; Kinn stumpf, Protuberanz schwach entwickelt. Alveolarteil des Unterkiefers vollständig; Zahnbogen halbkreisförmig, geschlossen; Biß gerade, scharf artikulierend; Zahnkronen groß, relative Größe der einzelnen normal; Kaufläche horizontal mäßig abgekaut. Gebiß: alveodentale Prognathie.

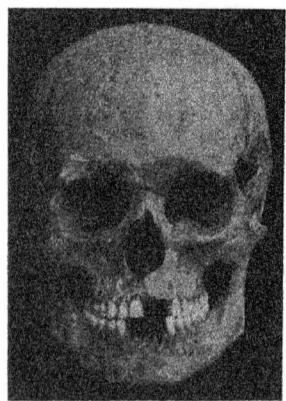 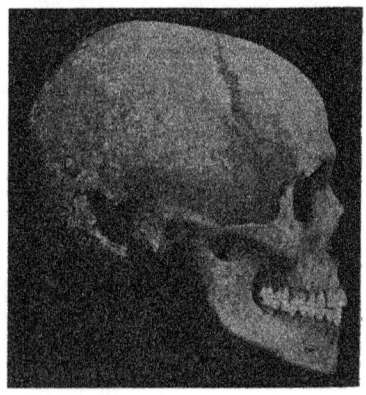

Fig. 140. ¹/₄.

*) Herr Schachtmeister Mayer aus Dürrenberg war schon Tags zuvor bei Klopfleischs Ausgrabung anwesend gewesen.

$$\frac{8\ 7\ 6\ 5\ 4\ 3\ \ 2\ \ 1\ |\ [1]\ [2]\ 3\ 4\ 5\ 6\ 7\ 8}{8\ 7\ 6\ 5\ 4\ 3\ [2]\ [1]\ |\ [1]\ [2]\ 3\ 4\ 5\ 6\ 7\ 8}$$

Zahnsteinansatz. — Gaumen mittelhoch gewölbt, medianer Gaumenwulst höheren Grades, einzelne Höckerchen am Gaumen. Gaumenlänge 5,0, Gaumenmittelbreite 4,1, Gaumenendbreite 3,9. Brachystaphylin (Index 94,0). — Alveolarfortsatz des Oberkiefers mittelhoch, gegen die Horizontale schräg gestellt, Juga alveolaria stark ausgeprägt, sehr dünn auf der rechten Seite; Fossa canina sehr tief. — Wangenbein nach vorn vortretend; Tuberositas malaris stärker ausgeprägt, hinterer Rand des Proc. frontal. des Jochbeins leicht flügelförmig ausgezogen; Jochbogen abstehend. — Nasenbeine schmal, viereckig; Nasenrücken im Seitenprofil eingesattelt, hochgewölbt im Querschnitt. Nasenöffnung lang, oval; Nasenstachel sehr lang, spitz; unterer Nasenrand schneidend scharfkantig. Nasenhöhe 4,4, gr. Breite der Nasenöffnung 2,2. Mesorrhinie (Index 50,0). — Augenhöhlen groß, rundlich, Querachsen wenig abfallend. Augenhöhleneingang größte Breite 3,7, horizontale Breite 3,6, größte Höhe 3,4 = Vertikalhöhe. Hypsikonchie (Index 91,8). — Gesicht erscheint im ganzen etwas breit. Stirn etwas nach hinten gedrückt. Glabella und Arcus superciliares mäßig entwickelt. Gesichtshöhe 10,7, obere Gesichtshöhe 6,15, Gesichtsbreite nach Virchow 8,85, nach v. Hölder 11,4. Jochbreite 13,45. Schmalgesichtig (Index 102), schmales Obergesicht (Index 67,5). Gerade Länge des Schädels 17,9 = größte Länge, Intertuberallänge 17,5, größte Breite 14,0, kleinste Stirnbreite 9,5. Ohrhöhe 11,6, vertikaler Querumfang 31 cm, horizontaler Umfang 51, sagittaler Umfang 35 cm. Koronalnaht zahnreich, Sagittalnaht und Lambdanaht grobzähnig. Am Vereinigungspunkt des Scheitelbeins, Schläfenbeinschuppe, Wespenbeinflügel, rechterseits ein gezackter Schaltknochen. Proc. mastoid. klein, Hinterhauptsschuppenmuskelleisten wenig entwickelt.

Vom übrigen Skelett vorhanden:

Das vollständige Männerbecken mit herzförmigem Beckeneingang, spitzer Symphyse; beide Femora, beide Tibiae, rechte Scapula, beide Humeri, beide Ulnae, rechter Radius.

„Das Skelett war 1,62 lang, hatte rechts eine Nadel, wie es scheint, in der rechten Hand."

40) „3." Alter Mann von ca. 60 Jahren.
Wieder zusammengesetzter, beinahe vollständiger Schädel (No. 1580). Fig. 141. Gerade Länge 20,0 = größte Länge, Intertuberallänge 19,3, größte Breite 14,0, kleinste Stirnbreite 10,5, Ohrhöhe 11,3, Hilfsohrhöhe 11,6, Horizontalumfang 55,3, Stirnbeinhöhe in Sagittalnaht 15,0, vertikaler Querumfang 32,6. Der Schädel ist dolichocephal (Index 70,0), chamäcephal (Index 56,0). Gesichtsbreite nach Virchow 10,0, nach v. Hölder 11,8, Jochbreite 13,4. Gesichtshöhe 11,0, obere Gesichtshöhe 6,5. Das Gesicht ist schmal (Index 110,0), auch das Obergesicht (Index 65,0). Stirnbein schwärzlich braun, ebenso Nasenbein und linke Hälfte des Oberkieferalveolarfortsatzes. Glabella flach, Arcus supercil. wenig entwickelt. Kleine Exostose auf der linken Stirnbeinhälfte nahe dem Stirnbeinhöcker. — Augenhöhleneingang abgerundet viereckig, größte Breite 4,5, horizontale Breite 4,3, größte Höhe 3,4 = Vertikalhöhe. Chamäkonchie (Index 75,5). Wangenbeinteil der Orbita nach unten außen ausgebaucht, Quer-

achse nach außen abfallend. — Nasenhöhe 4,8, 'größte Breite der Nasenöffnung 2,64. Platyrrhinie (Index 55,0), Nasenbeine viereckig, Nasenrücken eingesattelt, breit, Nasenöffnung oval, unterer Rand der Nasenöffnung stumpfkantig, Nasenstachel spitz, lang. Wangenbeine seitlich gestellt; Fossa canina links flach; in der rechten

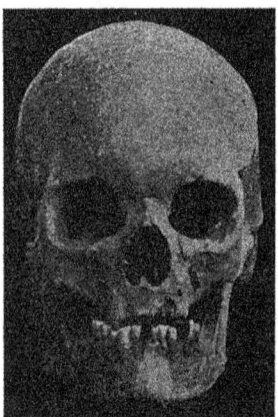 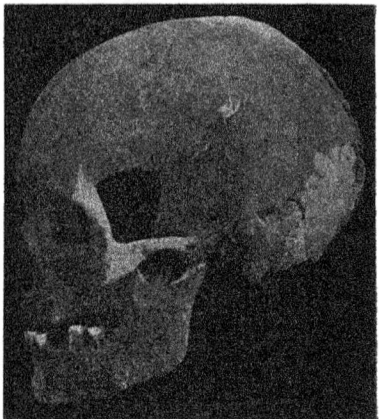

Fig. 141. $^1/_4$.

Fossa canina eine groschengroße, höckerig unebene, neugebildete Knochenpartie, die sich deutlich von der normalen Umgebung abhebt; in die Neubildung ist der untere Rand des Foramen infraorbitale mit hineingezogen; dadurch erscheint das Foramen sehr groß. Auch die Innenfläche der rechten Kieferhöhle ist an der pathologisch veränderten Stelle höckerig uneben. Alveolarfortsatz des Oberkiefers mittelhoch; Fistelöffnung an der Wurzel des rechten Eckzahns, ebenso am linken Eckzahn; Alveolarcyste ziemlicher Ausdehnung am linken kleinen Schneidezahn. Gebiß sehr schlecht im Oberkiefer.

(8) (7) (6) (5) (4) 3* (2) [1][1] [2] [3] [4] (5) (6) (7) (8)
[8] [7] 6 5 4 3 2 [1] 1 2 3 [4] (5) 6 7 (8)

Im Unterkiefer links ist der 2. Bicuspis vermutlich auch durch eine Knocheneiterung zu Grunde gegangen. Der daneben stehende erste Molar ist disloziert, seine mesiale Fläche durch Anwendung von Gewalt bis tief in die Wurzel glatt abgesprengt, wohl bei Extraktionsversuchen des kranken Prämolaren. Die Sprengfläche ist glänzend schwarz, ein Folgezustand, der häufig eintritt bei Freilegung des gesunden Zahnbeins. Zahnstein unten links. Zahnbogen parabelförmig. Unterkiefer vorbeißend, gerader Biß, Zahnkronen mittelgroß, untere Zähne mäßig abgekaut, horizontal, der eine erhaltene Zahn im Oberkiefer sehr stark abgekaut, da er längere Zeit der einzig artikulierende gewesen. Durch diese Abkauung ist die Pulpahöhle eröffnet, durch Gangrän der Pulpa eine alveoläre Zahnfleischfistel entstanden. Unterkiefer massiv, hoch, Muskelansätze kräftig. Unter-

kieferwinkel 118°, Distanz der beiden 10,2; unterer Rand des Unter-·
kieferkörpers dick, ausgeschweift; Kinn stumpf, breit, Protuberanz
stark entwickelt. — Gaumenlänge 4,5, Gaumenmittelbreite 4,1.
Brachystaphylin (Index 91,0). Gaumen flach; an Stelle des Foram.
incisiv. großes rundes Loch mit glatten Wänden; starke mediale
Kämme längs der Vasa palatina. — Koronalnaht zartlinig, ebenso
Sagittalnaht. Muskelansätze der Hinterhauptsschuppe kräftig hervortretend, auch die Linea nuchae suprema.

Vom übrigen Skelett sind erhalten: Die rechte Beckenhälfte
(ein großes Becken), der rechte und linke Femur, sehr lang, die
rechte und linke Tibia.

Notiz zu E 3. „Skelett 1,77 m lang, wenig erhalten; bei der
linken Hand ein Messer."

41) „E 4." Ältere Frau.

Unterkiefer. Zähne stark abgekaut, unregelmäßig.

[7]	6	(5)	4	3	2	1	[1]	[2]	3	4	[5]	(6)	[7]

Notiz zu E 4. „Unterkiefer allein."

42) Kind 3. 6 Jahr alt.

Unterkieferfragment mit Zähnen, Kinnpartie mit rechter Zahn-
bogenhälfte, etwas von der linken. Unterer Rand des Kieferkörpers dick.

6	V	IV	III	$\widehat{2}$ $\widehat{1}$	$\widehat{1}$	$\widehat{2}$

Die bleibenden Schneidezähne sichtbar bis zum Rand der
Alveole.

43) Kind 1. Ca. 15 Monate alt.

Oberkiefer. Die zweiten Milchmolaren sind noch nicht durchgebrochen, die Schneidezähne postmortal ausgefallen, in den Alveolen
die Anlagen der bleibenden Zähne sichtbar. Gaumen breit, Nasenstachel spitz.

**F. Fortsetzung der Ausgrabung durch Schacht-
meister Mayer.**

44) „F 1." „IX F 1." Ungefähr 18-jährige Frau.

Vollständiger, gut erhaltener Schädel (No. 1573). Fig. 142.
Schädelmaße: Gerade Länge 17,6, größte Länge 18,1, Intertuberallänge 18,5, größte Breite 13,2, kleinste Stirnbreite 9,05. Ganze
Höhe 14,0, Hilfshöhe 14,0, Ohrhöhe 11,3, Hilfsohrhöhe 11,1. Länge
der Schädelbasis 12,0, Breite der Schädelbasis 10,4. Horizontalumfang des Schädels 50,0, Sagittalumfang 37,0, vertikaler Querumfang
29,5. Gesichtsbreite (Virchow) 9,3, 10,9 (v. Hölder). Ganze Gesichtshöhe 10,4, obere Gesichtshöhe 6,3, Profillänge des Gesichts 9,75.
Schädel im ganzen klein, dolichocephal (72,0), Hochschädel
(77,0), schmalgesichtig (112,0). Unterkiefer dementsprechend klein,
zierlich, Muskelansätze mäßig entwickelt. Kieferast dünn, stumpfwinklig 121°, Distanz der Kieferwinkel 9,2, Gelenkfortsatze klein,
Achsen derselben schräg gestellt; Koronoidfortsatz klein, Incisur
rechts flach, links etwas tiefer, unterer Rand des Unterkieferkorpers
mitteldick, leicht ausgeschweift, Kinn vorstehend, Kinnprotuberanz
mittelstark. Alveolarteil vollständig erhalten. Gebiß:

7	6	5	4	3	[2]	[1]	[1]	2	3	4	[5]	6	7
7	(6)	5	4	2	[2]	[1]	[1]	[2]	[3]	4	5	6	7

.Alveolen erhalten, nur der erste Molar rechts unten extrahiert (wenigstens 2 Jahr vor dem Tod), Alveole oblitteriert. Weisheitszähne fehlen noch. Zahnbogen halbelliptisch; normaler Biß, scharfe

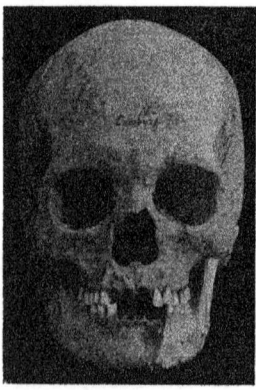 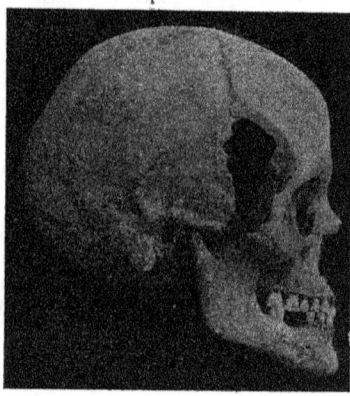

Fig. 142. $^1/_4$.

Artikulation; Zahnkronen mittelgroß, relative Größe normal, leicht schräg bukkalwärts abgekaut, keine Caries.

Gaumenlänge 4,9, Gaumenmittelbreite 4,2, Gaumenendbreite 4,2, Mesostaphylin (Index 85,0), Gaumen flach; Alveolarfortsatz des Oberkiefers niedrig, sehr schräg gegen die Horizontale gestellt (prognath). Juga alveolaria stark ausgeprägt, besonders am Eckzahn. Fossa canina sehr tief. Wangenbein massiv, stark vortretend, schnell umbiegend, hinterer Rand des Proc. front. des Jochbeins leicht flügelförmig, Jochbogen zierlich, leicht ausbauchend. Nasenbeine viereckig, seitlich etwas ausgeschweift, Nasenrücken steil dachförmig, schwach konkav eingesattelt, Nasenöffnung oval, rechts tiefer ausgemuldet als links, Nasenstachel fehlt, unterer Nasenrand verstrichen. Nasenhöhe 4,8, gr. Breite der Nasenöffnung 2,7. Platyrrhinic (Index 56). Augenhöhlen abgerundet viereckig, Querachse wenig nach außen abfallend, unterer Rand vorspringend. Augenhöhleneingang: gr. Breite 3,9, horizontale Breite 3,7, gr. Höhe 33,0, Vertikalhöhe 3,4, Mesokonchie (84,0). Stirnbein schmal, hoch, steil gestellt, kugelig gewölbt, auf der linken Hälfte nahe der Mittellinie linsengroße Exostose. Stirnhöcker hervortretend, Glabella flach, Arcus superciliares angedeutet. Koronalnaht zahnreich, Scheitelbeinhöcker wenig ausgeprägt, Linea temporalis suprema links deutlich. Occipitalschuppe schaufelförmig, hier Nackenlinien angedeutet, Prot. occipit. fehlend. Lambdanaht sehr reichzähnig, mit zwei größeren Schaltknochen am rechten Schenkel. Foramen magnum langoval, gr. Breite 2,9, gr. Länge 3,4. Richtung auf die Choanen. Länge der Pars basilaris des Hinterhauptbeins 3,4.

Notiz zu F 1. „Skelett 1,60 m lang, Knochenüberreste mangelhaft, bloß der Schädel gut. In der rechten Hand ein Messer."

45) „F 2." Ein Erwachsener.
Schädelreste. Os frontis, Parietalia, Occiput, rechtes Schläfenbein.

Notiz zu F 2. „Skelett 1,80 m lang, schlecht erhalten, Schädel gut; in linker Hand ein Messer, am Halse 3 Perlen."

46) Frau von 30—40 Jahren.
Halber Gesichtsschädel (No. 1579), kleinste Stirnbreite 10,0. Glabella und Arcus supercil. mäßig entwickelt. Gesichtsbreite nach Virchow 9,6, Gesichtshöhe 11,1, obere Gesichtshöhe 6,9. Gesicht im ganzen schmal (Index 129), ebenso Obergesicht (Index 80). Augen- höhleneingang abgerundet viereckig, gr. Breite 3,8 = horizontale Breite, gr. Höhe 3,2, Vertikalhöhe 3,4. Mesokonchie (Index 84). — Nasenhöhe 4,9, gr. Breite der Nasenöffnung 2,4. Mesorrhinie (Index 48,9), Nasenöffnung langoval, unterer Nasenrand scharfkantig, spitzer, langer Nasenstachel. Fossa canina flach. Wangenbein seitlich ge- stellt, Jochbogen wenig aushauchend. Alveolarfortsatz des Ober- kiefers niedrig, fast gerade gestellt gegen die Horizontale. Gebiß:

$$\frac{8\ [7]\ 6\ 5\ 4\ 3\ [2]\ [1]}{[7]\ 6\ [5]\ [4]\ [3]\ [2]\ [1]\ \big|\ [1]}$$

Zähne gut; der Weisheitszahn ist einwurzelig und verlängert, weil keine Antagonist vorhanden war. Biß gerade, scharfe Artiku- lation, Zahnkronen klein, zierlich, sehr schmale Zahnhälse, mäßige Abkauung horizontal. — Unterkieferwinkel 118°. Kieferast sehr breit, dick. Kinn spitz, unterer Rand des Kieferkörpers dick, geradlinig. Keine sonstigen Skelettreste.

47) Kräftiger Mann.
Nur der Unterkiefer (No. 1592) vorhanden. Derselbe ist sehr kräftig, breit. Unterer Rand des Unterkieferkörpers sehr dick, grad- linig, Kinn vorspringend. Gelenkfortsätze klein, Incisura flach. Kon- dylus breit, mit mittlerer Einschnürung. Unterkieferwinkel lateral- wärts schaufelartig ausladend. Unterkieferwinkel 120°, Distanz der- selben 12 cm. Gebiß:

$$\frac{}{8\ 7\ [6]\ [5]\ 4\ 3\ 2\ 1\ \big|\ 1\ 2\ 3\ 4\ 5\ 6\ 7\ 8}$$

Zahnbogen fast halbkreisförmig, Zahnkronen groß. Abkauung unregelmäßig, einzelne höher, einzelne tiefer.
Notiz zu F 3. „Skelett lag sehr flach, daher alles zerfallen, 1,50 m lang, nur der Unterkiefer gut, rechts ein Messer."

48) Kind 5. 6 Jahr alt.
Schädel in Bruchstücken: Stirnbein, (linke Ecke schwärzlich braun gefärbt durch Brand), Parietalia, Hinterhauptsbein, Schläfen- beine, Oberkiefer (linke Seite schwärzlichbraun), Unterkiefer. Der linke Ast fehlt. Gebiß:

$$\frac{7\ 6\ V\ IV\ [III]\ [II]\ [I]\ \big|\ [I]\ [II]\ [III]\ IV\ V\ 6\ 7}{6\ V\ IV\ III\ [II]\ [I]\ \big|\ [I]\ [II]\ [III]\ IV\ V\ 6}$$

Notiz zu F 4. Kinderskelett, Schädel defekt, sonst nichts vom Körper; beim Schädel zwei ganze Perlen, eine in drei Stücken."

49) „Camburg 5." Frau von ca. 30 Jahren.
Schädel (No. 1578) fast vollständig erhalten. Fig. 143. Gerade

Länge 18,2, größte Länge 18,5, Intertuberallänge 18,6, größte Breite 13,6, kleinste Stirnbreite 10,0, Ohrhöhe 11,2 = Hilfsohrhöhe. Horizontal-umfang 51,7, Sagittalumfang 37,4, vertikaler Querumfang 31,0. Der Schädel ist dolichocephal (Index 73,0), flach (Index 61). Gesichts-

 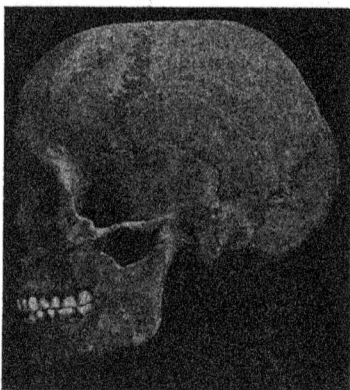

Fig. 143. $^1/_4$.

breite nach Virchow 9,6, nach v. Hölder 10,9, Gesichtshöhe 11,5, obere Gesichtshöhe 7,1. Das Gesicht ist schmal (Index 119), auch im Obergesicht (Index 73,9). Stirnnaht in ganzer Ausdehnung erhalten, in der hinteren Hälfte zahnreich. Glabella flach, Arcus superciliares eben angedeutet, ebenso Stirnhöcker. Augenhöhleneingang gr. Breite 3,7, horizontale Breite 3,5; gr. Höhe 3,4, vertikale Höhe 3,7. Hypsikonchie 91,8, Nasenhöhe 5,0, gr. Breite der Nasenöffnung 2,4, Mesorrhinie (Index 48,0). Nasenbeine sehr schmal, viereckig, Nasenöffnung langoval, unterer Nasenrand scharfkantig, Nasenstachel mittellang. Nasenrücken kaum eingesattelt. Fossa canina mäßig tief. Jochbeine seitlich anliegend, Jochbogen kaum ausgebaucht. Alveolarfortsatz des Oberkiefers hoch, sehr wenig gegen die Horizontale schräg gestellt. Zähne gut erhalten, Zahnkronen des Oberkiefers senkrecht gestellt, leicht einwärts geneigt. Gebiß:

$$8\frac{3}{3} \quad 7 \quad 6 \quad 5 \quad 4 \quad 3 \quad 2 \quad 1 \quad | \quad 1 \quad 2 \quad 3 \quad 4 \quad 5 \quad 6 \quad 7 \quad 8$$
$$8 \quad 7 \quad 6 \quad 5 \quad 4 \quad 3 \quad 2 \quad [1] \quad | \quad [1] \quad 2 \quad 3 \quad 4 \quad 5 \quad 6 \quad 7 \quad 8$$

Keine Caries, nur wenig Zahnstein. Zahnbogen in Parabelform. Biß gerade, obere Schneidezähne überbeißend, scharfe Artikulation, Zahnkronen schmal, klein, wenig abgekaut, horizontal. Gaumen hoch gewölbt, schmal. Unterkieferwinkel 115°, Distanz der Kieferwinkel 9,2. Kinn spitz, Protuberanz mäßig entwickelt, Rand des Unterkieferkörpers mitteldick, geradlinig. — Koronalnaht stark gezackt, ebenso Sagittalnaht und Lamdanaht, zwei kleine Schaltknochen im linken Ast derselben. Hinterhauptsschuppe leicht aushauchend. Muskelleisten mäßig entwickelt. Warzenfortsatz lang.

Vom übrigen Skelett nichts erhalten.

Notiz zu F 5. „Skelett 1,55 m lang, die Knochen ganz unbrauchbar, Schädel aber gut, dabei zwei Ohrgehänge, ein Eimerhenkel.“
50) „F.“ Frau mittlerer Jahre.
Unterkiefer (No. 1598) mit gutem Gebiß, keine Caries. Zahnkronen klein, wenig abgekaut, horizontal. Kinn spitz, rechte Unterkieferhälfte schwarz gefleckt von Branderde. Kieferäste abgebrochen.
Gebiß:

$$\overline{8\ 7\ 6\ 5\ 4\ 3\ 2\ [1]}\,\big|\,\overline{1\ 2\ 3\ 4\ 5\ 6\ 7\ 8}$$

Der linke Eckzahn hat zwei Wurzeln.
Vom übrigen Schädel erhalten in einem Stück, aber seitlich
von links her sehr verdrückt: Os frontis, Ossa parietalia, Os occipitis
zum Teil.
Sonst keine Skelettreste.
Notiz zu F 6. „Skelett 1,68 m lang, Knochen unbrauchbar,
Schädel gut; in linker Hand ein Messer.“
51) „F 7.“ Frau von ca. 40 Jahren.
Schädel (No. 1591) vollständig bis auf rechtes Schläfenbein und
Unterkiefer, zusammengesetzt, im ganzen zierlich. Fig. 144.

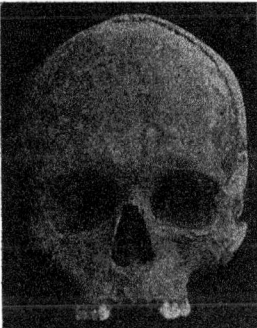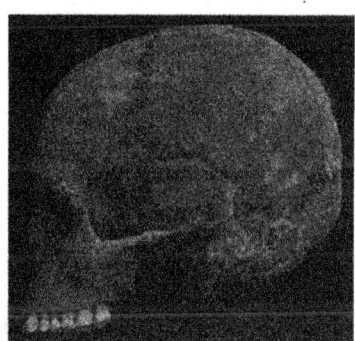

Fig. 144. ¹/₄.

Gerade Länge 18,3 = größte Länge, Intertuberallänge 13,0,
kleinste Stirnbreite 9,6. Ohrhöhe 11,8 = Hilfsohrhöhe. Breite der
Schädelbasis 11,2, Horizontalumfang 51,0, Sagittalumfang 38,3. Der
Schädel ist dolichocephal (Index 71), chamäcephal (Index 64,2).
Stirnhöcker wenig entwickelt. Starker Supraorbitalwulst, Glabella
vorgewulstet, Nasenrücken eingesattelt. Gesichtsbreite nach Virchow
9,5, v. Hölder 11,1. Obere Gesichtshöhe 6,4, schmales Obergesicht
(Index 67,3).
Augenhöhleneingang abgerundet viereckig, größte Breite 3,9,
horizontale Breite 4,75; gr. Höhe 3,1 = Vertikalhöhe. Chamäkonchie
(Index 79). — Nasenbeine viereckig, dachförmig aneinandergestellt.
Nasenhöhe 4,3; gr. Breite der Nasenöffnung 2,3. Platyrrhinie
(Index 53,0). Fossa canina mäßig tief. Jochbeine seitlich gestellt,
Jochbogen wenig ausgebaucht. — Alveolarfortsatz des Oberkiefers

sehr schräg gestellt gegen die Horizontale, ziemlich lang. Gebiß gut, keine Caries.

$$8\ 7\ 6\ 5\ 4\ 3\ [2]\ [1]\ |[1]\ [2]\ 3\ 4\ 5\ 6\ 7\ 8$$

Die ersten Molaren stark abgekaut schräg nach innen, die anderen fast gar nicht. Zahnbogen parabolisch. Gaumen flach, vom Foram. incisivum schräg nach der Ecke der mittleren Schneidezähne zu verlaufende feinlinige Nähte. Gaumenlänge 5,1, Gaumenmittelbreite 4,2, Gaumenendbreite 4,1. Mesostaphylin (Index 80,0). Nähte grobzackig, am linken Schenkel der Lambdanaht zwei reich- und langzackige Schaltknochen. Scheitelbeine in der Sagittalnaht flach dachförmig aneinanderstoßend. Parietalhöcker deutlich hervortretend. Muskelleisten der Hinterhauptsschuppe gering. Spitzer dreieckiger Schläfenschuppenfortsatz bis beinahe an das Stirnbein linkerseits. Linke Kopfseite schwarz gesprenkelt durch Aufliegen auf Branderde.

Keine weiteren Skelettteile.

Notiz zu F 7. „Weibliches Skelett 1,54 m lang, Knochen defekt; im linken Arm ein Kind (s. folgende No.). Dicht dabei zur Linken am Hals Bruchstücke von Perlen."

52) Kind 8. 1¹/₂ Jahr alt.

Zusammengesetzter Schädel (No. 1590), es fehlt das mittlere Gesicht. Fig. 145.

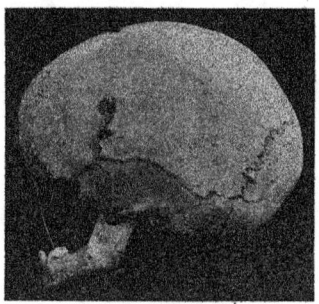

Fig. 145. ¹/₄.

Größte Länge 16,2, Intertuberallänge 16,3, größte Breite 11,3, kleinste Stirnbreite 7,6, Hilfsohrhöhe 10,8. Horizontalumfang 44,2, Sagittalumfang 32,0, wovon 11,0 auf Stirnbein entfallen. Stirnhöcker stark hervortretend, Stirnnaht bis auf einen kleinen Rest auf der Glabella obliteriert, Parietalhöcker kräftig. Länge der Sagittalnaht 11 cm. Bemerkenswert: spitzdreieckiger Fortsatz der Schläfenschuppe links bis ans Stirnbein, Scheitelbein und Wespenbeinflügel trennend. For. magnum spitzoval, 2,2 cm breit. Oberer Teil der Hinterhauptschuppe kräftig ausgehaucht, relativ schmal. Länge der Schädelbasis 8,5. Der Schädel ist dolichocephal.

Unterkiefer vollständig, Unterkieferwinkel 135°, Distanz der beiden 6,1. Gebiß normal, Stellung der Zähne gerade.

$$\overline{6\ \bar V\ IV\ \widehat{III}\ [II]\ I}\ |\ \overline{I\ II\ \widehat{III}\ IV\ \bar V\ 6}$$

V und 6 beiderseits tief liegend. Kinn stumpf, kräftige Protuberanz, parabolische Zahnkurve.

Lag beim vorigen Skelett.

53) „F 8.“ Ältere Frau.

Unterkieferhälfe (No. 1606): Kinn vorspringend, Zahnkronen klein, weiß, ohne Zahnstein, stark abgekaut, unregelmäßig. 2. Molar bei Lebzeiten verloren, Alveole atrophiert und bei Extraktion zerbrochen, da der 1. Molar eine hoch freistehende distale Wurzel hat.

Notiz zu F 8. „Skelettknochen ganz untauglich, 1,66 m lang, in der rechten Hand ein Messer.“

54) „F 9.“ Erwachsene Person.

Schädelrest in einem Stück zusammenhängend: Stirnbein, Scheitelbeine, Hinterhauptsbein, Schläfenbeine, Wespenbein. Arcus superciliares und Glabella gewulstet. Schädel oval, regelmäßig.

Keine Beigaben.

55) „F 10.“ Ältere Frau.

Sehr gut erhaltener Schädel (No. 1587), im ganzen zierlich. Fig. 146.

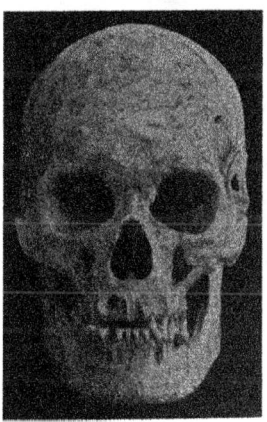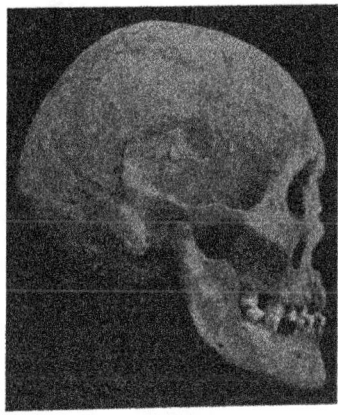

Fig. 146. ¹/₄.

Gerade Länge 17,8, größte Länge 18,0, Intertuberallänge 17,5. Größte Breite 12,7, kleinste Stirnbreite 9,05. Ganze Höhe 13,7, Hilfshöhe 13,6, Ohrhöhe 11,5 = Hilfsohrhöhe. Länge der Schädelbasis 10,8. Breite der Schädelbasis 11,1. Horizontalumfang 50,0, Sagittalumfang 34,5. Vertikaler Querumfang 29,5. Dolichocephalie 70,0. Orthocephalie 75,0. Glabella und Arcus superciliares mäßig entwickelt.

Das Gesicht ist schmal (Index 126), auch das Obergesicht (Index 79). Gesichtsbreite nach Virchow 9,1, nach v. Hölder 11,2, Jochbreite 13,1, Gesichtshöhe 11,5, obere Gesichtshöhe 7,2. Nasenrücken gerade, Nasenbeine viereckig, steil dachförmig aneinanderstoßend. Nasenöffnung ulmenblattförmig, unterer Nasenrand stumpfkantig. Nasenhöhe 5,05, gr. Breite der Nasenöffnung 2,4. Leptorrhinie (Index 47). — Augenhöhleneingang abgerundet viereckig, gr. Breite 3,9 = horizontale Breite; gr. Höhe 3,3 = Vertikalhöhe. Querachsen wenig nach außen unten geneigt. Mesokonchie (Index 84). — Fossa canina flach. Wangenbeine etwas nach vorn gedreht. Alveolarfortsatz des Oberkiefers mittelhoch, tiefes erbsengroßen Loch über der Wurzel des rechten lateralen Oberkieferschneidezahn (Cyste). Gebiß:

$$\frac{8\ (7)\ 6\ 5\ 4\ [3]\ [2]\ [1] \mid [1]\ 2\ 3\ 4\ 5\ (6)\ 7\ [8]}{8\ 7\ (6)\ 5\ 4\ [3]\ 2\ 1 \mid 1\ 2\ 3\ 4\ 5\ (6)\ (7)\ 8}$$

Zahnstein in stärkerem Maße. Durch das Fehlen vom 2. rechten oberen Molaren hat sich der 1. Molar dem Weisheitszahn derart genähert, daß sich die Lücke um mehr als die Hälfte verringert hat und dadurch eine unregelmäßige, aber scharfe Artikulation zu stande gekommen ist. Kleine Zahnwurzeln. Zahnbogen im Unterkiefer eine Parabel, im Oberkiefer Halbkreis, Biß gerade. — Gaumenlänge 5,2, Gaumenmittelbreite 4,4, Gaumenendbreite 3,8. Leptostaphylin (Index 73). Unterkiefer hoch, unterer Rand des Unterkieferkörpers mitteldick, leicht geschweift. Kinn etwas vorspringend, stumpf. Protuberanz wenig entwickelt. Muskelansätze ziemlich kräftig. Kieferwinkel 131°, Distanz der beiden 10,1. Koronalnaht reich gezackt, Sagittal- und Lambdanaht labyrinthisch verschlungen. Am Lambda großer Schaltknochen, Muskelansätze der Hinterhauptsschuppe wulstig, oberer Teil der Schuppe kapselförmig vorspringend. Länge der Pars basilaris 3,1, Foramen magnum langoval, 3,0 breit, 3,8 lang. Profillänge 10,3.

Keine weiteren Skelettreste.

Notiz zu F 10. „Skelett 1,60 m lang, Knochen unbrauchbar, Schädel gut, in linker Hand ein Messer."

56) Sehr alte Person.

Vom Schädel sind erhalten: Das Mittelstück des Unterkiefers, ohne Zähne, die postmortal ausgefallen, ein Stück vom Oberkiefer mit drei stark abgekauten, kariösen Zähnen (2. Prämolar rechts und links, Eckzahn), alle übrigen Zähne sind intra vitam verloren.

Anmerkung: Über das slavische Gräberfeld finden sich kurze Notizen in:

1) Korrespondenzblatt der deutsch. Ges. für Anthropologie, Ethnologie, Urgeschichte 1871. No. 6—10.

2) Ebenda 1872. No. 6. S. 46.

3) Schaaffhausen, Sur quelques trouvailles faites en Allemagne. Congrès international d'Anthropologie et d'archéologie préhistorique Compt. rendu de la 7ᵉ session. Stockholm 1874. Tome II. p. 841—850.

4) Korrespondenzblatt der deutsch. Ges. für Anthropologie, Ethnologie und Urgeschichte 1876. No. 9. S. 76—84.

5) Supplement des Berliner Katalogs v. J. 1880. S. 29.

6) E. Eichhorn, Grafschaft Camburg.

7) Regel, Thüringen, T. II. S. 516—517.

8) R. Lehmann, Beiträge zur prähistorischen Chirurgie nach Funden aus deutscher Vorzeit.

Zum spezielleren Studium standen mir zur Verfügung aus dem Germanischen Museum zu Jena:

Ein Brief von Dr. Bender an Klopfleisch vom 2. April 1869 (Act. des Germ. Mus. Jena.

Lose Blätter aus einem Notizbuch Klopfleischs 1871. 1872).

Ein kurzer Bericht von Schachtmeister Mayer an Klopfleisch.

Zwei Tafeln mit Zeichnungen von Klopfleisch.

Eine Wandtafel im Germ. Museum zu Jena No. 57. (1891. Wandtafel No. XXIX.)

Reste vorgeschichtlicher Wohnplätze.
a) An der neuen Ziegelei.

Trichterförmige Abfallgruben, die Reste vorgeschicht. licher Siedelungen, entdeckte Heim westlich der Stadt bei der neuen Ziegelei an der Straße nach Döbritschen. Er fand in denselben Urnenreste mit Tupfenleisten, neben nicht ornamentierten Gefäßscherben; ferner einen Klopf. stein, halbkugelförmig, stark beschädigt, von 10 cm Breite; einen Mahlstein (Läufer) mit abgeplatteter, rauher Fläche von 24 cm Breite, auf der Gegenseite in der Mitte mit kreisförmiger Vertiefung. (Die Funde sind jetzt im B.V.M. IIb 2640 a—d). In seiner jetzigen Privatsammlung besitzt Heim ein ca. 15 cm langes, im Querschnitt abgestumpft dreieckiges Steingerät von cylindrischer Gestalt, mit Rille, was ebenfalls an der neuen Ziegelei gefunden wurde.

Aus „Thielemanns Ziegelei" ferner einen Randscherben eines großen Tongefäßes, dessen Masse mit Quarzstückchen reichlich durchsetzt ist; der 7 cm hohe glatt gestrichene Hals ist leicht nach außen ausladend, der sich anschließende Bauchteil rauh, mit einem senkrecht nach unten verlaufenden schmalen, nasenförmigen Ansatz versehen. Die Krümmungsverhältnisse des Scherben lassen auf ein Gefäß von wenigstens 25 cm Höhe schließen.

b) An der Chaussee nach Schmiedehausen.

Bei Ausgrabungen an der Chaussee nach Schmiedehausen auf Camburger Gebiet förderte Heim Urnenreste zu Tage, die unverziert waren.

XXII.   22

Einzelfunde.

Nähere Bezeichnung der Fundstelle finden sich nur bei wenigen Einzelfunden.

Im Henneberger Haus in Meiningen liegt ein Bruchstück eines ca. 7 cm breiten keilförmigen Steinbeils, das beim Bau der Niederlage des Kaufmann Stürze gefunden worden ist.

Bei einer sechsflächigen facettierten rötlichen Perle ist als Fundstelle der Flurname „Lischwig" angegeben.

(H. H.)

An Einzelfunden auf Camburger Stadtflur ohne speziellere Angaben bewahrt das Henneberger Haus in Meiningen:
Eine ca. 10 cm lange, schuhleistenförmige gewölbte Steinhacke; eine kleinere, hochgewölbte Steinhacke mit zugespitztem Bahnende;
einen faustgroßen Reibstein aus Porphyr;
zwei apfelgroße Glättsteine;
einen kleineren Glättstein.

Ein kleines vierkantiges Steinbeil, grau mit schwarzer Sprenkelung, mit gerader Ober- und Unterseite, leicht gewölbten Seitenwangen, zugespitztem Bahnende, von 8,6 cm Länge, 15 cm größter Breite besitzt das Germanische Museum zu Jena.

Eine polierte, mit Bohrloch versehene Steinaxt aus Camburg aus der Sammlung des Oberstabsarztes Dr. Schwabe in Weimar — war 1880 auf der Ausstellung prähistorischer und anthropologischer Funde in Berlin ausgestellt (Katalog der Ausstellung S. 542).

In den Mitteilungen der G. und A. G. des Osterlandes zu Altenburg I. B. wird ein mündlicher Vortrag des Mühlenverwalters Brauer in Camburg am 15. April 1840 erwähnt über Ausgrabungen von Altertümern (Vasen, Schalen, Knochen, Reifen etc.) in der Camburger Gegend und unter den Altertümern, die die genannte Gesellschaft besitzt, 1841 in den Mitt. I. B. S. 27 erwähnt unter anderen:
„Ein halber steinerner Streithammer (sog. Donnerkeil);
vier eiserne schmale Reifchen nebst eisernem Bügel;
Bruchstücke einer Aschenurne, Scherben von Vasen."
Alles im Amtsbezirk Camburg aufgefunden (Mühlenverwalter Brauer daselbst)." Es erinnern diese Funde an die Beigaben des 1871 ausgebeuteten slavischen Gräberfeldes.

Einen schön polierten, polygonal (elfflächig) facettierten Axthammer mit Schaftloch, Länge 14 cm, größte Breite 5,3 cm, Höhe 3 cm, besitzt Heim in seiner jetzigen Sammlung.

Einzelfunde aus Camburg im Berliner Völkermuseum:

Steinbeil, sehr gut poliert, vierkantig, nach dem Bahnende sich leicht verjüngend, obere und untere Schmalseite geradflächig, Schneide etwas gebogen, Seitenwangen flach gewölbt, Bahnende geradflächig. Länge 11 cm, Schneidenhöhe 5,5 cm. K II b. 133.

Steinbeil, meist gut poliert, vierkantig, nach dem Bahnende sich leicht verjüngend, obere und untere Schmalseite geradflächig, Seitenwangen sehr flach gewölbt, Schneide schief verlaufend, Bahnende abgerundet. L. 7,7 cm, Schneidenhöhe 4,9 cm. K II b. 134.

Steinbeil, leicht facettiert, vierkantig, nach dem Bahnende sich etwas verjüngend, obere und untere Schmalseite geradflächig, Seitenwangen sehr flach gewölbt. Schneide gebogen, Bahnende schräg abfallend, ohne Sorgfalt behandelt. L. 11,0 cm, Schneidenhöhe 5,5 cm. K II b. 1122.

Steinbeil, vierkantig, aus schwärzlichem Gestein, Schmalseiten geradflächig, Seitenwangen flach gewölbt, Bahnende abgerundet, Schneide gebogen. L. 8,0, Schneidenhöhe 5,0. K II b. 1160.

Steinbeil, vierkantig, nach dem Bahnende sich etwas verjüngend, aus grauem Gestein, die obere und untere Schmalseite geradflächig, Seitenwangen sehr flach gewölbt, Schneide fast gerade. L. 7,0, Schneidenhöhe 4,0. II b. 1279.

Steinbeil, beschädigt, aus grauem Gestein, nach dem Bahnende zu sich verjüngend, flach gewölbte Schmalseiten und Seitenwangen. L. 8, Schneidenhöhe 4,8. II b. 1532.

Steinbeil, vierkantig, nach dem Bahnende sich etwas verjüngend, aus grauem Gestein, Schneide gebogen, Schmalseiten geradflächig, Seitenwangen flach gewölbt, Bahnende abgerundet. L. 9,0, Schneidenhöhe 4,8. II b. 1534.

Steinbeil, vierkantig, aus grauem Gestein, nach dem Bahnende sich etwas verjüngend, Schneide gebogen, Seitenwangen gewölbt, obere und untere Schmalseite geradflächig, Bahnende abgerundet. L. 14,0, Schneidenhöhe 7,0. II b. 1704.

Steinbeil, nach dem Bahnende sich etwas verjüngend, vierkantig, aus grauem Gestein, unvollständig, Schneide gebogen, obere und untere Schmalseite annähernd geradflächig. L. 7,0, Schneidenhöhe 5,0. II b. 1855.

Steinbeil, beschädigt, vierkantig, aus schwärzlichem Gestein, nach dem Bahnende sich etwas verjüngend, Schneide leicht gebogen, schief verlaufend, Seitenwangen sehr flach gewölbt, Bahnende abgerundet. L. 7,5, Schneidenhöhe 4,5. II b. 1856.

Steinbeil, beschädigt, vierkantig, nach dem Bahnende sich etwas verjüngend, aus grauem Gestein, Schneide kaum gebogen, Schmalseiten geradflächig, Seitenwangen sehr flach gewölbt, Bahnende abgerundet. L. 5,5, Schneidenhöhe 4,5. II b. 1857.

Steinbeil, beschädigt, vierkantig, nach dem Bahnende sich etwas verjüngend, Schneide kaum gebogen, Schmalseiten geradflächig, Seitenwangen sehr flach gewölbt, Bahnende abgerundet, aus dunkelgrauem Gestein. L. 5,5, Schneidenhöhe 4,0. II b. 1858.

Steinbeil, vierkantig, nach dem Bahnende sich etwas verjüngend, Schmalseiten geradflächig, Seitenwangen flach gewölbt, Schneide gerade, Bahnende abgerundet, aus grünem Gestein. L. 4,0, Schneidenhöhe 3,0. II b. 1859.

Steinbeil, vierkantig, nach dem Bahnende sich etwas verjüngend, Schneide leicht gebogen, Schmalseiten geradflächig, Seitenwangen sehr flach gewölbt, Bahnende abgerundet, aus grauem Gestein. L. 6,5, Schneidenhöhe 4,0.   II b. 2202.

Steinbeil, vierkantig, nach dem Bahnende sich etwas verjüngend, Schneide gerade, Seitenwangen flach gewölbt, Bahnende schräg. L. 6,5, Schneidenhöhe 4,0.   II b. 2203.

Steinbeil, vierkantig, nach dem Bahnende sich wenig verjüngend, Schneide wenig gebogen, Schmalseite gerade, Bahnende fehlt. Länge des erhaltenen Stückes 9,2.   II b. 2424.

Steinbeil, vierkantig, etwas beschädigt, nach dem Bahnende sich wenig verjüngend, Schneide leicht gebogen, Schmalseiten geradflächig, Seitenwangen flach gewölbt, Bahnende abgerundet. L. 8,5.   II b. 2425.

Steinbeil, vierkantig, nach dem Bahnende sich verjüngend, Schneide stark gebogen, Seitenwangen flach gewölbt, Bahnende abgerundet. L. 8,5.   II b. 2468.

Steinbeil, vierkantig, facettiert, gut erhalten, nach dem Bahnende sich etwas verjüngend, Schneide gebogen, Schmalseiten geradflächig, Seitenwangen flach gewölbt, Bahnende gerade. L. 6,2.   II b. 2799.

Steinbeil, stark beschädigt, nach dem Bahnende sich etwas verjüngend, Schneide gebogen, Seitenwangen flach gewölbt, Bahnende abgerundet. L. 7,0.   II b. 2800.

Steinbeil, mit spitzem Bahnende, Schneide gebogen, Seitenwangen gewölbt, in spitzem Winkel aneinanderstoßend, rauhe Oberfläche. L. 8,0, Schneidenhöhe 5,0.   II b. 1123.

Steinbeil, das spitze Bahnende abgebrochen, aus schwarzem Gestein. L. 6,0, Schneidenhöhe 8,5.   II b. 1241.

Steinbeil, vierkantig, aus grauem Gestein, mit spitzem Bahnende, flach gewölbten Seitenwangen, gebogene, an der einen Ecke beschädigte Schneide. L. 10,0, Schneidenhöhe 5,0.   II b. 1533.

Steinbeil, vierkantig, aus grauem Gestein, mit spitzem Bahnende, flach gewölbten Seitenwangen. Gebogene Schneide. L. 9,0, Schneidenhöhe 6,0.   II b. 2107.

Steinbeil, aus Flint, nach dem Bahnende zu sich zuspitzend, Schneide gebogen. L. 6,1.   II b. 2422.

Steinbeil mit spitzem Bahnende, sehr gut erhalten, die gewölbten Seitenwangen in scharfer Kante spitzwinklig aneinandertretend, Schneide gebogen. L. 19,0.   II b. 2638.

Steinhacke, hochgewölbt, schuhleistenförmig, aus grauem Gestein. L. 14,0, größte Breite 4,5.   II b. 1124.

Steinhacke, breit, flach, vierkantig, aus schwarzem Gestein, die gebogene Schneide in scharfem Winkel an die geradflächigen Schmalseiten angrenzend. L. 11,0, gr. Br. 6,8.   II b. 1159.

Steinhacke, breit, flach, facettiert, am Bahnende beschädigt, Schneide gebogen, allmählich in die Schmalseiten übergehend, aus grauem Gestein. L. 7,0, gr. Br. 7,9.   II b. 1239.

Steinhacke aus dunkelgrauem Gestein, breit, flach, vierkantig; die geradflächigen Schmalseiten abgerundet in die gebogene Schneide übergehend, am Bahnende etwas beschädigt. L. 7,0, gr. Br. 4,0.   II b. 1240.

Steinhacke aus grauem Gestein, flach, breit, die gebogene Schneide abgerundet in die Schmalseiten übergehend. L. 6,8, gr. Br. 6,5.   II b. 1242.

Steinhacke aus grünlichem Gestein, facettiert, vierkantig, die gebogene Schneide in scharfem Winkel an die geradflächigen Schmalseiten angrenzend. L. 12,5, gr. Br. 5,0.   II b. 1535.

Steinhacke aus schwärzlichem Gestein, flach, breit, mit abgerundeter, allmählich bogenförmig in die Schmalseiten umbiegender Schneide. L. 8,4.   II b. 2466.

Steinaxt aus grünlichem Gestein, mit Schaftloch, mit hochgestellter, scharfer Schneide, Bahnende breit, wenig bearbeitet. L. 11,0, gr. Br. 6,2.   II b. 1238.

Steinaxt aus grauem Gestein, plumpe Form, mit Schaftloch, horizontaler Querschnitt dreieckig, vertikaler unregelmäßig rechteckig, Bahnende breit, abgerundet. L. 10,0, gr. Br. 7,0. II b. 1408.

Steinaxt aus grauem Gestein, beschädigt, mit Schaftloch. Die Schmalseiten in einer Schneide unter spitzem Winkel sich vereinend, Bahnende schräg. Horizontalschnitt dreieckig, Vertikalschnitt rechteckig. L. 13,0, gr. Br. 4,5.   II b. 1675.

Steinaxt mit Schaftloch. im Horizontalschnitt dreieckig, im Vertikalschnitt rechteckig. Die Schmalseiten unter einem spitzen Winkel zu einer scharfen Schneide sich vereinend, Bahnende breit, abgerundet. L. 13,5.   II b. 2639.

Steinaxt aus schwärzlichem Gestein, mit Schaftloch, leicht facettiert, im Horizontalschnitt dreieckig, im Vertikalschnitt rechteckig. Die Schmalseiten unter spitzem Winkel sich zu einer scharfen Schneide vereinend, zum Bahnende allmählich umbiegend, Bahnende abgerundet. L. 10,0, gr. Br. 4,0.   II b. 1901.

Schöner polygonal facettierter Axthammer aus schwärzlichem Gestein, im Horizontalschnitt fünfeckig. Die Schmalseiten zu beiden Seiten des Schaftloches in leichter Biegung zu einem Kamm ausgezogen, Bahnende breit, abgerundet. Von der Seite betrachtet ist der axtförmige Teil nach unten verbreitert, so daß die Schneide höher als der übrige Hammerteil ist. L. 15,0, gr. Br. 4,8.   II b. 1705.

Große hochgewölbte, schuhleistenförmige Hacke aus grauem Gestein, quer durchlocht. L. 22,0, gr. Br. 6,0. II b. 1413.

Hirschhornhammer mit kreisrundem Schaftloch, mit breitem Bahnende, Schneidenteil fehlt. L. des erhaltenen Stückes 12,5, gr. Br. 6,5.   II b. 1031.

Klopfstein, würfelförmig, abgerundet. mit zentraler Vertiefung auf den Seiten. Mittlerer Durchmesser 6 cm.   II b. 1413.

Klopfstein aus granem Gestein, von annähernder Kugelform mit einzelnen Kanten. Mittl. Durchm. 7 cm.   II b. 1854.

Klopfstein aus rötlichem Gestein, kugelförmig. Mittl. Durchm. 7,5 cm.   II b. 2031.

———————

Reiber von Halbkugelform, gr. Br. 9,0 cm.   II b. 2426.

———————

Feuersteinspan, L. 3,4, gr. Br. 3,0.   II b. 1536.

Zwei weitere Feuersteinspäne.   II b. 1537.

Feuersteinmesser, doppelschneidig und zugespitzt, 7 cm lang, 2 cm breit, im Vertikalschnitt flach dachförmig. II b. 1860.

Feuersteinmesser, doppelschneidig, 5 cm lang, 2 cm breit, auf der einen Schneide vielfach zahnförmig gemuschelt.   II b. 1902.

Miszellen.

II.

Mitteilungen aus Copialbüchern der Stadt Naumburg a. S.

Von Karl Schöppe.

Von einer eigenartigen Beleidigung, deren Bedeutung noch der Erklärung bedarf, handelt das folgende Leumundszeugnis des Naumburger Rates: „Wir burgemeister und geschworene ratmanne der stadt Naumburg bekennen hiemit gegen ydermänniglich, so dieser unser offene brief vorkumpt, den sehen oder hören lesen, und besunderlich gegen euch, fürsichtigen und ehrsamen herren burgemeistern und räten zu Eisenberg, daß auf heute montag nach St. Lorenzentage dieses 1521. jahrs vor uns, als wir nach gewöhnlicher verheischung ratsweise versammelt, persönlich erschienen ist der fürsichtige Lorenz Kune, gegenwärtigen briefs zeiger, etwa unser bürger, anzeigend, wie er nach seinem abschiede von uns und als er sich allhieher zu euch um seiner besserung willen gewandt, von etzlichen euren einwohnern mit schmähelichen worten, die ihm auch seine ehr und gut gerüchte letzen thäten, beschwerlicherweise beleidigt und geschmähet würde und u. a. ein achtundzwanziger von Naumburg gescholten würde, welches ihm zu merklicher verkleinung, hohn, schmähe und schande reichte, vertraulicher hoffnung, es möchte doch solches von ihm in wahrheit nimmermehr angezeigt, viel weniger rechtlich auf ihn erweist noch beibracht werden.“ Auf seine Bitte bescheinigt ihm nun der Rat, „daß uns nicht anders wissend sei, denn daß sich derselbige Lorenz Kune diezeit und allsolange er bei uns bürger gewesen, aufrichtig, frömmlich und wie einem gehorsamen bürger ziembt, wohl gehalten habe, also daß wir ihm, so es ihm fügsam gewesen, wohl länger bei uns hätten erdulden mögen“.

Von einer sonderbaren Wette erzählt ein Protokoll des Naumburger Rates von 1520: „Wir burgemeister und geschworene ratmannen der stadt Numburg bekennen hiemit gegen allermänniglich und besonderlich vor euch ehrbaren und ehrsamen weisen burgemeister und ratmannen der stadt Weida, daß auf heute freitag nach Invocavit dieses 1520. jahrs vor uns, als wir nach gewöhnlicher verheischung ratsweise versammlet, erschienen ist der fürsichtige, erfahrene meister Georg Schieferdecker, anzeigend, wie er sich allhie zu Weida mit einem bürger daselbst, der einem ehrbaren rate allenthalben und wohl bekannt, etzlichermaßen mit nachfolgendem eide in der meinung dergleichen worten begriffen und eine verpflichtung gegen einander gethan haben, also: Es solle derselbige euer bürger vor gewiß und wahr angezeigt und gehabt haben wollen, es waren

aus der behausung unsers bürgers Bastian Friedrichs seligen, eines
bäcken hinter dem rathause wohnhaftig, in nächstvergangenen
sterbenslaüften 9 personen verstorben, dargegen genannter Georg
Schieferdecker in wahrheit zu erhalten angezeigt, daß derselbigen
alsoviel aus solcher behausung nicht gestorben sein sollten und solche
verpflichtung bei 20 gulden verpönt, welcher darinnen fällig befunden,
dem gewinnhaftigen ohne alle rechtliche und ertrachtliche behelfe
die zu überreichen; mit emsiger bitte, ihm dieser versterbung und
wie es sich in wahrheit darum hielte, ergründte bekundschaftung zu
geben; stallte und brachte derhalb vor uns die ehrsamen, fürsichtigen Wolfen Caspar und Veiten Leuben, als nächste nachbar der
gelassenen witwen desselbigen Bastian Friedrichs seligen, desgleichen
auch sie, die witwe, selbst, die allenthalb sämtlich und jedes besondern, was ihnen um die anzahl der personen, so aus dieser behausung in nächstem sterben verschieden, zu befragen bittend. Dieweil wir uns die wahrheit nach vermögen zu fördern schuldig erkennen,
haben wir ihm solch sein bitten als ziemliches abzuschlahen nicht
gewußt, sondern demnach dieselbigen unse bürger, auch die witwen
selbst bei den pflichten, damit sie dem hochw. und hochgeborenen
fürsten unsern gn. herrn von Freising und Numburg und uns be-
haftet und zugethan, was ihnen um die zahl der personen, so aus
oft bemeldter behausung Bastian Friedrichs seligen in nächstem
sterben hingeschieden bewußt, die lautere wahrheit zu vermeiden mit
fleiß befragt.   Also haben sie darauf sämtlich und jeder besondern
ausgesagt und bekannt, daß daraus Bastian Friedrich der hauswirt
selbst und zu ihm 6 seiner erben und nicht mehr verstorben sein,
welches wir also vor uns geschehen hiemit bekennen und darauf
freundlichs fleiß bitten, Ihr wollet gemeldtem eurem bürger die billigkeit und daß er die verwilligte pön, damit sich der Eure gegen ihm
verbunden, keine weitere beschwerung bekommen möge und weitere
unkost derhalb nicht thun müsse."

Eine gar naive Bemerkung findet sich bei einem Schreiben
des Naumburger Rates vom Mittwoch n. Nik. 1538 an den Papier-
müller zu Glaucha, worin er ihm den Sohn des Ratsdieners Hans
Donner als Lehrling empfiehlt.   „Hans Donner", bemerkt der Stadt-
schreiber bei dem Entwurfe dieses Schreibens, „hat kein geld, aber
zur steuer (d. h. zu den Unkosten) hat er einen bogen papier kauft,
den will er — daß es nicht gar, wie er spricht, über uns gehen
darf — darzu geben."

Auf die Frage nach gewissen Handwerksbräuchen der
Tuchmacher gab der Rat zu Naumburg am Dienstag n. Quas.
1528 dem Dr. Joh. Rainboth, Amtmanne zu Leuchtenburg und
Orlamünde dem Schösser Seb. Wellner zu Jena folgende Auskunft: „Wenn jemand fremde tücher in die stadt Naumburg bringt,
so werden dieselbigen tücher durch die verordneten und geschwo-
renen meister besichtigt, und wenn ein tuch oder mehr zu geringe,
zn schmal oder sonst mit einem wandel ihren tüchern nicht gleich
befunden wird, dasselbige tuch seind sie versessen. Desgleichen wenn
unsere meister in andere städte kommen, da die tuchmacher innungen
oder zunft halten, müssen sie auch ihrer tücher, ob sie gleich ver-
siegelt sein, von denselbigen meistern nach ihrer handwerksübung
und gewohnheit besichtigung und erkenntnus leiden. Dazu gestatten
unsere tuchmacher iddermänniglich auf karren oder wagen tuch in

die stadt zu führen, auch ein, zwu adder drei nacht ihres gefallens darinne zu beharren, doch, daß dieselbigen tücher nicht mit der elle verschnitten werden."

Am Donnerstage Himmelfahrt 1522 mußte sich der Naumburger Rat mit folgendem Ersuchen an den Vorsteher des Klosters zu Roda wenden: „Es gieht uns unser bürger Georg Metze klagend zu erkennen, wie ihm seine tochter Agatha, welche noch nicht zu ihren vollkommenen jahren und beständiger vernunft kommen, durch eines priesters dienerin sunder sein bewußt, willen und vergunst ins kloster zu Roda mit guten, süßen worten aufgesprochen und geantwurt wurden sei, die er bisher anher durch vielfältig sein freundlich ansuchen und erinnern wiederum zu notdürftiger hilfe und handreichung seiner aufenthaltung und haushaltens nicht habe zu ihm brengen mugen. Mit emsiger bitte ihn derhalb und in ansehung, daß solches alles wider seinen willen und bewußt geschehen, auf meinung, daß ihm seine tochter als diejenige, so noch aus seinem, als ihres vaters gewalt nicht entledigt, wiederum folge, zu verschreiben. So wir dann solche seine bitte gar in nichts vor unbillig ermerken mögen, auch daß es ja billig, daß die kinder dem gewalt ihres vaters in allem ziemlichen gefolgig seien, schätzen, ist unser freundlich fleißig bitten, ihr wollet gemeldtem unserm bürger dieselbige jungfrau Agathen, seine natürliche und eheliche tochter, wiederum sonder alle weigerung überreichen und folgen lassen, und also zwänglich ihm vorzuhalten nicht gestatten, damit er derhalb fördere unkost und nachrichten nicht thun darf." Der arme Vater bekam aber darauf keinen Bescheid, weshalb der Rat am Montage n. Mar. Himmelfahrt 1522 den Herzog Johann von Sachsen bat, zu beschaffen, „daß die klosterjungfrau in beiwesen ihrer eltern und des klosters vorstehers, der domina und wer dies füglich zu thun und schaffen hat, um ihr gemüt, sinne und bewegung, warum sie wider ihrer eltern willen, gunst und verjahung in berührtem kloster zu bleiben und verharren gesinnt, notdürftiglich befragt und alsdann darauf die billigkeit zu geschehen gnädiglich gefehlen."

Literatur.

IV

Beschreibende Darstellung der älteren Bau- und Kunstdenkmäler der Provinz Sachsen. Herausgegeben von der Historischen Kommission für die Provinz Sachsen und das Herzogtum Anhalt. XXIV. Heft. Die Stadt Naumburg. Bearbeitet von Dr. Heinrich Bergner. Mit 162 in den Text gedruckten Abbildungen, 20 Lichtdrucktafeln und 1 Stadtplan. Halle a. S. (Hendel) 1903. 8°. (Preis 10 M.).

Dieser neue Band der Baudenkmäler der Provinz Sachsen erhält durch die Beschränkung auf die Stadt Naumburg einen einheitlicheren Charakter als ähuliche Kunsttopographieen — sehr zum Vorteil seiner Lesbarkeit — und bietet bei dem großen Reichtum Naumburgs an Denkmälern und Kunstwerken aller Jahrhunderte der Naumburger Vergangenheit ein geschlossenes Bild von dem Kunstleben einer nicht unbedeutenden deutschen Stadt. Der Kreis Naumburg ist in der Reihe dieser Publikation der Hist. Kommission schon lange vermißt worden; jetzt hat Herr Pfarrer Bergner in der kurzen Frist von 2 Jahren den vorliegenden Band fertiggestellt, dem ein zweiter für den Kreis außerhalb der Stadt folgen soll. Schon daß nun eine Beschreibung der Naumburger Kunstdenkmäler also endlich vorliegt, ist dankenswert, mehr noch die eingehende und lebhafte Art, wie B. den reichen Stoff behandelt hat. In der Serie, zu der es gehört, zeichnet sich das Werk vorteilhaft vor manchen anderen aus, namentlich durch die Detailliertheit und Gründlichkeit der Beschreibung, durch das eindringende Studium und die Analyse sonst meist vernachlässigter Teile, wie des romanischen und gotischen Ornaments, und durch das Bestreben, die Zusammenhänge und die innere Entwickelung dieses lokalen Kunstlebens überall zu erkennen und hervorzuheben. Daß dieses Bestreben ihn manchmal etwas zu weit, zu etwas gewaltsamer Vereinfachung und Systematisierung verleitet, sowie daß auch Irrtümer und Fehler untergelaufen sind, vielleicht zahlreicher, als Ref. bei der Lektüre, ohne Vergleichung der Originale, feststellen konnte, ist wohl begreiflich und entschuldbar. — Die Einleitung gibt in 3 Abschnitten von anerkennenswerter Knappheit eine Übersicht über die Topographie (geologischen Charakter, Wasserläufe, Umfang des Weichbildes, Straßen, Stadtanlage), die geschichtliche Entwickelung der Stadt, bez. des Hochstiftes, namentlich unter den älteren Bischöfen bis zum 14. Jahrhundert, und über die Literatur[1]).

Die Darstellung der Verwaltungs- und Rechtsverhältnisse im Mittelalter leidet an Ungenauigkeiten; dafür wäre Hoffmanns Buch über Naumburg im Zeitalter der Reformation heranzuziehen gewesen; es findet sich unter der Literatur nicht aufgeführt, wohl weil B. es nach seinem Titel, aber mit Unrecht, zu den „überaus zahlreichen Schriften zu Reformations- etc.-Geschichte" rechnete. — Den weitaus größten Raum nimmt natürlich der Dom mit seinen Denkmälern und zugehörigen Bauten ein, ihm folgen die anderen Kirchen, die Friedhöfe, die Profanbauten der Stadt, endlich die — zum großen Teil nur auf Abbildungen und historischen Nachrichten beruhende — Beschreibung der Befestigungen[2]).

Wie überhaupt B. den einzelnen Baulichkeiten vorausgehen läßt, was über ihre Baugeschichte zu sagen ist, so gibt er auch über den Dom zunächst die wenigen urkundlichen Daten bis zu der großen Restauration von 1876 ff. Dann folgt die Beschreibung der Bauteile, in der Hauptsache, wenn auch naturgemäß nicht streng im einzelnen, nach der Zeit ihrer Entstehung, beginnend mit der Krypta; die romanischen Ostteile (Vierung mit dem ursprünglichen Altarhaus, Querschiff, Osttürme), dann das Langhaus und der Unterbau der Westtürme; über die Bauzeit dieser Teile konnte nach Lüttichs Naumburger Gymn.-Progr. von 1902 nicht viel Neues gesagt werden; die dort mitgeteilten Resultate werden im wesentlichen gesichert; abgesehen von der mittleren Krypta, die der ersten Hälfte des 12. Jahrhunderts angehört, sind alle diese Teile das Werk der Bischöfe Udo II., Berthold II. und Engelhard (1161—1242); in dieser Zeit hat eine Änderung des ganzen Bauplans, der Übergang von einer Flachdeckbasilica zu dem erhaltenen Gewölbebau stattgefunden, dessen Ausführung nach der überall einheitlich wiederkehrenden reichen Ornamentik im spätesten romanischen Stil der Zeit Engelhards (1202—1242) zuzuschreiben ist. B. geht sehr genau auf die ornamentalen Einzelheiten ein und sucht in sehr dankenswerter und lehrreicher Weise die Motive des stilisierten Pflanzen- und Rankenwerkes dieser Kapitäle u. s. w. zu analysieren; ebenso interessant ist sein Versuch einer Charakteristik des Stiles und der persönlichen Eigenart des Meisters dieses Baues. Nach diesem aber setzt im Westchor unter Dietrich II. (1243—1272) mit einem Schlage die

---

1) Erwähnt sei, daß ein lautlicher Übergang von Wythawe zu Wichaw (Weichau) [S. 3] doch sehr unwahrscheinlich ist; die erstere Form der Urkunde von 1278, die nur abschriftlich vorliegt, ist doch wohl nur als naheliegende Verschreibung für Wychawe anzusehen. — Der „Rosengarten" (S. 5) ist wohl die nicht vereinzelte Bezeichnung der Straße des Frauenhauses. — Die Bestätigungsurkunde Papst Johanns XIX. (nicht XX.) von 1032 über die Bistumsverlegung ist eine spätere Fälschung (S. 8), nicht diese, sondern die echte Papyrusurkunde von 1028 ließ Engelhard erneuern (S. 9), d. h. in Rom transsumieren. — Bischof Bruno (S. 10) gehört zu der Familie v. Langenboge.

2) S. 302 ist zu korrigieren: Dietrich von Landsberg; natürlich verbandelt 1276 nicht Dietrich „der Bedrängte", der Vater Heinrichs des Erlauchten, sondern der Sohn des letzteren, mit Bischof Member.

volle Gotik in schönster Blüte ein; die Naturfreude, mit der diese
Künstler die heimische Blumenfülle hier für ihre Ornamente verwertet haben, läßt sich nur bei einer so eingehenden Erläuterung
der Architektur und ihrer Zierglieder ahnen, wie sie auch hier
wieder B. gibt. — Die Erweiterung des Ostchores will B. etwa 40—50
Jahre früher ansetzen, als man bisher annahm und als Lüttich
a. a. O. noch ausführte; er beruft sich dafür auf ein Türbogenfeld in
dem Ostchor, das erst von ihm überhaupt beachtet und von ihm als
letztes, unvollendetes Werk des Meisters der Stifterfiguren im Westchor angesehen wird und danach gegen 1280 angesetzt werden muß.
— Mehrere (von Lüttich angeführte) Urkundenstellen von 1323 und
1328, die sich nur auf diesen Teil der Kirche beziehen können, ergeben indessen, daß der Ostchor 1323 bereits begonnen und 1328
noch nicht vollendet war; demgegenüber kann jene neue Annahme
nicht bestehen, selbst wenn das Tympanon dem Meister der Stifterfiguren zuzuschreiben sein sollte, was Ref. sehr anfechtbar erscheint.
Mit diesem Meister, von dem natürlich auch der Diakon und die
Reliefs am Lettner, wie auch nach B.s Meinung die liegende Bischofs-
figur im Ostchor, herrühren, beschäftigt sich der Verf. natürlich
besonders und bemüht sich — auch unter Heranziehung der so nahe
verwandten Meißner Figuren — der Persönlichkeit dieses großen
Künstlers nahe zu kommen, und wenn auch dabei die wiederholte
Parallele zu Goethe etwas sonderbar anmutet, so ist doch die starke
Hervorhebung der Bedeutung dieses Mannes nur zu billigen. Sein
Einfluß wirkt in Naumburg noch lange nach, wie B. an den Wasser-
speiern des Westchors, an den Glasmalereien und an Grabdenkmälern
nachweist. — Sehr eingehend beschreibt B. weiter die Glasgemälde
der beiden Chöre, die Altäre, Grabsteine[1]) und Gemälde, die wenigen
Paramente des Domes, auch die im Besitze des Kapitels erhaltenen
8 großen Meßbücher, an deren Miniaturen und Drolerien er 3 oder
4 verschiedene Hände festzustellen sucht. Leider vermißt man bis-
weilen eine Angabe über den Aufstellungsort (z. B. S. 166 No. 10;
167 No. 11; 168 No. 12). Auf den Dom folgt die Beschreibung der
anstoßenden Baulichkeiten: Dreikönigskapelle, Marienkirche, Klausur
— meist auf Grund der Lüttichschen Untersuchungen; alle Fragen
sind auch da nicht zu lösen gewesen — die Kurien[2]), namentlich
die interessante Ägidienkapelle, deren Inneres wenigen bekannt sein
dürfte. — Ärmer an baulichem Interesse, wie an Denkmälern sind
St. Moritz, St. Otmar und die Marienkirche; doch lernen wir auch
hier noch manches bemerkenswerte und wenig bekannte Kunstwerk

---

1) Falsch angegeben ist die Jahreszahl des Grabsteins des
älteren Dechanten Günther v. Bünau (S. 189, No. 53), der das Jahr
1519, nicht 1512 zeigt; der Fehler stammt wohl aus Mitzschkes
„Naumburger Inschriften". Auch das Todesjahr des Kilian Meusel
(S. 192) muß wohl 1553 lauten. — Unrichtig angesetzt ist auch der
Teppich (S. 173, No. 3); nach den Wappen: Schleinitz und Merse-
burger Bistum und beide quadriert, ist der dargestellte Bischof der
Merseburger Vincenz v. Schleinitz (1526—1535).

2) An dem Giebel des jetzigen Landratsamtes, früher Kurie des
Dompropstes von Werthern, befindet sich nicht das Burgsdorfsche
(S. 214), sondern das Werthernsche Wappen.

kennen [1]). Interessanter ist als Bau die Wenzelskirche; Ref. vermag. aber nicht die Ansicht des Verf. zu teilen, nach der die beiden von ihm als „Chörlein" bezeichneten Seitenkapellen am Chor zur ursprünglichen Anlage gehören sollen (S. 239). Das Vorhandensein des Laubkapitäls bei dem rechten Ecksäulchen des südlichen „Chörleins" für einen Kielbogen, wie solche über die Seitenflächen des Chores unter den Fenstern gezogen sind, setzt doch auch an dieser Seite eine gerade Wandfläche statt des Polygons als ursprüngliche Anlage voraus; die „3 Knollen" an dem Kapitäl des linken Ecksäulchens sind übrigens Reste einer Tiergestalt, entsprechend dem Affen rechts und den Kapitälfiguren an dem anderen „Chörlein". Auch der Ansatz für den Anbau der Sakristei (vor dem Brand von 1517) steht doch auf schwachen Füßen. — Die Profanbauten sind, abgesehen von dem hochinteressanten Marientor und allenfalls dem Rathaus, ohne erhebliche Bedeutung; als den für Naumburg vorherrsehenden und charakteristischen Stil bezeichnet B. eine Mischung von Spätgotik und Renaissance, wie sie höchst originell schon der Hochaltar des Doms zeigte; daneben sind auch Zierformen des Barock und Rokoko, namentlich als Fensterumrahmung, sehr beliebt. — In einer kunststatistischen Übersicht läßt der Verf. zum Schluß, in kurzem Rückblick auf die Ergebnisse seines Buches, die Entwickelung der Naumburger Kunst in kirchlicher und weltlicher Baukunst, Bildnerei und Malerei noch einmal an uns vorüberziehen. Dabei geht er nur in dem Bestreben nach Zusammenfassung der mannigfachen Erscheinungen und nach Systematisierung mehrfach über das vorher Gesagte hinaus und kommt auch zu direkten Widersprüchen mit dem Text der Beschreibung, z. B. wenn er (S. 315, No. 2) dem von ihm so bezeichneten „Meister der Dreikönige" aus dem ersten Viertel des 15. Jahrhunderts den Altaraufsatz auf dem Hieronymusaltar, den er S. 162 durchaus zutreffend um 1350 ansetzt, zuschreiben will. Muß man ferner schon zweifeln, ob die — so schlecht erhaltene — Dreikönigsgruppe (Fig. 100, nicht 67, wie B. auf S. 315 zitiert) dem Meister der vortrefflichen Grabfigur des Bischofs Gerhard II. zugewiesen werden kann, so ist vollends die Annahme, daß das Schleinitzmonument und die gänzlich verhältnislose Figur des Günther v. Bünau im Westchor von einer und derselben Hand herrühren, wohl ganz haltlos. Auch die Annahme eines Urhebers für die Epitaphien des Münch, Draschwitz und Gottart, oder die Absicht. die doch wohl erheblich späteren Figuren der Caritas und Pietas in St. Wenzel dem Künstler des Cracauschen Holzepithaphs von 1606 im Dom zuschreiben zu wollen, scheint nur durch das Streben des Verf. nach Zusammenfassung veranlaßt zu sein. Immerhin lassen sich doch einzelne Künstlerpersönlichkeiten in dem reichen Schaffen des 16. Jahrhunderts unterscheiden. — Die Abbildungen sind ungleichmäßig, die Lichtdrucktafeln schon häufig nicht scharf und klar genug, namentlich aber meist zu klein im Maßstab, da zu viel Ausschnitte auf ihnen zusammengedrängt sind; die in den Text gedruckten Autotypien sind vollends schlecht; die Zeichnungen B.s selbst

---

1) S. 226 No. 3 ist zu lesen: des letzten Propstes statt Priors. S. 268 ist zu verbessern: 1493, statt 1494. — S. 270, Kelch No. 1 lautet die Jahreszahl des Schriftbandes doch wohl M°. CCCC. XVII° = 1417.

teilweise recht instruktiv, z. B. die verschiedenen Kapitälformen; man
bedauert dabei indessen, daß nicht alle besprochenen Kapitäle auch in
Abbildung vorgeführt werden, und daß die Beziehung des Textes auf
diese Abbildungen nicht eine genauere ist. Andere seiner Zeichnungen sind dagegen auch nur sehr flüchtig und oberflächlich, aber
doch nur selten so irreführend unklar, wie Fig. 120 linke Ecke.
Auch der Stadtplan ist nicht einwandsfrei; abgesehen davon, daß
z. B. die S. 214 No. 2 beschriebene Bischofskurie hier als Propst-
kurie fälschlich bezeichnet wird, so ist vor allem der Bezirk der
Ratsvorstadt viel zu weit abgegrenzt, so daß der Sprengel der Dom-
propsteigerichte, die Michaelis-, Moritz- und Medergasse umfassend,
überhaupt ausgefallen ist.

Magdeburg.   Dr. Rosenfeld.

V.

Beiträge zur Sächsischen Kirchengeschichte. Herausgegeben im
Auftrage der Gesellschaft für Sächsische Kirchengeschichte von
Fr. Dibelius und **Th. Brieger.** Leipzig, J. A. Barth. 17 Hefte,
1882—1904.

Seit dem Jahre 1882 gibt die Gesellschaft für Sächsische
Kirchengeschichte „Beiträge" heraus, die in gewissem Sinne als eine
Ergänzung zu dem Neuen Archive für Sächsische Geschichte gelten
können und, wie es bei der historischen Entwickelung der wettini-
sehen Lande nicht anders erwartet werden kann, auch für die
thüringische Geschichte von Bedeutung sind. Es sind Namen von
gutem Klange, deren Träger sich in den bisher erschienenen 17 Heften
hören ließen. Die beiden verantwortlichen Herausgeber, Fr. Dibelius und Th. Brieger, bürgen schon dafür, daß wirklich wissenschaftliche Aufsätze in den Heften zum Abdrucke gelangen, und neben
den Herausgebern haben Männer wie Buchwald, Clemen, Drews,
Flathe, Kanis, Knothe, Müller u. a. beigesteuert. Es darf nicht
Wunder nehmen, daß der Reformationsgeschichte der breiteste Raum
in den Heften eingeräumt wird, doch kommen auch Mittelalter und
neueste Zeit zu ihrem Rechte. Der Mehrzahl der Beiträge kommt
es zu gute, daß ihren Verfassern wertvolle archivalische Quellen zur
Verfügung gestanden haben; besonders sind die Schätze des wohl-
geordneten und vortrefflich verwalteten Hauptstaatsarchives in Dresden
benutzt worden. Es ist natürlich nicht angezeigt, an dieser Stelle
auf alle in den Beiträgen veröffentlichten Abhandlungen hinzuweisen,
es scheint aber geboten, einige unseres Erachtens hervorragende Arbeiten, zumal sie auch auf die Geschichte Thüringens Streiflichter
werfen, hervorzuheben. Wir stellen die umfangreiche, auf eingehenden
Quellenstudien beruhende „Verfassungs- und Verwaltungs-
geschichte der sächsischen Landeskirche" von Prof. Dr.
G. Müller, die die Hefte 9 und 10 (272 u. 320 SS.) füllen, voran.
Für Thüringen hat auch Bedeutung die Untersuchung Flathes
über „Römische Inquisition in Mitteldeutschland, insbesondere in

den sächsischen Ländern" (XI, 58 ff.). Wertvoll weiter ist Buch-wald s und Scheufflers Zusammenstellung der in Wittenberg ordinierten Geistlichkeit der Parochien des jetzigen Königreichs Sachsen (XII, 101 ff. u. XIII, 1—214) und die von Germann gelieferte Biographie „Sebastian Fröschel, sein Leben und seine Schriften" (XIV, 1—126). Eine prächtige Illustration unserer Kleinstaaterei bietet Kröbers Aufsatz „Wie Bocka mit seiner Kirche und deren Zubehör nebst zwei Gütern nach Sachsen gekommen ist" (XIV, 127 bis 148); für Thüringen wichtig ist Meusels Abhandlung über die Reußische oder Reußisch-Schönburgische Konfession von 1567 (XIV, 149—187), ferner Spalatins Verzeichnis der Pfarreien in Sachsen, Meißen, Thüringen und Voigtland (!), mitgeteilt von Planitz (XV, 1 ff.), Blanckmeisters Festrede „Karl von Hase" (XV, 265 ff.), Zimmermanns Untersuchung über „die Entwickelung der Kirchen-inspektionen 1530—1800" (XVI, 120—209), „Johann Tetzel" von Dibelius (XVII, 1 ff.); „Die Grenzen der Bistümer Naumburg, Merseburg und Meißen" von Bönhoff (XVII, 142—156) u. a. m.

Wenn jetzt auch in der Provinz Sachsen eine Zeitschrift für Kirchengeschichte zur Ausgabe vorbereitet wird, so kann man nur wünschen, daß die Herausgeber sich an den vortrefflichen Beiträgen zur Sächsischen Kirchengeschichte ein Muster nehmen mögen.

O. Dobenecker.

VI.

Mitteilungen der Vereinigung für Gothaische Geschichte und Alter-tumsforschung. Jahrgang 1903. Friedrichroda, Jac. Schmidt u. Co. [1903]. 136 SS. 8°.

Seit einigen Jahren läßt die Vereinigung für Gothaische Ge-schichte und Altertumsforschung an Stelle der Quartalheftchen Jahres-hefte erscheinen, deren Redaktion in den Händen des Oberbiblio-thekars Professor Dr. R. Ehwald liegt. Der Jahrgang 1903, der hier zur Besprechung steht, wird von einer rechtshistorischen Abhandlung über die Stadtrechte im Herzogtum Gotha aus der Feder v. Strenges eröffnet. Der Verfasser, der im Auftrage der Thüringischen Histori-schen Kommission die Herausgabe der Stadtrechte von Gotha und Eisenach vorbereitet, gibt wohl im Hinblick auf diese größere Arbeit zunächst einen Überblick über das, was bisher über diese Materie veröffentlicht worden ist, und zeigt, wo die Forschung einzusetzen hat, um das Recht der Städte des gothaischen Landes, das auf das sächsische Landrecht sich gründet, an das Magdeburg-Leipziger an-geschlossen und schließlich zu einzelnen Fällen zu förmlichen Stadt-ordnungen ausgebildet worden ist, zur Darstellung zu bringen. Ganz methodisch behandelt er somit zunächst die handschriftliche Über-lieferung des Stadtrechtes von Gotha, Ohrdruf und Waltershausen und geht schließlich auf einige Punkte des Stadtrechtes selbst ein. Als Anlagen fügt er einige archivalische Mitteilungen bei.

Unter den übrigen Abhandlungen sei zuerst auf die beiden Aufsätze des Herausgebers hingewiesen. Ehwald berichtigt einige

fehlerhafte Notizen zur „Druckgeschichte Gothas" und ediert S. 119
bis 130 die Konfession und das Passionale Johann Friedrichs des Großmütigen. Der Erforschung der Prähistorie dient Florschütz'
Untersuchung des Urnenfeldes auf dem Simmel bei Eischleben.
Heß unternimmt den schwierigen Versuch, die Grenzen der Mark
Lupnitz (Reg. d. Thuringiae I no. 638) zu bestimmen. Literarhisto-
risch ist der Beitrag Berbigs zur Geschichte des Hainbundes in
dem Aufsatze über Schack Hermann Ehwald und von allgemeiner
Bedeutung der Vortrag Felgners über „Herzogin Louise Dorothea
und ein Besitzstück der Herzogl. Bibliothek zu Gotha (Matinées
du roi de Prusse)".

Reichhaltig ist der Inhalt dieses Heftes, und mannigfach sind
die Anregungen, die der Leser bekommt. Man kann nur wünschen,
daß die folgenden Hefte auf der Höhe dieses Jahrganges bleiben.

O. Dobenecker.

VII.

Grössler, Hermann: Führer durch das Unstruttal von Artern bis
    Naumburg für Vergangenheit und Gegenwart. 2. vermehrte
    und verbesserte Auflage. (Mit einer Karte des Unstruttales).
    Freyburg (Unstrut), Joh. Finke, 1904. XVI u. 256 SS. Preis
    kartonniert 1 M. 75 Pf., gebunden 2 M. 25 Pf.

Ein Buch Größlers anzuzeigen ist eine Freude, denn man befindet sich von vornherein in der angenehmen Lage, es mit einem
gründlichen, echt wissenschaftlichen Forscher zu tun zu haben.
Größler kennt wie kaum ein zweiter die geographische und geschichtliche Eigenart des Unstruttales, des Schauplatzes so vieler für die
Geschichte des thüringischen Stammes und des ganzen deutschen
Volkes wichtigen Ereignisse, und verläßt sich nirgends auf das Urteil
anderer, sondern will alles selbst sehen, prüfen und abwägen. So
ist, wie wir vorausschicken wollen, in diesem Führer, der zuerst in
den von A. Kirchhoff herausgegebenen Mitteilungen des Vereins für
Erdkunde zu Halle a. S., Jahrg. 1892 und 1893 erschienen ist, etwas
Ausgezeichnetes zu stande gekommen.

Der Verf. gibt zunächst einen Überblick über die Bedeutung
des Unstruttales im allgemeinen, indem er die Etymologie des Namens
„Unstrut" untersucht, den Lauf des Flusses in der Diluvialzeit und
die geologische Gliederung des untersuchten Geländes beschreibt,
dabei auch der Erklärung der Namen fortgesetzt seine Aufmerksamkeit schenkt. Wie der Titel des Buches schon andeutet, will er das
Unstruttal und das Gelände zu beiden Seiten des Flusses von dem
Unstrutknie bei Artern bis zur Mündung verfolgen. In scharfer
Gliederung behandelt er zunächst den oberen Teil des Tales bis
Nebra. Wir besuchen unter seiner sachkundigen Führung von
Artern aus jene Gegend, wo König Heinrich I. „iuxta locum, qui
dicitur Riade" am 15. März 933 die wilden und räuberischen Ungarn
zu schmählicher Flucht gezwungen hat, wandern über Gehofen nach
Kloster Donndorf und nach Wiehe, dem Geburtsorte Rankes, von

da nach Kloster Memleben, wo die beiden größten Vertreter des sächsischen Königshauses, der Einiger der deutschen Stämme und der Erneuerer des römischen Kaisertums, ihren Tod gefunden haben, und besuchen auch das südliche und nördliche Gelände mit allen historisch wichtigen Punkten.

Im 2. Abschnitte der Wanderung gelangen wir von Nebra aus in das untere Unstruttal über Vitzenburg, wo einst ein alter Herrensitz und ein Kloster sich befanden, über Reinsdorf nach Burgscheidungen, jenem Ort, wo 531 das thüringische Königreich den von dem Verf. in Prosa, wie in poetischem Gewande beschriebenen Todeskampf gekämpft hat, besuchen auch die seitwärts gelegenen Orte, wie Bibra und Thalwinkel, und kommen über Laucha und Zscheiplitz nach Freiburg und dem alten Landgrafenschloß Neuenburg und von da nach Groß-Jena, dem alten Sitze der Ekkehardiner, der seit der ersten Hälfte des 11. Jahrhunderts von Naumburg, der Neugründung desselben Markgrafenhauses, überflügelt worden ist, und verfolgen den Unstrutlauf bis zur Mündung gegenüber Naumburg.

Gegenstand und Form der Darstellung fesseln uns bis zu den letzten Seiten, auf denen der Verf. das sonderbare in den Felsen gehauene Stammbuch, über welches er schon im Archiv für Landes- und Volkskunde der Provinz Sachsen I, 150—154 berichtet hat, beschreibt; denn das Buch bietet mehr, als sonst die Führer leisten, es ist eher eine die Geographie, Prähistorie, Sage, Kunstgeschichte und Geschichte berücksichtigende kleine Landeskunde des Unstruttales, die jedem, der dies schöne Stück Land Thüringens besucht, auf das wärmste zu empfehlen ist.   O. Dobenecker.

VIII.

Gröger, Johannes: Ein thüringisches Städtchen. Beiträge zur Geschichte Großbreitenbachs und der Umgegend, hauptsächlich auf Grund der Kirchenbücher zusammengestellt. Arnstadt, E. Frotscher, 1903. 150 SS. 8°.

Aus Vorträgen erwachsen und zum Teil auf einer handschriftlichen Ortschronik des früheren Bürgermeisters v. Hopffgarten beruhend, will diese Stadtgeschichte in ganz anspruchsloser Form die Entwickelung des hochgelegenen thüringischen Waldstädtchens den Bewohnern Breitenbachs schildern.

Großbreitenbach ist eine verhältnismäßig späte Siedelung in der Nähe des Rennsteiges. Erst im Jahre 1442 wird sie, soweit bis jetzt bekannt ist, urkundlich erwähnt, und zwar bereits als Besitz der Grafen von Schwarzburg. Im Jahre 1586 erhielt das Dorf das Recht, jährlich drei Märkte abzuhalten, und erst 1855 wurde es zur Stadt erhoben. Es liegt an alten Straßenzügen, von denen der eine von Ilmenau und Gehren über Breitenbach nach Olze führt, ein anderer, von Erfurt kommend, dem Rennsteig bei Neustadt zustrebt.

Der Verf. behandelt zunächst Ort und Flur im allgemeinen und erzählt dann von den Heimsuchungen des Ortes, wie Hungersnot, Seuchen und Bränden. Dieser Abschnitt hätte besser mit dem

Abschnitt VII „Großbreitenbach in Kriegszeiten" verbunden werden können. Das Pfarrarchiv enthält Kirchenbücher, die bis zum Jahre 1619 zurückreichen und für die Zeitgeschichte höchst wertvolle Eintragungen erhalten, die in ihrer Urwüchsigkeit àn Einerts Berichte in dem lesenswerten Buche „Ein Thüringer Landpfarrer im 30-jährigen Kriege" (Arnstadt, E. Frotscher, 1895) erinnern. Der Ort hat damals wiederholt schwere Heimsuchungen erfahren, besonders durch die bestialische Mordgier der Kroaten, jenes kaiserlichen Raubgesindels, das in ganz Thüringen im schlimmsten Andenken steht. Nicht Geschlecht und nicht Alter bewahrte vor Mißhandlung und schmählichem Tod. Die viehische Roheit der entmenschten Soldateska schonte nicht Kinder und nicht Greise. Da würgen diese Banditen einen einjährigen Knaben, dort morden sie eine 91-jährige Matrone. „Christina, Claus Tresselds des älteren hinterlassene Witwe, eine ehrliche Matron, welche nach Gottes Gnaden, weniger achte, hundert Jahre erlebt hat und doch auf ihrem Siechbettlein nicht sterben können, sondern hat vom Feinde einen schmählichen Tod leiden müssen, alt 91 Jahre", trägt der Pfarrer ein. Und welchen Jammer enthüllt der kurze Vermerk: „Mittlerweile ist hierum auf 2 Meilen Wegs keine Stadt, Flecken, noch Dorf bewohnt gewesen, und hat auch das Volk in den wüsten, weit abgelegenen Wäldern, Klüften und Höhlen nicht sicher sein können, ist allenthalben durchstreift und geplündert worden."

Auch im Nordischen Kriege, als im Jahre 1706 die Sachsen von Karls XII. Scharen über den Wald gejagt wurden, und im 7-jährigen Kriege durch die Preußen hatte der Ort mancherlei zu leiden.

Die Kapitel über Kirche, Schulen und Familien werden wiederum durch Mitteilungen aus den erhaltenen Kirchenbüchern wertvoll ergänzt. Für das Jahr 1620 ist sogar ein genaues Verzeichnis über die Häuser des Ortes und die Namen sämtlicher Bewohner dieses aufgestellt worden. Der Ort, der 1900 378 Häuser und 2898 Einwohner zählte, hatte im Jahre 1620 289 Häuser und 1314 Bewohner. Die Untersuchung über das Erwerbsleben in alter Zeit zeigt, daß die Bewohner wie in anderen Gebirgsorten genötigt sind, ihren Lebensunterhalt auswärts zu suchen, sei es als Fuhrleute, die bis Lüneburg und Hamburg fahren, sei es als hausierende Handwerker, die die Produkte ihres Gewerbefleißes selbst verkaufen; besonders bekannt sind die Breitenbacher Olitätenhändler. Schon 1648 wurden Glashütten angelegt, dazu kam Bergbau auf Silber, Kupfer u. s. f., der aber nicht recht lohnte; viel wichtiger wurde, wie schon Stieda in seinem gründlichen Werke über die Anfänge der Porzellanfabrikation auf dem Thüringerwalde[1]) S. 263 ff. gezeigt hat, die Porzellanfabrikation für den Ort.

Aber nicht allein die materielle Entwickelung hat Gröger zu erforschen gesucht; wie wir es von einem Geistlichen erwarten dürfen, hat er auch dem religiösen und sittlichen Leben seine Aufmerksamkeit geschenkt. Wiederum gaben ihm die Kirchenbücher dabei den besten Führer ab. So hat der Verf. die historische Entwickelung des Städtchens nach allen Richtungen verfolgt und kann versichert sein, daß sein Buch, das ja in erster Linie lokalgeschichtlichen Wert

---

1) Jena, G. Fischer, 1902.

hat, dazu beitragen wird, in den Bewohnern Großbreitenbachs Ver-
ständnis für die Vergangenheit ihrer Gemeinde und damit rechte
Heimatsliebe zu wecken. O. Dobenecker.

IX.

Die Pfarrei Mupperg. Topographisch und kirchengeschichtlich dargestellt von weil. Dr. **Gustav Lotz,** Kirchenrat, Pfarrer zu
Mupperg und Gefell. Neu herausgegeben von **Adolf Joch,**
Lehrer. Mit 3 Abb. Sonneberg, Druck von Gräbe u. Hetzer,
1903. Broch. 3 M., geb. 3 M. 50 Pf.

Das Dorf Mupperg südlich von Sonneberg (S.-Meiningen) wird
bereits im Jahre 1069 urkundlich als ein Dotalstück des von dem
Markgrafen Hermann von Vohburg und seiner Gemahlin Alberade
gegründeten Klosters Banz in der Diöcese Bamberg erwähnt. Die
Vogtei über den Klosterbesitz und damit auch über Mupperg lag
zunächst in der Hand des Gründers, ging dann auf die Herzöge
von Meran und nach dem Aussterben dieses Geschlechtes auf die
Henneberger über. Die Geschichte des Dorfes und der Pfarrei
Mupperg hat zu einer Zeit, als Dorfgeschichten eine große Seltenheit waren, der ehrwürdige Pfarrer Gustav Lotz in ganz geschickter
Weise und nach guten Quellen bearbeitet und 1843 auf eigene
Kosten in Coburg drucken lassen. Das 353 SS. 8° füllende, mit
urkundlichen Beilagen ausgestattete Buch ist sehr selten geworden;
es ist daher dankenswert, daß der Lehrer des Ortes, Adolf Joch,
eine 2. Auflage hergestellt hat. Pietätvoll hat er das Buch im ganzen
unverändert gelassen, natürlich aber bis zur Gegenwart fortgesetzt.
Die urkundlichen Beilagen hat er freilich bedeutend gekürzt, trotzdem ist die neue Auflage mit 275 SS. gr. 8° ein stattlicher Band
geworden. O. Dobenecker.

X.

Behr, Otto: Triebeser Schulchronik. Ein Beitrag zur Geschichte
der Landschulen in der Herrschaft Schleiz. Selbstverlag des
Verfassers. [Triebes] 1903. 43 SS. 8°.

Es ist ein erfreuliches Zeichen für einen gesunden historischen
Sinn, daß man mehr und mehr beginnt, das Wesen und die Bedeutung auch kleinerer Institutionen durch Untersuchung ihrer geschichtlichen Entwickelung zu studieren. Diese Betrachtungsweise wird
um so wertvoller, wenn für sie die rechten Quellen erschlossen werden
und wenn die Darstellung dadurch in die rechte Beleuchtung gerückt
wird, daß man sie in Zusammenhang mit der allgemeinen Entwickelung bringt. Beide Bedingungen sind in dem vorliegenden Hefte

erfüllt worden. **Der** Verfasser, der erst vor kurzem eine lesbare und dankenswerte Untersuchung der Geschichte des aufstrebenden **Ortes** Triebes und seiner Umgebung gegeben hat[1]), hat die **Schulchronik** wesentlich nach Archivalien, die er im Archive zu Schleiz, im Amtsgerichtsarchive zu Hohenleuben, im Pfarr- und Schularchive zu Triebes und im Archive des Rittergutes Weißendort gefunden hat, zusammengestellt. Die Darstellung ist gewandt und übersichtlich und verfolgt die lehrreiche Entwickelung der Schule von der **Reformation** bis zur Gegenwart. Sie wirft eine Menge **Streiflichter** auf die Geschichte des Vogtlandes und die allgemeine **Sitten-** und Kulturgeschichte und bleibt immer im Zusammenhang mit der allgemeinen Geschichte. Interessant sind Erscheinungen, wie der Burggraf, der seit 1550 Landesherr war und, obwohl Katholik und Bundesgenosse des Kaisers, in seinem Lande doch die evangelische Richtung zu fördern sich angelegen sein ließ. Wichtig ist auch der Nachweis, wie der politische und wirtschaftliche Aufschwung Deutschlands im Zeitalter Bismarcks selbst auf kleine und abgelegene **Orte** segensreich eingewirkt hat und als glänzendes Gegenstück zu der allgemeinen Depression in und nach der Zeit des 30-jährigen Krieges gelten kann.

Möchte die Geschichte auch anderer vogtländischer **Schulen** und Orte ähnliche Bearbeitung erfahren! O. Dobenecker.

XI.

Übersicht über die neuerdings erschienene Literatur zur thüringischen Geschichte und Altertumskunde.

Von O. Dobenecker.

Abriß, kurzer, der Geschichte des Herzogl. Lehrerseminars zu Altenburg. Festschr. Altenburg, Pierer, 1902. 56 SS.

Albrecht, O.: Mitteilungen aus den Akten der **Naumburger** Reformationsgeschichte. Theol. Studien u. Kritiken (1904). 32—82.

Derselbe: Geschichte der Marien-Magdalenenkirche in Naumburg. Naumburger Kreisblatt. 1902. No. 216—259.

Alt-Plauen in Wort und Bild. Aus Anlaß des 30-**jährigen** Bestehens des Altertumsver. zu Plauen herausg. vom Gesamtvorstande. Plauen im V., 1903. IV u. 60 SS. 4°.

Armbrust, L.: Neuigkeiten von 1384. Mit einem Anhange. [Nachrichten über das Verhältnis Hermanns d. Gelehrten, Lgr. v. Hessen, zum Erzbischof v. Mainz, dem Lgr. Balthasar v. **Thüringen** u. Herzog Otto d. Quaden v. Braunschweig-Göttingen.] **Hessenland,** XVII. Jahrg. No. 1 u. 2 (1903. Jan. 2 u. 16). S. 2—5 u. 18—21.

---

1) O. Behr, Bunte Bilder aus der **Geschichte** von **Triebes** und seiner Umgebung. (Triebes, Selbstverlag des Verfassers, 1903.) 55 SS. 8°.

Auerbach, F.: Das Zeißwerk und die Carl-Zeiß-Stiftung in Jena. Ihre wissenschaftliche, technische und soziale Entwickelung und Bedeutung für weitere Kreise dargestellt. Jena, G. Fischer, 1903. Mit 78 Abb. im Text,

Aus vergangenen Tagen. Nach den Tagebüchern eines Jenaischen Bürgers. Blätter f. Unterhaltung u. Belehrung. Sonntags-Beil. zur Jenaischen Ztg. 1903. No. 9, 10.

Bärwinkel: Die Bedeutung der Besitzergreifung Erfurts durch Preußen für die evang. Kirche in Erfurt. Dentsch-evang. Blätter. XXVIII, 203—215.

Bamberg, v.: Herzog Ernst d. Fromme u. seine kirchl. Friedensbestrebungen. Monatshefte der Comenius-Ges. XI, 258—272.

Bau- und Kunstdenkmäler Thüringens. Bearbeitet von P. Lehfeldt, herausg. von G. Voss. Heft XXIX. Herzogt. S.-Meiningen. Amtsgerichtsbezirk Hildburghausen. Jena, G. Fischer, 1903. S. 1—112. Mit 2 Lichtdrucken u. 12 Abb. im Texte. Gr. 8⁰. Heft XXX. Herzogt. S.-Meiuingen. Amtgerichtsbezirke Eisfeld u. Themar. S. 113—247. Mit 2 Lichtdr. u. 27 Abb. im Texte. Heft XXXI. Herzogt. S.-Meiningen. Amtsgerichtsbezirke Heldburg u. Römhild. Jena, G. Fischer, 1904. XVI u. S. 249—479. Mit 11 Lichtdrucktafeln u. 68 Abb. im Texte.

Behr, Otto: Bunte Bilder aus der Geschichte von Triebes und seiner Umgebung. (Triebes, Selbstverl. des Verf., 1903.) 55 SS. 8⁰.

Derselbe: Triebeser Schulchronik. Ein Beitr. zur Gesch. der Landschulen in der Herrschaft Schleiz. Selbstverl. des Verf., Okt. 1903. 43 SS. 8⁰.

Derselbe: Türkensorgen eines vogtl. Adligen ums J. 1600. Ein Beitr. z. G. derer von Metzsch. Unsere Heimat. Illustr. Monatsschr. f. d. gesamte Erzgebirge, Osterland u. Vogtland. II (1902/3), 243—246.

Beiträge z. Gesch. des 30-jährigen Krieges. (Aus Prof. Opels Nachlaß.) N. Mitt. hist.-ant. Forsch. Bd. XXI. H. 3 (Halle a. S. 1903). S. 291—320.

Benndorf, P.: Vier Tafeln vorgeschichtlicher Gegenstände aus Mitteldeutschland. Mit erläut. Text auf jeder Tafel. Leipzig, Brandstetter, 1903.

Berbig, G.: Die Deutsche Augsburgische Konfession nach der bisher unbekannten Coburger Handschrift. Zs. f. Kirchen-G. XXIV, 429—474.

Derselbe: Urkundliches zur Reformations-Geschichte. Theol. Studien u. Kritiken (1904), 1—31. Inh.: 1) Eigenh. Brief des H. Georg v. Sachsen vom Reichstag zu Augsburg 1530. 2) Spalatiniana.

Derselbe: Geschichte des Emsegrundes. Waltershausen, J. Waitz, o. J.

Derselbe: Kurf. Bestätigung des Konsistoriums zu Coburg v. J. 1542. Zs. f. Kirchen-G. XXIV, 150—152.

Derselbe: Zwei Vorladungen vor das Konsistorium zu Coburg in Ehesachen v. J. 1563. Ebenda XXIV, 153 f.

Derselbe: Eine Differenz Luthers mit dem Stadtrate zu Coburg im J. 1539. Ebenda XXIV, 154—164.

Bergner, H: Beschreibende Darstellung der älteren Bau- u. Kunstdenkmäler der Stadt Naumburg. A. u. d. T.: Beschr. Darst.

der älteren Bau- u. Kunstdenkmäler der Prov. Sachsen. Herausg. von der hist. Kommission für die Prov. Sachsen u. das Herzogt. Anhalt. H. XXIV. Die Stadt Naumburg. Halle a. S., O. Hendel, 1903. Mit 162 in den Text gedr. Abbildungen, 20 Lichtdrucktafeln u. 1 Stadtplan. VIII u. 322 SS. 8°.

Bericht über die Hauptversammlung des Gesamtvereins in Erfurt. Korrespondenzbl. des Gesamtvereins (1903). No. 10/11, 12; (1904). No. 1, 2, 3, 4/5.

Beyer, C.: Geschichte der Stadt Erfurt, fortges. von J. Biereye. Lief. 8 u. 9. Erfurt, Keysersche Buchh., 1903. S. 225—256 u. 257—288.

Bibra, Reinh. v.: Bodenlauben bei Bad Kissingen. Geschichte der Burg u. des Amtes. Mit 8 Abb. u. Plänen. Bad Kissingen, Fr. Weinberger (1903). 146 SS. 8°.

Blau, G.: Beiträge zur Geschichte der Gemeinde Großbodungen bis zum Beginn des 30-jähr. Krieges. Zs. z. Harz-V. XXXVI, 1—18.

Bönhoff: Die ursprüngliche Parochie Zwickau. Zwickauer Ztg. 1903. No. 15—17.

Derselbe: Die Grenzen der Bistümer Naumburg, Merseburg und Meißen unter einander. Beitr. zur Säehs. Kirchengesch. H. 17. (Leipzig, J. A. Barth, 1904). S. 142—156.

Bojanowski, El. v.: Louise, Großherzogin von Sachsen und ihre Beziehungen zu den Zeitgenossen. Nach größtenteils unveröffentlichten Briefen u. Niederschriften. Stuttgart u. Berlin, Cottasche Buchh., 1903. Mit einem Porträt. VIII u. 429 SS. 8°.

Bojanowski, P. v.: Das Weimar Johann Sebastian Bachs. Zur Erinnerung an den 8. April 1703. Mit einem Bilde: Die Schloßkirche zur Zeit Bachs. Weimar, Böhlaus Nachf., 1903. 50 SS. 8°.

Derselbe: Niederschriften des Herzogs Karl August von Sachsen-Weimar über den Schutz der Demarkationslinie, den Rennweg (1796) und die Defension Thüringens (1798). Mit einer Karte der Südgrenze Thüringens aus dem J. 1796 nach Güssefeld-Weimar. Weimar, H. Böhlaus Nachf., 1902. VII u. 73 SS. 4°.

Derselbe: H. Karl August u. der Pariser Buchhändler Pougens. Weimar, Böhlaus Nachf., 1903.

Brackmann, A.: Papsturkunden des östlichen Deutschlands. Ein Reisebericht. Nachr. von der Königl. Ges. der Wissensch. zu Göttingen. 1902. S. 193—223.

Brandenburg, E.: Politische Korrespondenz des Herzogs u. Kurfürsten Moritz von Sachsen. Bd. II. 1. Hälfte (1544 u. 1545). Leipzig, Teubner, 1903. 468 SS. 8°.

Brode, Reinh.: Der Schauplatz der Kaisermanöver 1903. Hist. Skizze aus Deutschlands Vergangenheit. Halle a. S., Gebauer-Schwetschke, 1903. XIV u. 155 SS. 8°.

Bruck, R.: Friedrich d. Weise als Förderer der Kunst. Mit 41 Lichtdrucktafeln u. 5 Textabb. (Studien z. d. Kunstgesch. H. 45.) Straßburg i. E., Huth, 1903. VIII u. 336 SS. 8°.

Brüll, J.: Die Anfänge des preußischen Eichsfeldes, 1902. 32 SS. 8°.

B[uchenau], H. Über einige thüringische Pfennige aus der Zeit Friedrichs d. Freidigen, Markgrafen von Meißen, und seiner Gemahlin Elisabeth von Lobdeburg. Bl. f. Münzfreunde (1904). No. 4. Sp. 3121—3126.

Derselbe: Kurzer Bericht über den um 1238 vergrabenen Schleusinger Fund. Ebenda Sp. 3126—3129.

Buchner, O.: Erfurt und die dortige kunsthistorische Ausstellung. Wartburgstimmen. I. Jahrg. Bd. I. S. 532 ff.

Derselbe: Das städtische Museum zu Jena. Ebenda I. Jahrg. Bd. I. S. 61 ff.

Buddeus, Th.: Szenen aus dem Kommandantenleben der Wachsenburg. Goth. Tagebl. 1902. No. 143, 145, 149, 153, 155.

Bühring, Johannes: Geschichte der Stadt Arnstadt 704 bis 1904. Im Auftrage der Stadt und unter Benutzung hinterlassener Vorarbeiten des Archivrats Hermann Schmidt dargestellt. Arnstadt, E. Frotscher, 1904. IV u. 212 SS. 8⁰. Mit vielen Abbildungen.

Derselbe: Die Rennsteigurkunde von 1519 im Sondershäuser Landesarchiv. Das Mareile. III. Reihe (1903, No. 11/12. S. 127.

Derselbe: Karl August u. der Rennsteig. Das Marcile. 1903. No. 7. S. 66—71.

Derselbe: Rennsteigvermessung mit dem Handmeßrad von Pretzsch. Ebenda S. 71—82.

Bürkner, R.: Herder u. Dresden. Ein Gedenkwort zur 100. Wiederkehr seines Todestages († 18. Dez. 1803). Dresdener Anz. 1903. No. 349. S. 2 f.

Derselbe: Herders Deutschtum. Wartburgstimmen. I. Jahrg. Bd. II. S. 119 ff.

Derselbe, Herder; sein Leben und Wirken. Berlin, Hofmann u. Co., 1903. 287 SS.

Clemen, O.: Ein Brief von Johannes Bernhardi aus Feldkirch (an Johann Lang in Erfurt). A. f. Reformationsgesch. I. Jahrg. H. 2. (Berlin, C. A. Schwetschke u. S.) 1904. S. 192 ff.

Derselbe: Beiträge zur Reformationsgeschichte aus Büchern u. Handschriften der Zwickauer Stadtschulbibl. Ebenda H. 3. Berlin, Schwetschke u. S., 1903). IV u. 115 SS. 8⁰.

Debes, H.: Aug. Trostbach, der Thüringer Pfarrer u. Dichter. Ev. Gemeindebl. f. d. Stadt Gotha. V, 19, 20, 21.

Derham, M. J.: Saxe et Thuringe. Situation économique en 1902. Extrait du recueil consulaire belge. Bruxelles, P. Weissenbruch, 1903. 30 SS. 8⁰.

Dermbach a. d. Feldabahn. Rhön-Sommerfrische. (Führer, Hofbuchdr. H. Kahle, Eisenach, 1903.) 10 SS. 8⁰.

Devrient, E.: Saalfeldische Historien von M. Caspar Sagittarius, im Auftrage der Stadt Saalfeld herausg. I. Teil: Bis zur Reformation. Saalfeld a. S., 1903. 189 SS. 8⁰.

Derselbe: Urkundenbuch der Stadt Jena u. ihrer geistlichen Anstalten. Bd. II. (1406—1525). Namens des Vereins f. Thüringische Geschichte u. Altertumskunde mit Benutzung des Nachlasses von Dr. J. E. A. Martin herausg. Jena, G. Fischer, 1903. XLIV u. 608 SS. 8⁰. A. u. d. T.: Thür. Gesch.-Qu. N. F. III. Bd. 2. Teil.

Dibelius, [Fr.]: Johann Tetzel. Beitr. zur Sächs. Kirchengeschichte. H. 17 (Leipzig, Joh. Ambr. Barth, 1904). S. 1—23.

Diemar, H.: Stammreihe des Thüringischen Landgrafenhauses u. des Hessischen Landgrafenhauses bis auf Philipp d. Großmütigen. Zs. d. V. f. hess. G. u. Lt. N. F. XXVII. S. 1—32.

Derselbe: Texte u. Untersuchungen zur verlorenen Hessenchronik. Ebenda S. 33—55.

Dobenecker, O.: Die Vermählung des Landgrafen Ludwig IV. mit Elisabeth von Ungarn. Wartburgstimmen. I. Jahrg. Heft 2. (Mai 1903). S. 169 ff.

Doebner, E.: Bausteine zu einer Gesch. der Stadt Meiningen. N. Beitr. z. G. des deutschen Altertums, herausg. v. Henneh. Altertumsver. zu Meiningen. Lief. XVII. Meiningen, Brückner. 112 SS. 8⁰.

D[oebner, E.]: Die Meininger Maler des 18. Jahrhunderts. Zur Einführung in die Pastellbilder-Ausstellung. in Meiningen. Meininger Tageblatt (1904). No. 112.

Döring, E.: Beitr. zur Kenntnis der Sondershäuser Mundart. T. I. Sondershausen, Prgr. 1903. 48 SS.

Döring, O.: Alte Fachwerkbauten der Provinz Sachsen. Mit 112 Lichtdrucktafeln u. 16 Tafeln in Photolithographie. Magdeburg, E. Baensch jun., 1903.

Duijnstee, Dominicar Fr. X. P. ord. erem. s. Aug.: Polemiea de s. s. Eucharistiae sacramento inter Bartholomaeum Arnoldi de Usingen O. E. S. A. ejusque olim in universitate Erfurdiana discipulum Martinum Lutherum anno 1530 etc. Würzburg, Stahel, 1903. VIII u. 98 SS. gr. 8⁰.

Ebart, P. v.: Gotha in den Oktobertagen 1806. Goth. Tagebl. 1902. No. 289, 291, 292, 293, 295.

Eckermann, J. P.: Gespräche mit Goethe in den letzten Jahren seines Lebens, herausg. von L. Geiger. Leipzig, Hesse, 1902.

Erbstein, J.: Medaille auf Herzog Christian I. v. Sachsen-Merseburg u. s. Gem. Christiana Prinzessin v. Schleswig-Holstein-Sonderburg-Glücksburg. Münz- u. Medaillenfreund. IV (1902). No. 47. Sp. 372—374.

Escherich, M.: Die kunsthistorische Ausstellung in Erfurt. Wartburgstimmen. I. Jahrg. Bd. 2. S. 27 ff. u. 105 ff.

Feier, Die, der Eröffnung des Städtischen Museums. Beil. zu No. 29 der Jenaischen Ztg., 4. Febr. 1903. (Reden des Prof. Dr. P. Weber u. des Oberbürgerm. Singer.)

Festgabe zur Hundertjahrfeier der Einverleibung des Eichsfeldes in die Krone Preußens. Heiligenstadt, F. W. Cordier, 1902. 20 SS.

Fischer, Ernst: Die Münzen des Hauses Schwarzburg. Heidelberg, Wintersche Universitätsbuchh. gr. 8⁰. Mit 16 Lichtdrucktafeln.

Fitte, S.: Johann Friedrich d. Großm. (geb. 30 Juni 1503). Vossische Ztg. 1903. Sonntagsbeil. No. 25 u. 26.

Förtsch, O.: Bronzezeitliche Gräber von Goseck. Jahresschr. f. d. Vor-G. der sächs.-thür. Länder. I, 62—74.

Francke, H. G.: Miszellen aus der Geschichte Weidas. Die Schicksale der Stadt im 30-jährigen Kriege. Weidaer Ztg. Jahrg. 1903. No. 4, 6, 9, 10.

Freidorf, v.: Der Püsterich von der Rotenburg (jetzt zu Sondershausen). Ein Beitrag zur Geschichte der Schrei- u. Gerüftewahrzeichen. Zs. f. Kulturgesch. (1902). S. 322—344.

Freysoldt, A.: Die fränkischen Wälder im 16. u. 17. Jahrh. Ein Beitrag zur Forstgeschichte des Meininger Oberlandes. Nach den Quellen bearbeitet. Mit einer Karte. Steinach S.-M., Selbstverlag des Verf., 1904. IV u. 162 SS. 8⁰.

Frieder ich, K.: Zur Münzgeschichte des fürstlichen Hauses Stolberg. I. Dresden, Selbstverl., 1903. 51 SS. u. 4 Tafeln.

Gedenkschrift zum 75-jährigen Stiftungsfest des Bürger- lichen Gesangvereins Jena, am 12.—14. September 1903. 115 SS. 8°.

Gensel, Jul.: Friedrich Preller d. Ä. Mit 134 Abb. u. einem Titelbild. Bielefeld u. Leipzig, Velhagen u. Klasing, 1904. 134 SS. 8°. (A. u. d. T. Künstlermonographien, herausg. von Knackfuß, 69.)

Gerard, Frances: A grandduchess. The life of Anna Amalia duchess of Saxe-Weimar-Eisenach and the classical circle of Weimar. Vol. I, II. London, Hutchinson u. Co., 1902. XXIV, 582 SS. 8°.

Göring, H.: Friedrich Fröbel. Wartburgstimmen. I. Jahrg. Bd. 1. S. 368 ff.

Goethes Briefe. Bd. XXVI—XXVIII: 24. Mai 1815 bis. Dez. 1817. Weim. Goethe-Ausg. (Abt. IV. Bd. 26—28).

Goethe-Briefe. Mit Einleit. u. Erläut. herausg. von Ph. Stein. Bd. III: Weimar u. Italien 1784—1792. Bd. IV: Weimar u. Jena 1782—1800, Bd. V, 1801—1807. Berlin, Elsner, 1903 u. 1904. 8°.

Götze: Das vorgeschichtliche Thüringen (Vortrag). Korre- spondenzbl. des Gesamtvereins (1904). No. 2. Sp. 62—68.

Grabitzsch, W.: Eisenach vor 200 Jahren. Thür. Monatsbl. X, 25—26, 105—108.

Greiner: Die kirchlichen Verhältnisse von Jüdewein. Pöß- necker Tagebl. 1904. No. 19 u. 20.

Greiner, Hugo: Aus alter Zeit. Volksschauspiel in einem Vorspiel u. vier Aufzügen. Festgabe zu Arnstadts Zwölfjahrhundert- feier. Arnstadt, K. Brettinger, 1904. 90 SS. 8°.

[Grimm. L.] Ausf. Nachricht von der am 6. April 1802 in Greiz leider erfolgten schrecklichen Feuersbrunst. Unsere Heimat. Ill. Monatsschr. f. d. gesamte Erzgebirge, Osterland u. Vogtland. II (1903) 87 ff.

Gröger, Joh.: Ein thüringisches Städtchen. Beitr. zur Ge- schichte Großbreitenbachs und der Umgegend. Arnstadt, E. Frot- scher, 1903. 150 SS. 8°.

Größler, H.: Die Entstehungszeit u. Geburtsstätte des Lutherliedes „Eine feste Burg ist unser Gott". Mansf. Blätter. XVII. Jahrg. (Eisleben 1903). S. 113—125.

Derselbe: Führer durch das Unstruttal von Artern bis Naumburg für Vergangenheit u. Gegenwart. 2. verm. u. verbesserte Aufl. Mit einer Karte des Unstruttales. Freyburg, J. Finke, 1904. XVI u. 256 SS. 8°.

Guttenberg, Frh. F. K. v.: Regesten des Geschlechts von Blassenberg u. dessen Nachkommen. A. f. G. u. A. v. Oberfranken. XXII. H. 1. S. 1—86.

Habbicht, H.: Zur Geschichte des Weimarischen Schul- wesens, Volksschule u. Gymnasium. Deutschland. 55. Jahrg. No. 163. (1903 Juni 17).

Derselbe: Das ehrbare Töpferhandwerk zu Eisenach. Ein Beitrag zur Geschichte des Zunftwesens. Beiträge zur Geschichte Eisenachs. XI. Hofbuchdr. Eisenach, Verl. von H. Kahle, 1902. 64 SS. 8°.

Habenicht, H.: Das Herzogt. Gotha. Proömium zu einer projektierten Heimatkunde. Goth. Tagebl. 1902. No. 296—298 u. 300.

Derselbe: Einen vergleichend erdkundlichen Beitrag zur Heimatskunde von Thüringen. Wartburgstimmen. I. Jahrg. Bd. 1. S. 68 ff.

Happel, E.: Die Burgen in Niederhessen, u. dem Werragebiet. Marburg, Elwert, 1903. 159 SS.

Hartmann, N. v.: Herder als Erzieher. Wartburgstimmen. I. Jahrg. Bd. 2. S. 114 ff.

Hasenclever, Ad.: Die Politik Kaiser Karls V. u. Landgraf Philipps v. Hessen vor Ausbruch des schmalkaldischen Krieges (Jan. bis Juli 1546). Marhurg i. H., Elwert, 1903. 88 SS. 8⁰.

Haupt, H.: August Trinius, der Thüringer Wandersmann. Thüringer Warte. I. Jahrg. No. 1. S. 37—40.

Hecker, Max F.: Wild- und Weidwerk in Goethes Dichtung. Die Vogeljagd. Wartburgstimmen. II. Jahrg. (Bd. 1). S. 164 ff.

Heese, B.: Sachsen-Weimar-Eisenach als Waldland. Beil. zu No. 234 der Jenaischen Ztg. (1903 Okt. 6).

Heimatgeschichte, Zur, (Naumburg a. S. im Okt. 1813). Beil. zu No. 78 des Naumburger Kreisblattes. 1903 April 2.

Helling, V.: Rudolf v. Habsburg u. die Wettiner. Kamerad. 1903. No. 11. S. 9.

Helmke, F.: Die Wohnsitze der Cherusker u. der Hermunduren. Emdener Prgr. (1903). 43 SS.

Herrmann, M.: Übersicht über die historische und numerische Entwickelung der römisch-katholischen Kirche in der Provinz Sachsen am Ende des 19. Jahrh. Herausg. vom Hauptverein des Evang. Bundes der Prov. Sachsen. Halle, Wischau u. Wettengel, 1902. 88 SS. 8⁰.

Hertel, L.: Kleine Landeskunde des Herzogtums Sachsen-Meiningen. Hildburghausen, F. W. Gadow u. S., 1903. 118 SS. 8⁰. 1 M.

Hertzberg, H.: Deutsch-sorbische Kulturzustände. Mitt. d. V. f. Erdk. zu Halle (1902). S. 1—7.

Heydenreich, Ed.: Städtische Archivbauten. Korrespondenzbl. des Gesamtvereins. 1902.

Hirschberg, L.: Ludwig Bechstein, zu seinem 100. Geburtstage (24. Nov. 1901). Zs. f. Bücherfreunde. V. Jahrg. S. 262—272, 312—320, 346—354.

Höfer: Archäologische Probleme in der Provinz Sachsen. Festgabe der hist. Kommission für die Provinz Sachsen u. das Herzogt. Anhalt. Halle a. S., O. Hendel, 1903. 31 SS. 8⁰.

Hofmann, A.: Kurf. Johann Friedrich d. Großm. v. Sachsen. Die Wartburg. II. Jahrg. No. 27 (3. Juli 1903).

Huxsel, A.: Ein Elgersburger Jubiläum. Thür. Monatsbl. X, 112—113.

Iber, Gesch. des Wiederherstellungsbaues der Marienkirche zu Mühlhausen i. Thür. Mühlhausen, 1903 (Selbstverlag).

Issleib, S.: Philipp v. Hessen, Heinrich v. Braunschweig u. Moritz v. Sachsen in den J. 1541—1547. Jahrb. des Geschichtsv. f. d. Herzogtum Braunschweig. II (1903). S. 1—80.

Derselbe: Moritz von Sachsen u. die Ernestiner, 1547—1553. N. A. f. Sächs. G. XXIV, 248—306.

Jahr, E. R.: Die Entwickelung des Verkehrswesens in Thüringen im 19. Jahrh. Leipzig, E. Glausch, 1903.

Jahresbericht der öffentlichen Lesehalle zu Jena für 1902. Beil. zu No. 64 der Jenaischen Ztg. 17. März 1903.

Jahresschrift für die Vorgeschichte der sächsisch-thüringischen Länder. Herausg. v. d. Provinzial-Museum der Provinz Sachsen in Halle a. S. Bd. I. Halle, O. Hendel, 1902. 258 SS. 8⁰. Mit 25 Taf. u. 4 Plänen.

Joch, Ad.: Die Pfarrei Mupperg, topographisch u. kirchengeschichtlich dargestellt von weil. Dr. S. Lotz, Kirchenrat, Pfarrer zu Mupperg u. Gefell, neu herausg. Mit 3 Abb. Sonneberg, Druck von Gräbe u. Hetzer, 1903. XV u. 275 SS. 8⁰. (Broch. 3 M., geb. 3,50 M.)

Johnson: Vogtl. Altertümer. CLIV—CLVI. Wirk. der Kämpfe zw. Welfen u. Staufen. CLVII. Eine Germanenburg b. Jocketa.. CLVIII. Das Ende der plauischen Herrsch. über das Ascher Gebiet. CLIX. Aus der Perrückenzeit. CLX. Sünderhauf. CLXI. Plauen als Bergort. CLXII. Vogtländer mit Luther in Worms. Vgtl. Anz. u. Tagebl. 1903. No. 67, 76, 86, 101, 118, 125, 129, 141, 165.

Jordan: Chronik der Stadt Mühlhausen in Thüringen. Bd. II (1526—1599 [1604]). Mit 4 Abb. u. einem Plane. Mühlhausen i. Thür., Danner, 1903. VII u. 200 SS. 8⁰.

Derselbe: Zur Geschichte der Stadt Mühlhausen i. Thür. H. 3. Beil. zum Jahresber. des Gymn. in Mühlhausen i. Thür. 1903. 48 SS. 8⁰.

Derselbe: Zur Geschichte der Stadt Mühlhausen i. Thür. Heft 4 „Zur Schlacht bei Frankenhausen." Hierzu ein Plan von Frankenhausen u. Umgegend. Mühlhausen i. Thür., Dannersche Buchdr., 1904. 52 SS. 8⁰. (S. 1—40 als Beil. zum O.Prgr. des Gymn. zu Mühlhausen i. Thür. 1904).

Derselbe: Aus der Franzosenzeit 1806—1807. In „Aus alter Zeit." Zwanglose Beiblätter zum Mühlhäuser Anzeiger. 1903. No. 47—51; 1904. No. 52, 53, 54, 55, 56. Mühlhausen i. Thür., Dannersche Buchdr.

Derselbe: Die Verwaltung der Stadt Mühlhausen i. Thür. unter dem Königreich Westfalen. Mühlhäuser Anz. CVII. Jahrg. (1903). No. 119—124 (23.—29. Mai).

Derselbe: Inscriptiones Mulhusinae. Sonderabdr. aus „Aus alter Zeit". Mühlhausen i. Thür., Danner, 1903. 33 SS. 8⁰.

Jubiläumsfeier, Zur 200-jährigen, des 3. Bataillons des 7. Thüringer Infanterie-Regiments No. 96. Rudolstädter Ztg. XXXIII. Jahrg. (1903). No. 191 u. 193.

Thüringer Kalender 1904. Inh: Trinius, A.: Ruine Liebenstein. — Voß, G: Dornburg b. Jena. — Loßnitzer: Gedenktag u. Gedenkstücke Herzog Bernhards v. Weimar. — Voß, G.: Greifenstein am Eingang des Schwarzatales. — Baethcke: Aus den Klosterruinen Georgentals. — Ehwald, R.: Die Gothaer Prachtbibel Ottheinrichs von der Pfalz. — Bornemann, G.: Mit Goethe auf dem Inselsberg. — Bojanowski, P. v.: Der Hornstein in Weimar. Zur 400-j. Gedenkfeier Johann Friedrichs d. Großm. — Voß, G.: Die Osterburg b. Weida. — Pick, B.: Porträt-Medaillon Johann Friedrichs d. Großm. — Eggeling: Im Dom zu Naumburg. — Kriesche: Die Liebfrauenkirche in Arnstadt. — Fritze: Das steinerne Haus in Meiningen. — Voß, G.: Das obere Schloß in Greiz.

[Ketelhodt, G. v.] Unsere Gesetzsammlung. 1. Beil. z. Schwarzb.-Rudolstädtischen Landeszeitung (1904). No. 14.

Kleinteich, H.: Kurzer Führer durch Kranichfeld u. s. Umgebung. Kranichfeld a. Ilm, G. Hahn, 1902. 16 SS. Mit 1 Karte.

Koch, Ernst: Die Jüdeweiner Kirche und die Kirche zu St. Bartholomäus in Pößneck. Pößnecker Ztg. 1904. März 2 u. im Pößnecker Tageblatt. 1904. März 2.

Derselbe: Die ehemalige Hospitalkirche zu Pößneck. Pößnecker Ztg. 1904. April 17.

Derselbe: Das Gemeindevermögen, die Einwohner u. Gebäude der Stadt Meiningen im Jahre 1650. Meininger Tagebl. 1904. No. 49, 55, 61, 67.

Derselbe: Nachrichten über die Stadtflur von Meiningen aus dem Jahre 1650. Meininger Tagebl. 1904. No. 73.

Krauth, S.: Untersuchung über den Namen u. die ältesten Geschichtsquellen der Stadt Erfurt. Erfurt, Druck von Fr. Bartbolomäns, 1904. Beil. zum Jahresber. des Realgymn. zu Erfurt. 36 SS. 4°.

Krebs, K.: Nach der Schlacht bei Jena am 14. Okt. 1806. Leipz. Tagebl. 1902. No. 521, 534. S. 7083 f. 7261 f.

Krieg, Thilo: Prinz Leopold von Coburg bei der Erfurter Kaiserzusammenkunft. Beil. zu No. 97 der Coburger Zeitung (26. April 1903).

Derselbe: Herzog Ernst I. v. Sachsen-Coburg-Saalfeld am napoleonischen Kaiserhofe 1807/8. Beil. zu No. 75 der Coburger Zeitung (29. März 1903).

Kück, Ed.: Die Erfurter Ausgabe des Katechismus der böhmischen Brüder. Mitt. d. Ges. f. d. Erzieh.- u. Schulgesch. XIII (Berlin, Hofmann u. Co., 1903). S. 86 f.

Kühn: Zur Geschichte der Stadt Eisenach. II. (Schluß der Ratsfasten. — Wandlungen der städtischen Verfassung). Eisenach. Jahresbericht über das Karl Friedrichs-Gymn. 1904. S. 3—23. 4°.

Kuntze, H.: Einladung zum Grabgeleite Ludwigs v. Wiehe auf Burgscheidungen vom 16. Febr. 1596. Mansf. Bl. XVI, 178—180.

Lane, M.: Sachsen u. Thüringen. Jahresberichte der Geschichtswissenschaft. 1901. II, 218—254.

Liebe, G.: Das Beginenwesen der sächsisch-thüringischen Lande in seiner sozialen Bedeutung. Archiv für Kulturgeschichte, herausg. von G. Steinhausen. I (1903), 35—42.

Liebe: Die Herausgabe von Kirchenvisitations-Protokollen. Korrespondenzbl. des Gesamtvereins (1903). S. 47—49.

[Liebmann, P.] Die geschichtliche Entwickelung und wirtschaftliche Bedeutung des Forstwesens im Fürstentum Schwarburg-Rudolstadt. Ein Beitrag zur vaterl. Geschichte. Schwarzb.-Rudolstädtische Landeszeitung (1903). No. 245, 251, 256 u. 262.

Lindner: Die Stellung Sachsens u. Thüringens in der deutschen Geschichte. Korrespondenzbl. des Gesamtvereins der deutschen Geschichts- u. Altertumsvereine. LI. Jahrg. No. 10/11. S. 202 f.

Linn-Linsenbarth, O.: Schiller u. der Herzog Karl August v. Weimar. Teil II. Prgr. Kreuznach, 1903. 44 SS.

Linz, W.: Beiträge zur Ortschronik von Apfelstädt. Apfelstädt 1902.

Lippert, W. u. Beschorner, H.: Das Lehnbuch Friedrichs des Strengen, Markgrafen v. Meißen u. Landgrafen v. Thüringen,

1349/1350. Mit 9 Tafeln in Lichtdruck. Leipzig, B. G. Teubner, 1903. CCLVIII u. 640 SS. 8⁰. (A. u. d. T.: Schriften der Königl. Sächsischen Kommission für Geschichte. Bd. VIII). (Besprechung folgt.)

Lippert, W.: Jahresanfang am 1. Januar in der meißnisch-thüringischen Kanzlei um die Mitte des 14. Jahrh. Mitt. d. Inst. f. öst. GF. XXIV, 302—309.

Derselbe: Studien über die Wettinische Kanzlei u. ihre ältesten Register im 14. Jahrh. NA. f. Sächs. G. XXIV, 1—42.

Löber, E: Aus einem Stützerbacher Patrizierhause. Thür. Monatsbl. X, 115—118.

Loreta, M.: Miedzy Jeną a Tylzią. Warschau, Laskauer u. Co., 1902. XV u. 165 SS.

Lüttich, S.: Zur Baugeschichte des Naumburger Doms u. der anliegenden Baulichkeiten. Prgr. des G. zu Naumburg a. S., 1902. 48 SS. 4⁰. Mit 4 Tafeln.

Derselbe: Dritter Beitrag zur Baugeschichte des Naumburger Doms und der anliegenden Baulichkeiten. Beil. zum Jahresber. des Dom-G. zu Naumburg a. S., H. Sieling, 1904. 62 SS. 4⁰. Mit einer Karte.

Lutze, G.: Aus Sondershausens Vergangenheit. Lief. 1—4. Sondershausen. Eupel, 1902. 128 SS. 8⁰.

Mansberg, Frh. v., Rich.: Erbarmanschaft Wettinischer Lande. Urk. Beitr. zur Obersächs. Landes- u. Ortsgeschichte in Regesten vom 12. bis Mitte des 16. Jahrh. I. Bd.: Das Osterland. Mit 6721 Regesten, 22 Taf. u. 66 Holzschn. Dresden, W. Baensch, 1903. IX u. 676 SS. 8⁰.

Meier, H.: Aus Schulprogrammen des Gymnasiums zu Nordhausen 1712—1722. Zs. des Harz.-V. XXXVI, 270—274.

Mensing, K.: Bilder aus der sächsischen Geschichte. II. Georg d. Bärtige u. Kurf. Moritz. Dresden, E. Zacharias, 1902. 96 SS. 8⁰.

Mentz, G.: Johann Friedrich d. Großmütige. I. Teil: Johann Friedrich bis zu seinem Regierungsantritt 1503—1532. Festschrift zum 100-j. Geburtstage des Kurfürsten namens des Vereins f. Thüringische Geschichte u. Altertumsk. herausg. von der thüringischen historischen Kommission. Mit dem Bildnis Johann Friedrichs als Bräutigam. Jena, G. Fischer, 1903. XII u. 142 SS. 8⁰. (A. u. d. T.: Beiträge zur neueren Geschichte Thüringens. Bd. I. Erster Teil.)

Derselbe: Zur Geschichte der Packschen Händel. A. f. Reformationsgeschichte. I. Jahrg. H. 2. Berlin, C. A. Schwetschke u. S., 1904. S. 172—191.

Derselbe: Die Briefe G. Spalatins an V. Warbeck nebst ergänzenden Aktenstücken. A. f. Reformationsgeschichte. I. Jahrg. H. 3 (Berlin, C. A. Schwetschke u. S., 1904). No. 3. S. 197—246.

Meurer, H.: Zum Regimentsjubiläum. Beitr. z. G. des Regiments „Großherzog von Sachsen" (1807—34). Weimar, Böhlaus Nachf., 1902. 28 SS.

Meyer, P.: Droyßig 1852—1902. Eine Festschrift. Breslau, F. Hirt, 1902. 168 SS. Mit 10 Tafeln.

Mitzschke, P.: Ungedrucktes vom Rennsteig. Das Mareile. III. Reihe (1903). No. 11/12. S. 122—126.

Mörtzsch, O.: Die „Erbar Manschaft" der Läuder Meißen,

Thüringen u. Sachsen i. J. 1445. Zs. f. hist. Waffenk. II (1902), 448—750; III (1902/3), 48—51.

Morgenstern, O: Hennebergica, Verzeichnis der alten Drucke aus der Gymnasialbibliothek, die sich auf die ehemalige Grafschaft Henneberg beziehen. T. I. Schleusingen, Prgr. 1903. 22 SS. 4⁰.

Mücke, R.: Aus der älteren Schulgeschichte Ilfelds. Prgr. der Klosterschule zu Ilfeld. 1902. 26 SS. 4⁰.

Naumann, L.: Die Ruinen des Schlosses Eckartsberga u. seine einstige Bedeutung als Festung. Eckartsberga, Verl. des Eckartshauses, 1902. 31 SS. 8⁰. Mit 3 Taf.

Derselbe: Das Schloß Eckartsberga, „Eckartsburg." H. 4 der Beitr. zur Lokalgeschichte des Kreises Eckartsberga. 3. Aufl. Eckartsberga, Verl. des Eckartshauses, 1902. 48 SS. 8⁰. Mit 1 Abb.

Nehmer, A.: Beiträge zur Landesk. des Eichsfeldes (mit 2 Karten u. 1 Profiltafel). A. f. L.- u. Volkskunde der Prov. Sachsen. XIII (1903). S. 77—127.

Nippold, Fr.: Der Kurfürst-Confessor Johann Friedrich. Rede, gehalten zu seinem Säkular-Jubiläum am 30. Juni 1903. Jena (G. Neuenhahn) 1903. 29 SS. 4⁰.

Derselbe: Zum 400. Geburtstage des Kurf. Johann Friedrich. Deutschland, Monatsschr. f. d. ges. Kultur. II, 493—507.

Oergel: Das Bursenwesen der mittelalterlichen Universitäten, insbesondere Erfurts (Vortrag). Korrespondenzblatt des Gesamtvereins (1904). No. 4/5. Sp. 151—159.

Opitz, W.: Über die Hersfelder Schrift: de unitate ecclesiae conservanda. Prgr. des RG. zu Zittau, 1902. 18 SS. 4⁰.

Overmann: Erfurt in Geschichte u. Kunst (Vortrag). Korrespondenzblatt des Gesamtvereins (1903). S. 237—244.

Polack, Fr.: Der Kreis Worbis in den hundert Jahren preuß. Herrschaft von 1802—1902. Worbis, C. Müller, 1902. 136 SS. 8⁰.

Posse, O.: Die Siegel des Adels der Wettiner Lande bis zum J. 1500. Im Auftr. der Kgl. Sächs. Staatsregierung herausg. I. Bd.: Grafen von Käfernburg-Schwarzburg, Vögte von Weida, Plauen und Gera. Adel Buchst. A. Dresden 1903. VII, 65 SS. 50 Taf. 4⁰.

Quantz, H.: Skelet-Gräber von Solkwitz in Ost-Thüringen. Nachr. über deutsche Altertumsfunde. XIII. Jahrg. (1902). H. 5. S. 67—71.

Raab, C. v.; Das Amt Pausa bis z. Erwerbung durch Kurf. August v. Sachsen im J. 1569 u. d. Erbbuch v. J. 1506. Beil. z. d. Mitt. d. Altertumsv. zu Plauen i. V. 16. Jahresschr. auf die J. 1903/4. Plauen i. V. 1903. 4 Bl. u. 115 SS. 8⁰.

Rademacher, O.: Die Merseburger Bischofschronik. Übersetzt u. mit Anm. versehen. T. I. Beil. z. Jahresber. des Dom-G. zu Merseburg, 1903. Merseburg (F. Stollberg). 74 SS. 8⁰.

Ranke, H.: Stammbaum der Familie Ranke. 12 Tafeln. Als Manuskr. gedruckt. München. 1901.

Ratzel, F.: Bruno Hassenstein†. Petermanns Mitteilungen. XLVIII (1902). Heft. 12. S. 1—5.

Rechnungslegung über die Ausgaben eines Jenenser Studenten in der Zeit vom 12. April 1589 bis zum 18. Mai 1590. Jenaische Zeitung. 1903. Juli 17.

Reglement und Wacht-Ordnung der Stadt Jena de anno 1757. Jenaische Ztg. Jahrg. 230. No. 100 (1903, April 30).

Reichardt, R.: Zum Wortschat d Nordthüringer Mundart. Zs. f. hochd. Mundarten. III, 354 z er 363.

Derselbe: Sagen aus Nordthüringen. Zs. d. V. f. Volkskunde.
XI, 68—73 u. XII, 66—72.

Derselbe: Die Grafschaft Hohenstein unter der Herrschaft
des Grafen Thun 1628—1631. Zs. des Harz.-V. XXXVI, 274—283.

Reimanu, K. E.: Wo ist Friedrich Hortleder geboren? NA.
f. Sächs. G. u. A. XXIV, 174—178.

Rodigast, G.: Ursprung und Alter der Schützengilde Jena
mit einer Original-Urkundentafel. Aus amtlich beglaubigten Thüring.
Geschichtsurkunden verschiedener Staatsarchive u. der Universitäts-
bibliothek Jena zusammengestellt. Gewidmet zum 600. Stiftungsfeste.
Jena, 28. Februar 1904. 16 SS. 8⁰. Mit einer Tafel.

Rühl, K.: Das obere Saaletal. 2. verm. Aufl. Ziegenrück, H.
Jentzsch, 1903. 132 SS. 8⁰.

Rühlmann, P.: Die öffentliche Meinung in Sachsen während
der Jahre 1806—1812. Gesch. Untersuchungen, herausg. von K. Lam-
precht. H. 1. Gotha, Perthes, 1902. 121 SS. 8⁰.

Sachsenklemme, Die (4. Aug. 1809). Unsere Heimat, illustr.
Monatsschr. f. d. gesamte Erzg. u. Vogtl. I (1902), 353 f.

Schenk au Schweinsberg, G. Frh.: Die drei thüringischen
Werraorte Breitungen. Quartalbl. des hist. V. f. d. Großh. Hessen.
NF. Bd. III. H. 5.

Derselbe: Bemerkungen zu neueren Urkundenbüchern (zu
Cod. d. Sax. r. I, 3). Ebenda NF. Bd. III. H. 7. S. 279 u. 280.

Schlüter, Otto: Die Siedelungen im nordöstlichen Thüringen.
Ein Beispiel für die Behandlung siedelungsgeographischer Fragen.
Berlin, H. Costenoble, 1903. Mit 6 Karten u. 2 Tafeln. XIX u. 453
SS. 8⁰. (S. a. Zs. der Ges. f. Erdkunde zu Berlin [1902]. No. 10. S.
850—874.)

Schmidt, B.: Die Reußen. Genealogie des Gesamthauses
Reuß älterer u. jüngerer Linie, sowie der ausgestorbenen Vogtslinien
zu Weida, Gera u. Plauen u. der Burggrafen zu Meißen aus dem
Hause Plauen. Im Auftrage Sr. Durchlaucht Heinrichs XIV. Re-
gierenden Fürsten Reuß j. L. und Fürstregenten Reuß ä. L. Schleiz,
F. Webers Nachf., 1903. IX u. 70 SS. Fol. (Besprechung folgt.)

Schmidt, C. F. L.: Heimatliche Kunst und Bauweise in
Sachsen und Thüringen (Vortrag). Korrespondenzblatt des Gesamtvereins (1904). No. 4/5. Sp. 169—175.

Schmidt, Erich: Luise, Großherzogin v. S.-Weimar. D.
Rundschau. XXX. H. 1.

Schmidt, Fr.: Die schwedische Invasion in Kursachsen u.
insbesondere im Herzogtum S.-Weißenfels in d. J. 1706 u. 1707.
Mansf. Bl. XVI (1902), 115—137.

Derselbe: Die Dinggrafen (Dinggrefe) von Sangerhausen.
Zs. d. Harz-V. XXXV, 443—447.

Schmidt, Kunhardt v.: Aus der Gesch. des 4. Rheinbund-
regiments Herzöge v. Sachsen. Militär-Wochenbl. 1902. No. 99, 105;
1903. No. 5, 12, 16, 21.

Schmidt, O. E.: Wolfg. Lazius, ein Geschichtsschreiber des
Schmalkald. Krieges. N. A. f. Sächs. G. XXIV, 111—133.

Schnehen, W. v.: Herders religiöse Weltanschauung. Wartburgstimmen. I. Jahrg. H. 2. S. 83 ff.

Schneider, M.: Die Einrichtung einer „deutschen Schul"
(d. h. Realabteilung) am Gymnasium zu Gotha durch Herzog Ernst
d. Fr. im J. 1662. Mitt. der Ges. f. d. Erziehungs- u. Schulgeschichte.
XIII. Jahrg. (Berlin, Hofmann u. Co., 1903). S. 34—41.

Schneider, W.: Querfurter Stadt- u. Kirchchronik. Querfurt,
W. Schneider, 1902. VII u. 575 SS. Mit 4 Taf.

Schöppe, K.: Das Vereinswesen in Naumburg. Naumburg
a. S., Druck von H. Sieling, 1903. 36 SS. 8⁰.

Derselbe: Zur Häuserchronik von Naumburg. (Gesch. verschiedener bemerkenswerter Häuser: Schloß, Schlößchen, Drei Lilien
u. a. m.). Naumburger Kreisbl. 1902. No. 100, 117, 143, 213.

Derselbe: Siegel aus dem Stifte Naumburg-Zeitz. Mit Siegel-
tafeln. Vierteljahrsschr. für Wappen-, Siegel- u. Familienk. Jahrg.
1903. S. 81—88.

Derselbe: Das Naumburger Kirschfest. Seine Geschichte u.
Bräuche. Naumburg a. S., H. Sieling, 1903. 16 SS. 8⁰.

Derselbe: Innungsartikel der Glaserinnung zu Naumburg
a. S. N. Mitt. hist.-ant. Forsch. Bd. XXI. H. 3 (Halle a. S., 1903).
S. 209—223.

Derselbe: Mittelalterliche Rechtsfragen. Ebenda S. 224—236.

Schrödel, H.: Ernst, Herzog von Sachsen-Altenburg. Festschrift zur Feier seines fünfzigjährigen Regierungsjubiläums am 3.
August 1903. 1. Geschichtliche Einleitung bis zum J. 1826 von Herm.
Schrödel-Friedrichstanneck. 2. Lebensbild des Herzogs von Gym-
nasialdirektor Prof. Dr. Moritz Geyer-Eisenberg. Eine Jubiläums-
gabe für die Schulen des Altenburger Landes. Friedrichstanneck
1903. 68 SS. 4⁰. Mit 12 Abb.

Schröder, Edw.: Der Epilog der Eneide. Zs. für deutsches
Altertum u. deutsche Literatur. XLVII. Bd. (Berlin 1903). S. 291
bis 301.

Scobel, A.: Thüringen. 2. Aufl. Bielefeld, Velhagen u.
Klasing, 1902. 160 SS. 8⁰.

Sehling, E.: Die evang. Kirchenordnungen des XVI. Jahrh.
I. Abt. Sachsen u. Thüringen nebst angrenzenden Gebieten. 2. Hälfte.
Leipzig, Reisland, 1904. VII u. 614 SS. 4⁰.

Seitz, O.: Der authentische Text der Leipziger Disputation
(1519). Aus bish. unbenutzten Quellen herausg. Berlin, Schwetschke
u. S., 1903. V u. 247 SS. 8⁰.

Siefert, G.: Zum Gedächtnis Gustav Richters. In Lehrproben
u. Lehrgänge. H. 79. (Halle a. S. 1904).

Stein, F.: Kulmbach und die Plassenburg in alter u. neuer
Zeit. Kulmbach, Rehm, 1903. 184 u. 17 SS.

Suphan, B.: Briefe von Goethe und Frau von Stein an Joh.
Georg Zimmermann. Wartburgstimmen. II. Jahrg. (Bd. I.). S. 171 ff.

Tangl, M.: Das Todesjahr des Bonifatius. Zs. d. V. für
Hessische G. u. Lk. NF. XXVII (1903). S. 223—250.

Techow: Zur Gesch. der Fischgerechtigkeit bei Kösen. Naumburger Kreisbl. 1902. No. 186.

Teichmann, E.: Zur G. der vogtl. Perlenfischerei. Unsere
Heimat, illust. Monatsschr. f. d. ges. Erzgeb. u. s. f. II (1902/3),
177—181.

Th„ R.: Der Hörselberg. Thür. Monatsbl. X, 1—3.

Derselbe: Ein Herbstthing auf dem Venusberg. Ebenda S.
13—15, 43—44, 77—80.

Thauß, G: Das Herzogl. Coburg-Gothaische Infanterie-Regiment in der Schlacht b. Langensalza am 27. Juni 1866. Langensalza, Wendt u. Klauwell.

Thiele: Die sprachliche Bedeutung unserer mitteldeutschen Urkunden und Handschriften (Vortrag). Korrespondenzblatt des Gesamtvereins (1904) No. 4/5. Sp. 142—150.

Thümmel: Herder als Leiter der weimarischen Landeskirche. Aus einem am 3. Dez. im Zweigverein des Evang. Bundes gehaltenen Vortrag. Jenaische Ztg. (1903). No. 290, 291 Dez. 11 u. 12).

Thüna, L. Frh. v.: Das löschpapierne Prinzchen im und beim Witthumspalais in Weimar. Nord und Süd. 1903. Juni. S. 321.

Thüringen in Wort u. Bild. Herausg. v. d. Thüringer Pestalozzivereinen. Bd. II. Leipzig 1902. III u. 492 SS.

Timpel, M.: Graf Gotter u. Schloß Molsdorf. Thür. Monatsbl. IX. Jahrg. No. 6.

Töpfer, H.: Der Püsterich in Sondershausen. A. f. L.- u. Volkskunde der Prov. Sachsen. XIII (1903). S. 62—74.

Trauer, Ed.: Chronik des Dorfes Marieney i. Vogtl. bis zur Einführung der Sächs. Landesverf. Plauen i. V., A. Kell, 1903. 111 SS. 8°.

Unstruttale, Aus dem. Heft 1—3. Langensalza, Wendt u. Klauwell, 1901/2. 52, 72 u. 96 SS. 8°. Inh.: 1. Ludendorff, Immobil. Erinnerungen eines Landwehroffiziers an die Schlacht b. Langensalza am 27. Juni 1866. — 2. Cramm, B. Baron v.: Aus Langensalza. Ein Erinnerungsblatt. — 3. Erinnerungen, Langensalzaer aus der Zeit vor u. während des tollen Jahres 1848/49 (von Prof. Dr. Wolf).

Voigt, R.: Der Landkreis Erfurt unter preußischer Herrschaft. Bericht über die Jahre 1802—1902. Erfurt, Selbstverl., 1902. 52 SS. 4°.

Voß: Thüringische Holzschnitzerei an der Schwelle der deutschen Renaissance. Thüringer Warte. I. Jahrg. No. 1. S. 2—15.

Wächter, A.: Das Rudolstädter Gymnasium sonst und jetzt, besonders in den letzten 6 Jahrzehnten, eine Überschau. Rudolstädter Ztg. 1904. No. 119 (22. Mai).

Derselbe: Wie Rudolstadt u. Umgebung unserm Schiller erschienen sind. 2. Beil. zu No. 79 (1904) der Rudolstädter Zeitung.

Weber, P.: Forschungen über mittelalterliche Grablenkmäler. Beil. zur Allg. Ztg. 1903. No. 117 (Mai 26).

Derselbe: Die Burgen des mittleren Saaltales. Eine bangeschichtliche Übersicht. Wartburgstimmen. I. Jahrg. H. 4.

Derselbe: Die Pflege unserer kirchlichen Altertümer. Eine kurze Handweisung für den thüringischen Pfarrer- u. Lehrerstand. Weimar, H. Böhlaus Nachf., 1903. 20 SS. 8°.

„Aus Weimars klassischer und nachklassischer Zeit", neu herausg. von Robert Kohlrausch. Memoirenbibliothek, R. Lutz, Stuttgart, 1904.

Wenck, K.: Zur Geschichte des Hessengaus. In Zs. d. V. f. Hess. G. NF. XXVI (1903). S. 227—276.

Derselbe: Landgraf Philipp d. Großmütige. Rede gehalten auf der 7. Jahresversammlung der historischen Kommission für Hessen und Waldeck am 7. Mai 1904. SA. aus der Zs. des V. f.

XXII.   24

hessische Gesch. u. LK. N. F. Bd. 28. Marburg, Elwert, 1904.
13 SS. 8⁰.

Derselbe: Berichtigungen zum Elisabeth-Aufsatz. Ebenda
S. 304.

Wenzel, A.: Das höhere Schulwesen in Langensalza seit dem
Übergang der Stadt an Preußen. Festschr. z. Feier des fünfzigjährig.
Jubiläums des Realgymnasiums. 1902. 76 SS. 8⁰.

Werthern, Alfr. Frh. v.: Gesch. des Geschlechts der Grafen
u. Freiherrn v. Werthern. T. I. Urkundl. Familiengesch. H. 1.
Älteste Familiengesch. bis 1501. Als Manuskript gedr. Naumburg,
Rietz, 1902. VI u. 133 SS. 4⁰.

Wieland, M.: Cistercienserinnenkloster Sonnenfeld. Cisterc.-
Chron. XIII.

Wilhelm, E.: Gustav Paul Richter. Im Jahresbericht über
das Großh. Gymnasium Carolo-Alexandrinum zu Jena. 1904. S. 4—6
(s. a. Jen. Ztg. 1904. No. 26).

v. Wintzingeroda-Knorr, Die Wüstungen des Eichsfeldes.
Verz. der Wüstungen, vorgesch. Wallburgen, Bergwerke, Gerichts-
stätten u. Warten innerhalb der landrätl. Kreise Duderstadt, Heiligenstadt, Mühlhausen (Land u. Stadt) u. Worbis. Halle, Hendel, 1903.
(A. u. d. T.: Geschichtsqu. der Prov. Sachsen. Bd. 40.) LXXXVIII u.
1280 SS. 8⁰.

Wispel, A.: Entwickelungsgeschichte der Stadt Naumburg
a. S. nebst einem Anhang: Abriß der G. von Freyburg a. U., Goseck,
Schönburg, Saaleck u. Rudelsburg. Naumburg a. S., A. Schirmers
Buchh., 1903. VI u. 120 SS. 8⁰.

Wolff-Beckh, Br.: Johann Friedrich Böttger, der deutsche
Erfinder des Porzellans. Mit Böttgers Porträt. Steglitz b. Berlin,
Wolff-Beckh, 1903. 48 SS. 8⁰.

Wolff, W.: Die Entstehung des Ortsnamens Eschwege, sprach-
lich u. geschichtlich erklärt. Eschweger Tagebl. 1901. No. 27.

Zemmrich, J.: Die vogtl. Landschaft von einst u. jetzt. Unsere
Heimat. II (1902/3), 105—110, 129—133.

Zimmer, H.: Herzog Ernst d. Fromme. Wartburgstimmen.
I. Jahrg. Bd. 1. S. 355 ff.

Zschiesche: Das vorgeschichtliche Erfurt. Korrespondenzbl.
des Gesamtvereins (1904). No. 3. Sp. 102—105.

Aus den coburg-gothaischen Landen. Heimatsblätter, unter
dem Protektorate Seiner Durchlaucht des Regierungsverwesers Erb-
prinzen Ernst zu Hohenlohe-Langenburg im Auftr. des schriftl. Aus-
schusses herausg. von R. Ehwald. Gotha, Perthes, 1903. IV u. 76 SS.
gr. 8⁰. Inh.: Baethcke: Die Gründung des Kl. Georgental. S. 1/18.
— Berbig, M.: Gotha im Mittelalter. Aus dem Tagebuche eines
fahrenden Schülers. S. 19/23. — Ehwald, R.: Drei Stücke aus dem
Briefwechsel Friedrichs d. Weisen. S. 24/31. — Gerbing, L.: Die
Thüringer Landwirtschaft bis zur Reformationszeit S. 32/41. — Krieg,
Th.: Erbprinz Herzog Ernst (H. Ernst I.) v. Sachsen-Coburg-Saalfeld im preuß. Lager 1806/7. S. 42/44. — Pabst, W.: Die Fußspuren

vorweltlicher Tiere in den Gesteinen der Umgegend von Friedrichroda, Tambach u. Kabarz in Thüringen. S. 45/51. — Pick, B.: Die ältesten Thüringer Münzen. S. 52/57. — Schäfer, H.: Was uns die Kalktuffe von Tonna erzählen. S. 58/63. — Trinius, A.: Schloß Tenneberg. S. 64/70. — Zahn, G.: Einheimische u. eingebürgerte Pflanzen als Heilmittel. S. 71/76.

Beiträge, Neue, zur Geschichte deutschen Altertums. Lief. 17. 1902. Inh.: Doebner, E.: I. Die Entstehung der Jahrmärkte u. die Wochenmärkte in Meiningen. II. Inschriften u. Denkmäler der Stadtkirche in Meiningen. III. Die Beziehungen des letzten Fürstbischofs von Würzburg zur Stadt Meiningen. IV. Die Gast- u. Unterkunftshäuser im alten Meiningen. V. Ein Leprahaus in Meiningen. VI. Meininger Gelehrte u. a. hervorragende Meininger Stadtkinder aus alter u. neuer Zeit. VII. Übersicht über Herkunft u. Bearbeitung der Meininger Straßennamen. VIII. Die Bevölkerungszahlen der Stadt Meiningen sonst u. jetzt. 111 SS. 8⁰. — Lief. 18. 1903. Inh.: Fritze, E.: Die Veste Heldburg (Abdr. aus den Bau- u. Kunstdenkm. Thüringens. H. 31.) 41 SS. gr. 8⁰.

Geschichtsblätter, Mühlhäuser. Zs. des Mühlhäuser Altertumsvereins Jahrg. IV (1903/1904). Mühlhausen i. Thür., Komm.-Verl. von C. Albrecht, 1903. 80 SS. gr. 8⁰. Inh.: Heydenreich: Gedenkblätter an die Feier der hundertjähr. Zugehörigkeit zum preuß. Staat 1902. S. 1/16. — Claes: Die Maßnahmen zur Bekämpfung der Pest in Mühlhausen 1683. S. 16/20. — Heydenreich: Regesten zu den im Archiv der Stadt deponierten Pergamenturkunden I. S. 20/24. — Acmiaius, H.: Die St. Kilianslinde zu Mühlhausen i. Thür. S. 24/25. — Heydenreich: Zum Erfurtianus Antiquitatum variloquus. S. 25/26. — Jordan: Zur Verfassungsgesch. der Stadt Mühlhausen i. Thür. im 18. Jahrh. S. 28/36. — Sellmann: Prähistorische Funde aus der Umgebung von Mühlhausen i. Thür. S. 36/39. — Jordan: Wie Molhawssen eyngenommen. S. 40/42. — Ders.: Aus dem J. 1813. S. 43/62 — Ders.: Der Sühnebrief von 1525 u. die Festungswerke der St. Mühlhausen. S. 63/66. — v. Kauffungen: Ein Altertumsfund in der St. Blasius (Untermarkts-)Kirche. S 66/67. — Die Gerichtslinde zu St. Kiliani. S. 67/68. — Jordan: Joachim ä Burgk u. der Rektor Matthaeus Zimmermann in Sondershausen. S. 68/69.

Jahrbücher der Königl. Akademie gemeinnütziger Wissenschaften zu Erfurt. N. F. H. XXIX. Erfurt, C. Villaret, 1903. 276 SS. 8⁰. Inh.: A. Abhandlungen: 1) Heinzelmann: Gedenkrede auf den verewigten Prinzen Georg v. Preußen. S. 1/16. — 2) Thiele: Archäol. Wünsche eines altkl. Philologen. S. 17/27. — 3) Köster: Über die Persönlichkeit des Horaz in seinen Oden. S. 29/57 — 4) Treitschke: Der Föhn der Alpen u. der deutschen Mittelgebirge. S. 59/87. — 5) Bithorn: Blicke in Bismarcks Seelenleben. S. 80/107. — 6) Axmann: Die Giftwirkung des Wassers. S. 109/123. — 7) Schwarzlose: Die geistlichen Schauspiele der Vergangenheit. S. 125/150. — 8) Kekule v. Stradonitz: Die Ahnen des Prinzen Georg v. Preußen. S. 151/170. — 9) Heinzelmann: Über den ethischen Beruf der Kunst. S. 171/200. — 10) Thiele: Philol. u. archäol. Studien. S. 201/225. B. Jahresbericht der Akad. S. 227/276. — H. XXX. 1904. Festschrift zur Feier des 150-jährigen Bestehens der Kgl. Akademie. 652 SS. gr. 8⁰. Mit einer Porträttafel. Inh.: Thiele R.: Die Gründung der Akademie nützlicher (gemeinnütziger) Wissenschaften zu Erfurt und die Schicksale derselben bis zu ihrer Wiederbelebung durch Dalberg (1754 bis 1776). Mit urkundlichen Beilagen. S. 1—138. — Oergel: Die Akademie nützlicher Wissenschaften zu Erfurt von ihrer Wiederbelebung durch Dalberg bis zu ihrer endgültigen Anerkennung durch die Krone Preußen (1776—1816). S. 139—224. — Heinzelmann, W.: Beiträge zur Geschichte und Statistik der Erfurter Akademie im neunzehnten Jahrhundert. S. 225—382. — Loth, R.: Das Medizinalwesen, der ärztliche Stand und die medizinische Fakultät bis zum Anfang des 17. Jahrhunderts in Erfurt. S. 383—466. — Lüttge, A.: Die Lebensarbeit eines Hohenzollern im Osten Europas. S. 467—509. — Hagen, Ed. v.: Die Transfiguration von Raffael. Ein Deutungsversuch. S. 511—541. — Baumeister, A.: Ein Vorschlag zur Neugestaltung des Geschichtsunterrichts in den obersten Klassen unserer höheren Schulen. S. 543—564. — Albrecht, O.: Luthers kleiner Katechismus nach der Wittenberger Ausgabe im J. 1540 zum ersten Male herausg. S. 565—600. — Hintner, V.: Beiträge zur tirolischen Namenforschung. S. 601—630. — Althof, H.: Gerald und Erchambald. Eine Untersuchung über ein Problem in der Walthariusforschung. S. 631—652.

Jahresbericht, 72. und 73. des Vogtländischen Altertumsf. Vereins zu Hohenleuben, herausg. von Diak. F. Thormann. 119 SS. 8°. Inh.: Auerbach, A.: Das Archiv des Vogtländ. Altertumsf. Vereins. S. 1—45. — Francke, H. G.: Die St. Peterskirche zu Weida. S. 46—76. — Behr, O.: Das Copial-Buch des Ernst Metzsch auf. Triebes. 1576. S. 77—82. — 72. u. 73. Jahresber. S. 83—96. — Verz. der Mitgl. S. 97—102. — Bücher-Katal. S. 103—119.

Mitteilungen des Geschichts- u. Altertumsf. Vereins zu Eisenberg. H. 19. Eisenberg, H. Geyer, 1904. 76 SS. 8°. Inh.: 1) Löbe, R.: Zur Gesch. des deutschen Zunftwesens während seiner Blütezeit, mit bes. Rücksicht auf die Städte Altenburg u. Eisenberg S.-A. S. 3/71. — 2) Bericht über die Tätigkeit des Vereins. S. 72 f. — 3) Verz. der Mitgl. S. 74/76.

Mitteilungen des Vereins f. d. G. u. A. von Erfurt. H. XXIV. 1. Teil: Vereinsnachrichten. Erfurt, 1903. 23 SS. — H. XXIV. 2. Teil. Mit 12 Tafeln, 1 Karte u. 4 Abb. im Texte. Erfurt 1903. 204 SS. (Festgabe für die Teilnehmer an der Generalversammlung des Gesamtvereins der deutschen Geschichts- u. Altertumsvereine zu Erfurt vom 27.—30. Sept. 1903.) Inh.: Eitner, Th.: Erfurt u. die Bauernaufstände im XVI. Jahrh. S. 3—108. — Peters. P.: Das Collegium maius zu Erfurt. S. 109—121. — Apell, Fr.: Zur Münzgeschichte Erfurts. S. 123—134. — Buchner, O.: Der Severi-Sarkophag u. s. Künstler. S. 135—157. — Oergel, G.: Das ehemalige Erfurtische Gebiet. S. 159—190. — Zschiesche: Funde aus der merovingischen Zeit in Erfurt u. der Umgegend. S. 191—204.

Mitteilungen des Vereins f. Geschichts- u. Altertumsk. zu Kahla u. Roda. Bd. VI. H. 2. Kahla 1904. 181 SS. 8°. Inh.: Lehmann, Fr.: Die Renovierung der Stadtkirche zu Kahla im J. 1791. S. 73—99. — Martin, M.: Nachrichten über Adelige aus den Kirchenbüchern der Parochie Reinstädt. S. 100—109. — Schaffner, S.: Aus dem Gerichtsbuch der Stadt Kahla, angefangen Michaelis 1527. S.

110—113. — Lommer, V.: Volkstümliches aus dem Saaltale. Sagen u. Erzählungen, Sitten u. Gebräuche. S. 114—181.

Mitteilungen der Vereinigung für Gothaische Geschichte u. Altertumsforschung. Jahrg. 1903. Friedrichroda, J. Schmidt u. Co. 136 SS. 8⁰. Inh.: v. Strenge: Stadtrechte im Herzogt. Gotha. S. 1/48. — Ehwald, R.: Ein Kuriosum aus der Druckgeschichte Gothas. S. 49/54. — Felgner, G.: Herzogin Luise Dorothee u. ein Besitz-stück der Herz. Bibliothek zu Gotha. S. 55/80. — Florschütz, G.: Das Urnenfeld auf dem Simmel b. Eischleben. S. 81/87. — Berbig, M.: Schack Hermann Ehwald. S. 88/111. — Heß, H.: Die Grenzen der Mark Lupnitz. S. 112/118. — Ehwald, R.: Zur Erinnerung an Johann Friedrich d. Großm. S. 119/130. — Jahresber. u. Lit. S. 131/136.

Schriften des Vereins für Sachsen-Meiningische Geschichte u. Landeskunde. Heft 43. Hildburghausen, Kesselringsche Hofbuchh., 1903. Inh.: Neue Landesk. des Herzogt. S.-Meiningen. H. 4. Geo-logie von Dr. E. Zimmermann. — Heft 44. Hildburghausen 1903. Inh.: Neue Landesk. des Herzogt. S.-Meiningen. H. 5. Klimatologie von Prof. Dr. Lehmann. — Heft 45. Inh.: Neue Landesk. des Herzogt. S.-Meiningen. H. 8. Zweiter Hauptteil: Die Leute. A. Vorgeschichtliches. Von Hofr. Dr. med. G. Jacob (†). Abdr. aus dem 24. Heft der Ver-einsschr. (1896), neu herausg. von Dr. L. Hertel 1903. 56 SS. 8⁰. — Heft 46. Neue Landesk. des Herzogt. S.-Meiningen. H. 9 B. Ge-schichtliches. Polit. G. von den frühesten Zeiten bis auf die Gegen-wart. 1. Teil. Thür. Geschichte. Von Prof. Dr. Hertel. 1903. H. 47. 2. Teil. Meining. Geschichte von 1680 bis zur Gegenwart. Erste Hälfte bis zum Regierungsanstritt Herzog Bernhards II. (1821). 1904.

An unsere Mitarbeiter und an die Pfleger der Thüringischen historischen Kommission.

Zur Förderung theatergeschichtlicher Forschungen, die in der Herstellung einer wissenschaftlich begründeten und jedem Gebildeten verständlichen Geschichte des deutschen Theaters gipfeln sollen, gibt seit diesem Jahre die Gesellschaft für Theatergeschichte ein „Archiv für Theatergeschichte" heraus. In der Ankündigung wendet sich der Herausgeber, einer Anregung Gaehdes in den Deutschen Geschichtsblättern Bd. II. Heft 6 u. 7 (März und April 1901) folgend, an alle Forscher, die, sei es um Einzeluntersuchungen zur Lösung wissenschaftlicher Fragen anzustellen, sei es, um im Interesse der Allgemeinheit ganze Archivbestände zu inventarisieren, in den Archiven arbeiten, und bittet sie, ihr Augenmerk auf sogenannte Komödiantenakten zu richten.

Im Interesse dieser Forschungen bitten wir unsere Mitarbeiter und besonders die Hauptpfleger und Pfleger der Thüringischen historischen Kommission, bei archivalischen Forschungen und besonders bei der Inventarisationsarbeit auch Theaterakten zu verzeichnen und auf Ratsprotokolle und auf Sammelbände gedruckter und handschriftlicher Veröffentlichungen dieser Art (Theaterzettel!) zu achten. Hinweise anf Archivfunde zur Theatergeschichte werden am besten direkt an den Herausgeber des Archivs für Theatergeschichte, Herrn Dr. Hans Devrient in Weimar, gerichtet.

Die Redaktion.

CPSIA information can be obtained
at www.ICGtesting.com
Printed in the USA
BVHW08s0852210918
528170BV00023B/728/P